Dictionary
of Modern
French
Literature

DICTIONARY OF MODERN FRENCH LITERATURE

From the Age of Reason through Realism

Sandra W. Dolbow

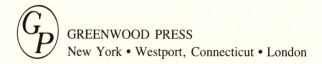

GREENWOOD PRESS
New York • Westport, Connecticut • London

Library of Congress Cataloging-in-Publication Data

Dolbow, Sandra W.
  Dictionary of modern French literature.

  Includes index.
    1. French literature—History and criticism—
Dictionaries. 2. French literature—Bio-bibliography—
Dictionaries. 3. Authors, French—Biography—
Dictionaries. I. Title.
PQ41.D65 1986   840'.3   85-15492
ISBN 0-313-23784-0 (lib. bdg. alk. paper)

Library of Congress Catalog Card Number: 85-15492
ISBN: 0-313-23784-0

First published in 1986

Greenwood Press, Inc.
88 Post Road West
Westport, Connecticut 06881

Printed in the United States of America

The paper used in this book complies with the
Permanent Paper Standard issued by the National
Information Standards Organization (Z39.48-1984).

10 9 8 7 6 5 4 3 2 1

To Steven R. Dolbow and our family

Contents

Preface

The nearly three hundred entries in this Dictionary and the bibliographical information following them aim to provide both the literature student and the reference librarian an introduction to the major writers, works, and literary movements that flourished during the 180 years from the dawn of eighteenth-century French literature through the age of realism, as well as a starting point for further research.

Biographical entries situate the writer's life, works, philosophy, and place in the history of French literature. Entries for literary works include synopses and discuss their significance or influence. Literary movements and terms such as "l'art pour l'art" or "beylisme" are presented in their historical context and evaluated for their contribution to the development of French literature. Wherever possible, bibliographies indicate books and articles, usually from 1980 through 1985, written in English, as sources for additional reading.

The eighteenth-century entries range from the neoclassical poets and playwrights of the Regency period (1715), through the philosophe movement of the mid-eighteenth century and the writers and orators inspired by the French Revolution of 1789. All major authors have been included. Entries for the nineteenth century continue the preromanticism of Rousseau, which began in the previous century and culminated in the romanticism of the 1830s and 1840s with its colorful and passionate poets, novelists, playwrights, historians, and philosophers. Again, all major preromantics and romantics are included. Along with representative realists, who reacted against romanticism primarily in the novel and on stage, and the Parnassians, who carried out the reaction in poetry, there are also the positivists, all of whom contributed to the demise of romanticism.

I chose the year 1880 as a cut-off date for nineteenth-century entries since it forms a natural division between the first literary currents of the century (romanticism and realism) and those that follow (naturalism and symbolism), which will be the beginning points of this work's forthcoming companion volume, *Diction-*

ary of Modern French Literature: From Naturalism and Symbolism to Post-Modernism. That year marks the death of the realist master, Gustave Flaubert. By 1880, Zola, who had published his first important novel, *L'Assommoir,* three years earlier, was the acknowledged leader of the naturalist school. In 1880, he formulated the esthetics of the movement in *Les Soirées de Médan,* a collection of stories by emerging naturalists. Early in the 1880s a large number of young, experimental poets gave rise to the symbolist movement. Finally, 1880 very nearly coincides with the establishment of the Third French Republic, which lasted from 1870 until 1946. To simplify matters, Zola and his novels, as well as those of other naturalists, including the Goncourt brothers and Maupassant, will fall under the purview of the next *Dictionary of Modern French Literature.* The realist drama of playwright Henry Becque is considered here. The next volume will pick up with André Antoine and his Théâtre libre.

Every effort has been made to ensure that the information included in the Dictionary is current and readily accessible. Entries are alphabetized, with cross-references to related entries indicated by asterisks. "Romanticism," for example, contains nearly twenty cross-references, leading the reader to entries on *Hernani,* Rousseau, preromanticism, realism, Chateaubriand, and more. A double asterisk denotes a name or term that will be covered in the companion volume. The bibliography following each entry lists books and articles. Bibliographical data has been arranged alphabetically according to the author's last name.

Two appendices should also prove helpful. One chronicles the history of France as well as significant literary events. A second appendix categorizes the entries according to century, genre, and context to provide access to the reader who is interested in a particular aspect of French literature.

It is my hope that this Dictionary will reveal the genius and individuality of French literature and inspire further explorations amid its mystery and beauty. And may it all endure.

Dictionary
of Modern
French
Literature

A

ADOLPHE (1816), Benjamin Constant's* masterful novel of self-analysis, details with classical precision and clarity the sad tale of a doomed love affair between a young aristocrat named Adolphe and a woman ten years his senior, Ellénore, the mistress of a family friend. Ellénore is an amalgam of several of Constant's lovers—Anna Lindsay, Julie Talma, Charlotte von Hardenberg, and Germaine de Staël.* Adolphe is clearly Constant himself. Antoine Adam writes in his introduction to the Garnier Flammarion edition of the novel that reading it is like listening to a man's confession. To avoid a scandal and the ire of Madame de Staël, Constant delayed publishing the novel, which was written in 1806, for ten years. When it finally appeared, it met with great success.

The story takes place toward the end of the eighteenth century in a small German principality where Adolphe occasionally resided. Adolphe, a young aristocrat of twenty-two, describes himself as "listless, careless and bored," one who feels isolated and misunderstood by a society he feels is inferior to him. He wants to be loved but sees no one to inspire love within him, until he meets Ellénore, whom he deems "a conquest worthy of me." He vows his love for her; after much protest, she eventually gives in, offering in return a love that confines him. Adolphe realizes that their liaison cannot endure, but afraid of hurting her feelings, becomes trapped by them. She sacrifices all for him—her arrangement with the count of P——, her children, and her dignity. Adolphe tries to repay her devotion but finds a hopeless void. "It is a frightful misfortune to not be loved when one loves," he writes. "But it is a much greater one to be loved passionately when one no longer does." Out of pity and weakness, he resolves to stay with her until she no longer needs him. He lives suspended, without home, family, career, and without love. He wants to break from her but is powerless and continually delays his final adieux. Ellénore learns of his plans to leave when the baron de T——, a friend of Adolphe's father, sends her a letter in Adolphe's hand promising to break as soon as possible. Ellénore falls ill and dies from the news. Adolphe is free at last, but alone, no longer loved, a stranger to the world.

As a novel, *Adolphe* has all the trappings of a classical tragedy. Its style is eloquent, controlled. It depicts a precise analysis of passion and weakness. However, as a character, Adolphe is purely romantic. His disenchantment, malaise, sadness, and introspection exemplify the mal du siècle* of his generation. Much of the emotion portrayed in the novel stems from Constant's seventeen-year liaison with Madame de Staël. Unlike Ellénore, she was married and possessed an intellect that attracted Constant, but like her, she enslaved her young suitor in a liaison which he eventually found stifling. Unlike Adolphe, Constant extricated himself. In his novel, however, he succeeds in painting in exacting detail the cruel dilemma of those who dream of liberty, but when freed, find freedom more terrifying than slavery. Unlike most of its predecessors, *Adolphe* paints the tragic ending of an affair, not its beginnings. The look is cold and hard but powerful and true.

For further information, see V. Brady-Papadopoulou, "The Killing of the 'Mother' in Constant's *Adolphe,*" *Nineteenth Century French Studies* 10 (January 1981): 6–14; C. P. Courtney, "The Text of Constant's *Adolphe,*" *French Studies* 37 (3) (July 1983): 296–309; M. N. Evans, "*Adolphe*'s Appeal to the Reader," *Romanic Review* 73 (3) (May 1982): 302–313; A. Fairlie, "Framework as a Suggestive Art in Constant's *Adolphe* (with Remarks on Its Relation to Chateaubriand's *René*)," *Australian Journal of French Studies* 16 (January–April 1979): 6–16; Fairlie, "The Shaping of *Adolphe:* Some Remarks on Variants," in *Mélanges de littérature française moderne offerts à Garnet Rees par ses collègues et amis,* C. E. Pickford, ed. (Paris: Minard, 1980), 145–164; G. C. Jones, "The Devaluation of Action in Constant's *Adolphe,*" *Australian Journal of French Studies* 16 (January–April 1979): 17–26; Jones, "The Para-Story in Constant's *Adolphe,*" *Nineteenth Century French Studies* 11 (1–2) (Fall–Winter 1982–1983): 23–31; R. J. Niess, "Disenchanted Narcissus: *Adolphe,*" *Nineteenth Century French Studies* 11 (1–2) (Fall–Winter 1982–1983): 16–22; C. L. Peterson, "Constant's *Adolphe,* James's 'The Beast in the Jungle,' and the Quest for the Mother," *Essays in Literature* 9 (2) (Fall 1982): 224–239; T. Unwin, "The Narrator and His Evolution in Constant's *Adolphe,*" *Swiss-French Studies/ Etudes Romandes* 3 (2) (November 1982): 60–86; D. Wood, "Benjamin Constant's First Novel," *Times Literary Supplement* (6 February 1981), 151.

ALEMBERT, JEAN LE ROND D' (1717–1783), mathematician, philosophe,* and coeditor, along with Diderot,* of the *Encyclopédie,* began his life as a foundling left in front of the church of St. Jean le Rond in Paris (hence his name) and was raised by a Madame Rousseau, wife of a glazier, who lived nearby. He was the illegitimate son of Madame de Tençin* and the chevalier Destouches, a lieutenant general in the artillery who never acknowledged his paternity but provided him a small annuity throughout his lifetime. He attended boarding school from age four through ten and then went to the Jansenist Mazarin College, where he revealed exceptional talent but was discouraged from his true loves, poetry and mathematics, which he taught himself after he left the college. D'Alembert lived with his foster parents for thirty years, studied law, medicine, and mathematics and frequented the salons of the day. In 1741 he was admitted to the Academy of Sciences, where he presented papers on integral calculus (1739) and the refraction of solid bodies (1741). Two years later he published his *Traité de dynamique* (*Treatise on Dynamics*), a revolutionary contribution to the science of motion; his *Réflexions sur la cause générale des vents* (*Reflections on the General Cause of Winds*), dedicated to Frederick II (1712–1786), was awarded a prize medal by the Academy of Berlin in 1746. He was offered the presidency of the Berlin Academy by King Frederick, which he refused, applying himself instead to the study of vibrating chords, the resistance of fluids, and the planets. In 1754, he entered the French Academy, becoming its perpetual secretary in 1772 and fostering a liberal and philosophical tenor; in 1756, d'Alembert received a pension from the French government.

In 1751, d'Alembert wrote the *Discours préliminaire* (*Preliminary Discourse*) for the *Encyclopédie,* a treatise that, according to Condorcet,* only two or three men in a century could produce. The *Discours* consists of three parts of which Diderot's *Prospectus* comprises the third. In the first part, d'Alembert reiterates John Locke's (1632–1704) principle that knowledge comes from the senses, with the corollary that man is not born with an innate idea of religion or morality but forms them from his experience. He classifies human faculties into memory, reason, and imagination, which in turn produce history, philosophy, and poetry, a system that has since been debunked as erroneous and misleading. In the second part, a history of the arts and sciences accords little importance to the Middle Ages, emphasizing, instead, the Renaissance, Francis Bacon (1561–1626), René Descartes (1596–1650), Isaac Newton (1642–1727), Locke, and Gottfried Leibnitz (1646–1716).

D'Alembert contributed literary articles to the first two volumes of the *Encyclopédie* and mathematical entries to the remaining ones. His controversial article "Genève" embroiled him with the Calvinists of that city and with J.-J. Rousseau,* leading eventually to his withdrawal from the *Encyclopédie.* Among his other works are *Eléments de philosophie* (*Elements of Philosophy,* 1759), a history of the members of the French Academy, and a study of music.

Though he was courted by King Frederick and Catherine of Russia (1729–1796), who sought his wisdom and knowledge for their domains, he was criticized by the Jesuits in their *Journal de Trévoux,* in anonymous pamphlets, and by Nicolas Moreau (1717–1803) and Palissot,* friends of Fréron.* D'Alembert lived, until his end, a quiet and simple life, colored only by his love, later in life, for Mademoiselle de Lespinasse (1732–1776). The acknowledged leader of the philosophe faction of the Academy after Voltaire's* death in 1778, d'Alembert died five years later.

For further information, see D. F. Essar, *The Language Theory of Jean LeRond d'Alembert* (Oxford: Taylor Institution, 1978); Essar, "Polemical Intent and Rhetorical Style in d'Alembert's *Eloges historiques,*" in R. Emerson, G. Girard, and R. Runte, eds., *Man and Nature: Proceedings of the Canadian Society for Eighteenth-Century Studies,* vol. 1 (London, Ontario: University of Western Ontario, 1982), 31–39; O. Ranum, "D'Alembert, Tacitus, and the Political Sociology of Despotism," in *Transac-*

tions of the Fifth International Congress on the Enlightenment, vol. 2 (Oxford: Taylor Institution, 1981), 547–558; J. Shklar, "Jean D'Alembert and the Rehabilitation of History," Journal of the History of Ideas 42 (October–December 1981); 643–664.

A REBOURS (Against the Grain, 1884), by Huysmans.** See Dictionary of Modern French Literature, from Naturalism and Symbolism to Post-Modernism.

ARNAUD, FRANÇOIS-THOMAS BACULARD D' (1718–1805). See Baculard d'Arnaud, François-Thomas.

ARSENAL, LA BIBLIOTHEQUE DE L' (Arsenal Library), a library situated in the former royal cannon and gunpowder arsenal, first opened to the public in 1797. It was created in 1757 by a great book lover and minister of war, Antoine-René d'Argenson (1722–1787), in the residence of a former artillery master and enlarged by the count of Artois (the future Charles X, 1757–1836). The library was the seat of the first romantic (see romanticism*) cénacle,* when Charles Nodier,* chief librarian from 1824–1844, received there such young illustrious writers as Lamartine,* Hugo,* Vigny,* Musset,* and Dumas père.* Toward the turn of the century, J.-M. Heredia's* Parnassian* salon met there. Today it houses more than 1.5 million volumes, 15,000 manuscripts and 120,000 prints.

L'ART POUR L'ART (Art for art's sake) is an early nineteenth-century literary movement best expressed in the work of Théophile Gautier* and culminated in the Parnassian* poets. The expression "l'art pour l'art" was first used by Benjamin Constant* in his Journal intime (Intimate Journal, 1804). It originated as a reaction against the Saint-Simonians* and the Fourierists (see Fourierisme*), who sought to enlist the poet and his work into social and political causes, especially during the time of the July monarchy. Hugo* was the first to rebel against this social romanticism,* stating in the preface of his Orientales (1829)* that it was his right as a poet to publish "a useless book of pure poetry tossed in the middle of the serious preoccupations of the public," although this was a position he later reversed. Gautier, whose preface to Albertus (1832) launched the movement, became its most stalwart advocate, taking his inspiration from Germans Immanuel Kant (1724–1804), Friedrich Hegel (1770–1831), and Friedrich Schiller (1759–1805). Madame de Staël,* Victor Cousin,* and Theodore Jouffroy (1796–1842) imported their ideas of ideal beauty and the autonomy of art into France.

Gautier believed that art should be completely independent of moral, social, political, and scientific considerations and devoid of romantic sentimentality and emotionalism. His preface to Mademoiselle de Maupin (1835) reinforced the idea that art is solely an instrument of beauty. "Everything that is useful is ugly," he wrote, "for usefulness expresses human needs, and they are base and debilitating." He believed that the only aim of art should be beauty and pleasure and sought with his pen to capture and idealize what he saw through his artist's eye. His poem "L'Art" expresses the ideal of the movement—that civilizations, philosophies, mankind, even the gods, are ephemeral; only art endures and gives meaning to life—and this became the manifesto of the Parnassians.

ARVERS, FELIX (1806–1850), a minor romantic (see romanticism*) poet and playwright who frequented the salon of Charles Nodier.* Other than light plays of little significance, he is best known for a sonnet inspired by Nodier's daughter, Marie ("Mon âme a son secret, ma vie a son mystère"—"My Soul Has Its Secret, My Life Has Its Mystery"), contained in his collection, *Mes Heures perdues* (*My Lost Hours,* 1833).

ASSOMMOIR, L' (1877), by Zola.** See *Dictionary of Modern French Literature, from Naturalism and Symbolism to Post-Modernism.*

ATALA (1801), by Chateaubriand,* is a short, lyric illustration of the "Harmonies of the Christian religion with scenes of nature and the passions of the human heart," a chapter of *Le Génie du Christianisme* which was to include the tale. However, *Atala* was published separately. Chactas, an old, blind Natchez Indian, tells the story to René, a young Frenchman much like Chateaubriand a few years earlier. Overcome by "passion and sadness," René is in the New World to find himself. (His story is related in *René,* published a year after *Atala.*) Chactas is a cosmopolitan Indian who has travelled to France, had an audience with Louis XIV, visited Versailles, and hosted Fénelon.* His tribe grants asylum to René, whom he adopts as a son and marries to an Indian maiden, Celuta. One evening during a beaver hunt, the old Indian tells René the story of his adventures.

When his tribe was defeated by its enemy, the Muscogulges, Chactas, a young boy of seventeen, fled to Saint Augustine, Florida, where he was raised by a kind Spaniard, Lopez, and his sister. He longed to return to his native land; when he did, nearly three years later, he was captured by the enemy and condemned to the stake. One night, however, Atala, daughter of the chief, untied him and followed him to the freedom of the forests. They travelled for weeks; Chactas fell in love with the beautiful but often sad young maiden. In their conversations, they discovered that Atala's father is Lopez, Chactas's Spanish benefactor. During a storm, they met a missionary, Father Aubry, who sheltered them in his cave. While Atala slept, Father Aubry took Chactas to the village of Christian Indians he had established. He wanted to convert Chactas and marry him to Atala. When they returned to the cave, however, they found Atala dying. She revealed her fatal secret and the cause of her sadness. As an infant she was near death and her mother consecrated her to the Virgin Mary, promising that if she could live, she would remain a virgin. Torn between keeping her mother's vow and her love for Chactas, she poisoned herself, learning too late that she could have been absolved. Atala dies. Her burial is a beautiful and moving scene.

Atala was originally intended as part of *Les Natchez,* Chateaubriand's American epic, and was completed during his London exile. It was included in the English version of *Le Génie du Christianisme*. Upon his return to France, Chateaubriand published it separately, a year before *Le Génie*, as *Atala or The Loves of Two Indians in the Desert*. The short tale conquered France and Europe with its noble simplicity, exoticism, and depiction of natural man and established Chateaubriand's reputation as a writer. It combined the dignity and form of the classics—prologue, narrative, epilogue—with a sensitive treatment of a romantic theme—the "troubles of love" versus "the calm of the deserts and the calm of religion." *Atala* has been criticized as naive and unrealistic; however, it endures as an eloquent testimony to the dawn of romantic (see romanticism*) literature.

For further information, see D. Kadish, "Symbolism of Exile: The Opening Description in *Atala*," *French Review* 55 (3) (February 1982): 358–366.

AUGIER, EMILE (1820–1889), popular author of social comedies who led, with Ponsard,* the "bon sens" ("common sense") school of drama against romanticism,* is best known for *Le Gendre de M. Poirier (Mr. Poirier's Son-in-Law*, 1854), written in collaboration with Jules Sandeau,* and *Maître Guérin (Master Guerin*, 1864). His first work, *La Ciguë (The Hemlock*, 1844), taken from antiquity and influenced by Ponsard, was followed by two verse comedies, *L'Aventurière (The Adventuress*, 1848) and *Gabrielle* (1849), which lashed out against the romantics' excessive passion and individualism and defended bourgeois values such as the sanctity of family, home, and marriage. After 1854 and the success of *Le Gendre de M. Poirier*, Augier was on his true course, writing comedies in prose extolling the morals and manners of the bourgeoisie. *Le Mariage d'Olympe (Olympia's Marriage*, 1855) condemns the courtesan; *Les Lionnes pauvres (The Poor Lionnesses*, 1858) chastises adultery and money as destructive to marriage; *Le Fils de Giboyer (Giboyer's Son*, 1862) attacks the clerical-legitimist party; *Maître Guérin* criticizes unscrupulous lawyers. *Madame Caverlet* (1876) is about divorce; *Les Fourchambault* (1878) focuses on illegitimacy. Augier's comedies are generally well-constructed representations of the bourgeois milieu, reminiscent of Molière (1622–1673), but they lack the master's style and imagination. They pleased the public for which they were written, but are less appealing today.

B

BACHAUMONT, LOUIS PETIT DE (1700?–1771), essayist and observer of the eighteenth-century social scene, is best known as editor of *Mémoires secrets pour servir à l'histoire de la république des lettres* (*Secret Memoirs to Serve the History of the Republic of Letters*, 1762–1789). He was host and secretary for Madame Doublet de Persan (1687–1771), whose salon or "parish" included Piron,* abbé Chauvelin (1685–1762), Charles Augustin d'Argental (1705–1788), abbé de Voisenon (1708–1775), and Riqueti Mirabaud (1715–1789). Their exchanges and gossip were the source for much of Bachaumont's observations. The *Mémoires*, also known as *Journal de Bachaumont* (*Bachaumont's Journal*, 1762–1789), contained news, witticisms, and literary criticism in the manner of Grimm's* more illustrious *Correspondance littéraire*. The *Mémoires* circulated in manuscript until a posthumous collection appeared in 1777. Pidansat de Mairobert (1727–1779) and others assumed editorship until the *Mémoires* grew to fill thirty-six volumes.

Bachaumont followed trends in the theatre, arts, manners, and fashion. Among his essays are memoirs on the Louvre, the opera, theatre, painting, architecture, and sculpture.

BACULARD D'ARNAUD, FRANÇOIS-THOMAS (1718–1805), novelist, poet, and playwright protected by Voltaire* and Frederick the Great, was the master of the macabre whose sensitivity and darkness anticipated the romantic (see romanticism*) melodramas of the next century. Two plays, *Le Comte de Comminge ou Les Amants malheureux* (*The Count of Comminge or The Unhappy Lovers*, written 1764, performed 1790) and *L'Euphémie* (1768) are set in crypts. Two others, *Falvey* (1770) and *Merinval* (1774), along with novels *Les Epoux malheureux* (*The Unhappy Spouses*, 1746) and *Fanni ou l'Heureux Repentir* (*Fanny or the Happy Penitent*, 1764), abound in horror and passion. His collected short stories include *Les Epreuves du sentiment* (*Trials of Sentiment*,

1773), *Les Nouvelles historiques* (*Historical Stories,* 1774) and *Les Délasse-
ments de l'homme sensible* (*Relaxations of a Sensitive Man,* 1783–1793). Besides creating the "genre sombre," d'Arnaud collaborated with Palissot* on
Fréron's* anti-philosophe publication, *L'Année littéraire.*

For further information, see R. L. Dawson, *Baculard d'Arnaud* (Banbury, Eng.: Voltaire Foundation, 1976).

BALLANCHE, PIERRE-SIMON (1776–1847), religious historian and philosopher, was a mystic and an illuminist who sought to restore religion to its rightful
place in the history of man's progress. He was born in Lyons, the son of a
printer, and was burdened with poor health, no doubt aggravated by his witnessing, at an early age, the horrors of the Revolution, which forced him and his
mother to flee to the countryside. In 1812, he met Madame Récamier (1777–
1849) and embarked on a platonic relationship that enriched the rest of his days.
At her urging, he moved to Paris, and in 1815 accompanied her to Italy. An
aspiring inventor, he worked on a number of projects, including a steam engine,
which failed. In 1833, he received a government pension. He entered the Academy in 1842.

His first major work, *Du sentiment considéré dans ses rapports avec la littérature et les arts* (*Concerning Sentiment Considered in its Relationships with
Literature and the Arts,* 1801) exalts sentiment rather than reason as the true
source of inspiration. *Antigone* (1814) is a modern interpretation of an ancient
myth. *Essai sur les institutions sociales dans leurs rapports avec les idées
nouvelles* (*Essay on Social Institutions in their Relationships with New Ideas,*
1818) seeks to synthesize political authority with individual freedom and Christianity with the notion of progress. His most important work, *Palingénésie
sociale* (*Social Palingenesis,* 1827–1829), attempts to interpret the working of
providence in history. Of this vast ensemble, only *Prolégomènes* (1827), *Orphée*
(1827), and *La Vision d'Hébal* (*Hebal's Vision,* 1831) are complete.

Ballanche considered humanity as fallen from the time of the original sin of
Adam and Eve and saw the history and progress of mankind as a series of
atonements for that sin which had culminated in the Revolution and the Empire.
His works have been criticized as verbose, obscure, and unsystematic but reveal
a depth of thinking that influenced Chateaubriand's* *Le Génie du Christianisme** and contributed to the rehabilitation of religious ideas badly shaken in
the eighteenth century.

BALZAC, HONORE DE (1799–1850), novelist and creator of *La Comédie
humaine** (*The Human Comedy,* 1829–1849), was born in Tours, the eldest of
four children, to Bernard-François Balzac, deputy-mayor of the town, and Anne-
Charlotte-Laure Sallambier. His father descended from a line of Gascon peasants
originally named Balssa. His elegant, beautiful mother, thirty-two years younger
than his father, came from the Parisian bourgeoisie. Her coldness resulted in
Balzac's longing for maternal affection in his sexual relationships and in his

writing. In 1807, he was sent to the Collège de Vendôme, where he received only the barest necessities and supposedly only one visit from his family during his six-year stay. His novel *Louis Lambert* (1832) details the harshness of his existence at this school. In 1814, in the grip of a constant fever, he returned to Tours, attended the lycée, then moved to Paris with his family, his father having been named director of military provisions. He attended two successive schools before receiving his degree in 1816. From 1816 to 1819, he studied law at the University of Paris while clerking in the chambers of Guyonnet-Merville, where he picked up the knowledge of wills and contracts, which later played significant roles in his novels. However, Balzac was more enamored of literature than law. In 1819, he installed himself for a two-year probationary period at his family's expense in a cold, leaky room at 9, rue Lesdiguières, in Paris, where he reread Pierre Corneille (1606–1684), Jean-Baptiste Molière (1622–1673), François-Marie Arouet Voltaire,* and Jean-Jacques Rousseau* and tried his hand at a verse tragedy (*Cromwell,* 1819), a hollow imitation of the classical tragedies then in vogue but a sincere attempt to support himself with his pen. It failed and Balzac turned to the historical novel à la Walter Scott (1771–1832), *Falthurne* (1820), and the epistolary novel, *Sténie ou Les Erreurs philosophiques (Stenie, or Philosophical Errors,* 1819). With his two-year trial nearly at a close, he met Auguste Le Poitevin (1791–1854) with whom he dashed off gothic novels, *L'Heritière de Birague (The Heiress of Birague,* 1822) and *Jean-Louis* (1822), under the pseudonym of Lord R'hoone. After *Clotilde de Lusignan* (1822), he assumed a new name, Horace de Saint Aubin, with *Le Centenaire (The Centenarian,* 1822) and *Le Vicaire des Ardennes (The Vicar of the Ardennes,* 1822). In 1822, he experienced his first love affair. Madame de Berny, whom he called "La Dilecta" ("Tender Love"), was twenty-two years his senior and the mother of seven children. Until her death fourteen years later, she offered Balzac her steadfast love, friendship, and guidance.

Materialistic by nature, Balzac was seeking to cement ties with the aristocracy, improve his finances, and reconcile his debts. Dissatisfied with his earnings as a writer, he invested his family's fortune, first in a publishing venture, next in a printing business, and finally in a new printing process, all of which failed and saddled him with debts totalling nearly 100,000 francs, which he would never repay. He turned to writing again to stave off his creditors, this time using his own name. Mindful of the example of Napoleon, he vowed, "What he achieved by the sword, I will accomplish with the pen."

The first novel to bear the name Balzac was *Les Chouans* (1829), written, as he stated in the preface, to "reproduce the spirit of an age." It is an historical and adventure novel about a peasant uprising in Brittany, which he documented with a research trip, extensive notes, and interviews. An immediate success, *Les Chouans* founded Balzac's reputation as a serious writer. It was followed later that same year by the completed version of *La Physiologie du mariage (The Physiology of Marriage,* 1829). Five months after that, two volumes of stories comprising *Scènes de la vie privée (Scenes from Private Life,* 1830) appeared.

Between 1830 and 1831, he turned out reams of short stories, novels, articles, and political pieces in all of the journals and periodicals on various topics, from the "Philosophie de la toilette" to the Saint-Simonians (see Saint-Simonisme*).

By 1830, Balzac had transformed himself into a dandy with a carriage and servants, thanks to his literary success and the influence of his sister, Laure Surville (1800–1871), and his mistresses. He became an habitué of the Paris clubs and salons, a friend of novelist Sophie Gay (1776–1852) and Madame Récamier (1777–1849); the confidant of Zulma Carraud, an artillery captain's wife who wanted to adopt him "as a son"; the intimate of the duchesse d'Abrantès (1784–1838), a Napoleonic aristocrat; and the suitor of the duchess de Castries, a member of the old nobility. Balzac cut a strange shape with his short, rotund body, his expensively tailored clothing, his devotion to luxury. He was eccentric in his work habits as well, writing from midnight until eight in the morning, working on galley proofs until five in the afternoon, wearing a monk's frock, sustaining himself with endless cups of strong coffee. In rapid succession, he produced the novels of the *Comédie humaine* at the rate of one or two volumes per year. The first novel by "de" Balzac, his self-given aristocratic surname, *La Peau de chagrin* (*The Fatal Skin* or *The Wild Ass's Skin,* 1831), was followed by *Louis Lambert* (1832), *Le Curé de Tours* (1832), *Le Colonel Chabert* (1832), *Les Marana* (1832–1833), *Le Médecin de campagne* (*The Country Doctor,* 1833) and *Eugénie Grandet** (1833).

Shortly before the publication of *Eugénie Grandet* in 1833, Balzac met Countess Eveline Hanska (1801–1882) in Switzerland, with whom he had corresponded for more than a year. She turned out to be the woman of his dreams, a wealthy Polish aristocrat with a husband twenty-five years her senior. To woo her in style, he contracted with a publisher for twelve volumes of a proposed *Etudes de moeurs au 19e siècle* (*Studies of the Manners of the Nineteenth Century*), which would include a new edition of *Scènes de la vie privée, Scènes de la vie de province,* and *Scènes de la vie parisienne* (*Scenes from Private Life, Scenes from Provincial Life,* and *Scenes from Parisian Life*).

By 1834, he had outlined the broad scheme of the *Comédie humaine* in a letter to Madame Hanska. The "Etudes de moeurs" ("Studies of Manners"), he wrote, would depict "all the repercussions of social conditions . . . every situation in life, every type of physiognomy, every kind of male and female character, every way of living, every profession, every social stratum, every French province, childhood . . . nothing is to be omitted." The "Etudes philosophiques" ("Philosophical Studies") would address the "origin of the emotions and of the motivating causes of life." Finally, the "Etudes analytiques" ("Analytical Studies"), including the *Physiologie du mariage* (*Physiology of Marriage*), would delve into the underlying principles.

After *Eugénie Grandet,* which met with resounding success, he travelled to Geneva to be near Madame Hanska and to complete the manuscript of *La Duchesse de Langeais* (1833–1834), the story of his adventure with Madame de Castries. Balzac's affair with Madame Hanska, on the other hand, was to remain a well-kept secret, as he plunged into the fever of work that brought forth *La Recherche de l'absolu* (*The Search for the Absolute*, 1834), *Séraphita* (1835), *Le Père Goriot** (1834–1835), *Un Drame au bord de la mer* (*A Drama by the Sea*, 1835), *La Fille aux yeux d'or* (*The Girl with the Golden Eyes*, 1834–1835), and *César Birotteau* (1837). At the same time, he collaborated on a play with Sandeau,* wrote his *Lettres aux écrivains français du 19e siècle* (*Letters to the French Writers of the Nineteenth Century*, 1834), exchanged passionate epistles with Madame Hanska, and kept his diaries. In 1835, at great expense, he travelled to Vienna to be near Madame Hanska, whom he was not to see again for seven years.

Upon his return, Balzac was greeted by increased personal and family debts, deadlines, and the failing health of his surrogate mother, Madame de Berny. However, Vienna had spawned the idea for *Le Lys dans la vallée* (*The Lily of the Valley*, 1835–1836), a novel that triggered a suit against Balzac's publisher. Buloz, in Balzac's absence, had sold the proofs of *Le Lys dans la vallée*, still in rough form, to a Russian review. Balzac, incensed, sued; Buloz countered for Balzac's nonfulfillment of contractual obligations and enlisted the aid of Dumas père,* Sue,* and other writers in his case. Only Hugo* and George Sand* refused to bow to Buloz's influence. The court ruled in Balzac's favor.

In 1836, dreaming of political power and a career in Parliament, Balzac acquired a journal, the *Chronique de Paris,* an ultraclerical and legitimist publication, which he filled twice a week with political and literary articles and short stories. It soon failed. Other publishers were demanding works Balzac had promised, debts continually mounted, and Balzac was forced again to hide from creditors. To satisfy his publisher, Béchet, and to avoid a fine, he completed the first part of *Les Illusions perdues* (*Lost Illusions*, 1837–1843) in eight days. Yet true to his nature, he continued the vicious cycle of debts and his enslavement to luxury by moving into an elegant dwelling on rue Cassini to impress his latest love interest, the beautiful Contessa Guidoboni-Visconti. In 1836, she financed his trip to Italy, which he took in the company of Caroline Marbouty, the bored wife of a court official in Limoges, whom the local aristocrats mistook for George Sand. He returned to the sad news of the death of Madame de Berny. The following year, the countess arranged a second Italian journey; again he returned to outstanding debts and unfilled writing obligations and lived in seclusion in the Contessa's house on the Champs-Elysées, where in two month's time he completed *La Maison Nucingen* (*The Firm of Nucingen*, 1838) and *La Femme supérieure* (*The Superior Woman*, 1838) and wrote the final episodes of *Contes drolatiques* (*Droll Stories*, 1832, 1833, 1837). By 1838, thanks to the generous contessa, who settled most of his accounts, and his growing literary reputation, Balzac was enjoying a modicum of financial stability.

But once again extravagance and foolishness took the upper hand. Balzac's dream of an idyllic rustic retreat away from the demands of life in Paris grew to mammoth proportions in Sèvres, where he bought a property and hired legions of workmen to construct a villa and plant 120 fruit trees. While the work was underway, Balzac went prospecting for silver in Sardinia on the advice of an Italian merchant, Guiseppe Pezzi. With funds borrowed from his mother, he set out on an arduous three-months' journey, only to find that Mr. Pezzi had beaten him to it. In 1838, he visited George Sand at Nohant. *Béatrix* (1839), the second part of *Les Illusions perdues* (1839), and *Une Fille d'Eve* (*A Daughter of Eve,* 1839) appeared the following year, as well as his *Mémoire sur le procès Peytel* (*Memoir on the Trial of Peytel,* 1839), a defense of a fellow journalist accused of murder.

In 1840, turning to the theatre, Balzac hired a collaborator to write a play that was refused by the director of the Théâtre de la Renaissance. Next, his drama *Vautrin* (1840), based on the master criminal of the *Comédie,* which had been readily accepted by the Théâtre Porte-Saint-Martin, failed dismally and was prohibited from being produced by the minister of the interior. Three others, *Les Ressources de Quinola* (*The Resources of Quinola,* 1842), *Paméla Giraud* (1843), and *La Marâtre* (*The Stepmother,* 1848), also failed. *Le Faiseur* (*The Businessman,* 1830, 1840), though slightly better than the others, was never produced during Balzac's lifetime and was later renamed *Mercadet.* He founded another journal, the *Revue parisienne* (*Parisian Revue*), which saw three issues. In it he attacked Sainte-Beuve* and praised Stendhal's* *La Chartreuse de Parme,** then an unknown book by an unknown author. Balzac was forced to sell his estate at Les Jardies at a loss. However, he saw the chance to pay his debts in 1841, when Madame Hanska's husband died, freeing her to at last marry Balzac, as they had vowed years earlier. She declined for practical and personal reasons. Not only did she need the permission of the tsar, she distrusted Balzac. On top of her rejection, he failed as a candidate to the Academy. In 1841, after a serious illness, he assembled the greater number of his novels into the *Comédie humaine.* The first edition appeared the following year. In 1843, he travelled to Saint Petersburg, where he finally joined Madame Hanska. He returned to Paris, wrote additional volumes of his *Comédie humaine,* and published *Les Paysans* (*The Peasants,* 1844). By 1844, his health began to deteriorate. The following year, he went to Dresden at Madame Hanska's request; they travelled to Germany, back to Paris, then to Italy, and across France, Holland, and Belgium. In anticipation of his marriage, Balzac began collecting antiques and works of art so that by 1847 he was beginning to feel weakened by overwork and mounting debts. His writing suffered. Progress on *Les Paysans* and *Les Petits Bourgeois* (*The Lower Bourgeois,* posthumous) stalled. In a flurry of rededication to his craft, he produced his final masterworks, *La Cousine Bette* (1846) and *Le Cousin Pons* (1847). During the winter of 1848–1849, he travelled to the Ukraine. By his return, the Revolution of February 1848 had erupted; later that year, he failed in his third attempt to join the Academy. He returned to the Ukraine the following year, where Madame Hanska was irritable and cool, stalling their marriage and preferring the company of her daughter. Balzac, discouraged and ill, suffered two heart attacks in 1849 before Madame Hanska finally consented, perhaps through pity, to marriage the following March. Weak, exhausted, and nearly blind, Balzac and his wife returned to Paris in May; he was extremely ill by July. Balzac died in August in the company of his mother and was buried at Père Lachaise Cemetery. Hugo delivered a moving speech on his behalf.

Balzac is situated at the confluence of the two great and opposing tides of thought running through the nineteenth century—romanticism* and realism.* In his youthful exuberance, his vitality and passion, his bountiful imagination, Balzac was a romantic. Yet his motivations were very much rooted in reality— the need for money, his desire for glory and love. Likewise, romanticism and realism weave the fabric of Balzac's *Comédie humaine*. In the ninety-one novels that comprise his magnum opus, Balzac the realist presents a living tableau of France from 1789 to 1848. He describes the peasants, the provincials, and the Parisians he had observed so often as they made their way through life. He depicts their homes and habits; he uncovers their passions. He introduced materialism and the lust for money and power into the novel. Balzac the romantic endowed the *Comédie humaine* with a vision that transcends the ordinary and elevates his characters into mythical incarnations. By the force of his fertile imagination, Balzac peopled his universe with unforgettable, larger-than-life representatives of the dark side of humanity—Father Grandet is the wretched miser, Rastignac the young arriviste, Vautrin the escaped prisoner. He showed the interplay of the individual and society and the dynamics of character. He didn't flinch before the ugly or vulgar but painted it in his giant social fresco. He created a world which became so real for him that he inhabited it. It is said that upon his deathbed he cried out for Horace Bianchon, a physician in his *Comedie humaine*.

Balzac's portrait of French society was as deep as it was wide, penetrating the imaginary, the mysterious, the fantastic, the philosophical elements of life. Balzac believed that thought is "the most vital cause of the disorganization of man," that "life diminishes proportionately as desires increase." His *Contes philosophiques* (*Philosophical Stories,* 1831) and other novels demonstrate the unfortunate social consequences of unbridled desire. A mystical search for God and questioning of human destiny pervades the philosophical novels.

Balzac is generally considered the father of realism. He led the way for the novels of Zola** and Edmond and Jules de Goncourt** with his attention to detail and the minute portraits of his characters. Baudelaire,** on the other hand, found him a "passionate visionary" whose stories are as "colorful as dreams." According to Maurois,** Balzac ranks with William Shakespeare (1564–1616) and Leo Tolstoy (1883–1945) as a writer able to depict the range of human passion. Henry James (1843–1916) called him the greatest of all novelists. Friedrich Engels (1820–1895) felt that despite his Catholicism and monarchist beliefs, he taught him more than all the historians, sociologists, and political analysts in the world. That opinion was shared by Nikolai Lenin (1870–1924).

Balzac's energy, his imagination, and his voluminous output dominates the literature of the nineteenth century. Though his work has been called uneven, his style pretentious, and at times tasteless, it has survived. His influence on the novel is unparalleled. Blaise Cendrars** wrote that "Balzac is the creator of the modern world. For that reason, every young author of today must pass through him."

For further information, see D. Adamson, *Illusions Perdues* (London: Grant and Cutler, 1981); J. Beizer, "Victor Marchand: The Narrator as Story Seller: Balzac's '*El Verdugo*,' " *Novel: A Forum on Fiction* 17 (1) (Fall 1983): 44–51; D. Bellos, *Honoré de Balzac, La Cousine Bette* (London: Grant and Cutler, 1980); R. Butler, *Balzac and the French Revolution* (Totowa, N.J.: Barnes and Noble, 1983); G. Besser, "Historical Intrusions into Balzac's Fictional World," *French Literature Series* 8 (1981): 76–84; H. Borowitz, "Balzac's Unknown Masters," *Romanic Review* 72 (4) (November 1981): 425–441; P. Brooks, "Narrative Transaction and Transference (Unburying *Le Colonel Chabert*)," *Novel* 15 (2) (Winter 1982): 101–110; W. Conner, "Albert Savarus and 'L'Ambitieux par amour,' " *Symposium* 37 (4) (Winter 1983): 251–260; S. Daugherty, "The Golden Bowl: Balzac, James and the Rhetoric of Power," *Texas Studies in Literature and Language* 24 (1) (Spring 1982): 68–82; E. Esrock, "Literature and Philosophy as Narrative Writing," in P. Ruppert, E. Crook, and W. Forehand, eds., *Ideas of Order in Literature and Film* (Tallahassee: University Press of Florida, 1980); S. Felman, "Rereading Femininity," *Yale French Studies* 62 (1981): 19–44; D. Festa-McCormick, "Paris as the Gray Eminence in Balzac's *Ferragus*," *Laurels* 51 (1) (Spring 1981): 33–43; N. Finlay, "Rodin's Monumental Head of Balzac," *The Princeton University Library Chronicle* 43 (Spring 1982): 234–240; A. Greet, "Picasso and Balzac: Le Chef-d'oeuvre inconnu," *Comparatist* 6 (1) (May 1982): 56–66; D. Kadish, " 'Alissa dans la vallée': Intertextual Echoes of Balzac in Two Novels by Gide," *French Forum* 10 (1) (January 1985): 67–83; Kadish, "Landscape, Ideology, and Plot in Balzac's *Les Chouans*," *Nineteenth Century French Studies* 12–13 (Summer-Fall 1984): 43–57; Kadish, "The Ambiguous Lily Motif in Balzac's *Le Lys dans la vallée*," *International Fiction Review* 10 (1) (Winter 1983): 8–14; D. Kelly, "What is the Message in Balzac's 'Le Message,' " *Nineteenth Century French Studies* 13 (2–3) (Winter–Spring 1985): 48–58; Kelly, "Balzac's l'Auberge Rouge: On Reading an Ambiguous Text," *Symposium* 36 (1) (Spring 1982): 30–44; P. Lock, "Text Crypt," *Modern Language Notes* 97 (4) (May, 1982): 872–889; D. Magette, "Trapping Crayfish: The Artist, Nature and Le Calcul in Balzac's *La Rabouilleuse*," *Nineteenth Century French Studies* 12 (1–2) (Fall–Winter 1983–1984): 54–67; H. Majewski, "The Function of the Mythic Patterns in Balzac's *La Recherche de l'absolu*," *Nineteenth Century French Studies* 9 (Fall–Winter 1980–1981): 10–27; B. McGraw, "The Function of Descriptive Utterances in the Balzacian text," *Semiotica* 3/4 (1981): 367–376; J. Mileham, "Group Names in Balzac's *Les Paysans*," *Romance Notes* 23 (2) (Winter 1982): 140–145; A. K. Mortimer, "Problems of Closure in Balzac's Stories," *French Forum* 10 (1) (January 1985): 20–39; A. Pasco, "Balzac and the Art of the Macro-Emblem in *Splendeurs et misères des courtisanes*," *Esprit Créateur* 22 (3) (Fall 1982): 72–81; I. Pickup, "Balzac and the Dynamics of Passion: The Case of Véronique Graslin," *Nottingham French Studies* 22 (2) (October 1983): 1–8; V. Pritchett, *Balzac* (New York: Harmony, 1983); K. Rivers, "The Swirl: Eroticism in Balzac and Flaubert," *French Literature Series* 10 (1983): 138–142; F. van Rossum-Guyon, "Aspects and Functions of Fictional Description: Balzac's *The Village Priest*," *Style* 17 (2) (Spring 1983): 209–233; L. Schehr, "The Unknown Subject: About Balzac's 'Le Chef d'oeuvre inconnu,' " *Nineteenth Century French Studies* 12–13 (Summer–Fall 1984): 58–69; Schehr, "Fool's Gold: The Beginning of Balzac's *Illusions perdues*,"

Symposium 36 (2) (Summer 1982): 149–165; C. Smethurst, "Balzac and Realism: An Essay," *Romance Studies* 1 (Winter 1982): 64–76; S. Stary, "Balzac's Cold-Hearted Coquettes: The Link between Foedora, Antoinette and Valérie," *Degré second* 6 (July 1982): 101–120; T. Steele, "Matter and Mystery: Neglected Works and Background Materials of Detective Fiction," *Modern Fiction Studies* 29 (3) (Autumn 1983): 435–450; W. Stowe, *Balzac, James and the Realistic Novel* (Princeton, N.J.: Princeton University Press, 1983); Stowe, "Intelligibility and Entertainment: Balzac and James," *Comparative Literature* 31 (1) (Winter 1983): 55–69; E. Sullivan, "The Novelists' Undeclared Assumptions: Balzac and Stendhal," *Laurels* 54 (1) (Spring 1983): 49–57; E. Talbot, "Pleasure/Time or Egoism/Love: Rereading *La Peau de chagrin*," *Nineteenth Century French Studies* 11 (1–2) (Fall–Winter 1982–1983): 72–82.

BANVILLE, THEODORE DE (1823–1891), considered by many to be the most gifted among the Parnassian* poets, was born in Moulins in the department of Alliers in the center of France to an impoverished but noble family. His father, a naval officer who became a government functionary, died early, leaving his young son in the care of his mother and sister. In Paris, he studied at Collège Bourbon and attended law school, but he found his true vocation early in poetry. His first work and one of his best, *Les Cariatides* (1842), was written between the ages of sixteen and eighteen years. In 1845, he began a career in journalism at *La Silhouette*. He also worked for *Le Pamphlet* (1848) and later wrote for *La Revue de Paris* (1852), where he met Gautier,* and *Le Figaro* (1855). In 1857, he was hospitalized with weak lungs and nervousness. Ill again in 1859, he spent the winter in Nice with actress Marie Daubrun, Baudelaire's** mistress. In 1863, he met the widowed Madame Rochegrosse, whom he married three years later. Other friends included young poets Mallarmé,** Glatigny,* and Rimbaud.** After 1880, he received few visits, except for those from his wife's son, painter Georges Rochegrosse. He died in Paris in 1891.

Banville's first poems, *Les Cariatides,* were filled with the lyricism of Musset* and Hugo* as well as his admiration for classical antiquity and myth. *Les Stalactites* (1846), his second collection, inspired by Ronsard and the German poet Heinrich Heine (1797–1856), repeats the theme of ancient Greece. Other collections include *Odelettes* (1856), *Odes funambulesques (Fantastic Odes,* 1857), *Les Exilés (The Exiled,* 1867), and *Idylles prussiennes (Prussian Idylls,* written after the war, 1870–1871). He also wrote two plays, a prose comedy entitled *Gringoire* (1866) and *Socrate et sa femme (Socrates and His Wife,* 1885). His *Petit Traité de poésie française (Little Treatise on French Poetry,* 1871) set forth the manifesto of the Parnassians. Banville wrote plays, *Florise* (1870), *Déidamia* (1874), *Le Baiser (The Kiss,* 1888), and *Esope* (1890). He tried his hand at the novel and stories with *La Vie d'une comedienne (The Life of an Actress,* 1855), *Contes féeriques (Fairy Tales,* 1882), *Contes héroïques (Heroic Stories,* 1884), *Contes bourgeois (Bourgeois Stories,* 1885), and *L'Ame de Paris (The Soul of Paris,* 1891), among others, and volumes of chronicles and memoirs.

Twenty years before the Parnassian poets, Banville expressed their ideal of enduring beauty in "Sculpteur, cherche avec soin . . ." ("Sculptor, seek with care . . ."), advising the artist to carefully "seek a flawless marble" before making a vase showing the calmness and purity of a procession of young Athenian women. "Le Saut du tremplin" ("The Somersault from the Springboard") compares the poet to an acrobat or clown who springs from the banal earth with its petty bourgeois in a flight to the stars. "L'Exil des dieux" ("Exile of the Gods") depicts man as a "vile murderer of the gods" who, as Christian, has exiled the pagan gods of Olympus to obscurity and forced the greatest poets, Ovid, Dante, and Hugo, to flee their native lands. Banville revived the lyric poetic forms of the Middle Ages—madrigals, ballads, rounds, triolets, and chansons—in the above-mentioned collections and two others, *Ballades joyeuses à la maniere de Villon* (*Joyous Ballads in the Manner of Villon*, 1873) and *Rondels à la manière de Charles d'Orléans* (*Rondels in the Manner of Charles d'Orleans*, 1875). He believed that medieval French poets truly possessed a sense of rhythm that was lost during the seventeenth century with the rules imposed by Nicolas Boileau (1636–1711) and François de Malherbe (1555–1628), writing in *Les Cariatides* that "when Malherbe came, poetry went."

Banville's *Petit Traité de poésie française* is considered a valuable handbook on Parnassian poetry, mainly for its praise of Hugo, though it was poorly received by Leconte de Lisle* and others. Banville would replace the poetry of the seventeenth and eighteenth centuries with that of the sixteenth, which was written by François Villon (1431–1463) and Pierre de Ronsard (1524–1585) and "perfected" by the great poets of the nineteenth. "Victor Hugo's *La légende des siècles*,"* he writes, "must be the Bible and Gospel of all French versifiers." Banville considered rime as the most important quality of a poem since "one hears in a verse only the word which rimes."

Banville was a poet to whom verse came easily. He wrote in his treatise on poetry that when the poet heard a word, its "rhyming twin" naturally followed. For him, "the poet thinks in verse and has only to transcribe what is dictated; he who is not a poet thinks in prose and must translate his thoughts into verse." The ideals of Gautier and de Lisle, however, provided the necessary discipline to shape his romantic, lyric inspiration into art that celebrates pure form, balance, and objectivity.

For further information, see A. Harms, *Théodore de Banville* (Boston: Twayne, 1983); R. Storey, "Pierrot 'Narcisse': Théodore de Banville and the Pantomime," *Nineteenth Century French Studies* 13 (2–3) (Winter–Spring 1985): 1–21.

BARANTE, BARON GUILLAUME PROSPER DE (1782–1866), historian, orator, and publicist for the doctrinaire (moderate) party and diplomat, was a contemporary of Thierry* and, like him, a writer of narrative history. The epitaph to his *L'Histoire des ducs de Bourgogne* (*History of the Dukes of Burgundy*, 1824–1826), by Quintilian (first century A.D.), summarizes Barante's philosophy of history, "scribitur ad narrandum, non ad probandum" ("One

BARBEY D'AUREVILLY, JULES 19

writes to tell, not to prove''). Barante believed that history should be, above all, "exact and serious" as well as "true and living." He attempted to "penetrate" the spirit of his sources and to reproduce their "color," while eliminating his own thoughts and judgments. His *L'Histoire des ducs de Bourgogne* is a conscientious rendition of the spirit of the fifteenth century.

BARBEY D'AUREVILLY, JULES (1808–1889), novelist and literary critic, was born to a wealthy bourgeois family at Saint-Sauveur-le-Vicomte, a village near Cherbourg in Normandy, where he spent most of his youth. He studied humanities with Maurice de Guérin* at Collège Stanislas and law at the university at Caen where his friend, Guillaume-Stanislas Trébutien (1800–1870) initiated him into liberal thinking. Though family misfortune forced him to take work as a journalist in Paris, he lived as a dandy and assumed the demeanor of an ancien régime aristocrat. He publicly adhered to Catholicism and monarchism; however, his private life and works attest to the influence of passion. He was strongly dependent on alcohol and drugs until 1852, when he was cured by a companion, a widowed baroness, Madame de Bouglon. After initial attempts at poetry, a novel, *L'Amour impossible* (*The Impossible Love*, 1841), and an essay, *Du dandysme et de George Brummel* (*On Dandyism and George Brummel*, 1845), he shocked Catholic and aristocratic circles with his violent novel, *Une Vieille Maîtresse* (*An Old Mistress*, 1851). *L'Ensorcelée* (*The Bewitched Woman*, 1854), *Le Chevalier des Touches* (1864), and *Un Prêtre marié* (*A Married Priest*, 1865) continued the violence and added the darkness and superstition of his native land. His best-known work is *Les Diaboliques* (*The Diabolics*, 1874), a collection of short stories depicting the battle between the forces of good and evil in the world. Others include *Une Histoire sans nom* (*Story without a Name*, 1882), *Ce qui ne meurt pas* (*That Which Does Not Die*, 1884), and an important critical work, *Le Dix-neuvième Siècle, les hommes et les oeuvres* (*The Nineteenth Century, Men and Works*, 1861–1865, 4 vols.). The publication of his works and letters is due primarily to his friends Trébutien and Louise Reid.

Barbey d'Aurevilly, with his romantic imagination, passion, expansive vision, his powerful evocations of the irrational and terrible, and his spiritualism, disliked the naturalists (see naturalism**), positivists (see positivism*), and Parnassians* of his day. He was admired by the symbolists (see symbolism**), who saw in him a precursor.

For further information, see D. Aynesworth, "The Telling of Time in *L'Ensorcelée*," *Modern Language Notes* 98 (4) (May 1983): 639–656; C. Bernheimer, "Female Sexuality and Narrative Closure: Barbey's '*La Vengeance d'une femme*' and '*A un diner d'athées*,'" *Romanic Review* 74 (3) (May 1983): 330–341; E. Mickel, "Barbey d'Aurevilly and Fromentin: Classic Esthetic Values in a Romantic Context," *Symposium* 35 (4) (Winter 1981–1982): 292–306; A. Moger, "Godel's 'Incompleteness Theorem' and Barbey: Raising Story to a Higher Power," *SubStance* 12 (4 [41]) (1983): 17–30; M. Scott, "Sexual Ambivalence and Barbey d'Aurevilly's *Le Chevalier des Touches*," *Forum for Modern Language Studies* 19 (1) (January 1983): 31–42.

BARBIER, HENRI-AUGUSTE (1805–1882), minor romantic (see romanticism*) poet, is the author of several collections of satirical poems. After studying law and working with novelist and later opera director Alphonse Royer (1803–1875) on a historical novel, *Les Mauvais Garçons* (*The Bad Boys,* 1830), he found immediate fame with "La Curée" ("The Rush for Spoils," 1830), a bitter satire against the profit-mongers after the revolution of 1830, which he published in the *Revue de Paris*. His first collection of poems, *Iambes* (1831), contained this and other well-known poems, "Quatre-vingt-treize" ("Ninety-three"), "L'Emeut" ("The Uprising"), "L'Idole" ("The Idol"), all directed against the politics and morals of the times. After *Il Pianto* (*The Weeper,* 1833), about Italy, and *Lazare* (1837), against English industrialism, he continued to write but never equalled the renown of his first poems.

Barbier continued the tradition of Chénier* in his political satire and indignation against corruption and immorality. His forceful, eloquent verses earned him accolades as the greatest political satirist of the 1830s. However, his glory was shortlived. Nearly forgotten, he died in 1882 in Nice.

BARBIER DE SEVILLE, LE, OU LA PRECAUTION INUTILE (*The Barber of Seville or Useless Precaution,* 1775), by Beaumarchais,* along with *Le Mariage de Figaro** (*The Marriage of Figaro,* 1784), with its gaiety, wit, intrigue, and satire, breathed freshness and vigor back into French comedy, which, for thirty years after the death of Marivaux,* had become stale and mediocre. While its subject matter, that of an old man tricked out of marriage right under his nose by the young woman he hoped to marry, is hardly original (the same theme is found in Molière's [1622–1673] *L'Ecole des femmes—School for Women,* 1662; and Paul Scarron's [1610–1660] *La Précaution inutile—Useless Precaution,* 1655), his presentation of scenes swiftly following one after another, unexpected turns of plot, and witty dialogue reveal a genius for comedy that is uniquely Beaumarchais's. He wrote in a letter to baron de Breteuil (1730–1807), "While surrendering myself to my true personality, I have tried, in the *Barbier de Séville,* to bring back to the theatre its former unrestrained gaity and unite it with the lightness, finesse, and delicacy of our present brand of humor." He adds to the comedy the social criticism indigenous to the eve of the Revolution and personified by the character of Figaro.

The play may have originated as a parade.* In 1772, Beaumarchais transformed it into an opéra-comique,* which was refused by the Comédie italienne, allegedly because its principal singer had been a barber and feared comparisons with Figaro. It was rewritten as a comedy in four acts and accepted by the Comédie-Française in 1773, but presentation was delayed because of Beaumarchais's lawsuit with Magistrate Goëzman. (Beaumarchais had attempted, in 1778, to bribe the judge in a dispute over a will. When the judge accused him of corruption, Beaumarchais countered with scathing attacks against lawyers in his pamphlets.) Meanwhile Beaumarchais expanded the play into five acts, according to the rules of high comedy, and when it was performed in February 1775, it met with resounding failure. Three days of revisions resulted in the four-act version whose immediate success has endured for more than two hundred years. *Le Barbier* has been hailed as the best conceived and best executed of Beaumarchais's comedies.

The plot revolves around the efforts of the Spanish count Almaviva, aided by his former valet-turned-barber, Figaro, to woo and marry a beautiful young orphan, Rosine, who is kept under lock and key by her elderly guardian and tutor, Bartholo, who also has designs on her. Calling himself Lindor, a bachelor, Almaviva serenades Rosine at dawn beneath her window; Rosine drops him a letter. Bartholo is apprised by Bazile, Rosine's music teacher, that Almaviva is in town and resolves to marry her on the morrow. Meanwhile, the count, disguised as a drunken cavalier, enters the house to ask for lodging and slips a letter to Rosine. Bartholo, suspicious, refuses the request and asks Rosine for the letter. Luckily, she substitutes another in its place. Almaviva enters again, this time disguised as Alonzo, student of Bazile, who sent him to replace the music master, who is allegedly sick. To gain Bartholo's confidence, he gives him a letter written by Rosine to the count. Rosine's music lesson turns into a love session at the piano while Bartholo dozes in the room. Figaro comes to groom Bartholo and divert him from the couple. When a healthy Bazile eventually shows up for the lesson, Figaro, the count, Rosine, and even Bartholo himself, in the comedy's most humorous and memorable scene, convince him, with a sum of money, to go back to bed. Finally, Bartholo, realizing that he has been duped, tells Rosine that Almaviva is actually an emissary of the count, who has betrayed her. Convinced, she reveals Almaviva's plans to visit her that night and promises to marry Bartholo. While he seeks the authorities, Almaviva arrives, followed soon after by Bazile and a notary, who marries them both. When Bartholo returns, it is too late. All of his precautions have, indeed, been useless.

BAUDELAIRE, CHARLES (1821–1867). See *Dictionary of Modern French Literature, from Naturalism and Symbolism to Post-Modernism.*

BAYLE, PIERRE (1647–1706), Protestant scholar and philosopher, lived most of his life in the seventeenth century yet incarnated the skepticism, the quest for truth, and the ideal of religious toleration of the next. He has been called the "first representative of the critical spirit of the eighteenth century" (Marcel Braunschvig, *Notre Littérature étudiée dans les textes* [*Our Literature Studied in Texts*] Paris: Armand Colin, 1921); and his major work, *Dictionnaire historique et critique* (*Historical and Critical Dictionary,* 1697), the "arsenal" from which the philosophes* of the eighteenth century freely drew (G. Lanson, P. Tuffrau, *Manuel d'histoire de la littérature française* [*History Manual of French Literature*] Paris: Hachette, 1931).

Bayle was born in Carla in the south of France. His father, a Protestant minister, taught him Latin and Greek; he studied at the Protestant academy of Puylaurens. He studied with the Jesuits in Toulouse, converted to Catholicism in

1669 but relapsed into Protestantism the following year. He fled to Geneva, where he completed his education. He became a tutor in Paris, then professor of philosophy at the Protestant Academy of Sedan in 1675. When that institution was closed in 1681, he and his colleague, Pierre Jurieu (1637–1713), professor of theology, fled to Rotterdam, where he taught philosophy and history at L'Ecole Illustre and did the bulk of his writing. His first work, *Pensées sur la comète de 1680* (*Thoughts on the Comet of 1680*, 1682), regarded the comet as a natural phenomenon, not as a miracle, as it had been traditionally regarded by poets and historians. Comets did not presage misfortune anymore than "a man's leaving his house is the cause of people passing in the street all day." Bayle's nascent scientific spirit questioned, in lengthy digressions, authority and superstition and fostered his belief that morality and religion were separate and that morality existed independent of religion. For Bayle, it was possible for atheists to help the poor, oppose injustice, be faithful to friends. *Commentaire philosophique sur ces paroles de Jesus-Christ: "Contrains-les d'entrer"* (*Philosophical Commentary on These Words of Jesus Christ: "Compel Them to Enter,"* 1686), a study of Luke's parable of a lord's inviting hesitant guests to his great supper, used by St. Augustine as a pretext for forced compliance with Catholicism, is a plea for religious toleration long before that of Voltaire.* Bayle reasoned that since it is impossible for us to know absolute truth, people should be permitted their own versions of it. "The main thing," he writes, "is then to act virtuously; and thus each one must use all his forces to honor God by a prompt obedience to morality." The *Dictionnaire historique et critique,* originally conceived to correct errors in Louis Moréri's (1643–1680) *Grand Dictionnaire historique* (*Great Historical Dictionary,* 1674), is a critical examination of historical and philosophical topics that reveals the errors, lies, and uncertainties propagated by unquestioning historians and philosophers. Couched in extensive notes and cross-references pertaining to the entries, a system later used by the Encyclopédists (see *L'Encyclopédie**), are attacks on religious dogma, superstition, and tyranny. According to Norman L. Torrey (in *Les Philosophes,* 1980), Bayle's dictionary "supplied both the weapons and methods with which the authoritarian principles of the Old Regime were destroyed."

Bayle's former colleague, Jurieu, worked to have him condemned as an atheist by Dutch Protestant authorities; he was removed from his university chair and lived his last years in poverty. His other works include *Critique générale de l'histoire du Calvinisme du P. Maimbourg* (*General Criticism of the History of the Calvinism of P. Maimbourg,* 1682); *Nouvelles de la république des lettres* (*News from the Republic of Letters,* 1684–1687), a review of contemporary literature and events; *La France toute catholique sous Louis-le-Grand* (*An Entirely Catholic France under Louis the Great,* 1685); *Avis aux réfugiés* (*Advice to Refugees,* 1690); and pamphlets on the revocation of the Edict of Nantes.

BEAUMARCHAIS, PIERRE-AUGUSTIN CARON DE (1732–1799), playwright best known for two comedies, *Le Barbier de Séville** (*The Barber of*

Seville) and *Le Mariage de Figaro** (*The Marriage of Figaro*), created one of the most unforgettable of French figures, Figaro. He was born in Paris; like J.-J. Rousseau's,* his father was a clockmaker. At age thirteen, he quit school to make watches and in 1753 invented a mechanism to improve them. When his invention was stolen by Jean Lepaute (1720–1787), his ingenuity and articulate defense of it before the Academy of Science won the admiration of the court and earned him the title of King's Watchmaker. In 1755, he bought the position of official clerk of the king's house (Contrôleur clerc d'office de la maison du roi) from Pierre-Augustin Francquet and married his widow when Francquet died a year later. Though his wife died within ten months, Beaumarchais took his name from one of her properties, the ''bois'' (woods) Marchais. A talented musician, he taught harp to the daughters of Louis XV. While at court, he met Lenormant d'Etiolles, husband of Madame de Pompadour (1721–1764), mistress of the king, for whom he wrote parades* between 1757 and 1763, notably *Les Députés de la Halle et du Gros-Caillou* (*The Deputies of La Halle and of Gros-Caillou*), *Colin et Colette, Jean bête à la foire* (*Jean the Fool at the Fair*). He also befriended Joseph Paris-Duverney (1684–1770), noted financier, and acquired a fortune in supplying arms to the royal army. In 1761, he bought the post of secretary to the king, thus entering the nobility; two years later, he became lieutenant general of the hunt. Thus he assured his social and financial position.

From 1764 to 1765, he went to Madrid on business with the Spanish government for Paris-Duverney (and in the process offered the king of Spain his own mistress) and to defend the honor of his sister, scorned by her intended, Spanish journalist José Clavijo y Fajardo (1726–1806), who refused to marry her. His fourth *Mémoire* (1774) relates his Spanish adventure, which Johann Wolfgang von Goethe (1749–1832) presented in his play *Clavigo* (1774).

Well entrenched in the Parisian upper-crust by this time, Beaumarchais turned to the theatre as a diversion from his business affairs and wrote two mediocre drames,* à la Diderot.* *Eugénie* (1767) was a failure but was saved by a rewrite of the last two acts. Its preface, *Essai sur le genre dramatique sérieux* (*Essay on the Serious Dramatic Genre*), summarized his belief in drama as the wave of future theatre. *Les Deux Amis ou Le Négociant de Lyon* (*The Two Friends or The Merchant from Lyon,* 1770), on the theme of business, also failed. He remarried in 1768; his second wife died two years later. Paris-Duverney also died in 1770, setting off a struggle with the comte Falcoz de La Blache, his legal heir. Beaumarchais won; La Blache appealed; and in 1773, the case came before Judge Goezman. Beaumarchais, afraid of losing the case, left prison (where he had been incarcerated after a quarrel with the duke of Chaulnes) and offered gifts of 100 louis and a watch to Madame Goezman. When he lost the case, Madame returned the gifts minus 15 louis, which had gone to a secretary. Beaumarchais, enraged, wrote four *Mémoires* against Goezman, read by all of Europe; the judge countered with charges of corruption. When the case was heard in 1774, both parties were blamed. Goezman was removed from office, his wife condemned, and Beaumarchais reprimanded. His *Mémoires* were ordered burned.

Though still a popular figure, Beaumarchais was forced to remain in the shadows. He became an undercover agent for the king and travelled to London to stop pamphlets against Madame du Barry (1743–1793), mistress of the aging Louis XV. He went to Holland and Vienna in pursuit of a government enemy and again to London to negotiate with the Chevalier d'Eon, who was threatening to blackmail the government. In 1775, he founded a fictitious business and navigational company, Roderigue, Hortalez et Cie, to supply arms to the American colonies. That same year he presented *Le Barbier de Séville,* after a two-year delay. By 1778, the judgment in his case against Goezman was overruled and Beaumarchais was reinstated by the king and new parliament. He continued to supply munitions to 25,000 American insurgents without being paid for them. In 1777, he founded the Society of Dramatic Authors for the protection of their rights, to which Marmontel* and Sedaine,* among others, belonged. He undertook the publication of the complete works of Voltaire,* known as the Kehl edition after its publication in Germany, which appeared from 1783 to 1790. Though he lost money in the enterprise, Beaumarchais succeeded in saving much of Voltaire's works. In 1784, *Le Mariage de Figaro* was finally performed at the Comédie-Française and enjoyed a rousing success after scrutiny by six censors and Louis XVI himself, who had declared a year earlier that it would never be played. Beaumarchais was jailed once again for badmouthing the philosophe* Jean-Baptiste Suard (1733–1817) but was released four days later by the comte d'Artois. In 1786, Beaumarchais remarried, this time to Mademoiselle de Willermaula, who outlived him until 1816. In 1787, his opera *Tarare,* based on an Oriental theme and written in collaboration with Antonio Salieri (1750–1825), was performed at the Theatre of the Royal Academy of Music (The Opera). In 1792, he presented *L'Autre Tartuffe ou La Mère coupable (The Other Tartuffe or The Guilty Mother)*, a disappointing drame* larmoyante (see comédie larmoyante*) (tear-jerker) after his two rousing successes.

By the outbreak of the Revolution, Beaumarchais was considered suspect, largely because of an ostentatious house he built directly across from the Bastille. He was jailed, barely missed being massacred, was saved by an influential mistress, and fled to Holland, London, and Germany, where he remained until 1796. He returned to France, old, deaf, and disappointed; yet he managed to reestablish his fortune before he died three years later.

It is often said that Beaumarchais's life itself reads like a novel. It provided a rich source for his writing. He turned to the theatre as a diversion from the exigencies of the life of an adventurer, courtier, and businessman. He began with the light-hearted parades performed for the salons. Indeed, *Le Barbier* may have its origins here. He soon turned, however, to drame, a serious, moralizing genre founded in realism,* which proved ill-suited to his genius. Comedy, rather, was his forte. Though he wrote only two, they were masterpieces that restored the "franche gaieté" (unrestrained gaiety) of Molière (1622–1673) to the theatre and added to it the social satire of the philosophes. His comedies transposed the undercurrent of social unrest into a comic spectacle enjoyed by everyone from the king to the bourgeoisie and down to the people. They lack the depth of character portrayal of the seventeenth-century master and have been criticized as unoriginal reruns of plays by Molière ("L'Ecole des femmes"—"School for Women," 1662), Paul Scarron (1610–1660), Sedaine, and others; however, his comedies excel in dialogue and plot, with comic situations following rapidly one after the other, and abound in surprise and ingenuity. The moderate satire of *Le Barbier*, directed primarily against doctors, writers, and judges, bursts into full flower in *Le Mariage*, where Figaro, the valet, outwits his master. Beaumarchais succeeded in portraying one character who has endured—Figaro—the incarnation of the people, their gaiety, wit, confidence, and ability to survive. For this, and for his own skepticism and audacity, Beaumarchais has been called a precursor of modern comedy.

For further information, see M.E.C. Bartlet, "Beaumarchais and Voltaire's *Samson*," *Studies in Eighteenth Century Culture* 11 (1982): 33–49; R. Runte, "Beaumarchais' *La Mère Coupable*," *Kentucky Romance Quarterly* 29 (2) (1982): pp. 181–189; J. Undank, "Beaumarchais' Transformations," *Modern Language Notes* 100 (4) (September 1985): pp. 829–870.

BECQUE, HENRY-FRANÇOIS (1837–1899), dramatic playwright whose play *Les Corbeaux** is a masterpiece of realism* in nineteenth-century theatre, was born in Paris, the son of a bank worker. He attended the Lycée Bonaparte and was employed variously as a clerk for the Chemins de Fer du Nord, in the Chancellery of the Legion of Honor, and in a stockbroker's office. None of his plays brought him financial success, and despite a government pension toward the end of his life, he lived most of his days in poverty. He died in 1899, a shock victim, after a fire in his bedroom.

Becque's first work was a libretto for the opera *Sardanapale* (1867). He wrote a vaudeville play, *L'Enfant prodigue* (*The Prodigal Son*, 1868) and a social play, *Michel Pauper* (1870), which failed along with his next, *L'Enlèvement* (*The Kidnapping*, 1871). *Les Corbeaux*, produced at the Théâtre Français in 1882, after a five-year struggle to bring it to the stage, shocked its audience with its harsh realism and pessimism but won a measure of success for its author. *La Parisienne* (*The Parisian Woman*), presented in 1885, pushed the realism even further, exposing mercilessly the duplicity behind a seemingly respectable marriage. After *La Parisienne*, Becque retired from theatre, writing only short sketches and articles. He began a final piece, *Les Polichinelles* (*The Marionettes*), about politics and high finance, which remains unfinished. Despite the paucity of his output, Becque exerted a tremendous influence over the development of French theatre. He spurned the "pièces bien faites" ("well made plays" of Augier* and Scribe*; he disapproved of naturalism** in the theatre. His plays are careful presentations of daily life and human nature, classic in their simplicity and restraint, but powerful and frank in their vision. Becque outdid Dumas fils* with his realism and prepared the way for André Antoine's** Théâtre libre (Free Theatre).

BERANGER, PIERRE-JEAN (1780–1857), popular and national songwriter who sang the praises of Napoleon and the common man, has been called the greatest French songwriter ever. He was born in Paris, abandoned by his father and mother, and raised by an aunt, an innkeeper, in Péronne in Picardy. A mediocre student, he left school at thirteen to become a printer's apprentice. He returned to Paris and around 1802 began writing poetry. In 1804, the poverty-stricken young poet sent some verses to Lucien Bonaparte, brother of Napoleon, who procured him a small pension and, five years later, clerical employment in a university. His early songs spread by word of mouth, as he often neglected to write them down. In 1813, he was elected to "Le Caveau," a literary club founded in 1729 by Piron* and the elder Crébillon.* In 1815, his first collection, *Chansons morales et autres* (*Moral Songs and Others*), appeared, containing his most famous piece, "Le Roi d'Yvetot" ("The King of Yvetot"), a satire against Napoleon's despotism. The first book escaped censure, but the next, *Chansons, 2e receuil* (*Songs, Second Collection,* 1821), did not. These daring, liberal verses against the Restoration cost Béranger his university post. He was fined and jailed but found imprisonment more comfortable than his normal life and while there composed a third collection of songs, *Chansons nouvelles* (*New Songs,* 1825). *Chansons inédites* (*Unedited Songs,* 1828) earned him another prison term for its Bonapartist sympathies. After *Chansons nouvelles et dernières* (*New and Last Songs,* 1833), directed against the July monarchy, Béranger retired. In 1848, he was elected to the assembly, but resigned soon afterward. He retired again but was not forgotten. He was visited by the literary and political giants of the age—Adolphe Thiers,* Pierre Laffitte (1823–1903), Chateaubriand,* Michelet,* Lamennais*—and loved by the people. His death was mourned by all of France.

Béranger's songs, "Le Vieux drapeau" ("The Old Flag"), "Le Roi d'Yvetot," and "Les Souvenirs du peuple" ("The Memories of the People"), ranged from mordant political satire to light-hearted pieces sung by the common man. A staunch republican, he kept the spirit of Voltaire* and the French Revolution alive well into the nineteenth century.

For further information, see H. Fremont, "General Lafayette and songwriter Béranger," *Gazette of the American Friends of Lafayette* (Lafayette College, Easton, Pa.: American Friends of Lafayette, April 1983).

BERNARDIN DE SAINT-PIERRE, JACQUES-HENRI (1737–1814), like his friend J.-J. Rousseau,* was a poet, painter, and apostle of nature. His works, especially *Etudes de la nature* (*Studies of Nature,* 1784) and *Paul et Virginie** (1787), evince the dawn of preromanticism.* He was born in Le Havre, travelled to Martinique at age twelve, and after his early education enrolled in the Ecole des Ponts et Chaussées (School of Bridges and Roadways, Engineering School). He became an engineer in 1758 and from 1761–1766 travelled to Malta, Holland, Russia, and Poland and spent two years (1769–1771) as the king's engineer in Maurituis. However, his temperament, given to dreams of founding an ideal republic, was ill-suited to the task. He returned to France, published his *Voyage à l'Ile de France* (*Voyage to Marituis,* 1773), aligned himself with the Encyclopedists* until he befriended Rousseau, and, thanks to a pension, dedicated himself to literature. With Rousseau's encouragement, he began his life's work in 1773, *Etudes de la nature*; its first three volumes appeared in 1784. The enormously successful *Paul et Virginie,* comprising its fourth and last volume, appeared in 1787. Bernardin's popularity, like that of his mentor Rousseau, grew to epic proportions. He published one other work, less successful than *Paul et Virginie, La Chaumière indienne* (*The Indian Cottage,* 1790). During the Revolution, he was named intendant of the Jardin des Plantes and professor of ethics at the Ecole Normale Supérieure. In 1795, he was elected to the National Institute (Academie française). He enjoyed the favor of Napoleon and King Joseph until his death in 1814.

Etudes de la nature illustrates Bernardin's Rousseauistic beliefs in the goodness of man and the perfection of nature (which exists to supply man's needs) and his dream of a more natural society. *Paul et Virginie* depicts the absolute happiness found in the innocence of primitive life in accordance with nature and virtue away from the evils of civilization. His story of two young lovers is now seen as naive and dated; his demonstrations of nature's goodness, puerile and silly. For example, he claims that nature illuminates rocks in the dark sea with white foam to prevent shipwrecks and, in *Harmonies de la nature* (*Harmonies of Nature,* written, 1796; published, 1815), that fruits are brightly colored for man to find easily amid their dark leaves. However, his descriptions of nature—its colors, sounds, smells, and exotic beauty,—creating a canvas with words instead of brushstrokes, remain eloquent and moving. Senancour* and Chateaubriand* appreciated his art, his love of solitude, ruins, and nature and stepped closer to romanticism* because of it.

Other works by Bernardin de Saint-Pierre include *L'Arcadie* (*Arcadia,* Book 1, 1788; Fragments of Books 2 and 3 published by L. Aimé-Martin, 1836); *Café de Surate* (1790); *La Vie et les ouvrages de J.-J. Rousseau* (*The Life and Works of J.-J. Rousseau,* posthumous, 1820); and *Les Voeux d'un solitaire* (*The Wishes of a Solitary Man,* 1790).

For further information, see L. Jordanova, "Natural Facts: A Historical Perspective on Science and Sexuality," in C. MacCormack and M. Strathern, eds., *Nature, Culture and Gender* (Cambridge: Cambridge University Press, 1980), 42–69; R. Runte, "*La Chaumière indienne*: Counterpart and Complement to *Paul et Virginie*," *Modern Language Review* 75 (October 1980): 774–780; Runte, "*La Chaumière indienne*: A Study in Satire," *French Review* 53 (March 1980): 557–565.

BERQUIN, ARNAUD (1749–1791), popular writer of idylls and romances, is best remembered for his collection of stories for children, *Lectures pour les enfants, ou Choix de petits contes et drames également propres à les amuser et à leur inspirer le goût de la vertu* (*Readings for Children, or Choice of Little Stories and Dramas Equally Suited to Amuse Them and Inspire Them with the*

Love of Virtue, 1784) and *L'Ami des enfants* (*The Friend of Children*, 1782). His stories, often imitated from the English or German, are noted for their naturalness and sensitivity. A twenty-volume complete edition of his works was published in 1803.

BERTRAND, ALOYSIUS (1807–1841, born Louis Bertrand), minor romantic (see romanticism*) poet who also dabbled in the theatre, is best known for his prose poems. He was born in Ceva in the Piedmont region of Italy, the son of a police captain and an Italian woman. In 1814, they settled in Dijon. In 1828, he went to Paris, where his poetry drew the attention of Hugo,* Nodier,* Sainte-Beuve,* and other members of the cénacle.* However, he was extremely poor, having no family wealth and little inclination to work. In 1830, finances forced him to leave Paris for Dijon; he returned only two years later. Details of his life upon his return are sketchy except for his poverty and tuberculosis. He died in 1841 of consumption.

Bertrand's prose poems found no publisher during his lifetime. A year after his death, Sainte-Beuve and painter David d'Angers (1788–1856) had them published as *Gaspard de la nuit, fantaisies à la manière de Rembrandt et de Callot* (*Gaspard of the Night, Fantasies in the Manner of Rembrandt and Callot*, 1842). The poems are divided into six parts, "École flamande" ("Flemish school"), going back to the sixteenth and seventeenth centuries; "Le Vieux Paris" ("Old Paris"), depicting medieval Paris; "La Nuit et ses prestiges" ("Night and its Marvels"); "Les Chroniques" ("Chronicles"); "Espagne et Italie" ("Spain and Italy"); and "Silves." These poems, inspired by the architecture and history of medieval Dijon, painted that illusory world midway between dream and reality and inhabited by angels and fairies, devils, magicians, sprites and dwarves, as well as people. Their lyrical incantations inspired Baudelaire,** who asked in the dedication of his *Le Spleen de Paris* (*The Spleen of Paris*, 1869), "Who among us has not dreamed, in his ambitious days, of a poetic prose, musical without rhythm or rhyme, supple and distinct enough to adapt to the lyrical movements of the soul, to the undulations of revery, to the quick movements of the conscience." Bertrand's poetry also influenced Mallarmé** and the surrealists (see surrealism*).

BEYLISM is the system devised by Stendhal* in which "the happy few" find happiness. The term comes from Stendhal's true name, Henri Beyle. Stendhal believed that only the "pursuit of happiness" mattered in life and that happiness could be found by the free exercise of one's intelligence and passions. Like the empirical philosophes* Helvétius* and Condillac,* Stendhal believed that the senses were the basis of all knowledge, that ideas and character come from our sensations. By rejecting traditional religion and morality, and obeying our reason, we gain power over nature and fellow man. Thus, knowledge can lead to happiness.

Those most likely to attain happiness are original nonconformist types, insulated from the exigencies of social interaction and unconcerned for others. They mistrust others, challenge authority, believe only that which they can verify for themselves. Facts are the only certainties in the world and must be ascertained without error. Yet, while a member of the elite unveils the mysteries of the hostile world, he must shroud himself with secrecy, hide behind a veil of hypocrisy, guile, and cunning in order to protect his independence and integrity. Introspection and self-study can determine the hurdles, social and personal, in the path to happiness. These can systematically be removed by inflexible will and intellectual independence. Happiness, for Stendhal, exceeded mere sensual pleasure. It consisted of intense emotion, intellectual satisfaction, and success.

French socialist critic Léon Blum (1872–1950) saw at the heart of Beylism a contradiction between Stendhal's method, which is logical and intellectual, and his goal, happiness, which is spontaneous and incomprehensible. This contradiction, the opposition between Stendhal's intellectual needs and those of his heart, is the essence of the author and his characters.

BLANC, LOUIS (1812–1882), journalist, politician, historian, and disciple of Saint-Simon,* interpreted history in terms of socialism. He participated in the provisional government of 1848, then exiled himself to Belgium and England, not returning to France until 1870. His most important work, *L'Organisation du travail* (*The Organization of Work,* 1840), advocated reorganizing private industry into social workshops. Other works include *Histoire de dix ans, 1830–1840* (*History of Ten Years, 1830–1840,* 5 vols., 1841–1844), written against the July monarchy; and *Histoire de la Révolution française* (*History of the French Revolution,* 12 vols., 1847–1862), which considered Robespierre* and the Reign of Terror as the climax of the Revolution.

BLOY, LEON (1846–1917). See *Dictionary of Modern French Literature, from Naturalism and Symbolism to Post-Modernism.*

BONALD, LOUIS-GABRIEL-AMBROISE, COMTE DE (1754–1840), political philosopher and statesman, supported the ideals of the ancien régime, the divine authority of the church and state. He was born in Rouergue near Millau in the south of France to the lesser nobility. He served in Louis XV's corps of musketeers and was mayor of Millau for ten years before emigrating to Heidelberg. He joined the prince of Condé's army of emigrés, not returning to France until the final days of the Directory under the name of Saint-Severin. In 1808, he was named a counselor to the Imperial University. After the Restoration, he served on the council of public instruction. In 1816, he entered the Academy. He became a deputy from 1815 until 1822. In 1822, he was named minister of state and became a peer the following year. After refusing his allegiance to the July monarchy, he retired from public life in 1830 to his home at Monna, where he died in November 1840.

Along with de Maistre* and Lamennais,* de Bonald was a vigorous supporter of the theocratic school. He believed in the divine origin of society, that God, as head of the monarchy and of the Catholic church, governs the world. Therefore the Revolution was a mistake, a crime against God, and that man's salvation lie in restoring the ancien régime. De Bonald proved the existence of God in man's language, the "first truth," a gift from God that led to "subsequent truths" such as man's capacity for knowledge, thinking, and the organization of his family, political, and social structures. His *Théorie du pouvoir politique et religieux dans la société civile* (*Theory of Political and Religious Power in Civil Society,* 1796) and *Essai analytique sur les lois naturelles de l'ordre social* (*Analytical Essay on the Natural Laws of the Social Order,* 1800) combatted, in the name of Catholicism, the revolutionary ideas of the eighteenth-century philosophes,* which he held responsible for the ills of France, and predicted the return of the Bourbons to the throne. His most important work was *Legislation primitive* (*Primitive Legislation,* 1802).

For further information, see W. Reedy, "Burke and Bonald: Paradigms of Late XVIIIth Century Conservatism," *Historical Reflections* 8 (Summer 1981): 69–93.

BOREL, PETRUS (1809–1859), a minor romantic (see romanticism*) poet and storywriter who called himself the Lycanthrope (werewolf), belonged to the frénétique* school and was, for a time, the leader of the radical petit cénacle.* He was born Joseph-Pierre Borel d'Hauterive in Lyon to the lesser nobility, studied architecture in Paris but preferred literature, finding the artists' studios and cénacles of the 1830s better suited to his nature. He wrote *Rhapsodies* (1831), a collection of poems filled with hatred and revolt; *Champavert, contes immoraux* (*Champavert, Immoral Stories,* 1833), a masterpiece of the frenetic; and a novel, *Madame Putiphar* (1839); none of which met with much success. He wrote newspaper articles, farmed, and edited small journals to keep hunger at bay. In 1846, with the help of Delphine de Girardin (1804–1855), he obtained a post as colonial inspector in Algeria. He was dismissed in 1855 and lived his final years in solitude in Mostaganem, an Algerian port. He died of sunstroke in 1859.

BOVARYSME is a term derived from Flaubert's* masterpiece, *Madame Bovary,* * depicting a state of mind incarnated in the main character of that novel, Emma Bovary, and experienced in real life by many others. Flaubert wrote that "my poor Bovary suffers and cries in twenty villages in France." Bovarysme describes a pessimistic romantic condition in which one seeks an ideal of unattainable perfection but eventually must come to grips with reality. Emma Bovary aspires toward an ideal of life and love that has been shaped by romance novels and the mysticism of her convent education. After marriage, she realizes her true condition—that she lives a boring life in a small town with a mediocre husband whose intelligence and sensitivity will never equal what she perceives as hers. The novel is the story of her desperate attempts to escape.

BRIZEUX, AUGUSTE (1806–1858), minor romantic (see romanticism*) poet, is best known for his verses about his native Brittany. He was born in Lorient, raised in Arzanno by his uncle after the death of his father, studied in Arras and later in Paris, where he became friends with Vigny* and Barbier.* He divided his time between Paris, Brittany, and Italy, which he adopted as a second home. He died in Montpellier of a chest ailment.

Marie (1831, revised in 1840), his most celebrated work, is a collection of rustic idylls of his youth in the Breton countryside. *Ternaires* (Ternaries), later entitled *Fleur d'or* (*Flower of Gold,* 1841), traces a "poetic voyage from a Breton town to the cities of Italy." *Les Bretons* (1845) is a rustic epic in twenty-four strophes on the customs and manners of the region. Other works include *Primel et Nola* (1852) and *Histoires poétiques* (*Poetical Stories,* 1855).

BUFFON, GEORGES-LOUIS LECLERC, COMTE DE (1707–1788), eighteenth-century naturalist whose *Histoire naturelle* (*Natural History*), published in thirty-six volumes from 1749 to 1788, epitomizes the spirit of inquiry and the love of learning that lies at the heart of the Age of Enlightenment. Buffon was born in Bourgogne (Burgundy) to a former peasant family that had slowly improved its position through medicine and bureaucratic charges. His father was councillor of the Burgundy parliament. Buffon, also destined for a career in law, studied with the Jesuits in Dijon but showed a preference for science and mathematics, which he pursued at the University of Angers. After a quarrel and duel with a young Englishman at Angers, he returned to Dijon where he befriended Lord Kingston and travelled with him and his tutor through the south of France, Italy, Switzerland, and England from 1730 to 1738. In 1732, he took the name "Buffon" from properties inherited from his mother. The following year he was elected to the Academy of Sciences. He translated Stephen Hales's (1677–1761) *Vegetable Staticks* into French in 1735 and Isaac Newton's (1642–1727) *Fluxions* in 1740. From 1739 until his death, he served as superintendent of the king's botanical gardens, which gave him access to documents, samples, and information from all corners of the world. He enlarged the royal collections, added to his personal property in Montbard, and divided his time between his provincial estate and Paris. His *Histoire naturelle* is a monument to his research and observations, a marriage of science and art that rivalled Diderot's* *Encyclopédie** in popularity and became one of the best-selling books of the century.

The work began as a *Catalogue raisonné du cabinet du jardin royal,* (*Descriptive Catalogue of the Collection of the Royal Garden*) but soon expanded, with the help of collaborators, into an intensive study and organization of the world of nature, zoology, biology, the history of man and of the universe. It includes three volumes on the theory of the earth (*Théorie de la terre*) and natural history of man (*Histoire naturelle de l'homme,* 1749); fifteen volumes on quadrupeds (1749–1767); nine volumes on birds (1770–1783); five volumes on minerals (1783–1788); and supplements written from 1774 to 1789, which include the famous *Epoques de la nature* (*Epoches of Nature,* 1778). Louis Daubenton (1716–1800) collaborated on the quadruped volumes; Guéneau de Montbéliard (1720–1785) and Abbé Bexon (1748–1784) assisted with birds; Faujas de Saint-Fond (1741–1819), minerals. Lacépède (1756–1825) completed the work in 1789 after Buffon's death a year earlier.

The *Histoire naturelle* is the work of a savant who advanced theories and hypotheses based on detailed observation of the world around him. It presents the vast tableau of the earth's history, its transformation from a fragment of the sun into a cold, solid mass capable of supporting a chain of life extending from the mineral to the vegetable to the animal and culminating in man. Buffon places man unequivocally in the center of the universe, a being superior to all others by his reason, vigor, and the spirituality of his soul. He advises him on healthful eating, how to find happiness, and in a multitude of practical areas. He presents a series of famous animal "portraits," exact descriptions of little scientific worth of the dog, the horse, the cow, the swan, which captures more the spirit of the animals than their anatomy. With *Epoques de la nature,* Buffon returns to the theories of the earth explained in his first volume. He traces seven ages or "époques" in the formation of the earth, equates nature with God, and subordinates man to both.

Contrary to his contemporaries, the philosophes,* Buffon was conservative in politics and religion. He believed in God. His *Histoire naturelle* explores a quality of life in harmony with God and nature. When the Sorbonne identified fourteen propositions in his *Théorie de la terre* counter to the teachings of the Bible, he yielded, publishing a foreword to his fourth volume renouncing "anything which could be contrary to the account of Moses." Censorship of the *Epoques de la nature* thirty years later was stalled by the king.

Buffon was elected to the French Academy in 1753, marking his reception into that body with his renowned "Discours sur le style" ("Discourse on style"), a treatise extolling his love of order and his respect for reason. He writes that style is more important than ideas or facts; that works written "without taste, without nobility, without genius, will perish. . . . Style is man himself. . . . Style is but the order and movement which one puts in one's thoughts." Writers can find examples of perfect order in nature where "each work is an entity and where it [nature] works on an eternal plan from which it never strays."

During his lifetime Buffon enjoyed a social and intellectual prominence second only to that of J.-J. Rousseau,* who admired his work, or Voltaire,* who scoffed that the *Histoire naturelle* was not "natural enough." He inspired Diderot, who read his work while in prison. Over time, some of Buffon's theories have proven false and parts of the *Histoire naturelle* have been criticized as pompous. Nevertheless, it remains a work respected for the perspicacity of its author and his lifelong dedication to the task. It announced the evolutionary theories of Jean-Baptiste Lamarck (1744–1829) and Charles Darwin (1809–1882). Most important, with his eloquence and imagination, Buffon elevated the field of science to an art.

For further information, see Daniel J. Boorstin, *The Discoverers* (New York: Random House, 1983), 446–457; G. Bremner, "Buffon and the Casting Out of Fear," *Studies on Voltaire and the Eighteenth Century* 205 (1982): 75–88; David Goodman, *Buffon's Natural History* (Stony Stratford, England: Open University Educational Enterprises, 1980); John Lyon and Philip H. Sloan, eds., *From Natural History to the History of Nature: Readings from Buffon and His Critics* (Notre Dame, Ind.: University of Notre Dame Press, 1981).

C

CABANIS, GEORGES (1757–1808), doctor and materialist philosopher belonging to the idéologue* school of thought, his *Traité du physique et du moral de l'homme* (*Treatise on the Physical and Moral Aspects of Man,* 1802) outlined the relationships between man's physical and his spiritual being. He believed that the brain produces thoughts through a psycho-physiological mechanism as naturally as the stomach produces digestive juice.

CANDIDE (1759), by Voltaire,* a philosophical tale in thirty chapters, is generally recognized as his masterpiece. Written shortly after the Lisbon earthquake and the Seven Years' War, which swiftly followed his personal disappointment at the death of Madame du Châtelet and his disillusionment at King Frederick's Prussian court, the story reflects Voltaire's increasing pessimism at his own circumstances and the world around him. In the face of the optimism of German philosopher Gottfried Wilhelm Leibnitz (1646–1716) and his disciple Jean Christian Wolff (1679–1754), Voltaire confronts his young and innocent hero with the evils of the world—physical, spiritual, and moral—and forces him to deal with them. Candide's resolution is a clarion call for mankind to do as he has done; to face up to the reality of the world and to work to change it.

Candide, so called for his "straightforward judgment" and "simple spirit," is exiled in the very first chapter of the story from the "best of all possible worlds," the Westphalian castle of the Baron of Thunder-ten-tronckh, for wooing Cunégonde, the Baron's beautiful young daughter. Tricked into serving in the Bulgarian army, Candide witnesses first hand the horrors of war. He escapes in Holland, where he meets his former tutor, the optimist Pangloss, now a miserable, pustular tramp despite his Leibnitzian belief that everything happens for the best. Pangloss informs him of the brutal deaths of the baron's family, including Cunégonde, and the destruction of the castle. An Anabaptist, Jacques, receives the two weary, homeless men and takes them to Lisbon. An earthquake wrecks their ship; Jacques is drowned trying to save a sailor who in turn lets him drown; only the sailor, Candide, and Pangloss survive. In Lisbon, they are condemned by the Inquisition for Pangloss's beliefs on original sin and liberty. Pangloss is hanged, Candide is saved by Cunégonde, who though brutally violated and sold into slavery, was miraculously spared the terrible fate of her family. However, Candide's joy at finding his beloved is shortlived—to free her, he kills Cunégonde's masters, the Grand Inquisitor and the Jew Don Issachar, and flees with Cunégonde to America. Accompanying them is an old woman, the daughter of a princess and a pope, who has been mutilated and sold into slavery. Nearly captured in Buenos Aires, Candide leaves Cunégonde in the hands of the governor, who is much attracted by her beauty, and flees with his valet Cacambo to the Jesuit rulers of Paraguay. To his surprise, Candide recognizes the Jesuit "commandant" as Cunégonde's brother, who warmly receives him but refuses to permit his marriage to Cunégonde because of Candide's lack of noble birth. Unwittingly, Candide draws his sword and kills him.

Disguised as a Jesuit, Candide escapes with Cacambo, kills two monkeys pursuing two Oreillon women, who surprisingly, turn out to be their lovers. The Oreillon tribe, enraged and believing Candide is a Jesuit, threatens to roast and eat the two men; however, Cacambo convinces them of their true identity and motives. Released, they brave the mountains, rivers, rapids, and reefs leading to Eldorado, the mythic land of gold-paved streets and beautiful, virtuous people, where neither priests, parliaments, nor prisons are necessary. After a pleasant stay, they leave with thirty sheep loaded with gold and jewels ("the rocks and mud of Eldorado"). The road is treacherous, all but two of the sheep die along the road to Surinam where they meet a half-clothed slave missing a leg and a hand. ("This is the price paid for the sugar you eat in Europe," the slave informs them.) Candide sends Cacambo to Buenos Aires to buy Cunégonde's freedom, is tricked out of his remaining two sheep by the Dutch merchant Vanderdendur, and finally sails for Venice after locating, among a boatload of contenders, the honest man who is "the most disgusted with his condition and the most unhappy in the land."

The pessimist and philosopher Martin who "had nothing to hope for" wins the prize of free passage to Bordeaux with Candide. Along the way, Candide recovers one of his stolen sheep; Candide and Martin endlessly "talk, exchange ideas and console each other." From Bordeaux, they go to Paris, where they attend the theatre; Candide is duped by a false Cunégonde and loses his money. He and Martin travel to Venice, witnessing the execution of Admiral Byng (for having "not killed enough people") in London along the way. In Venice, Candide, now desperate for Cunégonde, rediscovers Paquette, the Baron's former servant in Westphalia; visits Prococurante, a dissatisfied Venetian nobleman; and dines with six dethroned kings visiting the carnival to forget their disappointments.

Candide and Martin depart for Constantinople, meet Cacambo, now a slave, who informs them of Cunégonde's ill fate—she has become a horribly ugly slave—and find that Pangloss and Cunégonde's brother (whom Candide hadn't killed, after all) are galley-slaves. Candide sells the last of his diamonds to free them all, including the old woman; marries Cunégonde over the persistent objections of her brother (whom he happily returns to the galleys); and settles down on a small farm. They visit a local dervish, supposedly the best philosopher in Turkey, who slams the door on their questions about the meaning of life, and meet an old man on the way home, who encourages them to stop wasting their efforts on vain metaphysical speculation and to work, instead, for work dispels man's three greatest evils—boredom, vice, and need. Heeding his advice, they stop worrying and find happiness in working their farm.

Candide can be read as a novel of edification, the story of its hero's awakening to the reality of evil in the world and his response to it. It has been seen as a translation of the events of Voltaire's own life—his initial naiveté, his travels, education, and his retreat to Les Délices and Ferney, where he "cultivated his garden." Like other stories and treatises he has written, it is a philosophical tract. Satire on human nature, justice, war, religion, slavery, tyranny, prostitution, metaphysics, and the philosophy of optimism abounds. The rapidity and diversity of the action, the vivacity, irony, and humor relieve much of the horror Candide meets in life. Finally, *Candide* represents a positive response to that horror, a call to action, a belief that man can and should work to improve his lot, or in the case of Voltaire, the lot of humanity.

For further information, see D. DiOrio, "Narrative Geometry Compared in Voltaire's *Candide* and Diderot's *Jacques le fataliste,*" *Re: Artes Liberales* 9 (2) (Spring 1983): 11–14; C. Doyle and R. Unger, "Dr. Pangloss and Anne Greene of Oxfordshire," *Romance Notes* 24 (2) (Winter 1983): 174–178; R. Francis, "Prévost's *Cleveland* and Voltaire's *Candide,*" *Studies on Voltaire and the Eighteenth Century* 208 (1982): 295–303; J. Grieder, "Orthodox and Paradox: The Structure of *Candide,*" *French Review* 57 (October 1983): 485–492; P. Henry, "Sacred and Profane Gardens in *Candide,*" *Studies on Voltaire and the Eighteenth Century* 176 (1979): 133–153; P. Kivy, "Voltaire, Hume and the Problem of Evil," *Philosophy and Literature* 3 (Fall 1979): 211–224; C. Levin, "*Gulliver* and *Candide*: a Comparative Study of Narrative Techniques," in *Transactions of the Fifth International Congress on the Enlightenment,* vol. 3 (Oxford: Taylor Institution, 1981), 1317–1324; R. McGregor, "Heraldic Quarterings and Voltaire's *Candide,*" *Studies on Voltaire and the Eighteenth Century* 183 (1980): 83–87; McGregor, "Pangloss' Final Observation, an Ironic Flaw in Voltaire's *Candide,*" *Romance Notes* 20 (Spring 1980): 361–365; R. A. Nablow, "Voltaire, *Candide,* and a Couplet from Pope," *Romance Notes* 25 (2) (Winter 1984): 160–161; G. Reed, "*Candide*: Radical Simplicity and the Impact of Evil," in E. Kurzweil and W. Phillips, eds., *Literature and Psychoanalysis* (New York: Columbia University Press, 1983), 189–200; I. C. Ross, " 'Everyone to Cultivate his Own Garden': John Evelyn, Voltaire," *Notes and Queries* 226 (June 1981): 234–237; J. Sareil, "Teaching *Candide* in Translation," *Teaching Language Through Literature* 23 (1) (December 1983): 3–14; T. Scanlan, " 'Mais' in *Candide,*" *Literatur in Wissenschaft und Unterricht* 14 (March 1981): 22–28; M. Shanley and P. Stillman, "The Eldorado Episode in Voltaire's *Candide,*" *Eighteenth Century Life* 6 (January–May 1981): 79–92; A. P. Stabler, "Voltaire Misses the Point?" *Romance*

Notes 22 (Fall 1981): 124–125; P. Stewart, "Holding the Mirror Up to Fiction: Generic Parody in *Candide*," *French Studies* 33 (October 1979): 411–419; M. J. Temmer, "*Candide* and *Rasselas* Revisited," *Revue de littérature comparée* 56 (April–June 1982): 176–193.

CARMEN (1845), by Mérimée,* is a short novel of the passion of a handsome young soldier, Don José, for his gypsy mistress, Carmen. In typical Mérimée fashion, he tells the tragic tale coolly and objectively. The idea for the story was given to him by his friend, Madame de Montijo, mother of Empress Joséphine. It was written after a visit to her palace in Madrid in 1840 for financial reasons, supposedly in order to buy himself a pair of trousers. Carmen was immortalized in Georges Bizet's (1838–1875) opera, which premiered at the Opéra-Comique* in 1875.

The novel has but four chapters. The first finds Mérimée on an archaeological trip in Andalusia in 1830, where he first meets, in a leafy glade near Cordoba, the bandit Don José. Despite the apprehension of his guide, Mérimée offers him a cigar and some ham, which, he explains, establishes "hospitable relations" between them. They spend the night in a lowly inn. Despite Mérimée's efforts to dissuade him, the guide rides off during the night to alert the authorities and win the reward for his capture. Mérimée, however, awakens Don José and allows him to escape. In chapter 2, the author is in Cordoba, where the next week, he meets Carmen, the beautiful gypsy, who takes him to her home to read his fortune. Suddenly a man, whom he recognizes as Don José, bursts into the room, yells at Carmen, and asks him to leave. When Mérimée returns to Cordoba several months later, he learns that Don José is in prison for murder and is about to be executed. He visits him there and learns the story of his relationship with Carmen and his imprisonment, which is the subject of Chapter 3.

Don José tells his visitor that he descends from an ancient Basque family who had destined him first for the church. A quarrel over a game of pelota forced him to leave his home and enter the dragoons. Well-suited to the military, he was quickly promoted to corporal and assigned to guard duty at a tobacco factory in Séville where several hundred women rolled cigars. There he first meets the beautiful and seductive Carmen, hands on her hips, a flower in her mouth, who accosts him verbally on her way into the factory. A few hours later, Don José enters the factory to quell a disturbance in which Carmen has mutilated the forehead of a woman who had insulted her. On the way to prison, he lets her escape, for which he must spend thirty days in prison and is demoted to private. While there, he receives a gift of bread in which is hidden a file and a gold piece, but Don José is too honorable to escape. After his release, he is standing guard at his colonel's house when he sees Carmen again, all aglitter and bespangled in gold and ribbons, on her way to dance at the colonel's party. On leaving, she suggests he meet her at a restaurant. She spends a day and a night with him in payment for her escape. Several weeks pass before Don José sees her again. This time he is standing guard at the city wall. Carmen promises she will see him again if he lets through some smugglers. She misses their rendezvous, however, and Don José, obsessed with seeing her again, searches everywhere for her. He finds her, eventually, in the company of a young lieutenant, whom Don José kills in an argument while suffering a serious head wound himself. Carmen hides and cares for him and soon persuades him to join her band of smugglers. With his hopes for a military career dashed, Don José accedes to her wishes and leaves the city in disguise to meet with the chief smuggler, Le Dancaire, and his cohorts, including the ugly Garcia the One-Eyed, Carmen's first husband. Don José sinks deeper into the ways of the lawless—smuggling, stealing, and killing Garcia and an Englishman. But despite his outward bravado, he is saddened by Carmen, who is unfaithful to him, and disappointed in himself. Le Dancaire is killed and Don José is wounded in a scuffle, and while Carmen nurses him back to health, he asks her to go to America to start a new, honest life with him. Carmen refuses and mocks him. In Granada, she meets a young toreador, Lucas, and follows him to a bullfight in Cordoba, where he gallantly presents her with the "cocarde" of ribbons from his bull. Lucas is wounded, and Carmen doesn't return until two in the morning. Don José asks her once again to come to America, but she refuses. Don José walks to a nearby monastery and asks the priest to say a mass for "a soul who is probably going to appear before its Creator." He waits outside the church. He hopes that Carmen has fled in the meantime, but she has remained. They mount his horse and as they head for a solitary gorge, Don José asks again if she wants to follow him. "I will follow you unto death, yes," she replies, "but I will no longer live with you." Knowing what he is about to do, she refuses to love him and to renounce her freedom for any price and tosses his ring into the bushes. In a rage, Don José strikes her twice; she dies without a sound. He digs her grave, finds the ring, and buries it and a little cross with her. He turns himself over to the authorities, but refuses to divulge her grave site.

The book ends in a final chapter on gypsies, their looks, their life, their customs and rites, which Mérimée later appended to the original three chapters.

CARMONTELLE, LOUIS CARROGIS DE (1717–1806), son of a shoe-maker, became an eighteenth-century playwright, painter, garden designer, and reader to the duke of Orleans. He was blessed with a gift for detail, being able to reproduce in a few hours silhouettes and portraits of astonishing likeness. In the theatre, his flair for realism* manifested itself in the dialogue, costumes, and social conditions of his characters. He popularized the "proverbe dramatique,"* short pieces illustrating a point or proverb which make liberal use of parody, swiftly moving dialogue, and playfulness. Collections of his more than one hundred proverbs include *Proverbes dramatiques* (*Dramatic Proverbs,* 1768), *Amusements de société* (*Social Amusements,* 1769), and *Théâtre de campagne* (*Country Theatre,* 1775). One comedy, *L'Abbé de plâtre* (*The Abbot of Plaster,* 1779), was played by the théâtre Italien.*

CASANOVA DI SEINGALT, GIACOMO GIROLAMO (1725–1798), the Italian adventurer popularly renowned as a lover, bequeathed the world a witty account of his travels, conquests, and escapades in French in twelve volumes of

Mémoires. Initially published in German from 1826 to 1832 and followed by Paul Laforgue's version (1826–1838) in proper French but devoid of Casanova's vivacity and spirit, the original text remained unpublished until 1960, when it was produced by Brockhaus (Wiesbaden) and Plon (Paris). The *Mémoires* are a curious melange of truth and fiction, an elaboration upon the events in his life before 1774 as a seminarian, soldier, violinist, diplomat, bohemian, and libertine, with a bit of philosophy and social commentary as well. Besides his *Mémoires*, Casanova wrote a novel, *Isocaméron* (1788); a verse translation of the *Iliad*; and *L'Histoire de ma fuite des prisons de Venise* (*The Story of My Flight from the Prisons of Venice*, 1788).

For further information, see M. B. Alden, "The Distillation of an Episode: Casanova's *Mémoires*—a Source for Hofmannsthal's Der Abenteurer und die Sangerin," *The German Quarterly* 53 (March 1980): 189–198; Alden, "Schnitzler's Repudiated Debt to Casanova," *Modern Austrian Literature* 3 (1980): 25–32; J. Caplan, "Vicarious *Jouissances*: or Reading Casanova," *Modern Language Notes* 100 (4) (September 1985): 803–814; Millicent Marcus, "Fellini's Casanova: Portrait of the Artist," *Quarterly Review of Film Studies* 5 (Winter 1980): 19–34.

CAZOTTE, JACQUES (1720–1792), who wrote "contes fantastiques" ("fantasies") in an age enamoured with demons, genies, and sylphs, introduced mysticism and magic into the novel. He was born in Dijon, studied with the Jesuits, practiced law, frequented literary salons, and was named "Writer in Ordinary" and later "Principal Writer" to the navy. His first literary attempts were inspired by the Orient—*Patte du chat, conte zinzimois* (*The Cat's Paw, a Zinzimois Story*, 1741) and *Mille et une fadaises* (*A Thousand and One Bits of Nonsense*, 1742). He spent ten years in Martinique as naval commissioner, where he wrote ballads and *Olivier* (1763), a heroic-comic poem in prose. He returned to France and published poetry and short stories—*Le Lord impromptu* (*The Impromptu Lord*, 1770) and his masterwork, *Le Diable amoureux* (*The Amorous Devil*, 1772). He devoted the last years of his life to esoterica and became a fervent mystic and was visited by dreams and revelations. Nerval* later pointed out that Cazotte "took his own inventions too seriously. . . . That was, it is true, the misfortune and the glory of the greatest writers of that age." Tradition has it that he foretold the coming of the Revolution, which as a royalist, cost him his life. He died on the scaffold, despite the protests of his daughter and the public.

As a master of the mystic and mysterious (his *Diable amoureux* still intrigues today), Cazotte influenced the romantic (see romanticism*) novel. Nodier* and Mérimée* are indebted to him, as well as Nerval.

CENACLE is a term that derives its meaning from the gathering of Jesus's disciples for the Last Supper ("cena" in Latin means "meal"; "la cène" in French means the "Last Supper"; "la cénacle" in French means the room in which the Last Supper took place). More broadly, it signifies any reunion, coterie, or group having similar ideas and interests. In literary history, it refers to the two groups of poets in which the principles of the romantic (see romanticism*) movement were formulated. The first cénacle consisted of the conservative poets of *La Muse française** (the Deschamps brothers, Emile [1791–1871] and Anthony [1800–1869]; Alexandre Soumet [1788–1845]; Alexandre Guiraud [1788–1847]; Chênedollé [1769–1833]; Hugo*; and Vigny*) who later met with Lamartine,* Sainte-Beuve,* Paul-François Dubois (1793–1874), and Musset* at Charles Nodier's* salon at the Arsenal* from 1824 to 1834. The second, more revolutionary cénacle met at Victor Hugo's salon on the rue Notre-Dame-des-Champs from 1828 to 1830 and included the Deschampses, Sainte-Beuve, Vigny, Dumas père,* Musset, and Balzac* and artists David d'Angers (1788–1854), Ferdinand Delacroix (1798–1863), Louis Boulanger (1806–1867) and others. It was here that new works were read and the doctrines of the romantic movement emerged until quarreling and political disagreements dispersed the group. A "cénacle de Joseph Delorme" formed around Sainte-Beuve and a "petit cénacle" of radical young romantics formed in the 1830s around Pétrus Borel.* The petit cénacle met at the studio of sculptor Jean Duseigneur (1808–1866) and included engravers Celestin Nanteuil (1813–1873) and Joseph Bouchardy (1810–1870) and writers Jules Vabre, Théophile Gautier,* Gérard de Nerval,* Philothée O'Neddy,* Alphonse Brot (1809–?), and Auguste Maquet (1813–1888). They were outrageous, totally uninhibited, and engaged in shocking behavior, all in the name of Art.

CHALLES OR CHASLES, ROBERT (1659–c. 1721), author of the best example of the early realist (see realism*) novel—*Les Illustres Françoises* (*The Illustrious Frenchwomen*, published anonymously, 1713)—was virtually unknown and unappreciated by literary historians until the discovery and republication of his novel in 1959 by Frédéric Deloffre. Little is known of the author's life. He was well educated, with influential friends, notably Jean-Baptiste Colbert's son, marquis de Seignelay (1651–1690), who sponsored his Canadian expeditions. He served in the military, participated in the French colonization of Nova Scotia, and travelled frequently between France and Canada until his capture by the British. Seigneur de Saint-Evremond (1613–1703) was instrumental in securing his return to France. He served as record keeper aboard an East India Company ship from 1690 to 1691 and lived in Paris upon his return. Mystery surrounds his life from that time until his death sometime around 1721.

He is considered the author of the sixth volume in a series of lackluster sequels to Miguel de Cervantes's (1547–1616) *Don Quixote* (1713) and a posthumous *Journal d'un voyage fait aux Indes Orientales* (*Journal of a Voyage Made to the East Indies*, 1721), based on his travels. His *Mémoires* were published in 1831 and again in 1931. However, the seven tales comprising the *Illustres Françoises* remain most significant. A popular success in the early eighteenth century, the work enjoyed a number of editions until 1780, then lapsed into oblivion until the discovery by Deloffre in the library of the University of Leyden of the correspondence between Challes and the original publisher. The novel has since enjoyed widespread acceptance by critics for its place in the history of realism. Contrary to the burlesque novels and parodies that preceded it, Challes's novel is solidly realist. It limits the role of chance and the unbelievable and is supported with realistic references to Paris, French history, and social institutions as well as seasons, weather, time, geography, money, and names. The diverse characters, who reappear in the seven stories detailing the obstacles faced by seven couples in fulfilling their love affairs, offer multiple viewpoints and thus distinguish the work from the single point of view explored in similar novels. Its influence has been shown on Prévost* and Marivaux.* Henri Coulet (*Le Roman jusqu'à la Revolution* [*The Novel Before the Revolution*], 1967) called *Les Illustres Françoises* "the masterpiece of the realist novel in its time."

CHAMFORT (1741–1794), born Nicolas-Sebastien Roch, the illegitimate son of an Auvergne woman, became, along with Vauvenargues* and Rivarol,* one of the most significant moralists of the eighteenth century. He never knew his father. He studied at Collège des Grassins in Paris, showed remarkable aptitude, and became an abbé for a short time but turned to literature as an outlet for his intelligence. He assumed the name Chamfort and earned his keep by writing sermons, journal articles, sentimental comedies—*La Jeune Indienne* (*The Young Indian*, 1764) and *Le Marchand de Smyrne* (*The Merchant of Smyrne*, 1770)—and a tragedy, *Mustapha and Géangir*, in 1778. His *Eloge de Molière* (*In Praise of Molière*) was recognized by the French Academy in 1766; *Eloge de La Fontaine* (*In Praise of La Fontaine*) was recognized in 1774 by the Academy of Marseille.

Chamfort was blessed with beauty and wit, qualities that assured his success in literary circles and salon society. Poverty and poor health, on the other hand, forced him to accept pensions. He collaborated on a *Dictionnaire des théâtres* (*Dictionary of the Theatre*, 1776) and the *Mercure* and served as secretary to the prince of Conde, a post that bored him. He retired to the solitude of Auteuil and married, though his wife died within six months. He entered the Academy in 1781 and published, ten years later, a *Discours sur les Académies* (*Discourse on Academies*), which contributed to their temporary suppression from 1793 until 1795.

It was his friendship with Mirabeau* and enthusiasm for the coming revolution that fueled his polemics: "War in the castles, peace in the cottages." He provided the title for abbé Sieyès's (1748–1836) revolutionary pamphlet, "Qu'est-ce que le Tiers-Etat? Tout. Qu'a-t-il? Rien" ("What is the Third Estate? Everything. What does it have? Nothing"). However, the excesses of republicanism likewise felt his sting. He transformed its motto "Fraternité ou la mort" ("Fraternity or death") into "Sois mon frère ou je te tue" ("Be my brother or I'll kill you"). He was considered suspect, imprisoned, and later released, but fearing reimprisonment, he attempted suicide and died soon after from his wounds. His friend, Jean-Pierre Ginguené (1748–1816), posthumously published his most significant work, *Maximes et pensées* (*Maxims and Thoughts*) and *Caractères et anecdotes* (*Portraits and Anecdotes*), containing the bulk of his ideas, under the title *Produits de la civilisation perfectionée* (*Products of Perfected Civilization*, 1795).

Chamfort's *Caractères et anecdotes* captures the manners and conversation of the "beau monde" (society or the "fashionable set") with an occasional jab at its foolishness and pretention. His *Maximes et pensées*, however, delve beneath the artifice and superficiality to reveal tellingly and cruelly the corruption of the ancien régime. Pessimism and cynicism pervade his thoughts: "To be happy in this world, there are sides of one's soul which it would be necessary to paralyze entirely"; "We must begin human society again, just as Bacon said we must begin human understanding again."

Chamfort shared the acuity and pessimism of Jean de La Bruyère (1645–1696); however, his *Maximes et pensées* lacks the psychological depth of his seventeenth-century predecessor. Though more limited in scope than those of Vauvenarges, it is important as a daring and accurate depiction of salon life on the eve of the Revolution. Stendhal* admired Chamfort's work, and German philosopher Friedrich Nietzsche (1844–1900) was influenced by it.

For further information, see G. A. Kelly, "Conceptual Sources of the Terror," *Eighteenth Century Studies* 14 (Fall 1980): 18–36; R. S. Ridgway, "Chamfort: Voltairean 'Child of Rousseau,'" *Romance Notes* 25 (1) (Fall 1984): 41–46; Ridgway, "Camus' Favourite Moralist," in *Studies on Voltaire and the Eighteenth Century*, vol. 199 (Oxford, Eng.: Taylor Institution, 1981), 363–373; Ridgway, "Chamfort's *La Jeune Indienne*: the Moralist as Playwright," *Romance Notes* 21 (Spring 1981): 334–337.

CHAMPFLEURY (1821–1889), early realist (see realism*) theoretician and writer, was born in Laon as Jules Husson. In Paris, he frequented bohemian circles that included Baudelaire,** Banville,* Henri Murger (1822–1861), and realist artist Gustave Courbet (1819–1877). He later became conservator of the collections of the Musée de Sèvres (1872) and assistant administrator of the porcelain manufacturing company. In 1856, his *Gazette de Champfleury* became the official organ of the newly forming realist school but ceased publication after its second issue for lack of funds. The following year, he brought out a volume of critical discussions entitled *Le Réalisme* (*Realism*, 1857). Champfleury traced the origins of realism back to Robert Challes's* *Les Illustres Françoises* (*The Illustrious Frenchwomen*, 1713) and to Diderot.* He believed the novelist should document his works by notating facts and traits. Like Courbet, who believed that the artist must paint only what he can see, he felt the writer should transcribe reality as a daguerreotype. Yet he recognized that as an observer, a novelist can never be totally objective; his "moi" is always present. Therefore, he must limit his interference and write simply. He disapproved of the puerile idylls of the Fourierists (see Fourierisme*), the carelessness of Sue* and Dumas père,* the lyricism of Sand,* the fantasy of the romantics (see romanticism*). Above all, he idolized Balzac.*

As a novelist and story writer, Champfleury borrowed his themes and characters from his native Laon. His realist depictions include the commonplace and the vulgar. *Chien-Cailloux* (1847) is a simple story about an engraver; *Les Aventures de Mlle Mariette* (1851) recounts the tribulations of a young writer and details the harsh reality of bohemian life. *Les Bourgeois de Molinchart,* his best-known work (1854), portrays the provincial bourgeois life. Other works include *Les Excentriques* (*The Eccentrics,* 1852), *Les Souffrances du professeur Delteil* (*The Sufferings of Professor Delteil,* 1856) and *La Succession de Camus* (*The Camus Heritage,* 1860). At its best, Champfleury's writing was influenced by his talent for caricature and humor; at its worst, it is a poor imitation of Diderot and Balzac.

For further information, see D. Flanary, *Champfleury, the Realist Writer and Art Critic* (Ann Arbor, Mich.: UMI Research, 1980); M. Weatherilt, "Champfleury: a Little-Known Precursor of Zola," *Nottingham French Studies* 20 (May 1981): 22–29.

CHANTS DU CREPUSCULE, LES (*Songs of the Dusk,* 1835), a collection of poems by Victor Hugo,* adds to the intimacy and melancholy of the *Feuilles d'automne* (*Autumn Leaves*), the political poems that he purposely omitted from the former collection. Here Hugo externalizes his poetic sensitivity, turning the personal probing of his earlier poems to a careful consideration of his era, voicing his disappointment in the monarchy, glorifying Napoleon and the imperial past. The preface reveals Hugo's preoccupation with "that strange twilight state of the soul and of the society in the age in which we are living," of that "haze on the outside, that uncertainty within," that "half-lit indefinable something which surrounds us." The poems are classic in structure, Greek in inspiration, and recall the poetry of Pindar (522?–443 B.C.). In contrast to the *Odes and Ballades* (1828) of his youth, they are considered genuine odes.

"À la Colonne" ("To the Column"), dedicated to the Austerlitz column that Napoleon had made from captured Prussian and Austrian cannon and erected in 1810, recalls the glory of Napoleon and the First Empire. He castigates those politicians fearful of the emperor's memory and prophesizes the return of his ashes despite official refusal to permit transfer of the ashes to the column. "Napoléon II" relates the birth of Napoleon's son, his life, and early death; "Hymne" celebrates France and those who died for her. Besides the political poems, love poems to Juliette Drouet, his mistress, are also included.

For further information, see E. Kaplan, "Victor Hugo and the Poetics of Doubt: The Transition of 1835–1837," *French Forum* 6 (May 1981): 140–153.

CHARTREUSE DE PARME, LA (*The Charterhouse of Parma,* 1839), by Stendhal,* often called his most brilliant novel and, according to André Gide,** among the ten best French novels ever, was written in Paris in fifty-two days while Stendhal was on leave from his diplomatic post in Civitavecchia. It combines two characteristically Stendhalian themes, his love of Italy and his interest in contemporary politics, with his sentimental yearning for the past. Stendhal took his inspiration from a short account of the life and career of Alexandre Farnèse (1468–1549), who rose to the papacy as Paul III, largely due to the intrigues of his father's beautiful sister. He transposed the action into the nineteenth century, adding his memories, impressions, and dreams to create a novel of historical, autobiographical, and psychological importance.

The novel opens in 1796, as General Bonaparte makes his triumphant entry into Milan. Fabrice del Dongo, the protagonist, is the illegitimate son of Marchesa del Dongo and a young French lieutenant. He is raised by his mother and his beautiful aunt, Gina del Dongo, both Bonapartists, at the chateau Grianta on Lake Como. Fabrice admires Bonaparte too, and at sixteen, filled with hopes of military glory, sets out to join his army. With little money and a false passport, he goes to Paris, follows one of Napoleon's battalions, but is arrested and jailed as a spy. He escapes with the help of the jailer's wife, buys a horse, and joins Marshal Ney's Hussars at the Battle of Waterloo. He loses his horse to a general who commandeers it for his own, joins a French infantry troop, and retreating from Waterloo, kills a Prussian cavalier. He, in turn, is wounded and taken to an inn, but awakens the next day to find the inn in flames. He escapes, makes his way to Geneva, and learns that his elder brother has denounced him to the Italian police as a conspirator. He returns to Grianta where his mother and aunt help him escape. Their carriage is stopped along the way by police looking for General Conti, whom they soon meet. Fabrice notices immediately the beauty of Conti's young daughter as he helps her into the carriage. Fabrice is detained in Milan, but his aunt arranges for him to study theology in Naples, where he remains for four years.

In the meantime, his aunt marries, becomes the Duchess of Sanseverina and mistress of Count Mosca, the prime minister of Parma, and gains influence at court. When Fabrice returns to Parma, her love for him arouses Mosca's jealousy. Fabrice, however, despite his appointment as alternate for the archbishop, is more concerned with the affairs of the temporal rather than the spiritual world, He frequents the theatre, falls in love with an actress, Marietta Valserra, and kills her protector, Giletti. With Giletti's passport, Fabrice, wounded, escapes with Marietta to Bologna, where they spend many happy days together until Fabrice falls for a famous singer known as Fausta. He follows her back to Parma, is recognized and, despite Gina's efforts to the contrary, is imprisoned in Farnèse Tower, less for reasons of justice than to satisfy the political intrigues of Prince Ranuce-Ernest IV, who also is in love with Gina and wants to seduce her. Surprisingly, Fabrice finds true happiness in jail. He has fallen in love with Clélia Conti, the jailer's daughter, whose melancholy expression and angelic face give him so much happiness that he initially refuses to escape. With his aunt's and Clélia's help, he escapes from the tower and flees to Piedmont, though Clélia has vowed never to see him again. In the meantime, Gina has Prince Ranuce-Ernest poisoned and replaced with a new prince. When she and Fabrice return to Parma, he is named coadjutor by the archbishop. Clélia marries the wealthy Marquis Crescenzi, and Fabrice devotes himself to an austere life of religious retreat. He preaches moving sermons in the hopes of attracting her. When at last he spies her in the crowd of listeners, he loses his place in the sermon. Clélia had vowed to the Virgin Mary, however, never to see Fabrice again and would receive him only in the dark. They become lovers, even after Fabrice has become archbishop, and have a child. When the child dies, however, Clélia dies out of guilt at having broken her promise to the Virgin Mary. Fabrice, heartbroken, renounces his office and wealth and retires to the Charterhouse of Parma, a Carthusian monastery on the river Pô, where he finishes his days in quiet meditation. His death is swiftly followed by that of his aunt.

La Chartreuse de Parme is rich in psychological realism.* Handsome, courageous, and intelligent Fabrice incarnates Stendhal's ideal of Beylism*; he is passionate and lucid in his search for happiness. His aunt feminizes this ideal. She loves Fabrice fearlessly and plots ceaselessly to insure his protection and advancement. Clélia, on the other hand, is a sensitive, moral creature who incarnates that ideal of tender love which was lacking in Stendhal's own life. The novel, which is often ironic and, at times, humorous, as it exposes the intrigue, tyranny, and passions of court life, is also a historical, political, and social chronicle of his adoptive homeland. Stendhal's description of Waterloo is a masterpiece of irony and realist art. *La Chartreuse de Parme* contains valuable insights into Stendhal, whose energy and spirit pervades the novel and its characters.

For further information, see L. Brotherson, "Determining Influences of Childhood in *La Chartreuse de Parme*," *Australian Journal of French Studies* 20 (2) (May–August 1983): 139–146; H. Davies, "Waiting for Gonzo: Irony in *La Chartreuse de Parme*," *Nottingham French Studies* 21 (1) (May 1982): 1–8; A. Finch, *Stendhal: La Chartreuse de Parme* (London: Edward Arnold, 1984); J. MacCannell, "Oedipus Wrecks: Lacan, Stendhal and the Narrative Form of the Real," *Modern Language Notes* 98 (5) (December 1983): 910–940; G. Moskos, "Burning Books and Writing in *La Chartreuse de Parme*," *Neophilologus* 66 (3) (July 1982): 349–359; A. Tintner, "In the Footsteps of Stendhal: James's 'A Most Extraordinary Case' and *La Chartreuse de Parme*," *Revue de la littérature comparée* 218 (2) (April–June 1981): 232–238; N. Ward, "The Prisonhouse of Language: The Heart of Midlothian [W. Scott] and *La Chartreuse de Parme*," *Comparative Criticism, A Yearbook* vol. 2 (New York: Cambridge University Press, 1980), 93–107.

CHATEAUBRIAND, FRANÇOIS-RENE DE (1768–1848), author of *Atala*,* *René*,* *Le Génie du Christianisme*,* and *Mémoires d'outre-tombe*,* dominated the literature of the early nineteenth century and inaugurated a literary movement—romanticism*—that irrevocably altered the course of literature and survived well into the twentieth century. His adult life was bounded on either side by the political revolutions of 1789 and 1848; he set the wheels in motion for a third, the romantic revolution, which liberated literature from the strictures of classicism and instituted a new esthetic of beauty and sensitivity. His personal life combined the ideals of the old age with the aspirations of the new. As a

nobleman, he enjoyed the benefits of material prosperity and a classical education. He was an aristocrat to the core, proud and insensitive to the people; he
supported the return of the legitimate monarchy. As a writer, however, he
bequeathed a legacy of sentiment, nature, and religion that spoke to generations
to follow and revealed to the common man the beauty of his soul.

Born in Saint-Malo to an illustrious but impoverished noble Breton family,
Chateaubriand was the youngest and frailest of ten children. His father was cold
and distant; his mother, melancholy. Chateaubriand spent much of his youth
alone, cared for by his faithful servant Villeneuve and playing at the seaside in
the company of the "waves and the winds" and the local ragamuffins until
studies at the colleges of Dol and Rennes took him away. He went to Brest in
hopes of a naval commission that never materialized, completed humanities
studies at Dinan, and at sixteen, retired to Combourg with his father, mother, and
sister Lucile. Those solitary years (1784–1785) spent within the cold, stone
walls of the sombre feudal estate or rambling with Lucile about the grounds fed
his burgeoning imagination with fantasies and hallucinations and intensified his
melancholy temperament. In 1786, he entered the regiment of Navarre as a
second lieutenant until the death of his father that same year called him back to
Combourg. In 1791, thanks to his brother, the count of Chateaubriand, and his
sister Julie, Madame de Farcy, he was presented at court, but he preferred the
company of Lebrun,* Chamfort,* Evariste-Désiré de Parny (1753–1814), La
Harpe,* and Louis de Fontanes (1757–1821), frequenters of the salons and
literary circles. By 1791, with revolutionary fever at an all-time high, Chateaubriand decided that the time was right to travel. Under the pretext of discovering
the Northwest Passage, he embarked for America in April 1791 and remained
there until news of the king's arrest at Varennes in December. His journey
through Baltimore, Philadelphia, New York, Boston, and Niagara Falls (he soon
abandoned his intended polar expedition) is second only to his experiences at
Combourg as a rich source for his writing, especially *Le Voyage en Amérique*
(*American Voyage,* 1827), *Les Natchez* (1826), and *Atala* (1801). When he
returned in 1792, he married the beautiful, delicate, seventeen-year-old Céleste
Buisson de Lavigne, primarily for monetary reasons, and joined the Breton
regiment of the Army of Princes. He was badly wounded at Thionville, came
down with dysentery, and contracted either smallpox or chicken pox. He made
his way to Brussels, where he saw his brother, who was soon to be executed, for
the last time. He travelled to Jersey and finally London, where he experienced
firsthand poverty, hunger, and misery. During his seven-year stay (1793–1800),
his brother, sister-in-law, and her father, Malesherbes,* were guillotined; his
mother, wife, and sister Lucile were imprisoned but released at the end of the
Terror. In Beccles, Suffolk, Chateaubriand taught French to support himself and
courted the woman of his dreams, his "sylphide," the charming and demure
Charlotte Ives, until he confessed that he was already married. He returned to
London and in 1797 published his *Essai sur les révolutions* (*Essay on Revolutions*), a pessimistic, anti-Christian work written in the spirit of the en-

cyclopédists (see *L'Encyclopédie**), which brought him little financial relief but established him as an author in emigré circles. News of the death of his mother followed rapidly by that of his sister Julie precipitated a sudden return to the faith ("I cried and I believed," Chateaubriand claims in his *Mémoires d'outre-tombe*) and inspired his famous apologia of Christianity, *Le Génie du Christianisme,* which first appeared in London in 1800.

That same year, claiming to be "David de La Sagne" from Neufchâtel, Chateaubriand joined the flood of emigrés returning to their native soil, took a position on the *Mercure,* frequented the salon of Madame de Beaumont, and renewed contacts with Joseph Joubert (1754–1824), Fontanes, and Madame de Stael.* Thanks to Fontanes, who encouraged him to work on *Génie,* his name was soon removed from the list of emigrés. From 1800 to 1801, fragments of his *Génie* were published in the *Mercure* and in 1801, another episode, *Atala,* also published separately, took the country by storm. On 14 April 1802, four days after Napoleon's concordat with the pope establishing Catholicism as the official religion of France, *Le Génie,* including *René,* was published in its entirety. Its success, riding on the new wave of enthusiasm for religion encouraged by the emperor, was enormous. In 1803, Napoleon named him secretary of the Roman embassy and chargé d'affaires for the Swiss canton of Valais; however, he resigned the following year to protest the unjust execution of the Duke d'Enghien (1772–1804). Disgraced, he retired to private life. In 1806, he undertook a long voyage to the Orient through Italy, Greece, Constantinople, Palestine, Tunisia, Carthage, and Spain, a trip which formed the basis for his work on *Les Martyrs** (1809). Upon his return, in 1807, he found himself sole proprietor of the *Mercure,* which he used once again to denounce d'Enghien's execution. Napoleon promptly shut down the journal, and Chateaubriand retired to his newly purchased country estate of La Vallée-aux-Loups near Sceaux to work on his memoirs and *Les Martyrs,* his Christian epic poem in prose. He published *L'Itinéraire de Paris à Jerusalem (The Itinerary from Paris to Jerusalem),* a travelogue based on his Oriental voyage, in 1811. That same year, he was elected to the Academy to fill the seat of Marie-Joseph Chénier*; however, his acceptance speech denouncing the Empire was censured. Chateaubriand never publicly received the seat.

Restoration politics dominated his life during the years 1814–1830, beginning with his anti-Bonapartist pamphlet, *De Buonaparte et des Bourbons (On Buonaparte and the Bourbons,* 1814), whose publication, according to Louis XVIII, was worth "an army of 100,000 men" to him. He was named minister of the interior of Louis XVIII's government in exile; in 1815, he was named a peer of France; he entered the "ultra-royalist" opposition and wrote, a year later, *La Monarchie selon la Charte (The Monarchy according to the Charter,* 1816), expounding his ideas on constitutional monarchy and criticizing the king. That same year he was removed as minister and was forced, because of finances, to sell his Vallée-aux-Loups. With Bonald,* Jean-Baptiste Villèle (1773–1854), Jules Auguste Armand, prince de Polignac (1780–1847), Nodier,* and Lamennais,* he founded *Le Conservateur* (*The Conservator*) in 1818, the opposition's journal for the next two years. To remove him after the assassination of the duke of Berry (b. 1778) in 1820, Louis named him ambassador to Berlin and then to London, where he was known for his sumptuous receptions. He represented France at the Verona Congress and in 1823 was named minister of foreign affairs, in charge of the armed effort to maintain Bourbon King Ferdinand on the Spanish throne. He was removed from the position a year later and back in the midst of financial difficulties. To alleviate his money problems, he proposed to the publisher Charles Ladvocat (1790–1854) an edition of his complete works, including the unpublished *Les Natchez* (1826), *Les Aventures du dernier Aben-cérage* (*The Adventures of the Last Abencerage,* 1826), and *Le Voyage en Amerique* (1827). The venture took five years to complete, from 1826 to the publication of his *Etudes historiques* (*Historical Studies*) in 1831. He returned to his beloved Rome as ambassador in 1828 but resigned a year later under the antiliberal prime minister Polignac. After the revolution of 1830, he resigned as peer, refusing to pledge his allegiance to the new king, Louis-Philippe, support-ing instead the "shadow cabinet" of the exiled widow of the duke of Berry. Her efforts to regain the throne were thwarted, and Chateaubriand was placed under temporary house arrest. In 1832, he repaired to Geneva; Madame de Berry was imprisoned. He returned to Paris in 1832 to publish a pamphlet in her defense. "Madame, your son is my king," he courageously wrote, but to no avail. Despite Chateaubriand's help, her son never attained his legitimate power.

Chateaubriand spent his final years completing his memoirs, which he sold in 1836 to alleviate his continual financial problems. The publishers, Sala and Delloye, printed them in serial form in *La Press* from 1848 to 1850. His later works include *La Vie de Rancé* (*The Life of Rancé,* 1844), written about the Trappist reformer at the instigation of his confessor; *Mémoire sur la captivité de la duchesse de Berry* (*Memoir on the Captivity of the Duchess of Berry,* 1833); *Essai sur la littérature anglaise* (*Essay on English Literature,* 1836), and *Con-grès de Vérone* (*Verona Congress,* 1838). After the death of his wife in 1847, he proposed marriage to Madame Récamier (1777–1849) whose salon he fre-quented. She refused, but they shared daily visits for his remaining year of life; he was half-paralyzed and she was blind. Upon his death, Chateaubriand was interred alone at his favorite spot at the point of the island of Grand-Bé at Saint-Malo facing the sea.

Chateaubriand's life was marked by deeply felt solitude and melancholy, feelings inspired by the sea and his lonely youth at Combourg and expressed in René's mal du siècle*—his feeling, since childhood, of "languor," of "distaste for life," which fostered his boredom and despair. Chateaubriand found solace in his imagination, in the perfection and beauty he cultivated and preferred to reality. His rich inner life gave him his "sylphe," his ideal of femininity; his *Génie du Christianisme,* his ideal of religion; *Les Martyrs,* his illustration of Christian morality and history; *Les Natchez,* his ideal of natural man; and culmi-nated in his *Mémoires,* the ideal self he created as he rewrote the story of his life.

His work is permeated by his sense of dignity and pride, his legacy from his upbringing and the classics. At times, it is marred by clichés and rhetoric. His characters, Chactas, René, Eudore, have been criticized as inferior. However, his depictions of America and the Middle East paint the beauty, the poetry, the mystery of nature with the sensitivity of J.-J. Rousseau.* Like him, Chateaubriand sensed the correspondence between nature and the soul; he expressed the wonder, the fear, the sadness of the forests, autumn, ruins, focusing on the individual and his sensitivities rather than on the universalities of the classics. At times, his writing sings with the harmony, rhythm, cadence, and sound of music; it dazzles with color, imagery, and versatility, revealing the magnificence of nature, the landscape of a reverie, or the melancholy of a soul.

Chateaubriand's influence on his contemporaries was significant. Through *Le Génie du Christianisme,* his religious reawakening spread throughout France, reestablishing the respectability and influence of the church. He restored interest in old churches, gothic architecture, the history of France and of ancient civilizations. Rene's mal du siècle spawned a generation of malcontents, whom the haughty Chateaubriand disdained. His themes of nature, melancholy, death, the infinite became the hallmarks of a generation. Through his influence on the young Victor Hugo,* Lamartine,* and George Sand,* Chateaubriand prepared the way for one of the most significant literary movements of all time—romanticism.

For further information, see A. Cancogni, "My Sister, Do You Still Recall?: Chateaubriand/ Nabakov," *Comparative Literature* 35 (Spring 1983): 140–166; H. Redman, "Chateaubriand and Washington, Chateaubriand and Napoleon: Some New Perspectives," *French Literature Series* 8 (1981): 53–64; M. Riffaterre, "Descriptive Imagery," *Yale French Studies* 61 (1981): 107–125.

LES CHATIMENTS (*Punishments,* 1853), by Victor Hugo,* unleashes in more than 6,200 lines of verse the ire and vengeance of the transplanted poet and his dashed dreams of liberty. Written in exile in Brussels and Jersey and directed against Louis-Napoleon (Napoleon III, 1808–1873) and the Second Empire, the poems combine satire in the tradition of Juvenal (60–140 A.D.), whom Hugo greatly admired, with Hugo's lyricism, imagery, and cosmic vision. The collection, with more than one hundred odes, popular songs, hymns, and narrative poems, was first published in Brussels by Henri Samuel; numerous copies were smuggled into France. A definitive edition with five new poems, including "Au moment de rentrer en France" ("As I am about to Return to France"), appeared in 1870, shortly after Hugo's triumphant return to his homeland. The poems are divided into seven "books" and, except for the last, bear the Empire's slogans as ironic titles; 1. "Society Is Saved," 2. "Order Is Re-Established," 3. "The Family Is Restored," 4. "Religion Is Glorified," 5. "Religion Is Sacred," 6. "Stability Is Assured," and 7. "The Saviors Will Save Themselves."

The opening poem, "Nox," describes the dire preparations for the emperor's coup d'état the night of 1 December 1851. Those following portray the tyranny of an emperor who deserves the stings of the bees embroidered on his royal cloak ("Le Manteau impérial"—"The Imperial Cloak") and the death he unmercifully inflicted on his enemies, even innocent children caught in crossfire ("Souvenir de la nuit du 4"—"Memory of the Night of the Fourth"). "L'Expiation" ("The Expiation"), perhaps the best known of the poems, draws an unflattering comparison between Napoleon III and his predecessor, Napoleon I (1769–1821). For Hugo, the Second Empire is a punishment more cruel than the snowy retreat from Russia, defeat at Waterloo, or the exile on Sainte-Helene suffered by Napoleon-le-Grand. "Ultima Verba" ("The Last Words") is Hugo's pledge to oppose the tyranny of the "abominable deceiver" to the finish, "And if there remained but one [enemy], I would be the one." "Stella," lacking the satire of the other poems but evoking a mystic image of light and liberty, is a rarity here. Finally, "Lux" balances the misery of the introductory "Nox" with a note of hope, a prophesy of peace and liberty. "Oh! See! Night is lifting./ On the world which is becoming free. . . . vast wings of peace are opening in the azure sky."

Les Châtiments, a work born in the face of combat that gave full rein to his indignation, outrage, and horror, is Hugo's response to tyranny. Yet he transcends his anger to achieve a vision of progress, a belief in peace and brotherhood, a call for human freedom that will be heard again in *Les Contemplations** (*Contemplations*) and *La Légende des siècles** (*The Legend of the Ages*).

CHATTERTON (1835), by Vigny,* is a prose drama in three acts based loosely on the life of a poverty-stricken young English poet who at age eighteen commits suicide to escape his misery. Vigny, the poet of symbols, found in the young man a symbol of "spiritualistic man smothered by a materialistic society, where the greedy calculator pitilessly exploits intelligence and hard work" (Preface). Vigny, the poet of ideas, created in this play a "drama of thought" in which he pleads the case before God of the "perpetual martyrdom and the perpetual immolation of the poet . . . the right which he would have to live . . . the bread which he wasn't given . . . the death which he was forced to give himself" (Preface).

The story takes place in 1770 in the home of John Bell, a rich London industrialist, where the young poet, Chatterton, is renting a meager room. Mr. Bell, authoritarian and cruel, adheres to a code of justice that is based on the law but often self-serving and brutal. Act 1 finds him refusing to rehire a worker injured in his plant and chastising his wife, Kitty Bell, for an error of a few shillings in her account book. The idealistic Chatterton is the antithesis of his host. He lives for his art and defends his right to die for it. "Poetry," he exclaims (act 1, scene 5), "it is everywhere; it gives me everything and takes it all away; it charms and destroys everything for me; it has saved me . . . it has lost me!" Kitty Bell is a kind soul who pities the sensitive and poor poet. Act 2 reveals that Chatterton had once been rich and attended Oxford before he lost his fortune. He is in reality a well-known poet who fears recognition. While walking with his friend the Quaker, he crosses paths with a former schoolmate, Lord Talbot, who visits him at Bell's house. Kitty is the butt of some crude remarks by Talbot's friends. After they leave, she confesses her affection for Chatterton to the Quaker. He throws her into a frenzy by telling her of Chatterton's plans for suicide. Act III opens with Chatterton alone in his room, writing and contemplating Kitty Bell, his poetry, his predicament since his identity has been revealed, his father, and suicide. He hears the Quaker approach his room and leaves his vial of opium in full view. The Quaker, trying to dissuade him from drinking it, reveals Kitty's love for him and argues that, if he commits suicide, she will die of sadness. Talbot returns with the news that a creditor wants Chatterton arrested and that a critic is accusing him of plagiarism. Bell wants to evict the penniless poet; Talbot offers to defend and protect his friend. Chatterton replies that he has written to the lord-mayor for help. "The lord-mayor is the government in my eyes," he declares, "and the government is England, my lord; it is England I am counting on." In the end, it is England that disappoints him. The lord-mayor arrives and advises Chatterton to stop writing poetry. Poetry is good for nothing, he says, and a good Englishman must serve his country. He informs him that he has been found a plagiarist and offers him a position as chamber valet. In his deepest despair, Chatterton swallows the opium and destroys his manuscripts. Kitty admits her love for him, but it is too late. He falls dead; Kitty follows suit moments later, and the curtain falls with the Quaker on his knees praying to God to receive the two martyrs.

The theme of the poet as a social outcast long interested Vigny. He took up the subject three years earlier in a novel, *Stello*. The play is classic in its simplicity of plot. Most of the action is psychological rather than physical. Vigny wrote that *Chatterton* is the "story of a man who wrote a letter in the morning and is waiting until evening for an answer; it comes and kills him." However, its thesis is firmly romantic (see romanticism*), the concern for the poet and his social role. The play was a critical and popular success with the role of Kitty Bell brilliantly played by Vigny's friend, Marie Dorval. If it is somewhat dated today, *Chatterton* remains a fine example of romantic theatre at its best.

For further information, see R. Buss, *Vigny: Chatterton* (London: Grant and Cutler, 1984).

CHENIER, ANDRE (1762–1794), the most original and influential of the eighteenth-century poets, was born in Constantinople where his father was consul general. He was brought to Paris at an early age by his mother, a Hellene about whom little is known other than that her intelligence and inspiration created within her son an abiding appreciation of his Greek heritage. A brilliant student, Chénier studied at the Collège de Navarre in Paris, where his poetic talent soon surfaced. He disliked the army in which he briefly served, preferring the pursuit of love and poetry and the company of Palissot,* Florian,* Jean-Baptiste Suard (1733–1817), l'abbe Barthélemy (1716–1795), and the painter Louis David (1748–1825), habitués of his mother's salon. Chénier travelled to

Switzerland and later to Italy in hopes of reaching Greece but both his travels and romances along the way were curtailed by ill health in Rome. In 1788, he went to London as secretary to the ambassador. Liking neither the climate nor the English poets, he returned after a year to a Paris seething with the Revolution, which, as a believer in liberty, he supported. With his friends, Louis and Michel Trudaine, he founded La Société de 1789, which eventually became La Société des amis de la Constitution (Society of the Friends of the Constitution) and published an ode celebrating the Oath of the Tennis Courts ("Le Serment du jeu de paume," 1791). However, believing in moderation and justice as well as liberty, he protested in numerous articles in *Le Mercure* and in *Le Journal de Paris* the excesses of the Jacobins and satirized the triumphant return of the mutinous Swiss soldiers of Chateauvieux. He prepared, with Malesherbes,* the defense of Louis XVI. Suspect because of his views, Chénier repaired to Versailles where, momentarily escaping the heat of the Terror, he found a measure of happiness and wrote his "Pièces à Fanny" ("Poems to Fanny"), poems for Madame Le Coulteux, whom he met there. He was mistakenly arrested shortly thereafter at Passy and imprisoned at Saint-Lazare, where he wrote his odes and iambs on scrap paper and smuggled them out to his father with the laundry. A few months later and two days before the fall of Robespierre,* Chénier was denounced as an enemy of the people and died on the scaffold.

From 1790 on, Chénier was known primarily as a journalist. Except for "Le Serment du jeu de paume" and a hymn dedicated to Chateauvieux's mutinous Swiss soldiers (1792), his poetry remained unpublished during his lifetime. "La Jeune Tarentine" ("The Young Tarentine") appeared in *Le Mercure* shortly after his death. The manuscripts scattered, although poets Charles Millevoye (1782–1816) and Chateaubriand* had access to them. Henri de Latouche published the first edition in 1819, followed by editions by Becq de Fouquières in 1862, Gabriel de Chénier in 1874, and P. Dimoff from 1908 to 1919.

Chénier's love for his Greek heritage and especially the poetry of Homer (8th century B.C.), Aristophanes (448–380 B.C.), Theocritus (3d century B.C.), and Anacreon (572–488 B.C.) resulted in the literary doctrine set forth in his "Epître à Lebrun" ("Epistle to Lebrun," 1785). From these "ancient masters of perfection," Chénier freely borrowed ideas, images, and verse to fashion a poetry that imitated their formal beauty, clarity, and harmony, but which was also personal and lyric. The *Bucoliques* (*Bucolics*) or *Idylles* (*Idylls*) best illustrate this doctrine. Inspired by the third-century bucolics of Theocritus, they flow directly from Chénier's Greek soul. Consisting of "petits tableaux" or "little pictures," these pastoral poems depict the mythology and legends of Greece, its countryside, and history, especially the harmony, naiveté, and sense of moderation and proportion inherent in its life and art. "L'Aveugle" ("The Blind Man"), an epic in the style of Homer, recounts the themes of ancient Greek poetry; "La Liberté" ("Liberty") is a dialogue between a shepherd and a slave. Mythic evocations such as "Bacchus," "Jupiter et Europe," and "L'Enlèvement d'Europe" ("The Abduction of Europe") honor the gods, while "Le Jeune malade"

("The Ill Young Man"), "La Jeune Tarentine," and "Néaere" are sentimental portrayals of youth, love, and death. Models of grace and beauty, the *Bucoliques* paint a picture, sculpt a pose, or capture a movement in verse, making Chénier's poetry "plastic" like the ancient works he admired.

"L'Invention" ("The Invention"), written in London from 1787 to 1790, takes his doctrine of imitation one step further. While still holding the ancients as models, Chénier calls for the poet to "make antique verse based on new ideas," like those of Evangelista Torricelli (1608–1647), Isaac Newton (1642–1727), Johannes Kepler (1571–1630), and Galileo (1564–1642), to celebrate the discoveries, beliefs, and ideas of the present. Chénier himself outlined two such poems but never completed them. "L'Hermès" was to be an epic of nature, man, and society similar to Buffon's* *Histoire naturelle,* which would describe in the first canto the physical system of the earth and the appearance of the animals; in the second, the appearance of man and society; and in the third, the establishment of a "social contract" and the invention of science. "America" would recount the explorations and colonization of the New World, showing its habits and people.

Other poems he planned or partially wrote include "Suzanne," a biblical poem in six cantos; "L'Art d'aimer" ("The Art of Loving"); "La République des lettres ou Les Cyclopes littéraires" ("The Republic of Letters or Literary Cyclops"), a satire against poor poetry; poems on superstition and astronomy; and four hymns.

If Chénier's poetry falls prey at all to the mediocrity of his contemporaries, such as Lebrun* or Evariste-Désiré Parny (1753–1814), it is in his elegies, which he began writing at nineteen and resumed in his final years. His themes echo those of the day—love, the rustic life, epicurian delights. Besides his "Pièces à Fanny," the most poignant and one of his final poems is "La Jeune Captive" ("The Young Captive") which was written in the shadow of death in Saint-Lazare about fellow-captive Aimée de Coigny (1769–1820) and expresses his melancholy farewell to life.

On the other hand, the *Iambes,* like the *Bucoliques,* imitate an ancient poetic form but explode with anger and sadness at the injustices of the times. Written at Versailles and Saint-Lazare at the height of the Terror, their satire and indignation are urgent appeals for liberty, dignity, justice, and virtue. Their emotion and outrage anticipate Hugo's* *Les Châtiments.**

Chénier's superiority over the spurious imitations of the classics typical of his day lies primarily in his genuineness, manifest in the Grecism of the *Bucoliques,* and in his passion, manifest in the fervor of the *Iambes.* The result is a lyricism, a depth of meaning, that the others lack. His odes and elegies, when finally published, were enthusiastically received for their melancholy, sensitivity, and sincerity by a budding generation of romantic (see romanticism*) poets. The purity of his style and the "plastic" quality of his verse were seen again in the Parnassians.*

Chénier has been called the first of the romantic poets yet he was very much a man of his times. His pastorals reflect a Rousseauesque (see J.-J. Rousseau*) desire to return to nature, to the simplicity and happiness of the countryside. Like Voltaire,* however, he envisions in "L'Invention" the possibility of an intellectual poetry based on his enthusiasm for science and his faith in man's progress. Unfortunately, Chénier died at thirty-one, before he could explore either path to the fullest.

For further information, see J. Mills, *The Iambs of André Chénier: Poetic Innovation and Moral Commitment* (Salt Lake City: University of Utah, 1980); Mills, "The Iambes of André Chénier: A Manifesto of Poetic Engagement," *Selecta* 4 (1983): 17–22.

CHENIER, MARIE-JOSEPH (1764–1811), poet and dramatist, younger brother of André Chénier,* was the voice of the Revolution in his odes, hymns, and tragedies. Like André, he was born in Constantinople and served briefly in the army. A deputy to the National Convention (one of the assemblies formed during the Revolution), he voted for the death of Louis XVI, whom his brother defended. He was named inspector general for studies and though later opposed to the Empire, he received, nevertheless, a pension from Napoleon in his final years.

Chénier's patriotic hymns, such as "Chant du départ" ("Song of Departure," 1794), "Chant du 14 juillet" ("Song of the Fourteenth of July," 1790), and "Hymne à la victoire" ("Hymn to Victory," 1793), were popular though of little poetic merit and not very original. He also wrote satire and epistles but is best known for his tragedies, *Henri VIII* (1791), *Calas* (1791), and *Charles IX ou La Saint-Barthélemy* (*Charles IX or Saint-Bartholomew,* 1789), which attacked royalty and the clergy and inspired the theatre of the Revolution. However, as Chénier's zeal for the Revolution mollified, so did his plays. *Caïus Gracchus* (1792) and *Fénelon* (1793) called for moderation and humanity, "laws and not blood." *Timoléon* (1794) indicated the horrors of the Revolution. It was forbidden by Robespierre* and not presented until after his fall on 27 July 1794 (known as the ninth day of Thermidor—the eleventh month on the Republican calendar).

Accused of neglecting to save his brother, who died just two days before the fall of Robespierre, Chénier wrote "Epître sur la calomnie" ("Epistle on Calumny," 1797) in self-defense.

COLLE, CHARLES (1709–1783), a lawyer's son and cousin of Regnard,* made his way into eighteenth-century society by writing songs, parades,* comedies, and comic operas (see opéra-comique*). He was well respected at the court of the regent, where he was appointed reader and secretary to the duke of Orleans and a favorite with the ladies. His plays, written for the duke's exclusive circle, rely on innuendo and illusion; their tone is uninhibited. His best-known, *La Partie de chasse de Henri IV* (*Henry IV's Hunting Party,* 1764), considered a threat by the less popular Louis XV, remained unperformed publicly until Louis XVI granted permission to the Comédie-Française to perform it ten years later.

He also wrote a *Journal historique* (*Historical Journal*, 1748–1772, published posthumously, 1807). His correspondence was published in 1864.

For further information, see J. Van Eerde, *"The King and the Miller* in England, France and Italy," *Francia* (April–June 1981): 41–51.

COLLIN D'HARLEVILLE, JEAN-FRANÇOIS (1755–1806), poet and comic author reminiscent of Regnard,* Piron,* and Gresset,* was born in Maintenon, the son of a lawyer turned farmer and architect. He turned from law to writing light poetry and comedy in the classic tradition. His plays, consisting primarily of superficial plots, fantasy, grace, and delicate verse, are unmarked by the revolutionary period during which they were written. His best known, *Le Vieux Celibataire* (*The Old Bachelor*, 1792), details in five acts the attempts of a housekeeper and nephew to ingratiate a rich old man. Other plays include *L'Inconstant* (*The Fickle One*, 1786), *L'Optimiste* (*The Optimist*, 1788), *Les Châteaux en Espagne* (*Castles in Spain*, 1789), and *M. de Crac dans son petit castel* (*Mr. Crac in his Little Castle*, 1791). Like those of his predecessors, his comedies lack the vigor and originality of the preceding century, which was achieved in the eighteenth century only by Beaumarchais* and Marivaux.*

COLOMBA (1840), written by Mérimée* after a two-month Corsican visit in 1839, like *Mateo Falcone,** is set in Corsica. *Mateo Falcone,* however, was documented from secondary sources. *Colomba* was first published in the *Revue des deux mondes* in 1840 and appeared in book form the following year. It has since been published in numerous editions and translations and is one of the most widely read French novels of all time. *Colomba* is said to possess the perfect balance between the romantic and the classic. It is romantic in its exotic setting and depiction of the passionate, lawless nature of the Corsicans. It is classic in its clear, concise writing and restrained, sombre style.

Colomba is a novel of revenge. Its central figure is a beautiful, young girl who is obsessed with avenging the death of her father in a centuries-old feud. Her primitive ways contrast with the civilized European justice that her brother, Orso, has learned as a student and soldier on the Continent. As the story opens, Orso is returning to Corsica after serving in the Battle of Waterloo. While crossing the Mediterranean, he befriends Colonel Nevil, an Irishman who fought opposite him at Waterloo, and his daughter, Lydia, who are traveling to Corisca in search of excitement and good hunting. After a few pleasant days with the Nevils in Ajaccio, Colomba arrives to escort her brother to their native village, Pietranera, where she hopes he will uphold the honor of their family and kill their father's murderers. Orso, however, has spent too many years abroad to harbor the animosities of his kin. He believes that his rivals, the Barricini family, had been rightfully cleared. Like Lydia, he feels that the law should decide such matters. When the prefect tries to convince Colomba and Orso of the Barricinis' innocence, Colomba has a bandit friend testify that the man found guilty of the murder had been bribed by the Barricinis. Orso, suddenly convinced of their guilt, promises to fight the two Barricini sons. Orlanduccio Barricini draws his stiletto, and the prefect barely averts the fight. In a letter, he challenges Orlanduccio to a duel. Orlanduccio refuses, however, and forwards the note to the prosecutor as evidence of a threat. The next night, Colomba steals into the garden to slit the ear of Orso's horse. He suspects Orlanduccio, but filled with disgust for his enemies, refuses to lower himself to fight with them, deferring to the police and jailers. After warning his sister and her cohorts against further violence, he leaves with an escort to meet the Nevils who are en route to Pietranera. Along the way, he is ambushed and injured by the Barricini brothers, whom he in turn shoots and kills. Though innocent, he goes into hiding. Lydia and the colonel reach the village and fear for Orso's fate until Orso and Lydia learn that he is safe. Colomba and Lydia visit him at his hideout. As they declare their mutual love, the police arrive on the scene. Orso is forced to flee; Colomba and Lydia are taken to the prefect, who by then is convinced, largely by Colonel Nevil's testimony about the number of shots fired, that Orso had killed the Barricini brothers in self-defense. His name cleared, Orso bids adieux to his two bandit friends and leaves for Italy. In the final chapter, Orso and Lydia, now married, and the colonel and Colomba are near Pisa when Colomba happens upon a sickly and senile Mr. Barricini, father of the two men Orso killed, living in a farmhouse. Recognizing Colomba, he asks, "Why both of them. . . ? You should have left me one." Colomba replies in a low voice in her Corsican dialect, "I needed them both." As she leaves the farm, satisfied that justice had been met, the farmer's wife remarks that Colomba has "the evil eye."

COMEDIE HUMAINE, LA (*The Human Comedy*, 1842–1848), by Balzac,* that vast panorama of French society from the Revolution through the Empire, the Restoration, and the July monarchy, consists of more than eighty novels and short stories. It grew from Balzac's notion in 1833 that his novels, previously written independently of each other, could be integrated into a larger study of contemporary life and manners. The characters of the *Comédie humaine* reappear in the various novels, forming a collective society interconnected by family, social, business, and professional ties. Balzac grouped this vast body of work into *Etudes philosophiques* (*Philosophical Studies*), *Etudes analytiques* (*Analytical Studies*), and *Etudes de moeurs* (*Studies of Manners*). The *Etudes de moeurs* are subdivided into *Scènes de la vie privée* (*Scenes from Private Life*), *Scènes de la vie de province* (*Provincial Life*), *Scènes de la vie parisienne* (*Parisian Life*), *Scènes de la vie politique* (*Political Life*), *Scènes de la vie militaire* (*Military Life*), and *Scènes de la vie de campagne* (*Country Life*). In 1842, he chose *La Comédie humaine* as the overall title for the collection, probably with Dante's *Divina Comedia* (1307–1321) in mind.

    The foreword to the 1842 edition outlines the scientific basis for the *Comédie humaine*. Like naturalist Geoffroy de Saint-Hilaire (1772–1844), Balzac believed in the unity of all species. "The Creator used one and the same pattern for all organized beings," he wrote. Moreover, just as different animal species evolve according to their conditions and milieux, man evolves according to his environment and is inseparable from it. Thus, the differences between a "soldier, worker, administrator, lawyer, idler, scholar, statesman, businessman, sailor, poet, poor man, and preacher" are as "considerable" as those between various animal species. The *Comédie humaine* illustrates the interdependence between individuals and their environment and the unwritten laws in these various social sectors. Balzac hoped to achieve for society what Buffon's* monumental *Histoire naturelle* (1749–1788) had accomplished for the animal kingdom. He borrowed his technique from Walter Scott (1771–1832), that "modern poet" who Balzac claimed "raised the novel to the philosophical value of history," adding "drama, dialogue, portrait, landscape, and description" to the "spirit of ancient times." Balzac regretted only that Scott didn't link his novels into a complete history. As the self-appointed "secretary" of society, Balzac aimed to inventory the "vices and virtues," the "passions" and "characters," while writing that story "forgotten by so many historians, that of manners." Balzac claimed that he wrote by the light of "two eternal truths, religion and monarchy."

Many of the novels in the *Comédie humaine* were published before the idea of organizing them into a network of interrelated stories and episodes was born. *Les Chouans* (1829), a historical novel written under the influence of Scott and later included as one of the *Scènes de la vie militaire,* was conceived as early as 1827. *La Physiologie du mariage* (*The Physiology of Marriage*), a light-hearted Rabelaisian (1494–1553) consideration of marriage, female psychology, and the problems of conjugal life belonging to the *Etudes analytiques,* was written in 1829. The first two volumes of his *Scènes de la vie privée,* which included six stories, *La Maison du Chat-qui-pelote* (*At the Sign of the Cat and Racket*), *Le Bal de Sceaux* (*The Sceaux Ball*), *La Vendetta* (*The Vendetta*), *Une Double Famille* (*A Second Home*), *La Paix de ménage* (*The Peace of a Home*), and *Gobseck,* appeared in 1830. Balzac wrote many of the novels of the *Scènes* and *Etudes* before he formulated these divisions of his oeuvre. *Le Curé de Tours* (*The Vicar of Tours,* 1832), originally included in the *Scènes de la vie privée,* later became part of the provincial scenes. *La Peau de chagrin* (*The Magic Skin,* 1831), a fantastic novel with supernatural elements, was written in 1831; the autobiographical and philosophical *Louis Lambert,* from 1832 to 1833. Both eventually became part of the *Etudes Philosophiques.*

Balzac wrote that his *Etudes de moeurs* would "represent all the social effects" such that "no life situation, no physiognomy, no man's or woman's character, no way of life, no profession, no social zone, no part of France, nor anything of infancy, old age, nor of maturity, politics, justice or war would be forgotten." The novels of the *Scènes de la vie privée* deal primarily with morality, the love of a young girl for a writer whom she has never met but corresponds with (*Modeste Mignon,* 1844) or a young man's start in life (*Un Début dans la vie,* 1842). *Le Père Goriot,** *La Maison du Chat-qui-pelote, La Femme de trente ans* (*The Woman of Thirty,* 1831–1842), *Le Colonel Chabert* (1832) are important novels in this category. The *Scènes de la vie de province* illustrate unforgettable provincial types: Gaudissart, the crafty, boastful travelling salesman; Félix Grandet, the sordid, tyrannical miser. Besides *L'Illustre Gaudissart* (1834) and *Eugénie Grandet*,* Balzac's notable provincial novels include *Ursule Mirouët* (1841), *Les Illusions perdues* (*Lost Illusions*, 1837–1843), *Le Curé de Tours*, and *La Rabouilleuse* (*A Bachelor's Establishment*, 1841–1842). *Scènes de la vie parisienne* include *La Duchesse de Langeais* (*The Duchess of Langeais*, 1833–1834), *La Fille aux yeux d'or* (*The Girl with the Golden Eyes*, 1834–1835), *L'Histoire de la grandeur et de la décadence de César Birotteau* (*The Rise and Fall of Cesar Birotteau*, 1837), *La Maison Nucingen* (*The Firm of Nucingen*, 1838), *Splendeurs et misères des courtisanes* (*Scenes from a Courtesan's Life*, 1839–1847), *La Cousine Bette* (*Cousin Betty*, 1846), *Le Cousin Pons* (*Cousin Pons*, 1847). *Un Episode sous la Terreur* (*An Episode under the Terror*, 1830), *Une Ténébreuse Affaire* (*The Gondreville Mystery*, 1841), *Le Député d'Arcis* (*The Deputy from Arcis*, 1847), and *Z. Marcas* (1840) comprise the *Scènes de la vie politique; Les Chouans* and *Une Passion dans le desert* (*A Passion in the Desert*, 1830), *Scènes de la vie militaire.* The four novels of *Scènes de la vie de campagne, Les Paysans* (*The Peasantry*, 1844), *Le Médecin de campagne* (*The Country Doctor*, 1833), *Le Curé de village* (*The Village Rector*, 1833–1839), and *Le Lys dans la vallée* (*The Lily of the Valley*, 1835), complete Balzac's sweeping study of the manners and morals of his times.

Balzac's philosophical novels attempted to uncover the causes for the social effects depicted in the *Etudes de moeurs.* He wrote, "I will have painted for you in the *Etudes de moeurs* the sentiments and their play, life and its demeanor. In the *Etudes philosophiques* I will tell the 'why' of the sentiments. . . ." *Etudes philosophiques* include *La Peau de chagrin, La Recherche de l'absolu* (*The Search for the Absolute*, 1834), *Louis Lambert*, and *Séraphita* (1835).

The *Etudes analytiques* (*Analytical Studies*) were to uncover the "principles" governing the effects and causes of the other novels. Comparing his plan to the theatre, Balzac wrote that "the manners are the play, the causes are the wings and the stage effects. The principles are the author." The *Etudes analytiques* consists of two works, *La Physiologie du mariage* (1829) and *Petites Misères de la vie conjugale* (*Petty Troubles of Conjugal Life*, 1845), a witty and frivolous study of the marriage of Adolphe and Caroline de Chodoreille detailing their mutual vexations, disillusions, and estrangement. Balzac is sympathetic to the female faced with her husband's infidelity, her altruism, and her self-denial.

Thanks to Balzac's careful research, the *Comedie humaine* is a valuable historical and social document. He observed his fellow man, visited the towns and sites used as the settings for his novels, interviewed individuals and specialists, and relied on his own experience and intuition to describe minute details of setting, examine character, and re-create the atmosphere of the times in his novels. The cities and towns of his settings have not only picturesque value, but historical and geographical significance. Balzac carefully documented their influence on the masses and individuals who inhabited them. The novels reveal the passions and interests of the people—Mr. Grandet's avarice, Father Goriot's paternal devotion, Baron Hulot's need for women, Vautrin's criminality, Birotteau's social ambitions, Claes's scientific passion.

The novels also treat the philosophical problems of the time. The animal skin of *La Peau de chagrin* symbolizes the destructive capabilities of man's desires and his need for power. As the magic skin grants each of its young possessor's wishes, it shrinks, its energy depleted. The novel is an allegory of the waste and debauchery of the society of 1830. *Louis Lambert* details the metaphysical discoveries of a student at the Collège de Vendôme who is endowed, as Balzac was, with a prodigious memory, a vivid imagination, and a rich fantasy life. It is a valuable document on Balzac's beliefs about instinct, intelligence, will, and thought and the development of his mysticism. Under the influence of Emanuel Swedenbourg (1688–1772), Louis Claude de Saint-Martin (1743–1803), and the illuminists, Balzac believed in the correspondences between the visible and invisible worlds. He envisioned a fluid that emanated from the brain in the form of human thought. "They are like myriads of stars," he wrote. "They also live outside. They assail us; we are obsessed by them, as they act, now one by one, now in groups." *Le Lys dans la vallée* is filled with sentimental mysticism; *Séraphita* is a Swedenborgian tale; *Ursule Mirouët* has spiritualist overtones.

Through Balzac's novels we traverse the various milieux of the early nineteenth century—the Parisian upper and middle classes, the clergy, the civil service, the military, law, finance, the tradesmen and lower bourgeoisie, doctors, artists, journalists, the peasantry. He was the first French writer to portray the power of money and the motive of gain. Beneath it all is a naturalistic and metaphysical substratum in which Balzac questions the meaning of the universe and human destiny. His view was broad and sweeping yet penetrating as it revealed both his external world and his own consciousness.

The style of the novels has been criticized as hasty, negligent, lacking the refinement of Flaubert* or the subtlety of Stendhal* or Proust.** Balzac's descriptions of background detail and character occasionally seem overwrought, superfluous, burdensome. These faults diminish, however, in comparison to Balzac's powerful imagination, his immense knowledge of his country and its social history, its social and political attitudes, and his prophetic vision. He has been called an observer and a visionary, a realist and a romantic, but he remains above all an artist who created and inhabited a *Human Comedy* that is universal and enduring.

For further information, see J.-P. Barricelli, "The Social and Metaphysical Rebellions of Vautrin and the 'Innominato,' " *Comparatist* 5 (May 1981): 19–29; J. Bruneau, "Reality and Truth in *La Comédie humaine*," in A. Tymieniecka, ed., *The Philosophical Reflection of Man in Literature: Selected Papers* (Dordrecht, Netherlands: Reidel, 1982); J. Manalan, "Interior/Exterior Movement in *La Comédie humaine*," *Paroles Gelées* 1 (1983): 31–44; M. McCarthy, *Balzac and His Reader: a Study of the Creation of Meaning in La Comédie humaine* (Columbia: University of Missouri Press, 1982); J. Mileham, *The Conspiracy Novel: Structure and Metaphor in Balzac's Comédie humaine* (Lexington, Ky.: French Forum Monographs, 1982); I. Pickup, "Causality and Determinism in

Balzac: The 'Law' of Diminishing Possibilities,'' *Modern Languages* 62 (4) (December 1981): 196–200; Mileham, "Numbers in the *Comédie humaine*," *Romance Notes* 22 (1) (Fall 1981): 48–52.

COMEDIE LARMOYANTE, or tearful comedy in verse, was written in the early eighteenth century by Baculard d'Arnaud* and Nivelle de la Chaussée,* its chief practitioner, who, though he never set down rules for the genre, purported to offer "a school where youth may learn with enjoyment lessons of wisdom and virtue." La Chaussée's *Le Préjugé à la mode* (*Fashionable Prejudice*) and *Mélanide* depicts virtuous young women in the throes of misfortune. In the first, a faithful wife is socially maligned, yet because of social convention, unable to receive the affections and support of her husband; Mélanide is ruefully separated from her husband and family. Comédie larmoyante was influenced by the novels of the time, Prévost's* *Manon Lescaut** and Samuel Richardson's (1689–1761) *Pamela* (1740), which Prévost translated. It is marked by excessive tragedy, sensitivity, and poor versification, making it irrelevant and uninteresting today. Yet, its treatment of domestic life and family relationships and its appeal to emotion represent an important step from the laughter and fantasy of Marivaux* toward the development of drama, which Diderot,* with his "drame bourgeois" (tearful comedies in prose), and Sedaine* would expand.

For further information, see T. Braun, "From Marivaux to Diderot: Awareness of the Audience in the 'Comédie,' the 'Comédie Larmoyante' and the 'Drame,'" *Diderot Studies XX* (Geneva: Droz, 1981), 17–29.

COMTE, AUGUSTE (1798–1857), eminent social philosopher who conceived the philosophical system of positivism* to cure the social ills of the early nineteenth century, was born in Montpellier to a conservative, Catholic, middle-class family. After brilliant studies at the lycée at Montpellier, he attended the Ecole Polytechnique from 1814 until 1816, when he was expelled for demonstrating against one of the schoolmasters. He was sent home but returned to Paris later in 1816 to live by giving lessons in mathematics. At twenty, he met philosopher Saint-Simon,* who employed him as secretary and "launched him," according to Comte, "in the philosophic direction." They separated in 1824, when Saint-Simon attempted to usurp Comte's work. Comte married in 1825; it was a stormy union of almost twenty years' duration. He contributed occasional articles to *Le Producteur* and, in 1826, delivered a course of lectures in his own rooms, which were his first exposition of his positivist philosophy. In April, after the third lecture, he suffered an attack of cerebral derangement and was hospitalized until December. A severe case of depression followed, culminating with a suicide attempt. Comte was rescued after throwing himself into the Seine from the Pont des Arts. The lectures resumed in 1828 and were published in six volumes from 1830 until 1842 as *Cours de philosophie positive* (*Course of Positive Philosophy*). He separated from his wife in 1842 and lost his appointment at the Ecole Polytechnique. John Stuart Mill (1806–1873) and other English admirers supported him financially until Comte's arrogance deterred them. He subsisted for the remaining nine years of his life on a fund collected by his disciple, Emile Littré (1801–1881), author of the famous *Dictionnaire de la langue française* (*Dictionary of the French Language,* 1863–1872). In 1844, he fell passionately in love with Clotilde de Vaux (1815–1846) who awakened a mysticism in the positivist thinker. Comte's *Système de politique positive* (*System of Positive Politics,* 4 vols., 1851–1854), which advocates a "religion of humanity," attests to her influence. In 1857, Comte died of cancer.

Comte's philosophy descended from the philosophes* of the eighteenth century, especially from Condorcet.* His preoccupation with science ushered in an age of positivist thinking that influenced the development of realism* in literature. From Comte, it is but a short step to the positivism of Taine* and Renan.*

For further information, see O. Marti, "August Comte and the Positivist Utopia," in E. Sullivan, ed., *The Utopian Vision: Seven Essays on the Quincentennial of Sir Thomas More* (San Diego: San Diego State University Press, 1983), 93–114; J. McLaverty, "Comtean Fetishism in *Silas Marner,*" *Nineteenth Century Fiction* 36 (3) (December 1981): 318–336; A. Standley, *August Comte* (Boston: Twayne, 1981); T. Wright, "From Bumps to Morals: The Phrenological Background to George Eliot's Framework," *Review of English Studies* 33 (129) (February 1982): 35–46.

CONDILLAC, ETIENNE BONNOT DE, abbé de Mureaux (1715–1780), the eighteenth-century philosophe* and younger brother of political theorist Mably,* is best known as a disciple and disseminator of John Locke's (1632–1704) psychological and philosophical doctrines. Few details of his life survive. Born into a family of Grenoble aristocrats, the serious and dignified Condillac entered a religious order at an early age, though he supposedly celebrated only one mass. As a youth, he associated with J.-J. Rousseau,* Diderot,* and other luminaries of his day and was often quoted in, but never directly contributed to, the *Encyclopédie.** In 1768, he was elected to the French Academy of Sciences. Condillac remained a spiritualist throughout his life and was one of the few Enlightenment philosophers faithful to the church.

Condillac's *Essai sur l'origine des connaissances humaines* (*Essay on the Origin of Human Knowledge,* 1746) focuses on the origin of our ideas. Like Locke, he believed that the mind is born tabula rasa and is formed from the senses. *Traité des systèmes* (*Treatise on Systems,* 1749) examines and argues against the philosophical systems of Nicolas de Malebranche (1638–1715), Gottfried Leibnitz (1646–1716), and Baruch Spinoza (1632–1677) and validates only that philosophy, Locke's, which is based in concrete experience. *Traité des sensations* (*Treatise on Sensations,* 1754) develops his theory of "sensualism," showing how "all our knowledge and all our faculties come from the senses, or more exactly, from sensation." According to Condillac, man's knowledge, feelings, and ideas derive from the combination and interaction of various senses. He envisioned man as an "homme-statue," a statue-man, devoid of ideas, who is granted one by one the five senses until he is able to survive.

As preceptor to the duke of Parma, grandson of Louis XV, Condillac composed a thirteen-volume *Cours d'études* (*Course of Study,* 1755) consisting of "Grammaire" ("Grammar"), "L'Art d'écrire" ("The Art of Writing"), "L'Art de raisonner" (*"*The Art of Reasoning"), "L'Art de penser" (*"*The Art of Thinking"), "L'Histoire ancienne" (*"*Ancient History"), "L'Histoire moderne" (*"*Modern History"), "L'Etude de l'histoire" (*"*The Study of History"), and "Traité des animaux" (*"*Treatise on Animals"). *Le Commerce et le gouvernement* (*Commerce and Government,* 1776), his contribution to the science of economics, developed the idea of commerce or exchange and studied its relationship with government. *La Logique* (*Logic*) was published in 1780, and *La Langue des calculs* (*The Language of Mathematics*) appeared posthumously in 1798.

Bernardin de Saint-Pierre* summarizes Condillac's philosophy and contrasts it with that of René Descartes's (1596–1650) "I think, therefore I am" as "I feel, therefore I am." Despite its occasional inconsistencies and exaggerations, Condillac's sensationalist philosophy was well received by his fellow freethinkers and provided a springboard for the materialism and later atheism of philosophes Diderot, Holbach,* and Helvétius.*

For further information, see A. Bewell, "Wordsworth's Primal Scene: Retrospective Tales of Idiots, Wild Children, and Savages," *Journal of English Literary History* 50 (2) (Summer 1983): 321–346; L. Bongie, ed., *Condillac. Les Monades* (Oxford: The Voltaire Foundation, 1980); Bongie, "A New Condillac Letter (10 June 1750) and the Genesis of the *Traité des sensations,*" *Journal of the History of Philosophy* 16 (January 1978): 83–94; J. J. Chambliss, "The Educational Significance of 'Nature' and 'Conduct' in Condillac's *Logic,*" *Paedagogica historica* 17 (1) (1977): 50–61; E. McNiven Hine, *A Critical Study of Condillac's Traité des systèmes* (The Hague: Nijhoff, 1979); M. F. O'Meara, "The Language of History and the Place of Power: Male and Female Versions of Condillac's *Histoire ancienne et moderne,*" in R. Chambers, ed., *Discours et pouvoir* (Ann Arbor: Department of Romance Languages, University of Michigan, 1982): 177–204; Aldo Scaglioni, "Direct vs. Inverted Order: Wolff and Condillac on the Necessity of the Sign and the Interrelationship of Language and Thinking," *Romance Philology* 33 (May 1980): 496–501.

CONDORCET, MARIE-JEAN-ANTOINE-NICOLAS DE CARITAT, MARQUIS DE (1743–1794), distinguished mathematician, economist, and

philosopher, continued the Enlightenment spirit of truth, tolerance, and humanity until his death at the hands of captors during the French Revolution. He was born at Ribemount in Picardy to an ancient family and was educated at the Jesuit College in Reims and at the Collège de Navarre in Paris. Possessing a brilliant mind, he successfully supported a geometry thesis before mathematicians d'Alembert* and Alexis Claude Clairaut (1713–1765) at age sixteen; at twenty-two he composed a treatise on integral calculus; at twenty-six he entered the Academy of Science, becoming its perpetual secretary four years later. He wrote several mathematical dissertations and a theory of comets (1777), which was well received in Berlin. He frequented the salons of Madame du Deffand (1697–

1780) and Mademoiselle de Lespinasse (1732–1776) and befriended Buffon,*
Benjamin Franklin (1706–1790), and d'Alembert, who encouraged his collaboration, under the pseudonym of Schwartz, on the *Encyclopédie*.* His *Eloges
des académiciens de l'Académie Royale des Sciences morts depuis 1666 jusqu'en
1699* (*In Praise of Academicians of the Royal Academy of Sciences Who Died
between 1666 and 1699*, 1773) established his reputation as a writer.

Politics and social reform fascinated Condorcet as well as mathematics. He
defended Turgot* and the free internal trade of corn in *Lettre d'un laboureur de
Picardie à M. Necker* (*Letter from a Picardie Laborer to M. Necker*, 1775). In
the spirit of his friend Voltaire,* he attacked Christianity in his *Lettres d'un
théologian à l'auteur du Dictionnaire des trois siècles* (*Letters from a Theologian to the Author of the Dictionary of the Three Centuries*, 1772) and in his
Eloge de Pascal (*In Praise of Pascal*, 1773). He pleaded for tolerance in his
Eloge de Michel de l'Hospital (*In Praise of Michael de l'Hospital*, 1777), *Réflexions sur l'esclavage des nègres* (*Reflections on Negro Slavery*, 1781), and *Recueil de pièces sur l'état des protestants de France* (*Collection of Articles on the
State of Protestants in France*, 1781). In 1782 he entered the French Academy.

An ardent republican, Condorcet supported the Revolution with pamphlets and
politics as a member of the municipality of Paris, the Legislative Assembly, and
the National Convention. He wrote addresses and helped frame the constitution,
but when another was adopted, his criticism of it, along with his more moderate
policies, resulted in his condemnation. Outlawed, he fled to the home of
Madame Vernet, where he composed his masterwork, *Esquisse d'un tableau
historique des progrès de l'esprit humain* (*Outline of a Historic Tableau of the
Progress of the Human Mind*, published posthumously, 1794), without benefit of
reference books or notes. Believing her in danger, he fled Madame Vernet's
house and wandered in the woods for three days and nights until his capture in a
village tavern. He was immediately tossed into prison where he died during the
night, either from exhaustion and exposure or by poisoning himself.

Marcel Braunschvig (*Notre Littérature étudiée dans les textes*, 1932) called
the *Esquisse d'un tableau historique des progrès de l'esprit humain* "a synthesis
of philosophic thought in the eighteenth century"; J. H. Brumfitt, "the last great
testament of Enlightenment thought." It details Condorcet's belief in the perfectibility of human nature and the boundless possibilities for human progress and
traces the evolution of science and civilization through ten ages from primitive
times through the age of the philosophes* until the foundation of the French
republic. It envisions a utopian future based on equality between men and nations
and the attainment of the Enlightenment ideals of liberty, truth, justice, and
happiness. Two other works of note are Condorcet's *Vie de Turgot* (*Life of
Turgot*, 1786) and *Vie de Voltaire* (*Life of Voltaire*, 1787).

For further information, see K. M. Baker, *Condorcet* (Chicago, London: University of
Chicago Press, 1975); B. Brookes, "The Feminism of Condorcet and Sophie de Grouchy,"
Studies on Voltaire and the Eighteenth Century 189 (Oxford: Taylor Institution, 1980),
297–361; H. Dippel, "Franklin and Condorcet: Revolution and Social Order, Some

Remarks on Their Social Thought," in *La Révolution américaine et l'Europe* Colloques internationaux du Centre National de la Recherche Scientifique No. 577 (Paris, Toulouse, 1978), 431–447; C. V. Michael, "Condorcet and the Inherent Contradiction in the American Affirmation of Natural Rights and Slaveholding," in *Transactions of the Fifth International Congress on the Enlightenment,* vol. 2 (Oxford: Taylor Institution, 1981), 768–774; Charles B. Paul, *Science and Immortality: The Eloges of the Paris Academy of Sciences, 1699–1791* (Berkeley and Los Angeles: University of California Press, 1980).

CONFESSIONS, LES (*The Confessions*) by Jean-Jacques Rousseau,* published posthumously in 1782 (part 1) and in 1789 (part 2), are perhaps the most widely read of all of his works both for their literary and autobiographical value. They were composed on the run from 1765 to 1770 in Switzerland, Paris, and London (where Rousseau fled after the condemnation of *Emile** in Paris) and written largely in response to charges of child abandonment levelled against him by Voltaire* in an anonymous brochure, *Sentiment des citoyens* (*Feelings of the Citizens,* 1764). Rousseau's *Confessions* trace his life—his early childhood, education, his sojourns at Charmettes with Madame Warens (1700–1762) and at the Hermitage with Madame d'Epinay (1726–1783)—and bear witness to all that made him what he was—his love of nature and solitude, his pride, his sensitivity, his genius. Feeling haunted, persecuted, betrayed by his friends, Rousseau hoped to leave a true record of his life for all to read, "the only sure monument to my nature which has not been defaced by my enemies." Most important, while defining himself, the *Confessions* constitute an apology; they satisfy Rousseau's need to exonerate his sins before God and his fellowman and to console himself.

The *Confessions* are divided into two parts, each containing six books. Part 1 covers the first thirty years, from his birth until his departure for Paris in 1742. It evokes the charm, insouciance, and rusticity of his youth. Part 2 is bitter, detailing the period from his entrance into Parisian literary circles until his departure for England in 1765, including his quarrel with Madame d'Epinay, his rupture with the philosophes,* and his break with society. Both parts reveal a concern for truth that Rousseau felt was his best defense against his enemies, "I want to show my fellowmen a man in all the truth of nature; and that man will be me."

By its lyricism and melancholy, its sensitivity to nature and the soul, the *Confessions* announce the attitude of the romantics (see romanticism*), who were deeply influenced by Rousseau.

For further information, see M. Bullitt, "Rousseau and Tolstoy: Childhood and Confession," *Comparative Literature Studies* 16 (March 1979): 12–20; F. V. Bogel, "Crisis and Character in Autobiography: The Latter Eighteenth Century," *Studies in English Literature* 21 (Summer 1981): 499–512; J. M. Coetzee, "Confession and Double Thoughts: Tolstoy, Rousseau, Dostoevsky," *Comparative Literature* 37 (3) (Summer 1985): 193–232; T. L. Hollard, "Sources of Lyricism in Rousseau's Autobiographical Writings," *New Zealand Journal of*

French Studies 2 (May 1981): 34–55; S. Larkin, ''Jean-Jacques Rousseau, the *Histoire de Cleveland* and the *Confessions,*'' in *Transactions of the Fifth International Congress on the Enlightenment,* vol. 3 (Oxford: Taylor Institution, 1981), 1295–1297; J. A. Perkins, ''Contexts of Autobiography in the Eighteenth Century: France and America,'' in A. Bingham and V. Topazio, eds., *Enlightenment Studies in Honor of Lester G. Crocker* (Oxford: Voltaire Foundation, 1979), 231–241; H. Witemeyer, ''George Eliot and Jean-Jacques Rousseau,'' *Comparative Literature Studies* 16 (1) (June 1979): 121–130.

CONSTANT, HENRI-CONSTANT DE REBECQUE, BENJAMIN (1767–1830), liberal politician and writer best known as the author of *Adolphe,** a masterpiece of early romantic (see romanticism*) literature, was born in Lausanne to a French family transplanted to Switzerland after the revocation of the Edict of Nantes. His mother died shortly after his birth. Constant was raised by his father, a Swiss army colonel in the service of Holland, who exposed him to travel and a succession of mediocre tutors. From 1774 to 1780, Benjamin lived in Brussels, Holland, and his native Lausanne. In 1780, he went to London and Oxford, then back to Holland and Lausanne a year later. He attended the University of Erlangen in 1782 and the University of Edinburgh from 1783 to 1785. In 1785, he moved to Paris with the Suard family and met leading Parisian liberals and philosophes.* From 1787 to 1794, he travelled to England, Scotland, Holland, and Switzerland, experiencing various love affairs and a brief marriage (1789–1795) with Wilhelmina von Cramm along the way. The year 1794 marks the beginning of a long and stormy liaison with Germaine de Staël* and a turn in his political and literary career. In 1795, he and Madame de Staël settled in Paris, where he became a member of the moderate republican party; that year his first article, published anonymously, appeared in Suard's journal, *Les Nouvelles Politiques* (*Political News*). At Madame de Staël's estate at Coppet, while she was writing *De l'influence des passions* (*On the Influence of the Passions,* 1796), Constant wrote *De la force du gouvernement actuel de la France et de la nécessité de s'y rallier* (*On the Force of the Present Goverment of France and the Need to Join It,* 1796). In 1797, he helped found the *Cercle constitutionnel* (*Constitutional Circle*) and published *Des réactions politiques, Des effets de la terreur* (*Of political Reactions, Of the Effects of the Terror*). In 1799, he was elected to the Tribunat, becoming a leading member and eloquent orator of the liberal opposition until expelled by Napoleon in 1802. He accompanied Madame de Staël, expelled from Paris on political grounds in 1803, to Germany. In Weimar in 1804, he met Johann Wolfgang Goethe (1749–1832), Friedrich Schiller (1759–1805), and Christoph Martin Wieland (1733–1813) and renewed a former liaison with Charlotte von Hardenberg, whom he secretly married in 1808. From 1805 until 1807, however, still under the protection of Madame de Staël, he wrote his masterwork, *Adolphe*. In 1807, he began his adaptation of Schiller's dramatic trilogy, *Wallenstein* (1796–1799), which had appeared in 1798–1799. His version, called *Wallstein,* with a preface entitled

"Quelques réflexions sur la tragédie de Wallstein et sur le théâtre allemand" ("Some Thoughts on the Tragedy Wallstein and on German Theatre"), was published in 1809. Two years later, he definitively ended his seventeen-year liaison with Madame de Staël. In 1814, he published numerous political tracts and returned briefly to Paris in 1815 where, in hopes of a liberal empire, he assisted Napoleon during the Hundred Days. After the defeat of Waterloo, he fled to England. An apologia for his actions inspired Louis XVIII to revoke his exile. The following year, in 1816, *Adolphe* was published in London and Paris, as well as *De la doctrine qui peut réunir les partis en France* (*Of the Doctrine which Can Reunite the Parties in France,* 1816), which was well received. A proponent of constitutionalism, he fought the reactionary measures of the government. He collaborated on political journals including *Débats,* the *Mercure de France,* and *La Minerve française.* In 1819, he was elected deputy for the Sarthe region. As one of the leaders of the liberal party, he spoke for freedom of the press and against the slave trade. He was elected deputy for Paris in 1824 and 1827, deciding the second time to represent Strasbourg. By 1829, his health had seriously deteriorated and he died a year later and received a national funeral.

Constant was remembered by his contemporaries primarily as a politician. However, he dedicated almost his entire life to the study of religion, producing two works, *De la religion, considérée dans sa source, ses formes et ses développements* (*On Religion, Considered in its Source, its Forms and its Developments,* 5 vols., 1824–1831) and *Du polythéism romain, considéré dans ses rapports avec la philosophie grecque et la religion chrétienne* (*On Roman Polytheism, Considered in Its Relationships with Greek Philosophy and Christian Religion,* 2 vols., published posthumously, 1833), which have virtually been ignored until relatively recently. These volumes trace the evolution of religious ideas throughout history, delving beneath the exterior of religion, its dogmas, beliefs, practices, and ceremonies, to examine the essence of religion, which is unchanging and universal.

Constant is best known for his novels and journals. *Adolphe* is an autobiography in disguise; *Le Cahier rouge* (*The Red Notebook,* 1907) is the elegant and cynical memoirs of his youth; *Journaux intimes* (*Private Journals,* 1887) recounts the events of his life, especially his unhappy love affair with Madame de Récamier. His novel *Cécile* (written 1813, discovered in 1948 and published in 1951), which he never completed, reveals his love for Charlotte von Hardenberg. The novels are personal and psychological, belonging to the early romantic school with their introspective analysis of the romantic state of mind. Constant personified in his life and works the spirit of liberalism that was rampant at the turn of the century. His steady stream of love affairs earned him the epithet "Constant L'Inconstant" ("Constant the Un-Constant"). He strove eloquently for freedom in parliament and in political tracts. His novels study the psychology of freedom and slavery in love. While the political tracts gather dust on the shelves, his novels and journals continue to be read. *Adolphe* reveals the mal du siècle* gripping so many of the young people at the turn of the century—the need for solitude, liberty, passion—and its underside—vanity, melancholy, boredom, weakness. His autobiographical works provide a glimpse of Constant himself, a curious blend of intellect and emotion, classicism and romanticism, trying to understand himself. Contrary to the works of his friend, Madame de Staël, which are read primarily for their historical significance, Constant's works continue to speak to the modern conscience.

Other works include *Cours de politique constitutionelle* (*Course on Constitutional Politics*, 4 vols., 1818–1820); *De l'esprit de conquête et de l'usurpation* (*On the Spirit of Conquest and Usurpation*, 1813), *Mélanges de littérature et de politique* (*Miscellany on Literature and Politics*, 1829).

For more information, see *Annales Benjamin Constant*, vol. 3 (Oxford: The Voltaire Foundation, 1983); C. P. Courtney, "Benjamin Constant Seen by his Father: Letters from Louis-Arnold-Juste to Samuel de Constant," *French Studies* 39 (3) (July 1985): 276–284; Courtney, "Isabelle de Charrière and the 'Character of H. B. Constant': A False Attribution," *French Studies* 36 (3) (July 1982): 282–289; Courtney, *A Bibliography of the Writings of Benjamin Constant to 1833* (London: The Modern Humanities Research Association, 1981); G. H. Dodge, *Benjamin Constant's Philosophy of Liberalism: A Study in Politics and Religion* (Chapel Hill: University of North Carolina Press, 1980); A. Fairlie, "Suggestions on the Art of the Novelist in Constant's *Cécile,*" in C. A. Burns, ed., *Literature and Society: Studies in Nineteenth and Twentieth Century French Literature Presented to R. J. North* (Birmingham: University of Birmingham, 1980): 29–37; A. Fairlie and M. Bowie, eds., *Imagination and Language: Collected Essays on Constant, Baudelaire, Nerval and Flaubert* (Cambridge: Cambridge University Press, 1981); G. Kelly, "Constant Commotion, Avatars of a Pure Liberal [Chronique]," *The Journal of Modern History* 54 (September 1982): 497–518; D. K. Lowe, *Benjamin Constant. An Annotated Bibliography of Critical Editions and Studies 1946–1978* (London: Grant and Cutler, 1979); J. Vuillemin, "On Lying: Kant and Benjamin Constant," *Kant-Studien* 4 (1982): 413–424; D. Wood, "Constant's *Cahier Rouge:* New Findings," *French Studies* 38 (1) (January 1984): 13–29.

CONTEMPLATIONS, LES (*Contemplations*, 1856), by Victor Hugo,* usually considered the culmination of his lyric poetry, is a spiritual autobiography, the "memoirs of a soul" (Preface), relating "all the impressions, all the memories, all the realities, all the vague phantoms, smiling or dismal, which a consciousness can contain." The 157 poems in the collection were written over a period of twenty-two years; the earliest, "Mon bras pressait ta taille frêle" ("My arm squeezed your tiny waist"), dates back to 1834, but most were composed in exile in Jersey or Guernsey between 1852 and 1855. All were influenced by Hugo's interest in the occult, begun in Jersey. The collection is divided into two parts, "Autrefois" ("Formerly") and "Aujourd'hui" ("Today"), divided by the death of Hugo's newly wed daughter, Léopoldine, in a boating accident with her husband on 4 September 1843. Each part contains three "books" tracing the span of Hugo's life, thoughts, and feelings from the "enigma of the cradle" to the "enigma of the grave." Together they constitute his mystical voyage through life and death, joy and sadness, to the "infinite," the "abyss," the "darkness," beyond the grave.

Book 1, "Aurore" ("Dawn"), reiterates the themes of previous collections, *Les Chants du crépuscule** and *Les Voix intérieures**—Hugo's childhood, enthusiasm for family life, and his poetic inspiration. "A propos d'Horace" ("Regarding Horace") relates school memories; "Lise," initial stirrings of love; "Vere novo," the beauty of spring. "Réponse à un acte d'accusation" ("Reply to an Act of Accusation"), recalling the opposition to *Hernani** and other early dramas, enumerates Hugo's poetic innovations, justifies his "war" on rhetoric and "peace" on syntax in the theatre and the resulting romantic (see romanticism*) revolution. ("And all of '93 broke out," Hugo wrote in this poem, referring to the Reign of Terror in 1793.) "Mes Deux Filles" ("My Two Daughters") expresses Hugo's joy in his daughters, Léopoldine and Adèle; "La Fête chez Thérèse" ("Festivities at Therese's") paints a charming, springtime tableau à la Watteau or Fragonard of feminine beauty and love. Book 2, "L'Ame en Fleur" ("The Soul in Bloom"), is dedicated to love and Juliette Drouet, the sites they visited ("Lettre"), the emotions she inspired ("Viens, une flûte invisible . . ."—"Come, An Invisible Flute . . ."). Book 3, "Les Luttes et les rêves" ("Struggles and Dreams"), more dramatic than the first two, is colored by sadness, suffering, and questioning before the paradox of the universe. "Mélancholia" presents the misery of the wife of an alcoholic, a fallen woman, a corrupt judge, a scoffed genius, exploited children, a horse dying from maltreatment, an old soldier. "Magnitudo parvi" ("The Greatness of the Small") juxtaposes two distant lights discovered by Léopoldine on a seaside walk, that of a shepherd's fire and that of a glittering star, two "worlds" that Hugo explores, that of the inexplicable, vast cosmos and that of the solitary, peaceful heart of a simple shepherd. Their light is forged by God into the "two wings of prayer."

Book 4, "Pauca Meae" ("A Few Words For My Daughter"), sets a tone of grief pervading much of the poetry of part 2. Hugo is haunted by the memory of his daughter and continually questions the meaning of life and what lies beyond the grave. The poems relate the love he felt for her ("Elle avait pris ce pli . . ."— "She Had This Habit"); his extreme anguish upon her death ("Oh! Je fus comme un fou . . ."—"Oh! I was like a Madman"); his dedication to her memory ("Demain, dès l'aube"—"Tomorrow, at Daybreak"). Other poems reveal his resignation before God, destiny, and death ("A Villequier"—"To Villequier," one of the most famous poems of the collection, and "On Vit, on Parle"—"We Live and Speak"). "Veni, Vidi, Vixi," taken from Caesar's pronouncement, "I came, I saw, I conquered," outlines his discouragement, his willingness to "disappear through the doors of night." In book 5, "En marche" ("On the March"), Hugo tries to pull himself up by his poetic bootstraps and get on with his odyssey. He finds solace in the beauty and "poetry" of nature in "Mugitusque Boum" ("The Cattle's Lowing") and "Pasteurs et troupeaux" ("Shepherds and Flocks"); satisfaction and a glimpse of the sublime in sheltering a poor man ("Le Mendiant"—"The Mendicant"). "Paroles sur la dune" ("Words on the

Dune''), however, reveals his abiding sadness in his exile, his recurring doubt and weariness on the path through life. In the final book, ''Au bord de l'infini'' (''On the Brink of the Infinite''), he achieves his quest, an apocalyptic vision of the world beyond taken from the Bible and Hugo's own dabbling in the occult. He spreads his wings in ''Ibo'' and will learn the truths of the ''unfathomable . . . terrible tabernacle'' of the heavens, regardless of how high he must fly. ''Eclaircie'' (''Enlightened'') echoes the faith in nature expressed in earlier poems, affirms the continuity and unity of life in a scene where all is ''calm, happy, at peace'' with God watching. ''Les Mages'' celebrates his divine mission as a poet ''blessed by the hands of God in the shadows of the cradle,'' along with the artists, visionaries, savants, inventors, and philosophers. This book ends with the optimism of ''Ce que dit la bouche d'ombre'' (''What the Mouth of the Shadow Said''), depicting a world in which ''everything is a voice and everything is a perfume . . . all speaks . . . all is filled with souls;'' all will be reconciled in a new beginning, death will perish along with tears, weapons, mourning, and fear. The volume closes with a dedication to his daughter, ''A celle qui est restée en France'' (''To She Who Remained in France''), whose death inspired his deepest despair but also led him to ''contemplate'' life before and after the grave. Thus she inspired a lyric masterpiece that endures among the most beautiful and meaningful poetry ever written in the French language and that speaks to us all, as Hugo claimed in his Preface, ''When I speak to you of myself, I am speaking to you of you.''

For further information, see W. Greenberg, ''Structure and Function of Hugo's Condensed Metaphor,'' *French Review* 56 (December 1982): 257–266; John P. Houston, ''Design in *Les Contemplations*,'' *French Forum* 5 (May 1980): 122–140; S. Nash, *''Les Contemplations'' of Victor Hugo: An Allegory of the Creative Process* (Princeton: Princeton University Press, 1976).

CONTRAT SOCIAL, LE (*The Social Contract*, 1762), by Jean-Jacques Rousseau,* along with *La Nouvelle Héloïse** and *Emile,** offers a program of reform for the ills of civilization that Rousseau had outlined in earlier works. While *La Nouvelle Héloïse* depicts an ideal of family life and *Emile* an ideal of education, *Le Contrat social* deals with an ideal state devoid of injustice and tyranny that would restore man to his natural freedom. ''Man is born free, and everywhere he is in chains,'' he declares in book 1. Rousseau would establish ''a form of association which defends and protects with common force the individual and the possessions of each associate, and by which each one, uniting with each other, obeys himself and remains as free as he had been before.'' This association would be ratified by means of a contract or ''social pact'' in which each individual subordinates himself, his power, and his rights to the whole community and totally integrates himself as a ''citizen'' into a new form of public union, which Rousseau calls a ''republic'' or ''political body.'' In relinquishing his natural liberty for civil liberty, man reestablishes and reinforces his freedom and equality, for ''each man, in giving himself to all, gives himself to nobody.''

In book 2, Rousseau defines sovereignty as "nothing less than the exercise of general will," which is inalienable and indivisible. He distinguishes between the "will of all," which takes private interests into account, and the "general will," which considers only the common interest. Individual citizens are bound to surrender immediately to the state that which it demands, but the state, on the other hand, is bound to be fair and "cannot exceed the limits of general conventions." Citizens must be ready, if necessary, to give their lives for the state and obey its laws. Book 3 discusses forms of government—democracy, which Rousseau declares that in its true form never has and never will exist for it goes against nature; aristocracy; and monarchy. The best government, however, is that in which the people multiply. Book 4 deals with voting, by which the majority rules, and religion, which Rousseau feels is necessary to reinforce morality and one's sense of duty, but which should otherwise be left up to the individual.

In defining and setting limits to the powers of government, Rousseau, more than any other philosophe,* influenced the politics of France, which declared in 1789 the sovereignty of the people, and the revolutions of the United States and Russia. His criticism of private property provides the basis for socialism and communism. *Le Contrat social* has been called "one of the most remarkable treatises of political theory that has ever been written" (Niklaus, *A Literary History of France*, 1970).

For further information, see S. Ellenburg, "Rousseau and Kant: Principles of Political Right," in R. Leigh, ed. *Rousseau after Two Hundred Years: Proceedings of the Cambridge Bicentennial Colloquium* (Cambridge: Cambridge University Press, 1982), 3–35; H. Gildin, *Rousseau's Social Contract: The Design of the Argument* (Chicago: University of Chicago Press, 1983); R. Ginsberg, "Rousseau's *Contrat social* in Current Contexts," *Transactions of the Fifth International Congress on the Enlightenment*, vol. 1 (Oxford: Taylor Institution, 1981), 252–258; A. Kalleberg, "The Structure of Argument in Political Theory," in A. Kalleberg, J. D. Moon, and D. Sabia, eds., *Dissent and Affirmation: Essays in Honor of Mulford Q. Sibley* (Bowling Green, Ohio: Popular, 1983), 224–246; J. Lough, "*The Encyclopédie* and *The Contrat social*," in S. Harvey, M. Hobson, D. Kelley, and S. S. B. Taylor, eds., *Reappraisals of Rousseau in Honor of Ralph A. Leigh* (Totowa, N.J.: Barnes and Noble, 1980), 64–74; L. McKenzie, "Rousseau's Debate with Machiavelli in *The Social Contract*," *Journal of the History of Ideas* 43 (2) (April–June 1982): 209–228; J. B. Noone, Jr., *Rousseau's Social Contract: A Conceptual Analysis* (Athens: University of Georgia Press, 1980).

COPPEE, FRANÇOIS (1842–1908), Parnassian* poet and dramatist, distinguished himself as a poet of the people. A child of Paris, he lived there all of his life except for a few excursions. His father was a humble functionary in the war department, which François also entered when a lack of funds forced him to curtail his education. Through a friend he met Catulle Mendès* and became acquainted with the Parnassian milieu, whose esthetics he adopted in his first volumes of poetry. He remained on the sidelines until his play, *Le Passant* (*The Passer-By*, 1869), which starred Sarah Bernhardt (1844–1923) at the Odéon

Theatre, catapulted him to fame. In 1870, he became underlibrarian of the senate in the Luxembourg Palace. He was named archivist at the Comédie-Française in 1878 and entered the Academy in 1884, which enabled him to devote himself full time to literature. After a serious illness, he returned to the Catholicism of his youth. His support for the nationalists, or "anti-Dreyfusards," during the highly publicized Dreyfus affair (1894–1899), brought him the condemnation of many of his friends and caused him much pain. He died in Paris in 1908.

Coppée's first collection, *Le Reliquaire* (*The Reliquary,* 1866), with its concerns of poetic form, philosophy, and praise of Leconte de Lisle,* is steeped in Parnassianism. *Intimités* (*Intimacies,* 1868), written, as its title indicates, more in the vein of Sully-Prudhomme,* is intimate and sentimental and aimed at the literate Parisian bourgeoisie. In 1869, his poetry began the course that made him famous. *Les Humbles* (1872), *Le Cahier rouge* (*The Red Notebook,* 1874), *Promenades et intérieurs* (*Walks and Interiors,* 1875), and *Les Récits et les elégies* (*Narratives and Elegies,* 1878) depict realistically and passionately the Paris he knew and loved and the soul of its people. "La Petite Marchande de fleurs" ("The Little Flower Girl") portrays a poor seven-year-old girl selling flowers in the cold November air; "Un Fils" ("A Son") is about a boy's devotion to his sick mother; "Les Parfums" ("Perfumes") evokes the smells of the city—its oranges, firewood, steaming asphalt. The poems reveal the resignation and the courage of the common people as well as the sensitivity and nostalgia of the poet and won him the hearts of many.

Coppée's contributions to the theatre include *Le Luthier de Crémone* (*The Violin-Maker of Cremone,* 1876), *Severo Torelli* (1883), *Les Jacobites* (1885), and *Pour la couronne* (*For the Crown,* 1895), among others. His novel *La Bonne Souffrance* (*The Good Suffering,* 1898) reflects his religious conversion.

CORBEAUX, LES (*The Crows,* 1882), by Becque,* is a masterpiece of realist (see realism*) drama about the exploitation of a widow and her three daughters by the avaricious "vultures" who descend upon them after the sudden death of her husband. Its bitter, pessimistic depiction of their helplessness and one daughter's sacrifice for her family marked the beginning of modern theatre.

The play begins on a pleasant note as Madame Vigneron and her daughters are reviewing plans for an engagement party that evening. The youngest daughter, Blanche, is about to marry Georges, a young man from a poor but noble family. Mr. Vigneron, napping on a couch, awakens to his daughters' concerns about his health, which is declining because of overwork at his firm, Teissier, Vigneron, and Co. He repeats the story of his rise in business, thanks to Monsieur Teissier, whom Blanche describes as "old, ugly, coarse and miserly." Vigneron leaves for work and the afternoon progresses as guests arrive for the dinner—Madame de Saint-Genis, Blanche's future mother-in-law; Merckens, music teacher of Judith, the eldest daughter; Teissier; Bourdon, a notary; Mr. Lenormand; Georges de Saint-Genis; General Fromentin; and Gaston, the Vignerons' son. As the act closes, a doctor arrives with the news that Vigneron has died suddenly of apoplexy. Act 2 begins with Madame de Saint-Genis warning Madame Vigneron of the motives of others, especially Teissier and the notary. Teissier informs her that her husband's estate is worth only 50,000 francs. Marie, the middle sister, tells Blanche of their potential financial ruin and the probable annulment of her marriage plans. Blanche, astounded, says she will die or go crazy if the plans fail. Bourdon, in league with Teissier to swindle the women, recommends they sell their land to meet their debts. Lefort, the architect, suggests that they finish the construction that Vigneron had begun there. This act ends with Madame Vigneron and her daughters discussing their alternatives as a servant delivers a number of bills to be paid.

By act 3 Teissier is slowly winning control, lending the Vignerons money, and showing interest in Marie. Bourdon brings news of additional debts and the need to sell their factory. Teissier proposes that Marie come to live at his house, where she will have food, lodging, and a "little sum" besides. She refuses, preferring to remain with her family and devoted servant, Rosalie. Madame de Saint-Genis, convinced of the Vignerons' poverty, breaks her son's wedding plans. Blanche, however, sure that Georges loves her, believes he will marry her out of duty. When she says she would rather be his mistress than the wife of another, Madame de Saint-Genis has moral grounds to destroy their relationship forever. Blanche faints into the arms of Rosalie, calling herself a "fallen woman," and Madame Vigneron decides to accept Bourdon's terms. Act 4 finds the family reduced to poverty; Blanche has suffered a nervous breakdown. Judith entertains ideas of teaching music or entering the theatre to support her family but Merckens discourages her. At Bourdon's insistence and against her better judgement, Marie accepts Teissier's proposal and marries the unscrupulous man responsible for her family's misery to restore a measure of their financial stability.

CORBIERE, TRISTAN (1845–1875). See *Dictionary of Modern French Literature, from Naturalism and Symbolism to Post-Modernism.*

COURIER, PAUL-LOUIS (1772–1825), liberal thinker and writer, is best known for his pamphlets in which he exposed injustice and satirized his contemporaries. He was born into a wealthy bourgeois family, was well-educated, and served in the army under the Republic and the Empire but spent most of his time haunting Italian libraries. He resigned in 1808, reenlisted a year later, then resigned for good after the battle of Wagram in July 1809. After travels and marriage in 1812, he settled at his country estate, La Chavonnière, in Touraine, where he observed the local scene and wrote most of his pamphlets. He met a violent death at the hand of a disgruntled former farmhand in 1825.

Courier was a classical scholar with a lifelong passion for Greece. While in the military in Florence, he discovered a manuscript of a novel, *Daphnis et Chloé*, by Greek novelist Longus (A.D. third or fourth century). He translated Xenophon's (434?–355? B.C.) *Traité de l'equitation* (*Treatise on Equitation*, 1813) and *Sur le commandement de la cavalerie* (*On Commanding the Cavalry*,

1813) and works by Plutarch (A.D. 46?–120?) and Herodotus (fifth century, B.C.). But he is remembered as a polemicist who directed his ire and irony against individuals such as the French scholar who claimed he intentionally spilled ink on the only surviving copy of an ancient manuscript (*Lettre à M. Renouard, libraire, sur une tache faite à un manuscrit de Florence* [*Letter to Mr. Renouard, Bookseller, on a Spot Made on a Manuscript from Florence*], 1810), or against the Institute (*Lettre à messieurs de l'Académie des Inscriptions et Belles-Lettres* [*Letter to the Gentlemen of the Academy of Inscriptions and Humanities*], 1820). One petition decried the actions of the "White Terror," led by the royalists against so-called revolutionary traitors; another denounced a national subscription to hand over the 12,000 acres of the Chambord estate to the duke of Bordeaux, aged two months. In writing that was witty and elegant, often in the manner of Voltaire,* he exposed the excesses of the clergy and Restoration politics and worked for the rights of the peasants.

COURTILZ DE SANDRAS, GATIEN DE (c. 1644–1712), storywriter, political journalist, pamphleteer, and historian, published a number of anonymous pseudo-memoirs around the turn of the century, notably the *Mémoires de M.L.C.D.R.* (*Memoirs of M.L.C.D.R.*, 1687), thought to stand for Monsieur le Comte de Rochefort, 1687); *Mémoires de M. D'Artagnan* (*Memoirs of Monsieur D'Artagnan*, 1700), remembered as the source for Dumas père's* *Les Trois mousquetaires* (*The Three Musketeers*, 1844); and *Mémoires de M. de B.* (*Memoirs of Mr. B.*, 1711). Although of little interest now, his depictions of life during the ministries of Cardinal Richelieu (1585–1642) and Jules Mazarin (1602–1661) were immensely popular in their day. Though based in fact, Courtilz embellished them with anecdotes of his own, thus bridging the gap between the authentic memoir and the fictional one and preparing the way for the novels of Prévost* and Marivaux.*

COUSIN, VICTOR (1792–1867), historian and philosopher, was the son of a watchmaker, like J.-J. Rousseau.* He was born in Paris at the time of the founding of the new republic. He received a classical education at the Lycée Charlemagne and exhibited an early interest in letters and Greek literature. He attended the Ecole Normale, where he was attracted to the teaching of Royer-Collard* and Maine de Biran.* From 1815 until 1820, he taught philosophy at the Ecole Normale and the Sorbonne. He was influenced by German philosophers Immanuel Kant (1724–1804) and Friedrich Hegel (1770–1831). In 1817, he met Hegel in Heidelberg; the following year, he met Friedrich Schelling (1775–1854) in Munich. In 1820, his course, considered too liberal by the Restoration, was suppressed. From 1821 to 1822, he travelled to Germany, where he developed his philosophical doctrine in his *Fragmens philosophiques* (*Philosophical Fragments*, 1826) and *Cours de l'histoire de la philosophie* (*Course on the History of Philosophy*, 1827). With the enlightened and tolerant spirit of the year 1828, Cousin was called back to the university along with his illustrious colleagues, Guizot* and Villemain.* He distinguished himself as an eloquent lecturer. After the 1830 revolution, he espoused the causes of national liberty and constitutional rights. The bourgeois government of Louis-Philippe recognized his contributions and named him counsellor of state. In 1832, he was made a peer of France. In 1840, he became minister of public education and organized the primary instruction of France. The years of his official service, from 1830 until 1848, were spent revising his former lectures and studies. He also renewed his interest in seventeenth-century literature and society. By 1848, his political views had moderated. He published a pamphlet, *Justice et charité* (*Justice and Charity*), which was markedly antisocialistic, and withdrew from public life. He renewed his interest in seventeenth-century literature, publishing, among other things, *Etudes sur les femmes et la société du XVIIe siècle* (*Studies on the Women and the Society of the XVIIth Century,* 1853). Napoleon withdrew his seat on the council of public instruction but decreed him, along with Guizot and Villemain, honorary professor. He spent his final years in residence at the Sorbonne until his death in Cannes in 1867.

Cousin's philosophy of eclecticism was first inspired by the writings of Kant and Hegel, then expanded to include the truths of various philosophical systems. It is a synthesis of the best of ancient and modern teachings—sensualism, idealism, skepticism, and mysticism—with much emphasis on the history of philosophy and the relationship between "the two immortal sisters," philosophy and religion. Cousin's eclecticism, his need to synthesize, is characteristic of the romantic (see romanticism*) temperament, which his philosophy helped to formulate. Sainte-Beuve,* Balzac,* Stendhal,* and Michelet* attested to his influence. Cousin's most important work is *Du vrai, du beau, du bien* (*Of the True, the Beautiful, the Good,* 1837 and 1853). His principal disciple was Théodore Jouffroy (1796–1842), who became a professor at the Sorbonne and the Collège de France and wrote a *Cours de droit naturel* (*Course on Natural Law,* 1835–1842) and *Cours d'esthétique* (*Course on Esthetics,* 1843).

CREBILLON, CLAUDE-PROSPER JOLYOT DE (1674–1762, also spelled Crais-billon) after Voltaire,* was the principal writer of tragedies in the eighteenth century. Born in Dijon, he came to Paris as a law clerk but soon turned to the theatre, encouraged by his lawyer-patron and the beneficence of the Regency and several noblemen. After the death of his wife in 1711, he spent much of his time alone, listless, bohemian, accompanied often only by his ten cats and 22 dogs. Well-respected nevertheless, he was named royal censor in 1733 and censor of the police in 1735.

Crébillon achieved renown first with *Idoménée* (1705), *Atrée and Thyeste* (1707), and *Electre* (1709) and reached his height with *Rhadamist and Zénobie* (1711); with *Xerxès* (1714) and *Sémiramis* (1717) his influence waned. At the behest of the government, he abandoned his *Cromwell* and remained silent until *Pyrrhus* (1726) nine years later.

The poet of horror, Crébillon is credited with saying, "Corneille has taken the heavens, Racine the earth; for me there is hell.'' His aim, according to the preface to *Atrée and Thyeste,* was to ''move the spectator to pity through terror.'' Thus in *Idoménée,* a father kills his son; in *Atrée and Thyeste,* a father drinks his son's blood; in *Rhadamist and Zénobie,* a father kills his son and then himself. But in accordance with the classical precept of ''bienséance'' or good taste, the horror takes place accidentally, the result of a bizarre turn of plot, or is committed in ignorance. Unfortunately, the brutality and action on stage take precedence over the psychology of the characters, resulting in melodramatic, often poorly written travesties of the masterpieces of Pierre Corneille (1606–1684) and Jean Racine (1639–1699). Crébillon never achieves the status of his rival, Voltaire, who emerges with *Zaire** and *Mérope** as the only tragedian of merit in the eighteenth century.

CREBILLON, CLAUDE-PROSPER JOLYOT DE (1707–1777), son of Crébillon* (Voltaire's* rival in writing tragedies) and therefore known as Crebillon Fils, wrote novels and dialogues steeped in the libertinism of the eighteenth-century aristocracy to which he belonged. His parents wed two weeks before his birth; he traded the rigors of a Jesuit education for the pleasures of the theatre, epicureanism, and licentious literature. First, he wrote letter-novels, *Le Sylphe* (*The Sylphe,* 1730) and *Les Lettres de la marquise de M____ au comte de R____* (*Letters from the Marquise of M____ to the Count of R____,* 1732). His second novel, *L'Ecumoire* (*The Ladle,* 1732), with thinly disguised attacks on the Duchess of Maine (1676–1753), the Cardinals Rohan (1734–1803) and Dubois (1656–1723), and the papal bull *Unigenitus,* resulted in a short term in Vincennes prison. His masterwork, *Les Egarements du coeur et de l'esprit* (*Aberrations of the Heart and Mind,* 1736), depicts the initiation of a young aristocrat into socially acceptable promiscuity. *Le Sopha* (*The Sofa,* 1740), blatantly licentious, was branded obscene, and Crébillon fils was exiled from Paris two years later. Oddly enough, upon his return in 1747, he was appointed royal censor for ''belles lettres'' by Madame de Pompadour (1721–1764); a year later he married a wealthy Englishwoman who, impressed by his novels, offered herself in marriage. A competent public official and loyal husband, Crébillon fils filled both roles respectfully. In 1774, he was named police censor. Other works include *Ah! quel conte!* (*Ah! What a Story,* 1751), *Les Heureux Orphelins* (*The Happy Orphans,* 1754); his dialogues, *La Nuit et le moment* (*The Night and the Moment,* 1755) and *Le Hasard du coin du feu* (*Fate in the Corner of the Fire,* 1763); and *Lettres de la duchesse de ____ au duc de ____* (*Letters from the Duchess of ____ to the Duke of ____,* 1768) and *Lettres athéniennes* (*Athenian Letters,* 1771).

Crébillon fils' novels deal exclusively with Parisian aristocrats and their permissiveness during the Regency. Long misunderstood, especially *Les Egarements,* they are only recently being assessed as objective exposés of the corrupt mores and potentially damaging sexual warfare playfully waged by the idle rich. Crébillon, at last, has been recognized as distinct from his characters. He analyzes their minds rather than their sentiments, as Marivaux* or Prévost* had. And though not as accomplished as Laclos,* with whom he shares a common theme and approach, Crébillon fils' writing is lucid; his psychology, deep; his influence on the letter-novel and the use of third-person narrative, significant.

For further information, see P. Conroy, "Real Fiction: Authenticity in the French Epistolary Novel," *Romanic Review* 72 (November 1981): 409–424; J. Undank, "Contagions of Truth: Language and History in *Les Egarements du coeur et de l'esprit,*" *Esprit Créateur* 22 (3) (Fall 1982): 59–71; T. Vessely, "Innocence and Impotence: The Scenario of Initiation in *l'Ecumoire* and in the Literary Fairy Tale," *Eighteenth Century Life* 7 (1) (October 1981): 71–85.

CROS, CHARLES (1842–1888). See *Dictionary of Modern French Literature, from Naturalism and Symbolism to Post-Modernism.*

D

DANCOURT, FLORENT CARTON (1661–1725), actor, director, and playwright, continued the influence of Molière (1622–1673) in the early eighteenth century. Born at Fontainebleau into a noble family of magistrates and financiers, he studied law, which he abandoned in 1685 for a wife and career in the Comédie-Française. Partly in collaboration with Saint-Yon, a minor dramatist about whom little is known, he composed more than fifty plays in the grand style of the classic comedy of Molière—five-act, prose pieces with well-planned plots and characters. His comedies, though considered today superficial and uncreative, are significant for their realism and satire in portraying customs, corruption, and coquetry of the bourgeoisie without concern for moralizing. His best play, *Le Chevalier à la mode* (*The Fashionable Chevalier,* 1687), depicts an unscrupulous adventurer who deceives three women in hopes of advancing in society; *Les Bourgeoises à la mode* (*The Fashionable Bourgeoises,* 1692) weaves a comedy around the deceptions planned by two young women bored with their bourgeois husbands. Before Lesage,* Dancourt discerned the growing importance of money to the bourgeoisie. Other comedies include *Le Tuteur* (*The Tutor,* 1695), *Les Bourgeoises de qualité* (*Bourgeoises of Quality,* 1700), and many more. Dancourt also wrote several comédies-vaudeville, with song and dance.

DANTON, GEORGES JACQUES (1759–1794), orator and influential revolutionary, was a deputy to the National Convention from 1792 until his execution two years later. He was born in Arcis-sur-Aube to a modest family, received a solid education in law and, in 1787, acquired the position of advocate on the royal council. He was president of the Cordeliers, an extremist group based in his district, which he founded in 1790 with revolutionary journalists Jean-Paul Marat (1743–1793) and Camille Desmoulins.* Though never proven, it is believed he had some part in instigating the insurrection of 1792 and the fall of the monarchy, after which he became minister of justice. Likewise, his role in the massacre of hundreds of prisoners has long been suspected but never documented. At the convention, he voted for the death of the king and belonged, for a short while, to the committee for public safety, which under the direction of Robespierre,* orchestrated the Reign of Terror. On 30 March 1794, the committee, filled with his enemies, had him arrested. Danton was guillotined with Desmoulins, Fabre d'Eglantine,* and thirteen others six days later.

As an orator, the passion and inspiration of his words and his powerful physical presence recall that of Mirabeau*; however, less eloquent and logical, more vulgar and impetuous, he was called the "Mirabeau of the people." His cry before the Legislative Assembly on 2 September 1792 at the seige of Verdun has echoed through the centuries; "To vanquish them [the Prussians who were advancing on Verdun], Sirs, we need courage, more courage, always courage and France will be saved."

DAUDET, ALPHONSE (1840–1897). See *Dictionary of Modern French Literature, from Naturalism and Symbolism to Post-Modernism.*

DE BELLOY, born Pierre-Laurent Buirette (1727–1775), the son of a lawyer, orphaned at an early age, began his career as an actor but met with fame and fortune with his patriotic tragedies. His best, *Le Siège de Calais* (*The Siege of Calais,* 1765), based on a war that was currently being fought with the English, won the support of the government, which organized free public performances, and the enthusiasm of the people. Other tragedies include *Titus* (1759), *Zelmire* (1762), *Gaston et Bayard* (1771), *Pierre le cruel* (*Peter the Cruel,* 1772), and *Gabrielle de Vergy* (1777). He entered the French Academy in 1771.

DELILLE, JACQUES (1738–1813), poet and translator, sustained the pseudo-classicism prevalent in the poetry of the eighteenth century (that of Houdar de la Motte,* Pompignan,* and J.-B. Rousseau*) with his didactic poems but added a new dimension more in the vein of Jean-Jacques Rousseau* and the preromantics (see preromanticism*)—a love of and communion with nature.

Delille's didacticism was partially inspired by the ancients. He was a professor of Latin poetry at the Collège de France and translated Virgil's (70–19 B.C.) *Georgics* (1769), the *Aeneid* (1804), and John Milton's (1608–1674) *Paradise Lost* (1805). Translating the *Georgics* gained him entry into the salons and the Academy in 1774. Though later granted the title "Abbé," he was arrested during the Reign of Terror and fled to England and Germany. Upon his return, paralytic and soon blind, he resumed his chair at the Collège de France, where he continued to write until his death in 1813.

The best known of his poems, *Les Jardins ou L'Art d'embellir les paysages* (*The Gardens or The Art of Embellishing Scenery,* 1780) and *L'Homme des champs ou Les Géorgiques françaises* (*The Man of the Fields or The French Georgics,* 1800), evoke the melancholy of autumn, the beauty of the forest, a sense of isolation and communion with nature. "I love to mingle my sorrow with the sorrow of nature," he wrote in *Les Jardins*. Although often mediocre, monotonous, or contrived, the descriptive, picturesque poetry of Delille influenced Chenier* and the coming generation of romantic (see romanticism*) poets.

DE MAISTRE, JOSEPH (1754–1821), political philosopher who with de Bonald* upheld the absolute authority of the church and the king, was born in Chambéry in the duchy of Savoy, which at that time belonged to the kingdom of Sardinia. His father was president of the senate at Savoy, which de Maistre himself entered until the annexation of Savoy by the French in 1792. He fled to Turin, then to Geneva and Lausanne. He held a diplomatic post in Sardinia from 1799 until 1803, when King Victor-Emmanuel named him minister to Russia. He lived in Saint Petersburg for fourteen years, where, without his family, he wrote most of his major works. He returned to Turin in 1817, his health seriously impaired, and died four years later in 1821.

De Maistre believed in the sovereignty of God and that nothing in this world happens without his will, including the French Revolution. He believed that man is by nature evil and is redeemed by severe tests, such as war and execution, orchestrated by a just and wrathful God to punish and purify him. Like de Bonald, he refuted the philosophes* of the eighteenth century, especially J.-J. Rousseau* and Voltaire,* and supported the absolute authority and infallibility of the pope and a monarchy with limitless power and control. These thoughts are contained in *Du Pape* (*Concerning the Pope,* 1819) and *Les Soirées de Saint Petersbourg* (*Evenings in Saint Petersburg,* 1821), a treatise in dialogue form between three people, an emigré French knight, a Russian senator inclined toward mysticism, and the author himself, in the guise of a Savoyard count.

De Maistre was a powerful force in the restoration of the church after the blows it was dealt in the eighteenth century. His other works include *Considérations sur la France* (*Considerations on France,* 1796), *Essai sur le principe générateur des constitutions politiques* (*Essay on the Generative Principles of Political Constitutions,* 1810), and *De l'eglise gallicane dans son rapport avec le souverain pontife* (*Concerning the Gallican Church in its Relations with the Sovereign Pontiff,* 1821).

DESBORDES-VALMORE, MARCELINE (1786–1859) was a minor romantic (see romanticism*) poet whose passionate poems and plaintive elegies were admired by Sainte-Beuve,* Baudelaire,** Verlaine,** and Mallarmé.** Verlaine included her in his gallery of *Poètes maudits* (*Accursed Poets,* 1884). She was born in Douai, the daughter of a painter of coats of arms who was ruined by the Revolution. She grew up in poverty and knew misery intimately throughout her life. At fifteen, she travelled with her mother to Guadeloupe in search of a better life with a relative there, but her mother died. She returned to France and supported herself as a costume seamstress and later as a singer and actress in theatres in Lille, Rouen, Paris, and Brussels. In 1817, she married a mediocre actor, Valmore. Six years later, she gave up the theatre for her true vocation, poetry, but never succeeded in keeping poverty and sadness at bay.

Much of her poetry stems from an ardent and mysterious love for a man, supposedly Henri de Latouche (1785–1851), writer and editor of the literary review *Le Mercure de France au XIXe siècle,* who fathered and abandoned a child who died before the age of five. Her verse is musical, delicate, sensitive, and sincere, as it transposes her suffering, her love for her children, her passion for her beloved, and her religious yearnings. Her works include *Elégies, Marie et romances (Elegies, Marie [A Prose Tale] and Romances, 1819), Poésies* (1820), *Elégies et poésies nouvelles (Elegies and New Poetry,* 1825), *Poésies* (1830), *Les Pleurs (Tears,* 1833), *Pauvres fleurs (Poor Flowers,* 1839), *Bouquets et prières (Bouquets and Prayers,* 1843), and a posthumous collection of unedited poems published in 1860.

DESMOULINS, CAMILLE (1760–1794), revolutionary journalist and deputy to the National Convention, his shift from Robespierre* to a moderate position cost him his life. He was born in Guise in Picardy, studied law at the Collège Louis-le-Grand in Paris, and became an advocate of the Parisian Parliament in 1785. He started the wheels of the Revolution moving on 12 July 1789 by jumping on a table of a Palais Royal café and urging the people to arms at Louis XVI's dismissal of Jacques Necker (1732–1804) as France's financial director. The storming of the Bastille took place two days later. Desmoulins's forte, however, was political writing. He won Mirabeau's* attention and support with his treatise, *La France libre (Free France),* published in that pivotal month, July 1789. His *Discours de la lanterne aux Parisiens (Discourses from the Street Lamp to the Parisians,* 1789) fanned the emotions of the people. His news weekly, *Révolutions de France et de Brabant (Revolutions of France and of Brabant),* which he produced alone from November 1789 until July 1790 and with the assistance of Louis Fréron (1765–1802, son of Elie Fréron*) until publication was suspended in July 1792, brought him renown and long overdue financial security. The paper reflected the changing mood of Paris in the early years of the Revolution and praised its ardor and excesses.

Early in 1791, Desmoulins switched his allegiance from Mirabeau to Danton* and served as secretary general when Danton became minister of justice. Later that year, he represented Paris at the National Convention where, as a "montagnard," or extremist, he allied himself with Robespierre and voted the death of the king. His journal, *Tribune des patriotes (Tribune of the Patriots,* 1792), met with little success; *Jean-Pierre Brissot démasqué (Jean-Pierre Brissot Unmasked,* 1792), directed against the Girondin leader Brissot de Warville (1754–1793), led to his *Histoire des Brissotins (History of the Brissotins,* 1793) and the eventual fall of the moderate party. Desmoulins's most significant publication, *Le Vieux Cordelier (The Old Franciscan,* 1793), reflected his move from his extreme position. Taking its title from a club Desmoulins founded in 1790, it expressed eloquently and passionately, in seven issues, his disgust with the excesses of the Terror and an appeal for a committee of clemency. "Open the prisons for the two thousand citizens which you call suspect," he wrote at great personal risk. By now, he was totally alienated from Robespierre who ordered his publication burned and Desmoulins, Danton, and several others arrested. They were guillotined six days later; his wife, shortly thereafter.

Desmoulins's journals were the most distinguished among the bevy of publications spawned by the Revolution. *Le Vieux Cordelier* reveals his erudition and wit, sincerity and courage, in the face of certain death.

DESTINEES, LES, POEMES PHILOSOPHIQUES (*Destinies, Philosophical Poems*, 1864), by Vigny,* is a posthumous collection of eleven poems renowned for their austere beauty, eloquence, philosophy, and symbolism. Six of the poems first appeared in the *Revue des deux mondes* between 1843 and 1854. After his death, Vigny's friend, Louis de Ratisbonne (1827–1900), published them as *Les Destinées*. Vigny called them his "philosophical poems," the subtitle of Ratisbonne's edition. These eleven poems, as they explore the human condition, represent the culmination of Vigny's thought.

The title poem, "Les Destinées" ("Destinies," written 1849), which opens the collection, establishes the theme and tone of those to follow. Here Vigny pessimistically questions man's freedom and rejects the notion that Christianity liberated man from the clutches of the three Fates of the ancient Greeks. The Christian concept of "grace," which is the means of salvation, and the words "It is written" merely loosened the chain of man's bondage. "La Maison du berger" ("The Shepherd's Cottage," written between 1840 and 1844) invites an unknown and symbolic woman named Eva to abandon the bustle of city life for the solitude and peace of the countryside, an invitation also made by Des Grieux in *Manon,* by Chateaubriand,* Musset,* and English poet Lord Byron (1788–1824). The poem reproaches industrialization and the railroads and sings the praises of nature, love, inspiration, and poetry. However, unlike most other romantic poets, Vigny found nature beautiful but impassive, indifferent, and cold. "La Colère de Samson" ("Samson's Anger"), written in 1839 following his liaison with actress Marie Dorval (1798–1849), expresses his disillusionment with love and bitterness toward women. "La Mort du loup" ("Death of the Wolf," 1838), the earliest poem in the collection, was suggested by Byron's *Childe Harold* (1812). The wolf symbolizes Vigny's ideal of stoic honor and quiet resignation before suffering and death. In "Le Mont des Oliviers" ("The Mount of Olives," written between 1839 and 1843), Christ himself symbolizes the poet and suffering humanity against the silence of God. "La Bouteille à la mer ("The Bottle at Sea," 1847), taken from a passage by Bernardin de Saint-Pierre,* extolls the stoicism of the sailor who confronts certain death at sea with the toss of a bottle containing the ship's log, charts, and a message. For Vigny, a book is like a bottle tossed into the sea containing the message, "Attrape qui peut" ("Catch if You Can"). "L'Esprit pur" ("The Pure Spirit"), written in the final months of his life, is Vigny's spiritual testimony, an act of faith in the nobility of man's soul and his ability to progress. Other poems in the collection include "La Flûte" ("The Flute," 1840); "La Sauvage" ("The Savage," 1842), and "Wanda."

Les Destinées is characterized by a tone of despair that Vigny had experienced firsthand. He felt rejected by God, woman, and nature. But through his poetry, he formulated an ideal of stoicism that turned human suffering into majesty and loneliness into superiority. Though your task be "long and heavy . . . do it well," he implores. "Then afterwards, like me, suffer and die without speaking" ("La Mort du loup"). The poems are careful renditions of his thought and are supported by symbols and a formal beauty that have secured their place in the history of French literature as a precursor of symbolism** and Parnassian* poetry.

For further information, see S. Haig, "The Double Register of *Les Destinées*," *Studi francesi* 64 (January–April 1978): 104–106.

DESTOUCHES, PHILIPPE NERICAULT (1680–1754), belongs to that early phase of the eighteenth century that, still influenced by the classics, fostered an imitative art both in verse and on stage. It was an age concerned with "sensibilité," or emotion, and morality. Destouches, along with Dancourt,* Lesage,* Piron,* and Marivaux,* followed in the footsteps of Molière (1622–1673).

Destouches was born in Tours but left his family at seventeen to join a troupe of actors. In Paris, he gained the favor of the duchesse de Maine (1699–1753). In 1717, he accompanied abbé Dubois (1656–1723) to England as secretary to the embassy and remained as chargé d'affaires. Upon his return, he was admitted to the Academy (1723) but retired soon after to Melun to devote himself to his writing. In all, he penned twenty-seven plays of which nineteen were presented at the Comédie-Française.

His first attempts, *Le Curieux Impertinent* (*The Curious, Impertinent One,* 1716), *L'Ingrat* (*The Ingrate,* 1712), *L'Irrésolu* (*The Irresolute One,* 1713), and *Le Médisant* (*The Liar,* 1715), are character studies in the style of Molière that, despite their classic perfection of form, lack the depth of his comedies. Destouches's "noble" comedies, inspired by the English novels of the time, instruct as well as entertain in order to "correct morals, attack the ridiculous, discredit vice. . . ." (Preface to *Le Glorieux*). In the best, *Le Philosophe marié* (*The Married Philosophe,* 1727) and *Le Glorieux* (*The Vainglorious,* 1732), virtue triumphs, vice is punished, while the esthetic demands of emotion and sensitivity are met. Others, *Les Philosophes amoureux* (*The Amorous Philosophes,* 1721) and *La Belle orgueilleuse* (*The Proud Beauty,* 1741), are imbalanced and moralize to excess.

While his plays are not known for their sparkling wit or humor, they are important for their purity of style and an occasional well-struck verse: "Criticism is easy; art is difficult" or "Chase away the natural and it comes back at a gallop'' (*Le Glorieux*). The emotionalism of Destouches's plays influenced La Chaussée* and la comédie larmoyante.* Their realism and moral value prepared the way for the drame* of Diderot.*

DESTUTT DE TRACY, ANTOINE-LOUIS-CLAUDE, COMTE (1754–1836), member of the idéologues* and disciple of Condillac,* was born in Bourbonnais to a noble family of Scottish descent. He attended the University of Strasbourg, entered a military career, and at the outbreak of the Revolution, took an active part in the provincial assembly and was elected deputy to the states general. He was imprisoned during the Terror for nearly a year. He became a senator during the Empire and a peer during the Restoration. In 1808, he entered the Academy and, in 1832, became a member of the Academy of Moral Sciences.

Destutt de Tracy was a ''sensualist'' who believed that our four faculties of conscious life—perception, memory, judgment, will—are all varieties of sensation. To think is to feel. He combined his various writings into the *Eléments d'idéologie* (*Elements of Ideology*) and *Principes d'idéologie* (*Principles of Ideology,* 1804), a guide to the philosophy of the ideologues, and wrote a commentary on Montesquieu's* *De l'esprit des lois.**

For further information, see E. Kennedy, *A Philosophe in the Age of Revolution: Destutt de Tracy and the Origins of 'ideology'* (Philadelphia: The American Philosophical Society, 1978); Kennedy, ''Destutt de Tracy and the Unity of the Sciences,'' *Studies on Voltaire and the Eighteenth Century* 171 (1977): 223–239.

DIALOGUES OU ROUSSEAU JUGE DE JEAN-JACQUES (*Dialogues or Rousseau, Judge of Jean-Jacques,* written, 1776; published, 1780), by Jean-Jacques Rousseau,* expresses in a series of three dialogues the anguish and obsessiveness of his later years. Believing himself the object of a conspiracy led by Diderot,* David Hume (1711–1776), and Grimm* to discredit and humiliate him before all of mankind, Rousseau retired from active life into a solitude pierced only by, he believed, carriages bound to hit him in the streets, inksellers who sold him ''white ink,'' and spies who watched his every move. The *Dialogues* translates these experiences into a work of telling madness and genius.

The *Dialogues* take place between a ''Frenchman,'' a representative philosophe* who prejudiciously attacks ''Jean-Jacques,'' and ''Rousseau,'' who defends him, revealing his soul, his feelings, his philosophy. The ensuing debates are eloquent and imaginative, strange and tormented, flowing from the pen of a man at odds with himself and with the world. Rousseau attempts to place the *Dialogues* on the altar of Notre-Dame cathedral and finds its gate closed. Feeling abandoned by the God to whom he had dedicated the work, he turns to the streets, distributing a pamphlet entitled ''A tout Français aimant la justice et la vérité'' (''To all Frenchmen who love justice and truth'') to worthy-looking passers-by.

The *Dialogues,* though not a major work, are important for the haunting beauty and clarity of their style and their insights into the mind of Rousseau.

DICTIONNAIRE PHILOSOPHIQUE PORTATIF (*The Portable Philosophical Dictionary*, 1764), also known as *La Raison par alphabet* (*Reason by Alphabet*), by Voltaire,* is a collection of short articles summarizing his ideas on aesthetics, literary criticism, philosophy, religion, society, and politics. Editors later enlarged the book to include *Questions sur l'Encyclopédie* (*Questions on the Encyclopedia*, 1771–1773) and *Opinion par alphabet* (*Opinion by Alphabet*, which never appeared separately in print). Originally a small volume compared to Diderot's* grandiose *Encyclopedie,** it consisted of seventy-three articles, alphabetically arranged from "Abraham" to "Virtue," and included topics such as "The Soul," "Beauty," "Glory," "War," "Man," "Laughter," "Style," and "Tragedy."

Essentially an attack on religious dogma and the Bible, the dictionary was immediately condemned by the authorities and has since been criticized as biased, prejudiced, propagandist, and anti-Semitic and hailed by others as containing the essence of Voltairianism.

For further information, see B. E. Schwarzbach, "The Problem of the Kehl Addition to the *Dictionnaire philosophique:* Sources, Dating and Authenticity," *Studies on Voltaire and the Eighteenth Century* 201 (1982): 7–66; R. Shoaf, "Science, Sect and Certainty in Voltaire's *Dictionnaire philosophique.*" *Journal of the History of Ideas* 46 (1) (January–March 1985): 121–126; C. Todd, *Voltaire, Dictionnaire philosophique* ["Critical guides to French texts"] (London: Grant and Cutler, 1981).

DIDEROT, DENIS (1713–1784), the eighteenth-century philosophe,* writer, dramatist, and art critic best known as editor and director of the *Encyclopédie** and author of *Jacques le fataliste et son maître** (1773–1774) and *Le Neveu de Rameau** (1778), was born in Langres, the son of a master cutler. Destined for a career in the cloth, Diderot was tonsured at the age of twelve. He studied first with the Jesuits at Langres, where he revealed himself a gifted, though free-spirited student, then at the Collège de Harcourt in Paris, attaining a master of arts degree in 1732. Ten years of Parisian bohemianism and independence followed in which Diderot renounced his faith, frequented literary cafés such as the Procope, the Laurent, and the Régence, earned his keep variously as a tutor, translator, and sermon-writer, and acquired the friendship of Condillac,* Grimm,* and J.-J. Rousseau.* Rousseau's *Confessions** (1765–1770) would later testify to Diderot's influence on him. In 1743, against his family's wishes, he married Antoinette Champion, a pretty but simple fabric worker who, though uninterested in her husband's intellectual pursuits, blessed him with a daughter, Angélique, the object of his unremitting love and joy.

Diderot's translation of Englishman Anthony Shaftesbury's (1671–1713) *Essay on Merit and Virtue* (1745) and the publication of his *Pensées philosophiques* (*Philosophical Thoughts*) a year later launched him into the raging philosophical fray, first as a deist, then as a partisan of natural religion who rejected the church and its doctrine. "Destroy these walls which restrict your ideas," he wrote in 1746; "Enlarge God. See him wherever he is, or say that he does not exist." The deist became the skeptic who wrote *La Promenade du sceptic* (*The Promenade of the Skeptic,* 1747), describing three paths through life—the path of thorns (religion), that of flowers (sensual pleasure), and that of the chestnut trees (philosophy). In 1749, his *Lettre sur les aveugles** (*Letter on the Blind*), a discussion of blindness and the cataract operations recently performed by René Réaumur (1683–1757), put forth the idea that since knowledge comes from the senses, the blind, who are unable to see nature, cannot possibly know God. The *Letter*'s atheism earned Diderot several months' incarceration in Vincennes, where he received the now famous visit of a young Rousseau contemplating his first discourse (see *Discours sur les sciences et les arts**).

As editor of the *Encyclopédie* (1745–1772), which he had been asked by publisher André-François Le Breton (1708–1779) to direct in 1746, Diderot wrote, edited, revised, and saw to completion more than twenty years later the gargantuan enterprise envisioned by the philosophes as the repository of knowledge for the entire century. At the same time, his expansive mind sought other challenges. He explored developments in the burgeoning field of natural science, developed his philosophy of materialism, formulated a theory of drama, inaugurated a new style of art criticism, and wrote plays, essays, and novels. After Vincennes, a less audacious Diderot published anonymously his *Lettre sur les sourds et muets* (*Letter on the Deaf and Dumb,* 1751) dealing with communication, gesture, semantics, and word symbolism. *Pensées sur l'interprétation de la nature* (*Thoughts on the Interpretation of Nature,* 1754), also published anonymously, examines scientific method and, in the spirit of Francis Bacon (1561–1626), emphasizes empiricism, inductive reasoning, the importance of scientific investigation and anticipates the evolutionary theories of Jean-Baptiste Lamarck (1744–1829) and Charles Darwin (1809–1882).

Sometime near 1755, Diderot met Louise-Henriette Volland (1725–1784), whom he called "Sophie," and for whom he felt an enduring affection and with whom he maintained a lifelong correspondence. His letters to Sophie chronicled intimate details of his personal and social life and reveal his sensitivity and passion and his capacity for love.

Besides a letter writer, Diderot was a brilliant conversationalist and master of dialogue who recognized the theatre's potential as a moral force. He strove to liberate it from the influence of Pierre Corneille (1606–1684) and Jean Racine (1639–1699) and to restore truth and nature on stage with realistic scenery, action, gestures, dialogue, and prose, rather than verse. Though his two plays, *Le Fils naturel* (*The Illegitimate Son,* 1757) and *Le Père de famille* (*Father of the Family,* 1758), met with little critical success, they inaugurated a new form, "drame bourgeois" (bourgeois drama), which, as an intermediary between comedy and tragedy, dealt with the concerns of daily bourgeois life. "Man does not always find himself either in sadness or in joy. There is a point between the comic and the tragic which I call the serious," he wrote in *Entretiens sur le fils naturel ou Dorval et moi* (*Dialogue on the Illegitimate Son or Dorval and I,* 1757). He called for the depiction of "conditions" or professions, such as politician, philosopher, businessman, judge, lawyer; or family relations, such as husband, sister, brother, father, rather than classical depictions of character. Theatre should be "honest," or moral, teaching by means of living portraits or scenes rather than unbelievable theatrical coups and tirades. Another play, *Est-il bon? Est-il mechant? (Is he Good? Is he Bad?)* remained unedited until 1834 and unperformed until the twentieth century.

The years following his theatrical attempts were further complicated with personal loss—the final break with his friend J.-J. Rousseau in 1757, the resignation of d'Alembert* (1758) as coeditor of the *Encyclopédie,* the condemnation of the *Encyclopédie* by the parliament of Paris and the king's council (1759), the death of his father (1759), and the personal attack by Palissot* in his play, *Les Philosophes (The Philosophes,* 1760). Only de Jaucourt,* d'Holbach,* and Grimm remained faithful. Disillusioned and discouraged, Diderot restored his self-confidence as an art critic for Grimm's journal, *Correspondance littéraire (Literary Correspondence).* The nine Paris art salons Diderot reviewed for Grimm from 1759 to 1781 instituted a new form of criticism. His literary rather than technical approach sought the meaning and moral of art. He admired Joseph Vernet (1714–1789) and Jean-Baptiste Greuze (1725–1805) for moving spectators to fear, pity, or sadness; appreciated Maurice Quentin de La Tour (1704–1788) and Jean-Baptiste Chardin (1699–1779) for their verity, naturalness, and simplicity; and deplored François Boucher's (1703–1770) unnaturalness and superficiality. The imagination and enthusiasm of the salons, together with essays on painting (written, 1765; published, 1796) and *Encyclopédie* article "Beauty," earned him renown as France's first modern art critic.

While Diderot publicly espoused truth and nature on the stage and in art, he realized his theories most successfully in stories and novels that were written privately and published posthumously—*La Religieuse (The Nun,* written, 1760; published, 1796); *Le Rêve de d'Alembert** (written, 1769; published, 1830); *Jacques le fataliste (Jacques the Fatalist,* written, 1773; published, 1796), and *Le Neveu de Rameau (Rameau's Nephew,* 1762–1778; not definitively published until 1891). Two early attempts, *Les Bijoux indiscrets (The Indiscreet Jewels,* 1747) and *L'Oiseau blanc (The White Bird,* published 1798), are interesting, licentious failures. He was influenced by Englishmen Samuel Richardson, 1689–1761 (he wrote *Eloge de Richardson, In Praise of Richardson,* 1761), and Laurence Sterne (1713–1768), especially in *Jacques the Fatalist.* Though characters such as Jacques have been criticized as mere puppets or mouthpieces for his ideas, the novels abound in lively dialogue and realistic detail—the essence of drama, truth, and life that Diderot sought to portray on stage. *La Religieuse,* based on a true story and written as a joke against the marquis de Croismare, relates the story of a young woman sequestered against her will and attacks religious fanaticism and the unnaturalism of the convent. *Le Rêve de d'Alembert* illustrates his materialist philosophy and definition of man; *Jacques le fataliste* questions man's destiny; *Le Neveu de Rameau,* a personal and social satire, addresses the questions of genius, talent, and social corruption.

During his twilight years, Diderot wrote essays and moral tales. *Paradoxe sur le comédien** (*Paradoxe on Acting,* 1773), declares that great poets, actors, and "perhaps in general all great imitators of nature, whoever they might be, endowed with a beautiful imagination, great judgment, tact and a very sure taste, are the least sensitive beings." He emphasizes the importance of lucidity rather than emotion in rendering an honest portrayal of life, nature, and truth on the stage or in any creative endeavor. *Regrets sur ma vieille robe de chambre* (*Regrets on My Old Dressing Gown,* 1772) confesses the dangers of wealth. *Sur les femmes* (*On Women,* 1772) relates his ideas on the psychology, physiology, and sociology of women based on his experiences with his wife, his thirty-year affair with Sophie Volland, as well as others of shorter duration, and his daughter, Angelique, whom he revered his entire life. *Entretien d'un philosophe avec la maréchale de____* (*Conversation with a Christian Lady,* 1777), a model of eighteenth-century salon conversation, deals with religion and morality. *Entretien d'un père avec ses enfants* (*Dialogue between a Father and His Children,* 1770–1771) illustrates his love for his father and the relationship between law and justice. *Les Deux Amis de Bourbonne* (*Two Friends from Bourbonne,* 1770) is a realistic tale of friendship with social and political overtones. *Supplément au voyage de Bougainville* (*Supplement to the Voyage of Bougainville,* written, 1772; published, 1796) praises the freedom of the noble savage of Tahiti. Two final tales, *Ceci n'est pas un conte* (*This is Not a Story,* 1772) and *Madame de la Carlière,* portray the maliciousness and fickleness of love.

Diderot's reputation, thanks primarily to the *Encyclopédie* and contributions to Grimm's *Literary Correspondence,* spread across the continent to Russia's Catherine II, who bought his library, retained him as its custodian for life, and invited him to Saint Petersburg. Lasting more than five months, their daily, private conversations on law, justice, absolute government, and divorce are reported in *Entretiens avec Catherine II* (*Conversations with Catherine II,* 1773). Back in Paris, he wrote *Refutation de l'ouvrage d'Helvétius intitulé L'Homme* (*Refutation on a Work by Helvetius Entitled Man,* 1773–1774). He elaborated discussions with Catherine on education into a *Plan d'une université pour le gouvernement de Russie* (*Plan for a University for the Government of Russia*). He collaborated on abbé Raynal's* anticolonial *Histoire des deux Indes* (*History of the Two Indies*) and wrote *Eléments de physiologie* (*Elements of Physiology,* 1774–1778) and his final works, *Essai sur Sénèque le philosophe* (*Essay on Seneca the Philosopher,* 1779) and *Essai sur les règnes de Claude et de Néron* (*Essay on the Reigns of Claude and Nero,* 1782).

Diderot's lifelong appreciation for and understanding of science, anatomy, physiology, mechanics, geometry, and mathematics, along with his belief in natural religion, evolved into his philosophy of materialism. Diderot determined that God and the soul are nonexistent, that matter is the only reality and that all matter, being one and the same, is interconnected. "Each animal is more or less man; each mineral is more or less plant; each plant is more or less animal . . . . Do you not agree that all is interconnected in nature and that there cannot be a break in the chain?'' He believed that matter consisted of molecules, was sensitive and in constant movement; that species of animals, plants, and minerals evidence this composition in their ability to change and evolve; that man, a mere link in this great chain of matter, is determined by the laws of nature.

For Diderot, morality and religion were distinct; he believed that man can be moral independent of religion, that (like Rousseau) man is inherently good, and that (unlike Rousseau) he is entitled to happiness that does not interfere with the social structure and welfare of others. "There is only one virtue," he writes, "justice; only one duty, to make oneself happy." Thus he condemns political tyranny, privilege, and fanaticism as interfering with the general order of things.

In the eighteenth century the disparate paths of reason and sensitivity, materialism and idealism, realism* and romanticism* temporarily converged in Diderot, forming a lively intersection of genius and poetry, science and emotion. His life and works point philosophy, drama, and the novel toward the nineteenth century, where they would forge new in-roads in the realm of romanticism, realism, and later in the socialism of Jeremy Bentham (1748–1832), John Stuart Mill (1806–1873) and Herbert Spencer (1820–1903). Though he was the driving force behind the greatest publishing venture of the decade, when he died in 1784 his master works remained unpublished and unappreciated by his peers. Only now, two hundred years after his death, is Diderot being properly assessed, perhaps by the generations for whom he was writing all along.

For further information, see D. J. Adams, "A Diderot Triptych Re-Examined (*Ceci n'est pas un conte, Mme de la Carlière, Supplément au voyage de Bougainville*)," *Modern Language Review* 76 (January 1981): 47–59; V. Brady-Papadopoulou, "Separation, Death and Sexuality: Diderot's *La Religieuse* and Rites of Initiation," in *Transactions of the Fifth International Congress on the Enlightenment,* vol. 3 (Oxford: Taylor Institution, 1981), 1199–1204; L. Carr, "Painting and the Paradox of the Spectator in Diderot's Art Criticism," in *Transactions of the Fifth International Congress on the Enlightenment,* vol. 4 (Oxford: Taylor Institution, 1981), 1690–1698; M. Cartwright, "Diderot's Connoisseurship: Ethics and Aesthetics in the Art Trade," in *Studies in Eighteenth Century Culture,* vol. 10 (Madison: University of Wisconsin Press, 1981), 227–237; R. Champagne, "Words Disguising Desire: Serial Discourse and the Dual Character of Suzanne Simonin," *Kentucky Romance Quarterly* 4 (1981): 341–350; J. Chouillet, "Diderot and America," *Studies in Eighteenth Century Culture* 12 (1983): 223–230; H. Cohen, "Jansenism in Diderot's *La Religieuse,*" *Studies in Eighteenth Century Culture* 11 (1982): 75–91; Cohen, "The Intent of the Digressions on Father Castel and Father Porée in Diderot's *Lettre sur les sourds et muets,*" *Studies on Voltaire and the Eighteenth Century* 201 (1982): 163–183; W. T. Conroy, Jr., *Diderot's "Essai sur Sénèque"* (Banbury: Voltaire Foundation, 1975); L. Crocker, "The Idea of a 'Neutral' Universe in the French Enlightenment," *Diderot Studies* 21 (1983): 45–76; C. A. Durham, "The Contradictory Becomes Coherent: *La Religieuse* and *Paul et Virginie,*" *Eighteenth Century* 23 (Autumn 1982): 219–237; Durham, "Fearful Symmetry: The Mother-Daughter Theme in *La Religieuse* and *Paul et Virginie,*" in E. Crook, ed., *Fearful Symmetry: Doubles and Doubling in Literature and Film* (Tallahassee: University Press of Florida, 1982), 32–40; R. Feigenbaum-Knox, "Aesthetics and Ethics: A Study of Sexuality in Denis Diderot's Art Criticism," *Proceedings of the Annual Meeting of the Western Society for French History,* vol. 9 (1982), 226–237; *Diderot Studies XX,* ed., O. Fellows and D. Guiragossian Carr (Geneva: Droz, 1981); O. Fellows, *Diderot* (Boston: Twayne, 1977); Fellows, "Diderot's *Est-il bon?* Rediscovered," in *Enlightenment Studies in Honor of Lester G. Crocker,* A. Bingham and V. Topazio, eds. (Oxford: Voltaire Foundation, 1979), 87–109; P. France, *Diderot* (Oxford; Oxford University Press, 1983); R. Goldberg, *Sex and Enlightenment. Women in Richardson and Diderot* (Cambridge: Cambridge University Press, 1984); D. Goodman, "The Structure of Political Argument in Diderot's *Supplément au voyage de Bougainville,*" *Diderot Studies* 21 (1983): 123–137; J. Robert Loy, "Richardson and Diderot," in *Enlightenment Studies in Honor of Lester G. Crocker,* A. Bingham and V. Topazio, eds. (Oxford: Voltaire Foundation, 1979), 145–150; J. Mehlman, *Cataract: A Study in Diderot* (Middletown, Ct.: Wesleyan University Press, 1979); V. Mylne, *Diderot: La Religieuse* (London: Grant and Cutler, 1981); Mylne, "What Suzanne Knew: Lesbianism and *La Religieuse,*" *Studies on Voltaire and the Eighteenth Century* 208 (1982): 167–173; R. Niklaus, "Denis Diderot: Search for an Unattainable Absolute of Truth," *Ultimate Reality and Meaning* 3 (1) (1980): 23–49; L. Peer, "Fielding and Diderot in the History of Novel Theory: Some Considerations," *Actes du VIIIe congrès de l'Association internationale de littérature comparée,* Budapest I (Stuttgart: Bieber, 1980); 305–312; M. Perkins, *Diderot and the Time-Space Continuum: His Philosophy, Aesthetics and Politics* (Oxford: Voltaire Foundation, 1982); W. Rex, "Secrets from Suzanne: The Tangled Motives of *La Religieuse,*" *The Eighteenth Century* 24 (3) (Fall 1983): 185–198; L. A. Russell, "Challe and Diderot: Tales in Defense of Woman," *Proceedings of the Annual Meeting of the Western Society for French History* 9 (1982): 216–225; E. Sanders, *The Z-D Generation* (Barrytown, N.Y.: Station Hill, 1981); T. Scanlon, "The Functions of Writing and Prayer in Diderot's *La Religieuse,*" *South Central Bulletin* 40 (4) (Winter 1980): 160–162; Scanlon, "Humanity, Society and Utopia in Diderot's *La Religieuse,*" *Francia* (July–December 1981): 20–24; L. Schwartz, *Diderot and the Jews* (Rutherford/Madison/Teneck: Fairleigh Dickinson University Press, 1981); C. Sherman, *Diderot and the Art of Dialogue* (Geneva: Droz, 1976); Sherman, "Diderot's Speech-Acts: Essay, Letter and Dialogue," *French Literature Series* 9 (1982): 18–29; W. Stowe, "Diderot's Supplement: A Model for Reading," *Philological Quarterly* 62 (3) (Summer 1983): 353–365; V. Swain, "Conventional Wisdom and Conventional Acts: The Narrative Content in Diderot's *Ceci n'est pas un conte,*" *Eighteenth Century Studies* 17 (1) (Fall 1983): 14–27; S. Taylor, "The Moral and Social Significance of Diderot's Drames," *Forum for Modern Language Studies* 14 (April 1978): 129–142; J. Undank, *Diderot, Inside, Outside and In-Between* (Madison: Coda, 1979); A. Vartanian, "Diderot's Rhetoric of Paradox, or the Conscious Automaton Observed," *Eighteenth Century Studies* 14 (Summer 1981): 379–405; Vartanian, "La Mettrie and Diderot Revisited: An International Encounter," *Diderot Studies* 21 (1983): 155–197; Vartanian, "The Politics of *Les Bijoux indiscrets,*" in *Enlightenment Studies in Honor of Lester G. Crocker,* A. Bingham and V. Topazio, eds. (Oxford: Voltaire Foundation, 1979), 349–376; S. Werner, *Diderot's Great Scroll* (Banbury: Voltaire Foundation, 1975); A. M. Wilson, "Reflections upon Some Recent Diderot Discoveries," in R. Trousson, ed., *Thèmes et figures du siècle des Lumières: Mélanges offerts à Roland Mortier* (Geneva: Droz, 1980), 329–340.

DIERX, LEON (1838–1912), Parnassian* poet, who like his friend Leconte de Lisle* was born on the island of Réunion, came to France at an early age. He attended the Ecole Centrale, returned to his native home for a short time, then settled definitely in Paris, where he worked in the ministry of public education. Thanks to his dedication to the ideals of Parnassianism, he was elected "Prince of Poets," by the readers of *La Plume* and *Le Temps,* in 1898 to succeed Mallarmé.** He died in Paris in 1912.

Dierx's first poems, *Les Aspirations* (*Aspirations,* 1858) were influenced by the romantics (see romanticism*). With *Poèmes et poésies* (*Poems and Poetries,* 1864), he fit his work into the Parnassian mold. His best-known collection, *Les Lèvres closes* (*Closed Lips,* 1867), contains an important preface. Like those of his literary master, his themes are pessimistic but gradually become oriented to the music and sensuality of the symbolists (see symbolism**). Other works include *Paroles d'un vaincu* (*Words of a Conquered One,* 1871), *Amants* (*Lovers,* 1879), and a one-act play, *La Rencontre* (*The Meeting,* 1875). His complete works appeared in 1888 and a posthumous edition appeared in 1912.

DISCOURS SUR LES SCIENCES ET LES ARTS (*Discourse on the Sciences and the Arts,* 1750), by Jean-Jacques Rousseau,* is the work that catapulted the young music copyist and author of an earlier opera, *Les Muses galantes* (*The Gay Muses,* 1744), to intellectual prominence. The discourse was conceived in the summer of 1749 on the way to a now-famous visit with Diderot* (incarcerated in Vincennes prison for his *Lettre sur les aveugles** [*Letter on the Blind,* 1749]), when Rousseau read in the *Mercure de France* of a competition offered by the Academy of Dijon on "whether the revival of the sciences and arts have fostered the improvement of morals." Overcome by palpitations and tears, he fell beneath a tree and outlined his answer, so he relates in a subsequent letter to Malesherbes* on the incident. Whether such is the case or whether it was suggested to him by Diderot will probably never be known.

After a short preface in which Rousseau states that he is writing to please neither "the witty nor the fashionable," the *Discours* consists of two parts which support his thesis that "our souls have been corrupted in proportion to the advancement of our sciences and arts toward perfection." The first part would have us consider Egypt, Greece, Rome, and China as historical proof and contrasts them with the simplicity, innocence, and virtue of the first Persians, the Scythians, the Germans, and the savages of America. Part Two gives the logical basis for his argument—the sciences, "born in idleness, nourish it in turn;" the arts, as well, encourage corruption and decadence. "Oh virtue," Rousseau implores, "sublime science of simple souls, is so much trouble and apparatus necessary to know you? Are not your principles engraved in all our hearts? and is it not sufficient, to learn your laws, to look within oneself and to listen to the voice of one's conscience in the silence of the passions. That is the true philosophy. . . ."

Rousseau's first discourse translated his own unhappiness at living in a society that he considered perverted by luxury and material progress into a system of thought which would emerge more fully in his *Contrat social**. For the present, it shocked his more "enlightened" contemporaries and launched him on an irreversible course as a man who would find happiness in the simple life and as a philosopher who would find meaning only in virtue.

For further information, see L. Thielemann, "The Thousand Lights and Intertextual Rhapsody: Diderot or Mme Dupin?" *Romanic Review* 74 (3) (May 1983): 316–329; R. Wokler, "The *Discours sur les sciences et les arts* and its Offspring: Rousseau in Reply to His Critics," in S. Harvey, M. Hobson, D. Kelly, and S. S. B. Taylor, eds., *Reappraisals of Rousseau in Honor of Ralph A. Leigh* (Manchester: Manchester University Press, 1980), 250–278.

DISCOURS SUR L'ORIGINE DE L'INEGALITE (*Discourse on the Origin of Inequality,* 1755), by J.-J. Rousseau,* represents the second step in his attack on the social institutions of his day. His first discourse, *Discours sur les sciences et les arts,** condemned the arts and sciences as responsible for man's moral decay; the second, written in response to a second question proposed by the Academy of Dijon—''What is the origin of inequality among men, and is it authorized by natural law?''—attacks society itself as immoral. On the basis of his own logic rather than the teachings of religion or history, Rousseau hypothesizes the development of man from his primitive state to civilization and shows how inequality is a natural consequence of society, knowledge, and power.

Following an exceedingly complimentary dedication to the city of Geneva, the Preface raises the fundamental and paradoxical question of how we can ever know natural man, when the more we learn, the more we remove ourselves from our original state of nature. This knowledge is necessary if we are to formulate just and natural laws or to evaluate our present ones. In a short, but important introduction, Rousseau distinguishes between natural or physical inequality, which stems from age, health, bodily and intellectual strength, and social inequality, which consists in "the different privileges that some men enjoy to the prejudice of others." He exhorts men of all nations to listen to their story as it is found "not in the books of your fellowmen, which are liars, but in nature, which never lies." Part One describes the happiness of man as he existed in a state of nature—a physically strong, morally healthy individual not much different from an animal who followed the dictates of nature and his instinct for self-preservation. Part Two elaborates the ascension of independent, primitive man through the various stages leading to the present-day social animal that he is. The introduction of metallurgy and agriculture, with its subsequent division of labor and property, gave rise to the acquisition of material goods and wealth; man, removed from his original state of natural goodness, becomes proud, avaricious, and warlike. Wealthy men devise laws to legitimize the system. Social abuse, inequity, and eventually war become inevitable. Rousseau concludes his treatise with the thought that just as it is unnatural for a child to command an old man or for a fool to lead a wise man, so it is for "a handful of men to abound in luxury while the starving masses lack the necessary."

Rousseau's *Discours sur l'origine de l'inégalité* is an indictment of an unjust social system that has denaturalized and corrupted man. It was judged too revolutionary to merit a prize from the Academy. Undaunted, however, Rousseau launched another attack three years later in his *Lettre à d'Alembert sur les spectacles** (*Letter to d'Alembert on the Theatre*) and proposed his solutions to man's moral degeneracy in three later works, *Emile,* La Nouvelle Héloïse,** and *Le Contrat social.**

For further information, see C. Anschetz, "The Young Tolstoi and Rousseau's *Discourse on Inequality*," *The Russian Review* 39 (October 1980): 401–425; J. Derrida, "The Linguistic Circle of Geneva," *Critical Inquiry* 8 (4) (Summer 1982): 675–691; M. Plattner, *Rousseau's State of Nature: an Interpretation of the Discours on Inequality* (De Kalb, Ill.: Northern Illinois University Press, 1979).

DOMINIQUE (1862), by Fromentin,* is a psychological novel, partly autobiographical, based on the author's love for Jenny-Léocadie Chessy, a Creole girl of seventeen, while he was still a youth in Saint-Maurice and La Rochelle. Her marriage to another man and premature death inspired the novel, which is filled with the disappointment of unfulfilled love.

In the novel, Dominique de Bray relates the story of his life to one of his friends. Orphaned as a child and raised in the country, Dominique attends college and befriends Olivier d'Orsel, a classmate who introduces him to his two cousins, Madeleine and Julie. Dominique falls madly in love with Madeleine, who is older than he is and marries another man. She discovers his passion and attempts to cure it but falls in love with him herself. In desperation, she returns to her husband's estate and asks Dominique not to see her again. He turns to politics and literature as an outlet. They are briefly reunited in a three-day idyll in which they control their passion and finally say good-bye. She returns to her husband, and Dominique resumes his seignorial duties and marries.

Dominique continues the vein of the romantic (see romanticism*) novel in its lyric and introspective depiction of melancholy, guilt, passion. Its careful descriptions of nature and the countryside of Charente reveal Fromentin's artistic eye at work in his writing. While the novel's elegance and controlled style is reminiscent of *La Princesse de Clèves* (1678) or *Adolphe,** in its complexity and realism,* it hints at the modern novel.

For further information, see R. Lethbridge, "Fromentin's *Dominique* and the Art of Reflection," *Essays in French Literature* 16 (November 1979): 43–61; G. Martin, "The Ambiguity of Fromentin's *Dominique*," *Modern Language Review* 77 (1) (January 1982): 38–50; J. Toyama, "*Dominique* or How to Transcend Mediocrity," *The University of Southern Florida Language Quarterly* 20 (Spring-Summer 1982): 32–33, 38.

DRAME, or drama, an intermediary between the classic genres of "la comédie" (comedy) and "la tragédie" (tragedy), was born in the eighteenth century by Diderot,* who formulated its rules in his *Entretiens sur le fils naturel* (*Dialogues on the Illegitimate Son,* 1757) and *De la poésie dramatique* (*On Dramatic Poetry,* 1758). As a philosophe,* Diderot believed that the theatre could depict common man as well as kings and heroes, and that his daily life, feelings, and especially his "condition" as a professional person or family member, in addition to his "character," was stageworthy. Drame is serious but not tragic. It is engaging, yet stops short of the "grand rire" (great laughs) of Molière (1622–1673). It replaced verse and lengthy monologues with realistic, fast-paced dialogue and occasional pantomime. It is realistic, socially relevant, and emotionally piquant in revealing the lives, loves, and morality of the bourgeoisie.

Though Diderot was integral in establishing the rules of the drame, his drames, *Le Fils naturel* (*The Illegitimate Son*) and *Le Père de famille* (*The Father of the Family*, 1758), are uninspiring. Mercier* and Beaumarchais* attempted the genre. Drame failed, however, as a literary force. It was quickly dated and lacked psychological depth. Only Sedaine* succeeded with *Le Philosophe sans le savoir* (*The Unsuspecting Philosophe*, 1765), which would influence the drama of Augier* and Dumas fils* a century later.

For further information, see G. Adams, "The Eighteenth-Century Playwrights and the Question of Calvinist Emancipation," in J. Browning, ed., *The Stage in the Eighteenth Century* (New York: Garland, 1981), 23–39; T. Braun, "From Marivaux to Diderot: Awareness of the Audience in the 'Comédie,' the 'Comédie larmoyante' and the 'Drame,' " *Diderot Studies XX* (Geneva: Droz, 1981), 17–29.

DUCIS (1733–1816), a minor eighteenth-century playwright with no knowledge of English, adapted several Shakespearian tragedies for the French theatre. Relying on translations by Pierre-Antoine de la Place (1707–1793) and Pierre Le Tourneur (1736–1788), he produced *Hamlet* (1769), *Roméo et Juliette* (1772), *Le Roi Léar* (1783), *Macbeth* (1784), *Jean sans terre* (*John without Land*, based on *King John*, 1785), and *Othello* (1792). Despite the tide of anglomania sweeping the country, the French were not receptive to William Shakespeare's (1564–1616) on-stage violence and "barbarianism." Voltaire,* though he introduced English culture to Paris in his *Lettres philosophiques*,* called Shakespeare a "savage drunk" in a letter to the Academy. Ducis's adaptations, often ridiculed by the Théâtre Italien,* are considered insipid melodramas bearing little resemblance to the originals. Vigny,* early in the next century, would render more faithful translations.

Aside from his Shakespearian adaptations, Ducis wrote *Oedipe chez Admète* (*Oedipus with Admetus*, 1778), *Oedipe à Colone* (*Oedipus at Colone*, 1797), *Fédor et Vladimir* (*Fédor and Vladimir*, 1798), and his most original play, *Abufar ou La Famille arabe* (*Abufar or The Arabian Family*, 1795).

For further information, see P. V. Conroy, Jr., "A French Classical Translation of Shakespeare: Ducis' *Hamlet*," *Comparative Literature Studies* 18 (March 1981): 2–14.

DUCLOS (1704–1772), born Charles Pinot or Pineau, a wealthy Breton bourgeois, was in his day a respected historian, grammarian, moralist, and novelist. He studied law, frequented literary cafés, and was admitted to the Académie des Inscriptions et Belles-Lettres (Academy of Inscriptions and Humanities, founded in 1663 by Colbert) in 1739. His *Histoire de Louis XI* (*History of Louis XI*,

1745–1746) assured his seat in the French Academy in 1747 (he became its permanent secretary eight years later) and his succession to Voltaire* as royal historiographer in 1750. As a liberal, he worked to establish the philosophe* faction in the Academy. He collaborated on the fourth edition of the *Dictionnaire de l'Académie* (*The Academy Dictionary*, 1762) and wrote an *Essai sur les ponts et chaussées, la voirie et les corvées* (*Essay on Civil Engineering, Highways, and Labor*, 1759). Today, Duclos is remembered as a novelist and moralist of secondary importance. In the style of Crébillon fils,* his *Histoire de Madame de Luz* (*Story of Madame de Luz*, 1740) and *Les Confessions du comte de___* (*The Confessions of the Count of ____*, 1742), the latter containing a memorable portrait of Madame de Tençin,* depict the libertinism of the age. *Considérations sur les moeurs de ce siècle* (*Considerations on the Mores of this Age*, 1750), written in the spirit of Jean de la Bruyère (1645–1696), but less critically, record social and moral attitudes. Two volumes, *Mémoires secrets sur les règnes de Louis XIV* and *Louis XV* (*Secret Memoirs on the Reigns of Louis XIV* and *Louis XV*), drawing upon the *Mémoires* of Saint-Simon,* appeared posthumously in 1790. A prolific writer, his collected works, published in 1806 and 1821, total ten volumes.

DUFRESNY, CHARLES-RIVIERE (c. 1648–1724), author, playwright, and probably the gifted but illegitimate descendant of Henry IV (1553–1610), wrote comedy in the style of Molière (1622–1673) in the era bridging the seventeenth and eighteenth centuries. While the comedy of Dancourt,* Lesage,* and Piron* emphasized realism and satire and that of Destouches* and Gresset* focused on moralizing, Dufresny, with his contemporary and collaborator Regnard,* was concerned chiefly with comedy as pleasure. Besides short plays for the Théâtre Italien,* he wrote *Le Négligent* (*The Negligent One*, 1692); *Le Chevalier joueur* (*The Gambling Chevalier*, 1697), whose idea he claimed Regnard stole in *Le Joueur* (*The Gambler*, 1696) and vice versa; *La Malade sans maladie* (*The Sick Woman without a Sickness*, 1699), reminiscent of Molière's *Le Malade imaginaire* (*The Imaginary Illness*, 1673); *L'Esprit de contradiction* (*The Spirit of Contradiction*, 1700); *Le Double Veuvage* (*The Double Widowhood*, 1702), and others. Despite his ingenuity, his plays are flawed and uneven. Dufresny is best known for his *Amusements sérieux et comiques d'un Siamois à Paris* (*The Serious and Comic Amusements of a Siamese in Paris*, 1707), a decided influence on Montesquieu's* *Lettres persanes* (see the Persian letters*). He served the court as director of the Royal Gardens and edited the *Mercure galant* for a short time after the death of its founder, Donneau de Visé (1638–1710).

DULAURENS, HENRI-JOSEPH (1719–1797), a defrocked monk who detested the church and was condemned to prison (where he died insane) for sacrilegious writings, contributed two novels, *Imirce ou La Fille de la nature* (*Imirce or The Daughter of Nature*, 1765) and *Le Compère Mathieu* (*Comrade Matthew*, 1766), to the stockpile of libertine works being produced by the likes of Crébillon fils,* Denon,* and Louvet de Couvray.* His novels echo the cynicism of Voltaire* toward the church and the priesthood, yet display a licentiousness and vulgarity foreign to *Candide*.* Diderot* is said to have borrowed from *Le Compère Mathieu,* a long novel detailing the picaresque adventures of a band of rogues with satire and philosophic overtones.

DUMAS FILS (ALEXANDRE) (1824–1895), illegitimate son of the novelist Alexandre Dumas père,* made his name in the theatre with *La Dame aux camélias* (*The Lady with the Camelias,* 1852), based on his novel of four years earlier, and the "thesis" play. He had an irregular youth characterized by poverty and custody battles between his mother, Catherine Labay, and his free-wheeling father, who had a bevy of mistresses. Dumas père placed him in a boarding school where he was tormented by the other boys for his dishonorable birth, leaving emotional scars that surfaced in the moral values he depicted in his plays. From his father, he inherited spirit and imagination; from his mother, a sense of honor and love. He eventually reconciled himself with his father, writing, "My father is like a great big child whom I had when I was a little boy."

In 1844, he met Marie Duplessis (1824–1847), the courtesan who inspired his main character, Marguerite Gautier, the lady of the novel and play on which his fame rests. *La Dame aux camélias,* one of the most successful plays of the nineteenth century, treats a romantic theme, the redeeming love of a courtesan, sensitively and realistically. He wrote poetry, *Pechés de jeunesse* (*Sins of Youth,* 1847), and additional novels, *Le Roman d'une femme* (*The Novel of a Woman,* 1848), *Diane de Lys* (1851), *La Dame aux perles* (*The Lady in Pearls,* 1853), and *La Vie à vingt ans* (*Life at Twenty,* 1856), as well as comedies of manners, *Diane de Lys* (1853) and *Le Demi-monde* (*The Demi-monde,* 1855). He found his true vocation in the "pièce à thèse" ("thesis play"), depicting moral truths in an effort to reform society. *Le Fils naturel* (*The Illegitimate Son,* 1858) portrays the social problem of the illegitimate child; *Les Idées de Madame Aubray* (*The Ideas of Madame Aubray,* 1867), the seduced woman and the question of marriage and divorce; *La Princesse Georges* (1871), adultery. He entered the Academy in 1875.

Dumas fils sought to reform social ills, the disintegration of the family, the corruption of money, prejudice, and passion. His belief in utilitarian theatre contributed to the rise of serious, realistic drama in the mid-nineteenth century. "All literature," he wrote, "which does not have in view perfectibility, moralizing, the ideal, the useful, is, in a word, a literature full of rickets, unhealthy and stillborn." If his thesis plays are considered dated and contrived, *La Dame aux camélias* still enchants with its simplicity and romanticism.*

For further information, see S. Braun, "Dumas fils: Forerunner of Zionism," *Nineteenth Century French Studies* 13 (2–3) (Winter-Spring 1985): 105–112.

DUMAS PERE (ALEXANDRE) (1802–1870), popular romantic (see romanticism*) novelist immortalized by international successes such as *Les Trois*

Mousquetaires (*The Three Musketeers,* 1844) and *Le Comte de Monte-Cristo* (*The Count of Monte-Cristo,* 1844), has been called one of the most remarkable characters of the nineteenth century and the greatest French romantic novelist. His drama *Henri III et sa cour* (*Henri III and his Court,* 1829) was the first romantic drama performed on stage and prepared the way for Hugo's* *Hernani** a year later. He was such a prolific writer that it is said that no one has read all of his works but that most of mankind has read part. A complete edition of his works probably does not even exist. In all, he filled hundreds of volumes.

He was born in Villers-Cotterêts to Marie Labouret, an innkeeper's daughter, and General Dumas, who had served under Napoleon. Dumas's father, the mulatto child of the Marquis Davy de la Pailleterie and a Haitian Negro slave, died when Alexandre was four, leaving his widow with no pension. As a child, Dumas received little formal education, learning to read and write from his mother and sister and spending most of his days poaching in the immense forest surrounding his village. In his late teens, he became a clerk for a local solicitor. A performance of Ducis's* *Hamlet* convinced him to become a playwright. From 1820 to 1821, he collaborated with a young Swedish friend, Adolphe de Leuven (1807–1884), on three one-act vaudeville sketches, *Les Abencerrages, Le Major de Strasbourg* (*The Major of Strasbourg*), and *Le Dîner d'amis* (*Dinner with Friends*). In 1823, a visit to Paris convinced him to seek his fortune there, where, thanks to General Foy, a former friend of his father, and his own exquisite penmanship, he obtained a position in the household of the Duke of Orleans, the future King Louis-Philippe. In his spare time, he rounded out his education, read the classics, attended the theatre, and fathered a child, also named Alexandre (see Dumas fils*), by a seamstress, Catherine Labay. In 1825, his first play, *La Chasse et l'amour* (*The Hunt and Love*), a light farce written with Leuven, was produced. The next year, *La Noce et l'enterrement* (*The Wedding and the Burial*), a comedy written with a co-worker, E. H. Lassagne, appeared.

Dumas's first serious attempt at the theatre, *Christine* (1828), a romantic and historical drama, was influenced by the Shakespearean plays performed in Paris by the English players the previous year—*Romeo and Juliet, The Merchant of Venice, Othello. Christine* was accepted by the Comédie Française, probably through the influence of the Duke of Orleans, but not performed until 1830. His next attempt, *Henri III et sa cour* (*Henry III and His Court,* 1829), called the first great triumph of the romantic drama in France, catapulted the young dramatist to fame. Hugo and Vigny* attended its premiere; Charles Nodier* opened his Arsenal* to him. Dumas's next play (*Antony,* 1831), capped his success. It was performed 130 times in Paris alone. However, Dumas's rapid rise among the romantics was stalled by the revolution of 1830. An ardent republican sympathizer, he led a group of militants on an attack against the Hôtel de Ville and requisitioned munitions from an arsenal in Soissons. After the revolution, he repaired to Trouville, where he wrote *Charles VII chez ses grands vassaux* (*Charles VII with his Great Vassals,* 1831), a moderate success; later that year, his next play, *Richard d'Arlington*, restored Dumas's faith in himself. *Teresa* (1832) contained a part for young actress Ida Ferrier, who became Dumas's mistress, and in 1840, his wife. In 1832, he succumbed to the cholera epidemic that held Paris in its grip. Upon his recovery, he reworked a rough draft by Frédéric Gaillardet (1808–1882), a lawyer and minor playwright, into one of his most enduringly popular dramas, *La Tour de Nesle* (*The Tower of Nesle*, 1832), about the orgiastic revels of the queen of France in the early fourteenth century. The play set off a bitter dispute over collaboration in which his enemies claimed that all of Dumas's plays were plagiarisms. After a duel between the two authors, in which neither was hurt, Dumas set out for Switzerland, where he met Chateaubriand* and brought back lively, colorful ''travel impressions'' to fill five volumes. With the failure of his latest play, *Le Fils de l'émigré* (*The Son of the Emigre*, 1832), produced while he was away, he turned to history, writing *Gaule et France* (1833). In 1835, he travelled to Italy, bringing back three more dramas, a verse translation of the *Divine Comedy*, and several volumes of travel impressions. By 1836, Dumas's interest in drama was waning. After the relative failures of *Don Juan de Marana* (1836) and *Caligula* (1837) and the success of *Kean* (1836), about the great English actor, he returned to comedy with an enormous success, *Mademoiselle de Belle-Isle* (1839), *Un Mariage sous Louis XV* (*A Marriage under Louis XV*, 1841), and *Les Demoiselles de Saint-Cyr* (*The Damsels of Saint-Cyr*, 1843). Dumas continued to write for the theatre but produced infrequent and unimportant works. By 1839, he was agitating to be named to the Academy. Hugo's election in 1841 spurred him on, but he never attained his wish.

In 1838, he tried his hand at the serial novel with *Capitaine Paul*, which increased subscriptions to the newspaper, *Siècle*, by 5,000. The following year, through working with Gérard de Nerval* on two unimportant plays, *L'Alchimiste* (*The Alchemist*) and *Léo Burckhart*, he met twenty-five-year-old Auguste Maquet (1813–1888), who was to become the principal collaborator on the reams of novels that would bear his name. Dumas revised Maquet's play, *Bathilde* (1839); he reworked and lengthened his novel, *Le Chevalier d'Harmental* (1842), whose success encouraged Dumas down the path of the historical novel. Their next attempt—*Les Trois Mousquetaires* (*The Three Musketeers*, 8 vols., 1844), followed swiftly by *Le Comte de Monte-Cristo* (*The Count of Monte-Cristo*, 18 vols., 1844–1845)—sealed their fame and ushered in the most fruitful years of Dumas's life. Dumas moved to Saint-Germain-en-Laye and dispatched his wife to Florence, never to see her again. A spate of novels followed—*Vingt Ans après* (*Twenty Years after*, 1845); *Le Vicomte de Bragelonne* (*The Viscount de Bragelonne*, 1847); a Valois trilogy—*La Reine Margot* (*Queen Margaret*, 6 vols., 1845), *La Dame de Monsoreau* (*The Lady from Monsoreau*, 1846), *Les Quarante-cinq* (*The Forty-five*, 1848); *Les Mohicans de Paris* (*The Mohicans of Paris*, 1854). Dumas's vast output induced the ire of other writers aspiring to be published. In 1845, Eugène de Mirecourt's (1812–1880) pamphlet, *Maison Alexandre Dumas et compagnie, fabrique de romans* (*A Factory for Novels, the*

House of Alexandre Dumas and Company), attacked Dumas's work and vilified the man himself, his Negro ancestry, and his wife. Dumas sued and Mirecourt was condemned to a fortnight in prison. Throughout the affair, Maquet remained loyal.

In 1846, Dumas set out for Algeria, stopping in Spain for the Duke of Montpensier's marriage to Infanta Luisa. He recalled the voyage in two travel pieces, *De Paris à Cadix* (*From Paris to Cadiz,* 1848) and *Le Véloce* (*Tales of Algeria; or, Life Among the Arabs,* 1848–1851). Upon his return, his extravagant chateau, the Monte-Cristo, on the banks of the Seine, was complete. However, his use of a government vessel as his private transport caused a scandal. He also faced lawsuits with seven journals for failing to provide installments for his serialized novels.

Over the years, Dumas steadily dissipated his life; now, his personal fortune lay in ruins. Dumas's Théâtre Historique, founded principally for showcasing his works, fell into bankruptcy during the 1848 revolution. Building and maintaining his chateau amassed mountains of debts. With Louis-Napoleon's coup d'etat, Dumas exiled himself in Belgium, evading his debts, but living in luxury, all on credit, until he settled into a pattern of rigorous writing. He returned to Paris in 1853, founded a newspaper, *Le Mousquetaire* (*The Musketeer*), published until 1857. In 1858, he went to Russia, the source of seven volumes of travel notes entitled *En Russie* (*In Russia,* 1860) and *Le Caucase* (*The Caucasus,* 1859). He returned to Paris and poverty. In 1860, he set sail for Syria and Palestine, assisted Giuseppe Garibaldi (1807–1882) in driving the Bourbons from Naples, and in exchange was named director of antiques. Dumas supervised excavations at Pompeii and founded a newspaper, *L'Indépendante* (*The Independent*). He wrote eleven volumes of a history of the Bourbons in Naples, his memoirs, and a novel, *La San-Félice* (1864). In 1864, Dumas returned to Paris, somewhat restored financially. The following year he revived one of his more successful dramas, *Les Gardes Forestiers* (*The Forest Guards*) at the new Great Parisian Theatre. He spent much time in the provinces and abroad, visiting Italy, Germany, Austria, and Hungary. Despite ill health, he managed to raise a scandal by taking a young and beautiful mistress at the age of sixty-five. He died in Dieppe in 1870.

Dumas forged his plays from passion, melodrama, and elements of realism* into a series of actions that captivated audiences with their energy and intensity. Their sources are diverse—translations, adaptations, his own romances, historical tableaux. Most are written in prose; most are historical; crime and horror abound. Dumas's trademark, his swash-buckling historical novels, derive their enduring fame from their sense of adventure and entertaining style. Like his plays, they make no pretense of being psychological. Most relegate history to a secondary role, a framework within which his story can unfold. As Dumas's fame and commercial success grew, his work became increasingly formulized, collaborative, and unoriginal. Despite his initial promise as a serious, gifted playwright, he was overshadowed by Hugo, the true father of romantic theatre, the artist, poet, and philosopher who Dumas never was and never pretended to be.

For further information, see F. W. J. Hemmings, *Alexandre Dumas. King of Romance* (New York: Scribner's, 1979); L. Johnson, "Delacroix, Dumas and Hamlet," *The Burlington Magazine* 123 (December 1981): 717–721; D. Munro, "Two 'Missing' Works of Alexandre Dumas, père," *Bulletin of the John Rylands University Library of Manchester* 66 (1) (Autumn 1983): 198–212; M. Ross, *Alexander Dumas* (North Pomfret, Vt.: David and Charles, 1981).

EDUCATION SENTIMENTALE, L' (*Sentimental Education*, 1869), by Flaubert,* is a masterpiece of realism* which portrays the sentimental education of its young hero against the historical and social backdrop of Paris in the 1840s. It is a novel about failure, the unconsummated love of Frédéric Moreau for Madame Arnoux, and the political failure of the 1848 revolution. The love story stems from Flaubert's lifelong passion for Elisa Schlésinger (1810–1888), a married woman eleven years his senior whom he met at age fourteen in Trouville and visited as a law student in Paris. She influenced his life and many of his works, including *Mémoires d'un fou* (*Memoirs of a Fool*, 1838), which recounts their meeting at Trouville; *Novembre* (1842), where she is depicted as a prostitute; and the first version of *L'Education sentimentale*, written in 1843. From April 1864 until May 1869, Flaubert reworked the initial version into its final form, an arduous task that is documented, as is the development of *Madame Bovary,** in his correspondence.

The novel's subtitle, "Histoire d'un jeune homme" ("Story of a Young Man"), indicates that it is the story of a young man—Frédéric Moreau, from age eighteen to forty-seven, especially the eleven years from 1840 until 1851, during which he learns of life, love, friendship, and ambition. The story opens in 1840 on a river boat traveling from Paris to Nogent-sur-Seine. Frédéric has just completed his baccalaureate and is going home for two months before beginning law studies in Paris. On board he meets wealthy art dealer Jacques Arnoux and falls in love at first sight with his beautiful wife. He receives a warm welcome at home and sees his friend, Deslauriers, who also plans a career in law. In Paris, he calls on Mr. Dambreuse, a wealthy industrialist, giving him a letter from the Moreaus' neighbor in Nogent, Mr. Roque. Unhappy in Paris, Frédéric visits an old friend, Martinon, who is destined for a magistrate's career and cannot understand his distress. Gradually, his passion for Madame Arnoux wanes, and Frédéric associates with other young Parisians, journalist Hussonnet, who introduces him into the Arnoux household; painter Pellerin; the liberal office worker Dussardier; socialist intellectual Sénécal; Régimbart; and Deslauriers, who finally arrives in Paris. A dinner at Arnoux's rekindles his love for his wife. Frédéric, lovelorn, fails his exams and spends a lonely summer in Paris. Arnoux introduces him to the life of the boulevards, but Frédéric's mind is never far from Madame Arnoux. He eventually passes the bar and returns to Nogent, where he finds his mother in dire financial straits. He works in a law office until an inheritance from his uncle permits him to return to Paris and resume a life of leisure. Once again he frequents the Arnoux's, whose position is less secure financially than previously. Mr. Arnoux now sells porcelain and has sold his art journal to Hussonnet. Frederic renews his friendship with Deslauriers, who has failed his exam. Arnoux takes Frederic to a masquerade ball and introduces him to the courtesan, Rosanette, also known as "La Maréchale." Frédéric visits the Dambreuses' each week and feels Madame Dambreuse's attraction to him; he, on the other hand, feels attracted to Rosanette as well as Madame Arnoux. Finding himself succeeding with neither woman, Frédéric's thoughts turn to Louise Roque, his neighbor at Nogent. Madame Arnoux's jealousy at Frédéric's mistresses and proposed marriage suggests her true feelings for him and their relationship deepens but remains platonic. Frédéric arranges to spend an afternoon with her in an apartment he has rented, but when she doesn't show because of her young son's illness, he takes La Maréchale. The Revolution breaks out during the night and Frédéric descends into the streets to follow the action at the Palais-Royal and the Tuileries. In June, on Dambreuse's advice, Frédéric and Rosanette repair to the safety and tranquility of Fontainebleau until Frédéric learns that Dussardier has been wounded. He returns to Paris and visits Madame Arnoux. Rosanette appears on a business pretext and tells him there is a cab waiting for them, confirming Madame Arnoux's suspicions. Furious, Frédéric wants to break with her, but she tells him she is pregnant. He stays, realizing that it is injurious to his relationship with Madame Arnoux. He consoles himself with Madame Dambreuse, whom he finds interesting and amusing. They become lovers, and when her husband dies, she proposes marriage. Rosanette wants to marry him, also. The Arnouxes, meanwhile, are bankrupt and, despite Frédéric's efforts to save them, must leave the capital. In sympathy, he abandons Rosanette and breaks his engagement with Madame Dambreuse. He travels, has other loves, but none are permanent. All is overshadowed by his true passion for Madame Arnoux. He wastes his days in idleness and inertia. Sixteen years later they meet, reminisce, and console each other. In an epilogue, Frédéric and Deslauriers recall a brothel incident of their youth. "That was the best that we had," Frédéric concludes. Deslauriers agrees.

If Frédéric fails at love and life, it is because he, like his generation, is doomed to failure. In this novel, as in *Madame Bovary*, Flaubert castigates the romantic attitude, the "bovarysme"* it engenders. It paints a pessimistic view of the bourgeois world of the 1840s, one filled with the self-serving, the vain, dreamers, and pleasure-seekers. Only two redeem themselves, the kindly and sympathetic Madame Arnoux and Dussardier, who dies for his beliefs. The novel's desperate outlook, no doubt, accounts for its lukewarm critical and popular reception. It remains, even today, less read than *Madame Bovary*. It is, nonetheless, a profoundly original work. It is a realistic account of political events Flaubert witnessed first-hand or carefully researched by reading Proudhon,* Fourier (see Fourierisme*), Lamennais,* Saint-Simon,* and others. It portrays an attitude Flaubert knew intimately and feared for all of its devastating historical, political, and social consequences. Flaubert carefully details his narrative, bringing to life 1840s Paris and its inhabitants. He depicts the nuances of Frédéric's soul, his inertia, disillusionment, ennui, in language which is deliberately monotonous, controlled, passive, sorrowful. The novel profoundly influenced the naturalists (see naturalism**), who appreciated its pessimism. Many modern readers consider it superior to *Madame Bovary*.

For further information, see D. Aynesworth, "The Poetry of Violence in *L'Education sentimentale*," *Nineteenth Century French Studies* 11 (3–4) (Spring–Summer 1983): 285–301; M. Danahy, "Chronoscapes in *L'Education sentimentale*," *Australian Journal of French Studies* 15 (5) (September–December 1978): 253–265; Danahy, "A Critique of Recent Spatial Approaches to Flaubert and Related Theory of Fiction," *Nineteenth Century French Studies* 10 (3–4) (Spring–Summer 1982): 301–316; A. Sonnenfeld, "Flaubert's *Education sentimentale*: A Century of Relevance," *Laurels* 53 (1) (Spring 1982): 45–56.

EMILE (1762), by Jean-Jacques Rousseau,* presents an ideal of education based on nature and freedom that, together with *La Nouvelle Héloïse** and *Le Contrat social,** constitutes Rousseau's response to the social and political corruption of his day. Realizing that his social reforms depended on just and virtuous individuals raised in accordance with nature, Rousseau outlined in five books a plan that would foster the natural unfolding of a young boy's physical, moral, and intellectual attributes without the negative influence of civilization.

"All is well as it comes from the hands of the Author of things; all degenerates in the hands of man," begins book 1, underscoring Rousseau's contempt for society and the necessity of reform. Book 1 emphasizes infant Emile's need for maternal breast-feeding and unswathed freedom of movement. Until the age of five, Emile's physical needs are met and his senses developed. From five until twelve, in book 2, Emile continues to evolve naturally as a person in an environment of controlled freedom. Sports and physical activity are encouraged, sensory perceptions are refined, book learning and reading, except for *Robinson Crusoe* (Daniel Defoe, 1719), are prohibited. For Rousseau, the most important rule of pedagogy is not to make the most of one's time, but to "waste" it in happiness and freedom. "The first education must therefore be purely negative, to teach neither virtue nor truth," but rather to "protect the heart from vice and the intellect from error." Between ages twelve and fifteen, in book 3, Emile learns by observing and experiencing nature. Under the guidance of his tutor, he "invents" science for himself, deducing laws of geography, astronomy, and physics. To assure his freedom, he learns a trade: "The artisan depends only upon his work; he is free, as free as the field hand is enslaved."

Book 4, often published separately as "La Profession de foi du Vicaire Savoyard" ("The Vicar of Savoie's Profession of Faith"), constitutes Emile's moral and religious education, received between the ages of fifteen and twenty. Natural passions such as kindness, friendship, and pity are encouraged; ancient history provides lessons on man and government. Most important, however, is the natural religion expressed by the vicar who speaks "in good faith" of the "wise and powerful will which governs the world," which he calls "God": "I know with certainty that he exists and that he exists by himself; I know that my existence is subordinate to his and that all the things which I know are absolutely in the same case. I perceive God everywhere in his works; I feel him in me; I see him all about me . . . but as soon as I want to find him . . . he escapes me." He encourages fellow man to find justice and virtue in his conscience, that "divine instinct . . . that infallible judge of good and evil which makes man resemble God."

The last book deals with the education of Sophie, the ideal bride, who is taught to "please," "serve," "be loved and honored by," "raise," "care for," "advise," "console," and "make life pleasant and sweet" for Emile.

As an educational novel, *Emile* offered many practical hints in the area of childrearing and fostered a love of nature among French aristocrats. Though it has been touted as a landmark in modern educational theory, with its emphasis on sensitivity and freedom, it is nonetheless dated and at times, impractical. It was denounced as dangerous to Christianity by the archbishop of Paris and ordered burned. Rousseau, banished from France, became obsessed with justifying himself before his contemporaries and posterity. *Emile*'s religious influence was felt in the nineteenth century in Chateaubriand's* sentimental and romantic *Génie du Christianisme.**

For further information, see R. Grimsley, "Rousseau and his Reader: The Technique of Persuasion in *Emile,*" in R. Leigh, ed., *Proceedings of the Cambridge Bicentennial Colloquium* (Cambridge: Cambridge University Press, 1982), 225–238; J. F. Hamilton, "Rousseau's *Emile et Sophie:* A Parody of the Philosopher King," *Studi Francesi* 22 (May–December 1978): 392–395; P. Jimack, *Rousseau: Emile* (London: Grant and Cutler, 1984); R. Robison, "Victorians, Children and Play," *English Studies* 64 (4) (August 1983): 318–329; T. M. Scanlan, "Patterns of Imagery in Rousseau's *Emile,*" in *Transactions of the Fifth International Congress on the Enlightenment,* vol. 3 (Oxford: Taylor Institution, 1981), 1381–1387; N. Senior, "Aspects of Infant Feeding in Eighteenth Century France," *Eighteenth Century Studies* 16 (4) (Summer 1983): 367–388.

ENCYCLOPEDIE, L' (*The Encyclopedia,* 1751–1772), edited by Diderot* and d'Alembert,* constitutes, in seventeen volumes of text and eleven volumes of engravings, the greatest publishing enterprise in the eighteenth century and is considered the grandparent of the modern encyclopedia. An army of more than 160 contributors, including civil servants, professionals, clerics, and authors, contributed 23,135 pages on science, philosophy, arts, and trades. Yet the *Encyclopédie* provided more than a storehouse of information. As an arm of the philosophes,* it encouraged man's progress and reason and attacked social, religious, and political institutions.

The *Encyclopédie* originated as a translation of Ephraim Chambers's (1680–1740) *Cyclopedia* (1727), begun in 1743 by John Mills who applied to the king's printer, André-François Le Breton (1708–1779), to publish the work. Through cunning, Le Breton obtained the privilege and engaged Jean Paul de Gua de Malves (1713–1785), professor of philosophy at the Collège de France, as editor, but soon replaced him with Diderot, whose recent translation of Dr. Robert James's *Universal Dictionary of Medicine* (1746–1748) proved him better suited for the task. Diderot soon persuaded the publishers to undertake a more original and comprehensive work, engaged his friend d'Alembert to edit the mathematics, and enlisted twenty-one additional contributors. In 1750, Diderot's *Prospectus* announced the aim of the *Encyclopédie* and drew 2,000 subscribers. His imprisonment in Vincennes delayed but did not stop the printing of the first volume, which was a *Discours préliminaire* (*Preliminary Discourse*) by d'Alembert; it appeared in July 1751. The second volume appeared in January 1752.

Though the *Encyclopédie* was enthusiastically received by the public, it sustained repeated attacks by the Jesuit publication, *Journal de Trévoux,* which denounced certain articles and accused it of plagiarism. In January 1752, the Jesuits denounced the thesis, "A la Jérusalem céleste," defended before the Sorbonne a few months earlier by a friend and collaborator of the encyclopedists, the abbé de Prades (1720–1782), labelling it "blasphemous, heretical, erroneous, favorable to materialism" and condemned it to fire. The encyclopedists and Diderot, who wrote an apology for the abbé de Prades, were suspected of conspiracy in the affair, perhaps to infiltrate the ranks of the Sorbonne with one of their own freethinkers. Finally, in February of that same year, an arrest from the council of the king suppressed both volumes as erroneous, corrupt, and irreligious. Manuscripts were seized, and rumors flew that the Jesuits would continue the publication.

During the next three years, the support of d'Argenson, to whom the *Encyclopédie* was dedicated, Madame de Pompadour, who was the king's mistress and an enemy of the Jesuits, and the liberal policies of Malesherbes,* the director of publications, assured the future, for a time at least, of the *Encyclopédie*. With tacit government approval and stricter censors, the next five volumes, through the letter "G," appeared from 1753 to 1757, one each year. Subscriptions mounted, editions were reprinted, and the encyclopedists swelled their ranks.

By 1757, the seventh volume containing d'Alembert's controversial article "Genève," which praised Protestantism and encouraged the establishment of the theatre in that city, launched a new storm of protest. Nicolas Moreau (1717–1803), a lawyer, coined the term "Cacouacs" (1757) to ridicule the philosophes, comparing them to the savages of the Caribbean in an article for the

October issue of *Mercure de France*. Palissot's* antagonistic pamphlet, "Petites lettres sur les grands philosophes" ("Little Letters on Great Philosophers") attacked d'Alembert, who deserted the encyclopedist camp in 1758. Duclos* and Marmontel* soon followed. Later that year, the publication of Helvétius's* *De l'esprit* (*Concerning the Mind*) proposing a "science of morality," was condemned and linked with the encyclopedists in a conspiracy of corruption, materialism, and independence. In 1759, Helvetius's book, along with the *Encyclopédie* and six others, were condemned; *De l'esprit* was burned; sales of the *Encyclopédie* were suspended, and a commission of nine was formed to examine its volumes until it was finally suppressed on the grounds of "irreparable damage . . . in regards to morality and religion by the king." Undaunted by another tide of criticism, stemming this time from Fréron,* le Franc de Pompignan,* and Palissot's play, *Les Philosophes* (*The Philosophes*), Diderot, tired and in ill health, continued his work behind locked doors, abandoned by all but de Jaucourt.* He prepared eleven volumes of plates from 1762 to 1772. To his horror, Diderot discovered in 1764 that Le Breton had secretly removed and burned offending material from the remaining ten volumes of text, which finally appeared without opposition in 1765.

Diderot, writing and editing more than 1,000 articles on philosophy ("Eclectisme"), literature and aesthetics ("Beau"), social theory ("La Loi naturelle"), morality, religion, politics, economics, and the applied arts, provided the lifeblood for the *Encyclopédie* for more than twenty years. D'Alembert wrote chiefly on science and mathematics; de Jaucourt, at great personal expense, edited articles on politics, history, and natural and physical science; d'Holbach* edited scientific and theological articles supporting the doctrine of materialism; Voltaire* contributed the articles "Elégance," "Eloquence," "Esprit" and "Imagination"; Montesquieu* wrote the article "Goût" ("Taste"). Other contributors include Mably* and Raynal* (politics); Quesnay,* Turgot,* and J.-J. Rousseau* (economics); abbé Morellet,* abbé de Prades (1720–1782), abbé Yvon (1714–1791), and abbé Mallet (1713–1755) (theology); Theodore Tronchin (1709–1781) and Paul Joseph Barthez (1734–1786) (medicine); Louis-Jean-Marie Daubenton (1716–1799) (natural science); Duclos (morality, art, and history); Marmontel (literature).

As a promulgator of knowledge from A to Z, the *Encyclopédie* fulfilled the need of the times to systematize and spread the ever-growing body of information to an ever-mindful body of eighteenth-century would-be scholars. D'Alembert acknowledged in his *Discours préliminaire* that "as an Encyclopedia, it must set forth, as much as possible, the order and the sequence of human knowledge; as a Rational Dictionary of the sciences, arts, and trades, it must contain for each science and each art, whether liberal or mechanical, its general, fundamental principles and the most essential details which comprise its body and substance."

Despite the inevitable contradictions and errors in such a mammoth enterprise, the *Encyclopédie* is testimony to the awakening of Enlightenment man's intellect and growing spirit of dissatisfaction with the ancien régime. Praise of science, reason, and progress pervades its pages, supported by an undercurrent of political, social, and religious criticism. Couched in the philosophe's hypocritical examination of dogmas and traditions or hidden within an intricate system of cross-references lay attacks on authority, tradition, and faith. Though politically conservative and favoring a liberal, limited monarchy, the *Encyclopédie* supported the sovereignty of the people and their rights—personal liberty and freedom of thought and expression. It condemned torture and war and encouraged education as a safeguard against abuse. It spread Diderot's materialist philosophy, his belief in natural man's goodness and sociability. With its emphasis on economics, the *Encyclopédie* fostered a new appreciation for technical advances and the new machinery of the growing bourgeoisie.

Diderot claimed in his article "Encyclopédie" that "It is befitting only of a philosophical age to attempt an encyclopedia . . . . One must examine everything, turn everything over without exception and without caution." Thus the *Encyclopédie* incarnates his ideals and those of his age.

For further information, see P. Coleman, "The Idea of Character in the *Encyclopedia*," *Eighteenth Century Studies* 19 (Fall 1979): 21–47; R. Darnton, "A Bibliographical Imbroglio: Hidden Editions of the *Encyclopédie*," in *Cinq Siècles d'imprimerie genevoise*, vol. 2 (Geneva: Société d'histoire et d'archéologie, 1981), 71–101; Darnton, *The Business of Enlightenment. A Publishing History of the Encyclopedia* (Cambridge, Mass.: Harvard University Press, 1979); Darnton, "Philosophers Trim the Tree of Knowledge: The Epistemological Strategy of the *Encyclopédie*," in his *The Great Cat Massacre and Other Episodes in French Cultural History* (New York: Vintage Books, 1985); P. N. Furbank, *The Encyclopédie* (Milton Keynes, England: Open University Educational Enterprises, 1980); R. Hahn, "Science and the Arts in France: the Limitations of an Encyclopedic Ideology," in *Studies in Eighteenth Century Culture*, vol. 10 (Madison: University of Wisconsin Press, 1981), 77–93; K. Hardesty, "Thomas Jefferson and the Thought of the *Encyclopédie*," *Laurels* 52 (1) (Spring 1981): 19–31; F. Kafker, *Notable Encyclopedias of the Seventeenth and Eighteenth Centuries: Nine Predecessors of the Encyclopédie* (Oxford: Taylor Institution, 1981); L. Kerslake, "The Sources of Some Literary Articles in the *Encyclopédie*," *Studies on Voltaire and the Eighteenth Century* 215 (1982): 139–161; John Lough, "The *Encyclopedia* and Chambers' *Cyclopedia*," *Studies on Voltaire and the Eighteenth Century* 185 (1980): 221–224; C. V. McDonald, "The Utopia of the Text: Diderot's *Encyclopédie*," *The Eighteenth Century: Theory and Interpretation* 21 (Spring 1980): 128–144; J. A. Perkins, "Gardening in the *Encyclopedia*," *Diderot Studies* 19 (1979): 145–162; T. Scanlon, "The Family as Depicted in the *Encyclopedia*," *Trivium* 14 (1979): 155–166; R. N. Schwab, "Sleuthing in the *Encyclopedia*," in *Studies in the French Eighteenth Century Presented to John Lough*, D. Mossop, G. Rodmell, and D. Wilson, eds. (Durham: University of Durham, 1978), 229–247; A. Simowitz, *Theory of Art in the Encyclopédie* (Ann Arbor: University of Michigan Research Press, 1983).

ESPRIT DES LOIS, DE L' (*The Spirit of the Laws,* 1748), by Montesquieu,* written in thirty-one books and six major parts, is the culmination of more than twenty years of research and firsthand observation of laws, constitutions, and social systems from classical antiquity to eighteenth-century Europe, from America to the Orient. Montesquieu's method was scientific: "I have laid down principles, and I have seen particular cases submit to them . . . ." (Preface). His goal was to uncover the "soul" of the laws which govern man.

In book 1, Montesquieu defines law as "the necessary relationships which derive from the nature of things." Just as the physical universe has its "invariable laws," so too there exists a moral code, or "natural law," derived from prerational man's desires for peace, food, sex, society, and religion. Yet rational man, with his free will and passions, violates the law; with his reason, man establishes "positive laws" to maintain order. "Positive laws" or manmade laws, therefore, vary from one nation to another, for "they must belong to the people for whom they are made, such that it is a great coincidence if those of a nation are able to suit another." They relate first to the nature and principle of the government, then to the physical nature of the land, the way of life of its inhabitants, their degree of liberty, their religion, inclinations, prosperity, number, commerce, morals, and customs. All of these relationships form the "spirit of the laws."

Books 2 and 3 define three forms of government—the republican, where "the people as a body [Montesquieu later terms this form of republic a democracy] or only a part of the people [an aristocracy] have supreme power"; the monarchy, "where one alone governs, but according to fixed and established laws"; and the despotic, where "one alone, without law and without rule, leads all by his will and his whims." Each of the three forms of government operates according to certain principles or "human passions" that make the government work. Democracy is founded on virtue; aristocracy, on moderation; monarchy, on honor; despotism, on fear.

Books 4 through 8 discuss the importance of laws on education (4), constitutional law (5), penal law (6), and sumptuary law (7) in order to maintain the "principle" of government, which is where corruption takes root: "The corruption of each government begins, almost always, by that of its principles" (book 8). Democracy is prey to corruption by ambition ("the spirit of inequality") and insubordination ("the spirit of extreme equality"). Monarchy disintegrates when "intermediary powers" such as the nobility, clergy, and parliament are suppressed. Despotism, on the other hand, continually corrupts itself, because it is by nature corrupt. Books 9 and 10 discuss the importance of military law to maintain the state.

Book 11, entitled "Laws which Form the Political Liberty in its Relationship with the Constitution," examines the English constitution and its distribution of power, such that, "by the arrangement of things, power impedes power." Separation into executive, legislative, and judicial branches disperses power among the king, representatives of the people, and judges and results in fair and reasonable government. Book 12 considers the political liberty of citizens, proscribing abuses of punishment for heresy, writing, and speech; book 13 discusses taxation.

From book 14 on, Montesquieu examines the law in relation to physical and social factors such as the terrain of the land (book 18), morals and customs (book 19), commerce (books 20 and 21), currency (book 22), population (book 23), religion (books 24 to 26), Roman law (book 27), French civil law (book 28), composition of the law (book 29), and French feudal law (books 30 and 31). Book 14 contains his famous theory of climate, in which Montesquieu attempts to prove scientifically that climate determines man's temperament such that in cold climates, "the frigid air contracts the extremities of the exterior fibers of our bodies, which increases their elasticity and encourages the return of the blood from the extremities toward the heart." Therefore, inhabitants of cold climates are more vigorous, stronger, more self-confident, and more aware of their superiority. Observing and freezing a sheep's tongue leads him to conclude that because the taste buds contract when frozen, citizens of frigid climes have "little sensitivity for pleasure. . . . one must flay a Moscovite to give him feeling." Book 15 contains his eloquent argument against slavery.

Though it has been criticized for its complexity, superficiality (Madame du Deffand [1697–1780] termed it "Spirit on the Laws"), contradictory analytical methods (rationalism, determinism), and hastily drawn conclusions (such as relating the physiology of a sheep's tongue to the temperament of an entire nation), *De l'esprit des lois* ranks with the most important books of its century. Its analyses initiated the fields of historical and political science; its theory of climates influenced Madame de Staël,* Taine,* and the criticism of the nineteenth century. Above all, it constitutes a testament to reason and humanity. By seeking to understand "the general spirit" of what governs man—climate, religion, laws, government maxims, historical examples, morals, manners, and the relationship of that spirit to man's nature, *De l'esprit des lois* prepares the way for wise legislation, liberty and justice for the citizen, and prosperity for the nation. Its influence extended beyond France and its constitution of 1791 to Americans Benjamin Franklin (1706–1790), Thomas Jefferson (1743–1826), and James Madison (1751–1836), who embraced its principles as a safeguard against tyranny and as the foundation of democracy.

For further information, see D. W. Carrithers, "Montesquieu, Jefferson and the Fundamentals of Eighteenth-Century Republican Theory," *The French-American Review* 6 (Fall 1982): 160–188; S. Gearhart, "Reading *De l'Esprit des lois*. Montesquieu and the Principles of History," *Yale French Studies* 59 (1980): 175–200; G. Klosko, "Montesquieu's Science of Politics: Absolute Values and Ethical Realism in *L'Esprit des Lois*," *Studies on Voltaire and the Eighteenth Century* 189 (1980): 153–177; R. Shackleton, "John Norse and the London Edition of *L'Esprit des Lois*," in *Studies in the French Eighteenth Century Presented to John Lough*, D. Mossop, G. Rodmell, and D. Wilson, eds. (Durham: University of Durham, 1978), 248–259; J. Shklar, "Virtue in a Bad Climate: Good Men and Good Citizens in *L'Esprit des lois*," in *Enlightenment Studies Presented in Honor of Lester G. Crocker* (Oxford: Voltaire Foundation, 1979).

ESSAI SUR LES MOEURS ET L'ESPRIT DES NATIONS (*Essay on Manners and the Spirit of Nations*, 1756), by Voltaire,* generally called *Essai sur les* *moeurs,* represents the culmination of his thoughts on the history of the world from the time of Charlemagne to Louis XIV. Originally conceived in 1740 at Cirey for the edification of Mme du Châtelet and published in Holland in 1753 and again in 1756, Voltaire worked on its seven volumes the rest of his life. Comprised of 197 chapters, the book begins with the first civilizations—those of China, India, Persia, Arabia, Italy—and the origins of Christianity. Then, proceeding chronologically from the age of Charlemagne, it divides the history of the world into important periods—after Charlemagne, the Norman Conquests, the tenth and eleventh centuries, wars of the papacy, the crusades, the wars of Philippe-le-Bel, the Great Schism, the Hundred Years' War, the thirteenth and fourteenth centuries, the Turks, Louis XI and Charles the "Temeraire," the age of chivalry, the fifteenth century, Charles V and Francis I, the sixteenth century, the Reformation, the age of great discoveries, Philippe II, the Wars of the Roses in England, the wars of religion in France, Louis XIII and Richelieu, and the seventeenth century.

Besides the history of civilization, *Essai sur les moeurs* presents the development of the human spirit against a backdrop of Voltaire's ideas on religious fanaticism, persecution, violence, and his faith in reason and progress. He states in the preface that he will survey nations "who live on the earth and desolate it." From its first pages to its last, the book titillates with gems of wisdom and satire on individuals, events, and institutions over the course of a thousand years. The final chapter summarizes his view of history as "little else than a long succession of useless cruelties. . . . a collection of crimes, follies and misfortunes, among which we have seen some virtues, some happy times, just as we sometimes see habitations scattered here and there in barren deserts."

Yet Voltaire clings to his notion of progress. "In the midst of these ravages and destructions which we observe in the space of nine hundred years," he writes, "we see a love of order which secretly animates human nature and which has prevented its total ruin." Children's respect for their parents; the law's respect for the family; curbs placed on arbitrary power by law, custom, or manners; religious precepts of morality, all serve to unify human nature "from one end of the universe to the other." The arts are the true healers of the desecration. "When a nation knows the arts, when she is no longer subjugated and carried off by strangers, she rises easily from her ruins and reestablishes herself forever."

The work of an artist and historian-philosopher, Voltaire's *Essai sur les moeurs* retains its place as a masterpiece of Enlightenment literature.

EUGENIE GRANDET (1833), by Balzac,* belongs to the *Scènes de la vie de province (Provincial Scenes)* of the 1843 edition of the *Comédie humaine.** It is the story of one man's passion for money and how it destroys his family and himself. Originally conceived as a short story, its first chapter appeared in 1833 in the periodical *L'Europe littéraire (Literary Europe).* After a disagreement with the publisher, the work appeared in book form later that same year as the first volume of Balzac's proposed *Etudes de moeurs au XIXe siècle* (*Studies of the Manners of the XIXth century*).

The story unfolds in the provincial town of Saumur. After a careful description of the town, its manners, inhabitants, and the melancholy Grandet house, Balzac introduces Monsieur Grandet, a well-off cooper, fairly well educated and mayor of the town, who is more interested in enlarging his land holdings and acquiring gold than anything else. Grandet's avarice is so great that he is often likened to Molière's (1622–1673) Harpagon in *L'Avare* (1668). "He seemed," Balzac writes, "to economize everything, even movement." A man of simple habits and manners, he rarely spoke and always dressed the same. Even his face betrayed his passion. His miserly ways victimized his wife and daughter, Eugénie. His only callers were the families of his banker, Monsieur des Grassins, and that of his notary, Monsieur Cruchot. Both hoped to win Eugénie's hand for their sons.

The action begins in mid-November 1819 on the evening of Eugénie's birthday, with the des Grassins and the Cruchots in attendance, when Eugénie's cousin, Charles Grandet, arrives from Paris. Charles is an elegant young dandy the likes of which the modest and pious Eugénie has never seen before. He bears a letter from his father, Monsieur Grandet's brother, informing him of his bankruptcy and plans for suicide. Charles, genuinely grieved by his father's death, incites the pity of Eugénie, who is moved to give him her collection of rare gold coins. He, in turn, gives her a gold dressing case and pledges to marry her upon his return from the Indies, where he must go to seek his fortune. Selfish Grandet, on the other hand, plots to clear his brother's debts at the least possible cost to himself. He explodes with anger when he learns that Eugénie has given her coins to Charles and confines her to her room with a diet of bread and water. Madame Grandet, ill with fright and sadness, is near death when Grandet learns that when she dies, Eugénie can claim her portion of the estate. Out of selfishness, he is reconciled with his daughter. Under his training, she learns to manage her father's affairs. Paralyzed and near death, Grandet's main concern is his treasures. He dies trying to snatch his priest's gilded crucifix.

Upon her father's death, Eugénie finds herself at the head of a fortune valued at 17 million francs. She grants her faithful servant, Nanon, a lifelong annuity and faithfully awaits Charles's return. Charles makes his fortune in the Indies as a slave trader, contracts a marriage with the daughter of an illustrious family, and will become a marquis. He reneges on his father's debts, which are generously paid by Eugénie to clear his name and assure his marriage. With her hopes of marriage to Charles dashed, she consents to marry Monsieur de Bonfons. It will be a short, platonic marriage, stunted by Eugénie's demands that it not be consummated and by Bonfons's early death. Eugénie, wealthier than ever, continues her simple existence and dedicates her fortune to charitable works.

Eugénie Grandet met with immediate popular success. It has retained its place among the great masterpieces of literature. This is due partly to the author's skill as a storyteller. Balzac, in a letter to Madame Hanska in 1833, called the novel "one of my most accomplished tableaux." It has been called a masterpiece of realism, hailed for its classic depiction of Grandet's avarice and Eugénie's transformation from her father's prisoner to an independent, sensitive, generous woman. Most important is the novel's social significance. It pits the forces of money and power against those of love and sentiment, illustrating the role of money in early nineteenth century France and its devastating effects on family and social ties.

For further information, see A. Fischler, "Show and Rumor: The Worldly Scales in Balzac's *Eugénie Grandet*," *International Fiction Review* 8 (2) (Summer 1981): 98–105; J. Gale, " 'Sleeping Beauty' as Ironic Model for *Eugénie Grandet*," *Nineteenth Century French Studies* 10 (Fall–Winter 1981–1982): 28–36; L. Lynch, "People, Animals and Transformations in *Eugénie Grandet*," *International Fiction Review* 10 (2) (Summer 1983): 83–90.

F

FABRE, PHILIPPE-FRANÇOIS-NAZAIRE, who called himself Fabre d'Eglantine (1755–1794), after winning in 1775 the "églantine" (wild rose) prize in the "Jeux floraux," the famed Toulousian poetry contest, wrote comedies, poetry, and songs during the period of unrest and change following the French Revolution. He was born in Limoux and entered the religious order of the Brothers of Christian Doctrine in Toulouse, which he left for the actor's life in Paris. Though his first attempts (*Les Gens de lettres ou Le Provinçial à Paris— The Writers or The Provincial in Paris,* 1787; *Augusta,* 1787) were unsuccessful, he established himself as a playwright with *Le Philinthe de Molière ou La Suite du 'Misanthrope'* (*Moliere's Philinthe or The Continuation of 'The Misanthrope,'* 1791), in which an aged and egotistical Philinthe is contrasted with a kind and generous Alceste, who understands and sympathizes with the Revolution. *L'Aristocrate ou Le Convalescent de qualite* (*The Aristocrat or The Convalescent of Quality,* 1791) depicts a marquis's postrevolutionary awakening to the loss of his privileges and servants who are his equals. Later plays, *L'Intrigue épistolaire* (*The Letter Scheme,* 1791), *Les Précepteurs* (*The Tutors,* posthumous, 1800), *Le Présomptueux ou L'Heureux imaginaire* (*The Presumptuous One or The Imaginary Happy Man*), and others today are dated and artificial but retain a measure of comedy.

As a poet he wrote odes, satires, romances, and didactic poems. His song, "Il pleut, il pleut bergère" ("It Is Raining, It Is Raining, Shepherdess," 1780), announced the Revolution, which he supported as a member of the Paris Commune and as deputy to the National Convention. He devised much of the nomenclature of the republican calendar. Fabre d'Eglantine opposed the Terror, however, and was accused of corruption. On 5 April 1784, along with Danton* and Desmoulins,* he was guillotined.

FAUSSES CONFIDENCES, LES (*False Confessions*), presented in 1737 at the Théâtre Italien,* is the last and, along with *Le Jeu de l'amour et du hasard,** one of the most important of Marivaux's* love comedies. The critic Oscar Haac finds the originality of the play in its combination of sentiment and humor in a realistic setting. Besides its realism, *Les Fausses Confidences* differs from the other love comedies in its serious tone and mature characters. Like *Le Jeu de l'amour et du hasard,* it has social overtones, foreshadowing, according to Kenneth McKee (*The Theatre of Marivaux,* 1958), the social drama of the nineteenth century. Dubois, the scheming valet, prefigures Figaro in the comedies of Beaumarchais.*

The plot is complicated but revolves basically around the actions and falsehoods perpetrated by the wily Dubois to win the heart of Araminte, a beautiful, wealthy widow, for his handsome, though impoverished former master, Dorante, who with the help of his uncle has become her business manager. Dubois plays on the widow's sympathy, convincing her that Dorante is incurably crazy with love for her. She agrees to employ him, despite the objections of her mother, Mme Argante, who, though ignorant of Dorante's motives, finds him not only too good-looking for the post but unwilling to falsely advise Araminte in a legal suit against Count Dorimont. Mme Argante, a brazen social climber, wants Araminte to marry the count not only to end the litigation between the two families but to add to her fortune and enter the nobility.

In the second act, Dubois has a portrait, supposedly painted by Dorante as a sign of his love for her, fall into Araminte's hands; in act 3, he has Dorante write a letter to a friend admitting his passion for Araminte and his need, therefore, to leave the country, a letter which, like the portrait, finds its way to Araminte. Araminte, furious that Dorante's love is now public knowledge, grants him one last interview in which she reveals her love for him. He admits his deceit and she forgives all. The play concludes with marriage imminent, becoming the first, according to McKee, ever to end with a marriage that cuts across social lines.

The play has been attacked on moral grounds, for the unethical behavior of Dubois toward Araminte, and for Dorante's participation, though passive, in it. Yet it continues to be praised for its originality, wit, and its presentation of love and the female heart.

For further information, see G. Rodmell, *Marivaux: Le Jeu de l'amour et du hasard and Les Fausses Confidences* (London: Grant and Cutler, 1982).

FENELON, FRANÇOIS DE SALIGNAC DE LA MOTHE (1651–1715), eminent seventeenth-century churchman, is best known as author of *Télémaque* (1699). As tutor to the duke of Bourgogne (1682–1712), grandson of Louis XIV, who died before ascending to the throne, Fénelon wrote a mythological tale of the education of Télémaque, son of Ulysses, in the morality and politics of being a king. Besides tracing Télémaque's adventurous Mediterranean search for his father and exposing him to good and bad forms of government, the tale sets forth Fénelon's political and moral ideas and indirectly criticizes those of Louis XIV. Fénelon was opposed to war, luxury, and despotism, all embodied in the reign of the Sun King. The philosophes* admired his ideals, his daring, and originality.

Fénelon entered the Academy in 1693 and was named archbishop of Cambrai in 1695 but fell into disgrace for embracing "quiétisme" (a form of mysticism) and for the satire seen by Louis XIV in *Télémaque*. He spent his last years exiled in his diocese and died unpardoned and disappointed.

Other works by Fénelon include *Lettre à Louis XIV ou Lettre secrète (Letter to Louis XIV or Secret Letter,* 1694), also critical of the political system; *Tables de Chaulnes (Tables of Chaulnes,* 1711), plans, never realized because of his death a year later, for the government of the duke of Bourgogne written with the duke of Chevreuse. In a different vein, he wrote *Dialogues sur l'éloquence (Dialogues on Eloquence,* written, 1680?; published, 1718); *Traité de l'éducation des filles (Treatise on the Education of Girls,* 1687); *Les Fables (Fables)* and *Dialogues des morts (Dialogues of the Dead),* both written for the duke of Bourgogne in 1700; *Explication des maximes des saints (Explanation of the maxims of the Saints,* 1697); and *Le Traité de l'existence de Dieu (Treaty of the Existence of God,* 1712, 1718).

For more information, see M. Cor, "The Shield of *Télémaque," Romance Notes* 23 (1) (Fall 1982): 17–21; B. Fink, "Utopian Nurtures," [Fénelon, Mercier, Morelly, Sade], in *Transactions of the Fifth International Congress on the Enlightenment,* vol. 2 (Oxford: Taylor Institution: 1981), 664–671; B. Warnick, *Fénelon's Letter to the French Academy,* with an introduction and commentary (New York, London: University Press of America, 1984).

FEUILLES D'AUTOMNE, LES (*Autumn Leaves,* 1831), a collection of poems written by Victor Hugo* at the height of his glory as head of the new romantic (see romanticism*) movement, continues the lyric tradition of his earlier *Odes et Ballades* and *Les Orientales** but is marked by a sadness missing from his previous poems. The death of his father three years earlier, marital discord, religious doubt, and the changing political climate account for the somberness of the poems. Hugo indicates in his preface that he is offering "fallen leaves, dead leaves, like all the leaves of autumn . . . not the poetry of tumult and din; these are serene and peaceful verses of the family, home, private life; verses of the interior of the soul." In these poems, Hugo casts a melancholy glance on "that which is and especially, that which was."

The first poem, "Ce siècle avait deux ans" ("This Century Was Two Years Old"), evokes his childhood and his family, his mother's immeasurable love and the source of his inspiration, "Each breath, each ray of light, whether favorable or fatal/ Illuminates and vibrates my soul of crystal." "A M. Louis B." ("To Mr. Louis B.") is a meditation on his father's death suggested by two lines from Virgil's *Aeneid.* "La Pente de la Rêverie" ("The Slope of Reverie"), which depicts the "imperceptible" slope leading "from the real world to the invisible sphere" where his soul swims "alone and naked," announces the visionary poet of *La Légende des siècles,** as Hugo creates an imaginary land peopled with his friends and throngs of strangers and witnesses the entire spectacle of human history in the form of an ever-growing Tower of Babel. "La Prière pour tous"

("Prayer for All"), addressed to his daughter Léopoldine, asks her to pray for her parents, for the blind, for the suffering, for all of humanity, and for God himself. "Lorsque l'enfant paraît" ("When a Child Appears") is a beautiful and sincere expression of Hugo's joy in children. He writes, "When the child comes, joy arrives and lightens us."

Les Feuilles d'automne expresses with lyricism and sensitivity Hugo's most intimate thoughts on childhood, home, and family life; it constitutes the first step away from the early romanticism* of his Odes and Ballades. Its themes were echoed and expanded to include politics over the next ten years in Les Chants du crépuscule,* Les Voix intérieures,* and Les Rayons et les ombres.* With these collections, Hugo embarked on a poetic voyage that culminated in the auto-biographical, mystical, and epic poems of his later years, Les Contemplations* and La Légende des siècles.

FLAUBERT, GUSTAVE (1821–1880), the author of Madame Bovary,* L'Education sentimentale,* Salammbo,* and a few other carefully wrought novels and stories, dedicated his life to the pursuit of beauty and art. His years of work resulted in novels that are considered technically perfect and earned him renown as the master of the realist (see realism*) novel.

Flaubert was born and raised in the Hôtel-Dieu, the principal hospital in Rouen, where his father was chief surgeon. He enjoyed a comfortable if lonely childhood in a family that was cultivated and respected. The sterility of the hospital perhaps contributed to the occasional morbid nature of his realism. Illness, suffering, and death were familiar to Flaubert, who as a child spied upon bodies awaiting dissection in the morgue. In 1832, he entered the Collège Royal de Rouen, a distinguished secondary school, where he was an undistinguished student, preferring above all the romantic literature of Johann Wolfgang von Goethe (1749–1832), George Byron (1788–1824), William Shakespeare (1564–1616), Hugo,* Chateaubriand,* and Dumas père.* His penchant for writing surfaced early with stories, Rêve d'enfer (Dream of Hell, 1837), Passion et vertu (Passion and Virtue, 1837); drama, Loys XI (1838); and journalism, editing a student journal, Art et progrès (Art and Progress) and collaborating on Colibri, a Rouennais journal. At fourteen, while vacationing at Trouville, he was thunderstruck by Elisa Schlésinger (1810–1888), a married woman eleven years his senior who engendered a mystical ideal of love in the young boy, which influenced the youthful Mémoires d'un fou (Memoirs of a Fool, 1838), Novembre (1842), and especially both versions of L'Education sentimentale. Smarh, a preliminary sketch written between 1838 and 1839 for La Tentation de Saint Antoine (The Temptation of Saint Anthony, 1874), is a dialogue between Satan and an old hermit.

He passed the baccalaureate in 1840 and travelled to the Pyrenees and Corsica with a friend of his father, Dr. Jules Cloquet. It was a journey that introduced him to the Mediterranean and the architecture of the ancient world as well as to certain pleasures with the opposite sex. The following year, at his family's insistence, he entered law school in Paris but returned to Rouen, possibly for health reasons, to prepare for his exams and write a novella, *Novembre*. By late autumn 1842, he moved to the Latin Quarter, attended law classes, and prepared for the bar. In 1843, he met journalist and novelist Maxime Du Camp (1822–1894), his intimate and literary confidant for the next ten years, renewed his acquaintance with the Schlésingers, and visited friends, the Collier family, which he had met in Trouville, and sculptor James Pradier (1752–1852) and his wife. In January 1844, en route from Deauville with his brother, Flaubert suffered a seizure, the first manifestation of a nervous disorder that induced him to renounce his law career for literature. He retired to the family estate at Croisset on the Seine below Rouen, which his father had bought that same year, and began writing the first version of *L'Education sentimentale*.

In 1845, his sister married, and the family accompanied the couple to Italy. The following year, his father died and he lost his sister in childbirth. He lived virtually the rest of his life with his mother and little niece at Croisset, devoting himself to reading, study, writing, and the friendship of Alfred Le Poittevin (1816–1848), Maxime Du Camp (1822–1894), and Louis Bouilhet (1821–1869). In 1846, at Pradier's studio, he met Louise Colet (1810–1876), a romantic poetess about ten years his senior who soon became his mistress. Their correspondence over the next ten years is a meaningful record of his progress on *Madame Bovary* and *L'Education sentimentale*. The following year, he and Du Camp embarked on a three-month walking tour through Touraine and Brittany, which they captured in a joint writing venture, *Par les champs et par les grèves* (*Over Field and Shore*, posthumous).

In 1848, he witnessed the outbreak of the Revolution in Paris with Bouilhet. In May, he began his first version of *La Tentation de Saint Antoine*, a long, dramatic monologue inspired by Pieter Breugel's (1564–1637 or 1638) painting of the same name, which had impressed him profoundly the year before in Genoa. A work of enormous proportions, documented by more than sixty ancient texts, it took thirty-two hours to read to Du Camp and Bouilhet. To his dismay, they panned the work, advising him to harness the lyric flights of his romantic imagination. After a journey with Du Camp through Egypt, Palestine, Greece, and Syria that lasted from the fall of 1849 until 1851, Flaubert returned to Croisset in June, renewed relations with Louise Colet in July, and in September, began *Madame Bovary*, his work for the next five years. Progress was painfully slow, with only occasional diversions in Paris with Louise Colet and Sunday visits by Bouilhet, who served as Flaubert's mentor for the project. By 1856, the text was complete, and Du Camp consented to publish it, with the infamous cab scene cut, in his *Revue de Paris*. It met with moral outrage and a suit against Flaubert, which he won. The novel appeared in book form the following year. *Madame Bovary* is a realistic evocation of provincial manners and character, particularly that of Emma Bovary, so carefully wrought, that it brought its author immediate and enduring literary renown. It was exalted by Sainte-Beuve,* whom Flaubert met in Paris along with Gautier,* Edmond and Jules de Goncourt,** Renan,* Feydeau,** and Baudelaire.** He frequented the salons and befriended Sand,* Taine,* and Ivan Turgenev (1818–1883).

After completing *Madame Bovary,* Flaubert revised *La Tentation de Saint Antoine* and began *Salammbô,* a historical novel about ancient Carthage, which satisfied his desire to write about the Orient. He brought an inordinate amount of documentation to the task, spending the winter of 1856–1857 ensconced in the libraries of Paris and an enormous amount of time in planning and writing, which occupied him from March 1857 through April 1862. He set out for Carthage in April 1858 to complete his research, travelling to Tunisia, Carthage, and Utica. When *Salammbô* was completed nearly four years later, it met with great success.

The years from 1864 to 1869 were devoted to the completion and revision of *L'Education sentimentale,* with stays in Paris breaking up long periods of hard work. This novel marks a return to the realism of *Madame Bovary.* It is a study in personal and political failure, that of Frédéric Moreau and his generation. In 1866, Flaubert travelled to London; in August he was nominated to the Legion of Honor. George Sand* visited him at Croisset twice that year.

One month after completing *L'Education sentimentale,* he began his final revision of *La Tentation de Saint Antoine,* which continued until 1873. This work, partly inspired by Faust and the legend of the Wandering Jew, is a spectacle of the temptations, those of the flesh and the philosophic, of this holy man and of all mankind.

Flaubert's final years were filled with bitterness, sadness, and financial troubles. He felt the absence of his friends. Louis Bouilhet and Sainte-Beuve died in 1869, Théophile Gautier in 1872, and Ernest Feydeau in 1873. In 1870, with troops stationed at Croisset, Flaubert and his mother fled to Rouen. He feared the future after the defeat of 1870. His mother died in 1872. In 1873, he tried his hand at a comedy, *Le Candidat,* which failed. The following year, *La Tentation de Saint Antoine* met with a cool reception. In 1875, to aid Ernest Commanville, husband of his niece, he sold his farm at Deauville, nearly impoverishing himself. In September of that year, the peace and calm of Concarneau, which he visited with naturalist Georges Pouchet, unleashed the first of his *Trois contes* (*Three Stories,* 1877), *La Légende de Saint Julien l'Hospitalier* (*The Legend of Saint Julian the Hospitaller*), based on the life of a hermit who transports people across a dangerous river to expiate a past crime. The story is depicted in the windows of the cathedral of Rouen, which Flaubert had seen many times. Early the next year, he began *Un Coeur simple* (*A Simple Heart*), which took him to Pont-l'Evêque and Honfleur. It is, as Flaubert said, "the story of an obscure life." Félicité is a kind and devoted servant who centers her life first, on a man, then on her mistress's children, her own nephew, an old man, and a parrot, who die one by one. When at last she dies, she confuses the parrot with the Holy Ghost. By 1877, Flaubert had completed *Hérodias,* the last of the three stories about John the Baptist.

In 1874, Flaubert had travelled to Switzerland to research his next project, *Bouvard et Pécuchet.* In 1877, after the success of the *Trois contes,* he returned to the manuscript. The story of the two clerks of the title took his mind off the financial stress of his last years, but it is unfinished. Well-meaning friends, who campaigned to have him named head of the Mazarin library, secured an honorary stipend from the government instead. In 1880, after a final trip to Paris, he began the final chapter of *Bouvard et Pécuchet*. In April, he received his naturalist* friends Zola,** Daudet,** Edmond de Goncourt, Maupassant,** and George Charpentier at Croisset. A visit to Paris in May never materialized. Flaubert died the day before his proposed departure, on 8 May 1880, of a cerebral hemorrhage.

By nature a romantic, Flaubert was given toward emotion and lyric flights of imagination. However, a profound pessimism about himself and humanity pervades his personality and his writing. This conflict lies at the heart of his masterpieces, *Madame Bovary* and *L'Education sentimentale*.

Flaubert possessed the means and the desire to dedicate his life to the pursuit of Truth, Art, and Beauty. He conformed his existence to the necessities of writing, confining himself to his study at Croisset and limiting interruptions to an occasional day in Rouen or a few weeks each year in Paris. He strove for perfection by working in a slow, laborious manner, which resulted often in only a few written pages but in a perfection of style for which the exact word had been found, the precise detail had been rendered, the harmony and rhythm of style achieved, and his own presence effaced. Flaubert believed that artistic beauty led to truth. Hence his struggle to eliminate himself and his passions and prejudices from his work in order to capture objective reality. "The artist in his work must be like God in creation, invisible and all powerful," Flaubert wrote. "Let his presence be felt everywhere, but let him not be seen." He equated truth with morality. "If the reader does not derive from a book the morality that ought to be there, it is because the reader is an imbecile or because the book is false from the point of view of exactitude. From the moment that a thing is true, it is good."

Although Flaubert disliked the term, his name has been rightfully linked with realism. While that other great realist, Balzac,* bequeathed the movement with the imaginative world of the *Comédie humaine*,* Flaubert dignified realism with a technical perfection that elevated it to the level of art and pointed the way to the modern novel. His emphasis on objectivity and documentation and his doctrine of scientific and impersonal art link him to Zola and the naturalists (see naturalism*), who admired his work. His concept of formal literary beauty is close to the Parnassian* doctrine of "art for art's sake" ("l'art pour l'art"*).

Flaubert's correspondence with Louise Colet and his friend Alfred Le Poittevin and others has been called the most important of that of any man of letters of the nineteenth century for what it shows us of his work and life.

For further information, see W. Berg, M. Grimaud, and G. Moskos, eds., *Psychocritical Approaches to Flaubert's Art* (Ithaca: Cornell University Press, 1982); C. Bernheimer, *Flaubert and Kafka: Studies in Psychopoetic Structure* (New Haven: Yale University Press, 1982); C. Carlut, P. Dube, and J. Dugan, *A Concordance to Flaubert's La Tentation de Saint Antoine* (New York: Garland, 1979); Carlut, Dube, and Dugan, *A Concordance to Flaubert's Trois Contes* (New York: Garland, 1979); E. Donato and M.

Logan, "Historical Imagination and the Idioms of Criticism," *Boundary* 8 (1) (Fall 1979): 39–56; J. Finlay, "Flaubert in Egypt," *The Hudson Review* 36 (3) (Autumn 1983): 496–509; M. Ginsburg, "Representational Strategies and the Early Works of Flaubert," *Modern Language Notes* 98 (5) (December 1983): 1248–1268; S. Haig, "The Substance of Illusion in Flaubert's *Un Coeur Simple*," *Stanford French Review* 7 (3) (Winter 1983): 301–315; Y. Hervouet, "Aspects of Flaubertian Influence on Conrad's Fiction," *Revue de Littérature Comparée* 57 (1) (January–March 1983): 5–24; E. Jackson, "Flaubert in America: A Bibliographical Review 1857–1977," *The French-American Review* 6 (2) (Fall 1982): 260–282; D. LaCapra, "Intellectual History and Defining the Present as 'Postmodern,' " in Hassan, ed., *Innovation/Renovation: New Perspectives on the Humanities* (Madison: University of Wisconsin Press, 1983), 47–63; J. Logan, "Flannery O'Connor and Flaubert: A French Connection," *Notes on Contemporary Literature* 13 (5) (November 1983): 2–5; M. Lowe, " 'Rendre plastique . . .': Flaubert's Treatment of the Female Principle in *Herodias*," *Modern Language Review* 78 (3) (July 1983): 551–558; M. MacNamara, "Description, Rhetoric and Realism in *Bouvard et Pécuchet*," *Nottingham French Studies* 22 (2) (October 1983): 9–19; S. Maloff, "The Family Idiot," *Commonweal* 107 (15) (29 August 1980): 469–471; A. McKenna, "Writing in the Novel: Remarks on *Bouvard et Pécuchet*," *Language and Style* 14 (2) (Spring 1981): 83–91; H. Oliver, "Flaubert and Julie Herbert: A Postscript," *Nineteenth Century French Studies* 12 (1–2) (Fall–Winter 1983–1984): 116–123; D. Paul, "The Two Flauberts," *The New Criterion* 2 (1) (September 1983): 54–60; C. Peterson, "The Trinity in Flaubert's *Trois Contes:* Deconstructing History," *French Forum* 8 (3) (September 1983): 243–258; C. Prendergast, "Flaubert: Quotation, Stupidity and the Cretan Liar Paradox," *French Studies* 35 (3) (July 1981): 261–277; S. Richards, "The Historical Figure as Palimpsest: Flaubert's *La Tentation de Saint Antoine*," *French Literature Series* 8 (1981): 85–93; J. Robertson, "The Structure of *Herodias*," *French Studies* 36 (2) (April 1982): 171–182; A. Schoenholtz, "The Temptations of Truth: Imagination, Doubt and the 'Imposing Completeness of a Delusion' in Keats and Flaubert," *Modern Language Notes* 96 (5) (December 1981): 1051–1065; N. Schor and H. Majewski, eds., *Flaubert and Post-Modernism* (Lincoln: University of Nebraska Press, 1984); S. Selvin, "Spatial Form in Flaubert's *Trois Contes*," *Romanic Review* 74 (2) (March 1983): 202–220; F. Steegmuller, ed., *The Letters of Gustave Flaubert* (Cambridge: Harvard University Press, 1981); T. Sumberg, "Flaubert Against the Enlightenment," *College Language Association Journal* 26 (2) (December 1982): 241–250; L. Uffenbeck, guest ed., *Flaubert. Nineteenth Century French Studies* 12 (3) (Spring 1984); T. Unwin, "Flaubert and Pantheism," *French Studies* 35 (4) (October 1981): 394–406; Unwin, "Flaubert's Early Philosophical Development: The Writing of *Smarh*," *Nottingham French Studies* 21 (2) (October 1982): 13–26; Unwin, "Flaubert's First *Tentation de Saint Antoine*," *Essays in Foreign Literature* 16 (November 1979): 17–42; Dr. Vinoda, "Saul Bellow and Gustave Flaubert," *Saul Bellow Journal* 1 (1) (Fall 1981): 1–5; R. Waring, "Irony and the 'Order of Discourse' in Flaubert," *New Literary History* 13 (2) (Winter 1982): 253–286; E. Zants, "Flaubert's *Bouvard et Pécuchet:* A Socio-Political Critique," *Folio* 14 (December 1982): 41–48.

FLEURS DU MAL, LES (*Flowers of Evil*, 1857–1861), by Baudelaire.** See *Dictionary of Modern French Literature, from Naturalism and Symbolism to Post-Modernism.*

FLORIAN, JEAN-PIERRE CLARIS DE (1755–1794), dramatist, novelist, poet, practiced most of the genres, especially the fable and pastoral novel. Born in Languedoc, he lost his mother after one year and was raised in part by his uncle, the marquis of Florian. He spent some time in Switzerland near Ferney, the home of his great-uncle, Voltaire,* who encouraged his studies and writing. The young chevalier became a page to the duke of Penthièvre (1725–1793), then an officer of the Dragoons, and soon enjoyed success on stage with comedies such as *Le Baiser* (*The Kiss,* 1780) and *Jeannot et Colin* (1780) as well as in the salons. He wrote novels, short stories, and *Numa Pompilius* (1786), a long, sentimental, philosophical prose poem, but excelled in the pastoral novel. Both *Galatée* (1783), which he borrowed from Miguel de Cervantes (1547–1616), and *Estelle* (1787) drew upon and idealized his experience as a youth in the Cévennes and celebrate the peasantry, virtue, and innocence of life in the country.

Florian also published a collection of eighty-nine fables written in the tradition of Jean de la Fontaine (1621–1695) but without the art and ingenuity of the master poet. *Mémoires d'un jeune Espagnol* (*Recollections of a Young Spaniard*) recalls his youth.

Except for some of the fables, Florian lacks the satire and wit of his great-uncle. The pastorals, especially, evoke a Rousseauesque return to nature and the happiness it offers, a theme that also recurs in Chénier* and Bernardin de Saint-Pierre.*

FONTENELLE, BERNARD LE BOUVIER DE (1657–1757), playwright, philosopher, popular scientist, academician, and "bel esprit," was born and bred of the classicism of the seventeenth century. However, his skepticism, clear thinking, and methodical doubt anticipate the rationalism of the Enlightenment. He has been called the first "encyclopedist" (see *Encyclopédie**) (Proust, *Diderot et l'Encyclopédie,* 1962). He was born in Rouen, the nephew of the Corneille brothers, Pierre (1606–1684), the renowned dramatist, and Thomas (1625–1709), who oversaw his education. He became a lawyer but soon forsook law for the salons of Mesdames de Lambert, de Tençin,* and du Maine and the company of intellectuals such as mathematician Pierre Varignon (1654–1722) and astronomer Philippe de la Hire (1640–1718). In 1677, his literary career began with poetry for the *Mercure galant,* edited by Thomas Corneille and Donneau de Visé (1638–1710); he wrote an opera (*Psyché,* 1678) and tragedies, including *Aspar* (1680). *Dialogues des morts* (*Dialogues of the Dead,* 1683), written in the style of Greek satirist Lucian (2d century A.D.), debates human nature, astronomy, geometry, literature, the ancients, and the moderns.

Fontenelle turned to science and philosophy with *Relation de l'île de Bornéo* (*Report on the Island of Borneo,* 1686), a daring defense of the Protestants, which almost led him to the Bastille. The short but pote..tially dangerous *De l'origine des fables* (*On the Origin of Fables,* written, 1684; published, 1724) studies primitive man's belief, out of ignorance, in fables, which Fontenelle considers "the story of the errors of man's thinking." This work opened the way for the philosophes'* criticism of the Christian's belief in miracles and the supernatural. *Histoire des oracles* (*History of the Oracles*, 1686), a seemingly "innocent criticism" of the faith of the ancients and their oracles, constitutes, according to Gustave Lanson and Paul Tuffrau (*Manuel d'histoire de la littérature française*, 1931), the "first attack which the scientific spirit directs against the foundation of Christianity." An adaptation of a pedantic treatise by Dutch doctor Van Dale, it questions the early Christian belief that the pagan oracles were the work of demons, that certain oracles announced the advent of Christ, and that they ceased with his coming. He warns against superstition and blind acceptance of prophesy, advising, "If, along with the true certifications of our religion they [the first Christians] have left us others which may be suspect, it is for us to receive from them only that which is well-founded. . . ." *Entretiens sur la pluralité des mondes* (*Dialogues on the Plurality of the Worlds*, 1686) discusses astronomy and the concepts of Nicolaus Copernicus (1473–1543) in layman's terms, bringing an understanding of the cosmos to the people. The dialogues present, charmingly and clearly, in terms "not too dry for the people and not too light for the intellectuals" (Preface), the earth, the moon, the planets, the sun, and the stars in a series of five (and later, six) "soirs," or "evenings," in the marquise de G's garden. "Imagine a German named Copernicus," he writes in the first soir, "who makes a clean sweep of the various circles and of these solid heavens which had been imagined by antiquity. He destroys the one and shatters the others in pieces. Seized with the noble fury of the astronomer, he takes the earth and sends it far from the center of the universe where it was placed and in this center places the sun, to which this honor is more befitting." *Digression sur les anciens et les modernes* (*Digression on the Ancients and the Moderns*, 1688) sides with the moderns in their battle with the ancients and secured his election to the Academy in 1691. He served as perpetual secretary to the Academy of Science from 1699 to 1740 and captured the lives and spirit of many of his fellow academicians in the *Eulogies* (1708–1719), which includes pieces on Sébastien le Prestre de Vauban (1633–1707), Joseph Pitton de Tournefort (1656–1708), Gottfried Wilhelm Leibnitz (1646–1716), Nicolas de Malebranche (1638–1715), and others. His writing career closed in 1733 with a history of the Academy of Sciences.

In his *Caractères* (1694), Jean de la Bruyère (1645–1696) deprecated Fontenelle as an egotistical "composite of the pedantic and precious." However, his intellectual curiosity and intelligence soon took hold, revealing the first sparks of Enlightenment thought. His popularization of astronomy in *Mondes* predates the spirit of the *Encyclopédie;* his skepticism toward religion and his belief in reason became more pronounced with Voltaire* and the philosophes. His search for truth and his scientific method, seen again in Buffon* later in the century, are hallmarks of modern thinking.

For further information, see Charles B. Paul, *Science and Immortality: The Eloges of the Paris Academy of Sciences, 1699–1791* (Berkeley and Los Angeles: University of California Press, 1980).

FOUGERET DE MONBRON, LOUIS-CHARLES (1706–1760), a man of irascible temperament who spent most of his life carousing and traversing Europe, wrote two novels—*Margot la ravaudeuse* (*Margot the Mender,* 1750) and *Le Cosmopolite* (*The Cosmopolitan,* 1753)—which reflect the cynicism and libertinism of their author. The first is the story of a young prostitute who becomes a maid at the opera; the second is based on his travels.

FOURIERISME is a socialist system devised by Charles Fourier (1772–1837), which like Saint-Simonisme,* developed in France in the early nineteenth century and sought to reduce the disparity between the classes and eliminate the exploitation of the poor. Believing that the "well-being of the rich is founded on the 'poor-being' of the poor," Fourier proposed a social system in which people would be grouped into departments or "phalanges," numbering about 100 families or 1,600 persons. According to his plan, each phalange would belong to a "phalanstère," a common building or buildings, each with a plot of soil to cultivate. Though the system would be primarily agricultural, individual members could belong to the "série" or "groupe" whose occupation best suited them. Fourier did not wish to abolish private property or the privacy of family life but merely to lessen the distance between the rich and the poor, who would be living in close proximity. Each member would be guaranteed a minimum level of subsistence.

Fourier distrusted civilization and put his faith in man's passions, believing that they came from God as "guides for man and all creatures" and that they should not be repressed. His work, *Théorie des quatre mouvements* (*Theory of the Four Movements,* 1808), demonstrated that uninhibited indulgence of human passion is the only possible way to attain happiness and virtue and that misery and vice result from unnatural social constraints. He argued that this "harmony of the passions" is found in four great areas—society, animal life, organic life, and the material universe—and advocated a reorganization of society to facilitate cooperation and the harmonious evolution of human nature. Other works by Fourier include *Le Nouveau Monde industriel et sociétaire* (*The New Industrial and Corporate World,* 1820) and *Traité de l'association domestique agricole* (*Treatise on the Domestic Agricultural Association,* 1822). His principle disciple was Victor Considérant (1809–1893).

Fourier's ideas were of limited practical use. However, his trust in the power of human passion strikes a chord at the heart of romanticism.* He was admired by Zola** and socialist theoreticians Karl Marx (1818–1883) and Friedrich Engels (1820–1895). His theory of harmony influenced Hugo* and Baudelaire**; André Breton** considered him a forerunner of surrealism.**

For further information, see A. Fein, "Fourierism in Nineteenth Century America: A Social and Environmental Perspective," in Allain, Mathé, eds., *France and North America: Utopias and Utopians* (Lafayette: University of Southwestern Louisiana, 1928), 133–148; L. Goldstein, "Early Feminist Themes in French Utopian Socialism: The St.-Simonians and Fourier," *Journal of the History of Ideas* 43 (1) (January–March 1982): 91–108; M. Spencer, *Charles Fourier* (Boston: Twayne, 1981).

FRENETIQUE (frenetic) is a term coined by Charles Nodier* to describe a genre or school of writing that developed in the 1820s during the early phase of romanticism.* Frenetic writing sought to shock the reader by an excessive use of terror and violence. Its themes, handed down by the Marquis de Sade,* the "satanic" poetry of Lord Byron (1788–1824), and the French Revolution, which had left an indelible imprint of horror on the minds of the public, were bloodshed, executions, vampires, and monsters. Hugo's* *Han d'Islande* (1826), *Bug-Jargal* (1819, 1826), and *Le Dernier jour d'un condamné* (*The Last Day of a Condemned Man*, 1829); Balzac's* *Le Centenaire* (*The Centenary*, 1822); and Nodier's *Smarra* (1821) contain elements of the frenetic. By the 1830s, the frenetic had become the trademark of a new generation of young writers that included Petrus Borel* and Philothée O'Neddy.* Its influence pervaded romantic literature, from *Notre-Dame de Paris** (1831) to *Le Rouge et le noir** (1830); it greatly influenced Baudelaire,** the surrealists (see surrealism**) and endures in the modern age.

FRERON, ELIE (1719–1776), eighteenth-century journalist and critic, he championed the anti-philosophe movement in his pamphlets and journal, *L'Année littéraire* (*Literary Annual*), along with Palissot,* Pierre François Guyot, abbé Desfontaines (1685–1745), Abraham-Joseph de Chaumeix (c. 1730–1790), and Nicolas Moreau (1717–1803). A brilliant student educated by the Jesuits, at age twenty he was named to the Jesuit faculty of Louis-le-Grand, then contributed to Desfontaine's *Observations sur les ecrits moderns* (*Observations on Modern Writings*, 1735–1743). Upon Desfontaine's death in 1745, he published *Lettres sur quelques écrits de ce temps* (*Letters on Some Writings from These Times*,) until starting *L'Année littéraire* six years later. A widely read literary review appearing every ten days, the journal's collaborators included Baculard d'Arnaud,* Claude Joseph Dorat (1734–1780), and Palissot. It is best remembered as the voice of the anti-philosophes, the organ that expressed Fréron's fear of the freethinkers and his faith in the ancien régime.

Fréron's antiphilosophical attacks incurred the wrath of Voltaire,* who ridiculed him as "Frelon" ("Wasp") in his play *Le Café ou L'Ecossaise* (*The Café or the Scotswoman*, 1760) and in a notable epigram relating an imaginary incident in which Fréron is bitten by a serpent. "What do you think happened?" Voltaire wrote. "It was the serpent who died."

With Malesherbes's* support, Fréron's journal continued until 1776, when its privilege was finally revoked. Fréron died later that same year and his son, Louis Stanislas Fréron (1754–1802), continued the publication until 1790.

FROMENTIN, EUGENE (1820–1876), artist and author of *Dominique,** was born in La Rochelle and spent most of his youth in Saint-Maurice, a nearby village. There he experienced the beauty of nature and fell in love, at fourteen, with a neighbor's daughter, Jenny-Léocadie Chessy, a young Creole three years his senior. *Dominique* is based on this affair. Miss Chessy married a stockbroker in 1834 and died ten years later, inspiring the novel on which Fromentin's fame rests.

To assuage the pain of his love, Fromentin studied law and tried his hand at poetry and painting. He travelled to Algeria and the Orient, a voyage which provided the basis for his African art and two travel pieces, *Un Été dans le Sahara* (*A Summer in the Sahara*, 1857) and *Une Année dans le Sahel* (*A Year in the Sahel*, 1859). *Dominique* appeared in the *Revue des deux mondes* in 1862 and in book form a year later. In 1869, Fromentin was invited, along with his friend Théophile Gautier* and Louise Colet (1808–1876), to attend the opening of the Suez canal. *Les Maîtres d'autrefois* (*Masters from Before*, 1876), published shortly before his death, contains his thoughts on the art museums of Belgium and Holland.

For further information, see E. Mickel, *Eugène Fromentin* (Boston: Twayne, 1981).

FUSTEL DE COULANGES, NUMA-DENIS (1830–1889), along with Michelet,* is generally considered the outstanding historian of the nineteenth century and founder of historical science. He was born in Paris and educated at the Ecole Normale and Ecole d'Athènes. His life centered on the academic and the pursuit of knowledge. He taught in the lycées, then at the Faculté de Strasbourg, the Ecole Normale, where he served as director from 1880 to 1883, and at the Sorbonne. The rigors of scholarship took their toll, necessitating an early retirement from the Sorbonne. He died in Paris in 1889.

Ancient Greece provided his first topics in *Mémoire sur l'île de Chio* (*Memoir on the Island of Chios*, 1857) and *Polybe* (*Polybius*, 1858). His masterpiece, *La Cité antique* (*The Ancient City*, 1864), demonstrated the influence of religious and moral beliefs on the founding of the family, tribe, and city-state. *Histoire des institutions de l'ancienne France* (*History of the Institutions of Ancient France*, 1875–1891) considered the development of feudalism in France.

Fustel de Coulanges defined his method in *Recherches et nouvelles recherches sur quelques problèmes d'histoire* (*Research and New Research on Some History Problems*, 1885, 1891) and in *Questions historiques* (*Historical Questions*, posthumous, 1893). He brought to the study of history the rigor and objectivity of de Tocqueville.* However, under the influence of positivism,* he emphasized scientific method and the need to eliminate preconceived notions and subjective thinking. When studying the ancients, for example, the truth must come from the ancients themselves.

Today, many of Fustel de Coulanges's historical conclusions have been disproven. However, in the spirit of positivism, he inaugurated a scientific study of history that is worthy and practical.

G

GAUTIER, THEOPHILE (1811–1872), poet, novelist, journalist, art and literary critic, is best known as the founder of the "l'art pour l'art"* school of thinking, which upheld beauty as the sole aim of art. He was born in Tarbes in the Pyrennees, where his father was a civil servant. At three, his family moved to Paris, where he later attended Lycée Louis-le-Grand and the Collège Charlemagne. He studied art at the studio of Louis Rioult (1790–1855) and was torn between art and poetry. He opted for poetry and along with his schoolmate Gérard de Nerval,* engraver Celestin Nanteuil (1813–1873), and writer Petrus Borel,* formed the radical petit cénacle.* In 1829, Nerval introduced him to Hugo* and other romantics* with whom he attended the raucous premiere of *Hernani** wearing a flaming red vest and disheveled long hair.

Gautier's first works were steeped in romanticism. *Poésies* (1830) consisted of poems à la Hugo and Musset.* These were lyrical and sincere but not very original. The poem *Albertus ou L'Ame et le peché* (*Albertus or The Soul and the Sin,* 1830), a theological legend about a young painter who falls prey to a witch, captivated his fellow romantics. Its preface formulated the essential principles of art for art's sake. By 1833, he tired of the excesses of romanticism and satirized his contemporaries in the humorous stories of *Les Jeunes-France* (*The Young Romantics*).

In 1835, Gautier scandalized the Parisian literary scene with the preface to his first novel, *Mademoiselle de Maupin.* He lashed out against the hypocritical bourgeoisie, denounced the utilitarian value of art, and maintained that pure beauty is the aim of art. The novel itself reveals the pessimism and fear that he masked from his friends, a theme which he would take up again in his poem *La Comédie de la mort* (*Comedy of Death,* 1838). He formed a new cénacle at the Hôtel du Doyenné with Nerval and Borel, where eccentricity and insouciance aimed at outraging the bourgeoisie were the order of the day. In 1836, he became the art critic and later drama critic for the daily paper, *La Presse,* beginning a journalism career that would occupy most of his life. In his spare time he wrote poetry and stories, including *Fortunio* (1837), the tale of a Hindu prince in Paris, which later influenced Flaubert* and Huysmans's** *A rebours.*** In 1840, he lived in Spain for six months. *Tra los montes* (1840–1843) describes the Spain he found in the towns and countryside; the poems of *España* (1840–1845) relate the impressions and dreams that his travels inspired and transpose into words the grace and color of the monuments, sculptures, and paintings he found there. Later travels to Italy, Greece, Russia, and Turkey awakened a profound nostalgia, which he wrote about in stories and novels. *Arria Marcella* (1852) takes place in ancient Pompeii; *Le Roman de la momie* (*The Story of the Mummy,* 1858), in ancient Egypt. *Le Capitaine Fracasse* (1863) is the story of a young baron during the time of Louis XIII who out of love joins a troupe of actors; *Spirite* (1866), the most moving of the tales, is based on his love for a singer, Carlotta Grisi, and depicts the paradise genius attains when it has for wings faith and love.

His masterpiece is *Emaux et camées* (*Enamels and Cameos,* 1852), a collection of poetry to which he added throughout his life, whose perfection of form and rhythm exemplified the principles of art for art's sake. Gautier envisioned each poem as a miniature "enamel," requiring minute detail, or as a precious "cameo," which has been delicately sculpted into an object of beauty. The opening poem, "Affinités secrètes" ("Secret Affinities") expresses the harmony, beauty, and love Gautier experienced in the marble of monuments, the perfection of the pearl, the song of the ringdove, and the color of the rose. "Symphonie en blanc majeur" ("Symphony in White Major") attempts to evoke various shades of the color white and the different feelings and impressions it inspires. "L'Art" is his artistic credo, the culmination of his thoughts on the lasting value of art as opposed to the transitoriness of mankind and his civilization. "The gods themselves die," he writes, "But sovereign verses remain/ Stronger than brass."

Gautier dedicated his life and work to the principles of art for art's sake. He turned his back on the romanticism he initially admired and imitated, preferring the purity of art to sentimentality, false exoticism, and social purposes. He shut his eyes against the social and political problems of his time and refused to admit them into his work. As a painter, he saw the outside world as a source of line, shade, color, and form, which he transposed into the written word. He idealized his world in rhythm, rhyme, and sound. For Gautier, art was superior to nature. "Art is something more beautiful, more powerful than nature; nature is stupid; it is not conscious of itself . . . it needs a creative soul to endow it with animation," he wrote in "Salon de 1837," (*La Presse,* 1837). His work led the way to the poetry of Leconte de Lisle* and the Parnassians,* and his ideal of art for art's sake influenced Baudelaire,** who dedicated his *Les Fleurs du mal* ** to Gautier.

Gautier was a prolific writer who filled more than one hundred volumes with his works as a poet, novelist, storywriter, and journalist. Besides those above, worthy of mention are *Histoire du romantisme* (*History of Romanticism*, 1874), *Histoire de l'art dramatique* (*History of the Dramatic Arts*, 6 vols., 1858), numerous travel accounts, and pieces of art and literature criticism. He died in Neuilly after a long illness in 1872. His daughter, Judith Gautier (1846–1917), was also a novelist and the first woman admitted to the Goncourt Academy.

For further information, see J. Berben, "The Romantic Traveler as Questing Hero: Theophile Gautier's *Voyage en Espagne*," *Texas Studies in Literature and Language* 25 (3) (Fall 1983): 367–389; D. G. Burnett, "The Architecture of Meaning: Gautier and Romantic Architectural Visions," *French Forum* 7 (May 1982): 109–116; Burnett, "The Destruction of the Artist in Gautier's Early Poetry," *Bulletin de la Société Théophile Gautier* 3 (1981): 49–58; S. Godfrey, "Mummy Dearest: Cryptic Codes in Gautier's 'Pied de Momie,' " *Romanic Review* 75 (3) (March 1984): 302–311; R. Killick, "Gautier and the Sonnet," *Essays in French Literature* 16 (November 1979): 1–16; J. G. Lowin, "The Dream-Frame in Gautier's *Contes fantastiques*," *Nineteenth Century French Studies* 9 (Fall/Winter 1980–1981): 28–36; R. Snell, *Théophile Gautier, a Romantic Critic of the Visual Arts* (Oxford: Clarendon Press, 1982).

GENIE DU CHRISTIANISME, LE (*The Genius of Christianity*, 1802), Chateaubriand's* eloquent defense of Christianity, was published four days before the concordat between Napoleon and the pope, which reestablished Catholicism as the national religion of France. Its thesis—that "of all the religions which have ever existed, the Christian religion is the most poetic, the most humane, the most favorable to liberty, to the arts, and to letters"—reflects the rising sentiment in favor of the church, whose influence had been eroded by Voltaire* and the encyclopedists (see *L'Encyclopédie**) during the preceding century. It revealed "le génie," the essence, of Christianity and thrust Chateaubriand to the helm of a religious renaissance. He abandoned the skepticism of his preceding *Essai sur les révolutions* (*Essay on Revolutions*, 1797), which asked, "What religion will replace Christianity?" and returned to the faith prompted, as he claims in the preface to *Le Génie*, ("I cried and I believed") by the death of his mother and sister during his London exile. Whether Chateaubriand acted as crass opportunist capitalizing on public events or underwent a genuine religious conversion has been long debated. Jean-Charles Herbin points out that he was married and living with a mistress when he wrote it (*Mémoires d'Outre-Tombe de Chateaubriand* [*Memoirs from Beyond the Grave, by Chateaubriand*] (Paris: Editions Pédagogie Moderne, 1980)).

The work has been criticized as theologically weak. Part One, "Dogmes et doctrines" ("Dogmas and Doctrines"), for example, exalts the beauty, rather than the meaning, of the church's mysteries, sacraments, and scriptures. It maintains that we must not attempt to prove that Christianity "is excellent because it comes from God, but that it comes from God because he is excellent" and demonstrates God's existence in the beauty of nature. Part 2, "Poétique du Christianisme" ("Poetics of Christianity"), establishes the superiority of Christian literature—Dante's *Divine Comedy* (1307–1321), Torquato Tasso's *Jerusa-*

lem Delivered (1575), John Milton's *Paradise Lost* (1667, 1674), and Voltaire's*
Henriade—over pagan works, since the idealism of Christianity and its doctrines
lend themselves readily to art and poetry. Chateaubriand writes, "There is more
magic in one of those tears which Christianity causes a believer to shed than in all
the pleasant mistakes of mythology." Book 3 of this part includes "Vague des
passions" ("The Wave of Passions"), depicting the melancholia of souls "disgusted with the times and frightened by their religion," and introduces *René,**
which follows.

According to Albert Thibaudet (1874–1936), part 3 of *Le Génie,* "Beaux-Arts
et littérature" ("Fine Arts and Literature"), inaugurated the best part of modern
criticism. It examines the beauty of Christian art—its gothic cathedrals; philosophers such as Francis Bacon (1561–1626), Isaac Newton (1642–1727), Gottfried
Wilhelm Leibnitz (1646–1716), Nicolas de Malebranche (1638–1715), Jean de
La Bruyère (1645–1696), and Blaise Pascal (1623–1662); historians and orators,
including Jean-Baptiste Massillon (1663–1742) and Jacques Bénigne Bossuet
(1627–1704). Book 4 of this part, "Harmonies de la religion chrétienne avec les
scènes de la nature et les passions du coeur humaine" ("Harmonies between the
Christian Religion and Scenes from Nature and the Passions of the Human
Heart"), introduces the theme of *Atala,** which follows. The fourth and final part
of *Le Génie* illustrates the beauty of the church's bells, songs, prayers; its tombs
and cemeteries; its clergymen and missionaries.

Where Chateaubriand's apologia fails theologically, it succeeds esthetically,
proving the existence of God in the beauty and harmony of nature and in Christian art and ritual, and restores religion's place in the literature of the nineteenth
century.

GERMINAL (1885), by Zola.** See *Dictionary of Modern French Literature,
from Naturalism and Symbolism to Post-Modernism.*

GERMINIE LACERTEUX (1865), by Edmond and Jules de Goncourt.** See
*Dictionary of Modern French Literature, from Naturalism and Symbolism to
Post-Modernism.*

GIL BLAS DE SANTILLANE, L'HISTOIRE DE (*The Story of Gil Blas de
Santillane,* 1715–1735), the best-known work of Lesage,* was written in three
installments. The first six books appeared in 1715; the next three in 1724; the last
three in 1735. Taking its inspiration from the Spanish picaresque tradition, the
novel relates, on the one hand, the adventures and education of its central
character. On the other, it portrays and satirizes the habits and customs of
contemporary France. More than a mere adventure novel, *Gil Blas* is remembered for its realism* and satire. Gustave Lanson (1857–1934) called it the first
realist novel; Vivienne Mylne (*The Eighteenth Century Novel*), the first "roman
de moeurs" ("social novel").

The story begins with Gil Blas, a youth of seventeen, on his mule with a few ducats in his pocket, leaving his modest home in Oviedo, where his father is an equerry and his mother a chambermaid for the University of Salamanca. He is promptly intercepted by a band of "picaros," vagabonds, which he joins, setting him off on a course of adventures that continues throughout his life. He escapes and becomes a lackey, serving in turn, a canon, a doctor, several noblemen, actors, and an archbishop. He eventually becomes secretary and confidant to the duke of Lerme, the first minister. He achieves power and riches but, by selling his influence, is disgraced. He returns to Don Alphonse, a worthy nobleman, marries, and is widowed. Once again, he regains his fortune, returns to Madrid as secretary to the count of Olivarès, and finally retires to his manor, where again he marries and finishes his life in peace.

Ironically, Gil Blas never reaches the university but is educated in the living of life. He begins as an innocent fool who is duped by the first people he meets. Yet as he gradually traverses various social levels and milieux, he slowly learns through observing his surroundings that things are not always what they seem— that monks can steal; that noblemen and ministers can cheat; that justice is not always fair. He adapts, molding his character to fit the needs of the situation. He writes false letters, befriends a monkey, condemns a former protector. Unfortunately, in his course through life, Gil Blas emerges not as a leader, but as a follower; not as an actor, but as a reactor; never a hero, but a modest, humble man who recognizes, "I do not do the good that I love. And I do the bad which I hate." Eventually he does achieve a sense of right from wrong that he is able to apply.

Despite its Spanish setting, the substance of the novel is French. Noblemen, courtiers, clergymen, bourgeoisie, doctors, writers, valets, bandits, and peasants are realistically presented in costume, gest, attitude, and speech, always with the intention of satirizing. According to Jacques Vier (*Histoire de la Littérature Française,* vol. 2 (Paris: Armand Colin, 1970)), Lesage's global vision links him to Honoré d'Urfé (1567–1625), Balzac,* and Proust**; René Jasinski (*Histoire de la Littérature Française* (Paris: Nizet, 1966)) calls the novel a short version of *La Comédie humaine.**

Criticism has been levelled against the length of the book, the number of substories contained within, the weak characters who remain types rather than full-blown individuals, the dispassion of Gil Blas and others. *Gil Blas* achieves its merit essentially as a realistic social novel, representing, as Lesage states at the beginning, "life as it is."

For further information, see M. P. Laden, "Lesage's *Gil Blas:* Double Imitation, Duplicitous Writing," *Degré Second* 7 (July 1983): 1–25; V. Mylne, *The Eighteenth-Century Novel* (Cambridge: Cambridge University Press, 1981); P. Stewart, *Rereadings. Eight Early French Novels* (Birmingham, Alabama: Summa, 1984).

GLATIGNY, ALBERT (1839–1873), minor Parnassian* poet, strongly influenced by Banville* and Leconte de Lisle,* was born in Lillebonne near Le Havre, the son of a policeman. He earned his meager living variously as a travelling actor, prompter, improvisor, and vagabond. At seventeen, his love of poetry was awakened by Banville's *Odes funambulesques*. He published three volumes of poetry, *Les Vignes folles* (*The Foolish Vines*, 1857), *Les Flèches d'or* (*The Golden Arrows*, 1864), and *Gilles et Pasquins* (1871) and comedies, *Vers les saules* (*Toward the Willows*, 1870), *Le Singe* (*The Monkey*, 1872), and *L'Illustre Brizacier* (*The Illustrious Brizacier*), based on his stage life. Glatigny himself is the subject of a comedy by Mendès* (*Glatigny*, 1906).

GLOBE, LE (1824–1832), a journal founded by Paul-François Dubois (1793–1874), rallied around romanticism* in 1826 and became its principle liberal organ. Sainte-Beuve* was one of its principle collaborators, along with Stendhal* and Mérimée.* In the name of literary freedom, it opposed the tenets of the old school, the tyranny of rules and called for a "fourteenth of July in art."

GOBINEAU, JOSEPH-ARTHUR, COMTE DE (1816–1882), author and diplomat, was born in Bordeaux, served in the ministry of foreign affairs, and filled diplomatic posts in Bern, Tehran, Athens, Rio de Janeiro, and Stockholm. Travels with the emperor of Brazil took him to Sweden and Russia. He retired in Rome in 1877 and died in Turin in 1882.

He wrote poetry (*Les Adieux de don Juan—Don Juan's Good-byes*, 1844; *L'Aphroessa*, 1869), treatises on cuneiform writing and on the religions and philosophies of central Asia, histories, and travel impressions, but he is best known as the author of *Essai sur l'inégalité des races humaines* (*Essay on the Inequality of the Human Races*, 1853–1855, 3 vols.). This essay, which upheld the superiority of the Aryan race, was later used by the Germans as propaganda for their racism. Its principles are central to his later works, *L'Histoire des Perses* (*History of the Persians*, 1869), about a branch of the Aryans; *Les Pléiades* (*The Pleaides*, 1874), about a Frenchman, an Englishman, and a German who meet while on a voyage and consider themselves, as opposed to the rest of humanity, "sons of kings" and an honor to their race; and *Nouvelles asiatiques* (*Asian Stories*, 1874), a collection of stories about "what became of the first civilizers of the world, the first conquerers, the first savants, the first theologians which the world knew."

GONCOURT, EDMOND (1822–1896) AND JULES DE (1830–1870). See *Dictionary of Modern French Literature, from Naturalism and Symbolism to Post-Modernism.*

GRAFFIGNY, FRANÇOISE D'ISSEMBOURG D'HAPPENCOURT, MADAME DE (1695–1758), wrote one of the most popularly successful novels, along with Rousseau's* *La Nouvelle Héloïse,*' in the eighteenth century. Born in Nancy, the daughter of a major of the duke of Lorraine's gendarmerie and great-niece of the renowned engraver Jacques Callot (1592–1635), she married at a young age François-Hugues de Graffigny, chamberlain to the duke of

Lorraine and a brutal man who finished his days in prison. She befriended Voltaire* and Madame du Châtelet (1706–1749) and stayed at Cirey until accused of sending to friends, without authorization, a canto of Voltaire's *La Pucelle.* Without resources, she found refuge in the residence of the maréchal de Richelieu (1696–1788). Friends in high society encouraged her to write; she opened a salon. She rose to prominence with her *Lettres d'une Péruvienne* (*Letters by a Peruvian,* 1747), which recounts in letter-form the anguish and confusion of Zilia, a simple, young Peruvian girl stolen by European conquerers from her beloved country and from her fiance, Aza, on the day of their wedding. She brings to civilization the sensitivity of Samuel Richardson's (1689–1761) Pamela, the naiveté of Montesquieu's* Usbek and Rica. Though the novel is sincere and realistic in its portrayal of emotion, it lacks the philosophical importance of the *Lettres persanes* (see the Persian letters*). The ideal of love presented in the seven final letters, added in 1752, presages that of Rousseau in *La Nouvelle Héloïse* a few years later.

Madame de Graffigny detailed life at Cirey in letters she wrote during her stay there, published as *Vie privée de Voltaire et de Mme du Châtelet* (*The Private Life of Voltaire and of Madame du Châtelet,* posthumous, 1820). She wrote two plays, one successful, *Cénie* (1750), and one unsuccessful, *La fille d'Aristide* (*Aristide's Daughter,* 1757), which, along with money problems, reportedly hastened her death.

For further information, see C. Cameron, "Love: The Lightning Passion in *Les Lettres péruviennes* of Madame de Graffigny," *Encyclia* 56 (1979): 39–45.

GRESSET, JEAN-BAPTISTE-LOUIS (1709–1777), poet and dramatist, the son of a magistrate in Amiens, studied with the Jesuits and entered their order at sixteen. He taught the humanities at various Jesuit colleges until forced to resign because of his poem "Vert-Vert" and other licentious verse mocking the order. In 1735, he went to Paris, married, wrote for the theatre, and was elected to the Academy in 1748. Three years later, he returned to Amiens, where he founded a literary society and lived a life of charity and devotion. In 1759, in his *Lettre sur la comédie* (*Letter on Comedy*), he disowned his poetry and denounced the theatre, inspiring Voltaire's* *Le Pauvre Diable* (*The Poor Devil,* 1760), which mocks his religious reversion.

"Vert-Vert" relates in four cantos the adventures of a parrot named "Vert-Vert" who is raised by the "Nuns of the Visitation" in a convent in Nevers and sent to Nantes to the "Visitandines" who wished to meet him. Along the way, much to the surprise of both convents, the bird learns to swear and is quickly returned to Nevers, where he is cured of his nasty habits, spoiled once again by the sisters, and finally dies of indigestion. Other poems, "Le Carême impromptu" ("The Impromptu Lent"), "Le Lutrin vivant" ("The Living Lectern"), and "La Chartreuse" ("The Carthusian," 1735), ridicule his room at Louis-le-Grand, where he studied for the monastery.

Although he tried his hand at tragedy (*Edouard III,* 1740) and drama (*Sidney,*

1745), his comedy *Le Méchant* (*The Bad One*, 1747) is far superior and responsible for his entry into the Academy. While relating the story of Cléon, who wishes to destroy the marriage of his friend Valère, Gresset attacks the libertinage and frivolity of the age in a lively style reminiscent of Molière.

GRIMM, FREDERIC-MELCHIOR (1723–1807), German-born author and friend of J.-J. Rousseau* and Diderot,* was a critic, correspondent, and chronicler of Parisian literary and intellectual life in his *Correspondance littéraire* (*Literary Correspondence*). The son of a poor Ratisbon minister, he studied at the University of Leipzig, suffered an early failure in the theatre, and came to Paris as tutor to the sons of the count of Schomberg, a Polish envoy to France. In 1749, he befriended Rousseau, who introduced him to Diderot and other encyclopedists (see *L'Encyclopédie**). He became a reader to the young hereditary prince of Saxe-Gotha and secretary to Count Friesen Grimm, gaining entry into the height of Parisian society, where he was soon accepted for his intellect and amiability. In 1753, he wrote a witty pamphlet in favor of Italian music, *Le Petit Prophète de Boehmischbroda* (*The Little Prophet of Boehmischbroda*), and assumed responsibility for abbé Raynal's* private newsletter, *Correspondance littéraire*. For twenty years, until he passed it on to the Swiss Jacques Henri Meister (1744–1826) (who continued the publication from 1773 to 1813), he chronicled the Parisian political, social, and cultural scene for the duke of Saxe-Gotha, the empress of Russia, the queen of Sweden, the king of Poland, and other European notables. Diderot contributed a number of works otherwise unpublished during his lifetime as well as reviews of annual salons, or art exhibitions, marking the beginning of art criticism as a literary form. In 1754, Grimm attached himself to Madame d'Epinay (1726–1783), a liaison she detailed in her *Histoire de Mme de Montbrillant* (*Story of Mme de Montbrillant*), written from 1756 to 1770, which led to his subsequent rupture with Rousseau and his unfavorable portrait in Rousseau's *Confessions.** He was named a baron of the Holy Roman Empire in 1772; a series of political appointments ensued until 1790, when the heat of the French Revolution precipitated his regretful departure from France to Brussels and Saint Petersburg. Catherine the Great named him Russian minister to Saxony. Grimm died bitter and impoverished in Gotha seven years later.

Sixteen volumes of Grimm's *Correspondance littéraire*, first published in 1812–1813, survive as a valuable, just, and penetrating record of prerevolutionary France. A definitive edition, entitled *Correspondance Littéraire, philosophique et critique (1753–1800) par Grimm, Diderot, Meister, etc,* (*Literary, Philosophical and Critical Correspondence (1753–1800) by Grimm, Diderot, Meister, etc.*) was published by Maurice Tourneux (Paris: Garnier) in 1886.

For further information, see A. Amoia, "Sixteen Unpublished Letters (1767–1776) of Baron Frederic Melchior Grimm to Albrecht Ludwig, Count of Schulenburg," *Diderot Studies* 19 (1978): 15–53; L. Schwartz, "F. M. Grimm and the Eighteenth Century Debate on Women," *French Review* 59 (2) (December 1984): 236–243.

GUERIN, MAURICE DE (1810–1839), a minor romantic (see romanticism*) poet who published practically nothing during his lifetime, is remembered for his journal, letters, and two prose poems. Born to an impoverished noble family, he was raised, after the death of his mother, by his devoted and pious sister Eugénie (1805–1848), at the chateau de Cayla near Albi in the Tarn region of France. Eugénie herself was a talented writer. As a child, Guérin was given to reverie to escape the austere, mournful atmosphere of the chateau. He was destined for the clergy and studied at the seminary in Toulouse, then at Collège Stanislas in Paris, where he met the future literary critic Barbey d'Aurevilly.* He published a few articles in Catholic journals and in 1830, with Lamennais* and his associates Lacordaire* and Montalembert,* founded a liberal, Christian journal, *L'Avenir* (*The Future*). In 1832–1833, he spent nine months with Lamennais at La Chesnaie in Brittany, where his religious questionings led him to abandon Christianity and experience deeply the beauty of the countryside. He returned to Paris, supporting himself by journalism and teaching while he wrote poetry. In 1837, he married the sister of one of his pupils, achieving financial security but not happiness. He died a year later of tuberculosis at his native Cayla; he had been reconciled to his faith.

Upon his death, Guérin's sister collected his manuscripts. In 1840, George Sand* published his prose poem, *Le Centaure* (*The Centaur*), in the *Revue des deux mondes* prefaced with Guérin's biography. In 1861, his friend G. S. Trébutien (1800–1870), conservator of the library at Caen, published in two volumes *Reliquiae de Maurice de Guérin* (*Relics of Maurice de Guerin*) with a preface by Sainte-Beuve.*

Guerin's prose poems, *Le Centaure* and *La Bacchante,* were perhaps part of a larger work never completed. *Le Centaure,* written about 1835, is a pantheistic expression of man and nature. It relates the life of a centaur named Macarée, the last of its race, as he tells it to a wizard, Mélampe. He recounts the happiness and freedom of his youth spent in the splendor of nature and later his anguish over the mystery of creation. The old centaur, Chiron, teaches Macarée the difference between good and evil. Evil is the need to know all, the search for infinite knowledge; Good is submission to the gods and the acceptance of work as liberating. The poem is written in a prose that has been called sensuous, lyric, and symbolic, reflecting Guérin's own religious crisis.

Besides his prose poems, Guérin left his journal, *Le Cahier vert* (*The Green Notebook,* July 1832–October 1835) and *Méditation sur la mort de Marie* (*Meditation on the Death of Marie*). He has been called a "poet with a pagan soul" and "the Andre Chénier* of pantheism."

For further information, see M. de Vest, "A Reappraisal of Maurice de Guérin's 'Glaucus,' " *French Review* 56 (3) (February 1983): 400–410.

GUIZOT, FRANÇOIS (1787–1874), professor, statesman, and historian, was born in Nimes to a Protestant bourgeois family but moved to Geneva at an early age with his mother to escape the Revolution. His father died on the scaffold in

1794. He came to Paris to study law in 1805, supporting himself by writing for Jean-Baptiste Suard's (1733–1817) journal, *Le Publiciste,* and other periodicals. In 1812, he was named professor of modern history at the Sorbonne. Under Louis XVIII, in 1814, he became secretary general to the minister of the interior but resigned during Napoleon's Hundred Days (1815). Under the second Restoration, he served as secretary general of the ministry of justice. In 1816, he became counsellor of state, but his support of a constitutional monarchy was ill-received by the royalists, who suspended his lectures from 1822 to 1828. Under Louis-Philippe, he became minister of the interior in 1830 and minister of public education from 1832 to 1837, where he introduced important reforms. He became ambassador to London in 1840 and minister of foreign affairs from 1840 to 1848. His conservative politics contributed to the revolution of 1848, after which he retired to his estate at Val-Richer and wrote his final histories and memoirs.

Guizot ardently defended the liberal cause under the Restoration but was a staunch supporter of Louis-Philippe's monarchy. He advocated a compromise between the liberties won by the Revolution and respect for tradition. He believed in order and liberty, the limitation of royal authority, and the danger of revolutionary democracy and sought examples in history to support his doctrine. His *Essais sur l'histoire de France* (*Essays on the History of France,* 1823), which he conceived as a continuation of Mably's* *Observations sur l'histoire de France* (*Observations on the History of France,* 1765), studies French political regimes up to the tenth century and the advantages of liberal principles. *Histoire de la révolution d'Angleterre* (*History of the English Revolution,* 1826–1856) treats the origins of English constitutional monarchy. *Histoire de la civilisation en Europe* (*History of European Civilization,* 1845) and *Histoire de la civilisation en France* (*History of French Civilization,* 1845) show the formation of modern societies, their political and moral progress, and emphasize the role of the statesman. Guizot's histories, reflecting his understanding of the evolution of French society and his political beliefs, were erudite and austere.

H

HALEVY, LUDOVIC (1834–1908), librettist and comic playwright, collaborated for more than twenty years with Meilhac* on comic operas set to music by Jacques Offenbach (1819–1880), such as *La Belle Hélène* (*Beautiful Helen,* 1865) and *La Vie parisienne* (*Parisian Life,* 1867), and stage comedies, notably *Froufrou* (1869) and *La Petite Marquise* (*The Little Marquise,* 1874). A complete edition of their works numbers eight volumes. They wrote a libretto for Georges Bizet's (1838–1875) *Carmen** and Charles Lecoq's (1832–1918) *Le Petit Duc* (*The Little Duke,* 1878) and *La Petite Mademoiselle* (*The Little Miss,* 1879). Halévy also wrote volumes of short stories including *Un Scandale* (*A Scandal,* 1860), *M. et Madame Cardinal* (1873), *Les Petites Cardinal* (*The Young Cardinals,* 1880), *L'Abbé Constantin* (1882), *La Famille Cardinal* (*The Cardinal Family,* 1883), *Mon Camarade Mussard* (*My Friend Mussard,* 1886), and *La Plus Belle* (*The Most Beautiful,* 1892). He entered the Academy in 1884.

HAMILTON, ANTOINE (1645 or 1646–1720), an Englishman who was raised in France and settled there permanently in 1688, wrote in French a number of stories and a popular biographical-historical novel, the *Memoires de la vie du comte de Grammont* (*Memoirs of the Life of the Count of Grammont,* 1713). Besides the memoirs of Hamilton's brother-in-law, the count of Grammont, the novel relates the adventures and intrigues of the courts in Savoy and England and brought to the eighteenth century a measure of understanding of life during the years 1639–1669. Though the work is interesting for its style and subject matter, it lacks the scope of the *Mémoires* of Saint-Simon* and has been criticized for omitting the court of Louis XIV.

HARMONIES POETIQUES ET RELIGIEUSES (*Poetic and Religious Harmonies,* 1830), by Lamartine,* published ten years after his *Méditations poétiques,** expresses with deep-felt Christian fervor the harmonies of nature, God, and man in poems that vibrate with the harmonies of language, music, and rhythm. Max Milner, in *Le Romantisme* (Arthaud, 1973), writes that never had a French poet, including Victor Hugo,* displayed his ''rhythmic virtuosity.''

Written in Italy from 1826 to 1830, the sixty-five poems are a hymn to God and his presence in the world. Rather than a precise religious credo, the poems reveal the hope and consolation Lamartine experienced in God and nature and within his own heart. ''Hymne du matin'' (''Hymn of the Morning'') echoes the early morning song of praise raised to God by his awakening creatures. The theme of adoration continues in ''Hymne de la nuit'' (''Hymn of the Night''), ''L'Infini dans les cieux'' (''The Infinite in the Heavens''), ''Poésie ou Paysage dans le Golfe de Gênes'' (''Poetry or Landscape in the Gulf of Genoa''), and ''L'Occident'' (''The West''). ''Le Chêne'' (''The Oak Tree'') celebrates God and life as it recounts the growth of an oak tree from its humble origins into a ''superb colossus.'' ''L'Idée de Dieu'' (''The Idea of God'') reveals God as the ''unique key'' to the mystery of the world: ''Remove this idea from the earth/ And reason vanishes!'' ''Milly ou La Terre natale'' (''Milly or The Native Land'') evokes the happiness of his childhood memories of Milly and his desire to return there. On a more sombre note, ''Novissima Verba'' (''Newest Words'') explores his fleeting life and sense of impending death but finds solace in God.

HELVETIUS, CLAUDE ADRIEN (1715–1771), eighteenth-century philosophe* and bon vivant most famous for *De l'esprit* (*Concerning the Mind,* 1758), descended from a Protestant German family of physicians that had migrated to Holland seventy-five years before his birth. His grandfather introduced the drug ipecacuanha to Paris; his father was inspector-general of the military hospitals and first physician to Queen Marie Leczinska, wife of Louis XV. Young Helvétius became a tax collector at Caen, where he was also elected to the Academy. At age twenty-three, thanks to the queen, Helvétius was appointed general tax collector, a position that earned him a hundred thousand crowns a year. A generous, charming, and intelligent young man, he resigned his office twelve years later, married, and purchased the office of maître d'hotel to the queen. He divided his time between the court and his estate of Voré in Le Perche and developed an interest in literature.

Though not a contributor to the *Encyclopédie,*ics* Helvétius became linked with it and Diderot* in 1758 with the publication of *De l'esprit,* a controversial treatise believed to represent the encyclopedists' philosophy. Pushing the sensationalism of Condillac* to the extreme, Helvétius regarded man as determined and educated solely by sensory perception, since his ethics stemmed neither from God nor a traditional morality but from pure self-interest. He emphasized education as a means of achieving social harmony. The work was condemned and burned; Helvétius relinquished his position at court, issued three retractions, and travelled from 1764 to 1765 to Germany and England. His remaining years passed quietly in the country among family and friends.

Other works include "Le Bonheur" ("Happiness"), a long unfinished poem in ten cantos, and a posthumous work, *De l'homme, de ses facultés intellectuelles et de son éducation* (*Concerning Man, His Intellectual Faculties and His Education,* 1772), which further develops *De l'esprit.*

Though critics consider his works of little significance, his ideas on self-interest are precursors of Jeremy Bentham's (1748–1832) utilitarianism and aspects of Marxism.

For further information, see D. Raynor, "Hume's Critique of Helvétius' *De l'esprit,*" *Studies on Voltaire and the Eighteenth Century* 215 (1982): 223–229; G. R. Silber, "In Search of Helvétius' Early Career as a Freemason," *Eighteenth Century Studies* 15 (Summer 1982): 421–441.

HEREDIA, JOSE-MARIA DE (1842–1905), disciple of Leconte de Lisle* and often considered the most accomplished Parnassian* poet, was born in Cuba in the mountainside village of Fortuna-Cafeyere near Santiago Bay to a wealthy Spanish father, reputedly descended from a conquistador who had been a companion of Christopher Columbus. Heredia's mother was French. He came to France at eight to pursue his education at the religious College de Saint-Vincent in Senlis. He returned to Cuba from 1859 until 1861, attended the University of Havana, but went back to France to study law and take courses at the Ecole des Chartes, a well-known school for archivists. His first verses appeared in 1862 in the *Revue de Paris* and other journals, including *Le Parnasse contemporain,* and drew the attention of Gautier.* He was the devoted friend and student of Leconte de Lisle and, upon his death in 1894, assumed his leadership of the Parnassians. He entered the Academy in 1894, shortly after the publication of his volume of poetry, *Les Trophées* (*Trophies,* 1893). He was named administrator of the Arsenal* library in 1901. He died four years later in 1905.

Heredia's major claim to literary fame is the collection of 118 impeccable sonnets contained in *Les Trophées.* The sonnets deal not with the subject of love, traditionally associated with the form, but rather with visions of history and nature that Heredia wished to immortalize or celebrate. They are divided into five groups: Greece and Sicily, Rome and the Barbarians, the Middle Ages and the Renaissance, The Orient and the Tropics, Nature and Dreams. The opening poem, "L'Oubli" ("Forgetfulness"), reveals the indifference of man to "the dreams of his ancestors," which seem to be remembered only by the "sweet and maternal Earth." Included in the collection are sonnets dealing with Hercules and the centaurs, Artemis and Perseus, and a trio of sonnets about Antony and Cleopatra—"Le Cydnus," "Soir de Bataille" ("Evening of Battle"), and "Antoine et Cléopatre." "La Trebbia" and "Après Cannes" ("After Cannes") deal with Hannibal, first on the morning of the great battle against the Romans on the banks of the Trebbia River and next after inflicting the greatest defeat ever against the Romans in Cannes. "Le Vitrail" ("The Window") depicts medieval lords and ladies captured "without voices, without movement, without hearing" in a stained-glass window. "Les Conquérants" ("The Conquistadors") is a sonnet about the adventure-seekers, like his paternal ancestor, who accompanied Columbus to the New World. "Sur le 'Livre des amours' de Pierre Ronsard" ("On Pierre Ronsard's 'Book of Loves'") underscores the transitoriness of all things (even love) except poetry, which alone confers immortality. Egypt comes alive in "La Vision de Khem" ("Ham's Vision") and Japan in "Le Samouraï." "Le Récif de corail" ("The Coral Reef") evokes the beauty of underwater nature; "Soleil couchant" ("Setting Sun") relates the dreamy silence of the end of day; "La Mort de l'aigle" ("The Death of the Eagle") depicts the sudden and brief death of an eagle in flight. Ten of the sonnets express the customs, traditions, and landscape of Brittany. "Maris Stella" ("Star of the Sea") shows the anguish of Breton women "under the linen coifs, arms crossed on their breasts" kneeling before the stormy sea as they raise their plaintive hymn to "the holy star of the sea." Also contained in the collection are a romantic ballad, "Romancero," based on the Spanish El Cid, and a minor epic about the Spanish conquistador, Pizzaro, "Les Conquérants de l'or" ("The Conquistadors of Gold").

The sonnets contained in *Les Trophées* are masterpieces of precision and control that realize the union of science and poetry desired by de Lisle and the Parnassians. They bring an erudition and concern for detail to the historical moments Heredia wished to preserve, which results in perfectly wrought gems of poems whose beauty endures to this day.

For further information, see R. Berrong, "The Image of the Hero and the Functions of the Poet in Heredia's *Les Trophées*," *Nineteenth Century French Studies* 11 (3–4) (Spring–Summer 1983): 278–284; M. Tilby, "A Letter of Thanks to Heredia from Edmund Gosse [10 avril, 1894]," *Parnasse* 2 (September 1982): 4–10.

HERNANI (1830), a verse drama in five acts by Victor Hugo*, fomented a veritable "battle" between the classicists and the romantics (see romanticism*) and crowned its young author the uncontested leader of the new school. It was presented on 25 February 1830, three years after Hugo's important *Préface de Cromwell,** which had articulated the esthetics of romantic theatre. It premiered at the Comédie-Française, the bastion of classic theatre, with Théophile Gautier,* Gerard de Nerval,* and other partisans of the "Jeunes-France," stomping and cheering their approval of the play over the objections of the wigged classicists. "For our generation," Gautier wrote, "*Hernani* was what *Le Cid* had been for the contemporaries of Corneille. All which was young, valiant, amorous and poetic was inspired by it." In accordance with Hugo's precepts, the play breaks with the classic tradition of unity of place and time. The action takes place in Saragosse, Aragon, and Aix-la-Chapelle over a period of several months. Its plot has been criticized as complex, melodramatic, improbable, and historically inaccurate. However, the beauty of its verses and their lyricism is considered, along with those of *Ruy Blas,** Hugo's best.

The play takes place in Spain in 1519. Both Hernani, an outlaw, and the king, Don Carlos (the future Charles V of the Holy Roman Empire), are in love with Doña Sol, the beautiful niece of Don Ruy Gomez, who is planning to marry her.

For her part, Doña Sol loves Hernani and is willing to forego riches and respectability for a life with him. Act 1 finds her awaiting Hernani in her room when Don Carlos unexpectedly arrives. Hidden in an armoire, he overhears Doña Sol and Hernani pledge their love and plan an elopement. He confronts the two and crosses swords with Hernani. Ruy Gomez arrives and is upset at finding two men in his niece's room. Don Carlos reveals his identity, saying that the German emperor is dead and that as king of Spain he is a candidate for the throne of the Holy Roman Empire. He tells Ruy Gomez that Hernani is one of his party. In act 2, Don Carlos attempts to dissuade Doña Sol from eloping with Hernani and offers to marry her himself. Hernani appears; his men have captured the king's troops. Out of honor, Don Carlos refuses to duel with a bandit; Hernani sets him free and gives him a cloak. Doña Sol and Hernani repeat their love; he flees to the mountains. Act 3 takes place in the mountains of Aragon at Ruy Gomez's chateau, where preparations for his wedding with Doña Sol are taking place. A religious pilgrim appears at the door and asks asylum. At the sight of Doña Sol in her marriage garb he reveals himself as Hernani, the rebel leader with a price on his head. Ruy Gomez forbids his servants to turn him in, since he is a guest at his house, and hides him from Don Carlos even though he has caught him in the arms of Doña Sol. The enraged king leaves, taking Doña Sol as hostage. Hernani and Ruy Gomez make a pact: since Ruy Gomez has saved him, his life is now his. He will avenge Doña Sol's virtue and kill the king; when Ruy Gomez sounds the horn, Hernani too will die. In act 4, in Aix-La-Chapelle, Don Carlos visits the subterranean grave of Charlemagne; the sound of cannon fire announces his election to the imperial throne. He leaves the grave and has his enemies, lead by Hernani and Ruy Gomez, arrested. Hernani reveals his true identity. He is actually Jean d'Aragon, a peer of Spain. As the new emperor, Charles V, Don Carlos pardons the conspirators and permits the marriage of Hernani and Doña Sol. Their happiness is shortlived, however. In act 5, Ruy Gomez comes to make good on his pact with Hernani. Off in the distance, on their wedding night, Hernani and Doña Sol hear the sound of the horn and recall Hernani's pledge. Both young lovers poison themselves, and Ruy Gomez stabs himself over their bodies.

For further information, see K. Wren, *Hugo, Hernani and Ruy Blas* (London: Grant and Cutler, 1982).

HOLBACH, PAUL-HENRI THIRY, BARON D' (1723–1789), philosophe,* devoted friend of the *Encyclopédie,** and staunch foe of the ancien régime, was born into a wealthy German aristocratic family about which little is known. The family did bring its young son to Paris for his education. Holbach married and settled in Paris in 1749, where he maintained open house either at rue Royale Saint-Honoré or at his chateau at Grandval for freethinkers Helvétius*, d'Alembert,* Condillac,* Turgot,* Buffon,* J.-J. Rousseau,* Raynal,* Marmontel,* and lifelong friends Diderot* and Grimm.* He wrote more than 450 articles for the *Encyclopédie* on chemistry, pharmacology, physiology, and medicine but is best known for the extreme, if not particularly original, materialism and atheism of his philosophic works. *Le Christianisme dévoilé (Christianity Unveiled,* 1767), published under the pseudonym Boulanger, labelled Christianity and religion as evil, a form of bondage inflicted by a self-serving priesthood, a deterrent to progress, and unnecessary for morality. He extolled education as the sure guide to virtue and social welfare. *Le Système de la nature (The System of Nature,* 1770), his best-known work, again denies God and the immortality of the soul, presents nature as matter and motion and legitimizes happiness rather than virtue as an aim of mankind. This work shocked his contemporaries, even Voltaire,* who refuted it in the article "Dieu" ("God") in his *Dictionnaire philosophique.**

Before his death in 1789, Holbach published numerous works either anonymously or under an assumed name, including *Bon Sens, ou Idées naturelles opposées aux idées surnaturelles (Good Sense, or Natural Ideas Contrasted with Supernatural Ideas,* 1772), *Système social (Social System,* 1773), *Politique naturelle (Natural Politics,* 1773–74), and *Morale universelle (Universal Morality,* 1776). Though his works are encumbered by a heavily pedantic, largely unreadable style, they are remembered as a sincere cry against religious and political tyranny.

For further information, see T. A. Hoagwood, "Holbach and Blake's Philosophical Statement in "the Voice of the Devil," *English Language Notes* 15 (March 1978): 181–186; A. C. Kors, *D'Holbach's Coterie. An Enlightenment in Paris* (Princeton: Princeton University Press, 1976); Kors, "The Myth of the Coterie Holbachique," *French Historical Studies* 9 (Fall 1976): 573–595; H. Rayss, "The Problems of Social Dynamics in Holbach's Philosophy," *Annales Universitatis Mariae Curie-Sklodowska,* Lublin, Sectio 1. *Philosophia-sociologia* 2 (1977): 33–47.

HOUDAR DE LA MOTTE, ANTOINE (1672–1731), also known as Lamotte-Houdart, bridged the seventeenth and eighteenth centuries with his life and works. He was born the son of a hatter, studied law with the Jesuits, but found his true vocation in literature and criticism. He was received, along with his friend Fontenelle,* at the salons of the duchesse de Maine (1676–1753) and Madame de Lambert (1647–1733) and continued to write long past the onset of blindness at age thirty. Like that of Pompignan* and J.-B. Rousseau,* his poetry continued the classical tradition of the preceding century; however, his theories advanced ideals for the literature of the new age.

In 1714, he rekindled the quarrel of the ancients and the moderns with an eighteenth-century, abbreviated version of Homer's (8th century B.C.) *Iliad,* much to the ire of Madame Dacier (1647–1720), who had herself published a lengthy, cumbersome, yet more faithful translation of it fifteen years earlier. She attacked Lamotte-Houdart with a pamphlet entitled *Des Causes de la corruption du gout (Causes for the Corruption of Taste);* he countered with *Réflexions sur la critique (Reflections on Criticism,* 1715). The field divided with Madame Dacier and the ancients on one side against Lamotte-Houdart, the salons, and the Academy on the other. Fénelon,* in his *Lettre à l'Académie* (*Letter to the Academy*, 1714), defended the ancients yet avoided directly criticizing Lamotte-Houdart. In the end, the moderns prevailed and Madame Dacier and Lamotte-Houdart reconciled in 1716.

Although he wrote verse, primarily odes that moralized in the seventeenth-century tradition on vanity, enthusiasm, and human nature, his critical works denounced versification as vain, even dangerous. His *Discours sur la poésie* (*Discourse on Poetry*, 1707), *Réflexions sur la critique* (*Reflections on Criticism*, 1715), *Oeuvres de théâtre avec plusieurs discours sur la tragédie* (*Works of Theatre with Several Speeches on Tragedy*, 1730), and *Suite de réflexions sur la tragédie* (*Continuation of Reflections on Tragedy*, 1730) advocate a poetry that is clear, simple, without ornamentation, consisting of "daring ideas, truthful images, and energetic expression." He claimed that the forced rhythms and rhymes of verse restrain the spirit, distort the judgment, and mask the thought.

He criticized the drama of his day, which was suffocating under the still heavy influence of Jean Racine (1639–1699). Rejecting the unities, the simplicity of action, the preeminence of love and gallantry, and the lengthy monologues, Lamotte-Houdart called for more action. He wrote one play, *Oedipe* (*Oedipus*, 1726), in prose rather than verse, all in an effort to please, for pleasure rather than instruction, he felt, was the goal of tragedy.

Despite the boldness of his theories, in practice, Lamotte-Houdart remained firmly attached to the seventeenth century. If his poems and plays are uninspiring, even mediocre, he prepared the way, along with Fontenelle, for a literature freed from the strictures of the classics, a literature that would voice the ideals and spirit of the Age of Enlightenment.

HUGO, VICTOR-MARIE (1802–1885), universally considered the greatest French lyric poet and the foremost literary figure of nineteenth-century France, produced a torrent of works in all genres—poetry, novels, theatre—but was first and foremost a poet. Albert Thibaudet (*Histoire de la littérature française de 1789 à nos jours*, 1967) called Hugo the "greatest phenomenon of our literature," an honor that he gained by virtue of his vast imagination, command of the language, and enduring popular appeal. Before reaching age thirty, he was the acknowledged leader of the romantic (see romanticism*) movement, the voice of the ideals and aspirations of his generation. He remained a respected figure throughout his lifetime, achieving a renown equal to that of Voltaire* a century earlier.

Hugo was born in 1802, in Besançon, the third son of Joseph Hugo, a Bonapartist soldier from Lorraine, and Sophie Trébuchet of Nantes. His was a happy, but unstable childhood spent in Paris, Italy, and Spain with parents who argued and separated and inculcated him with divergent allegiances. His father rose to the rank of general in the emperor's army and became a viscount and close associate of Joseph Bonaparte, Napoleon's brother. His mother, daughter of an arms supplier, was an ardent royalist who protected, under her own Parisian roof and at great personal risk, her friend General Lahorie, an enemy of the regime. Hugo's earliest years (1802–1804) were spent in Corsica and on the island of Elba; he lived with his mother and two older brothers, Abel and Eugène, in Paris at 24 rue de Clichy from 1804 to 1807, until they joined his father in Naples. They returned to Paris in 1809 to rue des Feuillantines, where he spent happy days playing in the garden or reading the classics with Lahorie, whose arrest in 1810 swayed young Hugo to the royalist cause and fostered his compassion for the oppressed. A few days after Lahorie's arrest, Madame Hugo and her sons left for Spain, where her husband was now general and majordomo of the palace of King Joseph. There, Hugo entered the College of the Nobles for a year until returning to Paris with Eugène. Despite his short stay, Spain's language and culture indelibly impressed the young boy. The hunchbacked concierge of his Spanish school later served as a model for Quasimodo; a classmate, one of the madmen in *Cromwell*. He retained a knowledge of Spanish the rest of his life. He returned to his beloved Feuillantines in 1812, taking up Latin with M. Larivière. In 1815, at his father's insistence, he left his local school for Pension Cordier, where, with his brother, he studied science and math at Collège-le-Grand and dabbled in poetry, writing a complete opéra-comique,* two verse tragedies (*Irtamène* and *Athélie*), and a prose drama, *Inez de Castro*. "I want to be Chateaubriand* or nothing," he declared in 1816. A year later, his poem on the advantages of study was awarded honorable mention by the Academy; in 1817, he won the first prize from the Academy of Jeux Floraux in Toulouse.

By 1818, Hugo had definitively renounced science for law, which he studied half-heartedly until 1821, preferring to write odes and satires. With his brothers, he produced a literary magazine, *Le Conservateur littéraire,* from December 1819 until March 1821. His "Ode on the Death of the Duke of Berry" resulted in his first royal pension and encouraged further official poems. Hugo began writing *Han d'Island,* published in 1823; he wrote his first volume of *Odes,* published in 1822. The *Odes* were royalist and religious, written, à la Chateaubriand and Lamartine,* in the classic mold. They revealed, however, the seeds of Hugo's burgeoning imagination and inherent poetic ability. Their important preface announced the poetic and political intentions of the young poet, "The domain of poetry is limitless. . . . Poetry resides not in the form of ideas but in ideas themselves. Poetry is that which is intimate in everything." A collection of new odes (*Nouvelles odes*), written in the same vein, was published in 1824 and in 1826. The odes were joined with the lighter ballads, inspired by the medieval form. A definitive edition of the *Odes et ballades* appeared in 1828. Thanks to his royal pension, Hugo married his childhood sweetheart, Adèle Foucher (1803–1868), in 1822 over the objections of their parents. Hugo had lost his mother in 1821; on his wedding day, he lost Eugène, who went mad from jealousy. Several years of conjugal bliss followed, resulting in the birth of Hugo's four children, Léopoldine (1824), Charles (1826), François (1828), and Adèle (1830).

Besides poetry, Hugo tried his hand at the novel and the theatre, slowly evolving more liberal literary and political allegiances until by 1827, with his revolutionary *Préface de Cromwell,** he emerged as the leader of the new romantic school. In 1823, he founded another literary review, *La Muse française** (*The French Muse*), which called itself a "collection edited by the elite of the young literature," and with the help of Emile Deschamps (1791–1871) and Alexandre Guiraud (1788–1847) outlined the tenets of the new movement. Along with Vigny* and Lamartine, he frequented the salon of Charles Nodier* at the Bibliothèque de l'Arsenal,* one of the early romantic cénacles.* However, the royalism and conservativism of the odes remained, earning him the Legion of Honor, bestowed in 1825 by Charles X, and an invitation to his coronation.

His early novels, however, were written in a different vein. The first, *Bug-Jargal* (first version, 1819; second, 1826), recounts the sinister story of a slave revolt in Santo Domingo; *Han d'Islande* (1823) combines the influence of the "roman noir" (black novel) and its ghouls and vampires with the tradition of Walter Scott (1771–1832) in a lurid tale of fantasy, love, and violence set in seventeenth-century Norway. Though unimportant as literary works, they reveal, like the odes, the scope of his creative imagination and, unlike them, his fascination with the macabre, which came to fruition later in *Notre-Dame de Paris*. By 1827, however, Hugo's allegiance to romanticism was manifest. The death of his mother freed him from the clutches of her royalism; he became increasingly liberal and adopted the allegiances of his father. His first play, *Cromwell* (1827), attempted to bring his romanticism to the theatre. Though it was long (7,000 verses) and essentially unworkable, it was preceded by an important preface, which became the manifesto of the young romantics. The *Préface de Cromwell* outlined the three ages of humanity and their corresponding literatures, from ancient to modern times, and a theory of drama based on freedom from the classical unities and restraints on genre. By now, the principal proponents of the new school, Vigny, Dumas Père,* Merimée,* Balzac,* Sainte-Beuve,* Nerval,* and Gautier,* grouped themselves around Hugo, forming the second important romantic cénacle.

In poetry, his new-found love of liberty resulted in *Les Orientales** (*The Orientals,* 1829). Taking his inspiration from a Parisian sunset and backing it up with solid research, he painted the beauty, the colors, the brilliance, and the fantasy of Oriental history, landscapes, and skyscapes. He evoked feelings of heroism, enthusiasm, love, and melancholy that touched the people and rendered the sun, the moon, the brilliance of the Orient, which fascinated his fellow poets and inspired a new school of "art for art's sake" ("l'art pour l'art"*). He returned to the novel with *Le Dernier Jour d'un condamné* (*The Last Day of a Condemned Man,* 1829), another work of imagination combined with humanitarianism and psychological insight. A further dramatic attempt, *Marion Delorme* (1829), was censured by the king and unperformed until 1831. It was his *Hernani** (1830), however, when it opened at the Comédie-Française, which dealt the final blow to the classics. Despite its excesses of lyricism and fantasy, its beauty and energy met with rousing success. "Racine is buried," the young romantics cried after the performance as they danced in the lobby. Hugo, barely twenty-eight years old, had attained the pinnacle of glory.

His first important novel, *Notre-Dame de Paris** (1831), a gothic tale set in medieval Paris, introduced romanticism into the novel and capped the popularity of the historical novel in France. It remains a masterpiece of romantic literature, a monumental work combining history, architecture, fantasy, and terror around its focal point, the cathedral.

Hugo's personal happiness was short-lived, however, and followed almost immediately by betrayal. His marriage fell apart, Adèle having embarked on a questionable relationship with Hugo's former friend, Sainte-Beuve; he turned to the beautiful and well-known actress Juliette Drouet (1806–1883) and began a lifelong liaison. Hugo wrote abundantly, producing four major poetic collections and several plays. The poetry bears witness to this turning point in his life, mirroring his pain and melancholy. The first collection, *Les Feuilles d'automne** (1831), deals sensitively and intimately with domestic life, Hugo's children, his father, himself. The remaining three, *Les Chants du crépuscule** (1835), *Les Voix intérieures** (1837), *Les Rayons et les ombres** (1840), are more diverse, taking their inspiration from politics, patriotism, society, history, art, nature, and philosophy as well as Hugo's personal life. The plays, except *Ruy Blas** (1838), are unexceptional; none achieved the success of *Hernani.* A verse drama, *Le Roi s'amuse* (*The King Has Fun,* 1832), immortalized in Verdi's (1813–1901) opera *Rigoletto* (1851), recounts François I's affair with Blanche, the daughter of his court jester. Three prose dramas, *Lucrèce Borgia* (1833), *Marie Tudor* (1833), and *Angelo, tyran de Padoue* (*Angelo, Tyrant of Padua,* 1835), wallow in melodrama. His best-known dramatic work of the period is *Ruy Blas,* often considered his best play. His final attempt, *Les Burgraves* (1843), met with resounding failure and marked the close of the romantic period in the theatre and Hugo's demise as leader of the younger generation. Henceforth, the moral, bourgeois comedy of Augier* and Dumas fils would command the public's favor.

In 1841, after three unsuccessful attempts, Hugo was elected to the French Academy and surprised his audience with an acceptance speech more political than literary, recalling the grandeur of Napoleon and advocating a reconciliation with Prussia. His poems written on the return of Napoleon's ashes to Paris, *Le Retour de l'empereur* (*The Return of the Emperor,* 1840), and his travel letters from the Rhine (1842) echo these themes. Soon, however, he abandoned literature, publishing nothing for the next ten years. In 1843, the unexpected death of his daughter, Léopoldine, in a boating accident on the lower Seine at Villequier plunged Hugo into colossal despair. Like Lamartine, he put down his pen for politics.

Politically, Hugo was a chameleon, changing colors as one government succeeded another. During the Restoration, he was a legitimist, supporting the Bourbons; in 1830, with the Orleans branch of the royal family in power, he switched his allegiance to Louis-Philippe (1773–1850), who named him a peer in 1845. In 1848, while Lamartine was calling for revolution, Hugo tried to maintain the monarchy in the form of Louis-Philippe's daughter-in-law. His failure led to his republicanism and a liberal, humanitarian brand of politics. He was elected to the constituent and to the legislative assemblies, where he called for freedom of the press and elimination of capital punishment. "I am of those who think and hope that misery can be suppressed," he pronounced. Initially, he favored Louis-Napoleon, the future Emperor Napoleon III, and published a newspaper, *L'Evénement* (*The Event*), in his support; however, his dictatorial ambitions clashed with Hugo's republican and democratic ideals. By mid-1850 the rupture was definitive; in July 1851, he denounced "Little Napoleon" before the assembly. After the coup d'état of December 1851, Hugo fled to Brussels, where he re-created his version of Napoleon's maneuver in two prose pieces, *L'Histoire d'un crime* (*The Story of a Crime*, published, 1877) and *Napoléon-le-Petit* (*Little Napoleon*, 1852), and vented his anger in the early poems of *Les Châtiments*.* Most of the poems in this collection were written in Jersey, the small island whose sea and landscapes reawakened the poet in Hugo, who had been exiled there from August 1852 until 1855. In 1853, a visiting friend, Delphine de Girardin (1804–1855), introduced Hugo to table-tilting and the occult. Two-thirds of *Les Contemplations*,* Hugo's lyric masterpiece, were influenced by Hugo's new-found obsession with death and the invisible, by his belief that the dead and God himself had spoken with him. Like Chateaubriand's *Mémoires d'outre-tombe*,* these poems are, as Hugo states, the "memoirs" of his soul from the cradle to the grave, a spiritual odyssey through the "abyss" to the world beyond.

In October 1855, Hugo left Jersey for Guernsey, where continued exile and solitude intensified his metaphysical questioning. He planned an epic of cosmic proportions, beginning with a collection of poems entitled "Dieu" ("God," published posthumously, 1886), which explored the infinite and ending with "La Fin de Satan" ("The End of Satan," 1891), which dealt with the problem of evil. However, at the suggestion of editor Pierre-Jules Hetzel (1814–1886), he set aside these two hallucinatory, philosophical poems and devoted himself for the next eighteen months to the middle section of his proposed trilogy, the monumental history of humanity and Hugo's epic masterpiece, *La Légende des siècles*.* He completed the first edition of the *Légende* in May 1859 and then retired to the Isle of Serk, where he wrote his *Chansons des rues et des bois* (*Songs of the Streets and the Woods*, 1865). Their youthful, light-hearted epicureanism provided an antidote to the hallucinatory visions of "Dieu" and "La Fin de Satan." The respite was brief, however, for by the end of 1860, Hugo was fast at work on his *Les Misérables*,* a work he had contemplated for twelve years and which echoed the themes of *La Légende des siècles*. Hugo's second great novel has been hailed as a masterpiece of popular literature, an epic poem in prose about God, humanity, and Hugo.

Hugo had refused amnesty in 1859, declaring, "When liberty returns, I shall return.'' After *Les Misérables*, he filled his remaining years in voluntary exile writing an essay on *William Shakespeare* (1864) and two novels, *Les Travailleurs de la mer* (*Toilers of the Sea*, 1866) and *L'Homme qui rit* (*The Man Who Laughs*, 1869). He returned to France, 5 September 1870, two days after the collapse of the Empire; however, his joy in the defeat of Napoleon III was short-lived. The poems of *L'Année terrible* (*The Terrible Year*, 1872) recount the events of 1871: Paris overcome first by the Franco-Prussian War and next by civil war. His wife had died in 1868; his son Charles died, weakened by starvation, in 1871. Hugo was elected to the National Assembly but soon resigned and left for Brussels. In 1872, he returned to Hauteville House on Guernsey for eleven months. He returned to Paris in 1873, the year his last novel, *Quatre-vingt-treize* (*1793*), about the French Revolution, was published. He was elected to the senate in 1876; *L'Art d'être grand-père* (*The Art of Being a Grandfather*), with its light verses inspired by Hugo's grandchildren, appeared the following year, as well as the second edition of *La Légende des siècles*.

In 1878, Hugo suffered a stroke that halted his writing; he published earlier works. *Le Pape* (*The Pope*, written between 1875 and 1878, published in 1878), about an imaginary pope, illustrates his ideal of religion. *La Pitié suprême* (*Supreme Pity*, written as early as 1857, published in 1879) exhorts us to love our enemies, the cruel tyrants who most need the healing powers of our pity and understanding. *Religions et religion* (*Religions and Religion*, begun in 1870, published in 1880) condemns established religion and summarizes his own spiritual convictions. *L'Ane* (*The Ass*, 1880) is a satire against man and science. *Les Quatre Vents de l'esprit* (*The Four Winds of the Spirit*, 1881) is a repertory of satire, drama, and lyric and epic poems written throughout his life but not included in previous collections. His drama *Torquemada*, about a fanatical monk who believed in purification by fire, written in 1869, was published in 1882. The following year, the definitive edition of *La Légende des siècles* appeared. Though Hugo retired from active political life, his status with the people continued to grow. All of Paris celebrated his eightieth birthday, and when he died four years later, the nation mourned. He lay in state under the Arch of Triumph and was buried 31 May 1885 in the Panthéon.

His posthumous works include *Toute La Lyre* (*The Entire Lyre*, 1888–1893), *Les Années funestes* (*The Fatal Years*, 1898), *Dernière Gerbe* (*Last Gleanings*, 1902), *Océan* (1942), and *Tas de pierres* (*Heap of Stones*, 1942). Part of his work remains unedited.

Victor Hugo was a mountain of physical and intellectual strength. He outlived his wife, his mistress, and three of his four children. He withstood the pain of a broken childhood home, the tragedy at Villequier, personal scandal, and political exile. He rose to prominence at an early age and became the acknowledged dean of the romantic movement before age thirty, first with *Hernani* and next in the novel with *Notre-Dame de Paris*. However, in poetry, he found the genre best suited to his genius and to the philosophy that sustained him in times of solitude and deprivation.

Hugo was in tune with humanity. He loved children, he loved the people, he loved the humble, even the lowly spider and nettle because others hated them. He felt the vibrations of people's souls within his own and translated their hopes and aspirations into a heartfelt poetry of love, life, death, and glory. He had the unusual ability to expand his compassion and understanding to encompass not only his own generation, but those who preceded him and those to come. He saw in the march of the generations a vision of progress, of hope, proceeding from the darkness to the light, from the beginning of the ages to the future, from the beginning of life, to that vast emptiness that lies beyond. He had the courage to face the unknown head on and to attempt to know it, not to flee, but to conquer. His poetry gave him strength, which he shared with the weak, the humble.

He believed in himself. As a poet, Hugo believed that he was endowed with a special mission as a prophet, a magi, a priest, an interpreter for the people of God, destiny, death, and whatever lay beyond. He became the "sonorous echo," the voice of his age. His early romantic collections celebrate life and its emotions with clarity and music. *Les Châtiments* lashes out tirelessly against Napoleon III, tyranny, and injustice. In *La Légende des siècles,* Hugo transcends the sentimentalism of the romantic age to create the greatest epic poem in the French language. *Les Contemplations* and *Les Misérables* testify to his humanitarianism. The body of his work reveals his enduring belief in God, in whom, as he wrote to George Sand* in 1862, he believed in more than in himself.

His work has been variously criticized as verbose, humorless, melodramatic, obscure, and superficial. Yet it endures. *Ruy Blas* changed the direction of nineteenth-century theatre. The novels *Notre-Dame de Paris* and *Les Misérables* continue to be read and viewed as films. In prose and verse, Hugo's myths and symbols of hope, charity, and love gave spiritual and emotional strength to the people. The imagery and music of his poetry retain their magic for the modern reader and guarantee Hugo's title as a literary giant.

For further information, see E. Ahearn, "Confrontation with the City: Social Criticism, Apocalypse and the Reader's Responsibility in City Poems ɔy Blake, Hugo and Baudelaire," *University of Hartford Studies in Literature* 10 (1) (1982): 1–22; D. Aynesworth, "Anonymity, Identity and Narrative Sovereignty in *Quatre-vingt-treize*," *Kentucky Romance Quarterly* 29 (2) (1982): 201–213; N. Babuts, "Hugo's *La Fin de Satan:* The Identity Shift," *Symposium* 35 (Summer 1981): 91–101; D. M. Betz, "Victor Hugo in Support of Paul Huet: an Unpublished Letter [à L. Vitet]," *Romance Notes* 20 (Spring 1980): 322–326; J. Brody, "Let There Be Light": Intertextuality in a Poem of Hugo," *Romanic Review* 75 (2) (March 1984): 216–229; V. Brombert, "Hugo's *William Shakespeare:* The Promontory and the Infinite," *The Hudson Review* 34 (Summer 1981): 249–257; Brombert, "Hugo's Condemned Man: Laughter of Revolution," *Romanic Review* 70 (March 1979): 119–132; Brombert, "Hugo's Waterloo: the Victory of Cambronne," *Stanford French Review* (Fall 1979): 235–242; N. Brown, *Hugo and Dostoyevsky* (Ann Arbor, Mich.: Ardis, 1978); R. L. Doyle, *Victor Hugo's Drama: An Annotated Bibliography* (Westport, Ct.: Greenwood Press, 1981); M. Gatti-Taylor, "The Sacred Sower in Hugo and D'Annunzio: 'Saison des semailles' and 'I Seminatori,'" *Romance Notes* 20 (Winter 1979–1980): 190–194; P. Gassier, "Goya and the Hugo

Family in Madrid,'' *Apollo* 114 (October 1981): 248–251; W. Greenberg, ''Extended Metaphor in 'On loge à la nuit,' '' *Romanic Review* 74 (4) (November 1983): 441–454; Greenberg, ''Symbolism and Metonymic Chains in Hugo,'' *Nineteenth Century French Studies* 13 (4) (Summer 1985): 224–237; G. Greenhill, ''The Jersey Years: Photography in the Circle of Victor Hugo,'' *History of Photography* (April 1980): 113–120; S. Guerlac, ''Exorbitant Geometry in Hugo's *Quatre-vingt-treize,*'' *Modern Language Notes* 96 (May 1981): 856–876; P. Horn, ''Victor Hugo's Theatrical Royalties during His Exile Years,'' *Theatre Research International* 7 (Spring 1982): 132–137; J. Janc, ed., *Les Deux Trouvailles de Gallus* (Lanham, Md.: University Press of America, 1983); E. Kaplan, ''Victor Hugo and the Poetics of Doubt: The Transition of 1835–1837,'' *French Forum* 6 (May 1981): 140–153; J. Kessler, ''Art, Criminality and the 'Avorton': The Sinister Vision of Hugo's *L'Homme qui rit,*'' *Romanic Review* 75 (3) (May 1984): 312–334; Kessler, ''Babelic Ruin, Babelic 'Ebauche': An Introduction to a Hugolian Problematic,'' *Stanford French Review* 7 (3) (Winter 1983): 285–299; J. Mehlman, *Revolution and Repetition. Marx/ Hugo/ Balzac* (Berkeley: University of California Press, 1977); R. Mitchell, ''Poetry of Religion to Religion of Poetry: Hugo, Mallarmé and the Problematics of 'Preservation,' '' *French Review* 55 (March 1982): 478–488; S. Nash, ''Transfiguring Disfiguration in *L'Homme qui rit:* a Study of Hugo's Use of the Grotesque,'' in *Pre-Text. Text. Context. Essays on Eighteenth-Century French Literature,* R. L. Mitchell, ed. (Columbus: Ohio State University Press, 1980); S. Petrey, *History in the Text, 'Quatrevingt-treize'' and the French Revolution,* Purdue University Monographs in Romance Languages, vol. 3 (Amsterdam: John Benjamins, 1980); M. C. Rifelj, ''Diction and Figure in Hugo's *Réponse à un acte d'accusation,*'' *Romanic Review* 70 (November 1979): 346–356.

HUYSMANS, JORIS-KARL (1848–1907). See *Dictionary of Modern French Literature, from Naturalism and Symbolism to Post-Modernism.*

IDEOLOGUES, a group of intellectuals that gathered in Paris at the end of the eighteenth century and included Condorcet,* Destutt de Tracy,* Cabanis,* Volney,* and others who followed the thinking of Condillac* and dedicated themselves to formulating a science of ideas and psychology. They met at the home of Madame Helvétius (see Claude Andre Helvétius*) in Auteuil and later at the home of Madame Condorcet and the Institute of France, founded in 1794 by the National Convention. Like the philosophes* before them, they believed in reason and progress and the perfectibility of the human race. They supported the Revolution, opposed despotism of any sort, disagreed with the Concordat of 1801, which reestablished Catholicism as the church of France, and expressed their views in *La Décade philosophique, litteraire et politique* (*The Philosophical, Literary and Political Decade*), a review founded by Pierre-Louis Ginguené (1748–1816) in 1794, which merged with *Le Mercure* in 1807. They sought to understand the operations of the human spirit, to give a physical foundation to psychology. Their work influenced Stendhal,* then was overshadowed by romanticism,* but was rediscovered by the positivists (see positivism*), notably Taine.*

For further information, see C. Welch, *Liberty and Utility. The French Ideologues and the Transformation of Liberalism* (New York: Columbia University Press, 1984).

J

JACQUES LE FATALISTE ET SON MAITRE (*Jacques the Fatalist and His Master,* 1773–1774), by Diderot,* combines fiction, philosophy, and satire in what has been alternately hailed as the first modern novel or decried as a fictional failure. Jacques, who believes in Fate, is travelling with his master on horseback to an unknown destination. ("Do you ever know where you are going?" Diderot asks his reader.) Along the way he relates his life and loves but is constantly interrupted either by his master, a fictional narrator, or by one of many intervening incidents or adventures. Two captains who are mortal enemies as well as inseparable friends, the immoral abbé Hudson and the chevalier de Guerchy, provide a few of the diversions, while in the long episode detailing Madame de la Pommeraye's revenge against her unfaithful lover, even the interruptions are interrupted.

Besides the dialogue between valet and master, Diderot the master conversationalist initiates an on-going dialogue with the reader concerning the novel itself, its form, and intentions, while Diderot the philosopher questions man's freedom and morality in a universe determined by the laws of nature.

"All the good and bad which happens to us here is written above," is Jacques's response to events on his trip through life. A counterpoint to Voltaire's* optimistic *Candide,*' Jacques's fatalism depicts him and his fellow travelers as caught in the machinery of the universe. Though Diderot himself believed in scientific determinism, the question of whether Jacques's philosophy mirrors his beliefs or satirizes them is still open to debate. What is certain is that the story of Jacques's life and loves is but a pretext for a philosophical quest for truth and freedom in life and in literature.

For further information, see C. V. McDonald, "Fractured Readers," *Modern Language Notes* 97 (May 1982): 840–848; M. O'Dea, "Freedom, Illusion, and Fate in Diderot's *Jacques le fataliste,*" *Symposium* 39 (1) (Spring 1985): 38–48; D. O'Gorman, "Hypotheses for a New Reading of *Jacques le fataliste,*" *Diderot Studies* 19 (1978): 129–143.

JANIN, JULES (1804–1874), journalist and literary critic who was generally favorable toward romanticism,* was known as the "prince of the critics." He was born in Saint-Etienne, the son of a lawyer, and studied humanities at Lyon and Paris, where he gave up law for literature. He wrote for a number of newspapers, *Le Figaro, La Quotidienne* (*The Daily*), and *Le Messager* (*The Messenger*). After gaining public attention with his shockingly erotic novel, *L'Ane mort et la femme guillotinée* (*The Dead Ass and the Guillotined Woman,* 1829), a parody of the frenetic (see frénétique*) novel, he joined the *Journal des débats* (*Debate Journal*), a respected daily newspaper staffed by leading historians and critics reporting on discussions at the national assembly, literature, drama, and the stock exchange. Janin contributed literary feuilletons and dramatic criticism that have been collected and published as *Histoire de la littérature dramatique* (*History of Dramatic Literature,* 6 vols., 1851–1855) and *Variétés littéraires, portraits contemporains* (*Literary Varieties, Contemporary Portraits,* 2 vols, 1859). He also wrote stories, including *Contes fantastiques* (*Fantastic Stories,* 1832) and *Contes nouveaux* (*New Stories,* 1833).

For further information, see G. Williams, "Pushkin and Jules Janin: A Contribution to the Literary Background of the Queen of Spades," *Quinquerème* (July 1981): 206–224.

JAUCOURT, LOUIS, CHEVALIER DE (1704–1780), who belonged to one of the oldest families of France, dedicated his life and personal fortune to the cause of the *Encyclopédie.** A Protestant like Grimm* and well educated, he possessed an encyclopedic mind and studied theology as a youth in Geneva, mathematics at Cambridge, and medicine at Leyden, where he became a medical doctor. He wrote *Histoire de la vie et des oeuvres de Leibnitz* (*History of the Life and Works of Leibnitz,* 1734) and a six-volume universal dictionary of medicine that was lost at sea. He is best known as the unselfish supporter and most ardent collaborator of the *Encyclopédie,* for which he penned countless articles on politics, history, medicine, literature, law, and the physical and natural sciences. Diderot* claimed in a letter to Sophie Volland (1725–1784), that de Jaucourt spent "six or seven years surrounded by six or seven secretaries, reading, dictating, working thirteen to fourteen hours a day and this position had not yet tired him." De Jaucourt became a fellow of the Royal Society in London in 1756 and was highly respected throughout his life for his intelligence and integrity.

For further information, see J. Lough, *The "Encyclopédie" in Eighteenth Century England and Other Studies* (Newcastle: Oriel Press, 1970); R. A. Nablow, "Jaucourt's indebtedness to Addison in the *Encyclopédie*," *Romance Notes* 21 (Winter 1980): 211–214; George Perla, "The Unsigned Articles and Jaucourt's Biographical Sketches in the *Encyclopedia*," *Studies on Voltaire and the Eighteenth Century* 171 (1977): 189–195.

JEANNE D'ARC (*Joan of Arc,* 1841), by Michelet,* is the work with which he is most frequently associated. It originally appeared in volume five of his seventeen-volume *Histoire de France* (*History of France,* 1833–1867) and was published separately in 1853 with an introduction and six parts. Michelet found in

Saint Joan's (1411–1431) piety and heroism the purest representation of the French soul. "In her appeared at the same time the Virgin . . . and already the nation," Michelet wrote. She became his symbol for the emerging France. He recounts her childhood from the age of twelve in the village of Domrémy in the Vosges, her historic meeting with Charles VII at Chinon, her liberation of Orleans, the coronation of Charles VII at Reims, her betrayal by the duke of Burgundy, her trial and death at the hands of the English in Rouen in 1431. It was a story, Michelet said, that would make a grown man cry. It is an example of romantic history at its finest. Her story is also the basis of Voltaire's* *La Pucelle* (*The Maiden,* 1755), Péguy's** *Le Mystère de la charité de Jeanne d'Arc* (*The Mystery of the Charity of Joan of Arc,* 1909), Claudel's** *Jeanne au bûcher* (*Joan at the Stake,* 1935), Anouilh's** *L'Alouette* (*The Lark,* 1953), and a biography (1908) by Anatole France.**

JEU DE L'AMOUR ET DU HASARD, LE (*The Game of Love and Chance*), first performed at the Théâtre Italien* in 1730, is considered by many to be Marivaux's* masterpiece. Gautier,* in his *Histoire de l'art dramatique* (*History of the Dramatic Arts,* 1858), compared the charm of the play to the "fresh air" of William Shakespeare's (1564–1616) *As You Like It.* Jacqueline Casalies, in her preface to the Nouveaux Classiques Larousse edition (1966) of the play finds that it progresses with the well-orchestrated symmetry of a ballet. Yet the play's careful examination of the "surprise" of love in the hearts of its young characters is balanced by its plot of double disguise and its social implications. Paul Gazane, in *Marivaux par lui-même* (*Marivaux by Himself,* 1954), considers Marivaux a psychologist, philosopher, sociologist, and revolutionary.

The play relates the story of Silvia and Dorante, who have been promised to each other by their fathers and who both wish to study one another before finalizing marriage plans. Unknowingly, each trades places with a servant to freely observe the other. However, when Dorante's valet, Arlequin, arrives on the scene as Dorante, the trouble begins.

Silvia, disguised as her servant Lisette, believing Arlequin to be her intended, finds him despicable and prefers, much to her horror, his servant Bourgignon. Bourgignon, who in reality is Dorante, is in turn so attracted to the servant girl (Silvia in disguise), that he ignores the girl he believes to be his future wife. The real servants, disguised as masters, also fall in love with one another. Dorante, by the second act, is beside himself with passion and reveals his true identity. Silvia withholds hers until he declares his love for her servant-girl disguise, risking the rage of his father, his inheritance, and society's disapproval. When at last he does, Silvia, victorious, reveals her identity and all ends well.

This play, like many others of Marivaux, is first and foremost a comedy of love, tracing each minute step from love's first awakening to its final declaration. Bourgignon, ever a gentleman, is honest, sincere, and suffering in his love for a girl beneath his station. Silvia, armed with her intelligence and pride, combats her feelings and becomes one of the most complex, rich, and delicate characters to be portrayed on stage.

Underlying the love theme is the theme of social rank and status. The love between Arlequin and Lisette parodies that of their superiors, who remain educated, sensitive, and refined, despite their disguise. The boundaries of rank are fixed and not crossed, with the marriages of servants and masters, but not to each other.

Le Jeu de l'amour et du hasard remains a masterpiece enjoyed today for its complexity, relevance, and gaiety. In 1920, reviewer Antoine (his review is now part of the dossier on Marivaux in the Arsenal* library) wrote that no other comedy of the eighteenth century is so modern.

For further information, see R. Halsband, "The First English Version of Marivaux's *Le Jeu de l'amour et du hasard," Modern Philology* 79 (1) (August 1981): 16–23; G. Rodmell, *Marivaux: Le Jeu de l'amour et du hasard and Les Fausses confidences* (London: Grant and Cutler, 1982).

JOCELYN (1836), a narrative poem in more than 10,000 lines by Lamartine,* was originally conceived as an "episode" of his enormous epic poem on the destiny of man. According to Lamartine, the idea for the epic came to him like a thunderbolt in January 1821; he refined the plan over time to encompass the various stages, or "épisodes," of mankind's journey to God. Besides *Jocelyn,* Lamartine completed *La Chute d'un ange* (*The Fall of an Angel,* 1838), the first episode of the epic. However, tracing the lives that the fallen angel is forced to live, from the time of the flood through judgment day, proved too overwhelming and time-consuming for the politically active and socially committed poet. "Every poet, every age, may perhaps write but a page," he wrote in the preface to *Jocelyn,* bequeathing posterity with his burden.

Taking his inspiration for *Jocelyn* from his childhood priest and teacher, abbé Dumont, and adding his own memories of youth and love, Lamartine weaves a narrative in nine "époques" around Jocelyn, a country curate, and his sacrifice of love and happiness for God. The prologue sets the scene: The poet, who has come to visit his friend Jocelyn, learns that the old man has died and is to be buried the next day. The curate's journal, found in the attic, is the basis for the story. In 1786, as a young man of sixteen, Jocelyn defers his happiness to that of his sister, offering her his meager inheritance to increase her dowry and assure her marriage. He enters the seminary. When the seminary is threatened at the outbreak of the Terror, he flees to an Alpine cave, Grotto of the Eagles, where two refugees cross his path. The eldest, wounded by pursuers, soon dies, leaving his young son, Laurence, in Jocelyn's care. They soon develop a fondness for each other and a love for God and the nature in which they live. One day Laurence is injured in a fall and while convalescing, Jocelyn discovers that she is really a girl. They continue their idyllic existence as brother and sister until the height of the Terror (Lamartine mistakenly gives the year as 1795; Robespierre* actually fell from power a year earlier), when the bishop of Grenoble, imprisoned and condemned to death, sends for Jocelyn and ordains him so that he can hear his confession and give him the last sacraments. Despite his protestations, he submits, is ordained, hears and absolves the bishop's confession, and accompanies him to the scaffold. Her hopes of marriage dashed, a horrified Laurence flees the grotto. Jocelyn, alone, tries to make sense of his sacrifice. He spends two years in a house of retreat, then is nominated curate of the village of Valneige. His mother's death sends him home to pay his respects and relive memories of his youth. Afterwards, he accompanies his sister to Paris, where the spirit and vitality of the city excites and terrifies him. He attends a mass and to his surprise sees Laurence collecting the offering; he learns that she has become a dishonorable woman. Hurt and offended, he watches her hotel, confirms his suspicions, and retreats to his mountain hamlet, where he resumes with renewed dedication his life of humility, work, and prayer. One winter's night, he is called to give absolution to a young, beautiful, dying woman—Laurence, repentant and obsessed with visiting the Grotto of the Eagles and Jocelyn. She dies; Jocelyn buries her in a scene reminiscent of Chateaubriand's* Atala.* The epilogue relates the sad end of the tale. Jocelyn, caring for the sick, himself becomes infected, dies, and is buried by the villagers near his beloved Laurence.

Though it was hailed as a resounding success upon publication, especially for a work in verse, by and large, *Jocelyn* is a poem of little interest for the modern reader. The story is long, unrealistic, full of historical error, and dependent on coincidence. Its melodic evocation of nature and exaltation of love in the fourth epoque and its praise of God in the eighth echo the romanticism* of Lamartine's previous works, *Méditations poetiques et religieuses** and *Harmonies poetiques et religieuses**; the ninth, touting the value of labor and the social rewards of a return to the soil, reveals his evolving political and social beliefs. Its personalism, lyricism, idealism, and spiritualism are pure Lamartine.

JULIE OU LA NOUVELLE HELOISE (*Julie or the New Heloise*, 1761). See *La Nouvelle Héloïse*.

L

LABICHE, EUGENE (1815–1888), popular author of more than 160 farcical comedies including *Le Voyage de M. Perrichon* (*Mr. Perrichon's Voyage*, 1860), was born in Paris, studied law, and began his literary career in 1834 by contributing to journals such as *L'Essor* (*Flight*), *Chérubin*, and *La Revue du théâtre* (*The Theatre Review*). His first play, *La Cuvette d'eau* (*The Wash-Basin*, 1837), has been lost. After *L'Avocat Loubet* (*Loubet the Advocate*, 1838), he tried his hand at a novel but quickly returned to the stage. His first major work appeared in 1848, *Un Jeune Homme pressé* (*A Hurried Young Man*). Highlighting his repertory are *Un Chapeau de paille d'Italie* (*A Straw Hat from Italy*, 1851), *Le Misanthrope et l'Auvergnat* (*The Misanthrope and the Man from Auvergne*, 1852), *La Poudre aux yeux* (*Powder in the Eyes*, 1861), *La Cagnotte* (*The Hypocrite*, 1864), *Chemins de fer* (*Trains*, 1867), and *Le Plus Heureux des trois* (*The Happiest of the Three*, 1870). He entered the Academy in 1880.

Labiche is a direct descendant of vaudeville in the manner of Scribe* and is considered the most important comic author of the nineteenth century. His comedies, light-hearted and gay, amuse with plays on words, comic asides, surprise endings, misunderstandings, and occasional social satire. His characters move puppetlike, their dialogue spontaneous and swift, through situations and adventures seemingly too ridiculous to be real but that derive their humor from a germ of truth. They represent all walks of life: the bourgeoisie, nobility, servants, soldiers, and industrialists and treat social themes, marriage, adultery, and money. They shed light on the Paris of the July monarchy and Second Empire but are remembered mostly for their genuine humor and comic style.

For further information, see L. Pronko, *Eugène Labiche and Georges Feydeau* (London: Macmillan, 1982).

LA CHAUSSEE, PIERRE-CLAUDE NIVELLE DE (1692–1754), eighteenth-century poet, playwright, and socialite, is remembered principally as the originator of the *comédie larmoyante** or tearful comedy in verse aimed at social and moral edification. He was born in Paris to a wealthy family, met Voltaire,* frequented the salons and libertine societies, and generally led a dissipated life. He lost his fortune in the ruin that followed the financial reforms of John Law (1671–1729), yet maintained a social and literary prominence.

He began his literary career by jumping into the quarrel between the ancients and the moderns on the side of the ancients with his anonymous *"Lettre de la marquise de L___ sur les fables nouvelles"* (*Letter by the Marquise de L___ on the New Fables*, 1719) attacking the doctrines and fables of Houdar de La Motte.* *Epitre à Clio* (*Epistle to Clio*, 1731) defends the poetry of the ancients and attacks once again La Motte's antipoeticism. Early in 1730 he composed parades* for his society friends before finding his true vocation in the theatre. He wrote more than twenty plays, including twelve for the Comédie-Française, two for private theatres, and two for the Théâtre Italien.* Though he tried his hand at tragedy (*Maximien*, 1738), he found success on stage with the hardly laughable comédies larmoyantes, which pierced the spectator directly in the heart by portraying virtuous ladies in distress. His moralizing in the tradition of Destouches* secured his election to the Academy in 1736.

Except for Piron* and Collé,* who sarcastically labelled him "le Reverend Père La Chaussée" (The Reverend Father Chaussée), the public was touched and flocked to his plays. Chief among the comédies larmoyantes are *La Fausse Antipathie* (*False Aversion*, 1733); *Le Préjugé à la mode* (*Fashionable Prejudice*, 1735); *L'Ecole des amis* (*School for Friends*, 1737); *Mélanide* (1741), his masterpiece; *L'École des mères* (*School for Mothers*, 1744); *La Gouvernante* (*The Governess*, 1747); and *Paméla*, an adaptation of Samuel Richardson's (1689–1761) novel (1743). Though melodramatic and emotional, poorly versified, and irrelevant today, La Chaussée's comédies larmoyantes capitalized on the rising tide of sensitivity during the early to mid-eighteenth century and prepared the way for the drama of Sedaine* and Diderot.*

LACLOS, PIERRE CHODERLOS DE (1741–1803), artilleryman, military officer, and fortifications strategist, wrote one major work—*Les Liaisons dangeureuses* (*Dangerous Liaisons*, 1782)—which fulfilled his wish to write an extraordinary piece that would "echo on earth after he had left it." Born into a newly ennobled family of aristocrats, Laclos entered the artillery rather than a more prestigious branch of the military, where he had an undistinguished career in provincial outposts—La Rochelle, Toul, Strasbourg, Grenoble, Besancon, Valence, Rochefort, and the islands of Aix and Ré—never surpassing the rank of captain until he was made a general in 1799 by Napoleon. He wrote poetry, generally considered mediocre, and adapted Madame Riccoboni's* novel *Ernestine* into a comic opera (see opéra comique*) (1777), which was a dismal failure. Beginning in 1783 and continuing over the next ten years, he outlined his thoughts on women in an essay written but never submitted for a competition offered by the Academy of Chalons-sur-Marne on "What would be the best means to improve the education of women?" He portrayed woman as denaturalized and imprisoned by a male-dominated society; to survive and manipulate man, she developed the art of coquetry, a talent Laclos fully explores in *Les Liaisons*. In `1786, he married Marie-Souland Duperré, the mother of his two-year-old son and, unlike Valmont of his novel, was a devoted husband and father. He compromised his military career with "Sur l'eloge de Vauban," ("On the Praise of Vauban"), written for the Paris Academy in 1786, which dared attack the theories of the great seventeenth-century fortifications specialist. He was censured and relegated to the minor leagues of the military. He spent much time in Paris and allied himself with the revolutionary sympathizer, the duke of Orleans (1747–1793), serving as his secretary and accountant. In 1790, he joined the Jacobins and edited their publication, *Journal des amis de la constitution* (*Journal of the Friends of the Constitution*), and wrote a number of political articles defending the duke and the Jacobins. Both were arrested by Robespierre* in 1793; the duke was beheaded and Laclos incarcerated in various prisons until 1794. Released, he was named general-secretary of mortgages in Paris, associated with the Bonapartists, was named brigadier general by the emperor, and was sent to Italy. He died in Naples, old and tired by a lackluster military career, with one novel to his credit. That novel assured his place in the history of French and European literature.

Though frustrated and bored in his military career, Laclos orchestrated on paper the most imaginative and intelligent battle between the sexes waged in the eighteenth century. Written to dispel the boredom of securing fortifications on the islands of Aix and Ré, *Les Liaisons dangereuses* is a novel of intrigue, power, and seduction, whose meaning has beguiled the likes of Sade,* Stendhal,* Baudelaire,** Proust,** Giraudoux,** and Malraux.** It remains timely and relevant in its analysis of the human mind, its ambition, vanity, and capacity for evil.

It is the most technically accomplished of the bevy of letter novels written in the late eighteenth century. The 175 letters reveal intimate thoughts, actions, and aspirations, each with a tone unique to its writer and a different point of view. They follow the carefully planned and executed conquest of two ladies, young Cécile de Volanges and the married and devout Présidente de Tourvel, by the Marquise de Merteuil and her co-conspirator, the vicomte de Valmont. Cécile has just left a convent school and is promised in marriage to the Comte de Gercourt. Merteuil, jealous of Gercourt for leaving her, launches a scheme to have Cécile unfaithful to him before their marriage, convincing Valmont, another former lover, to assist her. Valmont is unprincipled; he seduces Cécile while still trying to win over the Présidente; he succeeds in that as well. A ruined Cécile retires to a convent; the Présidente dies of shame. Valmont is killed in a duel, and Merteuil, disfigured by smallpox and penniless, flees.

Though his motives remain suspect, Laclos insisted on the moral "usefulness" and "truth" of his book. The novel coldly lays bare the corruption of idle aristocracy in the wake of the Revolution; it details stage by stage the humiliating game of the libertine and his prey.

For further information, see J. Birkett, "*Dangerous Liaisons*: Literary and Political Form in Choderlos de Laclos," *Literature and History* 8 (1) (Spring 1982): 82–94; J.

Bloch, "Laclos and Women's Education," *French Studies* 38 (2) (April 1984): 144–158; S. Diaconoff, *Eros and Power in the Liaisons Dangereuses* (Geneva and Paris: Droz, 1977); S. Dunn, "Education and Seduction in *Les Liaisons dangereuses*," *Symposium* 34 (Summer 1980): 127–137; Dunn, "Valmont, Actor and Spectator," *French Review* 56 (1) (October 1984): 41–47; J. E. Flower, "Mask and Morality: Laclos' Theatrical Novel *Les Liaisons dangereuses*," *Quinquerème* (July 1980): 183–192; R. Frautschi, "Addenda to a Recent Bibliography on Laclos," *Romance Notes* 25 (2) (Winter 1984): 153–159; L. R. Free, ed., *Critical Approaches to Les Liaisons Dangereuses* (Madrid: Studia Humanitatis, 1978); M. Gutwirth, "Laclos and 'Le sexe': the Rack of Ambivalence," *Studies on Voltaire and the Eighteenth Century* 189 (1980): 247–296; S. Jones, "Literary and Philosophical Elements in *Les Liaisons dangereuses:* The Case of Merteuil," *French Studies* 38 (2) (April 1984): 159–169; F. Meltzer, "Laclos' Purloined Letters," *Critical Inquiry* 8 (3) (Spring 1982): 515–529; C. V. Michael, *Choderlos de Laclos. The Man, His Works, His Critics. An Annotated Bibliography* (New York, London: Garland Publishing, 1982); N. K. Miller, *The Heroine's Text* (New York: Columbia University Press, 1980); R. Nelson, "I, Eye and Aye: Points of View in Pascal and Laclos," *French Forum* 7 (2) (May 1982): 101–108; R. C. Rosbottom, *Choderlos de Laclos* (Boston: Twayne, 1978); R. Roussel, *The Conversation of the Sexes. Seduction and Equality in Selected Seventeenth and Eighteenth Century Texts* (Oxford: Oxford University Press, 1985); Roussel, "The Project of Seduction and the Equality of the Sexes in *Les Liaisons dangereuses*," *Modern Language Notes* 96 (May 1981): 725–745; P. Stewart, *Rereadings. Eight Early French Novels* (Birmingham, Ala.: Summa, 1984).

LACORDAIRE, JEAN-BAPTISTE-HENRI (1802–1861), a lawyer who entered the priesthood in 1827, became, for a while at least, an advocate of social Catholicism along with Lamennais* and Montalembert.* He was the principle collaborator on Lammenais's journal, *L'Avenir* (*The Future*), and worked for the establishment of his socialist ideals. He broke with Lamennais after his condemnation by Rome and moderated his liberal convictions. In 1840, he entered the order of the Dominicans, or "preaching brothers," which he worked to reestablish in France. He preached at Notre-Dame and in the provinces at Toulouse, Lyon, Grenoble, and Nancy. In 1848, he was elected deputy from Bouches-du-Rhône. He entered the Academy in 1860. He spent his final years directing the collège de Sorèze in the Tarn region of France, where he wrote *Lettres à un jeune homme sur la vie chrétienne* (*Letters to a Young Man on the Christian Life*, 1857) and *Vie de sainte Marie-Madeleine* (*The Life of Saint Mary-Madeleine*, 1860).

LAFORGUE, JULES (1860–1887). See *Dictionary of Modern French Literature, from Naturalism and Symbolism to Post-Modernism.*

LA HARPE, JEAN-FRANÇOIS DE (1739–1803), minor playwright, critic, and eighteenth-century man of letters, is perhaps best known for *Lycée*, his course in literature offered at rue Saint-Honoré from 1786 until 1798. A Swiss of humble origin, he attended the Collège de Harcourt and wrote a mediocre collection of *Héroïdes* (1759); however, it was his tragedy *Warwick* (1763) that opened the salons and gained him the support of Voltaire.* Three failures, *Timoléon* (1764), *Pharamond* (1765), and *Gustave Wasa* (1766), followed. He turned to drama with *Mélanie, ou La Religieuse* (*Melanie, or The Nun,* 1770), a criticism of the church, which consequently never was performed but which secured his election to the Academy. From 1770 to 1778, he was critic for the *Mercure,* where he perpetrated his classical ideals, politics, and philosophy. His analyses of works by Pierre Corneille (1606–1684), Jean Baptiste Racine (1639–1699), Molière (1622–1673), and Voltaire remain relevant. He published *Eloges de Fénelon* (*Praises of Fenelon,* 1771), *Eloges de Racine* (*Praises of Racine,* 1772), and *Eloges de Catinal* (*Praises of Catinal,* 1775), and abridged Prévost's* *Voyages* (1780). He wrote poetry, including a six strophe "Le Triomphe de la religion ou Le Roi martyr" ("The Triumph of Religion or the Martyr King"), published posthumously in 1814. Originally a supporter of the Revolution, La Harpe was imprisoned in 1794; he converted to Catholicism and the monarchy. The publication of his sixteen-volume *Lycée ou Cours de littérature* (*Lycée or Literature Course,* 1799–1805), offered from 1786 to 1798 at the Lycée on rue de Valois, and his literary correspondence with the grand duke of Russia occupied his final years.

LAMARTINE, ALPHONSE DE (1790–1869), early romantic (see romanticism*) poet and politician whose poems, by his own admission, were incidental to his political career. A fervent democrat and eloquent leader, he assisted the revolution of 1848, became minister of foreign affairs and head of the provisional French government. Poetry, for him, was as natural and necessary as prayer. He died, however, forgotten, his political power displaced by Napoleon III (1808–1873). It is his poetry—*Les Méditations poétiques,** *Les Harmonies poétiques et religieuses,** and *Jocelyn**—for which he is remembered.

He was born in Mâcon, the son of the chevalier de Lamartine, a lesser aristocrat imprisoned during the Revolution and who instilled in him the traditional values of the ancien régime. His mother, a sensitive and intelligent Christian, oversaw his intellectual and emotional education. After the village school, he studied with abbé Dumont, curé of Bussières. Later, the Fathers of the Faith in Belley schooled him in the humanities. In 1808, he returned to Milly, the family estate, unwilling to serve the "Usurper," Napoleon I (1769–1821). He read, he dreamed, he travelled to Italy (1811–1812) and became enamoured with its countryside and climate. With the restoration of the Bourbons, Lamartine found himself a military officer, an honor that he quickly abandoned for the solitude and indolence of Milly. He nurtured his intellect by reading Voltaire* and J.-J. Rousseau,* fostering his skepticism, and producing his first poems, feeble attempts that he mostly relegated to the fireplace. In 1816 in Aix, he met Madame Charles, the young wife of an elderly doctor, whose love and death a year later largely inspired his *Méditations*. Published in 1820, the lyricism, the sensitivity, the beauty, of these twenty-four poems met with resounding success and established Lamartine's reputation as a writer. "Le Lac" ("The Lake"), written at Aix in 1817 and contained in this collection, recalling his love for Madame Charles on the shores of Lake Bourget the previous summer, is his best-known poem. She died shortly after it was written.

From 1820 to 1830, Lamartine served as a diplomat at numerous posts in Italy. He married a young English woman, Elizabeth Birch, and published in 1823, *Nouvelles Méditations* (*New Meditations*), less original and striking than the first. The most memorable poems in this collection include "Bonaparte," written upon the death of the emperor; "Le Poète mourant" ("The Dying poet"), a melancholy poem about death written in 1817 and revised in 1823; "Les Préludes," written in Florence and described by Lamartine himself as a "literary sonata"; and "Le Crucifix," a hymn to Christ and the cross and the apex of Christian poetry, inspired by the crucifix sent him by Madame Charles. Also in 1823, he published "La Mort de Socrate" ("The Death of Socrates"), an 800-line didactic poem; "Le Dernier Chant du pèlerinage d'Harold" ("The Last Strophe of the Pilgrimage of Harold"), a completion of Byron's *Childe Harold* (1812) dedicated to the English poet and relating his skepticism and death. Lamartine's growing religious fervor, revealed in these rather mediocre poems, climaxed in *Harmonies poétiques et religieuses* (*Poetic and Religious Harmonies,* 1830).

Lamartine was elected to the Academy in 1830. In June 1832, he embarked for the Orient; however, the death of his daughter in Beirut six months later shortened the trip. Elected deputy from Bergues in the north during his absence, he entered the chamber of deputies in 1834, beginning a political career that would endure until 1851. At first loyal to the ministry, he gradually supported the opposition, proposing social reform aimed at improving the poor proletariat. By 1843, he headed the leftist opposition; the revolution of 1848 saw him head of the provisional government.

Paralleling his political rise was a poetic reform. His "Réponse à *Némésis*" ("Reply to *Nemesis*," 1831—*Nemesis* was a weekly newspaper) along with "Des destinées de la poésie" ("Of the destinies of poetry," 1834), enunciated the political and social mission of the poet: "Poetry will be reason put to music . . . it will be philosophical, religious, political, social, like the ages which humankind will achieve." In this vein, he abandoned the personal, lyrical poems of his youth. He published *Ode sur les révolutions* (*Ode on Revolutions,* 1831), beckoning the people to heed the call of political and social progress. He envisioned a sweeping religious and national epic depicting the "destiny of man . . . the stages which the human spirit must traverse to attain its ends by the ways of God." Ten great ages of humanity were to be depicted including the flood, the Patriarchs, Socrates, Jesus Christ, the Middle Ages, the French Revolution, the coming of the Anti-Christ. However, *Jocelyn* (1836) and *La Chute d'un ange* (*The Fall of an Angel,* 1838) are the only two that Lamartine had time to complete. The first met with mixed critical reaction but enjoyed popular success; the second was a complete failure, which Lamartine unsuccessfully attempted to rectify a year later with *Les Recueillements poétiques* (*Poetic Contemplations*, 1839), his last collection of poems. Most important among those included are "Ode à M. Felix Guillemardet" and "Utopie," poems that express his ideals of democracy, fraternity, and religious unity. *Histoire des Girondins* (*History of the Girondins*, 1847), his eloquent evocation of the final days of the revolution of 1789, fanned the sparks of a new revolution that would place him at its head. His glory was short-lived, however; the ascension of Louis-Napoleon to the presidency marked his political demise.

Lamartine finished the remaining twenty years of his life in penury and "forced literary labor." After *Histoire de la revolution de 1848* (*History of the Revolution of 1848*, 1849), he turned to his past with *Confidences* (1849); *Graziella* (originally included in *Confidences* and later published separately), depicting his love affair with a Neapolitan girl during an early stay in Italy; *Raphaël* (1849), a thinly disguised idealization of his love affair with Julie Charles; and *Nouvelles Confidences* (1851), which picks up where *Confidences* left off. Attempts at social novels followed with *Geneviève, histoire d'une servante* (*Genevieve, Story of a Servant*) and *Le Tailleur de pierres de Saint-Point* (*The Stone Cutter of Saint-Point*), both published in 1851. He wrote periodicals, *Le Conseiller du peuple* (*Advisor to the People*, 1849–1851) and *Les Foyers du peuple* (*Foyers of the People*, 1851–1853), and historical treatises on the Restoration (1851–1853), Mirabeau* and the Constituent Assembly (*Histoire des Constituants*, 1854), Turkey (1854–1855), and Russia (1855). *Le Civilisateur* (*The Civilizer*, 1852–1854) offered biographies of leading historical figures. *Le Cours familier de littérature* (*Informal Literature Course*), published from 1856 until Lamartine's death in 1869, relayed in twenty-eight volumes a literary panorama and contained a veritable lyric masterpiece, "La Vigne et la maison" ("The Vine and the House," 1857).

Despite his dogged persistence and voluminous output, poverty remained. Lamartine sold Milly and accepted a government pension and lodgings. He died solitary, exhausted, and forgotten.

Lamartine steeped his Muse in the ancients, the Bible, Ossian (3d century Gaelic bard), Lord Byron (1788–1824), Jean Baptiste Racine (1639–1699), Rousseau, Saint-Pierre,* and Chateaubriand.* His careful education, idyllic youth, and Christianity engendered his sensitivity and ideals of happiness, immortality, hope, and faith. Though his later poems translated his social and political aspirations, the harmony, lyricism, and personalism of the *Méditations* remain his hallmark. The ninth "époque" of his *Jocelyn*—"Les Laboureux" ("The Laborers")—ranks among the most beautiful verses ever written in the French language. If his poems seem imperfect, unstudied, that is what they were—impromptu chansons of nature, love, melancholy, and God effervescing from the wellsprings of his heart. His acceptance, however, is far from unanimous. Though praised by his contemporaries as a "Chateaubriand in verse," the Parnassians* criticized his sentimentalism; the naturalists (see naturalism**) disdained him. Modern opinion remains divided. Nevertheless, Lamartine endures, along with Vigny,* Musset,* and Hugo,* as one of the truly great romantic poets.

For further information, see M. E. Birkett, "Lamartine and the 'Poetic' Painting of L. Robert," *Symposium* 33 (Winter 1979): 299–311; Birkett, *Lamartine and the Poetics of Landscape* (Lexington, Ky.: French Forum Monographs, 1982); W. Fortescue, *Alphonse de Lamartine: A Political Biography* (New York: Saint Martin's Press, 1983); J. Lafontant, "Lamartine and the Negro," *Nineteenth Century French Studies* 11 (1–2) (Fall–Winter 1982–1983): 83–95; C. Lombard, *A Pilgrimage to the Holy Land* (Delmar, N.Y.: Scholars' Facsimiles and Reprints, 1978); S. Sider, "Lamartine's 'La Mort de Socrate' and Plato's Phaedo," *Romance Notes* 20 (Fall 1979): 58–64; R. Winegarten, "In Quest of Lamartine: A Poet in Politics," *Encounter* 59 (2) (August 1982): 22–29.

LAMENNAIS, FELICITE-ROBERT DE (1782–1854), liberal Catholic philosopher and political writer, was born at Saint-Malo, the son of a wealthy merchant and shipowner. The death of his mother and loss of his father's fortune placed him in the hands of his well-educated if eccentric uncle, who lived in the chateau of La Chesnaie near Dinan. His brother taught him Latin; he learned Greek, Hebrew, and modern languages, read J.-J. Rousseau,* and at an early age exhibited a religious skepticism that delayed his first communion until the age of twenty-two. He entered the clergy at thirty-four. His first work, *Réflexions sur l'état de l'eglise de France pendant le XVIIIe siècle et sur sa situation actuelle* (*Reflections on the State of the French Church during the Eighteenth Century and on Its Present Situation*, 1808), published anonymously in Paris, questioned the concordat of 1801 between France and the Holy See and advocated papal supremacy, much to the ire of Napoleon, who had the book seized. He rose to prominence with his *Essai sur l'indifférence en matière de religion* (*Essay on Indifference in the Matter of Religion*, 4 vols., 1817–1823), which denounced the religious passivity that leads to atheism and spiritual death and advocated a restoration of belief in a God whose existence he proved by "universal consent." Lamennais believed that the church must divorce itself from government and work for social justice. *De la religion considérée dans ses rapports avec l'ordre politique et social* (*On Religion, Considered in its Relationship with the Political and Social Order*, 1825) attacked the subordination of religion to politics and called for the separation of church and state. *Progrès de la révolution et de la guerre contre l'eglise* (*Progress of the Revolution and the War against the Church*, 1829) denounced the church's refusal to support the liberal movement. With his disciples Lacordaire*, Montalembert,* and de Guérin,* he founded *L'Avenir* (*The Future*), a journal subtitled "Dieu et la liberté" ("God and Freedom"), which advocated freedom for the people, their right to organize, and the freedom of the press. In 1832, the Vatican, shaken by his notion of freedom, condemned his works in a papal encyclical, *Mirari vos*. Lamennais retreated to La Chesnaie and after careful consideration, countered with *Paroles d'un croyant* (*Words of a Believer*, 1834), his best-known work, which restated his belief in liberty, equality, and fraternity and in a social system based on love and justice. It condemned kings, armies, the rich, even the church, for their repression of the people and abuse of power. In 1834, a second encyclical, *Singulari nos* censured Lamennais and his *Paroles*. Lamennais openly broke with the church but continued to support the cause of the people. *Livre du peuple* (*Book of the People*, 1836) and *Esquisse d'une philosophie* (*Outline of a Philosophy*, 4 vols., 1841–1846) outlined his views. Though imprisoned in 1841 for the beliefs expressed in *Le Pays et le gouvernement* (*The Country and the Government*, 1841), he supported the revolution of 1848 in two short-lived journals, *Le Peuple constituant* (*The Constituent People*) and *La Révolution démocratique et social* (*The Democratic and Social Revolution*), and innumerable pamphlets. In 1848, he was a member of the constitutional convention and an ardent supporter of republican aims and the sovereignty of the people. He retired after the coup d'état of 1851 dashed his hopes of popular freedom and occupied himself with a translation of Dante until his death. He refused to be reconciled with the church and was buried at Parisian cemetery Père La Chaise without funeral rites.

Throughout his life, Lamennais worked to involve the church in the social concerns that many of the romantic (see romanticism*) writers and historians from 1830 to 1848 were trying to address. His *Paroles d'un croyant* is a masterpiece of romantic imagery, rhythm, and rhyme, which echoes the poetry of the Bible as it taught his ideal of Christian socialism. He believed that the Gospel was the source of democracy; he adopted its style to communicate his ideals to the people. His influence on Vigny,* Hugo,* George Sand,* and Lamartine* was great.

LA METTRIE, JULIEN OFFRAY DE (1709–1751), eighteenth-century physician and philosopher whose materialism influenced Diderot* and Holbach,* was educated by the Jansenists but abandoned religion for medicine. He studied anatomy at Leyden with Herman Boerhaave (1668–1738), reputed to be the greatest physician of his time, and translated many of his medical works into French. He practiced in his native town of Saint-Malo and was appointed surgeon to the guards in Paris. La Mettrie's radical treatise, *Histoire naturelle de l'âme* (*Natural History of the Soul*, 1745), which introduced his theory that psychological phenomena were effects of physiological changes in the brain and nervous system, cost him his position and forced his return to Holland. There he elaborated his materialism in *L'Homme-machine* (*Man a Machine*, 1748) and *L'Homme-plante* (*Man a Plant*, 1748). Using "experience and observation" as his guides, he defined natural law in *L'Homme-machine* as a "feeling which teaches us what we should not do, because we would not wish it to be done to us," the human body as a "complicated machine which winds itself up, the living image of perpetual motion," and the universe as a "single substance with various modifications." He was forced to flee once again, this time to Frederick II in Berlin, where he resumed his medical career, was appointed court reader, and accepted into the Academy of Sciences before his death three years later.

La Mettrie's other works, *Discours sur le bonheur ou L'Anti-Sénèque* (*Discourse on Happiness or Anti-Seneca,* 1748), *Système d'Epicure* (*Epicurus' System,* 1750), and *L'Art de jouir* (*The Art of Enjoyment,* 1751) express his epicurian ideal of sensual pleasure and self-love. His belief in the correlation between mind and body, though innovative and influential, was considered extreme and immoral by his contemporaries, notably Voltaire* and Diderot, who preferred not to be associated with him. Today, however, La Mettrie's materialism and mechanistic psychology have been seen as a direct ancestor of the neurophysiological theories of the modern field of cybernetics and the "mechanical brain" (N. L. Torrey, *Les Philosophes*).

For further information, see J. Falvey, "Women and Sexuality in the Thought of La Mettrie," *Women and Society in Eighteenth Century France* (London: Athlone, 1979), 55–68; L. Honore, "The Philosophical Satire of La Mettrie," *Studies on Voltaire and the Eighteenth Century* 215 (1982): 175–222; L. Rosenfield, "La Mettrie and Quesnay: Physician-Philosophes of the Enlightenment," A. Bingham and V. Topazio, eds., *Enlightenment Studies in Honor of Lester G. Crocker* (Oxford: Voltaire Foundation, 1979), 263–282; A. Thomson, *Materialism and Society in the Mid-Eighteenth Century: La Mettrie's Discours préliminaire* ("Histoire des idees et critique litteraire"), vol. 198 (Geneva, Paris: Droz, 1981); N. Torrey, *Les Philosophes* (New York: Perigee Books, 1980).

LAUTREAMONT (1846–1870, born Isidore Ducasse), the gifted but troubled young author of *Chants de Maldoror* (*Maldoror's Songs,* 1869) who has been hailed as a forerunner of surrealism,** was born in Montevideo, Uruguay, to French parents. He studied at the Collège de Tarbes and Lycée de Pau before coming to Paris in 1867 to study for examinations at the Ecole polytechnique. There he did most of his writing before dying of consumption three years later in a Montmartre hotel at the tender age of twenty-four.

Lautréamont took his pseudonym from the hero of Eugène (Joseph) Sue's* historical novel, *Latréaumont.* It is said that he wrote at night, before his piano, fortified with cups of strong coffee and waking his neighbors with his shouts and music. The first stanza of the *Chants de Maldoror* was first published anonymously in 1868. Five more stanzas followed the next year, but publication was soon suspended by the editor because of the work's violence. Another work, *Les Poésies,* appeared in 1870. Interest was renewed in Lautréamont in 1874, when copies of *Chants de Maldoror* were sold in Brussels. His rise to prominence has been slow but steady, thanks to the efforts of the surrealists, notably André Breton.**

Chants de Maldoror is a lengthy prose poem about Lautréamont's war with society, with the almighty ("le tout-puissant"), and with himself. It depicts his longing for the infinite and his desire to be more than "the son of a man and a woman." For Maldoror and Lautréamont, poetry is a "fearless talisman," a means of combatting powerlessness. His poetry is violent, unflinching before the cruel, the ferocious, the evil, the erotic. Its hallucinatory vision earned the admiration of the surrealists and its esthetics contributed to the liberation of modern poetic form.

For further information, see L. Edson, *"Les Chants de Maldoror* and the Dynamics of Reading," *Nineteenth Century French Studies* 12 (1–2) (Fall–Winter 1983–1984): 198– 206; J. Mowitt, "Towards a Non-Euclidean Rhetoric: Lautréamont and Ponge," *Sub-Stance* 30 (1981): 63–84.

LEBRUN, PONCE-DENIS ECHOUARD (1729–1807), called Lebrun-Pin-dare after the Greek lyric poet, Pindar (522?–443 B.C.), wrote odes, elegies, verse epistles, and diverse poems and epigrams. His life and poetry spanned the century. He served as secretary to the prince of Conti (1717–1776), later wel-comed the Revolution, became a Bonapartist, and received a pension from the emperor. His odes celebrated Louis XV (1710–1774), Louis XVI (1754–93), the Revolution, the National Convention, Robespierre,* and Napoleon Bo-naparte (1769–1821).

His works, collected posthumously in 1811, comprise four volumes of various forms of verse, mostly odes. Despite their rhetoric, exaggeration, and excessive use of mythology, they are remembered for the sincerity of their emotion and enthusiasm, which was lacking in the earlier poetry of Lamotte-Houdart (see Houdar de la Motte*), Pompignan,* and J.-B. Rousseau.* His *Ode à Buffon* (*Ode to Buffon*) and *Ode sur les causes physiques des tremblements de terre* (*Ode on the Physical Causes of Earthquakes*) exemplify the scientific poetry of Ché-nier* in the later eighteenth century and by Sully-Prudhomme* in the nineteenth.

LECONTE DE LISLE, CHARLES-MARIE (1818–1894), called the "master of Parnassian* poetry" for the formal beauty and rigor of his verse, was born in Saint-Paul on the island of La Réunion, now called île Bourbon, which lies in the Indian Ocean to the East of Africa. His family, originally from Brittany, was named Leconte; the branch that settled in La Réunion added "de l'isle" ("from the island") to distinguish itself from the other. Leconte de Lisle spent his earliest years in Nantes. At ten, he returned to La Réunion, where his father, a former surgeon in the imperial army, owned a sugar cane plantation. He re-mained on the island until age eighteen, attending school at the Collège Saint-Denis de la Réunion. From 1837 to 1843, he returned to France, passed his baccalaureate, and attended law school at Rennes with a career in the mag-istrature looming in his future. De Lisle, however, preferred literature. He pub-lished verse in local papers and, with friends, founded a journal, *La Variété,* to which he contributed criticism, short stories, and poetry. At his family's request, he returned to law school, but never completed his degree. Homesick, he re-turned to La Réunion for eighteen months from 1843 until 1845, when he was offered an editorship with *La Démocratie pacifique* (*The Peaceful Democracy*) in Paris. There he met Hellenist scholar and chemist Louis Ménard,* who awak-ened De Lisle's interest in the Greek language and culture and introduced him to Baudelaire** and Banville.* From 1845 to 1847, de Lisle wrote poetry inspired by the heroic myths of ancient Greece but with a democratic message for the Fourierist (see Fourierisme*) review, *La Phalange*. He greeted the revolution of 1848 with enthusiasm for the socialists, worked for the abolition of slavery, much to his family's dismay, and spread democratic propaganda in Brittany. During the June riots, he spent two days in prison and, early in 1849, fled to Brussels to escape further imprisonment. He returned discouraged by the realities of politics, his socialist dreams shattered by Louis-Napoleon's coup d'etat. After 1851, he dedicated himself to literature, publishing *Poèmes antiques* (*Ancient Poems*, 1852), *Poèmes barbares* (*Barbarian Poems*, 1862), *Les Erinnyes* (1873), *Poèmes tragiques* (*Tragic Poems*, 1884), and *Derniers Poèmes* (*Final Poems*, posthumous, 1895). He earned his living by teaching and writing transla-tions, most notably of the *Iliad* (1866) and the *Odyssey* (1867), which earned him a pension near the end of the Empire. Under the Third Republic, he was named senate librarian, a position that alleviated his pecuniary difficulties. He entered the Academy in 1886, taking Victor Hugo's* seat. He died near Paris in 1894.

The preface to the *Poèmes antiques* attacks sentimental, romantic poetry in favor of a poetry based on knowledge, discipline, and scholarship. De Lisle himself had felt personally betrayed by the proclamation of the Empire in 1851 but masked his disillusionment and pessimism behind the erudition of these poetic evocations of ancient Greece, India, and his native island of La Réunion. Out of respect for tradition, he retained the original names of the Greek gods and heroes. Hercules figures in many of the poems, often inspired by Greek pastoral poet Theocritus (3d century B.C.): "La Robe du centaure" ("The Centaur's Robe"), "Héraklès au taureau" ("Hercules with the Bull"), "Héraklès so-laire" ("Hercules and the Sun"), "L'Enfance d'Héraklès" ("Hercules' Child-hood"). Others celebrate the plastic beauty of Greek art: "Vénus de Milo," "Hélène," "Niobé," "Hypatie." Hindu legends, including "Bhagavat," "La Vision de Brahma" ("Brahma's Vision"), and "Surya," bear witness to de Lisle's nihilism. "Dies irae" ("Day of Wrath") expresses disgust with the modern world; "Juin" ("June"), "Midi" ("Noon"), and "Nox" ("Night") evoke the sun-baked land of the ancients, the power and indifference of its landscape.

The vision of the *Poèmes barbares* is no less bleak than that of those above. Its preface called for a union of art and science. This time, de Lisle turned to Nordic myths and legends: "La Légende des Nornes" ("The Legend of the Nornes"), "Le Jugement de Komor" ("The Judgment of Komor"); Spain: "La Tête du Comte" ("The Count's Head"), "La Ximena"; and the Bible: "Qaïn" ("Cain"), "La Vigne de Naboth" ("The Vine of Naboth"). "Le Coeur de Hialmar" ("Hialmar's Heart"), taken from Xavier Marmier's (1809–1892) *Chants populaires du Nord* (*Popular Songs of the North*, 1842), recounts the warrior Hialmar's noble death before his comrades "asleep without tombs in the red snow," with classic simplicity and restraint. "La Fontaine aux lianes" ("The Fountain and the Liana Vines") recalls the beauty of his native island. The majesty of exotic, wild animals, superior to man in their natural habitat, is portrayed in "Les Eléphants," "Le Sommeil du condor" ("The Condor's Sleep"), "Le Jaguar." "Les Montreurs" ("The Showmen") is filled with scorn for the romantics (see romanticism*), who like animal exhibitors display their private lives to the crowds and dance on the "tawdry stage" of life. De Lisle's pessimism explodes with the violence and death wishes of "Le Voeu suprême" ("The Supreme Wish"), "Aux Morts" ("To the Dead"), and "La Dernière Vision" ("The Last Vision"). "Solvet saeclum" ("The World Dissolved") conjures up the end of the world.

The *Poemes tragiques* recall many of de Lisle's themes and present a harsher reality than that of earlier collections. He evokes the wisdom of the East in "Maya" and his hatred of Christianity in "L'Holocaust" and "Les Siècles maudits" ("The Cursed Centuries"). "L'Illusion suprême" ("The Supreme Illusion") is a pessimistic recollection of his youth on La Réunion. "L'Albatross" and "La Chasse de l'aigle" ("The Eagle's Hunt") continue the animal theme, while "Sacra fames" ("Sacred Hungers") discloses the universal law of hunger.

De Lisle's poetry was born of his dissatisfaction with the facile, sentimental verse of the romantics and of his pessimism toward the world in which he lived. Unlike Hugo, who saw history as a march toward progress, de Lisle considered humanity mired in an incurable and tragic barbarism that neither gods, men, nor nature could alleviate. He longed for the end of the universe or for his own absorption into nothingness. As a poet, he sculpted his fears, sadness, and bitterness into carefully wrought statements of his ideas on the world, humanity, and God. He upheld the beauty and perfection of classical antiquity as models for his art. His poetry was scholarly, dignified, controlled, sombre, the product of an intellectual rather than an imaginative mind. In the spirit of positivism,* he brought a wealth of research on all facets of antiquity to his poetry and hoped to unite art and science in his work. Each of his poems is based on a careful inquiry into the facts in which nothing is left to chance. De Lisle's poetry has been criticized as austere and impassive, poetry that requires effort on the part of the reader. However, it attained a technical perfection that continues to be recognized for its eloquence, rhythm, sonority, and beauty.

For further information, see I. McFarlane, "Pastoral and the Deprived Poet," in M. Bowie, A. Fairlie, and A. Finch, eds., *Baudelaire, Mallarmé, Valéry: New Essays in Honor of Lloyd Austin* (Cambridge: Cambridge University Press, 1982), 443–456.

LEGENDE DES SIECLES, LA (*The Legend of the Ages*, 1883) is the culmination of Hugo's* penchant for the epic as *Les Contemplations** is of his penchant for the lyric. It grew from the "Petites Epopées" ("Short Epic Poems"), written in exile in Jersey beginning in 1857, through additions and revisions into the grandiose French epic long-awaited and much contemplated by romantic (see romanticism*) poets since Lamartine.* Along with "Dieu" ("God") and "La Fin de Satan" ("The End of Satan"), *La Légende des siècles* was to reach cosmic proportions, uncovering the three aspects of God, the human, the evil, the infinite. However, Hugo never completed the other two parts of the triptyche.

Hugo's publisher, Pierre-Jules Hetzel (1814–1886), brought out the first series of *La Légende* in 1859; a second series in 1877; a third, in 1883. A definitive edition (1883) wove the beauty of the first, the emotions of the second, and the spirituality of the third into a single strand recounting man's progress, the "successive imprints of the human profile, from one age to the next, from Eve, mother of man, through the Revolution, mother of people" (Preface). Here history combines with fable, the Bible, the marvelous, and the supernatural and is transformed into legend. The poems echo man's collective consciousness, his sentiments and traditions from biblical times, ancient Greece and Rome, the Middle Ages, on down to the nineteenth century and provide a glimpse into the future. Hugo envisioned the world as a battlefield for the forces of good and evil. Here, he retraces man's path through the "labyrinthe" of progress, as the forces of good win out and humanity emerges from darkness into light.

"Vision d'où est sortie ce livre" ("Vision which Inspired this Book"), which opens the collection, recalls the earlier vision of "La Pente de la Rêverie" in *Les Feuilles d'automne*.* In gathering and reassembling the "debris" of the crumbled "wall of the ages," his vision of the human epic is born. The initial poems are biblic and well known: "Le Sacre de la femme" ("The Coronation of Woman") depicts the Garden of Eden and the birth of the human race; "La Conscience" ("Conscience"), the awakening of man's conscience in the story of Cain and Abel; "Booz Endormi" ("Boaz Asleep"), the beautiful and lyric evocation of Ruth and Boas so admired by Charles Péguy.** The heroic poems are inspired by Charlemagne ("Aymerillot"), Roland ("Le Mariage de Roland"—"The Marriage of Roland"), Le Cid ("Bivar"), and knights-errant ("Eviradnus"). Important Oriental poems, including "Zim-Zizimi" and "Sultan Mourad," relate the tyranny of the East. "L'Aigle du casque" ("The Eagle on the Helmet") and "Ratbert," the cycle of poems about Hugo's imaginary Italian king, symbolize the injustice and brutality of the Middle Ages. "Le Satyre" ("The Satyr") recounts the paganism of the sixteenth-century Renaissance and Hugo's hope for a reconciliation between man and nature; "La Rose de l'Infante" ("The Rose of the Infanta"), the dark side of the century, the Spanish Inquisition.

"Le Groupe des idylles" ("The Group of Idylls"), which includes "Aristophane," "Voltaire," "Beaumarchais," "Moschus," "Salomon," and "Virgile," are light love poems or pastiches that provide a transition from the darkness of the poems of the past to those of the present. Besides current themes and events (royalism in "Jean Chouan" and the revolutionary Paris Commune of 1871 in "Guerre Civile"), the modern poems express Hugo's hope, already found in *Les Contemplations,* for mankind's redemption. "Les Pauvres Gens" ("The Poor"), "Après la bataille" ("After the Battle"), and "Le Crapaud" ("The Toad") reveal the love and generosity of the poor, the charity of his father, the natural patience and compassion of animals, models for mankind. The poems "Pleine Mer" ("Out at Sea") and "Plein Ciel" ("Up in the Air") prophesy the progress, light, and hope of the twentieth century, where steamers are outmoded and airborne dirigible balloons lead humanity to its destiny, "the future, divine and pure, to virtue, science . . . , to abundance, to peace, to laughter . . . to fraternity . . . to love." The final poem goes beyond time. "La Trompette du jugement" ("The Trumpet of Judgment"), inspired by the Apocalypse, is Hugo's vision of judgment day, when the evil will receive their due.

These poems reveal Hugo at his finest. His imagination, his vision, and his technical skill as a poet are in full force and seemingly boundless. They have led to Hugo being called erudite, an apostle, a dreamer.

For further information, see D. Lotze, "The 'Poèmes d'humanité' of Guernsey and also Sztregova: Victor Hugo's *La Légende des siècles* and Imre Madach's *The Tragedy of Man*," *Neohelicon* 5 (2) (1977): 71–81.

LEMIERRE, ANTOINE-MARIN (1723–1793), minor eighteenth-century poet and playwright, was born in Paris, the son of an artisan. A brilliant student and the recipient of several academic prizes, he became a professor of rhetoric at the Collège de Harcourt, then secretary to tax collector Dupin. His poetry includes *Pièces fugitives* (*Short poems*, 1782), a poem on "L'Utilité des découvertes faites dans les arts et dans les sciences sous le règne de Louis XV" ("The Usefulness of the Discoveries Made in the Arts and Sciences during the Reign of Louis XV"), and two odes, "La Peinture" ("Painting," 1769) and "Les Fastes, ou Les Usages de l'année" ("Annals, or the Customs of the Year," 1779). He is best known for his philosophical tragedies in the style of Voltaire,* *Guillaume Tell* (*William Tell*, 1766), a protest against tyranny, and *La Veuve du Malabar* (*Malabar's Widow*, 1770), against the ancient Hindu custom of the "bûcher" (or "suttee"), in which a widow is burned alive after the death of her husband. Other tragedies include *Hypermnestre* (1758), *Térée* (1761), *Idoménée* (1764), and *Artaxerce* (1766). Lemierre purportedly died in a stupor brought on by the horrors of the Revolution.

LESAGE, ALAIN-RENE (1668–1747), eighteenth-century novelist best known for *Gil Blas*,* also wrote comedy and vaudeville. Born in Brittany to a bourgeois family, he studied law with the Jesuits and practiced in Paris. However, after his marriage he renounced law for letters, becoming one of the first French writers to earn his keep through writing without benefit of stipends or gifts. Obliged, therefore, to write quickly and abundantly, of his massive body of works, he wrote only one play, *Turcaret*,* and two novels of merit, *Le Diable boiteux* (*The Lame Devil*, 1707) and *L'Histoire de Gil Blas de Santillane* (*The Story of Gil Blas of Santillane*, 1715–1735). He spent his life in relative obscurity, apart from the salons and literati of his day, and died in 1747 in the calm of Boulogne-sur-Mer, where he had retired with his wife and son.

Initially, he translated Greek, then Spanish comedies by Francisco de Rojas (1607–1648), Lope de Vega (1562–1635), and Vélez de Guevara (1579–1644).

In 1707, at the Théâtre National, he presented *Crispin, rival de son maître* (*Crispin, His Master's Rival*), a one-act, prose comedy of manners in which Crispin the valet disguises himself to win a dowry. Drawing upon the comic tradition of Molière (1622–1673), the play depicts the antagonism between dishonest valet and master.

The realism and social satire of *Turcaret* carries the comedy of manners one step further. A violent satire against financiers and revenue collectors whom Molière had spared but La Bruyère (1645–1696) had attacked, the play pessimistically, if one-sidedly, exposes the immorality of the day.

After *Turcaret,* Lesage abandoned the Théâtre National for the théâtres de la foire,* writing between 1712 and 1735 more than 100 plays of uneven quality in the Italian tradition. In these plays, called vaudeville comedies because they were written in couplets and sung to familiar tunes, classic Italian characters such as Arlequin and Mezzelin join mythological and allegorical figures to satirize and parody in the same vein as the previous comedies. *Arlequin roi de Serendib* (*Arlequin King of Serendib,* 1713) and *Achmed et Almanzine* (1728), the master works of this period, along with others collected in Evariste Gherardi's (167?– 1700) *Théâtre italien* (1700) and *Théâtre de la foire* (1721–1737, 10 vols.), are characterized by their diversity, humor, and scathing satire.

The realism and satire of the comedies is manifest in the novels as well. In *Le Diable boiteux,* an imitation of Spanish author Guevara, a schoolboy is treated to an inside view of the homes of Madrid from the tower of San Salvador by the devil Asmodee, who lifts the roofs from the houses. Within this Spanish framework is revealed a panorama of society and manners, teaching the boy "perfect knowledge of human life."

L'Histoire de Gil Blas de Santillane is a more original work. Written as a Spanish picaresque novel, a form practiced in Spain since the end of the sixteenth century, it relates the adventures and education of "picaro" Gil Blas, who grows from ne'er-do-well adventurer to secretary to the first minister, achieving wisdom and respect along the way. Keen observation and plot movement redeem its psychological and emotional shortcomings.

Other novels by Lesage include *Les Aventures de M. Robert Chevalier, dit de Beauchêne* (*The Adventures of M. Robert Chevalier, called de Beauchêne,* 1732); *L'Histoire de Guzman d'Alfaroche* (*The Story of Guzman d'Alfaroche,* 1732); *L'Histoire d'Estevanille Gonzales, surnommé le garçon de bonne humeur* (*The Story of Estevanille Gonzales, Surnamed the Boy of Good Humor,* 1743).

Lesage advanced the classic comedy of manners with his insistence on detail. By rendering the truthfulness of his characters, their acts, words, gestures, he depicted not the psychological realism of Molière, but a reality that is more graphic. We remember Crispin for his bantering speech; Gil Blas, for his innocence and candor. Lesage's realism presages that of Diderot.* Yet at the heart of his comedies and novels lies the satire of French society, a commentary on Frenchmen and life. In that, he is heir to Molière.

For further information, see P. Baggio, "The Ambiguity of Social Characterization in Lesage's *Théâtre de la Foire,*" *French Review* 55 (5) (April 1982): 618–624; R. Runte,

"Parallels between Lesage's Theatre and His Novels," in A. Bingham and V. Topazio, eds., *Enlightenment Studies in Honor of Lester G. Crocker* (Oxford: Voltaire Foundation, 1979), 283–299.

LETTRE A D'ALEMBERT SUR LES SPECTACLES (*Letter to d'Alembert Concerning the Theatre*, 1758), by J.-J. Rousseau,* continues in the tradition of his first two discourses, *Discours sur les arts et les sciences** and *Discours sur l'origine de l'inégalité** in which the "Citizen of Geneva" blasts society and cultural advancement as dangerous and corrupt. This letter, written in three weeks at the Hermitage at Montmorency, is directed against the theatre, which Rousseau condemns as immoral. It was occasioned in 1757 by d'Alembert's* *Encyclopédie** article, "Genève," which praised the liberalism of certain Genevan pastors and hoped for the establishment of a theatre there. Voltaire,* for his part, was writing and producing propaganda plays at his nearby estate, Les Délices. Rousseau's *Lettre sur les spectacles* is a direct challenge to Voltaire and the liberalism and progress he embodied as well as an argument against the establishment of a theatre in Geneva. Its publication finalized his break with Voltaire and the philosophes* and left him to face squarely the consequences of his philosophy in the solitude of Montmorency.

The *Lettre* begins with a defense of the Genevan pastors, then exposes the dangers of the theatre. "The source of the interest which attaches us to what is honest and inspires us with aversion for what is evil, lies with us and not in the theatre," he writes. He condemns tragedy as pleasure-oriented and says that it acquaints man with vices that he should not know. Comedy, which is truer to life than tragedy, is "evil and pernicious . . . the pleasure of the comic being founded on a vice of the human heart." Rousseau ends his letter with the hope that a theatre will never see the light of day in Geneva, a city that is morally pure and better suited to entertainment such as military reviews and public festivals, psalm-singing and Maypole dancing.

For further information, see S. Ajzenstat, "Citizen Rousseau Banishes the Poets," in J. Browning, ed., *The Stage in the Eighteenth Century* (New York: Garland, 1981), 70–86; B. Berber, "Rousseau and Brecht: Political Virtue and the Tragic Imagination," in B. Barber, M. McGrath, J. Gargas, eds., *The Artist and Political Vision* (New Brunswick, N.J.: Transaction, 1982), 1–30; P. Coleman, *Rousseau's Political Imagination. Rule and Representation in the Lettre à d'Alembert* (Geneva: Droz, 1984).

LETTRES DE MON MOULIN, LES (*Letters from My Windmill*, 1869), by Daudet.** See *Dictionary of Modern French Literature, from Naturalism and Symbolism to Post-Modernism.*

LETTRES PERSANES, LES. See *PERSIAN LETTERS, THE.*

LETTRES PHILOSOPHIQUES (*The Philosophical Letters or English Letters*, 1734), Voltaire's* first major philosophical work, published secretly in London and Rouen, extolls the liberty, justice, and tolerance he experienced in England from 1726 to 1729 and criticizes, by contrast, French government and institutions. As a commoner, Voltaire was spurned in his native land; as a poet and dramatist, he was often imprisoned or banished from Paris for his writings. However, when sent to England following a confrontation with the chevalier de Rohan, he was received by political figures Henry St. John Bolingbroke (1678–1751), Charles Peterborough (1658–1735), and Robert Walpole (1676–1745); writers and philosophers Jonathan Swift (1667–1745), George Berkeley (1685–1753), and Samuel Clarke (1675–1729); poets Alexander Pope (1688–1744), John Gay (1685–1732), and Edward Young (1683–1765). He witnessed first-hand a government based on freedom—religious, political, philosophical, and literary—and the quality of life that it engenders. The *Lettres* idealizes the religion, politics, science, philosophy, and literature that Voltaire discovered there.

The first four letters relate the history, customs, and beliefs of the Quakers, whose straightforwardness, humility, and simplicity he admired and whose doctrines on baptism, communion, and the priesthood he shared. Letter 5 criticizes the ambitious Anglicans; letter 6, the intolerant Presbyterians; letter 7 praises the Sociniens, or Antitrinitarians. Letters 8 through 10 present England's political system—its civil liberty ("The English nation is the only one on earth which has succeeded in regulating the power of its kings while resisting them," 8), religious peace, constitutional monarchy, equitable taxation ("Each gives not according to his standing, which is absurd, but according to his income," 9), commerce ("which enriched the citizens of England, helped to make them free," 10), and the peasantry. Letter 11 presents smallpox inoculations as an act of philosophical freedom. Letter 12 praises Francis Bacon, the "father of experimental philosophy;" letter 13 debunks the metaphysical system if René Descartes (1596–1650) for the empiricism of John Locke (1632–1704); letters 14 through 17 present Isaac Newton's (1642–1727) theories of gravity and optics. Letters 18 through 21 deal with literature—William Shakespeare (1564–1616) ("He created the theatre; he had a genius full of force and fecundity, the natural and the sublime, without the slightest ray of good taste and without the least knowledge of the rules," 18), tragedy, comedy, poetry, literary academies. The final letter denounces the fanaticism and pessimism of Blaise Pascal (1623–1662) ("I dare to take the part of humanity against this sublime misanthrope; I dare to assert that we are neither so bad nor so unhappy as he claims," 25).

In its direct and implied criticism of Catholicism and absolute monarchy, the *Lettres* announces themes of Voltaire's future stories and pamphlets. Its style is witty and eloquent; irony abounds. Yet despite its enormous popularity (five editions were printed in 1734, followed by five more until 1739), it was banned and an order issued for Voltaire's arrest, forcing him to flee to Cirey chateau in Lorraine, where he remained with Madame du Châtelet for ten years. For the time being, Montesquieu* would reign as the major philosophic force; Voltaire would write tragedies (*Alzire,* 1736; *Zulime,* 1740; *Mahomet,* 1742; *Mérope,**

1743) and more poetry (*La Pucelle* [*The Maiden*], *Le Mondain* [*The Worldly Man*], 1736; and the seven *Discourses en vers sur l'homme* [*Discourses in Verse on Man*], 1738), until the latter half of the century, when as an activist and philosophe,* he would emerge as the dominant force of the Age of Reason.

For further information, see J. Epstein, "Voltaire's Ventriloquism: Voices in the First *Lettre philosophique*," *Studies on Voltaire and the Eighteenth Century* 182 (1979): 219–235; W. Hanley, "The Abbé de Rothelin and the *Lettres philosophiques*," *Romance Notes* 23 (3) (Spring 1983): 245–250; S. E. Jones, "Voltaire's Use of Contemporary French Writing on England in His *Lettres philosophiques*," *Revue de littérature comparée* 56 (April–June 1982): 139–156; M. Reisler, "Rhetoric and Dialectic in Voltaire's *Lettre philosophique*," *L'Esprit Créateur* 17 (Winter 1977): 311–324.

LETTRE SUR LES AVEUGLES (*Letter on the Blind*, 1749), by Diderot,* is a scientific and philosophical study of blindness and related religious and moral questions, which earned the daring young editor of the *Encyclopédie** several months imprisonment in Vincennes. Using John Locke's (1632–1704) theory in *The Essay on Human Understanding* (1690) that knowledge comes from the senses, Diderot examines how a person blind since birth comes to know the world in which he lives. Recent advances in the field of cataract surgery, which successfully restored sight to persons blind since birth, offered Diderot the opportunity to consider how their preconceived notion of the universe, derived primarily from a sense of touch, compared with their postoperative, sighted view. His ideas on touch as a teaching tool anticipated Louis Braille's (1809–1852) system in the following century.

Diderot examined the psychology of the blind and their reactions to the world around them in two case histories, that of a blind man from Puiseaux, and the blind mathematician Nicholas Saunderson (1682–1739). Most important for Diderot, however, was the moral issue at hand. In an imaginary deathbed scene, Saunderson mouths Diderot's evolutionary conception of the universe ("How many crippled, wasted worlds have vanished, are reformed, and vanish again perhaps each moment") and his arguments in favor of atheism ("If you wish me to believe in God, you must let me touch him with my finger"). A blind person, unable to see and thus know God, Diderot reasons, cannot believe in him and, most important, lives without religion. "It is very important (for a blind person) not to mistake hemlock for parsley, but not at all to believe or not to believe in God," he declares.

Lettre sur les Aveugles contained seeds of a materialist philosophy that Diderot would further develop in *Le Rêve de d'Alembert.** However, after his Vincennes experience, Diderot temporarily curtailed his philosophic excesses, publishing anonymously his *Lettre sur les sourds et muets* (*Letter on the Deaf and Dumb*, 1751) and turning to the theatre and the encyclopedia as a means of self-expression.

For further information, see M. Kelly, "Saying by Implicature: The Two Voices of Diderot in *La Lettre sur les aveugles*," *Studies in Eighteenth Century Culture* 12 (1983): 231–241.

LIAISONS DANGEREUSES, LES (*Dangerous Liaisons*, 1782). See Laclos.*

LORENZACCIO (1834), by Alfred de Musset,* a historical drama in five acts written in prose, is considered a masterpiece of romantic (see romanticism*) literature and one of the few that is still performed today. It contains the essence of romantic drama—action, historical and local color, freedom from classical constraints, variety of tone, melange of genre—which all combine to create a convincing historical tableau. It is the most Shakespearean of the romantic dramas and the most personal. Lorenzo's dilemma, his loss of innocence, his obsession with vice, is that of Musset himself.

Musset took his inspiration from two sources, *Storie Fiorentine* by Benedetto Varchi (1502–1562) and *Une Conspiration en 1537* (*A Conspiracy in 1537*, 1833), by his mistress, George Sand.* Musset enlarged the scope of Sand's drama, adding sixteen scenes, secondary episodes, and characters. It was first performed in 1896 in a condensed form at the Théâtre Sarah Bernhardt with the actress herself in the title role. A more complete version was staged in 1925 by Madame Falconetti. In 1927, it became part of the repertory of the Comédie-Française.

The play centers on the assassination, in 1537 of Alexander de Medici, the duke of Florence and ruler of the city, by his cousin, Lorenzo de Medici. Act 1 depicts Florence under Alexander's rule. He is debauched and cruel. The play opens as the duke lies in wait for his prey, a girl of fifteen. Lorenzo, called "Lorenzaccio" for his complicity in the duke's actions, is seemingly a loyal member of his entourage and partner in crime. The duke loves him, over the objections of the pope. Lorenzo embarrasses him, however, when he faints before a sword (scene 4). The act closes with Lorenzo's mother and young aunt lamenting the young man's sins as a group of men, banned by the government, is forming in a nearby field.

Act 2 introduces the Strozzi family, which is republican and an enemy of the duke. The Strozzis are outraged by an insult made to their daughter, Louise, by Julian Salviati, one of the duke's henchmen. Lorenzo visits the Strozzis (scene 5) where he learns Pierre Strozzi has wounded Salviati in revenge. In the final scene, the duke orders the arrest of Pierre and his brother Thomas.

Act 2 hints at Lorenzo's true political color. In scene 2, he asks a young artist why he remains in a city where he is subject to the whims of its ruler. He intimates to his mother that something "surprising" may happen soon and tells his uncle that the cut of his beard reveals his republican soul, but in a complete about-face, honors the duke when he enters the room (scene 4). Act 3 begins with Lorenzo sword fighting in his bedroom, accustoming his neighbors to its clatter. The younger Strozzis join forces with another family, the Pazzis (scene 2). Scene 3 is central to the entire play and reveals Lorenzo's true motives. With his sons arrested, Philippe Strozzi pleads for Lorenzo's aid. Lorenzo divulges his plan to kill the duke the following day. He remembers the purity of his youth, confides in him his oath to slay one of the tyrants of the land. He explains the tragic irony of his life—to gain Alexander's confidence, he had to become like him, vicious and shameful. Pessimistically, he advises Strozzi not to meddle, to remain pure. When he protests, Lorenzo wagers that after he kills Alexander neither the republicans nor the people will do anything. Then why commit this useless murder? Strozzi asks. "The world must know a little who I am and who he is," Lorenzo replies. The final scene of act 3 is a reunion of the entire Strozzi family, arranged by Philippe as a call to arms against the Medicis. Louise falls over dead, poisoned by a servant of Salviati's wife. Philippe, stunned, declares to the surprise of all that he is leaving for Venice, ignoring his own call to arms.

Act 4 builds slowly to Alexander's death. In the first scene, Lorenzo asks if the duke has found his missing armor and sets the murder site—a midnight rendezvous in his room of the duke and his young aunt, Catherine. When Alexander asks him if he is serious about the meeting, Lorenzo replies, "as serious as death itself." Lorenzo arranges for Scoronconcolo, his fencing partner, to return at midnight, then questions his motives for killing the duke in an ensuing monologue (scene 3). He learns that his mother fell ill when she learned of the duke's designs on Catherine (scene 5). Scene 6 reiterates the elder Strozzi's refusal to join the republican movement, even at the behest of François I. The movement dies without his help (scene 8). Lorenzo warns the republicans of his assassination plans (scene 7), but none believes him. Scene 9 recounts his final thoughts before the deed. The duke himself is warned to beware of Lorenzo (scene 10) but, undaunted, takes his place in Lorenzo's bed, where he meets death instead of Catherine (scene 11).

Act 5 relates the disappointing outcome anticipated by Lorenzo. Alexander is buried secretly, for fear of causing an outbreak of murders; Cardinal Cibo has Côme de Medici elected successor (Scene 1). Lorenzo, with a price on his head, is in Venice with Philippe Strozzi, to whom he presents the key to Alexander's death chamber (Scene 2). Despite attempts on his life, Lorenzo leaves for a walk but is attacked outside his door (scene 6). The final scene depicts the coronation of the next Medici.

Numerous subplots—Cardinal Cibo's attempts to manipulate the marquise and secure his influence over the duke; the tension between the Salviatis and the Strozzis; the duke's burgeoning interest in Lorenzo's Aunt Catherine—weave through the numerous scenes. Lorenzo's monologues add psychological depth. The quintessential romantic hero, he has been compared to Hamlet and Musset himself.

For further information, see B. Cooper, "Staging a Revolution: Political Upheaval in *Lorenzaccio* and *Léo Burckart,*" *Romance Notes* 24 (1) (Fall 1983): 23–29; C. Crossley, *Musset: Lorenzaccio* (London: Grant and Cutler, 1984); J. Lowin, "The Frames of *Lorenzaccio,*" *French Review* 53 (December 1979): 190–198; M. Maclean, "The Sword and the Flower: The Sexual Symbolism of *Lorenzaccio,*" *Australian Journal of French Studies* 16 (2) (January–April 1979): 166–181.

LOUVET DE COUVRAY, JEAN-BAPTISTE (1760–1799), politician, journalist, and author of a bawdy trilogy, *Les Amours du chevalier de Faublas (The Loves of the Chevalier de Faublas,* 1787–1790), belongs, along with Dulaurens,* Vivant Denon,* and Crébillon fils,* to the league of libertines writing near the close of the century. Louvet de Couvray's brand of libertinage, however, is distinguished by its humor as it leads Faublas through a maze of love affairs, disguises, rendezvous, deceptions, and boudoirs until he is united with his one true love, Sophie, at the end of the series. Béatrice Didier (*Littérature française,* 1976) sees the work as "a novel of education and the novel of a destiny." Louvet de Couvray also wrote *Emilie de Varmont* (1791), advocating marriage for priests and divorce, and fragments of his memoirs, published posthumously in 1889. A prominent political figure, he wrote political tracts—*Paris justifié (Paris Justified,* 1789) and *Sentinelle (Sentinel,* 1790)—joined the Jacobins, and voted for the death of the king. Later pamphlets attacked Robespierre,* and Louvet de Couvray joined with the more moderate Girondins. His political candor was costly—he fled Paris in 1793 and did not return until 1794. He died five years later, soured by politics, thankful "to be finished before the Republic."

For further information, see S. F. Davies, "Louvet as Social Critic: *Les Amours du Chevalier de Faublas,*" *Studies on Voltaire and the Eighteenth Century* 183 (1980): 223–237.

LUCIEN LEUWEN, by Stendhal,* published posthumously in 1855 as *Le Chasseur vert (The Green Huntsman),* the name of an inn mentioned in the novel, deals with many of the same themes of his masterpieces, *Le Rouge et le noir** and *La Chartreuse de Parme.** Lucien, like Julien and Fabrice, is motivated by typically Stendhalian passions. Lucien is considered the most autobiographical of his novels, and when Stendhal stopped working on it in 1835, it was to begin his actual autobiography, *La Vie de Henri Brûlard.* The novel also contains violent and direct political satire against the Orleanist regime. *Lucien Leuwen* remains unfinished and was never published during Stendhal's lifetime.

Stendhal took the idea for the story from reading the manuscript of a novel written by a friend, Madame Jules Gaulthier, in 1833. He envisioned the novel in three parts, set in Nancy, Paris, and Rome. It ends after the first two, with Lucien en route to Italy to assume his post as secretary in the French embassy in Rome. The story opens in Nancy at the beginning of the July monarchy. Lucien, the son of a wealthy Paris banker, is a young lancer lieutenant with republican leanings. He was expelled from the Ecole Polytechnique and had lived off the generosity of his parents until he entered the army to gain self-esteem. But in Nancy he is miserable. The town is depressing, his fellow officers boring, his commander resentful of Lucien's wealth. He finds diversion in cultivating the local aristocrats, fighting duels, and falls in love with a beautiful, wealthy, young widow, Bathilde de Chasteller. Their love is doomed because Lucien, a commoner, is beneath her class. The scheming Dr. du Poirier leads Lucien to believe that Bathilde secretly bears the child of another officer. Heartbroken, Lucien flees to Paris.

In Paris, through his father's influence, Lucien is released from the army and becomes master of petitions and secretary to the minister of the Interior. Fulfilling these posts is an education in the ways of political skulduggery. Lucien learns quickly how to make bribes and influence elections. His father arranges for the beautiful Madame Grandet to become Lucien's mistress in return for making her husband minister. Lucien is greatly upset when he learns that he did not win her on his own and quits the capital for a stay in the country. His father dies suddenly, leaving his estate in a shambles. Against all advice, Lucien pays off his father's debts and leaves Paris for a diplomatic post in Italy.

Lucien, like Julien and Fabrice, is a character morally alienated from the society in which he moves. The novel is the story of his attempt to embrace that world and the struggle between its demands and his ideals.

M

MABLY, GABRIEL BONNOT DE (1709–1785), eighteenth-century philosopher (like his brother Condillac*), historian, and moralist, is remembered primarily for his political reforms. Originally in favor of the monarchy, Mably served as secretary to Cardinal Tençin (1680–1758), wrote his cabinet speeches, and exerted considerable influence at court. A disagreement with the cardinal led to his withdrawal to a private life of studying Greek and Roman history, which irrevocably influenced his perception of French government. Mably's earliest treatise, *Parallèle des Romains et des Français (Parallel between the Romans and the French,* 1740), supported a strong monarchy. Later, *Le Droit public de l'Europe fondé sur les traités (European Public Law as Based on Treaties,* 1748), *Observations sur les Grecs (Observations on the Greeks,* 1749), *Observations sur les Romains (Observations on the Romans,* 1751), and *Entretiens de Phocion sur le rapport de la morale avec la politique (Phocion's Dialogues on the Relationship between Morality and Politics,* 1763) advocated simplicity rather than wealth and moral virtue rather than knowledge as the means of happiness. Other works, *De la législation ou Principes des lois (On Legislation or The Principles of Law,* 1776), *De la manière d'écrire l'histoire (How to Write History,* 1783), *Principes de morale (Principles of Morality,* 1784), and *Observations sur le gouvernement et les Etats-Unis d'Amérique (Observations on the Government and the United States of America,* 1784) directly inspired the Revolution with its ideals of the ancient republics—simplicity, liberty, and equality. His most audacious treatise, *Des droits et des devoirs du citoyen (Rights and Duties of the Citizen,* published posthumously, 1789), which appeared on the eve of the Revolution, called for the abolition of private property.

Mably is considered an early socialist for his beliefs in equality, justice, and humanitarianism.

For further information, see K. M. Baker, ''A Script for a French Revolution: the Political Consciousness of the Abbé Mably,'' *Eighteenth Century Studies* 14 (Spring 1981): 235–263.

MADAME BOVARY (1857), subtitled "Moeurs de Province" ("Provincial Manners"), along with *L'Education sentimentale,** is Flaubert's* greatest novel. Though it initially met with a lukewarm reception from the general public and resulted in a lawsuit on immorality charges for its author, it has since met with universal praise for the perfection of its style and the importance of its observations and analyses. It has been variously considered "the definitive model of the novel" (Zola**), "a masterpiece of the contemporary novel" (Gustave Lanson and Paul Tuffraut). It brought literary fame to its author and ushered the age of realism* into modern European literature.

Madame Bovary was written on the advice of Flaubert's friends and fellow writers Maxime du Camp (1822–1894) and Louis Bouilhet (1822–1869). They censured Flaubert's first attempt at fiction other than those of his youth, *La Tentation de Saint Antoine,* suggesting, in 1849, that he abandon the imaginative and lyrical elan of his youth for a more practical, domestic novel based on the lives of Eugène and Alice-Delphine Delamare. Eugène Delamare was a former medical student of Flaubert's father who became a health officer. Dependable and dull, like Charles Bovary, he married an older woman. Upon her death, he marries Delphine, the daughter of a prosperous farmer who soon commits adultery with a local man-about-town and a law clerk. In 1848, overcome by debt, she commits suicide at age twenty-seven, leaving a daughter and bereaved husband behind. He dies the following year. According to Gabrielle Leleu, Flaubert fashioned Madame Bovary's character from a former schoolmate, Louise Pradier, who also deceived her husband and accumulated enormous debts.

Flaubert worked fifty-five months, from September 1851, until April 1856, writing, revising, reading, and criticizing the work in the solitude of Croisset. His labors are documented in his correspondence with his mistress, poetess Louise Colet (1808–1876). Du Camp agreed to serialize the novel in his *Revue de Paris* in 1856, where it ran in six installments from October through December. Though it was attacked on grounds of immorality by the Imperial government, Flaubert and the novel were acquitted. It appeared in book form in 1857.

The novel is divided into three parts. Part 1 depicts Emma's marriage; part 2, her corruption; part 3, further debasement and death. Flaubert introduces first Charles Bovary as a new student in a boy's school at Rouen. His awkwardness and intellectual mediocrity is symbolized by his hat, a droll concoction that embarrassed and encumbered him. Through diligence and conscientiousness, he graduates from medical school and becomes a health officer in Tostes, thanks to his mother, who procures him a practice and a wife, Madame Dubuc, an austere widow who is jealous and demanding. One night, Charles is summoned to set the leg of Farmer Rouault, a simple, but prosperous farmer with a young daughter, Emma. She is beautiful and elegant, the antithesis of Bovary's wizened old wife, and tells Bovary her dislike of the country life. Charles visits regularly, and after the death of his first wife, works up the courage for a timid marriage proposal. After a lively country wedding and three-day feast, the couple leaves for Tostes,

Charles happy and proud of his new wife. But Emma, who had nurtured an ideal of love from romantic novels and ballads, is soon dismayed at married life and imagines another husband, one more handsome, intelligent, and dashing than her own. An invitation to a ball at a neighboring chateau whets her dreams of romance, wealth, and glamour. She assumes the airs of a lady, feels lonely, dissatisfied with the monotony of her existence, and eventually falls ill due to nerves. Charles decides to move to Yonville-l'Abbaye, a larger town where hopefully Emma will be happier. She is expecting their first child.

Part 2 begins with a description of Yonville and the Bovarys' arrival at the Lion d'or, where they meet Homais the pharmacist, Binet the tax collector, the shy clerk Léon Dupuis, and the priest. As they dine, Emma and Léon explore common interests, travel, music, and literature while Homais lectures Charles on Yonville. The pretentious Homais practices medicine without a license on most of the town's residents. Emma eagerly anticipates the arrival of her baby, names her Berthe after a woman at the ball, and places her with a wet-nurse outside of town. Despite her friendship with Léon, Emma remains unfulfilled, passing her days gazing out the window and visiting the Homais's. Léon, who is in love with her, secretly despairs over Emma, while she masks her desires behind feigned interest in home and family. The church turns a deaf ear to her appeal for moral support, and Emma's tension mounts. Finally, Léon moves to Paris to pursue a law career. Emma is miserable until she meets Rodolphe Boulanger, a wealthy, libertine bachelor who owns a nearby estate. He makes overtures in a memorable scene in which they observe the activities of the country fair from the second floor of town hall. Rodolphe disappears for six weeks, then declares his love while horseback riding. Emma surrenders and begins a passionate love affair, meeting him several times a week. When Rodolphe's passion cools, she buys him an expensive gift and begs him to elope with her and Berthe. Rodolphe stalls and finally abandons her, thinking, "It would have been too stupid." She glimpses him on his way out of town and falls into a fever for forty-three days. Her recovery is expensive, forcing Charles to borrow from the moneylender, Lheureux, at high rates. Well at last, she resumes her household and maternal chores with renewed vigor until a trip to the opera at Rouen reintroduces her to Leon and a life of deceit.

Part 3 recounts Emma's second affair and her eventual tragic end. Leon learns her address in Rouen and appears at her hotel the following day. Finding Emma alone, he confesses his love for her; she demurs, but agrees to meet him at the cathedral the next day. During the night, she writes a long letter ending the affair before it begins. She meets him at the cathedral and, to Léon's consternation, first she prays at the chapel, then they tour the cathedral, until in exasperation, Léon hails a cab. When Emma protests, his response, "It's done in Paris," with its "unassailable logic," wins. The carriage, "sealed tighter than a tomb," circulates Rouen's streets all day long, never stopping. Emr. a forgets the resolve of her letter and tosses it, in pieces, through the carriage window. She misses the coach to Yonville, catches up with it, and learns upon her return that her father-in-law has died of a stroke. She is too preoccupied with Léon to mourn with Charles and his mother. The moneylender Lheureux visits and suggests that Emma obtain power of attorney from Charles, which her trusting husband readily assigns her. On a legal pretext, Emma goes to Rouen, where she spends three days with Léon. She pretends to have music lessons there every Thursday, gradually becoming increasingly possessive of Léon and visiting him more frequently. Léon becomes frightened and resentful of this side of her character. In the meantime, Emma's money troubles mount as bill collectors appear at her door and she is forced to borrow money to pay them back. Charles's inheritance from his father is spent, and behind his back, Emma collects money from his patients. Emma ignores melancholy Berthe and spends most of her time reading in bed, anticipating her next meeting with Léon. After a night at a masquerade ball with Léon in Rouen, she returns to find a judgment ordering her to pay Lheureux 8,000 francs within 24 hours or forfeit her household goods. Lheureux assures her it is no joke. Emma travels to Rouen to seek help from bankers, all of whom refuse. Léon has no money for her, nor Rodolphe, whom she begs. Desperate, she rushes to Homais's, demands the key to his poison depository, seizes a blue jar of arsenic, and swallows the white powder. She returns home, writes a letter to Charles, and goes upstairs to die. Two additional doctors are called in, including Dr. Larivière, who realizes that all is hopeless. After a terrible agony, she succumbs and Charles is beside himself with grief. Faced with mountains of debts that he cannot pay and, aware, at last, of Emma's adultery, he stops working and withdraws into a world of remorse. After a chance encounter with Rodolphe, he dies of a broken heart, leaving Berthe in the care of a poor aunt, facing a future in a cotton mill. Homais, on the other hand, is prosperous and is awarded the Legion of Honor.

Madame Bovary portrays the vicissitudes of romanticism* in a realistic framework. Starting with the real-life tragedy of the Delamares, the novel depicts, in minute detail, Emma Bovary's disillusionment with the reality of her existence and her attempts to escape through adultery and financial deceit. Flaubert carefully documented every aspect of the novel, reading everything from Chateaubriand* to medical treatises on clubfeet and poison. He consulted experts and relied on his own keen powers of observation. Flaubert situated the novel so precisely in the village of Ry, (Yonville in the novel), where Delamare actually lived, that its places and characters have been positively identified by literary sleuths. Though he claimed that the characters are completely fictitious, Flaubert based the secondary characters on real-life models whom he knew or had observed. Dr. Larivière is supposedly a portrait of his father.

Though Flaubert consciously sought to absent himself from his work as an "impartial" observer and an objective writer, even such a genius as he could not entirely meet this goal. His contempt of the bourgeoisie, which he considered stupid and vulgar in its petty materialism and conformity, is evident as he paints the "moeurs de province" of the subtitle. Declaring "Madame Bovary, c'est moi," he realized that Madame Bovary's romantic longing to escape the mediocrity of her existence mirrored his own. His disgust with contemporary life, a common romantic trait, influences his portrayal of the despicable Homais. His imprint is most visible, however, in the perfection of the style of the novel, which he struggled for fifty-five months to attain. The rhythms, images, and esthetic details of the sentences he wrote, the harmony and precision of the words he chose, attest to his success as a writer and the enduring beauty of the novel.

For further information, see F. Bondy, "Thinking About Flaubert," *Encounter* 58 (4) (April 1982): 55–57; R. Butler, "Flaubert's Exploitation of the 'Style Indirect Libre': Ambiguities and Perspectives in *Madame Bovary*," *Modern Languages* 62 (4) (December 1981): 190–196; R. Cargo, "The Fruits of Love: An Image in Gustave Flaubert, George Sand and Guy de Maupassant," *Nineteenth Century French Studies* 11 (3–4) (Spring-Summer 1983): 350–353; P. Cohen, " 'Oil and Tar': An Allusion to *Madame Bovary* in The Waste Land," *American Notes and Queries* 21 (5–6) (January–February 1983): 75–77; J. Culler, "The Uses of *Madame Bovary*," *Diacritics* 11 (3) (Fall 1981): 74–81; I. Dash, "Emma Crosses the Channel," *Names* 31 (3) (September 1983): 191–196; B. Doering, "*Madame Bovary* and Flaubert's Romanticism," *College Literature* 8 (1) (Winter 1981): 1–11; E. Ermarth, "Fictional Consensus and Female Casualties," in C. Heilbrun and M. Higonnet, eds., *The Representation of Women in Fiction* (Baltimore: Johns Hopkins University Press, 1983), 1–18; S. Gurney, "The 'Dialectic of Desire' in *Madame Bovary* and *Le Grand Meaulnes*," *Romanticism Past and Present* 7 (1) (Winter 1983): 37–62; J. Hamilton, "*Madame Bovary* and the Myth of Androgyny," *The U.S.F. Language Quarterly* 19 (3–4) (Spring-Summer 1981): 19–22; N. Hernandez, "Emma, Ana and Religion: A Comparative Study of *Madame Bovary* and *La Regenta*," *Platte Valley Review* 9 (1) (April 1981): 74–78; P. Horn, "Art and Artifacts in *Madame Bovary*," *Lamar Journal of the Humanities* 8 (1) (Spring 1982): 6–12; D. LaCapra, *Madame Bovary on Trial* (Ithaca: Cornell University Press, 1982); A. Lajoux, "From Emma to Félicité: The Use of Hagiography in the Works of Gustave Flaubert," *Studies in Medievalism* 2 (2) (Spring 1983): 35–50; B. Paris, "Third Force Psychology and the Study of Literature, Biography, Criticism and Culture," *Literary Review* 24 (2) (Winter 1981): 181–221; J. Rhodes, "Homais, Capharnaum and *Madame Bovary*," *College Literature* 10 (1) (Winter 1983): 60–68; M. Riffaterre, "Flaubert's Presuppositions," *Diacritics* 11 (4) (Winter 1981): 2–11; L. Riggs, "Emma Bovary and the Culture of Consumption," *The U.S.F. Language Quarterly* 21 (1–2) (Fall-Winter 1982): 13–16; N. Schor, "For a Restricted Thematics: Writing, Speech and Difference in *Madame Bovary*," in H. Eisenstein, ed., *The Future of Difference* (Boston: Hall, 1980), 167–192; P. Tammi, "Some Remarks on Flaubert and Ada," *The Vladimir Nabakov Research Newsletter* 7 (Fall 1981): 19–21; L. Thornton, "Conrad, Flaubert and Marlow: Possession and Exorcism," *Comparative Literature* 34 (2) (Spring 1982): 146–156; H. Weinberg, "Irony and 'Style indirect libre' in *Madame Bovary*," *Canadian Review of Comparative Literature* 8 (1) (Winter 1981): 1–9.

MAINE DE BIRAN, MARIE-FRANÇOIS-PIERRE GONTHIER DE

(1766–1824, called Maine de Biran), philosopher and statesman, was born at Bergerac, the son of a physician. He entered the corps of body guards for Louis XVI and retired to Bergerac when the corps was dismantled in 1789, where, secluded from the horrors of the Revolution, he dedicated himself to philosophy.

He served as sub-prefect of Bergerac from 1806 to 1811. In 1813, he took part in the commission that expressed, for the first time, its opposition to the tyranny of the emperor. During the Restoration, he resumed the title of royal body guard, was named counsellor of the state, and sat in the chamber of deputies. He preferred living in the provinces to the hustle of city life. He died in Paris in 1824.

Maine de Biran was an original thinker who formulated his beliefs from a lengthy and profound self-examination. Originally a partisan of the idéologues,* he eventually opposed their materialism. His first work, *L'Influence de l'habitude sur la faculté de penser* (*The Influence of Habit on the Faculty of Thought*, 1803) distinguishes between "passive" sensation and "active" sensation in which the consciousness comes to know itself and acquire a sense of morality. He eventually realized that Condillac's* notion of "passive receptivity" or "sensation" as the source of knowledge was false. His metaphysical perceptions led him to a belief in God and an appreciation for the psychological side of existence. Other works by Maine de Biran include *Mémoire sur la décomposition de la pensée* (*Memoir on the Decomposition of Thought*, 1805), *Considérations sur les rapports du physique et du moral* (*Considerations on the Relationships between the Physical and the Moral*, 1811), *Les Perceptions obscures* (*Obscure Perceptions*, 1807–1810), and a richly introspective *Journal intime* (*Intimate Journal*, 2 vols., 1927, posthumous).

MAL DU SIECLE is a term that describes a sentiment of melancholy, worry, agitation ("mal"), which arose in the early nineteenth century ("du siècle") in the hearts and minds of the young, who felt deceived by the promises of the Revolution and disappointed in the Empire. It was expressed in the "vague des passions" ("wave of passions") of Chateaubriand's* *Génie du Christianisme**; the boredom, despair, inactivity of René,* Adolphe,* and Obermann.* The early romantic felt a vague sense of powerlessness and doubt against the dichotomy he perceived between the enormity of his hopes and passions and the emptiness of his world. Hypersensitive and superior, he sought resolve in love, nature, God, the infinite, and usually failed, turning more inward and feeling more disenfranchised, disenchanted, bored, melancholy, and sick. He felt distinguished by his hypersensitivity and convinced of his superiority, despite his incurable sadness. Chateaubriand found release in religion; Hugo* and Balzac,* in literature. For others, Lamartine,* Constant,* Sand,* and Michelet,* social and political involvement provided a remedy. The sentiment of mal du siècle pervades the literature of the romantics from *René* on and culminates in the tormented spleen baudelairien.**

MALESHERBES, CHRETIEN GUILLAUME DE LAMOIGNON (1721–1794), the tolerant and judicious director of the book trade from 1750 to 1763, during the storm of antigovernment and antireligious publications by the philosophes,* was minister and loyal defender of Louis XVI before the tribunal that ultimately guillotined them both. In keeping with family tradition, he became a lawyer and was appointed president of one of the tax courts of the Parisian parliament, a position purchased by his family. His father, as chancellor, entrusted him with the direction of the press, a duty that he fulfilled intelligently, balancing his desire for freedom of the press against the exigencies of the government. He wrote in his *Mémoire sur la liberté de la presse* (*Memoir on the Freedom of the Press*, published posthumously in 1809), "A man who only read those books which originally appeared with the express approval of the government, as prescribed by the law, would lag behind his contemporaries by almost a century." Thus, in a spirit of tolerance that became his hallmark, he granted publishing "privilèges" and "permissions" in the name of the king when possible, and "permissions tacites," when necessary, to foster the liberal exchange of ideas he believed was good for a society. He encouraged J.-J. Rousseau's* publication in Paris of *Emile** and saw to it that he was fairly paid. He communicated regularly with Diderot* and favored the continued publication of the *Encyclopédie** when, in 1752, the king's council threatened to revoke its license and the Jesuits wanted control of the enterprise.

Malesherbes entered politics in 1771 until his banishment to his estate at St. Lucie for criticizing Chancellor Maupeou's (1714–1792) system of justice. In 1775, as minister for Louis XVI, he worked to reform the prisons and the use of torture and to improve conditions for Protestants. Too radical for the queen and most of her courtiers, he was forced to resign nine months later. He returned briefly to the ministry in 1787, then repaired to Switzerland until asked, along with François Tronchet (1726–1806) and Romain Desèze (1748–1828), to defend the king. He then retired until his arrest, along with that of his family, in 1793. All were guillotined a year later.

Malesherbes wrote several scientific works, including *Observations sur Buffon et Daubenton* (*Observations on Buffon and Daubenton*, published 1798), and was elected to the Academy of Science and the French Academy.

For further information, see G. Kelly, "The Political Thought of Lamoignon de Malesherbes," *Political Theory* 7 (November 1979): 485–508; E. P. Shaw, "Censorship and subterfuge in 18th century France," in *Literature and History in the Age of Ideas* (Columbus: Ohio State University Press, 1975), 287–309.

MALLARME, STEPHANE (1842–1898). See *Dictionary of Modern French Literature, from Naturalism and Symbolism to Post-Modernism*.

MANON LESCAUT, fully titled *L'Histoire du chevalier des Grieux et de Manon Lescaut* (*The Story of The Chevalier des Grieux and of Manon Lescaut,* 1731), by abbé Prévost,* is the seventh volume of his larger novel, *Mémoires d'un homme de qualité qui s'est retiré du monde* (*Memories of a Man of Quality Who Has Retired from the World,* 1728–1731). This slim volume, which continues to be read, inspired the opera *Manon* by Jules Massenet (1842–1912) and ranks among the great love stories of all times.

The story, as told by Des Grieux to the Man of Quality, Mr. Renoncour, relates his all-consuming passion for Manon, from his first glimpse of her descending the coach in Amiens to their final moments as exiles in Louisiana. Des Grieux takes her to Paris in hopes of marriage, but the amoral coquette prefers money, pleasure, and her freedom above fidelity to her naive lover. She arranges his forced return to his father, who has him enter the seminary at Saint-Sulpice, where, as "abbé Des Grieux," he becomes a brilliant theologian. He appears completely cured of Manon until she appears in the seminary parlor one evening. Unable to resist her charms, Des Grieux flees with her to Chaillot. He learns to gamble and cheat to support Manon's taste for luxury. Both wind up in prison, escape, and are arrested again. This time Des Grieux's father has Manon deported to Louisiana with other women of loose morals. Des Grieux, unable to obtain her release, accompanies her. Though they wish to marry there, the governor has other plans; after a duel, Des Grieux, believing that he has killed the governor's son, escapes with Manon into the desert where she dies of exposure.

A masterpiece of passionate literature, according to Gustave Lanson (1857–1934), *Manon* presents a classic analysis of the ravages of emotion on a young man's soul and actions. Des Grieux sacrifices all—religion, family, morality, social status—for a coquette unworthy of his devotion. He is committed to an ideal of natural and perfect love. With Manon's feelings and motives largely unexplored, she assumes an aura of feminine mystique as the enigmatic and idealized object of Des Grieux's unfailing devotion. The plot is simple and unified, focusing on Des Grieux's social and moral conflict; the style is simple, the tone is somber. According to Robert Niklaus (*A Literary History of France, 1715–1789*, 1970), "the novel reads like a tragedy by Racine."

In focusing on the psychology of a sexual relationship, Manon belongs to the tradition begun with Madame de Lafayette's (1634–1693) *La Princesse de Clèves* (1678) and continued by Benjamin Constant's* *Adolphe*,* Fromentin's* *Dominique*,* and Gide's** *L'Ecole des femmes* (*School for Women*, 1929). Its autobiographical elements and emphasis on passion link it to Rousseau's* *La Nouvelle Héloïse** and the romanticism* of the nineteenth century.

For further information, see P. Brady, "Structuralist Perspectives in Criticism of Fiction," *Essays on "Manon Lescaut" and "La Vie de Marianne"* (Berne, Frankfurt, Las Vegas: P. Pang, 1978); J. R. Monty, "Narrative Ambiguity in *Manon Lescaut*," in *Enlightenment Studies in Honor of Lester G. Crocker*, A. Bingham and V. Topazio, eds. (Oxford: Voltaire Foundation, 1979), pp. 151–161; L. Rabine, "History, Ideology and Femininity in *Manon Lescaut*," *Stanford French Review* 5 (Spring 1981): 65–83; K. Ross, "The Narrative of Fascination: Pathos and Repetition in *Manon Lescaut*," *The Eighteenth Century* 24 (3) (Fall 1983): 199–210, P. Stewart, *Rereadings. Eight Early French Novels* (Birmingham, Ala.: Summa, 1984).

LE MARIAGE DE FIGARO OU LA FOLLE JOURNEE (*The Marriage of Figaro or The Crazy Day*, 1784), by Beaumarchais,* is a masterpiece of comedy, intrigue, and wit like its equally renowned predecessor, *Le Barbier de Séville.** The same spirit of playfulness and gaity prevails. However, this play is more complex, with added characters, a more complicated plot, and more pointed social satire. In a famous monologue (act 5, scene 3), Figaro attacks noblemen who "have troubled themselves only with being born"; earlier he jabs courtiers who know only how to "receive, take and ask" (act 2, scene 2) and politicians who "pretend not to know what they know and to know what they don't know" (act 3, scene 6). Judge Don Guzman Brid'oison, who cares more about "form" than fairness, is a caricature of Beaumarchais's enemy, counsellor Goëzman. The plot centers on Figaro's struggle with his master for the affections of the young and pretty Suzanne. His triumph over the count and the political and social satire of the work resulted in a ban on the play by Louis XVI for nearly three years. When finally publicly performed by the Comédie-Française, it enjoyed prodigious, enduring success. In 1786, Mozart transformed it into his opera, *Les Noces de Figaro*; in 1964, it entered the repertory of the Théâtre de France. Though Beaumarchais is generally not considered a revolutionary, his *Mariage de Figaro* echoed the political unrest of the day. It has been called revolutionary, a social and political vindication, a cry for a democracy of the spirit incarnate in Figaro. Louis Forestier, in his preface to the Nouveaux Classiques Larousse edition of the play, considers it the "last picture" of Beaumarchais's society and his age.

Three years have passed since the marriage of count Almaviva and Rosine in the *Barbier de Séville*. Figaro, now concierge of Almaviva's Spanish chateau, is about to marry Suzanne, Rosine's (now the countess) servant. Two obstacles, however, stand in his way. His most formidable opponent is the count, who has proven a wayward husband with a wandering eye, and plans to exercise his "droit du seigneur," his "right" as the seigneur, but only with her permission, on Suzanne's wedding day. The second obstacle is Figaro's agreement with Marceline, another servant, to repay a 10,000-franc loan or to marry her. Pretty and honest Suzanne reveals the count's intentions to the countess and Figaro, who plan to substitute Chérubin, a young page who adores the countess, for Suzanne in her garden rendezvous with the count. The count, sensing a conspiracy against him, enlists the help of Bazile, his lawyer, and Guzman Brid'oison, the judge, to effect Figaro's contract with Marceline. A turn of plot during the courtroom scene reveals that Figaro is Marceline's son by Bartholo and therefore cannot marry her; Suzanne offers to repay the debt with her dowry. The countess, meanwhile, has arranged to replace Suzanne herself in her rendezvous with the count; Figaro, believing himself duped by his beloved and ready for revenge, hides himself in the garden until he discerns what is happening. The countess succeeds in winning back her husband, and Figaro, triumphant, embarks on an honorable marriage.

For further information, see L. Las Gourgues, "*Le Mariage de Figaro:* Characters, Intrigue and Structure," *Australian Journal of French Studies* 16 (January–April 1979): 295–299; R. Niklaus, *Beaumarchais: Le Mariage de Figaro* (London: Grant and Cutler, 1983).

MARIVAUDAGE signifies not only the style of writing or conversing that characterized the love comedies of Marivaux,* but also an entire genre that is inextricably connected with the vision and genius of the eighteenth-century playwright. One definition of the term is found in *Larousse*: ''marivauder,'' the verb, means ''to imitate the style, the affectation of Marivaux; to make elegant, polite speeches [''galanteries raffinées''].'' More critical definitions appeared during Marivaux's lifetime: ''a strange mixture of subtle metaphysical and trivial locutions'' (La Harpe*); ''false badinage, formal and prolonged mischievousness, belabored and pretentious effervescence, finally, a sort of sprightly and pretty pedantism'' (Sainte-Beuve*).

Marivaudage is best understood in relation to Marivaux's vision of a fairylike realm inhabited by young and beautiful hearts free from the cares of the world who study their emotions and vent them in elegant conversations. Rather than mere ornamentation or affectation, the dialogue, as it reveals the minute workings of the human heart in its battle against the ''surprise'' of love, becomes the action of the play itself. Fredéric Deloffre, in his monumental study, *Marivaux et le marivaudage,* states that in this way the movement of the action is ''fractured to the point that not only each scene, but each reply, is a step forward. The action progresses, or rather evolves, by a series of infinitesimal, fortuitous word associations.''

Marivaux has been criticized for his excessive attention to detail; Voltaire* accused him of ''weighing flies' eggs in a spider web scale.'' However, Marivaux's playing with words and their shades of meaning is justified by his search for the truth in order to ''confess what one does not want to confess or to express what was previously inexpressible'' (Deloffre). In his quest, like Jean Baptiste Racine, he uncovered many of the mysteries of the human heart, and his influence can be seen in the theatre of Beaumarchais,* Musset,* and, in our century, in the drama of Giraudoux.**

For further information, see R. Aldington, ''Marivaux and Marivaudage,'' *The American Review* 216 (1922): 254–258; R. Girard, ''Marivaudage and Hypocrisy,'' *American Society Legion of Honor Magazine* 34 (1963): 163–174; A. Tilley, ''Marivaudage,'' *Modern Language Review,* 25 (1930): 60–77.

MARIVAUX, PIERRE CARLET DE CHAMBLAIN DE (1688–1763), best known for love comedies such as *Les Fausses confidences** and *Le Jeu de l'amour et du hasard,** also made his mark as a journalist and novelist with *La Vie de Marianne** and *Le Paysan parvenu.** Born in Paris, he spent his youth in Riom, where his father, of the lesser nobility, was director of the mint. He studied law in Paris and, along with Houdar de la Motte* and Fontenelle,* frequented the salon of Madame de Lambert (1647–1733), where he earned a reputation as a brilliant conversationalist. His predilection for literature surfaced early; he wrote his first comedy, *Le Père prudent et équitable* (*The Fair and Prudent Father,* 1709) while still a youth in Limoges. Several novels followed, *Les Effets surprenants de la sympathie* (*The Surprising Results of Affection,*

1713–1714), *Pharsamon* (written, 1714; published, 1736), *La Voiture embour-bée* (*The Stagecoach that Stuck in the Mud*, 1713), and travesties of the *Iliad* (1716) and of *Télémaque* (1714).

Marivaux's first articles appeared in the *Nouveau Mercure*, a publication partial to the moderns. "Lettres sur les habitants de Paris" ("Letters on the Inhabitants of Paris," 1717–1718) contained social and moral observations in the style of La Bruyère (1645–1696) and the French moralists; "Pensées sur différents sujets: sur la clarté du discours" ("Thoughts on Different Subjects: On the Clarity of Speech," 1719) defined his doctrine of suggestive rather than detailed writing and its effects on readers; "Cinq Lettres contenant une aven-ture" ("Five Letters Relating an Adventure," 1719–1720) recounted the follies of a coquette about to fall in love, a recurrent Marivaudian theme.

The bankruptcy of John Law's (1671–1729) financial system in 1720 con-sumed Marivaux's fortune as well as that of thousands of others and precipitated his turning to literature for a living. In 1721, he founded a periodical for moral observation, *Le Spectateur français* (*The French Spectator*), based on the *Spec-tator* of Joseph Addison (1672–1719) and Sir Richard Steele (1672–1729). Other journals he founded, none of which lasted very long (*Le Spectateur fran-çais* having the longest duration, 25 issues), include *L'Indigent Philosophe* (*The Indigent Philosopher*, 1727) and *Le Cabinet du philosophe* (*The Philosopher's Study*, 1734).

After an unsuccessful tragedy, *Annibal* (1720), Marivaux found his true voca-tion in the love comedy. His first, *L'Amour et la vérité* (*Love and Truth*, 1720), written in collaboration with the chevalier de Saint-Jory, like many of his later and better comedies, was not well received. It exists today as a fragment. His second comedy, *Arlequin poli par l'amour* (*Harlequin Polished by Love*, 1720), a pastoral fairy play, contains the germs of his later works. *La Surprise de l'amour* (*The Surprise of Love*, 1722), *La Double Inconstance* (*Two Cases of Infidelity*, 1723), *Le Prince travesti* (*The Prince in Disguise*, 1724), and *La Fausse Suivante* (*The False Servant*, 1724) continue his theme of love's awaken-ing in youth. The love comedies, all performed by the Italian troupe (see Théâtre Italien*), are known for their style "de jeu," of lightness, playfulness; their lively dialogues and tirades; their attitude of improvisation, disguise, coinci-dence, fantasy, and liberty, all of which were unheard of at the Théâtre National. They portray a world of surprise and chance where youth, beauty, and love triumph, a utopia where love eventually conquers all; they depict the warfare waged against love by the human heart, using hurt, denial, pride, and modesty as its weapons. The conflict of emotion and shades of feeling within Marivaux's characters surface in the dialogue of the play, resulting in a delicacy of ex-pression unique to the author, appropriately known as "Marivaudage."*

After 1725, Marivaux was attracted to the more prestigious Théâtre National and sought its approval as an established writer with two comedies written especially for it, *La Seconde Surprise de l'amour* (*The Second Surprise of Love*, 1727) and *Les Serments indiscrets* (*Oaths Too Rashly Taken*, 1732), both of which failed miserably. Once again, it was the Italians who were to perform what would become his masterworks, *Le Jeu de l'amour et du hasard* and *L'Heureux Stratagème* (*The Lucky Stratagem*, 1733) along with more original presentations intended to moralize, *L'Ile des esclaves* (*The Island of Slaves*, 1725), *L'Ile de la raison* (*The Island of Reason*, 1727), and *La Nouvelle Colonie* (*The New Colony*, 1729). He wrote mythological allegories, *Le Triomphe de Plutus* (*The Triumph of Plutus*, 1728) and *La Réunion des amours* (*Loves Reconciled*, 1731), which portray the evolution of mores and the power of money as well as love.

With *Le Petit-Maître corrigé* (*The Fop Reformed*), presented at the Théâtre National in 1734, Marivaux turned to themes other than love. A comedy of manners, it satirizes the ''petit-maître'' as a social type. *La Mère confidente* (*The Mother as a Confidante*, 1735) is a sentimental or bourgeois drama dealing with the conflict between generations and the financial requirements of marriage. *Le Legs* (*The Inheritance*, 1736), one of the most popular comedies performed at the Théâtre, is a light comedy without social or dramatic overtones. Finally, *Les Fausses Confidences* (*False Confessions*, 1737), written at the height of his career, restates the love theme of the earlier ''surprise comedies,'' yet adds the most daring, realistic portrayal of women in the eighteenth century.

From 1728 to 1741, Marivaux returned to the novel, writing *La Vie de Marianne* over a period of thirteen years and *Le Paysan parvenu* from 1735 to 1736. The two novels, his most successful, written as confessions and full of psychology, were never completed, although they inspired several imitations and false endings. Besides analyzing the shades of thought and feeling of Marianne and Jacob, both novels reflect the society of the time. In the first, Marianne is exposed to the perils of Paris; in the second, a peasant rises above them. However, the satire of Lesage* is lacking in these novels in which psychological realism and the truth and complexity of the human heart dominate.

Throughout his literary career, Marivaux frequented the salons; besides that of Madame de Lambert, he visited Madame de Tençin,* and later Madame du Deffand (1697–1780) and Madame Geoffrin (1699–1777). In 1742, with the assistance of Madame de Tençin, he was elected to the Academy, after which his literary output slowly subsided. *La Joie imprévue* (*Joy Unforeseen*, 1738), *Les Sincères* (*The Sincere Ones*, 1739), *L'Epreuve* (*The Test*, 1740), *La Commère* (*The Gossip*, 1741), *La Dispute* (*The Dispute*, 1744), and *Le Préjugé vaincu* (*Victory over Prejudice*, 1746) constitute his final dramatic works. He finished his days in relative obscurity under the watchful eye of Mademoiselle de Saint-Jean and died, nearly forgotten, in 1763.

Marivaux has been called the most original French dramatist of the eighteenth century, notably because of his departure from the classic tradition of Molière (1622–1673), which continued to dominate the theatre of the time. Farce, burlesque, and comic stock characters are absent in his work; neither the study of man's vices nor social reality takes precedence over his delicate treatment of love. He prided himself on his originality: ''I would rather be humbly seated on the last bench among the small troupe of original authors than proudly placed on the first line in the numerous stock of literary monkeys.''

If comparisons can be made at all, they are with Jean Baptiste Racine (1639–1699), who, like Marivaux, analyzed the complexities, the subtleties of love, especially within the feminine heart. Marivaux himself said, "I have searched within the human heart for all the different niches where love can hide when it is afraid to show itself; and the object of each of my comedies is to have it leave its niche." Yet he stops short of the intense passion, the tragic crises depicted by Racine. Marivaux's characters inhabit a pleasant fantasy world of gallantry and sensibility reminiscent of the paintings of Jean Antoine Watteau (1684–1721), a world where endings are always happy and real danger is always absent.

To his comedies Marivaux added a spirit of optimism and straightforward moralizing that resulted in his sophisticated style and dialogue. Although he was criticized by Voltaire* and others for his wit and esprit, the purity and lyricism of Marivaudage are unique to his age. Théophile Gautier* and Jules Lemaître (1853–1914) agree that "all of the poetry of the first half of the eighteenth century is in Marivaux."

Sadly, the complexity of Marivaux's works, his fine analyses of sentiment, and his grace and subtlety were not fully appreciated during his lifetime. The Italian troupe, which performed most of his works, was held in disregard, while the more prestigious Théâtre National performed them poorly. A century later, Musset* found in Marivaux a source for his plays, especially *On ne badine pas avec l'amour* (1834). In the twentieth century. Giraudoux** and Anouilh** once again uncovered the "paths of the human heart" as Marivaux had done two hundred years earlier.

For further information, see S. R. Baker, "Sentimental Feminism in Marivaux's *La Colonie*," in K. Hartigan, ed., *To Hold a Mirror to Nature: Dramatic Images and Reflections* (Washington, D.C.: University Press of America, 1982), 1–10; P. V. Conroy, "Marivaux's Feminist Polemic: *La Colonie*," *Eighteenth-Century Life* 6 (1) (October 1980): 43–66; D. J. Culpin, "Marivaux's Apology for Religion," *French Studies* 39 (January 1985): 31–42; R. J. Howells, "Marivaux and the 'fête': from Consuming to Narrating," *French Studies* 39 (April 1985): 152–165; P. Robinson, "Marivaux's Poetic Theatre of Love: Some Considerations of Genre," *Studies on Voltaire and the Eighteenth Century* 199 (1981): 7–24; F. Sturzer, "Exclusion and Coquetterie: First-Person Narrative in Marivaux's *L'Indigent Philosophe*," *French Review* 55 (4) (March 1982): 471–477; J. Whatley, "Nun's Stories: Marivaux and Diderot," *Diderot Studies* 20 (1981): 299–319.

MARMONTEL, JEAN-FRANÇOIS (1723–1799), eighteenth-century moralist, philosopher, and man of letters best known for his memoirs, was born of modest parents in Limousin. He studied with the Jesuits at Mauriac, taught at Jesuit institutions in Clermont and Toulouse, and, with Voltaire's* encouragement and assistance, came to Paris in 1745 to pursue a literary career. He tried his hand at tragedy (*Denis le tyran*, [*Dennis the Tyrant*, 1748]; *Aristomène*, 1749; *Cléopatre*, 1750; *Les Hérachides*, 1752; *Egyptus*, 1753), poetry, and comic opera (*Le Huron*, 1768; *Zémir et Azor*, 1771), all of which are generally considered tiresome and artificial today, but gained the attention of Madame de

Pompadour (1721–1764), Quesnay,* and the poet François-Joachim de Bernis (1715–1794). He frequented the salons of Madame de Tençin* and Madame Geoffrin (1699–1777), associated with Diderot* and d'Alembert,* and contributed literary articles to the *Encyclopédie.**

Marmontel achieved extraordinary success with his *Contes moraux* (*Moral Tales*), short moral stories of about forty pages in length, first published in the *Mercure de France* and printed as a collection in 1761. Written in the moralist tradition La Fontaine (1621–1695) employed a century earlier to entertain and instruct, they addressed issues clearly stated in an introduction and commentary by the author—wicked books in "Le Scrupule" ("The Scruple"), the dangers of the world in "Les Deux Infortunées" ("The Two Unfortunate Ones"), man's vanity in "Le Philosophe soi-disant" ("The Would-Be Philosopher"), and his infidelity in "Le Bon Mari" ("The Good Husband"). Marmontel wrote that the *Contes moraux* attempted "to paint either the manners of society or the sentiments of nature." Besides rendering a charming picture of French society under the reign of Louis XV, the contes taught prudence, moderation, respect for others and for solitude. By 1830, they had seen 110 editions, were produced on stage, translated into several languages, and had inspired imitations in prose and in verse by Bricaire de la Dixmerie, Madame Leprince de Beaumont (1711–1780), Berquin,* and Madame de Genlis (1746–1830).

Marmontel was appointed editor of *Le Mercure* in 1758. He published an academic *Poétique française* (*French Poetiques,* 1763) and two philosophical novels. *Bélisaire* (1767), relating the tale of the famous captain, unjustly blinded and reduced to misery by Justinian, who eventually recognizes his innocence, is remembered primarily for a chapter on tolerance that led to its condemnation by the Sorbonne and the archbishop of Paris. *Les Incas ou La Destruction de l'empire de Pérou* (*The Incas, or The Destruction of the Peruvian Empire,* 1773) constitutes a philosophical retort to the clerics, relating in two volumes the horrors of the Spanish conquest of Mexico, especially the religious fanaticism of the Roman Catholic invaders.

Further accolades followed, including election to the French Academy in 1763, of which he became perpetual secretary twenty years later. In 1771, Marmontel was named king's historiographer. At the age of fifty-six, he married Morellet's* niece, becoming a model husband and father. During the Revolution he retired to the countryside with his family, where he died in 1799.

Marmontel's many contributions to the *Encyclopédie* appeared collectively in a six-volume *Eléments de littérature* (*Elements of Literature,* 1787); he wrote a history of the regency of Philip of Orleans a year later. His masterpiece, however, is his *Mémoires,* written while in retreat in the country, which graciously evoke his youth, the encyclopedists, salon society, and literary and artistic life of the eighteenth century.

For further information, see A. Boime, "Marmontel's *Bélisaire* and the Pre-Revolutionary Progressivism of David," *Art History* 3 (March 1980): 81–101; M. Cardy, "The Literary Doctrines of Jean-François Marmontel," *Studies on Voltaire and the Eighteenth Century* 210 (1982): 1–182.

MARTIN, HENRI (1810–1883), historian strongly influenced by Thierry,* his chief work is a *Histoire de la France* (*History of France*), written from 1834 to 1836 and completed from 1837 to 1854. The work contains nineteen volumes which are generally considered well documented, impartial, and patriotic. It emphasized the Celtic influence in French history.

LES MARTYRS (*The Martyrs,* 1809), by Chateaubriand,* a prose epic in twenty-four cantos, exemplifies the superiority of Christianity over paganism as a literary force. Chateaubriand states in the preface, "I advanced in a previous work [*Le Génie du Christianisme**]* that the Christian religion seemed more favorable to me than paganism in the development of the characters and in the play of the passions in epic poetry. I said again that the 'marvelous' ("merveilleux") of this religion could perhaps compete against the 'merveilleux' borrowed from mythology. It is these opinions, which have been more or less contended, that I wish to support with an example."

The story takes place in Messina during Diocletian's third century persecution of the Christians. A young pagan girl, Cymodocée, daughter of Démodocus, is lost in the woods after a religious festival. She discovers Eudore, a young Greek Christian, asleep near a spring. He takes her home. When she and her father come to thank him the next day, he tells them the story of his life. At sixteen, he was taken hostage to Rome where he lost his religion in a life of debauchery with his friends Constantine (later the first Christian Roman emperor), Jérome and Augustin (before their conversions). He fought the Francs, was taken prisoner, was liberated, travelled to England, became governor of the ancient northwestern French region known as Armorica, and finally returned to Greece and resumed his religion. Cymodocée falls in love with Eudore and converts to Christianity to marry him. God, however, decides to sacrifice Eudore, in order to save the Christians who have become too weak. Diocletian begins the persecution; Eudore is arrested. Cymodocée, declaring herself a Christian, is also arrested, and dies with him in the lions' den.

Chateaubriand considered Christianity, with its morality, sacrifice, and ceremony, a rich source for poetry. However, *Les Martyrs* is a poor illustration of its thesis. When first written, critics denounced its mixing of paganism and Christianity, poetry and prose. Today, its plot, with divine and diabolic intervention, is considered contrived; its characters, superficial reincarnations of his "sylphe," his ideal woman, and himself; his style, coldly classical and occasionally tedious. However, at times *Les Martyrs* achieves vivid historical tableaux based on solid research and firsthand knowledge, which inspired Augustin Thierry's* love of history and future vocation. Like his other works, *Les Martyrs* abounds in lyricism, sensitivity, and beauty, the stamp of the romantic soul.

MATEO FALCONE (1829), by Mérimée,* a short tale of Corsican honor, along with *Colomba** and *Carmen,** is one of his best-known works and established his reputation as a writer. It first appeared in the *Revue de Paris* and was later included in *Mosaïque* (1833), Mérimée's first collection of stories. Its concision, careful composition, and characterizations sustain an emotional impact and energy throughout the narration. Mérimée captured the essence of Corsica, its primitivism, its customs and people, without having visited it, relying solely on secondary sources. It met with immediate success and later influenced realists Daudet** and Maupassant.** It endures today as a beautifully rendered tragic tale of classic simplicity and stark realism.*

The story begins with a short description of the "maquis" of Porto-vecchio whose rocks and ravines shelter Corsican bandits and shepherds. Nearby lives the shepherd Mateo Falcone, a "good friend as well as a dangerous enemy," whose ten-year-old son, Fortunato, is the "hope of the family." One autumn day, while Mateo and his wife are away, Fortunato hides and later betrays, for a gold watch, a bandit pursued by the local authorities. When Mateo returns and learns what his son has done, he takes his young life in payment. "This child is the first of his race to commit treason," he declares before shooting him in the name of justice.

For further information, see J. Hamilton, "Pagan Ritual and Human Sacrifice in Mérimée's *Mateo Falcone*," *French Review* 55 (1) (October 1981): 52–59.

MAUPASSANT, GUY DE (1850–1893). See *Dictionary of Modern French Literature, from Naturalism and Symbolism to Post-Modernism.*

MAUPERTUIS, PIERRE-LOUIS MOREAU DE (1698–1759), mathematician, astronomer, and scientific theorist, spent five years in the army as a musketeer before turning, at age twenty-five, to a career in math and science. He studied Newtonian physics, entered the Academy of Science in 1731, and published a *Discours sur les différentes figures des astres* (*Discourse on the Different Shapes of Stars*, 1732) in favor of Isaac Newton's (1642–1727) astronomy. In 1736, he was invited by the Academy to direct a scientific expedition to Lapland to measure the length of a degree of a meridian within the polar circle and thus establish the shape of the earth. Upon his return a year later he was welcomed into nearly all of the scientific societies of Europe. He visited Prussia in 1740 and was taken prisoner by the Austrians during the battle of Mollwitz. He returned to Paris, where he was named director of the Academy of Science in 1742. The following year he was elected to the French Academy. In 1746, he accepted the presidency of the Berlin Academy, joining Voltaire* and La Mettrie* in the "enlightened" court of Frederick the Great (1712–1786).

Maupertuis proffered his theories of genetics in *Vénus physique* (*Venus Physics,* 1745) and *Essai sur la formation des corps organisés* (*Essay on the Formation of Organic Bodies,* 1754). In Berlin he turned to epistemology and metaphysics in *Essai de cosmologie* (*Essay on Cosmology,* 1750) and *Recherches philosophiques sur l'origine des langues et la signification des mots* (*Philosophical Research on the Origin of Languages and the Significance of Words,* 1748). His *Essai de philosophie morale* (*Essay on Moral Philosophy,* 1749) addresses the question of morality.

Maupertuis's theory of the attraction between "maternal" and "paternal" molecules influenced the materialism of Diderot's* *Pensées sur l'interprétation de la nature* (*Thoughts on the Interpretation of Nature,* 1754) and led to Diderot's theories of evolution and transformation of the species. Though Maupertuis led the Berlin Academy to the height of its brilliance, his arrogance and querulousness earned him the enmity of Samuel Koenig (1712–1757), the mathematician, and of his former friend, Voltaire, who ridiculed him in *Diatribe sur Docteur Akakia* (1752) (resulting in Voltaire's arrest by Frederick) and in *Micromégas.** Maupertuis died lonely and discredited in Basel.

LES MEDITATIONS POETIQUES (*Poetical Meditations,* 1820), by Lamartine,* a slim volume of twenty-four lyric, intimate, evocative poems, reflected the emotions of the early nineteenth century and, after J.-J. Rousseau's* and Chateaubriand's* initial thrust, ushered in the age of romanticism.* The poems, largely inspired by his love for Julie Charles, mirror Lamartine's soul—his memories of his beloved, his remorse at her death, his awareness of the temporality and fragility of existence, his aspirations for the eternal—and the consolation he found in nature.

The best known of the poems depict his love and loneliness. "L'Isolement" ("Isolation") opens the collection with the loss that Lamartine felt upon the death of Madame Charles in 1817. "Un seul être vous manque, et tout est dépeuplé" ("One being is gone, and all is emptiness") crystallizes in one very poignant verse the depth of his emotional void. "Le Lac" ("The Lake") foreshadows his impending sorrow. With Madame Charles near Paris, extremely ill, Lamartine explores his powerlessness before the incessant march of time, the transience of life. "O temps, suspends ton vol!" ("O time, suspend your flight!") he cries in desperation and appeals to the fir trees and rocks surrounding Lake Bourget to guard the memory of their love. Nature, for Lamartine, provided solace, "silence" and "peace." In "Le Vallon" ("The Valley") he asks for "the 'shelter' of a day to wait for death." Several poems, "La Foi" (Faith), "La Semaine sainte" ("Holy Week"), "Le Chrétien mourant" ("The Dying Christian"), "Dieu" ("God"), "La Providence à l'homme" ("Providence to Man"), and "La Prière" ("The Prayer") express his religious beliefs. "L'Homme" ("Man"), addressed to Lord Byron, reproaches him for his skepticism and pride, his refusal to acknowledge the "truth" of his "divine slavery" to God.

A volume of *Nouvelles Méditations* (*New Meditations*) followed in 1823 containing 26 poems; however, with few exceptions—"Ischia," "Le Crucifix" ("The Crucifix")—they lack the originality of the first. The *Méditations* are landmarks of lyric poetry. Their music and imagery give rise to an ethereal quality, masking reality as gossamer mists rising from Lake Bourget, revealing glimpses of the illusive and intangible essence of Lamartine's soul and of poetry itself. His debt to Rousseau and Chateaubriand is evident as he carries the torch of romanticism into the nineteenth century.

For further information, see S. Godfrey, "Foules Rush In: Lamartine, Baudelaire and the Crowd," *Romance Notes* 24 (1) (Fall 1983): 33–42.

MEILHAC, HENRI (1831–1897), comic playwright and opera librettist, collaborated with Halévy* for more than twenty years. He worked for a bookseller and contributed to journals such as *Journal pour rire* (*Journal of Laughter*) and *La Vie parisienne* (*Parisian Life*). With Halévy, he produced a number of comedies including *Fanny Léart* (1868), *Froufrou* (1869), *Tricoche et Cacolet* (1873), and comic opera librettos to the music of Jacques Offenbach (1819–1880) such as the masterful *La Belle Hélène* (*Beautiful Helen*, 1865), a parody of the Trojan War, and *La Vie parisienne* (*Parisian Life*, 1866). He collaborated with others on some works and wrote alone comic operas *Mam'zelle Nitouche* (1883), *Manon* (1884), and *Rip* (1884). He entered the Academy in 1884.

MEMOIRES D'OUTRE-TOMBE (*Memoirs from Beyond the Grave*, 1848–1850), by Chateaubriand,* is the story of his life and times and a valuable source for the impressions of an impoverished aristocrat trying to seek his fortune in the face of political turbulence and personal uncertainty. Though it met with a chilly reception, it is now generally considered his greatest work. Opinions vary, but most agree that he conceived the idea for his memoirs in 1803, wrote sporadically from 1811 until 1826, dedicated himself to them upon his retirement from politics in 1833, finished in 1841, and continually revised them the remaining seven years of his life. Chateaubriand originally intended to publish his memoirs fifty years after his death; hence the title. However, he maintained a keen public interest on his progress by giving readings at Madame Récamier's (1777–1849) salon and publishing excerpts in the press. Out of necessity, in 1836 he sold publishing rights to Société Sala, which in turn sold rights to a daily paper, *La Presse,* to publish the work in serial form. Chateaubriand protested against the mutilation of his work, but little more than three months after his death, the first installment appeared and continued until 1850. The first edition appeared in 1849–1850 by Penaud frères. The number of revisions and corrected manuscripts gave rise to a number of editions: one by Lenormand in 1874 and another by Biré, in 1936. A definitive edition, culled from all known manuscripts, was published in 1948 by Maurice Levaillant. The sole existing manuscript, dating from 1847, was found in 1930.

Chateaubriand divided his memoirs into four parts corresponding with the stages of his life. Part 1 covers his youth and career as a soldier and traveller, beginning with descriptions of his father and mother, his birth and family history and continuing through his military service and years in exile. He describes his student life, his years at Combourg, his ''dungeon''; his favorite sister, Lucile; the first stirrings of his ''muse''; his ''sylphide,'' the phantom woman of his imagination whom he created from all the women he had seen and who transformed herself into various identities that he adored. His love of solitude, his timidity before the king, the outbreak of the Revolution, his voyage to America, his return to France and subsequent marriage fill the remaining books of part 1. Part 2 comprises his literary career, beginning with his return to France in 1800, the publication of the *Génie du Christianisme,* *Atala,* and *René.* It relates his meeting with Napoleon, his nomination and subsequent dismissal as secretary to the embassy in Rome, his travels to Jerusalem, the publication of *Les Martyrs*,* and his election to the Academy. His political career, that of Napoleon, the Bourbons, and the July revolution fill part 3. Part 4 relates his final career, a "mélange" of the previous ones—traveller, writer, and politician—his withdrawal from public life, his continuing pecuniary difficulties, the cholera outbreak in Paris in 1832, his unfruitful support of Charles X and the legitimate monarchy, his pessimistic assessment of present and future society. The *Mémoires* end in a reaffirmation of his Christian faith. "All I must do is seat myself on the edge of my grave," he writes. "Then I will descend bravely, a crucifix in my hand, into Eternity."

Chateaubriand's *Mémoires* have been praised for their beauty and lyricism, their ardor and temerity, for their revelation of the true René, their creation of a new one. His story is intertwined with that of his times; to read the one is to know the other through the optic of Chateaubriand's pride and sensitivity. Along with the nation's history, portraits—of Mesdames de Beaumont, de Duras, Récamier; Mirabeau,* Danton,* Charles Talleyrand; Louis XVIII, Charles X, Louis-Philippe, and Napoleon—abound. The work has been criticized for its subjectivity, its omissions and fabrication of the truth. It remains, however, a monument to the man and his imagination.

For further information, see L. Porter, "Chateaubriand's Revenge on History in the *Mémoires d'outre-tombe*," *Symposium* 35 (3) (Fall 1981): 267–280.

MENARD, LOUIS (1822–1901), early Parnassian* poet and scholar whose interest in Hellenism influenced Leconte de Lisle* and the direction of their newly forming school of poetry. He attended the Ecole Normale in 1842, brought out his first work, *Prométhée délivrée* (*Prometheus Freed*, 1844) under a pseudonym, practiced chemistry, and participated in the 1848 revolution. An ardent republican, his *Prologue d'une révolution* (*Prologue of a Revolution*), published in Proudhon's* *Le Peuple* (*The People*) in 1848–1849, earned him fifteen months in prison. On his release, he travelled to Brussels and London, where he met Karl Marx (1818–1883) and Friedrich Engels (1820–1895) and wrote more political pieces. He returned to France in 1852, studied ancient religions, and published *Poèmes* (1855), about ancient Greece. In 1860, he wrote a doctoral thesis, *La Morale avant les philosophes* (*Morality before the Philosophes*) and published a work on the religious philosophy he practiced, *Le Polythéisme hellénique* (*Hellenic Polytheism*, 1863). He found in polytheism a social and moral guide, a union of order and liberty in which reason, imagination, art, religion, and politics could flourish. His best-known work is *Rêveries d'un païen mystique* (*Reveries of a Mystical Pagan*, 1876), written in the manner of Diderot.*

Like his brother, René, with whom he wrote *De la sculpture antique et moderne* (*On Ancient and Modern Sculpture*, 1868) and *Le Musée de peinture et de sculpture* (*The Museum of Painting and Sculpture*, 1872), he was a painter.

He spent his last years as a professor at the Ecole des Arts Decoratifs in 1887 and taught universal history at the Hôtel de Ville in 1895. He published a number of histories, including works on the Orient (1882), the Israelites (1883), the Greeks (1884), Christianity (1894), and ancient and modern religions (1895).

MENDES, CATULLE (1843–1909), minor Parnassian* poet, also a novelist, playwright, and historian, helped found the Parnassian movement. He was born in Bordeaux, where his grandfather was a banker. His family travelled a great deal on business matters, settling in Paris in 1850. At eighteen, he founded the short-lived *Revue fantaisiste* (*Revue of Fantasy*), whose contributors included Daudet,** Banville,* and Baudelaire.** He admired Gautier* and married his second daughter, Judith (1846–1917), who became a writer in her own right. Mendès died in 1909, the victim of a train mishap in the gare Saint-Germaine.

His poetry was published in *Le Parnasse contemporain* (*The Contemporary Parnassian*) and in his own collections, *Poésies* (1876 and 1892), *Poésies nouvelles* (*New Poetry,* 1893), and *Choix de poésies* (*Choice Poems,* posthumous, 1925). His novels include *La Vie et la mort d'un clown* (*The Life and Death of a Clown,* 1879) and *Les Mères ennemies* (*Enemy Mothers,* 1880). Though his literary influence declined after 1876, he left two treatises, *Légende du Parnasse contemporain* (*Legend of the Contemporary Parnassian,* 1884) and *Rapport sur le mouvement poétique français* (*Report on the French Poetic Movement,* 1902), which are still read.

For further information, see N. Haxell, "The Rondeaux Parisiens of Catulle Mendès: Prose Poems Ancient and Modern," *Parnasse* 3 (1982): 21–35.

MERCIER, LOUIS-SEBASTIEN (1740–1814), prolific writer in all genres, notably drame,* helped prepare the way for the romantics (see romanticism*). The son of Parisian merchants, he attempted and soon abandoned poetry; he taught rhetoric at the Collège de Bordeaux; he wrote imitations of English and German drame. His *Essai sur l'art dramatique* (*Essay on Dramatic Art,* 1773) attacked the classics—Homer (8th century B.C.), Plautus (254?-184 B.C.), Jean Baptiste Racine (1639–1699), and Nicolas Boileau (1636–1711) and enlarged Diderot's* conception of drame, insisting that it "sing for virtue" and mold the citizenry in the national interest. Five years later his *Nouvel Examen de la tragédie française* (*New Examination of French Tragedy,* 1778) defined modern theatre in terms of truth and timeliness. He wrote thirty-one plays, including patriotic drama—*Jean Hennuyer* (1772), *La Destruction de la Ligue* (*The Destruction of the League,* 1782)—and bourgeois drama in the manner of Diderot—*Jenneval* (1769), *Le Déserteur* (*The Deserter,* 1770), *L'Indigent* (*The Indigent,* 1772), *Le Juge* (*The Judge,* 1774), *Natalie* (1775), and *La Brouette du vinaigrier* (*The Vinegar-Maker's Wheelbarrow,* 1787). Though they wallow in emotionalism and moralizing, the dramas were well received by the public.

Mercier proposed utopian political reforms in *L'An 2440 ou Reve s'il en fut jamais* (*The Year 2440 or A Dream if Ever There Was One,* 1770) and published a dictionary of neologisms (1801) introducing 3,000 new words to the French. Politically, he supported the Girondins but became reactionary and unsupportive of any government or authority. Mercier's most significant contribution to his age and ours is his twelve-volume *Tableau de Paris* (*Panorama of Paris,* 1781– 1788), a loosely organized collection of anecdotes and impressions of the social, political, and moral life of the capital, for which he was forced to flee to Switzerland. After the Revolution, he held a chair in history at the Ecole Centrale and was admitted to the newly founded Institute of France.

For further information, see B. Fink, ''Utopian Nurtures'' [Fenelon, Mercier, Morelly, Sade], in *Transactions of the Fifth International Congress on the Enlightenment,* vol. 2 (Oxford: Taylor Institution, 1981), 664–671.

MERIMEE, PROSPER (1803–1870), master of the short story whose literary fame rests on such tales as *Mateo Falcone,** *Colomba,** and *Carmen,** was also a historian and archeologist responsible for the preservation of many of France's historical monuments. He was born to cultivated, wealthy Parisian parents who exposed him at an early age to the value of art. His father was a painter and professor of art. His mother painted portraits, chiefly of small children; the granddaughter of Madame Leprince de Beaumont (1711–1780) who wrote *Beauty and the Beast* and other fairy tales, she was also a talented storyteller. Both of Mérimée's parents were agnostics, and he remained a nonbeliever throughout his life. An only child, Mérimée was solitary and timid and had no friends. At eight, he entered the Lycée Napoléon, later known as Collège Henri IV. At seventeen, he entered law school, where he showed a predilection for linguistics, philology, and, with his friend Jean-Jacques Ampère, son of the renowned physicist and mathematician, learned Spanish and read Ossian (3d-century Gaelic bard) and Lord Byron (1788–1824). He graduated in 1823. The previous summer, he met Stendhal,* twenty years his senior and recently returned to Paris from an extended stay in Italy, and embarked on a friendship that would endure the rest of Stendhal's life. Like Stendhal, Mérimée disliked the bourgeoisie and distrusted religion. He frequented the salons of the early 1820s, where he met middle-class liberals and associated with the young romantics, without committing himself too deeply. Mérimée's first literary attempt was a life of *Cromwell* (1822), very à la mode with the romantics, Balzac* having written a *Cromwell* in verse in 1819. Hugo* would have his turn in 1827. Mérimée's *Cromwell* is significant as an early application of his friend Stendhal's literary theories of *Racine and Shakespeare* (1823, 1825).

Early on, Mérimée developed an interest in the language and cultures of other lands. He spoke English fluently, had many English friends, and was well-versed in English history and literature. He loved Spain, publishing in *Le Globe,** in 1824 four articles on Spanish theatre. *Le Théâtre de Clara Gazul* (*The Theatre of Clara Gazul,* 1825), a collection of six plays attributed to a mythical Spanish actress and translated by ''Joseph l'Estrange,'' followed a year later. Her portrait on the frontispiece was actually Mérimée disguised in a Spanish mantilla. The

prologue to the collection again takes up the defense of French romanticism.*
Two years later, Mérimée worked a more successful hoax, *La Guzla* (an anagram
of Gazul), a supposed translation of Illyrian folk songs gathered in the Balkans,
which fooled many Slavic scholars. Aleksander Pushkin (1799–1837) actually
translated the work into Russian. The ballads sing of primitive Serbian customs
and folklore, offering realistic, dramatic tales of vengeance, courage, patriotism,
superstition, domestic life, bandits, mountaineers, and boatmen. Mérimée turned
to the Middle Ages with *La Jacquerie* (1828), the story of a medieval peasant
rebellion written in dialogue form, then back to Spain with a one-act melodrama,
La Famille de Carvajal (*The Carvajal Family*, 1828). He wrote a historical novel
in the vein of Vigny's* *Cinq-Mars* and Hugo's *Notre-Dame de Paris*.* *Chronique du règne de Charles IX* (*Chronicle of the Reign of Charles IX*, 1829) depicts
the political tension between the Huguenots and Catholics on the eve of the Saint
Bartholomew's massacre and reveals a coolness and restraint as well as a preference for detail that would become a hallmark of Mérimée's later stories and
novellas.

In 1829, Mérimée wrote three additional ballads for *La Guzla* and two plays
set in South America, *L'Occasion* (*The Occasion*) and *Le Carrosse du Saint-
Sacrement* (*The Carriage of the Holy Sacrament*), and most of the short stories
later published in his collection, *Mosaïque* (1833). *Mateo Falcone* (1829), a
brief, poignant, realistic tale of psychological skill and classical restraint, established his reputation in this genre. *Vision de Charles XI* (*The Vision of Charles
XI*) is a hallucinating tale of mystery and realism that depicts the horrific, prophetic vision witnessed by the king of Sweden and Norway. *L'Enlèvement de la
redoute* (*The Capture of the Redoubt, or Stronghold*) tells of the heroism and
pain of military assault. *Tamango*, about a slave revolt, reveals the cruelty and
injustice of the slave trade. In a lighter vein, *Federigo* is the irreverent tale of a
dissolute young lord granted three wishes by Jesus Christ. *Le Vase étrusque* (*The
Etruscan Vase*, 1830) details the tortured passions of a jealous lover. *La Partie
de trictrac* (*The Backgammon Game*, 1830) is also a study of passion.

Mérimée visited Spain in 1830, where he haunted museums, met gypsies and
bullfighters, and befriended the de Teba family (later known as Montijo), whose
daughter Eugénia (1826–1920), as the wife of Napoleon III (1808–1873), became
empress of the French. Upon his return, delayed partly by the July revolution,
Mérimée served in the National Guard, where he met Alexandre Dumas père.*
With the ascension of Louis-Philippe (1773–1850), Mérimée entered the civil
service in 1831 as secretary to a friend of Stendhal, the Count d'Argout. A
conscientious worker, he rose rapidly within the ranks, achieving, in 1834, the
position of inspector general of historical monuments. Along the way, he found
time to enjoy the company of Eugène Delacroix (1799–1863), Musset,* Stendhal,
and a number of mistresses and love interests. For the next eighteen years, he
devoted himself to the restoration of churches, abbeys, and structures throughout
France. After a period of unproductive dissipation, he brought forth two novellas,
La Double Méprise (*The Double Misunderstanding*, 1833), which divides critics

as to its merit, and *Les Ames du purgatoire* (*The Souls of Purgatory*, 1834), a modernized version of the Don Juan legend. In 1836, he entered a liaison with Madame Delessert, an intelligent, seductive woman portrayed as Madame Grandet in Stendhal's *Lucien Leuwen*.* Until 1846, he wrote most of his stories for her, including *Colomba,* and revised them according to her criticisms. *La Vénus d'Ille* (*The Venus of Ille,* 1837), about a statue that slays a man, deals with the fantastic, a theme which Mérimée took up again in one of his last stories, *Lokis* (1868).

In 1839, a visit to Corsica acquainted Mérimée with the habits and nature of these people as well as with an elderly manufacturer of cartridges who, along with her daughter, served as the basis for *Colomba.* Upon his return, Mérimée published *Notes de mon voyage en Corse* (*Notes from my Travel to Corsica,* 1840) and *Colomba* (1840), a long short story that appeared in the *Revue des deux mondes.* With a biography of Julius Caesar in view, he published two works, *Essai sur la guerre sociale* (*Essay on Social War,* 1841) and *La Conjuration de Catalina* (*The Conspiracy of Catalina,* 1843), about Caesar's early political career. Both volumes appeared as *Etudes sur l'histoire romaine* (*Studies on Roman History*), but the proposed third volume of the series, on the life of the Roman emperor, was never finished. In 1842, Mérimée's longtime friend, Stendhal, died. The following year, he submitted his candidature to the Académie des Inscriptions, which he entered in 1843. The day after his election to the French Academy in 1844, *Arsène Guillot,* about a courtesan, shocked the readers of the *Revue des deux mondes.* In 1845, *Carmen* was published by that same journal. *L'Abbé Aubain,* Merimee's last work of fiction for twenty years, appeared in the *Constitutionnel* in 1846.

He turned to the study of archeology, history, and translation. He wrote a meticulous *Histoire de Don Pédre I* (1847) and then embarked on a study of Russian literature and history, which would fill the next twenty years. He translated Pushkin's *La Dame de pique* (*The Queen of Spades,* 1849) and his prose poems, *Les Bohémiens* (*The Bohemians,* 1851) and *Le Hussard* (*The Hussard,* 1851), and published a long study of Russian novelist and dramatist Nikolai Gogol (1809–1852) for the *Revue des deux mondes;* he translated other Gogol works in 1853 and wrote *Les Cosaques d'autrefois* (*Cossacks from Long Ago,* 1865). He wrote two works about an impostor of the son of Ivan IV (1533–1584, known as "the Terrible"), *Les Débuts d'un aventurier* (*The Beginnings of an Adventurer,* 1852) and *Les Faux Démétrius* (*The False Demetriuses,* 1853), and met Russian novelist Ivan Turgenev (1818–1883) in 1857.

With Napoleon III at the helm of the Second Empire and married to Eugénie Montijo, the daughter of Mérimée's longtime Spanish friends, Mérimée was named, in 1853, by imperial decree, senator of the Empire, a position that allowed him to continue his archeological interests and to write his last stories. He travelled to Spain, England, Bavaria, and Scotland, became a favorite at Napoleon's court, served as vice president to the Commission of Historical Monuments, and helped Napoleon establish the Imperial Library (now the Bibliothèque Nationale). In 1866, he attained the post of grand officer of the Legion of Honor. Mérimée spent his last years wintering in Cannes, where he studied biology and practiced archery. He died of old age in Cannes shortly before the war of 1870, and though a lifelong agnostic, was buried by a Protestant minister. The following year, all of his belongings were burned by the revolutionary Paris Commune because of his association with the Empire. Mérimée's last stories were published in 1873, including *La Chambre bleue* (*The Blue Room*), written in 1866 for the Empress.

Throughout his life, Mérimée was drawn to exotic lands such as Corsica and Spain and was fascinated by outlaws and bohemians, which he depicted in his stories. Like his spiritual brother Stendhal, Mérimée masked his romantic inclinations behind his intelligence and restraint. Mérimée's stories, as opposed to the grandiose, sweeping works of Hugo and Balzac, are renowned for their objectivity, concision, and reserve. Merimee shared Stendhal's gift of observation but went further in the use of irony. His prose is clean and clear, a distillation of the sobriety of the classics, the acuity of the realists, and the intensity of the romantics. The action and passions of his characters serve as a powerful undercurrent. Mérimée's stories are milestones in the evolution of romanticism toward realism,* leading the way for the master Flaubert.*

For further information, see P. Cogman, "The Brother and the Beast: Structure and Meaning of Mérimée's *La Jacquerie*," *French Studies* 36 (1) (January 1982): 26–36; H. Collingham, "Prosper Mérimée and Guglielmo Libri. An Account of Mérimée's Role in the Affaire Libri with Five Unpublished Letters," *French Studies* 35 (April 1981): 135–147; K. Crecelius, "Fictional History in Mérimée's *Chronique du règne de Charles IX*," *French Literature Series* 8 (1981): 31–42; Crecelius, "Mérimée's 'Federigo': From Folktale to Short Story," *Studies in Short Fiction* 19 (1) (Winter 1982): 57–63; T. Hunt, "'L'Ironie du regard': Mérimée's *Arsène Guillot*," *Forum for Modern Language Studies* 17 (4) (October 1981): 351–360; L. Porter, "The Subversion of the Narrator in Mérimée's *La Vénus d'Ille*," *Nineteenth Century French Studies* 10 (3–4) (Spring–Summer 1982): 268–277; T. Siebers, "Fantastic Lies: Lokis and the Victim of Coincidence," *Kentucky Romance Quarterly* 28 (1) (1981): 87–93; R. Stephens, "Cable's Bras Coupé and Mérimée's *Tamango:* The Case of the Missing Arm," *Mississippi Quarterly* 35 (4) (Fall 1982): 387–405.

MEROPE (1743), by Voltaire,* illustrates his belief that emotions other than romantic love are valid in tragedy and are capable of moving the audience. Inspired by Scipione Maffei's (1675–1755) Italian version of the Greek tale, which was presented in Paris in 1717, the play is considered the most classic of his tragedies and was a resounding popular success.

A triumph of maternal love and courage, the play centers on Mérope, queen of Messina, whose husband Cresphonte and two sons were assassinated fifteen years earlier. A third son, Egisthe, was saved by the faithful Narbas and raised without knowledge of his royal blood; Mérope, in turn, knows nothing of his fate and upon his secret return believes him to be responsible for her lost son's death. Meanwhile, the ambitious Polyphonte, the actual murderer, hopes to seal his claim to the throne by marrying Mérope and killing Egisthe, if he can find him.

Mérope unwillingly agrees to marry Polyphonte, if she may be permitted first to murder the young man she feels responsible for her son's death, though the virtuous woman actually plans to take her own life immediately thereafter. In the temple, as she is about to kill him, the old Narbas intervenes, revealing the captive's true identity. To save her son, Mérope agrees at last to marry Polyphonte, whom Egisthe slays before the wedding altar, thus avenging his father and brothers and restoring Messina to its rightful rulers.

MICHELET, JULES (1798–1874), professor, philosopher, historian, wrote a voluminous *Histoire de France* (*History of France*, 1833–1867), of which *Jeanne d'Arc** originally comprised two chapters. Born in Paris the son of a poor printer, Michelet was personally acquainted with poverty and want at a tender age. From 1810 until 1812, he worked in his father's shop until it was suppressed by imperial decree. His family sacrificed in order to educate him, a debt he repaid by reaching the head of his class. He entered Collège Charlemagne in 1812, attained his doctoral degree in 1819 and his aggregate, a highly valued degree which enabled him to teach, in 1821. As professor of history at Collège Sainte-Barbe from 1822 until 1827, he met Victor Cousin* in 1824 and Edgar Quinet* in 1825 and published a *Précis d'histoire moderne* (*Précis of Modern History*, 1827). From 1827 until 1833, Michelet was professor of history and philosophy at the Ecole Normale Supérieure and came under the influence of French historian and philosopher Cousin, German philosopher Johann Herder (1744–1803), and Italian philosopher Giambattista Vico (1668–1744), whose *Scienza nuova* (1725) he translated as *Principes de la philosophie de l'histoire* (*Principles of the Philosophy of History*, 1827). From Cousin came the idea of synthesizing the various events of human history into a logical system. Vico instilled the notion of man's ability to create himself, "Man is its own Prometheus." Herder's works confirmed Vico. From these three, Michelet formulated his own philosophy of history, that of "man's war against nature, of spirit against matter, of liberty against fatality," which he first expressed in his *Introduction à l'histoire universelle* (*Introduction to Universal History*, 1831) and illustrated a few months later in his first masterwork, *L'Histoire de la république romaine* (*History of the Roman Republic*, 1831).

After 1830, Michelet began teaching the history of the Middle Ages and modern history; he was also named head of the historical section of the National Archives. These two fortuitous events lèd to his most important work, the *Histoire de France* (*History of France*, vols. 1–6, 1833–1843; vols. 7–17, 1855–1867). Michelet projected that his history of France would require four to six years' work, not realizing, when he began in 1833, that it would require nearly forty. From 1834 to 1836, he took over Guizot's* chair at the Sorbonne. In 1838, he became professor of history and ethics at the Collège de France.

In 1843, Michelet entered the political arena. Disillusioned with the July monarchy and its unfairness toward the common man, the democratic and humanitarian Michelet expressed his bitterness in his teaching and writing. He blasted the church as a repressive force in *Les Jésuites* (1843), written with Quinet. *Le Peuple* (*The People*, 1846) pleaded the cause of the peasants and workers, demonstrated their virtues, and discussed the mission of an egalitarian and democratic France. In 1847, he set aside his *Histoire de France* for an *Histoire de la Révolution française* (*History of the French Revolution*, 1847–1853, 7 vols.), which provided ground for lambasting kings, clergy, and nobility. He applauded the revolution of 1848 but was suspended from his teaching post a year later. After refusing to support the Empire, he lost his chair at the Collège de France in 1851 and at the Archives in 1852.

After 1852, he turned from politics back to history with the remaining ten volumes of his *Histoire de France* (1855–1867). He also found his voice in personal writing. *L'Amour* (*Love*, 1858) treats the subject of love, especially love in marriage, which is the foundation of social life. *La Femme* (*Woman*, 1859) would limit women's work to the home. *Nos Fils* (*Our Sons*, 1869) deals with education. *La Bible de l'humanité* (*The Bible of Humanity*, 1864) exalts certain nations, "the sons of humanity," which have contributed social ideals such as the family (India), manhood (Greece), and heroism (Persia). He also found inspiration in nature. The tranquility of Nantes and Le Havre, which he visited in 1853 and 1856, respectively, are found in *L'Oiseau* (*The Bird*, 1856). In 1856 and 1857, visits to Switzerland brought forth *L'Insecte* (*The Insect*, 1857). The Atlantic and the Mediterranean inspired *La Mer* (*The Sea*, 1861) and the Alps, *La Montagne* (*The Mountain*, 1868). He had envisioned future volumes on the sky and the plants, as well as a history of the nineteenth century, of which he wrote three volumes before time expired for him. He died at Hyères in 1874.

Michelet formulated a philosophy of history that integrated politics, war, geography, religion, language, art, and literature into an explanation of French civilization and the development of mankind. He worked to "resurrect" the history of French liberty in all of its complexity and to understand its implications for the present and future struggle for freedom. He sought the symbolism of historic characters such as Joan of Arc, Saint Louis, Georges Danton, and Martin Luther, and institutions and artifacts such as gothic architecture and the salons. He considered France "a person," a moral entity; his *Histoire de France* studies the development of its soul, its passions, its struggle against tyranny, its pursuit of liberty. His starting point is France's geography, which, according to Michelet, is fundamental to the history of any people. "As is the nest, so is the bird. As is the country, so is the man," he wrote in his *Tableau de la France* (*Tableau of France*), at the beginning of volume two of the *Histoire de France*.

Michelet's work embodies the spirit of positivism* in its authenticity and documentation. As director of the Archives, Michelet had access to dossiers, charts, memoirs, registers, and other firsthand sources, which provided essential information. However, Michelet's history is also the product of a romantic imagination and sensitivity that animated the facts with the conflicts, the hatred, the hopes, and dreams of the past. Later volumes of the *Histoire de France* are slanted by Michelet's vehemence against the ancien régime, his arguments for the oppressed and against the oppressor. When these two currents—positivism and romanticism*—are in balance, Michelet's history is a glorious monument to the country he loved, the work of a champion of democracy.

Other works by Michelet include *Procès des Templiers* (*Trial of the Knights Templars,* 1841–1852, 2 vols); *Les Femmes de la Révolution* (*Women of the Revolution,* 1854); *Les Soldats de la Révolution* (*Soldiers of the Revolution,* posthumous, 1878).

For further information, see J. Clarke, "Michelet and the Parnassians: Some Introductory Reflections," *Parnasse* 3 (1982): 50–59; O. Haac, *Jules Michelet* (Boston: Twayne, 1982); S. Kippur, *Jules Michelet: A Study of Mind and Sensibility* (Albany: State University of New York, 1981); J. Williams, "Jules Michelet and Medieval French Literature," *Res Publica Litterarum* 2 (1979): 347–358. Williams, "Michelet on Rabelais," in N. Lacy and J. Nash, eds., *Essays in Early French Literature Presented to Barbara M. Craig* (York, S.C.: French Literature Publications, 1982), 109–118.

MICROMEGAS (1752), a brief tale of interplanetary travel by Voltaire,* is primarily a philosophical journey into the realm of relativity and a satire on man. Written during Voltaire's Cirey retreat with Madame du Châtelet (1706–1749), though not published until thirteen years later, the story reflects his interest in Newtonian physics and astronomy.

Taking its inspiration from *Gulliver's Travels* (1726) by Jonathan Swift (1667–1745), whom Voltaire had met in England, and from François Rabelais's (1494–1553) *Gargantua,* and Fontenelle,* the story illustrates the travels of Micromégas ("little-big"), an inhabitant of the planet Sirius, who at age 450, still a young man, measures 120,000 feet tall. He is accompanied by the secretary of the academy of Saturn, only 6,000 feet tall and called "the dwarf," a man of "spirit," who, like Fontenelle, had never invented anything, but "understood well the inventions of others and wrote passable poetry and mathematics." After travelling to Jupiter and Mars, they encircle the earth in gigantic footsteps, balance a whale on their thumbnail, and view a boatload of philosophers and scientists with the aid of a microscopic diamond. Communicating through a horn fashioned from a fingernail clipping, the travellers form certain judgments on the nature of man—that he may be as insignificant in size as an ant living on a mudhill, but has intelligence and reason; that despite his intelligence and reason, he is evil, irrational, unhappy, and self-centered. As he departs, Micromégas presents man with a philosophy book containing "the reason for things;" however, the secretary of the Academy in Paris finds all the pages blank.

The story is a light-hearted reiteration of Voltaire's main themes—the criticism of philosophers René Descartes (1596–1650), Gottfried Leibnitz (1646–1716), and Fontenelle; the futility of metaphysics; the relativity of man in the universe; and the recognition of man's limitations.

For further information, see R. A. Nablow, "Was Voltaire Influenced by Lucian in *Micromégas?*" *Romance Notes* 22 (Winter 1981): 186–191.

MIGNET, FRANÇOIS (1796–1884), lawyer, journalist, history professor, and historian, like his friend Thiers,* wrote a *Histoire de la Révolution française de 1789 à 1814* (*History of the French Revolution from 1789 to 1814,* 2 vols., 1824). In 1830, he founded the liberal daily, *Le National,* with Thiers and Armand Carrel (1800–1836). Under Louis-Philippe, he became director of the Archives for the minister of foreign affairs. He served as perpetual secretary to the Academy of Moral and Political Sciences. His works include *Mémoires historiques* (*Historical Memoirs,* 1836–1848), *Antonio Perez et Philippe II* (1845), *Marie Stuart* (1851), *Charles Quint et son abdication* (*Charles V and His Abdication,* 1854), and *Rivalité de François I et de Charles Quint* (*The Rivalry between Francis I and Charles V,* 1875). Mignet wrote with precision, impartiality, and sobriety. His fatalistic attitude considered the Revolution inevitable, a necessary consequence of previous events. His *Histoire de la Révolution* has become a classic.

MIRABEAU, GABRIEL-HONORE DE RIQUETTE, COMTE DE (1749–1791), statesman and orator who rose to the presidency of the constitutional assembly in 1791, dominated the early years of the Revolution with his eloquence and physical presence. He was born near Sens in Provence, the son of author and political economist, marquis de Mirabeau (1715–1789), a tyrant of a father who frequently exercised his right to imprison his wayward son by ''lettre de cachet,'' an order under the king's private seal. In his youth, Mirabeau was a prodigious student, but an avid womanizer whose numerous conquests reaped scandal and lengthy stays, arranged by his father, on the isle of Ré and at the chateau d'If as well as three years in Vincennes prison. He had a short military career and was named captain of the dragoons. In 1772, he married a wealthy heiress but escaped to Holland with Marie-Thérèse de Monnier (''Sophie''), wife of a former president of the Dole chambre des comptes (accounting court). She inspired his passionate letters (published, among others, in *Lettres écrites du donjon de Vincennes—Letters Written from the Dungeon at Vincennes,* 1792), written, along with *Erotica Biblion* (1783) and *Ma Conversion* (*My Conversion,* 1777), while Mirabeau, like Sade,* was confined in Vincennes. Upon his release, he tried to obtain his wife's legal return and interfered in a Paris lawsuit between his mother and father, so angering the authorities that he fled to Holland, where he met Madame de Nehra, daughter of Dutch statesman Zwier van Haren. They travelled to England, where a more liberal climate greeted his treatise, *Des lettres de cachet et des prisons d'etat* (*Of Letters of Cachet and State Prisons,* 1783). A dispute with wealthy Parisian bankers over stock speculation dashed his hopes for a position as a government pamphleteer or diplomatic career; however, in 1786, he was secretly sent to Prussia, a mission he detailed in his *Histoire secrète de la cour de Berlin* (*Secret History of the Court of Berlin,* 1787). The trip was unsuccessful and, coupled with his *Dénonciation de l'agiotage* (*Denunciation of Stock Speculation,* 1789), outraged the king. Unwanted by the nobility as its representative at the states-general, which was summoned by Louis XVI in 1789, he attended as a representative of the Tiers Etat (the Third Estate, that is, the commoners) of the cities of Aix and Marseille. Over the next two years he rose to the helm of this changing and disparate body, preaching eloquently the necessity for action rather than idle theory. He amassed followers and formed a program of reform. He operated closely with the court and received a royal pension as a liaison between the queen and her advisors and for writing political treatises. He pronounced discourses favoring the king's power of absolute veto, his right to declare war and collect one-fourth of each citizen's income. Mirabeau's support of a limited monarchy was viewed by the people as treason; however, when he died in 1791, he was buried as a national hero.

Besides the works mentioned, Mirabeau wrote *Lettres du comte de Mirabeau à ses commettants* (*Letters from Count Mirabeau to his Constituents*), detailing the period from May to July 1789, and founded a newspaper, *Le Courrier de Paris* (*The Paris Courier*). Most important, however, are his discourses, renowned for their clarity, logic, and learning. His sense of cool and clear delivery, plus his ability to sense the emotion of his audience and capitalize upon it, far outweighs the fact that much of them was written and researched by a team of secretaries. Mirabeau's eloquence as an orator is the best of that inspired by the Revolution. It is marked by an earnestness and order which will not be felt again until the reign of Napoleon (1769–1821).

MISERABLES, LES (*The Miserable Ones,* 1862), Victor Hugo's* massive novel of human redemption, was begun in 1845 as *Les Misères* (*The Miseries*) but set aside for twelve years until 1860 because of Hugo's political involvement and subsequent exile. He completed the manuscript on a beautiful day in June 1861 and revised its various parts over the course of a year. The novel, in which he hoped to "cast all previous epics into a superior and definitive one" (Philosophical Preface), met with immediate and lasting success. Hugo stated that the work would present "the march from evil to good, from injustice to justice, from falsehood to truth, from lust to conscience, from decay to life, from bestiality to duty, from hell to heaven, from nothingness to God" (Philosophical Preface).

Les Misérables is the story of Jean Valjean, a simple peasant who, jailed in 1795 for stealing a piece of bread, is forever branded a criminal by an unjust system. The novel begins twenty years later, when Valjean, freed for four days, is taken in by Monseigneur Myriel, bishop of Digne, who calls him "sir" and gives him dinner and a bed for the night. Most importantly, he gives him his dignity and his soul when he defends Valjean, caught redhanded by the police with the bishop's silver. Valjean steals money from a child, then overcome with remorse, becomes an honest man. Under the name of Monsieur Madeleine, mayor of Montfermeil, a small village near Paris, he prospers and is charitable. Fantine, a worker in his factory, bears a child, Cosette, whom she is forced to abandon to the Thénardiers, innkeepers in the village, who abuse and overwork the child. Fantine is forced into prostitution to pay her upkeep. Monsieur Javert, the police inspector, believes Monsieur Madeleine is really Jean Valjean the convict, until a certain Champmathieu, arrested for stealing an apple, is said to be him. Valjean undergoes a crisis of conscience before surrendering. He promises Fantine, sick in the hospital, that he will always care for her daughter, then turns himself in to the authorities.

Valjean escapes that night, however, with the help of a nun, and heads for Paris. He is arrested again, escapes, and on Christmas Eve, finds Cosette, now eight years old, getting water from a well in the woods. He gives her a doll and a goldpiece and, after giving the Thénardiers 1,500 francs, takes her to Paris, where they live in hiding. With inspector Javert on his trail, Valjean takes a gardening job in the secluded convent of Petit Picpus as Monsieur Fauchelevent, and Cosette is educated there. They move to Plumet Street, where Cosette meets a poor student, Marius Pontmercy, who is the grandson of Monsieur Gillenormand, a bourgeois royalist, and son of a former officer of Napoleon's army. They fall in love; Marius, a republican, aids the revolutionaries. He is wounded in the insurrection of 1832, saved by Valjean (who also saves, during the uprising, the life of his endless pursuer, Javert), reconciled with his grandfather, and marries Cosette. Valjean reveals his identity to his new son-in-law who, overwhelmed, spurns him and keeps Cosette away. Thénardier tells him the truth, that Valjean did not steal the real Monsieur Madeleine's fortune, that he did not kill Javert (who committed suicide), and that it was Valjean who saved Marius's life during the uprising. A remorseful Marius and Cosette visit Valjean, who is dying but happy to see his beloved Cosette one last time.

Besides Jean Valjean, *Les Misérables* is the story of early-nineteenth-century France. Long chapters on Paris, Waterloo, the convent of Petit Picpus, and the insurrection of 1830 as well as the portraits of Bishop Myriel, Fantine, Gavroche, and Monsieur Gillenormand enrich the novel with realistic detail and historical and social significance. The various incidents and characters, at times seemingly disparate, form a complex network of interrelationships to enhance the mood and theme of the novel.

Les Misérables is a novel of the people. In it, Hugo pleads the cause of the downtrodden. Valjean incarnates man's ability to grow, to change, to become honest and charitable. At least twice, when faced with a difficult choice, Valjean chooses right and reveals his true identity. At the end, he is purified, justified, victorious.

Hugo hoped that *Les Misérables* would be one of if not *the* "principal summits" of his body of works. Despite its length, complexity, and occasionally unbelievable plot and characterization, it remains a masterpiece of popular literature. It anticipates Balzac* in its realism,* but in its flights of imagination and lyricism, its theme of redemption, and its melding of myth and history (it has been called a *Légende des siècles** in prose), it is uniquely Hugo.

For further information, see R. de la Carerra, "History's Unconscious in Victor Hugo's *Les Misérables*," *Modern Language Notes* 96 (May 1981): 839–855; John Gale, "Where History and Fiction Meet: Napoleon Bonaparte and Jean Valjean," *French*

Literature Series 8 (1981): 65–75; K. Grossman, "Hugo's Romantic Sublime: Beyond Chaos and Convention in Les Misérables," Philological Quarterly 60 (Fall 1981): 471–486; Grossman, "Jean Valjean and France: Outlaws in Search of Integrity," Stanford French Review 2 (Winter 1978): 363–374; F. Heck, "The Loaf of Bread in Les Misérables and in Zola's Travail," Romance Notes 25 (1) (Fall 1984): 254–258; R. Maxwell, "Mystery and Revelation in Les Misérables," Romanic Review 73 (May 1982): 314–330; A. Welsh, "Opening and Closing Les Misérables," Nineteenth Century Fiction 33 (June 1978): 8–23.

MONTALEMBERT, CHARLES-FORBES-RENE, COMTE DE (1810–1870), a gifted orator and proponent of liberal Catholicism, who, along with Lacordaire,* supported Lamennais's* socialist ideals. When Lamennais left the church, he became leader of the Catholic liberals. Named a peer of France in 1835, he fought for free education (which the minister Guizot* accorded to primary schools in 1833) and the freedom of the press. In 1844, he formed a committee for the defense of religious freedom. He represented Doubs at the assembly from 1848 to 1857. His writings include L'Histoire de sainte Elisabeth de Hongrie (The History of Saint Elizabeth of Hungary, 1836) and Les Moines d'Occident (The Monks of the West, 1860).

MONTESQUIEU, CHARLES-LOUIS DE SECONDAT, BARON DE (1689–1755), political theorist and writer best known for Les Lettres persanes (The Persian Letters,* 1721) and De l'esprit des lois* (The Spirit of the Laws, 1748), was born at the feudal castle of La Brède in Bordeaux to a 350-year-old succession of aristocratic landowners and parliamentarians. After initial studies in the classics at the Collège de Juilly near Paris, Montesquieu studied law at the University of Bordeaux. At age twenty-five, upon the death of his father, he became counsellor to the parliament at Bordeaux; two years later, his uncle bequeathed him the barony of Montesquieu and his presidency of the Bordeaux parliament. However, disinclined toward parliamentary matters, Montesquieu frequented the Academy of Bordeaux, where he presented historic treatises and scientific studies on the causes of echoes, the renal glands, the tides, and motion.

The Lettres persanes, published anonymously in 1721 in Amsterdam, brought him renown and entry into the most exclusive Parisian circles, such as the salons of Madame de Lambert (1647–1733) and Madame de Tençin,* the Club de l'Entresol, and the royal court. The slim volume, capitalizing on the popularity of the Orient, presented an exotic and licentious tale of harems and eunuchs as well as a thinly disguised satire of the social and political abuses of the end of the reign of Louis XIV and the Regency. No aspect of Paris escaped the critical eyes of Montesquieu's visiting Persians, from the pope to the starving poet, from the court to the cafes. The novel also contains the germs of many of the themes that Montesquieu developed in later works—law, government, justice, and virtue.

Dividing his time between Paris and Bordeaux, Montesquieu presented, in 1725, a treatise on duty to the Academy at Bordeaux and "The Temple de Gnide," a prose poem to entertain the court. The following year he sold his office in parliament; he entered the French Academy in 1728. More and more absorbed in the study of government, he departed that same year on a three-year tour of firsthand observations in Austria, Hungary, Poland, and Italy, spending time in Venice, Florence, and Rome. In Holland, he met Lord Chesterfield (1694–1773), who accompanied him to England, where he was presented at court, received into the Royal society, initiated into freemasonry, and came to understand and admire the writings of John Locke (1632–1704) and the workings of the English constitution.

Upon his return in 1731, Montesquieu sequestered himself at La Brède to study law and ancient constitutions and their relations to the societies he had observed. Interspersing long periods of work and reflection with visits to Paris, he produced, again anonymously, his *Considérations sur les causes de la grandeur des Romains et de leur décadence* (*Considerations on the Causes of the Grandeur of the Romans and of Their Decadence*, 1734), which, originally intended as a chapter of his *De l'esprit des lois,* was published separately because of its length and importance. He found in Rome an example of an empire that flourished because of its military discipline and political wisdom but perished in its success. As Rome expanded, its soldiers dispersed, dividing their loyalty; as its riches increased, religion suffered, corruption mounted, tyranny grew. As a historical tract, *Considérations* is significant for its rational structure, its explanation of the Roman history in terms of "general" and "particular" causes rather than fate or providence.

Twenty years of labor resulted in his masterwork, *De l'esprit des lois,* published in 1748 in Geneva. The depth and magnitude of this work exhausted and nearly blinded its author. A monumental study of the definition of law and its relation to "the nature of things," such as government, climate, religion, customs, and commerce, the book examines the "spirit" that derives from that relationship. It uncovers three forms of government—republic, monarchy, and despotism—and the principle unique to the operation of each—virtue, honor, and fear. The necessity of the clergy, nobility, and parliament to intermediate between the people and the king, and the theory of the separation of executive, legislative, and judicial powers of the government are also studied.

Despite its immediate success (22 editions appeared within a year and a half of publication), criticism from the Sorbonne, the Jesuits, and the Jansenists forced Montesquieu to write, despite his age and infirmity, a *Défense de l'esprit des lois* (*Defense of the Spirit of the Laws,* 1750). Nevertheless, the work was banned a year later.

His last work of importance, the novel *Arsace et Isménie* (1754), was followed by an essay on "Goût" ("Taste") for d'Alembert's* *Encyclopédie.** Montesquieu died, a semirecluse and totally blind, in Paris in 1755.

Both as a feudal lord and philosophe,* Montesquieu exemplified his century's ideal of reason. In his *Cahiers* (*Notebooks*), he wrote, "Let us try to accommodate ourselves to life; it is not up to life to accommodate itself to us"; and "Study has been for me the supreme remedy against the aversions of life, having never had vexations which an hour's reading had not removed." Though a nobleman, he warned of the abuse of power; he subordinated love of country to a global vision, writing, "I am a good citizen; but, in any country in which I had been born, I would have been one all the same" (*Cahiers*). His political analyses were logical, proceeding with scientific objectivity from the general to the specific. In *Considérations* he wrote, "It is not hazard which dominates the world. . . . If the fate of a battle, that is, a particular cause, has ruined a state, there had to have been a general cause which established that that state would perish by a single battle."

Despite occasional superficiality and hasty documentation, Montesquieu's political works have contributed to the development of numerous modern disciplines—political philosophy, jurisprudence, sociology. His quest to understand the workings of the ideal state, where man could flourish in accordance with laws that are just, influenced J.-J. Rousseau* and the political reforms of the constitution of 1791 and contributed to the liberalism of the following century. Yet liberty for Montesquieu did not consist of unbridled freedom and individual will but rather the "right to do all that the laws permit." In this, Montesquieu envisioned happiness and the ideal state.

For further information, see J. Appleby, "What Is Still American in the Political Philosophy of Thomas Jefferson," *William and Mary Quarterly* 39 (April 1982): 287–309; J. A. Baum, *Montesquieu and Social Theory* (Oxford: Pergamon Press, 1979); I. Cox, *Montesquieu and the History of French Laws* (Oxford: Voltaire Foundation, 1984); N. Hampson, *Will and Circumstance: Montesquieu, Rousseau and the French Revolution* (Norman: University of Oklahoma Press, 1983); M. Hulliung, *Montesquieu and the Old Regime* (Berkeley: University of California Press, 1976); Hulliung, "Montesquieu's Interpreters: a Polemical Essay," in *Studies in Eighteenth-Century Culture*, vol. 10 (Madison: University of Wisconsin Press, 1981), 327–345; J. Jones, "Montesquieu and Jefferson Revisited: Aspects of a Legacy," *French Review* (March 1978): 577–585; M. Masterson, "Rights, Relativism and Religious Faith in Montesquieu," *Political Studies* (June 1981): 204–216; J. McLelland, "Metaphor in Montesquieu's Theoretical Writings," *Studies on Voltaire and the Eighteenth Century* 199 (1981): 205–224; R. O'Reilly, "The Spurious Attribution of the *Voyage à Paphos* and an Appreciation of Montesquieu's *Temple de Gnide*," *Studies on Voltaire and the Eighteenth Century* 189 (1980): 229–237; M. Richter, *The Political Theory of Montesquieu* (London: Cambridge University Press, 1977); R. Shackleton, "Montesquieu, Suard and the Philosophes," in *Enlightenment Studies in Honor of Lester G. Crocker*, A. Bingham and V. Topazio, eds. (Oxford: Voltaire Foundation, 1979); W. Watson, "Montesquieu and Voltaire on China," *Comparative Civilizations Review* 2 (Spring 1979): 38–51; D. Young, "Montesquieu's View of Despotism and His Use of Travel Literature," *The Review of Politics* 40 (July 1978): 392–405.

MOREAS, JEAN (1856–1910). See *Dictionary of Modern French Literature, from Naturalism and Symbolism to Post-Modernism.*

MOREAU, HEGESIPPE (1810–1838), a minor romantic poet, is known primarily for a collection of stories and poems, *Les Myosotis* (1838). An illegitimate child, he was orphaned at an early age and grew up in poverty. He took a job as a proofreader in Provins, a village to the southeast of Paris, where he fell chastely in love with the printer's daughter. He returned to Paris, participated in the July revolution, and lived in abject poverty. He returned to Provins and founded a satirical journal, *Diogène,* modeled after Auguste Barthélemy's (1796–1867) *Némésis.* It failed. He returned to Paris, where he died in a charity hospital.

Moreau's short life, like that of his contemporary, Bertrand,* and Vigny's* *Chatterton,* * exemplifies the miserable lot of many a poor poet of his day. Like the young poet in the play, he died in poverty in Paris, seeking a place in the literary world. His songs and elegies are melancholy, delicate, inspired from his youth, as are "Dix-huit ans" ("Eighteen Years") and "L'Abeille" ("The Bee"), and occasionally bitter, inspired from his dire circumstances, as is "Ode à la faim" ("Ode to Hunger"). His best-known poem is "La Voulzie," written about the stream traversing Provins.

MORELLET, ABBE ANDRE (1727–1819), economist, writer, and last surviving member of the philosophe* coterie, was born in Lyons. He was educated there by the Jesuits, attended a seminary in Paris and finally the Sorbonne, where he met Turgot* and the abbé de Prades (1720–1782), who introduced him to Diderot.* Though he took holy orders, he earned his reputation as a writer, contributing articles on theology and metaphysics ("Fatality," "Figures," "Son of God," "Faith" and "Fundamentals") to the *Encyclopédie.* * His witty pamphlet *Préface de la comédie des philosophes (Preface to the Comedy of the Philosophes,* 1760), written in answer to Palissot's* antiphilosophical play, earned him two months' imprisonment in the Bastille. He frequented the salon of Madame Geoffrin (1699–1777) and, though not an atheist, that of Holbach.* He travelled to England on a diplomatic mission in 1772, met members of British government as well as Benjamin Franklin (1706–1790), received a government pension in 1784, and was elected to the French Academy in 1785. As its director, in 1792 when the Academy was suppressed, he safeguarded its papers, not returning them until 1803, after the danger of the Terror had passed. After the Revolution he supported himself as a translator, intervened on behalf of those families ruined or exiled by the war, and was elected to the legislative body in 1807. A year before his death, he published the four volumes of his *Mélanges de littérature et de philosophie au XVIIIe siècle (Miscellany of Literature and Philosophy of the Eighteenth Century).* His *Mémoires,* published posthumously in 1822, are a valuable record of the philosophe period.

Other works by Morellet include *Petit Ecrit sur une matière intéressante, la tolérance (A Short Examination of an Interesting Matter, Tolerance,* 1756), *Réflexions sur les avantages de la fabrication et de l'usage des toiles peintes (Reflections on the Advantages and the Use of Printed Cloth,* 1758), *Manuel des inquisiteurs (Manual on the Inquisitors,* 1762), a translation of Cesar Bonesana Beccaria's (1738–1794) *Traité des délits et des peines (Treatise on Crimes and*

Punishments, 1766), and numerous works on politics and commerce. He was a staunch defender of Turgot's* policy of free trade.

For further information, see D. Medlin, "Abbé Morellet and the Idea of Progress," *Studies on Voltaire and the Eighteenth Century* 189 (1980): 239–246; Medlin, "Abbé Morellet, Translator of Liberal Thought," *Studies on Voltaire and the Eighteenth Century* 74 (1978): 189–201; Medlin, "Thomas Jefferson, Abbé Morellet and the French Version of Notes on the State of Virginia," *The William and Mary Quarterly* 35 (January 1978): 85–99.

MORELLY, whose Christian names and dates of birth and death remain unknown, was a minor eighteenth-century philosopher and precursor of communism. Several works survive, including *Essai sur l'esprit humain* (*Essay on the Human Spirit,* 1745), *Essai sur le coeur humain* (*Essay on the Human Heart,* 1745), *Physique de la beauté ou Pouvoir naturel de ses charmes* (*The Physics of Beauty or the Natural Power of Its Charms,* 1748), *Le Prince, Les délices du coeur ou Traité des qualitiés d'un grand roi et système d'un sage gouvernment* (*The Prince, The Delights of the Heart or Treatise on the Qualities of a Great King and System of a Wise Government,* 1751). An allegorical poem in fourteen cantos, *Naufrage des îles flottantes à la Basiliade* (*The Shipwreck of the Floating Islands of the Basiliade,* 1763) describes a communist system more daring than Thomas More's (1478–1535) *Utopia* (1516). His *Code de la Nature* (*The Law of Nature,* 1755) advocates a social revolution based on a communistic egalitarianism that denounces property as the source of all evil. According to Morelly, nothing will belong to anyone except "those things which one will actually use either for his needs, his pleasures or his daily work. . . . Each citizen will be a public man, supported, or maintained and engaged at the expense of the public. . . . Each citizen will contribute his share to public service, according to his strength, his ability and his age." His ideas influenced revolutionary politician and writer François Emile Babeuf (1760–1797), nineteenth-century politican and historian Louis Blanc* (1811–1882), and social reformer Etienne Cabet (1785–1856) and anticipated the socialism of Karl Marx (1818–1883).

For further information, see F. D. Fergusson, "Morelly and Ledoux: Two Examples of Utopian Town Planning and Political Theory in Eighteenth Century France," *French Studies* (January 1979): 13–26; B. Fink, "Utopian Nurtures" [Fénelon, S. Mercier, Morelly, Sade], *Transactions of the Fifth International Congress on the Enlightenment,* vol. 2 (Oxford: Taylor Institution, 1981), 664–671.

MUSE FRANÇAISE, LA (The French Muse) was a literary journal published from July 1823 until June 1824, edited by Emile Deschamps (1791–1871) and written by a number of young poets, dramatist Alexandre Soumet (1788–1845), Alexandre Guiraud (1788–1847), Alfred de Vigny,* and Victor Hugo.* Lamartine* chose to subscribe but not contribute. A conservative periodical, its articles defended the monarchy and Christianity. While recognizing the need for a new literary movement, it envisioned romanticism* as an enlargement of classicism rather than a revolt against it. Its criticism exalted Lord Byron (1788–1824), Walter Scott (1771–1832), and William Shakespeare (1564–1616). As its contributors published more and more works (Hugo, *Bug Jargal* in 1820, *Odes* in 1822; Vigny, *Poèmes* in 1822; Soumet, *Clytemnestre* and *Saul* in 1822; Guiraud, *Poèmes et Elégies* in 1822), their authority increased, arousing the ire of the Academy and the remaining classicists. When *La Muse* ceased publication in 1824, its partisans gathered in the salon of Charles Nodier* at the Arsenal,* forming the first of the two cénacles* of the romantic movement.

MUSSET, ALFRED DE (1810–1857), nineteenth-century poet and playwright, represents youthful romanticism* in his passion, independence, and melancholy. He knew success and failure at an early age. At eighteen, he was an habitué of the cénacles,* charming and talented, a famous poet, a romantic child prodigy. By twenty, he was an alcoholic, and after the age of thirty he wrote little. The best of his poetry was born of sadness, his unhappy love affair with George Sand.* His life, though passionate and filled with wild abandon, was short and sad, characterized by physical and emotional despair.

Musset was born in Paris to upper-middle-class parents. His father, M. de Musset-Pathay, was an official in the ministries of war and the interior and had written a history of the life and works of J.-J. Rousseau* (1821, 1827) and edited a volume of his works (1818). Precocious Alfred was a brilliant student at Lycée Henri IV, where he met Paul Foucher, who in 1828 introduced him to his celebrated brother-in-law, Victor Hugo,* as well as Vigny,* Mérimée,* Sainte-Beuve,* and Charles Nodier.* A young dandy at heart, Musset preferred the company of rich friends, Alfred Tattet, Ulrich Guttinger, counts Belgiojoso and Alton-Shée. At the insistence of his family, he tried his hand at law, medicine, and music, but poetry was his first love. Until 1838, he filled the years with creative endeavors.

In June 1833 he met George Sand and embarked on perhaps the best-documented love affair in literary history. After an idyllic summer sojourn at Fontainebleau, they left in December for Italy. By February, Musset was gravely ill in Venice with typhoid but departed on March 29 for Paris after learning of Sand's unfaithfulness with his doctor. A brief reconciliation followed, but the couple parted ways definitively in March 1835. This unfortunate love affair is the source of Musset's most poignant verse—"La Nuit de mai" ("The May Night"), "La Nuit de décembre" ("December Night"), "Souvenir" ("Memory").

Before the age of twenty-five, Musset had written the best of his plays. On 1 January 1834, his comedy *Fantasio* was published in *Revue des deux mondes; On ne badine pas avec l'amour,* * also a comedy, appeared on July 1 of the same year; and *Lorenzaccio,* * in August. After Sand, he consoled himself in liaisons with fashionable ladies such as Aimée d'Alton, the Princess Belgiojoso, and various leading actresses and led a life of dissipation. Besides the "Nuit" poems (1835–1837), he wrote *La Confession d'un enfant du siècle (The Confession of a*

Child of the Age, 1836), several light comedies and proverbes dramatiques,*and *Lettres de Dupuis et Cotonet* (1836–1837), which affirmed his literary independence. In 1847, a French actress performed one of his comedies, *Un Caprice,* in Saint Petersburg and later at the Comédie-Française, igniting an interest in his comedies and dramas that has never waned. In 1852, he was elected to the Academy. However, for the most part, Musset's final years were spent in obscurity and sadness. He died in Paris in 1857.

Musset's first verse, written at fourteen, was a song for his mother. In 1828, his literary career began with an adaptation, of little consequence, of English essayist Thomas De Quincey's (1785–1859) *Confessions of an English Opium Eater* (1821). His first major work followed two years later, *Contes d'Espagne et d'Italie (Tales from Spain and Italy,* 1830), a series of tales that parodied romanticism's penchant for exoticism and local color in poems set in Spain and Venice, which Musset had never seen, as well as violent passion, irregular rhythms, and unexpected rhymes in the manner of Hugo. These poems, which met with immediate success, established their young author as the "enfant terrible" ("little terror") of romanticism who, though he enjoyed the spirit and freedom of the new movement, rejected its excesses. During the next three years, Musset broke with the cenacle and asserted his independence. His poem *Les Secrètes pensées de Rafaël (Rafael's Secret Thoughts),* published in 1830 in the *Revue de Paris,* affirms his admiration for the classics; *Namouna* (1832) reveals his disgust with the romantic's penchant for local color. The autobiographical poem *Rolla* (1833) recounts the story of a nineteen-year-old boy of "a noble but naive heart" given to debauchery, who has squandered his fortune and commits suicide after a final night of pleasure. Rolla's spiritual void and moral emptiness are his inheritance from the enlightenment for which Musset holds Voltaire* responsible.

After 1835, Musset published in the *Revue des deux mondes* some of his most beautiful verse—"Stances à Malibran" ("Stanzas for Malibran" [Spanish singer, 1808–1836], "La Lettre à Lamartine" ("Letter to Lamartine"), "L'Espoir en Dieu" ("Hope in God"), and the "Nuit" ("Night") poems. The "Nuit" poems ("Nuit de mai," 1835; "Nuit de décembre," 1835; "Nuit d'août," 1836; "Nuit d'octobre, 1837), generally considered his best, attempt through lyric dialogue to heal his wounded heart and end his suffering over George Sand, to enable him to live and write again and find a measure of peace. In the first and best known of his poems, the Muse visits and invites him to take up his lute and sing. She suggests themes and types of poetry and reminds him in a famous line that "The most desperate songs are the most beautiful." But the poet refuses, the sting of his love affair too recent. In the second poem of the series, Musset is haunted by a double, a "shadow friend" dressed in black, a tragic reflection of his misery and solitude. "La Nuit d'août" finds the poet trying to console himself in foolish love affairs rather than poetry. He tells the Muse that "After having suffered, one must suffer more/ After having loved, one must love more." In the final poem, confident that his wound has healed, the poet attempts to tell his story. When his hurt and passion once again erupt, the Muse quells his pain, and the poet vows to be reborn with the dawn of a new day. The "Nuit" cycle closes with "Souvenir" (1841), written after a visit to the forest at Fontainebleau where he had walked with George Sand. It is a poem that bears testimony to the healing, consoling power of time, which "carries off our tears, our cries and our regrets".

"La Lettre à Lamartine" (1836) pays homage to the poet with whom Musset felt a sentimental bond. Like Musset, Lamartine suffered in love, and Musset envied his spiritual faith. "Tristesse" ("Sadness," 1840) sets down his physical and emotional lassitude; "Une Soirée perdue" ("A Wasted Evening," 1840) reveals his admiration for Molière (1622–1673) and his criticism for his contemporaries.

Musset's first play, *Les Marrons du feu* (*Chestnuts in the Fire*), published in 1829, in *Les Contes d'Espagne et d'Italie* (*Tales from Spain and Italy*), parodied the themes and style of romantic drama. His next, a one-act comedy, *La Nuit vénitienne* (*The Venetian Night,* 1830), was a dismal failure that prompted him to limit his efforts to plays to be read only and enabled him to write more creatively, without concern for staging. Two years later, Musset published *Un Spectacle dans un fauteuil* (*An Armchair Spectacle,* 1832), a collection of plays to be read in the comfort of one's salon, which includes Namouna; a drama, *La Coupe et les lèvres* (*The Cup and the Lips*); and a comedy, *A quoi rêvent les jeunes filles* (*Young Girls' Dreams*). The next year another drama, *André del Sarto,* was published in the *Revue des deux mondes,* along with *Les Caprices de Marianne* (*The Whims of Marianne*), a comedy whose two male characters can be seen as opposite sides of Musset's personality. Coelio, a timid and melancholy aristocrat, is in love with Marianne, the wife of an elderly judge. His friend Octave, a happy-go-lucky libertine, assists him in his unfortunate quest for the capricious young woman. After *Fantasio* and *On ne badine pas avec l'amour,* other comedies were published in the *Revue des deux mondes*: *Barberine* (1835), *Le Chandelier* (*The Cicisbeo* [that is, the recognized lover of a married woman], 1835), *Il ne faut jurer de rien* (*One Musn't Swear About Anything,* 1836), and *Un Caprice* (*A Whim,* 1837). *Lorenzaccio* (1834), a prose drama in five acts that recounts the murder of Alexander de Medici (1510–1537) by his cousin Lorenzo, is considered a masterpiece of romantic theatre.

The presentation of *Un Caprice* in 1847 is considered a landmark in the history of the theatre. Musset at last found a public for his comedies and returned to the theatre with *Louison* (1849), *Carmosine* (1850), and *Bettine* (1851) and reworked some of his previous ones. In 1848, he rewrote *Il ne faut jurer de rien* and *Le Chandelier;* in 1851, *Les Caprices de Marianne;* and in 1853, *Barberine.* Only *Fantasio* and *On ne badine pas avec l'amour,* which along with the drama *Lorenzaccio,* were never played during his lifetime, remained untouched.

Musset's autobiographical novel, *La Confession d'un enfant du siècle,* an account of his affair with Sand, presents a telling description, in its long preface, of the moral malady prevalent at the time, le mal du siècle.* Other prose works include stories and tales—*Frédéric et Bernerette* (1838), *Le Fils du Titien*

(1838), *Pierre et Camille* (1844)—and *Lettres de Dupuis et Cotonet* (1836–1837), a critical work directed against romanticism's pretentiousness, which marked his definitive break with the cenacle.

Musset's poetry was published in two major collections. The first, *Premieres poésies,* includes poems written from 1829 to 1835, including *Les Contes d'Espagne et d'Italie, Le Saule* (*The Willow,* 1830), *Les Voeux stériles* (*Sterile Vows*), *Les Secrètes Pensées de Raphael, Un Spectacle dans un fauteuil,* and *Rolla.* This volume, published by Charpentier, first appeared in 1840 as *Poésies complètes.* A second volume of poetry written since 1833 appeared as *Poésies nouvelles* (1852). His stories have been collected as *Contes et Nouvelles;* the comedies and proverbes dramatiques were collected in one volume in 1840 and revised in 1853.

Musset was profoundly influenced by William Shakespeare (1564–1616), Lord Byron (1788–1824), Jean Racine (1639–1699) and Marivaux.* As a poet, Musset distanced himself from the romantic school, spurning the trappings of the movement and disagreeing with the principle that poetry should serve a social purpose. He admired the principles of classicism. In the theatre, he believed that the classical traditions of simplicity and truth could be combined with the freedoms of romantic form. He revolutionized playwrighting in France by breaking the unity of the act into short fragments and adding numerous interruptions into the action. His theatre is characteristically capricious, fanciful, lyric, and sad. Like his poetry, it portrays the deepest emotions of the human heart with sensitivity and sincerity and in that, he is genuinely romantic.

For further information, see S. Albuquerque, "A Brazilian Intermediary in the Transmission of European Romantic Ideas: Alvares de Azevedo," *Romance Notes* 23 (Spring 1983): 220–226; L. Bishop, "Musset's First Sonnet: A Semiotic Analysis," *Romanic Review* 74 (4) (November 1983): 455–460; Bishop, "Musset's 'Souvenir' and the Greater Romantic Lyric," *Nineteenth Century French Studies* 12–13 (Summer–Fall 1984): 119–130; D. G. Charlton, "Musset as Moral Novelist: *La Confession d'un enfant du siècle,*" in C. E. Pickford, ed., *Mélanges de littérature française moderne offerts à Garnet Rees par ses collègues et amis* (Paris: Minard, 1980), 29–46; G. Padgett, "Bad Faith in Alfred de Musset: a Problem of Interpretation," *Dalhousie French Studies* 3 (October 1981): 65–82; P. Siegel, *Alfred de Musset: A Reference Guide* (Boston: Hall, 1982).

N

NERVAL, GERARD DE (born Gérard Labrunie, 1808–1855), romantic poet and storywriter whose greatest works—*Sylvie* (1853), *Les Chimères* (1853), *Aurélia* (1853–1854)—were inspired by an ideal of love that eventually claimed his sanity and his life. He was born in Paris, the son of an army doctor. Nerval lived his formative years with his great uncle, Antoine Boucher, at Mortefontaine in the Valois, his mother having died when he was two. The forests and legends of this region of France and the early loss of his mother invested the young child with a sensitivity, imagination, and longing that are evident in his works. At eighteen, he enrolled in the Lycée Charlemagne, where he befriended Théophile Gautier,* and published a volume of political odes, *Elégies nationales* (*National Elegies*, 1826). He frequented Hugo's* cénacle* and Gautier's petit-cénacle, leading the carefree bohemian life he later described in *Petits Châteaux de Bohème* (*Little Bohemian Castles,* 1853) and *La Bohème galante* (*The Gallant Bohemian,* 1855). He steeped himself in German language, legend, music, and literature, especially Johann Goethe (1749–1832) and Ernst Hoffmann (1776–1822). In 1828, he published a translation of *Faust* that Goethe himself admired. He wrote the magical, humorous tale, *La Main de gloire* (*The Hand of Glory,* 1832) and poems à la Ronsard (1524–1585). In 1834, he travelled to Italy. But it was not until 1836, when he fell madly in love with actress Jenny Colon (1808–1842), that Nerval's literary and personal life came into focus. He founded a drama revue, *Le Monde dramatique* (*The Dramatic World*), which consumed his inheritance, and wrote dramas to aid her career. She married a musician in 1838, and Nerval was to lay eyes upon her but once more, at the Belgian premiere of his play, *Piquillo* (published, 1837). Nerval travelled to Belgium and Germany to assuage his pain but found peace instead in myth, transforming Miss Colon into a primordial, mystical incarnation of femininity that he worshipped to the point of losing touch with reality. He was institutionalized for eight months in 1841. After her death in 1842, Nerval transfigured her from a beautiful earthly creature into a full-blown celestial vision. The rest of Nerval's life and work were an attempt to come to terms with his dream and reality.

A trip to the Orient in 1843 gave a religious foundation to his fantasy. He borrowed the goddesses of Greece and Egypt as symbols of his ideal. He studied the illuminists (adherents of a mystical philosophy), especially Cazotte* and Restif de la Bretonne,* for whom he felt an affinity. He returned to France and made numerous excursions to the Valois of his youth. He was hospitalized again in 1851. With madness imminent, he composed *La Bohème galante, Lorely* (1852), and *Les Nuits d'octobre* (*October Nights,* 1852). From 1853 on, he juggled moments of sanity with periods of madness. From August until the following May, he stayed at the hospital of Dr. Emile Blanche in Passy. He had a brief respite in Germany, but returned to Dr. Blanche from August until October. At dawn on 26 January of the following year, Nerval was found hanged in a backstreet of Paris, either murdered or by his own hand.

Nerval's richest work was written in brief periods of lucidity while he held the growing cancer of madness at bay. *Le Voyage en Orient* (*Voyage in the Orient,* 1851) is the first expression of his hallucination, a travelogue of Nerval's interior landscape as much as an Oriental one. His itinerary is largely imagined; historical details are vague. But the trip awakened him spiritually and provided a basis for his own mythology "Yes, I felt pagan in Greece, Musulman in Egypt, pantheist amid the Druses, and devout on the seas of the astral-gods of Chaldea," he wrote.

Sylvie, the best of the stories contained in the collection, *Les Filles du feu* (*Daughters of the Fire,* 1853–1854), and perhaps the most significant of his works, was first published in the *Revue des deux mondes* in August 1853, just as Nerval was about to be institutionalized. It is a trip via Nerval's memory to the rustic landscape, villages, and people of his early years, a spiritual return to the stuff out of which his dreams were made and his fantasy spun; an exploration of Nerval's own consciousness and dreamworld, where reality and illusion, present and past commingle and his mystical woman was born of women he had loved. Sylvie is his first love, a pretty peasant girl who lives in a neighboring hamlet; Adrienne, a descendant of the kings of France, enchants a circle of children dancing outside her castle with her beauty and song before she is sent to a nunnery where she dies; Aurélie is an actress who perhaps is Adrienne reincarnated.

Les Chimères (1853) is a collection of twelve sonnets that were appended to *Les Filles du feu* and later augmented. Their themes continue those of the stories, his secret obsessions, his pursuit of the absolute, his confusion of dream and reality. "El Desdichado" ("Fatal Destiny"), "Myrtho," "Delphica," and "Artémis" relate his ongoing search for his mythical love; "Vers dorés" is dedicated to the wisdom of Pythagoras. The poems are dense and obscure, born of the legends of Egypt, India, Greece, Rome, and Christianity, but are considered among the summits of French poetry.

Aurélia (1855), his final work, written sporadically between 1842 and 1854 and edited during his stay with Dr. Blanche, is a diary of his madness, of his "descent into hell," which he promised in the preface of *Les Filles du feu*. It traces Nerval's anguish after losing his beloved, his unrelenting sense of guilt, his dreams and hallucinations of the mysterious, haunting phantom of Aurelia that "spill out" into reality. He deifies Aurelia, confounds her with nature, immortalizes her soul, and is united with her in eternity until he imagines a spiritual double of himself that punishes him by taking her away. He seeks pardon, sees visions, sinks lower into his abyss until Aurelia appears and reveals herself saying, "I am the same as Marie, the same as your mother, the same as all of the forms that you have always loved."

Nerval's works explored the nether world of the subconscious, that fantastic and mystical region of the brain where his genius resided before it finally claimed his hold on reality. His last words, found in his pocket when he hanged himself, explained that for him, dreams were a second existence, a passage through death to another life in the "invisible" and the world of the "Spirits." *Sylvie, Les Chimères,* and *Aurélia* chart his course through his subconscious, recording his memories and dreams with imagery which inspired Baudelaire,** Rimbaud,** and the surrealists (see surrealism**) who found in him a precursor.

For further information, see R. Chadbourne, "Gérard de Nerval's 'Essayism,'" *French Literature Series* 9 (1982): 35–42; S. Dunn, "Nerval: Transgression and the 'Amendment Riancey,'" *Nineteenth Century French Studies* 12 (1–2) (Fall-Winter 1983–1984): 86–95; D. P. Haase, "Gérard de Nerval's Magnum Opus: Alchemy in Literature and Life," *Kentucky Romance Quarterly* 29 (3) (1982): 245–250; Haase, "Nerval's Knowledge of Novalis: a Reconsideration," *Romance Notes* 22 (Fall 1981): 53–57; Haase, "Nerval's Revision of German Romanticism: Aurélia and Novalis' Heinrich von Ofterdingen," *Cincinnati Romance Review* 2 (1983): 49–59; S. Richards, "Alchemy as Poetic Metaphor in Gérard de Nerval's *Les Chimères*," *West Virginia University Philological Papers* 27 (1981): 34–41; N. Rinsler, "Nerval, Poe, Baudelaire: Transformations of an Image," *Parnasse* 1 (June 1982): pp. 5–17; R. Sieburth, "Nerval's *Lorely,* or the Lure of Origin," *Studies in Romanticism* 22 (2) (Summer 1983): 199–239; P. Thompson, "Sylvie: The Method of Myth," *Nineteenth Century French Studies* 12 (1–2) (Fall–Winter, 1983–1984): 96–104; R. Warren, "The 'Last Madness' of Gérard de Nerval," "Letter to Dumas," and "Octavie," *The Georgia Review* 37 (1) (Spring 1983): 131–138, 139–147, and 148–153.

NEVEU DE RAMEAU, LE (*Rameau's Nephew*), by Diderot,* a lively novel in dialogue form between a philosopher and a musician, is considered by many to be his masterpiece. Begun in 1762, finished in 1778, and circulated only among friends, the work remained unpublished until 1805 when it was translated into German by Johann Goethe (1749–1832) from a Saint Petersburg manuscript. It finally appeared in French in 1823 and gave rise to several versions until an original, signed copy came to light in 1891 along the quais of the Seine.

The dialogue takes place one evening after dinner at the Café de la Régence, a favorite gathering place, where Diderot meets a young musician, Jean-François Rameau, nephew of the famed eighteenth-century composer (Jean-Philippe

Rameau, 1683–1764). This "strange" young bohemian, an "original" blend of "the lofty and the low, good sense and foolishness," engages Diderot in a rambling philosophical discussion of society, genius, and music. Rameau "shakes," "agitates" and "brings out the truth" in the conversation, not unlike Diderot himself, who regaled salon guests with his vivacity and wit. Indeed, critics consider Jean-François a manifestation of Diderot's former ne'er-do-well self, who narrowly missed becoming the artistic, social, and moral failure that the young man represents. Philosophically, the dialogue externalizes the interior conflict between Diderot the liberal-thinking materialist and Diderot the sentimental idealist.

Besides his multifaceted portrait—physical, intellectual, and moral—of the eighteenth-century bohemian, Diderot, "Moi," and his foil, "Lui," pursue one thought after another, as young dissolutes following courtesans in the back streets of Paris ("My thoughts are my harlots," Diderot claims on the novel's first page). Still suffering from the personal attack of Pallissot's* play, Les Philosophes (The Philosophers), Diderot in turn satirizes a society that supports mediocrity and abandons originality and genius, epitomized by Rameau's nephew, which does not fit its mold. Besides social satire, the conversation addresses the role of genius, the education of children, musical theory, and moral problems.

The verve and animation of its dialogue, the free flow and resounding clash of ideas, the realistic detail, the importance of gesture and mime contribute to the originality of Le Neveu de Rameau and point the way not only to the coming political revolution but to the coming realist novels of Balzac* and Flaubert* as well.

For further information, see J. Creech, "*Le Neveu de Rameau*: the Diary of a Reading," *Modern Language Notes* 95 (May 1980): 995–1004; J. De Jean, "Intentions and Interventions in *Le Neveu de Rameau*," *Eighteenth Century Studies* 9 (Summer 1976): 511–522; S. B. Hammer, "The Dance of Dishonesty: Satiric Attack in *Le Neveu de Rameau*," *French Forum* 10 (1) (January 1985): 5–19; J. Kaplan, "Notes on *Le Neveu de Rameau*," *Romance Notes* 20 (Fall 1979): 68–74; A. P. Kouidis, *Le Neveu de Rameau and The Praise of Folly: Literary Cognates* (Salzburg: Inst. für Anglistik and Amerikanistik, University of Salzburg, 1981); Kouidis "The Praise of Folly: Diderot's Model for *Le Neveu de Rameau*," *Studies on Voltaire and the Eighteenth Century* 185 (1980): 237–266; J. Mall, "*Le Neveu de Rameau* and the Idea of Genius," *Eighteenth Century Studies* 11 (Fall 1977): 26–39; C. V. McDonald, "Dialogue and Intertextuality: the Posterity of Diderot's *Neveu de Rameau*," in *Pretext. Text. Context. Essays on Nineteenth Century French Literature*, Robert Mitchell, ed. (Columbus: Ohio State University Press, 1980); W. Rex, "Two Scenes from *Le Neveu de Rameau*," *Diderot Studies XX* (Geneva: Droz, 1981), 245–266; J. Siegel, "Lovelance and *Rameau's Nephew*: Roots of Poetic Amoralism," *Diderot Studies* 19 (1978): 163–74; R. P. Thomas, "Chess as Metaphor in *Le Neveu de Rameau*," *Forum for Modern Language Studies* 18 (January 1982): 63–74.

NISARD, DESIRE (1806–1888), literary critic and outspoken enemy of romanticism,* was born at Châtillon-sur-Seine. As a journalist, he jointed the staff of

Journal des débats (*Debate Journal*) in 1828 and *Le National* in 1832, after which he began an academic career smiled upon by the July monarchy and the Second Empire. In 1844, he became professor of Latin eloquence at the Collège de France; in 1852, professor of French eloquence at the Sorbonne; and in 1857, director of the Ecole Normale. He was named counsellor of state in 1836 and deputy in 1842. He entered the Academy in 1850 and in 1867 he was elected senator.

In 1833, he made his name with a famous manifesto published in *Le National* against historical novels and romantic plays, which he termed "la littérature facile" ("easy literature"). His *Etudes sur les poètes latins de la décadence* (*Studies on Latin Decadent Poets*, 1834) alludes to the decadence of the romantic poets, whom Nisard found lacking in good judgment and healthy doctrine. His most important work, *Histoire de la littérature française* (*History of French Literature*, 4 vols., 1844–1849), establishes a literary ideal of "French spirit," that is, "the expression of general truths in perfect language . . . perfectly conforming to the genius of the country which is speaking and to the human spirit." For Nisard, the seventeenth century is the perfect incarnation of his ideal. While Nisard's method confirmed the enduring beauty of the classical writers, it failed to consider evolving literary ideals of beauty and truth.

NODIER, CHARLES (1780–1844), poet, novelist, storywriter, Arsenal* librarian, and avid bibliophile throughout his life, was born in Besançon, the son of a lawyer who became mayor of that city. Details of his early life are sketchy, except that as a child he witnessed firsthand executions during the Reign of Terror presided over by his father as head of the criminal tribunal. These left an indelible impression upon him, which showed up later in his writings as a preoccupation with death and decapitation. He was librarian in his native town, then went to Paris, where he plunged into the literary scene. In 1802, he wrote *Les Proscrits* (*The Outlaws*), a novel dramatizing his early adventures, but fled Paris later that year after satirizing the emperor in an ode, "La Napoléone." He returned to Besançon and travelled to Dole and other places. The following year, inspired by *Werther* (Goethe, 1774), he wrote a sentimental novel, *Le Peintre de Salzbourg* (*The Painter of Salzburg*, 1803). His *Essais d'un jeune barde* (*Essays of a Young Bard*, 1804) are charming poems, written in the style of Ossian (3d century Gaelic bard); *Tristes ou Mélanges tirés des tablettes d'un suicide* (*Melancholies or Miscellanies Taken from the Notebooks of a Suicide*, 1806) reveals his preoccupation with death. In 1812, he left France under the protection of Joseph Fouché (1759–1820), a minister of the Empire and family friend, for Illyria, on the east coast of the Adriatic, where he was a librarian for several months in its capital, Laybach. When he returned, he published articles defending classicism in *Journal des débats* (*Debate Journal*). He wrote a historical novel, *Histoire des sociétés secrètes de l'armée* (*History of the Secret Societies of the Army*, 1815), another outlaw novel entitled *Jean Sbogar* (1818), *Thérèse Aubert* (1819), and *Adèle* (1820). Around 1820, his interests turned to horror and "la frénésie" (see frénétique*). He collaborated on a melodrama, *Le Vampire*

(*The Vampire,* 1820), and wrote the nightmarish *Smarra ou Les Démons de la nuit* (*Smarra or the Demons of the Night,* 1821). In 1821, he met Walter Scott (1771–1832) in Scotland. Upon his return, he wrote his masterpiece, *Trilby* (1822), less frenetic than *Smarra,* but still phantasmal and dreamlike. The following year, he was named librarian of the Arsenal.* The salon he held there from 1824 to 1834 for young poets was renowned as the literary hub of Paris. Around 1830, however, he suffered a depression. With Victor Hugo* the acknowledged leader of the romantic movement, Nodier's cénacle* at the Arsenal had lost its luster. He lamented the marriage of his daughter and had serious money problems. He resorted to dreaming and the world of his subconscious and, until he died, wrote more than thirty stories of dream-worlds, fantasy, and lunacy, including *Hélène Gillet* (1832), *Ines de las Sierras* (1837), and *La Fée aux miettes* (*The Fairy with Crumbs,* 1832).

Nodier was influenced by illuminism, an occult philosophy that attempts to uncover the meaning of the symbols of the world. For him, the unconscious world of dreams and sleep, where the spirit is free and in its proper element, was the true world, the most powerful one, the source of the myths of humanity and of its greatest thoughts. The story *Trilby,* about a boat-woman's happiness with a sprite who inhabits her cottage, evokes a dream-world until the sprite is exorcised and she commits suicide. *La Fée aux miettes,* perhaps his most beautiful story, is about a carpenter who inhabits a lunatic house in Glasgow and falls in love with an old, deformed beggar named "La Fée aux miettes." After a series of adventures, he marries her and at night she is transformed into Belkiss, the beautiful queen of Saba. He is finally caught and returned to the asylum. Nodier wrote in the preface to this story that "the good and true fantasy-story of an age without beliefs, cannot be suitably placed except in the mouth of a lunatic." Nodier's mysticism and fantasy, his probing of the subconscious, will be seen again in Nerval,* who acknowledged him as his "spiritual tutor," and point the way to the symbolism** of the later nineteenth century and the surrealism** of the twentieth.

For further information, see G. Crichfield, "The Alchemical Magnum Opus in Nodier's *La Fée aux miettes,*" *Nineteenth Century French Studies* 11 (3–4) (Spring–Summer 1983): 231–245; Crichfield, "The Romantic Madman as Hero: Nodier's *Michel le Charpentier,*" *French Review* 51 (May 1978): 835–842; D. Kelly, "The Ghost of Meaning: Language in the Fantastic," *Sub-stance,* 35 (1982): 46–55; B. Knapp, "*La Fée aux miettes:* an Alchemical Hieros Gamos," in *Pre-Text. Text. Context. Essays on Nineteenth Century French Literature,* Robert L. Mitchell, ed. (Columbus: Ohio State University Press, 1980); R.A.G. Pearson, "Poetry or Psychology? The Representation of Dream in Nodier's *Smarra,*" *French Studies* 36 (4) (October 1982): 410–426; L. M. Porter, "Hoffmanesque and Hamiltonian Sources of Nodier's *Fée aux Miettes,*" *Romance Notes* 19 (Spring 1979): 341–344; Porter, "Nodier and La Fontaine," *Neuphilologische Mitteilungen* 4 (1979): 390–398.

NOTRE-DAME DE PARIS (*Notre-Dame of Paris,* 1831), by Victor Hugo,* a historical novel set in fifteenth-century Paris, presents a tableau of medieval life under the reign of Louis XI and dominated by the towering, omnipresent figure of the cathedral. Against the gothic backdrop of the Middle Ages, with its religion, superstition, and customs, Hugo paints a somber tale of tragedy and cruelty. Written in the dawn of the romantic age, with its young author heavily influenced by Walter Scott (1771–1832), the novel marries the romantics' love for history, fantasy, and mystery with Hugo's imagination and creativity. It teems with life—the city, its gypsies and beggars, dark streets, and crowded festivals strain against the confines of the novel to produce a masterwork of romantic literature.

The plot centers around Esmeralda, a young and beautiful gypsy, and the three men who love her—the archdeacon Claude Frollo; the handsome captain of the Royal Archers, Phoebus de Chateaupers; and the hunchbacked bell-ringer, Quasimodo. The story opens in Paris on 6 January 1482, the day of the Festival of Fools. Esmeralda is dancing before the crowds at the Place de Grève. On Frollo's orders, Quasimodo kidnaps her, but she is rescued by Chateaupers. Frollo has Chateaupers killed at a secret rendezvous with Esmeralda who, left with the body, is accused of murder. Found guilty, she is condemned to die before the cathedral. Quasimodo, however, hides her in the cathedral; Frollo engages the help of the poet Gringoire and his fellow rogues and truants, who attack the cathedral at midnight. Quasimodo counters them single-handedly, while Frollo, disguised, persuades Esmeralda to flee with him. When she recognizes him, she refuses and he leaves her in the care of an old recluse while he goes off to denounce her to the authorities. The old woman realizes that Esmeralda is her daughter, stolen by gypsies as a baby. The authorities arrive, Esmeralda is hung, and her mother dies of remorse. From the top of the cathedral, Frollo happily watches Esmeralda die. Quasimodo pushes him off and goes himself to join in death his beloved gypsy dancer.

As a novel, *Notre-Dame de Paris* has been criticized for its lack of psychological depth, its difficult plot, its historical inaccuracies and digressions. As a novel written by the greatest poet of the nineteenth century and perhaps all of French literature, however, *Notre-Dame de Paris* has other virtues. Like the best of Hugo's poetry, it attains an epic vision that surpasses the confines of the written word to become a masterpiece of life and meaning. His research through historical archives and the works of historian Henri Sauval (1620–1676) are the point of departure for a grandiose evocation of an entire era. Hugo transforms gothic architecture into a symbol of medieval thought and expression. Realistic descriptions capture the medieval atmosphere and mirror the fatalism pervading the novel. The characters manifest the duality of natures set down in Hugo's *Préface de Cromwell** and explored throughout his life. *Notre-Dame de Paris* is a novel written by a poet who brought to it the force and creativity of genius and a vision and imagination uniquely his.

For further information, see V. Brady-Papadopoulu, "The Sun, the Moon and the Sacred Marriage: An Alchemical Reading of *Notre-Dame de Paris*," *Esprit créateur* 22 (Summer 1982): 11–17; K. Grossman, "Hugo's Poetics of Harmony: Transcending Dissonance in *Notre-Dame de Paris*," *Nineteenth Century French Studies* 11 (3–4)

(Spring–Summer, 1983): 205–215; S. Haig, "From Cathedral to Book, from Stone to Press: Hugo's Portrait of the Artist in *Notre-Dame de Paris*," *Stanford French Review* 3 (Winter 1979): 343–350; S. Nash, "Writing a Building: Hugo's *Notre-Dame de Paris*," *French Forum* 8 (2) (May 1983): 122–133; I. Zarifopol-Johnston, "*Notre-Dame de Paris*: The Cathedral in the Book," *Nineteenth Century French* Studies 13 (2–3) (Winter–Spring 1985): 22–35.

NOUVEAU, GERMAIN (1852–1920). See *Dictionary of Modern French Literature, from Naturalism and Symbolism to Post-Modernism*.

NOUVELLE HELOISE, JULIE OU LA (*Julie or The New Heloise*, 1761), by Jean-Jacques Rousseau,* weaves the author's fantasies, sensitivities, and philosophies into a novel of love and virtue, passion and purity. Written in the manner of Samuel Richardson's (1689–1761) *Clarisse Harlowe* (1747–1748) and conceived amid the idylls of L'Ermitage, where he had retreated in 1756 to complete works in progress, the novel encompasses "an ideal world which my creative imagination peopled with beings according to my heart" (*Les Confessions**).

The relatively simple plot, which can be divided into two sections of three parts each, recounts in an exchange of letters the love affair between a young Swiss noblewoman, Julie d'Etanges (an idealization of Rousseau's love, Madame d'Houdetot), and her tutor, commoner Saint-Preux, recalling the twelfth-century tale of Héloïse and her tutor, Abélard. Despite the young man's good qualities, Julie's father, the baron d'Etanges, refuses to consent to marriage. Saint-Preux and his friend Milord Edouard leave for Paris, and though still in love, Julie accedes to her father's will and marries Baron Wolmar. The rejected Saint-Preux considers suicide, but deterred by Edouard, undertakes a world voyage instead.

The second section of the novel describes the peaceful existence of the Wolmars at Clarens. The devoted wife confides in her husband the secret of her former indiscretions with Saint-Preux, and when he returns on the scene six years later, Wolmar, confident of his wife's virtue, generously invites him to stay with them. The two former lovers find the old flame still glowing as they return to familiar sites. Both resist. Julie vainly tries to match Saint-Preux with her widowed cousin Claire and steeps herself in religion until efforts to retrieve her drowning son from Lake Geneva result in her untimely death. Though she implores him in a final letter to marry Claire, Saint-Preux declines, dedicating himself instead to the education of Julie's remaining son.

La Nouvelle Héloïse enjoyed immediate popular success both in France and abroad, giving rise to nearly a hundred editions between its initial publication and the year 1800. Though modern critics consider its portrait of passion dated, verbose, and excessive, the novel contains the political and philosophical beliefs previously developed in Rousseau's early discourses and later enlarged upon in *Emile** and *Le Contrat social.** The moral and social corruption Saint-Preux finds in Paris contrasts with the beauty and morality of rustic Clarens. The

Wolmars themselves represent an ideal of simplicity and purity, emphasizing Rousseau's faith in the family as a primary social unit. Questions of religion and education are examined, as well as aspects of Parisian life—Saint-Preux and Julie exchange letters on the opera and theatre, duelling, suicide, and atheism. Above all, its sensitive portrayal of love, its lyrical descriptions of the rocks and mountains of le Valais and their rapport with the characters' emotions establish *La Nouvelle Héloïse* as an important forerunner to the nineteenth-century romanticism* of Chateaubriand,* George Sand,* Musset,* and Hugo.* Martin Turnell, in his *Rise of the French Novel* (1978), calls it the "first great Romantic novel."

For further information, see M. E. Birkett, "Rousseau and the Poetry of Mountaineering," in A. Singer, ed., *Essays on the Literature of Mountaineering* (Morgantown: West Virginia University Press, 1982); J. Charvet, "The Ideal of Love in *La Nouvelle Héloïse*," in R. Leigh, ed., *Rousseau after Two Hundred Years: Proceedings of the Cambridge Bicentennial Colloquium* (Cambridge: Cambridge University Press, 1982), 133–152; H. M. Davidson, "Dialectical Order and Movement in *La Nouvelle Héloïse*," in A. Bingham and V. Topazio, eds., *Enlightenment Studies in Honor of Lester G. Crocker* (Oxford: Voltaire Foundation, 1979); C. Duckworth, "Georgiana Spencer in France: Or the Dangers of Reading Rousseau," *Eighteenth Century Life* 7 (3) (May 1982): 85–91: C. Frayling, "The Composition of *La Nouvelle Héloïse*," in S. Harvey, M. Hobson, D. Kelly, and S. Taylor, eds. *Reappraisals of Rousseau. Studies in Honor of Ralph A. Leigh* (Manchester: Manchester University Press, 1980); J. F. Jones, Jr., "*La Nouvelle Héloïse*": *Rousseau and Utopia* (Geneva: Droz, 1978); D. Kadish, "Binary Narrative Structure and Moral Intent: Rousseau and Gide," in E. Crook, ed., *Fearful Symmetry: Doubles and Doubling in Literature and Film* (Tallahassee: University Press of Florida, 1982), 100–112; P. Kamuf, "Inside Julie's Closet," *Romanic Review* 69 (November 1978): 296–306; J. Lechte, "Fiction and Woman in *La Nouvelle Héloïse* and the Heritage of '1789,'" in F. Barker, J. Bernstein, P. Hulme, M. Iverson, and J. Store, eds., *1789: Reading, Writing, Revolution: Proceedings of the Essex Conference on the Sociology of Literature*, July 1981 (Colchester: University of Essex, 1982), 38–51; D. P. Webb, "Wolmar's 'Méthode' and the Function of Identity in *La Nouvelle Héloïse*," *Romanic Review* 70 (March 1979): 113–118.

O

OBERMANN (1804), by Senancour,* is a psychological portrait of the romantic (see romanticism*) soul, which he painted from his own experience of life. The novel consists of ninety-one letters written by Obermann to a friend, which chronicle the torment of his existence from the age of twenty when, unable to support the "intolerable ennui" of his life, he flees to Switzerland to escape his family's plans for him, until the age of twenty-five. In the land of J.-J. Rousseau,* he wanders amid the Alps. He returns to Paris, a city he finds also intolerable, where he spends a great deal of time, as did Senancour himself, in the forests of Fontainebleau. The dreams and thoughts on the vanity of life and his inability to find happiness unleashed on his walks are the subjects of most of the letters. After a few years, an inheritance permits him to return to Switzerland, where he embarks on a writing career.

Obermann was virtually ignored until George Sand's* discovery of it in 1833. After that, it was read and enjoyed by the romantics, who identified with his sadness, his social isolation, his dreams of impossible happiness, his questioning of destiny, his lyric outpourings on love, social pity, and nature. Like Senancour, Obermann is trying to resolve the mystery of his existence. He is seeking the meaning of life and a way to live without knowing the answer. He feels detached from God, detached from others, and painfully aware of the immense void within himself. Obermann seeks solace in the mathematics of Pythagoras or the philosophy of Swedish theologian Emanuel Swedenborg (1688–1772). Despite the occasional healing found in the beauty of nature, Obermann remains captive to his feelings of despair, passivity, uselessness, spiritual nonexistence. George Sand, in her preface to the third edition of the work in 1840, wrote that Obermann was like a bird "to whom nature had denied wings."

The influence of Rousseau on *Obermann* is evident—the personal confessions, the rapport between nature and soul, the lyric effusion. Obermann is distinguished, however, by his intelligence. He sought the meaning of his existence and the human condition on an intellectual level that speaks to the modern conscience facing the same questions.

For further information, see M. N. Evans, "The Dream Sequences in Senancour's *Obermann*," *Symposium* 32 (Spring 1978): 1–14.

O'NEDDY, PHILOTHEE (1811–1875, born Théophile Dondey), was a minor romantic poet and habitué of Borel's* petit cénacle.* He was born in Paris, lived all his life there, and, after a radical youth, settled down as a clerk in the Ministry of Finance to support his mother and sister. His one claim to fame is his collection of poems, *Feu et flamme* (*Fire and Flame*, 1833), which O'Neddy published himself with little success. The poems are irreverent and audacious and belong to the frénétique* genre yet contain an undercurrent of deeply felt desperation and pain. O'Neddy used the term "spleen" to describe his condition, along with "miasmes" and "dandysme." He wrote little else during his lifetime and died nearly forgotten, except by Baudelaire,** who found in him a source of inspiration.

ON NE BADINE PAS AVEC L'AMOUR (*Do Not Trifle with Love*, 1834), a comedy in three acts written by Alfred de Musset,* was written after his ill-fated romance with George Sand* in Italy and illustrates a tenet dear to his heart, that one should not play with love. For Musset, love and poetry ranked highest among the important things in life. The play was originally published in *La Revue des deux mondes* and not performed until 1861, after Musset's death, considerably altered by his brother Paul. It met with only moderate success. In 1918, the original text was performed for the first time.

The play was written in the tradition of the proverbe dramatique* a dramatic form that Musset admired and practiced. It evokes the fantasy world of William Shakespeare's (1564–1616) later comedies. The influence of Marivaux,* with his analyses of sentiment, is apparent. The play's originality stems from its counterpoint of dream and reality, comedy and drama. The principal players, Camille and Perdican, act out their drama of jealousy and pride against the backdrop of comic characters, the baron, Blazius, Bridaine, and Dame Pluche, often called marionettes. The tone becomes more somber as the play progresses, climaxing in the death of innocent Rosette. The play is important for its depiction of the human heart, and the drama it portrays is that of Musset himself.

Act 1 opens before the baron's castle, with a chorus of villagers signaling the arrival of the wine-drinking Maître Blazius, who announces the return of the baron's son, Perdican, a young man just come of age who has been named a doctor in Paris. Dame Pluche arrives next, with news of the arrival of Camille, the baron's niece, whom she describes as "a glorious flower of wisdom and devotion." In the following scene, the village cure, Maître Bridaine, denounces Blazius, but the baron, incredulous, reveals his plans to marry his son to Camille. The modest young woman refuses Perdican a kiss and is unmoved by his memories of their childhood together. Perdican goes to the village and finds

Rosette, Camille's pretty foster-sister, and invites her to dine at the castle, to his father's dismay.

In act 2, Camille tells Perdican that she doesn't want to marry and that she is returning the next day to the convent. Perdican says that he would welcome her friendship if he cannot have her hand in marriage. Camille asks Dame Pluche to convey a letter to Perdican, asking him to come at noon to the little fountain. Perdican courts Rosette, but thinks of Camille. At their rendezvous, Camille says that at the convent she learned to fear men, love, and marriage and plans to take her vows. Perdican replies that all men are liars, unfaithful, false, gossips, hypocrites, proud, and cowardly, and that all women are false, pretentious, vain, and depraved, but "there is one thing in the world which is holy and sublime, and that is the union of two of these imperfect and horrible beings."

Act 3 begins with the baron chasing Blazius from his chateau. Perdican questions whether or not he really loves Camille. He intercepts a letter written by Camille to a friend, saying that she has wounded him deeply by refusing him. Angry and wanting to make her jealous, he arranges to have her witness a love scene between him and Rosette. Camille understands that Perdican is acting out of spite and plans to spite him back. She tells Rosette that he will never marry her and hides her behind a curtain to spy on a scene that will prove it. When Perdican admits his love for Camille, she lifts the curtain to expose Rosette, who has fainted on a chair. Camille pretends to set up Rosette as an example of Perdican's inconstancy but becomes a victim of her own doing. Perdican vows to marry Rosette as soon as possible and is dissuaded neither by Camille's reproaches nor his father's anger. The final scene finds Camille in a chapel, asking God why he has abandoned her. Perdican has followed her there, and both finally admit their love for one another. As they embrace, they hear a cry from behind the altar. Rosette has overheard them and dies broken-hearted. Perdican beseeches God to revive her but to no avail. Rosette is dead and Camille departs.

For further information, see J. Hamilton, "From Ricochets to Jeu in Musset's *On ne badine pas avec l'amour*: A Game Analysis," *French Review* 58 (6) (May 1985): 820–826.

OPERA-COMIQUE, light comic opera comparable to twentieth-century musical comedy, developed early in the eighteenth century from the street entertainment of the théâtre de la foire.* Though rebuffed by the established Comédie-Française, the players, under the direction of impresario Jean Monnet since 1752, merged with the Théâtre Italien* ten years later to become the "Comédie Italienne" (though popularly called the "Opéra-Comique") and triumphed in its new home in the Hotel de Bourgogne. Initial presentations echoed or parodied offerings of the official opera. Eventually, the company produced spectacles of song and dance written especially for it by Charles Favart (1710–1792), who succeeded Monnet as director, and others by Sedaine,* Lesage,* and Piron.* The Italian element was completely absorbed, surviving today only in the name Boulevard des Italiens, and by 1780 the company, now officially the Opéra-

Comique, moved to Salle Favart. Two hundred years later, in December 1972, the theatre became "Centre national d'Art lyrique" (National Center for Lyric Art), and the company, still known as the Opéra-Comique or Salle Favart, as part of the Opera of Paris, is dedicated to presenting French music by French artists.

ORIENTALES, LES (*Oriental Poems*, 1829), by Victor Hugo,* is a collection of odes renowned for their vividness, lyricism, and innovative forms, which paint the beauty and exoticism of the Orient. The Greek war of independence from the Turks in 1821 stimulated a renewed interest in the Orient; for Hugo, the acknowledged leader of the romantic (see romanticism*) movement since 1827 and his *Préface de Cromwell*,* the war provided a forum for expressing his liberalism, both political and literary. Several of the poems depict his sympathy for the Greeks: "Canaris," "Navarin," and "L'Enfant" ("The Child"). The preface declares his freedom as a poet, "Everything is a possible subject; everything is in the domaine of art. . . . The poet is free."

Hugo had never visited the Orient, but solid research (Claude Fauriel's [1772–1844] *Les Chants populaires de la Grèce moderne*, 1824–1825; Abel Hugo's [1798–1855] translation of *Le Romancero;* Chateaubriand's* *Les Martyrs** and *L'Itinéraire* [1811]; the Bible; translations of Arabian and Persian texts and Lord Byron's [1788–1824] *Childe Harold* and *Giaour*), together with his powerful imagination and childhood memories of Spain, succeeded in capturing the ambiance of Greece, Arabia, Persia, Spain, Egypt, and Turkey. Some of the odes depict the violence and cruelty of the Orient ("Le Feu du ciel" ["The Fire from Heaven"]), its love of war ("Cri de guerre du mufti" ["The Mufti's War Cry"]), the injustices of the harem ("Claire de lune" ["Moonlight"], "La Sultane favorite" ["The Favorite Sultana"]). Others relate more generally to the Orient, "Mazeppa," "Rêverie," "Extase" ["Ecstacy"], "Grenade."

Hugo claimed that the idea for *Les Orientales* stemmed from watching, "like a painter," the colors of a Parisian sunset, which he witnessed during the summer of 1828. The poems are marked by their descriptive language, their use of color, shape, movement, and imagery. The best-known poem in the collection, "Les Djinns," describes the coming, arrival, and departure of a horde of evil spirits in verses that reflect the action of the poem. Though he states that *Les Orientales* was a "useless book of pure poetry," it was, in reality, a remarkable collection of forty-one poems whose beauty and originality instituted the notion of "art for art's sake" ("l'art pour l'art"*) and influenced Gautier,* de Lisle,* and the Parnassian* poets.

For further information, see R. Grant, "Sequence and Theme in Victor Hugo's *Les Orientales*," *Publications of the Modern Language Association* 94 (October 1979): 894–908; C. Stefanescu, "*Les Orientales* de Victor Hugo. An Imaginary Geography and a Programme Overcome," *Revista de istorie si teorie literara* 2 (1978): 219–229.

P

PAILLERON, EDOUARD (1834–1899), comic playwright in the manner of Augier* and Scribe,* whose fame rests essentially on one comedy of manners, *Le Monde où l'on s'ennuie* (*The World of Boredom*, 1881), a satire of literary circles and pedantic academic salons. He first published a collection of satires, *Les Parasites* (*The Parasites*, 1861), and verse plays, *Le Mur mitoyen* (*The Party Wall*, 1861), *Le Dernier Quartier* (*The Last Quarter*, 1863), *Les Faux Ménages* (*False Households*, 1869). He found his true vocation in prose comedies such as *Le Monde où l'on s'amuse* (*The World of Amusement*, 1868) and *Le Monde où l'on s'ennuie*. Pailleron was a careful observer of his contemporaries who prepared the way for realism* in the theatre.

PALISSOT DE MONTENOY, CHARLES (1730–1814), eighteenth-century playwright, journalist, and ardent enemy of the philosophes,* spearheaded the anti-encyclopedic movement directed against Diderot,* J.-J. Rousseau,* Voltaire,* and their cohorts. Aligned with Palissot were journalists Abbé Desfontaines (1685–1745), Abraham de Chaumeix (c.1730–1790), Nicolas Moreau (1717–1803), and Elie Fréron.* The precocious son of a counsellor to the duke of Lorraine and a brilliant student of rhetoric and philosophy, Palissot attained a master of arts degree at age eleven, wrote a number of unsuccessful plays, and finally distinguished himself with *Le Cercle* (*The Circle*, 1755), which cariacatured Rousseau, Voltaire, and Madame Gabrielle-Emilie du Châtelet. He wrote satirical pamphlets, including *Petites Lettres sur de grands philosophes* (*Little Letters on Great Philosophers*, 1757) against d'Alembert,* the philosophe "party," and Diderot's theory of drama as well as a poem in three cantos, *La Dunciade, ou La Guerre des sots* (*The Dunciade, or the War of the Fools*, 1764).

Palissot is best remembered, however, for his play *Les Philosophes* (*The Philosophes*, 1760), which, though considered superifical and of little intrinsic literary merit, is an important record of the social, religious, and political tempests raging at the time. Aimed particularly at Diderot, whom it disparaged as "Dortidius," the play also satirized d'Alembert, Helvétius,* Duclos,* Grimm,* and Rousseau, who as the valet Crispin, entered the scene on all fours with a head of lettuce in his pocket. Morellet* and Charles-Marie de la Condamine (1701–1774) reacted with satires; and Voltaire, though spared by Palissot, counterattacked with a satirical play, *Le Café ou L'Ecossaise* (*The Cafe or the Scotswoman,* 1760), directed against Palissot's supporter, Fréron. Palissot's *Philosophes* is said to have inspired Diderot's *Neveu de Rameau.**

Though Palissot enjoyed the protection of Louis XV, he later identified with the Revolution, sat in the Council of the Ancients from 1798 to 1799, and was an administrator of the Mazarin library. However, other than *Les Philosophes,* Palissot never fulfilled the promise of his genius.

PARADES, along with Proverbes dramatiques,* typify eighteenth-century "théâtre de société," light social theatre written to amuse the spectator. The parades originated as advertisements performed on the balconies outside the theatre hall to entice passersby to see the show. Spirited and often coarse dialogue and actions were intended to arouse the public's interest. Aristocrats such as Lenormand d'Etioles, husband of Madame de Pompadour (1721–1764), appreciated the ingenuity and spirit of the genre and encouraged their performance in private salons. Collé* popularized the genre; Beaumarchais's* *Jean Bête à la Foire* (*Jean Bete at the Fair,* written between 1757 and 1763), with its vivacity and satire, is an excellent example.

PARADOXE SUR LE COMEDIEN (*Paradox on Acting,* written, 1773–1778; published, 1830), by Diderot,* is an essay on acting and sensitivity written as a dialogue contrasting two opposing points of view. Having laid down the principles of drama twenty years earlier in *Entretiens sur le fils naturel* (*Dialogue on the Illegitimate Son,* 1757) and *De la poésie dramatique* (*On Dramatic Poetry,* 1758), Diderot establishes here, not only his conception of what constitutes superior acting but a relationship between sensitivity and creativity that applies to all forms of art.

Diderot defines the actor as a "marvelous puppet worked by the poet who holds his strings and indicates the actual position he must take," a puppet who, without emotion, must convey the illusion of emotion to the audience. The actor must "observe, study, and paint" rather than feel. "It is extreme sensitivity which makes mediocre actors, it is mediocre sensitivity which makes most bad actors, and it is the absolute lack of sensitivity which makes sublime actors."

Diderot himself was prey to his emotions ("If nature created a spirit sensitive to the impact of emotion, I am that man," he declared in the *Paradoxe*). However, the complexity and eloquence of his works testify to the power of his intellect and judgment, qualities he upheld as necessary in any creative endeavor.

For further information, see G. Bremner, "An Interpretation of Diderot's *Paradoxe sur le comédien,*" *The British Journal for Eighteenth-Century Studies* 4 (Spring 1981): 28–43; M. Cartwright, "Diderot and the Idea of Performance and the Performer," *Studies in Eighteenth Century French Literature presented to Robert Niklaus* (Exeter: University of Exeter, 1975): 31–42; J. Roach, "Diderot and the Actor's Machine," *Theatre Survey* 22 (1) (May 1981): 51–68; V. Swain, "Diderot's *Paradoxe sur le comédien:* The Paradox of Reading," *Studies on Voltaire and the Eighteenth Century* 208 (1982): 1–71.

PARNASSIANS, a group of poets that formed around Leconte de Lisle* between 1860 and 1866 and included Banville,* Heredia,* Sully-Prudhomme,* Coppée,* Ménard,* Mendès,* Dierx,* and others lasted until the Franco-Prussian War. The term "Parnassian," suggesting the mountain in southern Greece that was sacred to Apollo and the Muses, was proposed by Charles Marty-Laveaux (1823–1899), an obscure poet, to Alphonse Lemerre (1838–1912), who published its first collection of poems by thirty-seven young poets, *Le Parnasse contemporain: recueil de vers nouveaux* (*The Contemporary Parnassus: a Collection of New Verses,* 1866). Parnassian poetry grew from the "l'art pour l'art"* philosophy of Gautier,* adding a concern for scientific methodology and realist observation of the exterior world. It rejected the sentimentalism of Musset* and the social romanticism* of the 1830s for an ideal of beauty and art. The Parnassians stressed the need for autonomy in art. They upheld art as an absolute, an end in itself, from which beauty emanated as surely as manna from heaven. Their goal was to find and objectively express the enduring and visible beauty inherent in concrete reality. Unlike the romantics, their feet were firmly grounded in the physical rather than the spiritual world. Their poetry was formal, precise, impersonal, sober, and, in the face of human destiny, often profoundly pessimistic. It exalted Hellenistic perfection of form, equilibrium, and proportion.

Parnassian poetry was first published in a number of short-lived reviews, Mendès's *Revue fantaisiste* (*Review of the Fantastic,* February–November 1861), which extolled fantasy and art, and Xavier de Ricard's (1843–1911) *Revue du progrès* (*Review of Progress* (1863–1864), favoring scientific poetry. A third review, *L'Art* (November 1865–January 1866), also by Ricard, grew from the previous two and expressed the new ideal of poetry. When it ceased publication due to money constraints, the first edition of *Le Parnasse contemporain* appeared. A second edition followed in 1871, adding Victor-Richard de Laprade (1812–1887), Albert Glatigny (1839–1873), Anatole France,** and others to its contributors. In 1872, Banville's *Petit Traité de poésie française* (*Little Treaty of French Poetry*) outlined their technique. The third and final edition (1876) of *Le Parnasse contemporain* was a mere collection of the year's poetry with no unifying doctrine. The Parnassians met in the salon of the Marquise de Ricard, the mother of Xavier de Ricard, and at the home of de Lisle himself at 8 boulevard des Invalides.

Parnassian poetry constituted a definite rupture with the lyric, effusive, senti-mental, and socially conscious poetry of the romantics. It reflected the spirit of positivism* reigning in the 1850s and 1860s and served as a training ground for many young poets including Baudelaire,** Verlaine,** Mallarmé,** and Vil-liers de l'Isle-Adam,** who went on to distinguish themselves in symbolism** and other endeavors.

For further information, see *Parnasse. A Quarterly Journal Devoted to the Study of the French Parnassians and Their Influence,* Vol. 1, Nos. 1–4; Vol. 2, No. 1. (Oxford: Parnassian Study Circle, 1982, 1983).

PAYSAN PARVENU, LE (*The Peasant Who Gets Ahead in the World,* 1735–1736), by Marivaux,* written after the first two parts of *La Vie de Marianne* (*The Life of Marianne,* 1731–1741), is unfinished. Considered by many to be the male version of the longer and also incomplete memoir of *Marianne,* the novel recounts the rise of a humble vintner's son from Champagne to the world of wealthy Parisian financiers, petite bourgeoisie, and nobility. Capitalizing on his rustic good looks and simplicity, Jacob wiles the women of all social levels, from Genevieve, the chambermaid, to the aristocratic and pious Madame de Ferval. He marries Mademoiselle Habert, fiftyish, rich, and religious, who provides him not only with a name (Monsieur de la Vallée) and a life of ease, but with a sword, bedroom slippers, and other trappings of a gentleman. The fifth and final part of the novel finds Jacob at the theatre with Count d'Orsan, whose life he has just saved.

Like *Gil Blas,* Jacob's success story hinges often on chance and romanesque adventure; his ascension, however, is more rapid and assured. Jacob is more charming, more engaging in his simplicity, and more ingenuous than his pica-resque predecessors, and therein lies the key to his future.

Like *La Vie de Marianne,* the novel is important for its social realism* and analysis of Jacob's thoughts and feelings as he makes his way through the world.

For further information, see D. Coward, *Marivaux: La Vie de Marianne and Le Paysan parvenu* (London: Grant and Cutler, 1983); M.-P. Laden, "The Pitfalls of Success: Jacob's Evolution in Marivaux's *Le Paysan Parvenu,*" *Romanic Review* 74 (2) (March 1983): 170–182.

PERE GORIOT, LE (*Father Goriot,* 1834), by Balzac,* a novel in the *Scènes de la vie privée* (*Scenes from Private Life*) category of his *Comédie humaine,* originally appeared in *La Revue de Paris* (*The Paris Review*) and was published in book form the following year. It is dedicated to French evolutionist Geoffroy de Saint-Hilaire (1772–1844) as a token of Balzac's "admiration for his works and his genius." Under the influence of Saint-Hilaire, Balzac set out to depict representative social types similar to the species of the natural world. *Le Père Goriot* is the third of his studies of monomania, after Mr. Grandet's (see *Eugénie Grandet*) avarice and Balthazar Claes's (in *La Recherche de l'absolu,* 1834) passion for scientific research. Father Goriot represents the passion of all-consuming fatherhood. He loves his two daughters so much that he sacrifices all for them, even his self-respect.

The story takes place in Paris in 1819 where Goriot lives in a middle-class boardinghouse run by Madame Vauquer. The novel opens with a vivid description, a trademark of the Balzacian novel, of Madame Vauquer, her musty, old Latin Quarter establishment, and its seven lodgers. They are a curious mix: Eugène de Rastignac, a young, impoverished nobleman from Angoulême who, at great family expense, is studying law; Father Goriot, a retired noodle manufacturer; the mysterious Vautrin, a congenial man of about forty; the curious spinster, Mademoiselle Michonneau and her companion, Poiret; the young Victorine Taillefer, whose father has abandoned her to the care of Madame Couture, the widow of a commissary general. Several law and medical students, including Bianchon, dine there every evening. Father Goriot raises the suspicions of his fellow boarders by receiving chic female visitors, whom he claims are his daughters, into his quarters.

Young Rastignac is aware that the hopes of his entire family are pinned on his ability to succeed in Paris. Family connections enable him to penetrate the exclusive circle of his distant cousin, Madame de Beauséant. She teaches him the ways of the capital and how to succeed in it. "The more coldly you calculate, the further you will go," she says, advising him to seek the support of a "young, rich, elegant" woman. "If you have a true feeling, hide it like a treasure; let it never be suspected or you will be lost," she tells him. Rastignac has just learned Goriot's secret, that he has ruined himself and condemned himself to poverty so that his daughters may live in luxury. One daughter, Anastasie, married a gentleman of the ancien régime; Delphine married a banker named a baron during the reign of Napoleon. Both are embarassed by their father now, and he has banished himself from them. Madame de Beauséant suggests that Rastignac court Delphine, whose desires to frequent the old nobility could ingratiate her to him.

Back at the pension, Vautrin has sensed Rastignac's desire for success and suggests that Rastignac marry Victorine Taillefer. For 20 percent of her inheritance, Vautrin will kill her brother, making her sole heiress to her father's fortune. Rastignac refuses, swearing to earn his money honestly. He befriends Delphine de Nucingen, Goriot's daughter, and frequents the gaming tables. Vautrin, undaunted, has Victorine's brother murdered, but his true identity is revealed when he is drugged and the initials T.F. ("travaux forcés," "hard labor") appear on his shoulders. He is in reality Jacques Collin, the escaped convict known as "Trompe-la-mort" ("Death Cheater"). The police arrive on the scene and after a dramatic adieu, in which Vautrin condemns society as rotten, he is arrested.

Goriot, much to Madame Vauquer's despair, sets Rastignac and Delphine up in a charming little apartment. The next day at the pension, Rastignac overhears the two daughters relate their money problems to their father. Delphine's husband has his money invested in some shady speculations; she cannot secure her dowry from him. Anastasie has sold her husband's family's diamonds to settle the debts of her lover, Maxime de Trailles. Her husband has found out and is threatening her, and de Trailles is still in need of money. The two selfish girls argue vehemently, insulting each other, bringing an attack of apoplexy upon their father. Goriot, in the meantime, had sold his last pieces of silver for a thousand francs for a new dress for Delphine to wear to the Beauséant's ball. As his end draws near, Goriot sends for his daughters, but they refuse him. Anastasie is meeting with her husband, and Delphine is sleeping after the ball. Goriot, realizing that they will not come, chastises himself for spoiling them, acknowledging that if he had kept his fortune, they would be there at his side. Delphine arrives after Goriot has lost consciousness, deploring too late her behavior. Rastignac and Bianchon pay Goriot's funeral expenses. The empty carriages of his daughters follow the hearse to the gates of Père-Lachaise cemetery, where the young student, along with Christophe, the pension handyman, witnesses his solitary burial. At the cemetery, Rastignac, who has learned life's cruelty, cries his final tears as a youth. From the highest point of the cemetery, overlooking the beautiful, glittering Paris he hoped to conquer, he sends out his challenge, "A nous deux maintenant!" ("May the stronger of us win!") and goes to dine with Delphine.

Le Père Goriot depicts Balzac's vision of social corruption and the violence of passion. As it paints the portrait of Goriot's all-consuming paternalism, it presents the story of Rastignac's initiation into Paris society, his education in materialism and corruption. Rastignac learns that title, ambition, and sentiment are not enough; he needs the backing of a wealthy woman in order to succeed. Goriot sacrifices his entire worth to elevate his daughters into the social hierarchy.

Le Père Goriot is the first novel of the Comédie humaine to apply Balzac's idea of using recurring characters. Rastignac was already seen in La Peau de chagrin (The Wild Ass's Skin, 1831). He, along with Vautrin, will reappear in Illusions perdues (Lost Illusions, 1837–1843), Splendeurs et Misères des Courtisanes (Splendors and Miseries of the Courtesans, 1839–1847), and others. Similarly, other characters will be rewoven into the various threads of the novels. Though critics have disparaged its exaggerations, the novel enjoyed great popular success. Balzac was more pleased with it than he was with Eugénie Grandet.*

For further information, see R. Butler, "The Realist Novel as 'Roman d'education': Ideological Debate and Social Action in Le Père Goriot and Germinal," Nineteenth Century French Studies 12 (1–2) (Fall–Winter 1983–1984): 68–77; A. Pasco, "Image Structure in Le Père Goriot," French Forum 7 (3) (September 1982): 224–234; K. Rivers, " 'Cor-norama': Exclusion, Fathers and Language in the Society of Le Père Goriot," Stanford French Review 9 (Summer 1985): 153–168; W. Stowe, "Interpretation in Fiction: Le Père Goriot and The American," Texas Studies in Language and Literature 23 (2) (Summer 1981): 248–267; A. Tintner, "Henry James's 'The Pension Beaurepas': A Translation into American Terms of Balzac's Le Père Goriot," Revue de *littérature comparée*, 3 (July–September 1983): 369–376; P. Willis, " 'Angels' and 'Fillies' in *Le Père Goriot*," *Nineteenth Century French Studies* 12 (1–2) (Fall–Winter 1983–1984): 78–85.

PERSIAN LETTERS, THE (*Les Lettres persanes*) (1721), by Montesquieu,* published anonymously in Amsterdam, combines exoticism, social observation, and political theory into a loosely woven tale of oriental intrigue and philosophy. A thinly disguised satire of Parisian attitudes, customs, and politics, Montesquieu's first major work contains many ideas about justice, penology, law, and government further developed in *The Spirit of the Laws* (see *L'Esprit des lois**) (1748).

Two Persians, Usbek and Rica, visit France from 1712 to 1720. The story consists of their correspondence with friends on happenings back in their native Ispahan as well as their impressions of Europe, especially France. Usbek, the older Persian, has fled his country for political reasons, leaving his harem in the care of a black eunuch; Rica is younger and unburdened. During their absence, Usbek's wives rebel. Though he sends orders from afar, his commands are ineffectual in containing their revolt. His favorite, Roxane, reveals herself as unfaithful and poisons herself in the end, declaring in a final letter to him that though she has lived in servitude, she has always been free. "I have reformed your laws according to those of nature and my spirit has always maintained itself in independence" (Letter CLXI).

Interspersed among the letters dealing with the harem's delights and problems for its master are letters relating the essence of the book—Montesquieu's observations on French life and government through satire, allegory, and short essays on topics such as religion, government, justice, and morality. Montesquieu presents his ideas undogmatically, often tentatively, through bewildered Persian eyes that notice women without veils or eunuchs, houses "so high one would believe them inhabited only by astrologers;" and Frenchmen who "run" and "fly" through the streets (Letter XXIV). The Persians find the king a "great magician" who wills his subjects' minds, and the Pope "another magician," more powerful than the first, who owns his subjects' souls (Letter XXIV). Various letters portraying characters à la Bruyere satirize the tax farmer, the nobleman, the lackey, the starving poet, the coquette, and the retired soldier.

Besides social satire, the novel discusses theology, metaphysics, forms of government, colonies, law, divorce, the Romans, and suicide. The Troglodyte allegory relates Montesquieu's notion of freedom based on virtue and the burdens it imposes. When the virtuous Troglodyte nation, prosperous and growing, needs a king, the wise old man they choose accepts sadly, saying, "But realize that I shall die of grief to have seen Troglodytes born free and to see them today subjugated. . . . I see well what is happening, o Troglodytes! Your virtue is beginning to weigh you down. In your present state, without a chief, you must be virtuous in spite of yourself. . . . But this yoke seems too heavy; you prefer to be subjects of a prince and obey his laws, less rigid than your customs" (Letter

XIV). Usbek's harem, on the other hand, is an unnatural situation where individuals are repressed and despotism reigns. Montesquieu's ideal is that government which "accomplishes its aims at least expense" and "leads men in the manner most appropriate to their leanings and inclinations" (Letter LXXX).

The Persian Letters, like *The Characters* of La Bruyere, are witty and amusing, provocative and instructive. Its themes—justice, nature, humanity, and freedom—will be found again in Rousseau,* Diderot,* and Bernardin de Saint-Pierre.*

For further information, see P. Kra, "The Role of the Harem in Imitation of Montesquieu's *Lettres Persanes,*" *Studies on Voltaire and the 18th Century* 182 (1979): 273–283; S. Spruell, "The Metaphorical Use of Sexual Repression to Represent Political Oppression in Montesquieu's *Persian Letters,*" *Proceedings of the Annual Meeting of the Western Society for French History* 8 (1981): 147–158.

PHILOSOPHE is a term that designates eighteenth-century freethinkers such as Voltaire,* Montesquieu,* Diderot,* and J.-J. Rousseau,* who put their faith in reason above all else to cure the political, social, moral, and religious ills, not only of France, but of all Europe. Diderot defined the philosophe as "an honest man who acts in everything according to reason"; his *Encyclopédie* claimed that besides reading and observing, "to be a philosophe is to have solid principles and above all a good method in order to explain facts and to draw from them rightful results."

The philosophe's "good method" originated with the seventeenth-century philosopher René Descartes (1596–1650), whose *Discours de la méthode (Discourse on Method,* 1637) proposed that all the sciences are interconnected and therefore must be studied deductively; one must progress from the known to the unknown. His rationalism and method, together with an interest in science fueled by Isaac Newton's (1642–1727) physics and discoveries in chemistry and mathematics, led, by mid-century to the free examination of the very foundations of society. Religion, based in faith rather than reason, was considered arbitrary and superstitious; its dogma, hypocrisy; theological disputes and political power were considered immoral. D'Holbach,* La Mettrie,* and Diderot denied the existence of the soul; determinism, a direct descendant of Descartes's deductive thinking, took root. Voltaire, believing that religion was necessary only for the masses, opted for deism; Rousseau, for theism; Diderot, for pantheism. Atheism followed as a logical consequence.

Likewise, the monarchy, with its wars, heavy taxes, and financial difficulties, was considered corrupt. Though France was ostensibly the most powerful and richest nation in the world, this was due to its megalomaniac kings and corrupt ruling class. Supported by an intolerant and unjust church, the government extracted money and blood from a miserable, ignorant peasantry who enjoyed no freedom. Montesquieu compared the king to an Oriental despot in his *Lettres persanes* (see *Persian Letters**). His and Voltaire's search for the best government possible led to English empiricist John Locke (1632–1704) and English government as an ideal of liberty, equality, and tolerance.

As French thinking became more cosmopolitan, its literature, born of its enthusiasm for science and its empiricism, spread throughout the continent. Montesquieu studied the science of law; Buffon* wrote a monumental *Histoire naturelle* (1749–1788); Voltaire proclaimed Newton's law in prose and verse; a passage from Diderot's *Rêve de d'Alembert** anticipates Darwin's theory of evolution; Chénier,* at the end of the century, envisioned a scientific poetry.

By mid-century, the philosophes wielded a literature of action, progress, combat, an arm of the developing bourgeoisie. Stories, poems, letters, dialogues, and plays, brimming with ideas and imagination, actively combatted tyranny and injustice and promoted the philosophe's faith in reason and progress. In his pamphlets, plays, and philosophical stories, Voltaire denounced the abuses of the regime and the fanaticism of the clerics. Diderot's *Encyclopédie* unearthed traditional beliefs. Rousseau proposed new social and political models. Literature retained the form but not the substance of seventeenth-century classicism, looking outward to society and politics rather than inward to psychological conflict for its themes. It sought to instruct, persuade, and motivate change. Rousseau and Diderot cast off the final remnants of the classical age and found in themselves and nature a sensitivity that would reach full flower in the romanticism* of the next century.

Other philosophes include Condillac,* Turgot,* Condorcet,* Morellet,* Marmontel,* Helvétius,* and Raynal.* Many, including Voltaire and Diderot, were imprisoned for their audacity, their works condemned or publicly burned by the regime. Critics today occasionally find their didacticism sterile; their literature, sacrificing art for truth; their works, mere imitations of the classical masters. Yet the philosophe, with his belief in man's reason and capability for social, political, scientific, and moral progress, fostered a social and political upheaval that shook the foundations of his government, gave birth to the ideals of democracy, and revolutionized human thought.

For further information, see J. Barzun, "The Century of Light: Some Unanswered Questions," *Studies in Eighteenth Century Culture* 12 (1983): 3–10; H. S. Commager, *The Empire of Reason: How Europe Imagined and America Realized the Enlightenment* (Oxford: University Press, 1982); G. Cropp, "John McManners: Death and the Enlightenment," *New Zealand Journal of French Studies* 4 (2) (November 1983): 47–52; R. Darnton, *The Literary Underground of the Old Regime* (Cambridge: Harvard University Press, 1982); R. Graham, "The Revolutionary Bishops and the Philosophes," *Eighteenth Century Studies* 16 (Winter 1982–1983): 117–140; N. Hampson, "The Enlightenment in France," in Porter and Teich, eds., *The Enlightenment in National Context* (Cambridge: Cambridge University Press, 1981), 41–53; N. Torrey, *Les Philosophes* (New York: Putnam, 1980).

PHYSIOCRAT is a term that designates those eighteenth-century philosophers subscribing to a code of nature ("physio" = nature; "crat" = government) that considered the soil society's true source of wealth and the farmer its most valuable worker. Mirabeau* (author of *L'ami des hommes* [*The Friend of Man*], 1756–1760; *Philosophie rurale* [*Rural Philosophy*], 1763), the abbé Baudeau

(*Introduction à la philosophie economique* [*Introduction to Economic Philosophy*], 1771), Le Trosne Guillaume-François (1728–1780) (*De l'ordre social* [*On the Social Order*], 1777), Morellet,* Mercier de Larivière (1720–1793), Dupont de Nemours (1739–1817), Quesnay,* and Turgot,* as its principal proponents, are considered the founders of the science of economics. They sustained criticism by the philosophes,* especially abbé Mably* and Voltaire,* who ridiculed them in *L'Homme aux quarante écus* (*The Man with Forty Crowns,* 1768). The physiocrats believed in free trade, advocated political reforms, and worked to decrease the misery and poverty of the peasants. They defended democracy, education, and the aims of the French Revolution as a guarantee against despotism.

PIERRE ET JEAN (1888), by Maupassant.** See *Dictionary of Modern French Literature, from Naturalism and Symbolism to Post-Modernism.*

PIRON, ALEXIS (1689–1773), born in Dijon, the son of an apothecary, practiced all the genres, especially light verse, epigrams, and comedy. He studied law but never practiced it, preferring to release his mordant wit and humor in odes, epigrams, epistles, satires, and contes, which besides renown, won him many enemies, including Voltaire.* He gained fame in Paris at the théâtres de la foire* with his comedies, pastorals, and his one-man comic opera, *Arlequin-Deucalion* (1722). A tragedy, *Gustave Wasa* (1733), and his best-known work, *La Métromanie* (1738), were presented at the Comédie-Française. Despite his popular success, he was denied admission to the Academy because of the indecent "Ode à Priape" ("Ode to Priapus"), written in his youth. Piron became blind and devoted his later years to religious poetry.

   La Métromanie, a five-act comedy written in verse, recounts the humorous tale of Francaleu, an inveterate versifier who publishes poetry in *Le Mercure* under the pseudonym of Mademoiselle de La Vigne. A satire of himself and poets in general, especially Voltaire who had fallen prey to a similar scheme by the poet Paul Desforges-Maillard (1699–1772), the comedy is edifying in its satire, even if it lacks sufficient depth of character.

   For further information, see H. Hall, "From Extravagant Poet to the Writer as Hero. Piron's *La Métromanie* and Pierre Cerou's *L'Amant auteur et valet,*" *Studies on Voltaire and the Eighteenth Century* 183 (1980): 117–132.

PIXERECOURT, GUILBERT DE (1773–1844), playwright and creator of popular theatre, was known as the "Corneille of the Boulevards." A precursor of Hugo's* romantic (see romanticism*) theatre, he wrote comedies, comic operas (see opéra-comique*), vaudevilles, and melodramas, freed from the strictures of the classical unities, where genres were mixed and violence and the romanesque abounded. His more than one hundred works include *Le Château des Appenins* (*Apennine Castle,* 1798), *Coelina* (1800), and *L'Homme à trois visages* (*The Man with Three Faces,* 1801).

For further information, see W. D. Howarth, "Word and Image in Pixérécourt's Melodramas: The Dramaturgy of the Strip-Cartoon," in *Performance and Politics in Popular Drama: Aspects of Popular Entertainment in Theatre, Film and Television*, D. Bradby and L. James, eds. (Cambridge: Cambridge University Press, 1980), 17–32.

POEMES ANTIQUES ET MODERNES (*Ancient and Modern Poems*, 1826), by Vigny,* his first important collection of poems, contains the essence of his thought and established his reputation as a major romantic (see romanticism*) poet. It first appeared in 1826; a definitive edition was published in 1837. The collection includes nine of the poems of an earlier work, *Poèmes* (1822), a slim, anonymous volume written in the manner of Chénier* and Delille,* which passed almost imperceptibly through the literary scene of its day. The 1826 edition added six more poems and eliminated one; three more were added in 1829 and another two in 1837.

The poems are divided into three books. The first, the Mystical Book, contains three of his most significant poems. "Moïse" ("Moses"), with its plaintive refrain, "Let me sleep the sleep of the earth," echoes the moral and social isolation of the Hebrew leader. Moses represents a man of genius and superiority, misunderstood and estranged from those he is to lead. "Eloa" chronicles the loss of innocence and damnation of an angel born of a tear of Jesus at Lazarus's resurrection who tries to rescue Satan. "Le Déluge" ("The Flood") treats the theme of God's wrath and the suffering of the innocent. The second book, the Ancient Book, includes "La Fille de Jephté" ("The Daughter of Jephthah"), a short poem of a father's sacrifice of his daughter to God, and poems from antiquity written in the style of Chénier,* including "Symétha, "La Dryade" ("The Dryad"), and "Le Bain d'une romaine" ("A Roman Woman's Bath"). The Modern Book extends from the Middle Ages through the nineteenth century. "Le Cor" ("The Horn"), written in the Pyrenees, recalls Roland's return across the Pyrenees to France. "Paris," written in 1831, is dedicated to "the city which makes thrones fall."

Vigny drew heavily on the Bible and ancient history for many of his poems. Besides Chénier, he was heavily influenced by Chateaubriand* and Lord Byron (1788–1824). The chronological grouping of the poems suggests Hugo's* design for his *Légende des siècles** years later. By and large, the poems have been criticized as uneven. At this stage of his career, Vigny was vacillating between the formal beauty and eloquence of Chénier and the vestiges of eighteenth-century classicism and the burgeoning sentimentality of the romantics. The poems are important for introducing myth and symbolism into the realm of poetry, a distinction Vigny pointed out in the preface to the 1837 edition. "The only merit of these poems which has never been disputed," he wrote, "is that they have been the first in France, of any of this type, in which a philosophical thought is presented in an epic or dramatic form." Vigny's ability to present his thoughts via symbol and myth culminated in *Les Destinées.**

POMPIGNAN, JEAN-JACQUES NICOLAS LE FRANC, MARQUIS DE

(1709–1784) is best known for his religious poetry and as a defender of the faith in an essentially irreligious era. A successful lawyer and Counsellor of Honor at the parliament of Toulouse, he abandoned law for literature, writing a tragedy, *Didon* (1734), operas, several odes (of which the best is *Ode sur la mort de J.-B. Rousseau—Ode on the Death of J.-B. Rousseau,* 1741), and two volumes of poetry (1734 and 1763). In 1759, he was admitted to the Academy, where he immediately enraged the philosophe* faction in his acceptance speech, inciting their relentless ridicule, especially on the part of Voltaire,* who directed *La Vanité (Vanity,* 1760) and other satirical verses against him.

Inspired primarily by the Psalms and the prophets, Pompignan's poetry exemplifies the classic purity of style and verse that persisted well into the eighteenth century. If it often lacked inspiration and originality, it is important nonetheless as evidence that religious sentiment was not entirely defunct in the Age of Reason.

PONSARD, FRANÇOIS (1814–1867), writer of social comedies who with Augier* led the "école de bon sens" ("school of common sense") in theatre in the 1840s, found in classical tragedy an antidote to the excesses of romanticism.* He was born in Vienne in Dauphiné, trained as a lawyer, but made his literary debut with a translation of Lord Byron's (1788–1824) *Manfred* (1837). He burst upon the theatrical scene with the tragedy *Lucrèce* (Lucretia, 1843), presented a little more than a month after Hugo's* *Les Burgraves* marked the resounding failure of romantic drama. Its success is due as much to its principal actress, Mademoiselle Rachel (née Elisabeth Félix, 1820–1858), as to the worth of the play itself. Other tragedies, *Virginie* (1844), *Agnès de Méranie* (1845), *Ulysse* (1852), and *Galilée* (1857), were less successful. Besides *Lucrèce,* Ponsard wrote memorable social comedies in verse, *L'Honneur et l'argent* (*Honor and Money,* 1853) and *La Bourse* (*The Stock Exchange,* 1856), and two historical dramas in verse, *Charlotte Corday* (1850) and *Le Lion amoureux* (*The Amorous Lion,* 1866). Ponsard contributed to the demise of romantic theatre and is seen as a precursor to the bourgeois comedies of Augier.

POSITIVISM (positivisme) is a philosophy formulated by Auguste Comte* in the early nineteenth century, which upheld science as the means of transforming the political, social, and intellectual disorder following the French Revolution. It is based on a fundamental law that Comte discovered in his study of the development of intelligence, that "each of our principal conceptions, each branch of our knowledge, passes successively through three different theoretical states: the theological, or fictive, state; the metaphysical, or abstract state; the scientific, or positive state." Comte believed that positivism is the "veritable definitive state of human intelligence" and that it is achieved by passing through the theological and metaphysical states.

The aim of positivism is to bring the study of society from the realm of the theological and metaphysical into the scientific state. Comte believed that all phenomena, even the social, are subject to invariable, natural laws. When society has undergone the same scientific study as chemistry and physics, for example, its outworn, outdated theological and metaphysical preconceptions will be replaced with knowledge that will further human progress.

For further information, see T. Wright, "George Eliot and Positivism: A Reassessment," *Modern Language Review* 76 (2) (April 1981): 257–272.

PREFACE DE CROMWELL, LA (*The Preface to Cromwell*, 1827), by Victor Hugo,* is the lengthy preface to his first and unplayable romantic (see romanticism*) drama, *Cromwell*. Encumbered with its extreme length and multitude of characters, *Cromwell* has remained overshadowed by its preface, which, with characteristic Hugolian verve and panache, called for the abolition of classical theatre and set forth the principles of romantic drama.

The Preface begins with an analysis of the development of poetry through the ages. Poetry began with man himself in the time of Genesis; it was full of ecstacy and adoration; it was lyric. As history unfolded, by the time of Homer and the ancients, poetry recounted man's wars and heroism; it became epic. Finally, Christianity awakened in man a sense of his duality—the conflict between his desire for virtue and his instinct toward sin. This opposition is the essence of drama, the literature par excellence of the modern age. Drama is the literary union of these two aspects of human nature, the grotesque and the sublime, the beautiful and the ugly. "Complete poetry lies in the harmony of opposites," Hugo writes. The rest of the preface details his theory of drama. Contrary to the classical concept of the separation of genre, drama must portray both tragedy and comedy, tears and laughter, to remain integral and valid. Hugo dispels the unities of time and place as unrealistic and confining: "Every action has its own duration as well as its particular place." Only unity of action must be observed since "neither the eye nor the human spirit can grasp more than one unity at a time." History, geography, and local color are essential and must depict not the "beautiful," but the "characteristic," that which resides in "the very heart of the work." Romantic drama should be written in verse but more freely than the classical Alexandrine and with fewer tirades.

Most of Hugo's ideas were not new. Diderot's* drame* bourgeois had struck a blow at classical theatre. Madame de Stael's* *De l'Allemagne* (*On Germany*, 1810) praised Germanic and northern literatures quite foreign to the classic ideal. Stendhal's* *Racine et Shakespeare* (1823) demonstrated the superiority of Shakespeare over Jean-Baptiste Racine (1639–1699) and the relevance and enjoyability of romanticism as "the literature for today." Hugo's theory of the three ages of literature and humanity has been proven false, along with much of his criticism of the classics. However, he voiced his understanding of the complexity of human nature and the need for a corresponding drama with such conviction that his Preface became the manifesto of the romantic school and catapulted its young author to the head of the movement.

For further information, see J. Coates, "The Return to Hugo: A Discussion of the Intellectual Context of Chesterton's View of the Grotesque," *English Literature in Transition* 25 (2) (1982): 86–103.

PREROMANTICISM (preromanticisme) is a term often found in literary man-
uals that refers to the transitional period after the Age of Enlightenment when
many tendencies of the romantic (see romanticism*) movement surfaced and its
esthetic principles were formulated. The initial stirrings of preromanticism began
during the later half of the eighteenth century in a reaction against the excessive
intellectualizing and rationalism of the Enlightenment and a reawakening of the
sentiment and the love of nature. The salons of Madame du Deffand (1697–1780)
and Mademoiselle de Lespinasse (1732–1776), frequented by the philosophes*
(Voltaire,* Fontenelle,* and Montesquieu,* and later d'Alembert,* Turgot,*
Marmontel,* and others), developed a skepticism toward their ideas and a preference for affairs of the heart. Even Diderot,* the energetic, freethinking editor of
the *Encyclopédie** and defender of the philosophes, felt the stirrings of passion
and the need for creative freedom and expression in all genres, especially drama.
In 1773, his disciple, Sébastien Mercier,* outlined in his *Essai sur l'art dramatique* (*Essay on the Dramatic Art*), the principles of romantic theatre later formulated in Hugo's* *Préface de Cromwell.** The most important influence in this
early period of preromanticism was undoubtedly J.-J. Rousseau,* the acknowledged father of romanticism, who shunned his contemporaries and their world,
listened to his heart, and took refuge in his soul, his imagination, and nature,
whose landscape externalized his feelings and offered the ideal of simplicity and
purity he cherished. His disciple, Bernardin de Saint-Pierre,* elaborated his
sensitivity into lyric prose evocations of nature. Later, Senancour's* *Obermann**
lived in a reverie-world inspired, as Rousseau's "solitary walker" had been, by
the beauty of the Swiss countryside.

The soul-searching reveries Rousseau experienced as he communed with
nature spawned an introspective interest in oneself, one's loves, one's past, and a
mystical desire to attain the infinite, the absolute. Autobiographies, memoirs,
confessions flourished. Personal novels preoccupied with self-analysis explored
the passion, ideals, disenchantment, and arrogance of the burgeoning romantic
soul. The "mal du siècle"* experienced by Musset,* Nerval,* and Gautier* at
romanticism's fullest flush, had already been felt by J.-J. Rousseau, Constant,*
Senancour, and, a few years later, Chateaubriand* and Lamartine.* In the latter
half of the nineteenth century, this vague affliction would resurface in Baudelaire,** Leconte de Lisle,* Flaubert,* Fromentin,* and Taine.*

As the preromantic bared his soul, the principles of a new esthetic were being
haphazardly formulated which would provide the vehicle for the expression of
his ideas. Chateaubriand's *Génie du Christianisme** (*Genius of Christianity*,
1802) established Christianity, rather than the pagan mythology of the classics,
as his source of inspiration, writing that Christianity is "the most poetic, the
most human, the most favorable to liberty, arts and literature." An influx of
foreign literature, notably German, Swiss, and English, offered new literary
models. Anglomania was rampant. Ducis* translated William Shakespeare
(1564–1616), and everyone read Lord Byron (1788–1824) and Walter Scott
(1771–1832). From Germany came Salomon Gessner's (1730–1788) *Idylls*

(1754–1772), Johann Goethe's (1749–1832) *Werther* (1774), and Friedrich von Schiller's (1759–1805) dramas. Madame de Stael's* influential *De l'Allemagne (Of Germany,* 1810) imported German imagination and enthusiasm into France and defined romanticism as "poetry which originated in the songs of the troubadours, that which is born of chivalry and Christianity." Her *De la littérature (Of Literature,* 1800) praised the Gaelic poetry of Ossian (3d century Gaelic bard) and the north and founded the principle necessary for the viability of the new school—the idea of relativity in art and subjectivity in beauty. When this idea took hold, classic absolutes of perfection, which had dominated art since the reign of Louis XIV, were dealt a blow, and the growing romantic force gained credence and respectability. By 1830 and Hugo's triumphant *Hernani,* * romanticism was established as a full-fledged literary movement with the young poet at its head.

For further information, see J. Mehlman, ed., "Des Allemagnes: Aspects of Romanticism in France," *Studies in Romanticism* 22 (2) (Summer 1983): 156–161.

PREVOST, ABBE ANTOINE-FRANÇOIS (1697–1763), also known as l'abbé d'Exiles (the exiled abbot), led a life not unlike that of the heroes of his novels—romanesque, adventurous, passionate. Moreover, his ardor for life carried over into his literary career. Though best known as the author of *Manon Lescaut,* * he wrote more than fifty volumes of novels, twenty volumes of *Le Pour et le contre (For and Against),* a journal that he edited from 1733 to 1741, seventeen volumes of a *Histoire générale des voyages (General History of Travel),* and many volumes of English translations.

He was born in Artois, the son of a lawyer, and lived his early years under the strong influence of his father and the church, his mother and sister having died by the time he was fourteen. He was educated by the Jesuits at Hesdin but interrupted his studies around age sixteen (his exact age at the time is debatable) to join the War of Spanish Succession. Disillusioned with military life, he returned to Paris to study rhetoric at the Collège de Harcourt in 1713 and transferred to La Flèche in 1715, where the Jesuits received him as a novice. The details of his life after this point become sketchy and contradictory. Possibly, he reentered the army as an officer. Fearing his father's reprisals for his irregular life, he left France with a friend to visit Holland. After a life of dissipation and a sad love affair, he once again sought refuge with the Jesuits around 1719, but he left them after a year. He was received by the Benedictines at Saint-Wadrille near Rouen. In 1721, at the Abbey of Jumièges, he professed his faith and was sent to Rouen.

Despite his brilliance as a humanities teacher and student of theology and his renown as a fervent, gifted speaker, Prévost, weary from being buffeted from one abbey to another, became more and more disillusioned with the rigors of monastic life. Unknown to his superiors, he wrote the second part of *Les Aventures de Pomponius, cavalier romain (The Adventures of Pomponius, Roman Chevalier,* 1724), a satirical novel largely directed against the Jesuits and Benedictines. While he collaborated on the erudite *Gallia Christiana,* composed over a period of eighty years by legions of theologians, he was secretly writing the first two parts of his *Mémoires d'un homme de qualité qui s'est retiré du monde* (*Memoirs of a Man of Quality Who Has Retired from the World*).

He finally decided to break with the church in 1728, but unfortunately, he left before he had been granted permission. Considered an outlaw, he fled to England, where he converted to Protestantism and met the archbishop of Canterbury. He spent a year in London enjoying "all possible pleasures and the best company" (Roddier), forming his profound appreciation for the English. He tutored Francis Eyles, son of Sir John Eyles, former director of the Bank of England. However, seducing Sir John's daughter forced him to quickly leave England for Holland in the autumn of 1730. *Mémoires d'un homme de qualité* was finished in the spring of 1731; he quickly sold the first four volumes of *Le Philosophe anglais ou Les Mémoires de Cleveland* (*The English Philosopher or The Memoirs of Cleveland*) and finished translating *L'Histoire du Président de Thou* (*The History of the President of Thou*) into English. Besides the freedom to write, Holland offered Prévost the infamous Lenki Eckhardt, his mistress, who squandered his revenues and consumed his energy. Leaving considerable debts to publishers, Prévost and Lenki returned to London in 1733, where Prévost began working on his journal, *Le Pour et le contre*, published by Didot in Paris and modeled after Joseph Addison's (1672–1719) *Spectator*. His resources nearly exhausted, Prévost forged a note and was nearly hanged, but for the intervention of Sir John Eyles.

The following year, absolved by Pope Clement XII, he returned to France and entered a less austere Benedictine monastery. Though he underwent a second noviciate for a year at Croix-Saint-Leufroy near Evreux and was named chaplain to the prince of Conti in 1735, he continued to pursue worldly pleasures and the rigors of writing, rather than the life of a monk. He continued his journal, established himself with Voltaire,* produced the six volumes of *Le Doyen de Killerine* (*The Dean of Coleraine*) from 1734 to 1740, published *Histoire d'une Grecque moderne* (*Story of a Modern Greek*, 1741), *Histoire de Marguerite d'Anjou, reine d'Angleterre* (*Story of Marguerite of Anjou, the Queen of England*, 1742), *Mémoires de Monsieur de Montcal* (*Memoirs of Mr. Montcal*, 1741), and *Histoire de Malte* (*History of Malta*, 1741). He was forced once again to flee, this time to Brussels, because of a clandestine publication (and was assisted by Voltaire) but returned the following year.

From 1742 on, Prévost seems to have entered a wiser, more stable stage of his life. He translated Samuel Richardson's (1689–1761) *Pamela* (1742), Conyers Middleton's (1683–1750) *Cicero* (1743), *Letters from Cicero to Brutus and from Brutus to Cicero* (1744) and Cicero's (106–43 B.C.) *Familiar Letters* (1745). In 1744, *Les Voyages de Robert Lade* (*The Voyages of Robert Lade*) presaged his *Histoire générale des voyages* (*General History of Travel*, 1746–1761), the great work, according to H. Roddier in *L'Abbé Prevost* (Hatier-Boivin, 1955), about which Prévost had dreamed for so long. He retired to Chaillot in 1746 and finished his *Memoires d'un honnete homme* (*Memoirs of an Honest Man*, 1745). There he translated parts of Thomas Dyche's English Dictionary, which appeared as *Manuel lexique ou Dictionnaire portatif des mots français dont la signification n'est pas familiere a tout le monde* (*Lexic Manual or Portable Dictionary of French Words Whose Meaning Is Not Apparent to All the World* (1750); Richardson's *Clarisse Harlow,* under the title *English Letters* (1751); and Richardson's *Grandisson, or New 'English Letters'* (1755). He met Jean-Jacques Rousseau* in 1750, finished his travel history, and translated David Hume's (1711–1776) *History of the Stuarts.* The prince of Conti asked him to write the history of the houses of Condé and Conti. Finally overcome by the ravages of old age, Prévost acquired a small property near Chantilly and continued to write until his death in 1763.

According to Jeanne Monty in *The Novels of Abbé Prévost* (*Studies on Voltaire and the Eighteenth Century,* 1970), Prévost's entire body of works is seeking the answer to that eternal question, What is Man? a question that he eventually realized was unanswerable. If he believed, in his first novels, in the order of the world, the innocence of nature, and the power of reason, the more he advanced, the more aware he became of "disorder, obscurity, bad faith, and irrational contradictions."

Mémoires d'un homme de qualité qui s'est retiré du monde (1728–1731, 7 vols.) relates the suffering resulting from passion, the clash between the idealism of love and the realities of the outside world—order, reason, religion, morality, economics. *L'Histoire du Chevalier des Grieux et de Manon Lescaut* (1731) is a classic interpretation of man's conflict between heart and mind, between physical love and love of God, between duty and desire.

Le Philosophe anglais ou Histoire de M. Cleveland (*The English Philosopher, or The Story of Monsieur Cleveland* (1731–1739, 8 vols.) tells the story of a philosopher-hero, the fictional bastard son of Cromwell who, raised by his mother according to reason and nature, is unable to find happiness; *Le Doyen de Killerine* (*The Dean of Coleraine*) further explores the conflict between reason and happiness, the real and the ideal, and even hopes to resolve it, but does not. It is the story of a man who, despite his good intentions, is never able to understand his brothers and sister. He is stronger than the Man of Quality and Cleveland with his religion and principles but loses in the end because other people are not what they seem, and they act according to passion rather than the rules of logic. *L'Histoire d'une Grecque moderne,* the story of the relationship between a beautiful Greek slave and her liberator-lover, depicts the futility of trying to understand oneself and the feminine heart and the moral degradation that can result from it.

Though Prévost is remembered essentially in this century, as he was in the last, as the author of *Manon Lescaut,* his influence on the eighteenth century is considerably more vast. *Le Pour et le contre* strongly bears the imprint of Prévost's personality, especially his interest in science and the arts. The first volumes provided the philosophes* a storehouse of information on English culture and affairs. *Cleveland,* the most successful novel of his lifetime and admired by Rousseau and Diderot,* is considered a source for Rousseau's *Con-*

*fessions.** The twenty-one volumes of the *Histoire générale des voyages* (1745–1770), with its wealth of information on foreign people and customs, helped establish his reputation, provided source material for many of the philosophes, and paved the way for Buffon's* *Histoire naturelle.* His translations of Richardson not only influenced Rousseau but opened new vistas for the future of the novel in Europe; his translation of David Hume's *History of the Stuarts* inspired Rousseau's admiration for the great philosopher.

In his search for the meaning of life, Prévost introduced the theme of the individual versus society into the novel. While Marivaux's* Marianne (see *La Vie de Marianne**) was seeking her rightful place in the upper levels of Parisian society and Jacob was trying to forge one, Prévost's heroes, usually noble by birth, are thwarted by society's demands on them. Like the romantics (see romanticism*) of the next century, Prévostian heroes are sensitive and passionate; they long for order and balance but act according to their hearts rather than the dictates of society. The result can only be constant agitation and disorder.

Prévost has been called a "master of French sensitivity in the eighteenth century" (P. Trahard, cited in Ehrard's *Littérature Française*), and critics have linked him to the wave of preromanticism* beginning in the eighteenth century. However, Prévost remains essentially a man of his moment. In his quest for the meaning of life both the light and the darkness of the Age of Enlightenment prevail.

For further information, see R. A. Francis, "Prévost's *Cleveland* and its Anonymous Continuation," *Nottingham French Studies* (May 1984): 12–23; Francis, "Prévost's *Cleveland* and Voltaire's *Candide*," *Studies on Voltaire and the Eighteenth Century* 208 (1982): 295–303; L. Grossman, "Male and Female in Two Short Novels by Prévost," *Modern Language Review* 77 (January 1982): 29–37; J. Jones, "Textual Ambiguity in Prévost's *Histoire d'une Grecque moderne*," *Studi Francesi* 27 (2) (May–August, 1983): 241–256; S. Larkin, "The Abbé Prévost and David Hume's *History of Great Britain*," *The British Journal for Eighteenth Century Studies* 3 (Autumn 1980): 192–207; C. Lazzaro-Weis, "Feminism, Parody and Characterization of Prévost: the Example of the *Doyen de Killerine*," *Studies in Eighteenth Century Culture* 13 (1984): 143–154; Lazzaro-Weis, "Prévost's Comic Romance: *The Doyen de Killerine*," *Neophilologus* 67 (4) (October 1983): 517–524; P. J. Tremewan, "Narrative Point of View in Prévost's *Mémoires d'un honnête homme*," *Studies on Voltaire and the Eighteenth Century* 205 (1982): 45–56.

PROUDHON, PIERRE (1809–1865), social reformer and socialist philosopher, coined the statement, "La propriété, c'est le vol" ("Property is theft"). A true son of the people, he was born in Besançon, the birthplace of Fourier (see Fourierisme*) to a humble family. His father was a brewer. He began his formal education at the local college at sixteen. At nineteen, he went to work for a printer and proofread theological works. In 1838, he was awarded a prize by the Academy of Besançon. A year later, he went to Paris, where he lived the life of a poor student. He was influenced by the socialist ideas fomenting in Paris and published his first work, *Qu'est-ce que la propriété* (*What is Property?* 1840), which proposes the famous answer "Property is theft." His numerous treatises on economics and politics include *Principes d'organisation politique* (*Principles of Political Organization,* 1843), *Philosophie de la misère* (*Philosophy of Misery,* 1846), *Système des contradictions économiques* (*System of Economic Contradictions,* 1846), and articles in the *Représentant du peuple* (*Representative of the People*) and other journals. In 1848, he was elected to the assembly for the Seine department. The following year he attempted to found a Banque du Peuple (Bank of the People), but failed to raise the necessary capital. He was imprisoned for three years for articles against the prince-president (the future Napoleon III, 1808–1873). In 1858, his *De la justice dans la Révolution et dans l'eglise* (*On Justice in Revolution and in the Church*) earned him another prison term, which he escaped by fleeing to Brussels. He died soon after the publication of his last work, *Du principe fédératif* (*On the Federal Principle,* 1863). *Théorie de la propriété* (*Theory of Property*) appeared posthumously.

Throughout his life, Proudhon advocated economic justice, liberty, and equality. He strove for the establishment of a decentralized society in which workers freely divided labor and exchanged their products. He viewed private property as a means of exploiting the labor of others in the form of rent, interest, or profit that should be eliminated.

For further information, see P. Crapo, "The Anarchist as Critic: P.-J. Proudhon's Criticism of Literature and Art," *Michigan Academician* 13 (4) (Spring 1981): 459–473; Crapo, "Proudhon's Conspiratorial View of Society," *Journal of European Studies* 11 (3) (September 1981): 184–195; Crapo, "Proudhon's Romantic Rebellion," *Stanford French Review* 5 (2) (Fall 1981): 173–188; D. Matual, "The Gospel According to Tolstoy and the Gospel According to Proudhon," *Harvard Theological Review* 75 (January 1982): 117–128.

PROVERBES DRAMATIQUES, short, dramatic sketches that illustrate a point or proverb, along with parades,* originated in the salons of the eighteenth century. Carmontelle,* who wrote more than a hundred, defined the proverbe as "a sort of comedy written by inventing a theme or by using ideas from a short story, etc. The secret of the proverbe must be hidden in the action such that the spectators do not guess it; they must, upon being told, cry, 'Ah! That's true!' as when one is told the secret to a puzzle which one cannot solve." Carmontelle's proverbes are remembered for their detail, veracity, and satire and influenced Théodore Leclerq (1777–1851) and Musset* in the following century.

Q

QUESNAY, FRANÇOIS (1694–1774), eighteenth-century economist and founder of the physiocrat* school, was born in the countryside near Paris, the son of a poor lawyer. He was endowed with a love of learning but received little formal education in his early years. At sixteen he was apprenticed to a surgeon, then studied medicine in Paris. By 1718, he was a surgeon in Mantes with a privileged clientele including the queen; in 1730, he became perpetual secretary to the newly established Academy of Surgery and was named surgeon. Later, as physician to the king, he resided at Versailles. By mid-century, his interests turned to commerce and he associated with Vincent de Gournay (1712–1759), Victor Riquetti, the marquis de Mirabeau who was the father of the Revolutionary orator, Mirabeau (1715–1789), abbé Baudeau (1730–1792), Le Trosne, Morellet,* Mercier de Larivière (1720–1793), and Pierre-Samuel Dupont de Nemours (1739–1817), forming the economic school later known as the physiocrats because of their interest in agriculture rather than the production of luxury goods and free trade as a means of wealth.

Quesnay published medical works but is best known for the articles "Fermiers" ("Farmers") and "Grains," which he contributed to the *Encyclopédie,** his physics and agricultural journals and three treatises: *Le Tableau économique* (*The Economic Tableau,* 1760), *Maximes générales du gouvernement économique d'un royaume agricole* (*General Maxims for the Economic Government of an Agricultural Kingdom,* 1760), and *La Physiocratie ou Constitution naturelle du gouvernement le plus avantageux au genre humain* (*Physiocracy or The Natural Constitution of the Most Advantageous Government for Mankind,* 1768).

Quesnay enjoyed considerable influence during and after his lifetime. Adam Smith (1723–1790) recognized the work of the physiocrats in his *Wealth of Nations* (1776), and Karl Marx (1818–1883) hailed him as the founder of modern economics.

For further information, see G. Tonelli, "The Skepticism of François Quesnay," *International Studies in Philosophy* 11 (1979): 77–89.

QUINET, EDGAR (1803–1875), philosopher, historian, poet, was born in Bourg-en-Bresse in the department of Ain, where he led a lonely childhood strongly influenced by his mother. He was interested in literature and science, studied law and philosophy at the Ecole Polytechnique, and attended courses offered by Victor Cousin.* His first work, *Tablettes du Juif errant (Tablets of the Wandering Jew,* 1823), criticized contemporary philosophy and literature. His *Introduction à la philosophie de l'histoire de l'humanité (Introduction to the Philosophy of the History of Humanity,* 1825), a preface to his translation of the German philosopher Johann Gottfried Herder (1744–1803), earned him the friendship of Michelet,* his "soul brother" and supporter in his campaign against the church. He travelled to Germany and England and, in 1829, assumed a government post in Morea, which served as the basis for his *De la Grèce moderne et de ses rapports avec l'antiquité (On Modern Greece and Its Relationship with Antiquity,* 1830). He took up journalism upon his return, joining the staff of the *Revue des deux mondes.* A trip to Italy in 1832 inspired his first work of consequence, *Ahasvérus* (1833), a symbolic prose poem. He travelled to Germany where he married a German woman and wrote two epic poems in verse, *Napoléon* (1836) and *Prométhée* (1838), and a study of Germany and Italy. In 1839, he was named professor of foreign literature at the Faculté des Lettres de Lyon, where he began the brilliant course later published as the *Génie des religions (The Genius of Religions,* 1842), a study of various religions and their social consequences written in reply to Chateaubriand's* *Génie du Christianisme.* * In 1841, as professor of the history of the languages and literatures of southern Europe at the Collège de France, he used his professorial chair as a forum for his polemic against the church's interference with individual liberty. He was suspended by Guizot* in 1846, visited Spain, and resumed his teaching in 1848. He sat on the extreme left at the constituent and legislative assemblies and, as an arch opponent of the prince-president (the future Napoleon III, 1808–1873), he was exiled after his coup d'etat. Quinet lived in Brussels and Switzerland until the fall of the Empire. During this time, he wrote a second prose poem entitled *Merlin l'enchanteur (Merlin the Magician,* 1860), *Histoire de la campagne de 1815 (History of the Campaign of 1815,* 1862), and *La Révolution (The Revolution,* 1865). *L'Enseignement du peuple (Teaching the People,* 1850), *L'Esprit nouveau (The New Spirit,* 1874) and *La République (The Republic,* posthumous, 1881) demonstrate his belief in the education of the masses as the key to the future. He was elected to the Assemblée Nationale in 1871 and vigorously opposed the terms of the peace treaty between France and Germany. He died at Versailles in 1875.

Quinet's vast literary production sprung from his lifelong combat for liberty and progress. He was a historian with a republican conscience who studied the cause and effect of revolutions, a leader in the struggle against the power of the church, a visionary with an ardent faith in the future, and a romantic in the lyricism and symbolism of his writing.

For further information, see C. Crossley, *Edgar Quinet (1803–1875): A Study in Romantic Thought* (Lexington, Ky.: French Forum Monographs, 1983); Crossley, "Literary Opposition to the Second Empire: Quinet's *Merlin l'Enchanteur*," *Parnasse* 3 (1982): 36–49; Crossley, "The Treatment of Architecture in the works of Edgar Quinet published before 1851," in *Literature and Society. Studies in Nineteenth and Twentieth Century French Literature presented to R. J. North* (Birmingham: Goodman for University of Birmingham, 1980), pp. 13–22; Crossley, "The Young Edgar Quinet and the Philosophy of History," *Stanford French Review* 4 (Winter 1980): 405–415; B. Wright, "Quinet's *Ahasvérus:* an Alternative 'drame total'?" *French Studies Bulletin* 5 (Winter 1982–1983): 8–10.

R

RAYNAL, GUILLAUME THOMAS FRANÇOIS (1713–1796), minor eighteenth-century philosophe* who, along with Condillac,* Helvétius,* Grimm,* and Condorcet* supported the *Encyclopédie** with their ideas and friendship, but did not directly contribute to it. He was educated by the Jesuits, took orders, and did parish work in Paris but, preferring literature and secular life to ecclesiastical matters, left the priesthood, though he retained the title "abbé." From 1747 to 1751 and from 1754 to 1755, he authored *Nouvelles littéraires* (*Literary News*), a fortnightly confidential newsletter written for the duchess of Saxe-Gotha which he eventually passed on to Grimm, who expanded it into his influential *Correspondance littéraire*. He wrote historical and political works, including a history of Stadholder (1748), directed against the princes of Orange; a history of the English parliament (1748); and several volumes of literary, historical, and political anecdotes.

Raynal is best known for his four-volume *Histoire philosophique et politique des etablissements et du commerce des Européens dans les Deux Indes* (*Philosophical and Political History of the European Establishments and Trade in the East and West Indies*, 1770). Written with the help of Diderot,* Holbach,* and others, the treatise detailed the European colonialization of the Indies, attacking superstition, fanaticism, tyranny, slavery, and religion. Otis Fellows (*Diderot* [Boston: Twayne, 1977]) called the work "an anticolonial manifesto based on humanitarian principles close to the hearts of an elderly Diderot and his fellow encyclopediste the abbé." Though widely read, it was suppressed by the authorities, and Raynal was forced to flee the country. He returned in 1788, disavowed his revolutionary ideas, and became an ardent royalist until his death eight years later.

For further information, see C. P. Courtney, "The Abbé Raynal, Robert Orme and the *Histoire philosophique des deux Indes*," *Revue de littérature comparée* 54 (July-September 1980: 356–359; J. Salmon, "The Abbé Raynal, 1713–1796. An Intellectual Odyssey," *History Today* 26 (1976): 109–117.

RAYONS ET LES OMBRES, LES (*Rays and Shadows,* 1840), by Victor Hugo,* is the culmination of the lyricism and sensitivity expressed in other collections written in the 1830s (*Les Feuilles d'automne,* * *Les Chants du cré-puscule,* * and *Les Voix intérieures**). It develops the same themes—family life, nature, and love—more profoundly, with greater social and philosophical significance. "In *Les Rayons et les Ombres,*" Hugo writes, "perhaps the horizon is more wide, the sky more blue and the calm more profound."

A preliminary poem, "Fonction du poète" ("The Poet's Function"), elaborates upon an idea initially set down in the preface to *Les Voix intérieures,* the "civilizing mission" of the poet, and sets the tone for the poems that follow. The poet, "the sacred dreamer," must guide the people with his thoughts and visions; like the star of Bethlehem, he will guide the people to the truth. "Tristesse d'Olympio" ("Olympio's Sadness"), enlarging upon the theme of "Olympus" also found in *Les Voix intérieures,* recounts Hugo's nostalgic return in 1837 to Bièvre valley, two years earlier the site of an empassioned love sojourn with his mistress, Juliette Drouet (1806–1883). His sadness and disappointment in the site, which has erased the two lovers from its memory, encompasses nature ("Nature with your unruffled countenance, how you forget!") and God, who merely "lends" us the meadows and springs, the woods and the rocks, before snatching them back. "Oceano Nox" ("Night Over the Ocean"), inspired by a hurricane he witnessed at Saint-Valéry-en-Caux four years earlier, introduces the ocean as a reality into his body of poetry and relates the terror of a nighttime storm. "Ce qui se passait aux Feuillantines" ("What Happened at Les Feuillantines") recounts the happiness experienced as a child in his own backyard.

For further information, see R. Denommé, "The Palimpsest of the Poet's Remembrance in Hugo's 'Tristesse d'Olympio," *Kentucky Romance Quarterly* 29 (1) (1982): 15–24; W. Greenberg, "Symbolization and Metonymic Links in Three Poems from Hugo's *Les Rayons et les ombres,*" *Dalhousie Review* 62 (4) (Winter 1982–1983): 600–634; P. Ward, "Tristesse d'Olympio and the Romantic Nature Experience," *Nineteenth Century French Studies* 7 (Fall–Winter 1978–1979): 4–16.

REALISM is a literary movement that grew from and in reaction against the romanticism* of the early nineteenth century. The term was first used in the 1850s. Louis-Emile-Edmond Duranty's (1833–1880) review *Réalisme* appeared in 1856; the following year, Champfleury's* manifesto, *Le Réalisme,* appeared. Realism is the presentation of concrete details of everyday, contemporary life in literature. History and imagination, the mainsprings of romantic fiction, are relegated to the periphery of the realist novel or play. The romantics' melancholy, their need to idealize and to feel, was abandoned for a more objective, straightforward depiction of the world as it is. It is a verbal rendering of the world as it is seen, a transformation of the art of painting exterior reality into the art of writing it. Champfleury wrote in the preface to his *Contes domestiques* (*Domestic Stories,* 1852) that what he sees, "enters my head, descends into my pen and becomes what I have seen." In an article for the *Figaro,* he wrote, "the novelist doesn't judge, doesn't condemn, doesn't forgive. He exposes the facts.'' It presented unflinchingly the ugly, the popular, the modern, and the vulgar. It introduced new character types—the small investor, the failed artist, the worker—and objectively copied their speech, their habitats, their habits.

Realism stemmed in part from the dispassionate, realist paintings of Gustave Courbet (1819–1877). It grew, to an extent, from the romantics' appreciation for the commonplace, their love of local color and the primitive. Finally, it reflected the spirit of positivism* and an increased appreciation for and understanding of scientific fact, which was introduced by Comte* near the mid-century and propagated by Taine* and Renan.*

Realism found its ancestors in eighteenth-century writers such as Robert Challes*, Diderot,* and Restif.* It embraced Balzac* and Stendhal* as its more immediate relatives. It found its truest expression in Flaubert,* who passed on its heritage to Edmond and Jules de Goncourt,** Zola,** and Maupassant** in the nineteenth century, and in Jules Romains,** Martin du Gard,** Sarraute,** and Robbe-Grillet** in the twentieth.

For further information, see G. J. Becker, *Master European Realists of the Nineteenth Century* (New York: F. Ungar, 1982).

REGNARD, JEAN-FRANÇOIS (1655–1709), comedian and bon vivant, ushered the comic heritage of Molière (1622–1673) into the early eighteenth century, where it was imitated but never equalled by Dancourt,* Piron,* Gresset,* and Destouches.* Born in Paris to a rich bourgeois family, he was an excellent student and world traveller from the age of seventeen, who visited Constantinople, Italy, Algeria (where he was captured by pirates and sold as a slave), Holland, Denmark, Sweden, Poland, Hungary, and Germany. In 1682, he returned to Paris, starting his career as a writer for the Théâtre Italien* and from 1696 for the Théâtre Français. His principal comedies in verse include *Le Joueur* (*The Gambler*, 1696), *Le Distrait* (*The Absent-Minded*, 1697), *Démocrite* (1700), *Les Folies amoureuses* (*Follies of Love*, 1704), the *Ménechmes* (1705), and his principal work, *Le Légataire universel* (*The Heir*, 1708). He also wrote epistles, satires, and two novels based on his travels. Regnard died in 1709 at his chateau in Grillon.

While most of his comedies derive their theme, style, and characters from Molière, they lack the depth and understanding of the seventeenth-century master. However, their imaginative dialogue, word play, versification, and turns of plot result in a gaiety and frivolity characteristic of Regnard.

For further information, see G. Orwen, *Jean-François Regnard* (Boston: Twayne, 1982).

RENAN, ERNEST (1823–1892), writer and philosopher, was born in Tréguier in Brittany, the son of a sailor who died when Renan was five. He was raised by his mother, who ran a grocery store, and his sister Henriette, twelve years his elder. A diligent and intelligent student, he was destined for the clergy. Thanks to Henriette, he attended the seminary St. Nicholas du Chardonnet in Paris on a scholarship in 1838. In 1843, he entered Saint-Sulpice. The study of philology and biblical criticism led him to doubt the divine inspiration of the Bible and the teachings of Christianity. He left the church in 1845 and worked as a tutor at Collège Stanislas. He met the future chemist Marcelin Berthelot (1827–1907), who inspired his faith in science, and earned his philosophy degree in 1848. Renan taught in the lycées at Vendôme and Versailles and studied philology. In 1848, he wrote *L'Avenir de la science* (*The Future of Science*), which remained unpublished until 1890 on the advice of Augustin Thierry,* who found its belief that science alone "can resolve for man the problems for which his nature demands imperiously the solution" too audacious for the times. The following year, he went to Rome to explore French manuscripts in the Vatican for his doctoral thesis, *Averroès et l'Averroïsme* (1852). Back in Paris in 1851, he took a position in the manuscript department of the Bibliothèque Nationale. He published *Histoire générale et système comparé des langues sémitiques* (*General History and Comparative System of Semitic Languages*, 1855) and *Essai sur l'origine du langage* (*Essay on the Origin of Language*, 1858). In 1856, he entered the Académie des Inscriptions et Belles-Lettres (Academy of Inscriptions and Humanities, founded by Jean-Baptiste Colbert (1619–1683) in 1663) and he married.

In 1861, Renan went on an archeological mission to Syria and Palestine, where he retraced the life of Jesus. Upon his return, he was named professor of Hebrew at the Collège de France. His first lecture caused a scandal, when he referred to Jesus as an "incomparable" man who inspired some to call him God. His *Vie de Jesus* (*Life of Jesus*, 1863), the first volume in his *Histoire des origines du Christianisme* (*History of the Origins of Christianity*, 8 vols., 1863– 1883), enlarged this theme, calling Jesus "this sublime person who, as he presides over the destiny of the world each day, can be called divine, not in the sense that Jesus had absorbed all the divine, but in the sense that he is the individual who had made for his species the greatest step towards the divine." Though this work established his reputation, it raised storms of protest and cost him his professorial chair.

Renan's study of the history of Christianity occupied him for the next twenty years. He resumed his chair in 1870 and became an administrator at the Collège de France in 1883. He entered the Academy in 1876. In his later years, however, his enthusiasm for positivism* waned. The defeat of 1870 shook his moral idealism. His *Réforme intellectuelle et morale* (*Intellectual and Moral Reform*, 1871) advocated the return of the monarchy. He continued his search for truth but was less certain of its outcome. The *Dialogues philosophiques* (*Philosophical Dialogues*, 1876) and *Drames philosophiques* (*Philosophical Dramas*, 1878–1886) revealed the dangers and uncertainties of modern science in a form reminiscent of Plato (428–348 B.C.). He remembered his youth in *Souvenirs d'enfance et de jeunesse* (*Memories of Childhood and Youth*, 1883). Just before his death in 1892, he completed *L'Histoire du peuple d'Israël* (*History of the People of Israel,* 5 vols., 1887–1893), which extended his history of Christianity further back into time.

Renan's greatest contribution to the nineteenth century was his application of scientific method to the study of religious history. As a positivist, he discounted the miracle and mystery of religion as fiction and studied the origins of Christianity as historical fact. With Taine,* he led his generation further down the path of objective reality and gave credibility to realism* and naturalism** in literature.

For further information, see M. Reynolds, "Torn by Conflicting Doubts: Joyce and Renan," *Renascence* 35 (2) (Winter 1983): 96–118.

RENE (1802), by Chateaubriand,* was written, like *Atala,* for *Les Natchez,* but incorporated into *Le Génie du Christianisme.** This short tale illustrates that state of melancholy, boredom, and dissatisfaction known as "mal du siècle,"* which Chateaubriand invented and which became synonymous with romanticism.* It originally appeared in part 2, chapter 4 of *Le Génie,* after the chapter on the "Vague des passions" ("Wave of Passions"). It was published separately with *Atala* in 1805.

René is a young French aristocrat living with the Natchez Indians in America as an antidote to his unrelenting melancholy and aloofness. After hearing Chactas's story (*Atala*), he in turn relates the "secret feelings of his soul" to the old Indian and a missionary, Father Souel. He recounts his solitary youth with no mother ("I cost her her life in coming into the world," he begins his tale); a melancholy sister, Amélie; and distant father. Upon his father's death, he contemplated entering a monastery and travelled to Italy, Greece, and England, but neither religion nor the beauty of ancient ruins lightened the burden of his existence. He returned to Paris, a "vast desert of men." He was still miserable and therefore exiled himself to the countryside, where the "absolute solitude" and the "spectacle of nature" awakened a feeling of "overabundance of life . . . a crowd of fugitive sensations" that led him to thoughts of death. Amélie, concerned for her brother's well-being, spent several months with him, temporarily relieving his anxiety and thoughts of suicide; however, she changed temperament and abruptly abandoned him a few months later for a convent. As she took the veil, René learned the reason for her misery—she confessed her incestuous and "criminal" feelings for her brother. Filled with sadness, René departed for America, where he learned that Amélie had died aiding victims of a contagious disease.

Through Father Souel, Chateaubriand's message is clear. He chastises René: "I see a young man intoxicated with fancies, whom everything displeases and who has withdrawn from society in order to yield himself to useless reveries. . . . Solitude is bad for whoever lives in it without God." However, the message went unheeded by a generation of youths who saw in René the incarnation of their discontent. He became the symbol of the romantic soul who resided in that no-man's land between the real and the ideal, who fed on unattainable illusion and destined himself for failure. His relationship to Chateaubriand is apparent.

For further information, see E. Gans, "René and the Romantic Model of Self-Centralization," *Studies in Romanticism* 22 (3) (Fall 1983): 421–435; D. Knight, "The Readability of René's Secret," *French Studies* 37 (1) (January 1983): 35–46.

RESTIF, NICOLAS-EDMEE, (1734–1806) called de la Bretonne for his father's farm in Burgundy, is one of the most prolific authors of French literature, with more than two hundred books in all genres to his credit, many of which he printed himself and most of which are unmemorable. He took his inspiration from life—his rural youth in the village of Sacy near Auxerre, his later knowledge of Paris and its inhabitants, and his lifelong experiences as a libertine. The best of his works melded his memories with his genius and resulted in the "personal novel," a genre he helped inaugurate and which would rise to prominence in the nineteenth century.

Restif was born the eighth son of a well-to-do farmer and enjoyed a happy, rustic childhood. He resisted the Jansenist education provided by his father, apprenticed with a printer in Auxerre and, like the hero of his novel *Le Paysan perverti* (*The Corrupted Peasant,* 1775), was soon initiated into worldly ways—with the printer's wife. Four years later he went to Paris, where he worked for the royal publishers and broadened his experience as a young gallant. He returned to Auxerre four years later, married, and returned again to the capital. He launched his writing career with his first book, *La Famille vertueuse* (*The Virtuous Family,* 1767), which met with little success. He persisted, however, producing a spate of books, and succeeded with *Le Paysan perverti,* which he considered his best, and an idealized biography of his father, *La Vie de mon père* (*My Father's Life,* 1779). From 1780 to 1785, he wrote *Les Contemporaines* (*Contemporary Women*), a panorama of Parisian women from all walks of life. He filled sixteen volumes with his autobiography, *La Vie de Monsieur Nicolas* (*The Life of Mr. Nicholas,* 1794–1797), an erotic testimony to his life and the Parisian underworld. *Sara, ou La Dernière Aventure d'un homme de quarante-cinq ans* (*Sara, or The Last Adventure of a Forty-Five Year Old Man,* 1783), often considered his best work, recounts the sad tale of an older man's passion for a young girl. *Les Nuits de Paris* (*Paris Nights,* 1788) was inspired by his night roamings through the streets of Paris. *Idées singulières* (*Singular Ideas*), begun in 1769, comprises his ideas for regulating prostitution (Le Pornographe) and reforming the theatre (Le Mimographe), women (Le Gymnographe), men (L'Andrographe), laws (Le Thesmographe), language (Le Glossographe), and education (L'Edugraphe). Finally, disappointed and ruined by the Revolution, which he had looked to for reform, Restif died in misery and poverty at age 72.

Other works often cited include *Le Pied de Fanchette* (*Fanchette's Foot,* 1769); *La Paysanne pervertie* (*The Perverted Peasant Girl,* 1784), which was combined with *Le Paysan perverti* as *Le Paysan et la paysanne pervertis* (1787); *Mes Inscriptions* (*My Inscriptions,* written between 1780 and 1787 and discovered 1887); *Les Françaises* (*Frenchwomen,* 1786); *Les Parisiennes* (*Parisian Women,* 1787–1791); *La Femme infidèle* (*The Unfaithful Wife,* 1786); *Ingénue Saxancour* (1789); *L'Anti-Justine* (1798); and seventeen plays that were never presented.

Much of Restif's work is libertine and was long excluded from serious studies of literature as cynical, vulgar, and tasteless. However, his genius in recounting his experiences cannot be denied. His depiction of the country, the city, women, though often idealized and nostalgic, contains a realism* that comes only from intimate knowledge. He insisted that his novels were true. He wrote about the lower classes and simple, uneducated peasants, whose habits and dialects he knew and captured on paper. He created at least one memorable character, the villain Gaudet d'Arras, seen as a precursor of Balzac's* Vautrin. His love of the countryside and admiration for J.-J. Rousseau* (which earned him the dubious title, "Le Rousseau des ruisseaux—The Rousseau of the gutters") fostered his dream of a virtuous and egalitarian republic.

Restif de la Bretonne represents a curious amalgam of the idealist and the realist, the moralist and the libertine, the philosopher and the lover. Gerard de Nerval* hailed him as his "spiritual tutor." His vast imagination, his gift of observation, and his energy ally him with the likes of Balzac and Zola.**

For further information, see D. Coward, "Restif as a Reader of Books," *Studies on Voltaire and the Eighteenth Century* 205 (1982): 89–132; R. Veasy, "*La Vie de mon père:* Biography, Autobiography, Ethnography?" *Studies on Voltaire and the Eighteenth Century* 212 (1982): 213–224; P. Wagstaff, "Nicolas's Father: Restif and *La Vie de mon père,*" *Forum for Modern Language Studies* 16 (October 1980): 358–367.

REVE DE D'ALEMBERT, LE (*D'Alembert's Dream,* 1769), by Diderot,* a philosophical trilogy of three dialogues, exposes with characteristic wit and eloquence his most serious views on man, nature, and morality. At the insistence of friends, he decided against publication and gave the manuscript, unsigned, to Grimm's* *Correspondance littéraire* (*Literary Correspondence*). It was published posthumously in 1830.

In the first dialogue, Diderot debates the notion of materialism with his friend d'Alembert,* the illustrious mathematician and coeditor of his *Encyclopédie.** Recent scientific discoveries, along with Diderot's enthusiasm for anatomy, chemistry, physiology, and natural history, fueled his atheistic belief in matter as the sole basis for the existence of everything, from the smallest stones to mankind. Matter is sensitive, in constant motion, and provides the link between all things, animal, plant, and mineral.

The second dialogue relates d'Alembert's dream as it is recorded at his bedside by another friend, Mlle de Lespinasse, and discussed with a third, Dr. Bordeu, a physician known for his work on blood circulation. D'Alembert's delirium details Diderot's ideas on life and death ("Life is a series of reactions and actions. . . . To be born, to live and to die, is but to change forms"), liberty, and the notion of individuality ("All beings flow one into another . . . there is but one great individual which is the whole''). Bordeu agrees with the theory and concludes that such determinism negates the idea of virtue as well as liberty, a theme that Diderot takes up in *Jacques le fataliste et son maitre** as well. In the final dialogue Bordeu advances the subject of crossbreeding and other biological experiments as well as moral and sexual paradoxes that result from his materialism but urges Mlle de Lespinasse not to question his integrity.

The concept of matter expressed in *D'Alembert's Dream* anticipated later discoveries in the fields of molecular theory, biology, and evolution. More important, the work wed reverie and reality, the philosophical and the foolish, to produce a ''profound'' yet ''extravagant'' work that expressed the very essence of its author.

For further information, see C. J. Betts, ''The Function of Analogy in Diderot's *Rêve de d'Alembert*,'' *Studies on Voltaire and the Eighteenth Century* 185 (1980): 267–281; S. L. Pucci, ''Metaphor and Metamorphosis in Diderot's *Le Rêve de d'Alembert:* Pygmalion Materialized,'' *Symposium* 35 (Winter 1981–1982): 325–340.

REVERIES DU PROMENEUR SOLITAIRE, LES (*Dreams of a Solitary Walker,* written 1776–1778, published 1782), by Jean-Jacques Rousseau,* is the final and perhaps the most lyric of his works. The ten ''rêveries'' are important for the originality of their form, which lies somewhere between the classical ''meditations'' of René Descartes (1596–1650) and the ''essays'' of romantic English literature, and for the insights they provide into the mind and mood of Rousseau in his final months. According to Rousseau, they represent a ''faithful recording of my solitary walks and of the dreams which fill them when I allow my head to be totally free and my ideas to follow their inclination freely and without resistance.''

Written in Paris and its secluded environs, far from his enemies and the civilization he condemned as corrupt, the reveries convey the ''consolation, hope, and peace'' Rousseau experienced as he traversed the backwoods of the land and of his soul: ''I am consecrating my last days to studying myself and to preparing in advance my account which I will not delay reconciling,'' he writes in the first walk. The second walk describes a fall in Menilmontant, his unconsciousness, and subsequent awakening, in which he forgets his past and experiences the peace of rebirth, ''I knew not who I was nor where I was; I felt neither evil, nor fear, nor worry.'' The third walk retraces his moral development from his youth (''I became a Catholic, but I always remained Christian'') until his present pursuit of ''patience, kindness, resignation, integrity, and impartial justice.'' Walk four deals with morality, truth, and falsehood. The fifth walk is best known for its eloquent and lyric communion with nature during the two months he spent at Ile Saint-Pierre in 1765 as he collected and described plants of the island and rambled through its savage yet agreeable landscape. The sixth walk reexamines his conscience and his need for independence; the seventh, his love of botany and nature, the ''mother of all,'' his ''refuge.'' The eighth walk analyzes the reasons for his present happiness; the ninth, his love of children, despite having relinquished his own. The final walk, which is unfinished, recalls the "unique and short time of my life when I was myself completely, without mingling and without obstruction, and where I can truthfully say I experienced life," with Madame Warens (1700–1762).

The *Rêveries* represent Rousseau's final attempt at self-reconciliation, to find that innate goodness within himself that he experienced most fully in communion with nature. His walks amid forests, hillsides, groves, and vineyards inspired a lyricism, sensitivity, and self-revelation that anticipates Chateaubriand* and the romanticism* of the nineteenth century.

For further information, see E. Gans, "The Victim as Subject: The Esthetico-Ethical System of Rousseau's *Rêveries*," *Slavisticna Revija* 21 (1) (Spring 1982): 3–31; D. Williams, *Rousseau. Les Rêveries du promeneur solitaire* (London: Grant and Cutler, 1984).

RICCOBONI, MARIE-JEANNE DE LABORAS, MADAME (1713–1792), actress turned novelist whose works reveal an early feminism, was unhappily married to actor-playwright François Riccoboni, son of the famed director of the Théâtre Italien,* where she played from 1734 to 1760. After 1761, she supported herself by writing; her income, from 1772 on, was supplemented by a pension from the king. She wrote eight novels, six in letter form, including her best-known *Lettres de Mistress Fanni Butlerd* (*Letters of Fanni Butlerd*, 1757), supposedly translated from the English; *L'Histoire de M. le marquis de Cressy* (*The Story of Monsieur le marquis de Cressy*, 1758), and *Les Lettres de Milady Juliette Catesby* (1758). She also wrote probably the best conclusion among those offered to Marivaux's* unfinished *Vie de Marianne.**

Riccoboni's novels portray the fears, pains, loves, and happiness of the female heart and uphold an ideal of love similar to J.-J. Rousseau's*—a love rooted in mutual respect, confidence, and admiration. If such a love is difficult to grow, the fault, according to Riccoboni, lies with the male, who is unfaithful, mendacious, ambitious, and proud. Women should find solace in virtue or in "solid and true principles which make us capable of enjoying with moderation the blessings of fortune or help us to bear its privation." Her writing is founded in sensitivity and sincerity.

RIMBAUD, ARTHUR (1854–1891). See *Dictionary of Modern French Literature, from Naturalism and Symbolism to Post-Modernism.*

RIVAROL, ANTOINE DE (1753–1801), eighteenth-century moralist and author of epigrams and portraits, was born the eldest of sixteen children of a Languedoc innkeeper. He assumed various names and claimed ascension from Italian nobility before coming to Paris in 1777, where, like Chamfort,* his wit and intelligence opened the doors of salon society. His *Discours sur l'universalité de la langue française* (*Discourse on the Universality of the French Language*, 1784) resulted in his election to the Berlin Academy and a pension from

Louis XVI. In collaboration with a lesser-known writer, Louis-Pierre Quentin de Richebourg, Marquis de Champcenetz (1759–1794), Rivarol produced two satirical "almanacks." The first, *Petit Almanach des grands hommes pour l'année 1788* (*Little Almanack on Great Men for the Year 1788*), directed against minor writers—he had previously attacked Delille,* Beaumarchais,* and others in anonymous letters—won him many literary enemies. The second, aimed at the "Grands hommes de la Révolution" ("Great Men of the Revolution"), made political ones. A fervent royalist, he wrote for antirevolutionary journals, *Actes des apôtres* (*Acts of the Apostles*) and *Journal politique* (*Political Journal*). He was forced to emigrate to Brussels, London, and Hamburg. While in exile, he wrote political pamphlets and published, in 1797, the preface to his *Nouveau Dictionnaire de la langue française* (*New Dictionary of the French Language*), which he never completed. In late 1800, he travelled to Berlin where he died a few months later.

Rivarol's works, first collected and published by his friend Charles-Julien de Chênedollé (1769–1833), fill five volumes. He is remembered primarily for his *Discours sur l'universalité de la langue française* and his *Carnets* (*Notebooks*). The *Discours* praises the French language for the "order and construction" of its sentences based on "the natural logic of all men." The result is its "admirable clarity. . . . That which is not clear," according to Rivarol, "is not French." The *Carnets* reveal his mastery of the language, for the epigrams and portraits they contain reveal more of his skill as a writer than any deep perception of human nature. They ring with stylized statements of his morals and philosophy such as: "Words are exterior thoughts and thoughts are interior words"; "Mirabeau* was capable of anything for money, even of a good deed"; "Passions are the orators of large assemblies"; "The people gives its favor, never its trust."

Rivarol's *Cahiers* and the preface to his proposed dictionary reflect his disapproval of the Revolution and his disappointment in the philosophes.* Just as they had satirized church and state at mid-century, he in turn, pitted his wit against their false promises of liberty, equality, and fraternity and affirmed his belief in sentiment as supreme rather than reason.

ROBESPIERRE, MAXIMILIEN MARIE ISIDORE (1758–1794), revolutionary leader and orator who dominated the National Convention and perpetrated the Reign of Terror. He was born in Arras, educated in Paris at Collège Louis-le-Grand and returned to his native town as a lawyer in 1781. In 1789, he was elected to the states general, representing the third estate of Arras. There he won the support of the people of Paris and turned to the radical Jacobin Club as a forum for his ideas. His influence among the people grew; the Jacobins supported him ardently. In 1792, he became first deputy of Paris to the National Convention. He voted for the death of the king and led the opposition to the moderate Girondins. Two years later, he succeeded Danton* to the committee for public safety, consolidating his power and eliminating his enemies during the

Terror until overthrown on 27 July 1874. He and his supporters, including revolutionary writer and theorist Louis de Saint-Just (1767–1794), were executed the following day.

Robespierre, imbued with the teachings of J.-J. Rousseau,* sought to establish a France where the democratic ideals of the eighteenth-century philosophe* would flourish. He condemned atheism and instituted worship of a supreme being among the people. His speeches, less imaginative and passionate than other revolutionary orators, were well-written, logical testimonies to his convictions.

For further information, see G. A. Kelly, "Conceptual Sources of the Terror," *Eighteenth Century Studies* 14 (Fall 1980): 18–36.

ROLAND, MADAME (born Manon-Jeanne Philipon, 1754–1793), revolutionary writer and instrumental member of the moderate Girondist party, left a legacy of memoirs and letters written while she was in prison. She was born in Paris, the daughter of an engraver, and received a good education nourished by a love of reading, especially the Greek writer, Plutarch (c.50–c.125). She was married at twenty-six to Roland de la Platière (1732–1793), twenty-two years her senior, who became minister of the interior in 1792. They lived first in Amiens, then Lyons, where both established their interest in the Revolution. She edited the *Courrier de Lyons,* a political newsletter from the provincial city that won them friends and influence as far away as the capital. They came to Paris in 1791, where her salon on rue Guénégaud was a favorite meeting place for the Girondists, including Jean-Pierre Brissot (1754–1793), Pétion de Villeneuve (1756–1794) and Robespierre,* whose extremist faction, the "montagnards," had not yet broken away. A year later, however, both Rolands denounced the excesses of the Revolution, earning the enmity of Robespierre, Danton,* and other extremists. In June 1793, she was arrested and spent five months' imprisonment writing letters and her memoirs, *Appel à l'impartiale posterité (Appeal to an Impartial Posterity).* Her work is important not for its literary value as much as for the personal and historical insights of her final days. She was a valiant prisoner, retaining her independence and conscience. "I am more at peace with my conscience than my oppressors are with their domination. . . . Tyrants may oppress me, but swallow me? Never, never," she wrote to her Girondist friend, François Buzot (1760–1793). She was guillotined in November 1793, along with other Girondists. Her husband committed suicide upon the news of her death.

ROMANTICISM (romantisme) is a literary movement that began in France around the year 1820, culminated ten years later with the battle of *Hernani,* * and ended approximately in 1850, when it was succeeded by realism.* It grew from the pre-romanticism* of J.-J. Rousseau,* the "grandfather" of romanticism, who passed its torch onto Chateaubriand* and Madame de Staël.* Their novels (Chateaubriand's *Atala* * and *René*;* Stael's *Corinne* [1807] and *Delphine* [1802]) expressed imagination and sensitivity, the essence of romantic poetry.

Romanticism fed on the mal de siècle* that followed the fall of the Empire in 1815 and on the restoration of the Bourbons to the throne, when disappointment, dissatisfaction, and malaise were at an all-time high among a young generation who felt deceived by the promises of the philosophes.* It was influenced by English poets Percy Bysshe Shelley (1792–1822) and Lord Byron (1788–1824), the novels of Walter Scott (1771–1832), and the ballads of Germans Friedrich von Schiller (1759–1805) and Johann Wolfgang von Goethe (1749–1832). Its principal theoreticians were Madame de Staël, who defined romanticism as "born of chivalry and Christianity"; Stendhal,* who defined it as "the art of presenting to the people literary works which . . . are apt to give them the most pleasure possible"; and Hugo,* who identified the movement with the nineteenth century. The richness and disparity of the movement, however, is best witnessed in the works themselves.

Romanticism is characterized as a revolution against the classical principles of order and restraint, reason and tradition, that reigned in the seventeenth century and continued to endure, though less gloriously, in the eighteenth. Young romantic poets and playwrights proclaimed that art was free. Hugo, in his preface to *Hernani,* defined romanticism as "liberalism in literature." Romanticism emphasized the individual. Lyricism, emotion, and passion are its hallmarks, as love, hate, hope, despair, and sadness are confessed and scrutinized again and again in an attempt to define oneself and one's place in society. The romantics sought the mysterious, the fantastic, the infinite, the infernal, the invisible, and the supernatural; they examined the grotesque and the sublime, the ugly and the beautiful; they loved the humble, the familiar, the quaint, and original. They extolled the Middle Ages with its ideals of Christianity, chivalry, freedom, and justice; they despised the industrialized present and the materialistic bourgeois society that surrounded them; they adored nature, which they considered a mirror of their moods and emotions.

The poets tried new rhythms, fresh images and symbols. Their poetry was personal, subjective, lyric. Exoticism and local color abounded. Playwrights abandoned the classical unities of time and place and replaced them with a single unity of action or impression. They mixed genres, the comic and the tragic, the grotesque and the sublime, in an attempt to portray a complete, natural picture of modern life. William Shakespeare (1564–1616) and Friedrich von Schiller (1759–1805) were their models.

The romantics grouped themselves in cénacles,* first around Charles Nodier* at the Arsenal* along with Emile (1791–1871) and Anthony (1800–1869) Deschamps, Vigny,* Hugo,* and Musset.* A more ardently romantic second cénacle formed around Hugo at rue Notre-Dame-des-Champs and included Sainte-Beuve,* Nodier, Nerval,* Dumas père,* Gautier,* and painters Louis Boulanger (1806–1867), Eugène Delacroix (1798–1863), and Pierre-Jean David d'Angers (1783–1856). Romantic journals published their works—*Le Conservateur littéraire* (*The Literary Conservator*), founded by Hugo from December 1819 through March 1821; *La Muse française* (*The French Muse*)*; *Les Annales* *de la littérature et des arts* (*The Annals of Literature and of the Arts*, 1820–1827); *Le Mercure du XIXe siècle* (*The Mercury of the Nineteenth Century*, 1823–1830); and *Le Globe.**

Victor Hugo was the shining star of romanticism, the standard by which the others defined themselves. His *Préface de Cromwell** became the manifesto of the new school. The triumph of his *Hernani* marked the apex of the movement and the failure of *Les Burgraves* in 1843, its demise.

The romantics rediscovered a poetry that was personal and lyric, the poetry of the Middle Ages and of the modern age. Their insistence on liberty in art opened new avenues of expression in poetry, the novel, and on the stage, which laid the foundation for modern literature.

For further information, see J. S. Allen, "French Romanticism and the Origins of Modern Popular Literature in Paris," *Journal of Popular Culture* 15 (3) (Winter 1981): 132–141; Allen, *Popular French Romanticism. Authors, Readers and Books in the Nineteenth Century* (Syracuse: Syracuse University Press, 1981); D. G. Charlton, ed., *The French Romantics*, vols. 1 and 2 (Cambridge: Cambridge University Press, 1984); B. Daniels, ed., *Revolution in the Theatre: French Romantic Theories of Drama* (Westport, Ct.: Greenwood Press, 1983); K. Engelberg, ed., *The Romantic Heritage: A Collection of Critical Essays* (Copenhagen: University of Copenhagen, 1983); D. Erdman, ed., *The Romantic Movement. A Selective and Critical Bibliography for 1979* (New York/London: Garland, 1980); M. Iknayan, *The Concave Mirror: From Imitation to Expression in French Esthetic Theory 1800–1830* (Saratoga, California: Anma Libri, 1983); F. Kluck, "Charles Gleyre and the French Romantics," *Nineteenth Century French Studies* 10 (3–4) (Spring–Summer 1982): 228–243; G. Lanyi, "Debates on the Definition of Romanticism in Literary France (1820–1830)," *Journal of the History of Ideas* 41 (1980): 141–150; T. Raser, "Reference and Allegory in Romantic Description," *The Romanic Review* (January 1984); 35–50; N. Rogers, "The Wasting Away of Romantic Heroines," *Nineteenth Century French Studies* 11 (3–4) (Spring–Summer 1983): 246–256; E. N. Schamber, *The Artist as Politician. The Relationship between the Art and the Politics of the French Romantics* (Lanham, Md.: University Press of America, 1984); M. Shaw, "French Studies: The Romantic Era," *The Year's Work In Modern Language Studies* 42 (1980): 180–195; and 43 (1981): 171–182.

ROUGE ET LE NOIR, LE (*The Red and the Black*, 1830), by Stendhal,* was his first novel of literary significance. Subtitled "Chronique du XIXe siècle," it presents the politics, morals, and customs of Restoration France, from the village of Verrières to the aristocratic salons of Paris. Although it was written when the romanticism* of Hugo* and Vigny* was in full flower, the novel recalls in its style the restraint, precision, and detachment of the classics. Its historical veracity and attention to detail anticipates the realism* that Flaubert* would perfect later in the century. Its psychological realism would become the theme of Proust** and Sartre** in the modern psychological novel.

On one level, the novel parallels the newspaper account of Antoine Berthet, a peasant boy who was guillotined in 1828 for shooting his mistress, Madame Michoud, whose children he tutored. Likewise, Julien Sorel, the son of a carpenter, seduces Madame de Rênal, the wife of the mayor of Verrières, who has employed him as a tutor. Julien, a proud and ambitious boy, has realized that the defeat of Napoleon has weakened his chances in the army (Le Rouge) and turns to the clergy (Le Noir) to advance himself. Dismissed by M. de Rênal, he enters the seminary. There he wins the confidence of the superior, abbé Pirard, who places him as secretary to the Marquis de la Mole in Paris. Julien makes himself indispensable to the marquis and arouses the curiosity and love of his daughter, Mathilde. After seducing her, he obtains from her parents a title, a rank, and permission to marry. His triumph seems assured until Madame de Rênal, still in love with him and consumed with jealousy, denounces him as a schemer. In revenge, Julien returns to his village and wounds Madame de Rênal in church. He is arrested, condemned, and dies on the scaffold. Mathilde buries his severed head in the Juras. Madame de Rênal dies in the arms of her children a few days later.

Le Rouge et le noir is the story of characters caught in a web of history who reflect in their thoughts and actions the historical moment in which they live: Julien, the peasant, who succeeds through ambition and ruse in breaking through social barriers; M. de Rênal, the ultra-royalist mayor of the village; the aristo-cratic, conservative marquis; Mathilde, his bored, romanesque daughter.

The novel is important as a psychological study. Stendhal penetrates the mind of Julien, revealing his innermost thoughts as well as his rise up the social scale. Julien is alien, at war with society, a forerunner of the twentieth-century "etranger" ("stranger"). His weapons are his genius and hypocrisy. Forever isolated, he finds fulfillment only in prison and ultimately in death.

For further information, see P. Brooks, "The Novel and the Guillotine; or, Fathers and Sons in *Le Rouge et le Noir*," *Publication of the Modern Language Association* 97 (3) (May 1982): 348–362; K. Bulgin, "Love, Self-Esteem and Narrative Perspective in Stendhal's *Le Rouge et le Noir*," *Essays in Literature* 10 (1) (Spring 1983): 101–110; R. Buss, "Quick on the Draw? Stendhal's Lottery Ticket and Some Early Critics of *Le Rouge et le Noir*," *Literature and History* 8 (1) (Spring 1982): 95–107; A. Jefferson, "Stendhal and the Uses of Reading: *Le Rouge et le Noir*," *French Studies* 37 (2) (April 1983): 168–183; P. Pollard, "Colour Symbolism in *Le Rouge et le Noir*," *Modern Language Review* 76 (2) (April 1981): 323–331.

LES ROUGON-MACQUART (1871–1893), by Zola.** See *Dictionary of Modern French Literature, from Naturalism and Symbolism to Post-Modernism.*

ROUSSEAU, JEAN-BAPTISTE (1671–1741), considered by many to be the greatest poet of his time, spent nearly half of his life lonely and miserable in exile from France for declamatory verses that he claimed not to have written. Despite his early success and encouragement by Nicolas Boileau (1636–1711), failures in comedy and opera soured his personality. Pompous and vain, he disowned his shoemaker father and satirized the habitués of the Café Laurent, which he once frequented. Condemned to banishment for blasphemy in 1710, he followed the count of Luc to Switzerland and Vienna, refused letters of recall in 1716, and stayed in Belgium, England, and Holland. Later denied the right to return, he died, sick and morose, in Brussels.

Rousseau's epigrams reflect his bitterness and disappointment, but he is best known for his odes, rounds, and cantatas. Pompous and impersonal, written in the classical tradition, which continued to dominate but had lost its lustre, his odes are nonetheless pleasant, well-written examples of "noblesse" and "beau désordre" that Boileau so admired. The purity, rhythm, and movement of the odes were later found in the romanticism* of the nineteenth century, which converted Rousseau's "lyrisme impersonnel" into a lyricism that is personal, sincere, and spontaneous.

ROUSSEAU, JEAN-JACQUES (1712–1778), eighteenth-century philosopher and author, has inspired revolutionaries and romanticists around the world for the past two hundred years. He is known as the father of romanticism* and of the French Revolution and the grandfather of the Russian Revolution. While his contemporaries, notably Voltaire,* Diderot,* and the philosophes,* believed in enlightenment, man's reason and progress, Rousseau, the solitary dreamer and man of nature, denounced the immorality and materialism of the age. Rousseau's doctrine centered on one basic idea—that man is naturally good but has been corrupted by civilization.

Rousseau was born a Protestant in Geneva. His mother died in childbirth, leaving him in the hands of his father, a ne'er-do-well clockmaker, who taught his son to read but soon abandoned him to a lonely and irregular life in the care of others, which Rousseau relates in great detail in his *Confessions.** At fourteen, he was apprenticed to a notary and later to a printer. One night, returning from a walk, he found the gates of the city closed. The curé of a nearby village sent young Rousseau to Madame Warens (1700–1762), a Catholic convert in Annecy, who sent him to Turin to be baptized a Catholic. The next three years were filled with adventure as a footman in the seminary at Annecy and finally as a vagabond passing through Lyon, Fribourg, Lausanne, Neuchâtel, Bern, and Paris before returning to Madame Warens at Chambéry. Affectionately called "Maman" ("Mama") by Rousseau, the pretty young widow filled the maternal void in his life from 1732 to 1740 and fostered his love of music, reading, and nature. In 1737, she took a country house, Les Charmettes, near Chambéry, where they led an idyllic life until Rousseau left for Montpellier. Upon his return, he found himself replaced and left for Lyons as tutor to the children of M. Mably, the elder brother of Gabriel Mably* and Condillac.* Unhappy and unfit as a teacher, Rousseau left for Paris the following year.

In 1742, he unsuccessfully presented a new system of musical notation before the Academy of Sciences and was unable to obtain pupils. A year later he became secretary to the ambassador, M. de Montaigu, accompanying him to Venice. They argued, he returned to Paris in 1744, collaborated with Voltaire on an opera, and became, in 1746, secretary to Madame Dupin. He copied music, frequented the salons, befriended Diderot,* and contributed music articles to the *Encyclopédie,** which he later collected and published as a separate *Dictionary of Music* in 1768. He met Fontenelle,* Marivaux,* and Condillac, as well as Thérèse Levasseur, an uneducated servant girl who bore him five children, all of whom he abandoned to a foundling hospital.

The turning point in his life came in 1750 when, on his way to visit Diderot, who was incarcerated in Vincennes prison for his *Lettre sur les aveugles,** he read in the *Mercure de France* of the prize offered by the Academy of Dijon for an essay on the effect of scientific and artistic progress on man's morals. His award-winning and surprising answer in the *Discours sur les sciences et les arts** (1750) formulated in general terms the central idea of his doctrine, which stated that the arts and sciences have corrupted man's natural goodness and that scientific and cultural progress results in decadence and depravity. The quarrel still rages as to whether Rousseau himself planned his reply or whether it was Diderot who suggested it. A primitivist appeal for a return to nature, the discourse catapulted him to fame. Rousseau retired from society, dressed in homespun clothing, and copied music while he formulated more fully his system of thought. In 1752, his operetta *Le Devin du village* (*The Village Soothsayer*) was successfully performed at Fontainebleau; a comedy, *Narcisse*, failed a year later. Also in 1753, Rousseau published a *Lettre sur la musique française* (*Letter on French Music*), siding with the Italians in the Quarrel of the Buffons, the great debate over the superiority of French or Italian music.

Two years later, Rousseau's second major treatise, *Discours sur l'origine de l'inégalite** (1755), though not awarded by the Academy of Dijon, caused no less of a stir than his first for its attack on a society that requires man to relinquish his natural instincts and develop his reason instead. In search of property and riches, natural man loses his vigor, morality, happiness, and solitude; he becomes avaricious and domineering. Society splinters into the rich and the poor, tyrants and slaves; man's original equality is lost. Three years later, in his *Lettre à d'Alembert,** Rousseau condemned the theatre as immoral.

With his stance against the arts and sciences, the theatre, and the entire social system itself, Rousseau instituted a philosophy which was at opposite poles from that of his contemporaries. Diderot, at this time, was in Paris, knee-deep in publishing his monument to man's reason and ingenuity, the *Encyclopédie.** Their friendship ended in a quarrel over Madame d'Epinay (1726–1783) and Grimm.* In 1756, Rousseau sent Voltaire a *Lettre sur la Providence* (*Letter on Providence*) in reply to his *Poème sur la désastre de Lisbonne* (*Poem on the Lisbon Disaster,* 1756), in which Rousseau confirms his faith in the existence of an afterlife and a charitable Providence. Three years later, his *Lettre à d'Alembert* consummated the enmity between the two men with Voltaire firmly entrenched in the rationalism of the philosophes* and Rousseau alone with himself and his moral consciousness.

Rousseau had returned to Geneva in 1754, resumed his Protestantism, and became once again a citizen of the city he so loved. From 1756 to 1757, however, he repaired to the fertile tranquility of Madame d'Epinay's cottage near Montmorency outside of Paris, where he completed his music dictionary, wrote his *Lettre sur la Providence* to Voltaire and outlined his major works. He also fell in love with the young, though rather plain Madame d'Houdetot (1730–1813), sister-in-law of Madame d'Epinay, who inspired his sentimental novel, *La Nouvelle Héloïse.** He broke with Madame d'Epinay and spent four years in a small house named Montlouis in Montmorency and enjoyed the hospitality and support of the nearby duke of Luxembourg. There he outlined his three major works.

La Nouvelle Héloïse (1761), while recounting the love story of Julie and Saint-Preux through a series of letters, exalts nature as a purifying force in a rural setting where libertinage gives way to love, where truth, liberty, virtue, and happiness reign, where peace and serenity are restored.

Le Contrat social* (1762) presents Rousseau's plan to bring man from the isolation of nature into a society that approximates politically the freedom and equality of primitive man. In Rousseau's society man would subordinate his individual liberty by means of a social contract to the will of all, which would predominate. Thus, all men would be equal and self-ruling within the confines of laws based on popular consent rather than force. Rousseau's democratic thinking foresaw the Revolution of 1789; unfortunately, it also sowed the seeds of totalitarianism and nationalism by declaring the state almighty, demanding absolute allegiance, removing individual liberties, interest groups, political parties, and religious sects that might interfere with the unity of the state.

Rousseau outlined the education of his citizenry in *Emile** (1762). The ideal man, Emile, would be raised from infancy away from society and according to the laws of nature. Fortify the body, develop the senses and instinct, and respect the child's emerging personality are Rousseau's precepts. Emile finally emerges as a loving, sensitive, moral, and religious man. The fourth part of the book, "Profession de foi du vicaire savoyard" ("The Vicar of Savoy's Profession of Faith"), explains Rousseau's belief in natural religion and in a God who demands only "Look, admire and believe."

Despite the renown that these works brought to him, their antipolitical and antireligious doctrines aroused suspicion. In June 1762 *Emile* was condemned by the parliament of Paris and a warrant was issued for Rousseau's arrest. With the help of the duchess of Luxembourg (1707–1787) and the prince of Conti (1717–1776), Rousseau fled to Yverdon, then to Motiers in Neuchâtel. There, in the relative tranquility of this Protestant community, he wrote his *Lettre à Christophe de Beaumont* (*Letter to Christopher Beaumont*, 1762), outlining his religious convictions, to the archbishop of Paris who had issued a mandate against *Emile*. *Lettres de la montagne* (*Letters from the Mountain*, 1763) attacked the Genevan council and constitution. Voltaire, in turn, retaliated with a pamphlet, *Le Sentiment des citoyens* (*The Feelings of the Citizens*, 1764), rousing public opinion against Rousseau. His house was stoned in the middle of the night, and Rousseau fled to Ile St. Pierre until ordered to leave by the Bernese government six weeks later. He accepted the hospitality of David Hume (1711–1776) in England in 1766, where he wrote most of his *Confessions,* but a suspicious and quarrelsome Rousseau argued with his host. He returned to France a year later and lived on the run, finding haven first with the Marquis de Mirabeau (1715–1789), then with the prince of Conti; then on to Lyon, Grenoble, Bourgoin, and Monquin in Dauphiné. He finally returned to Paris, where he lived in solitude and poverty on rue Plâtrière (today known as rue Jean-Jacques Rousseau) with Bernadin de Saint-Pierre,* his only friend. He was always obsessed with the suspicion of a plot against him. To justify himself before God and the world, he finished his *Confessions* (1770), wrote the *Dialogues ou Rousseau juge de Jean-Jacques** (*Dialogues or Rousseau Judge of Jean-Jacques,* 1772–1776) and *Rêveries du promeneur solitaire** (*Dreams of a Solitary Walker,* 1776–1778). He finally accepted the hospitality of the Marquis de Girardin's (1735–1808) Ermenonville estate, where he died in 1778. He was buried in the nearby Ile des Peupliers until his remains were transferred to the Panthéon six years later.

Among the brilliant and renowned philosophers of the Age of Enlightenment, Rousseau is the only one to address the evils of the age with a coherent plan for social, educational, and political reform. Though his early works praised the freedom and morality of primitive man living in a state of nature, he realized that regression to such a state was impossible and undesirable. The reforms outlined in *La Nouvelle Héloïse, Emile,* and *Le Contrat social* were an attempt to reconcile his ideals with reality. Rousseau preferred the patriarchal, industrious, rural life of the Wolmar's in *La Nouvelle Heloïse;* he advocated a healthful and practical education; he feared a society based on might and power. The reforms outlined in *Le Contrat* directly influenced the thinking of Mirabeau,* Robespierre,* and Marat,* inspiring the French Revolution. Later the American and Russian revolutions followed suit. German political philosophers Immanuel Kant (1724–1804), Hegel (1770–1831), Fichte (1762–1814), and Karl Marx (1818–1883) were deeply influenced by his ideas.

Contrary to Voltaire, who extolled reason, and Diderot, who extolled instinct, Rousseau based his system on man's sensitivity. Rousseau shunned the society he despised, finding consolation in the beauty and goodness of nature and the sentiment, religion, and reveries it inspired. His solitude, his love of nature, his dreams culminated in his later works, his *Confessions, Dialogues,* and *Rêveries.* Descriptions of the lakes, mountains, and forests he traversed are melodious and eloquent, flowing from the pen of a man communing with nature and his innermost self. He transformed his emotions into a system of religion, literature, politics, and philosophy that was not only revolutionary, but contained the seeds of an entire literary movement—romanticism.

Throughout his life Rousseau was suspicious, unsociable, sensitive, and melancholy; some critics call him mad, others point to his ill health. For whatever reasons, he was generally misunderstood. His life and works continue to intrigue as scholars try to comprehend his genius.

For further information, see S. Axinn, "Rousseau Versus Kant on the Concept of Man," *The Philosophical Forum* 12 (Summer 1981): 348–355; F. Barnard, "National Culture and Political Legitimacy: Herder and Rousseau," *Journal of the History of Ideas* 44 (April–June 1983): 231–253; R. H. Bell, "Rousseau: the Prophet of Sincerity," *Biography* 3 (Fall 1980): 297–313; J. Bernstein, *Shaftesbury, Rousseau and Kant: An Introduction to the Conflict between Aesthetic and Moral Values in Modern Thought* (Madison: Fairleigh Dickinson University Press, 1980); M. Bloch and J. Bloch, "Women and the Dialectics of Nature in Eighteenth Century French Thought," in C. MacCormack and M. Strathern, eds., *Nature, Culture and Gender* (Cambridge: Cambridge University Press, 1980), 25–41; C. K. Blum, "Rousseau's Concept of 'Virtue' and the French Revolution," in *Enlightenment Studies in Honor of Lester G. Crocker,* A. Bingham and V. Topazio, eds. (Oxford: Voltaire Foundation, 1979), 29–48; S. Brodwin, " 'Old Plutarch at Auchinleck': Boswell's Muse of Corsica," *Philological Quarterly* 62 (1) (Winter 1983): 69–93; D. Buttry, "Perceptions of the Physical World: Jean-Jacques Rousseau, Knut Hamsum and Nature," *Scandinavian Journal of Literary Research* 6 (1981): 347–358; D. Cameron, "The Hero in Rousseau's Political Thought," *Journal of the History of Ideas* 46 (1) (January–March 1985): 397–420; R. Carter, "Rousseau's Newtonian Body Politic," *Philosophy and Social Criticism* 2 (1980): 143–167; H. Cell, "The Civil Religion Incarnate," *Swiss-French Studies/Etudes romandes* 2 (November 1981): 38–57; M. Cranston, *Jean-Jacques: The Early Life and Work of Jean-Jacques Rousseau, 1712–1754* (New York: Norton, 1983); L. G. Crocker, "Hidden Affinities: Nietzsche and Rousseau," *Transactions of the Fifth International Congress on the Enlightenment,* vol. 1 (Oxford: Taylor Institution, 1981), 119–141; P. de Man, *Allegories of Reading: Figural Language in Rousseau, Nietzsche, Rilke, and Proust* (New Haven: Yale University Press, 1982); E. Duffy, *Rousseau in England. The Context for Shelley's Critique of the Enlightenment* (Berkeley: University of California Press, 1979); S. Ellensburg, *Rousseau's Political Philosophy* (Ithaca: Cornell University Press, 1976); M. B. Ellis, *Rousseau's Socratic Aemilian Myths* (Columbus: Ohio State University Press, 1977); C. Eykman, " 'Souvenir' and 'Imagination' in the Works of Rousseau and Nerval," in A. Tymieniecka, ed., *The Philosophical Reflection of Man in Literature* (Dordrecht, The Netherlands: Reidel, 1982), 415–428; E. Gallagher, "Political Polarities in the Writings of Rousseau," *New Zealand Journal of French Studies* 2 (November 1981): 21–42; R. Godwin-Jones, "The Rural Socrates Revisited: Kleinjogg, Rousseau and the Concept of Natural Man," *Eighteenth Century Life* 7 (1) (October 1981): 86–104; R. Grady, "Bertrand de Jouvenel: Order, Legitimacy, and the Model of Rousseau," *Interpretation: A Journal of Political Philosophy* 9 (2–3) (September 1981): 365–383; J. C. Hall, *Rousseau: An Introduction to His Political Philosophy* (London: Macmillan, 1973); J. Hamilton, "Rousseau's *Préface de Narcisse:* An Essay in Self-Understanding," *French Literature Series* 9 (1982): 30–34; S. Harvey, M. Hobson, D. Kelly, and S. Taylor, eds., *Reappraisals of Rousseau* (Manchester: Manchester University Press, 1980); J. H. Huizinga, *Rousseau, The Self-Made Saint* (New York: Grossman, 1976); T. Kavanaugh, "Rousseau's *Le Lévite d'Ephraïm:* Dream, Text and Synthesis," *Eighteenth Century Studies* 16 (2) (Winter 1982–1983): 141–161; G. Kelly, " 'The Romance of Real Life': Autobiography in Rousseau and William Godwin," in *Man and Nature/L'Homme et la nature,* vol. 1 (London, Ontario: The University of Western Ontario, 1982), 93–101; W. Kumbier, "Rousseau's *Lettre sur la musique française,*" *Stanford French Review* 6 (2–3) (Fall–Winter 1982): 221–237; R. A. Leigh, ed., *Rousseau after Two Hundred Years: Proceedings of the Cambridge Bicenten-*

nial Colloquium (Cambridge: Cambridge University Press, 1982); J. MacAdam, M. Neumann, and G. Lafrance, eds., *Trent Rousseau Papers/Etudes Rousseau-Trent* (Ottawa: University of Ottawa Press, 1980); J. G. Merquior, *Rousseau and Weber: Two Studies in the Theory of Legitimacy* (London: Routledge, 1980); J. Miller, *Rousseau. Dreamer of Democracy* (New Haven: Yale University Press, 1984); E. Misenheimer, *Rousseau on the Education of Women* (Washington: University Press of America, 1981); A. Ridehalgh, "Preromantic Attitudes and the Birth of a Legend: French Pilgrimages to Ermenonville, 1778–1789," *Studies on Voltaire and the Eighteenth Century* 215 (1982): 231–252; A. Rosenberg, "Rousseau's View of Work and Leisure in the Community," *Australian Journal of French Studies* 18 (1) (January–April 1981): 3–12; T. Scanlon, "Manners, Morals and Maxims in Rousseau's *Lettre à Christophe de Beaumont,*" *Neophilologus* 65 (July 1981): 366–374; T. Siebers, "Ethics in the Age of Rousseau: From Lévi-Strauss to Derrida," *Modern Language Notes* 100 (4) (September 1985): 758–779; J. Starobinski, "Rousseau's Happy Days," *New Literary History* 11 (Autumn 1979): 147–166; J. C. Stewart-Robinson, "[Thomas] Reid's Anatomy of Culture: a Scottish Response to the Eloquent Jean-Jacques," in *Studies on Voltaire and the Eighteenth Century* 205 (1982): 141–163; J. Still, "Rousseau in *Daniel Deronda,*" *Revue de littérature comparée* 56 (January-March 1982): pp. 62–77; R. Teichgraeber, "Rousseau's Argument for Property," *History of European Ideas* 2 (2) (1981): 115–134; C. Thacker, "Rousseau's *Devin du Village,*" in *Das deutsche Singspiel im 18. Jahrhundert* (Heidelberg: Winter 1981), 119–124; H. Williams III, *Rousseau and Romantic Autobiography* (Oxford: Oxford University Press, 1983); N. Wilson, "Discourses on Method and Professions of Faith: Rousseau's Debt to Descartes," *French Studies* 37 (2) (April 1983): 157–167; R. Wokler, "Rousseau and Marx," in D. Miller, L. Siedentop, eds., *The Nature of Political Theory* (Oxford: Clarendon, 1983), 219–246.

ROYER-COLLARD, PIERRE-PAUL (1763–1845), professor, philosopher, and statesman, founded with Guizot* the doctrinaire party that, in the years following the Restoration of Louis XVIII, advocated a middle-of-the-road course ("le juste milieu") between the sovereignty of the king and the power of the people. He was born in Vitry-le-François near Châlons-sur-Marne, studied with the Brothers of the Christian Doctrine, taught school in the provinces, and by twenty was practicing law in Paris. He supported the Revolution and participated in the Paris Commune until 1792. He later separated himself from the excesses of the Revolution and aligned himself with the royalists. After trying to effect the restoration of the monarchy, he retired from public life, dedicating himself to philosophical pursuits during Napoleon's reign. He was a professor of the history of modern philosophy at the Sorbonne from 1811 to 1814, director of the government book trade from 1814 to 1815, elected to the chamber of deputies in 1815, and counsellor of state and president of the commission of public education. A popular leader with moderate royalist views, he was elected to the Academy in 1827 and became president of the chamber of deputies the next year. His influence declined after the July monarchy. He retired in 1842 to his estate at Chateauvieux near Sainte-Aignan, where he died in September 1845.

Royer-Collard was renowned as a political orator, spiritualist, and ardent opponent of the idéologues* who, influenced by the Scottish philosopher Thomas Reid (1710–1796), believed that the senses alone could not explain human knowledge and that substance, cause, space, and time must also be considered.

RUY BLAS (1838), by Victor Hugo,* a verse drama in five acts, along with *Hernani,* is one of the best known of his attempts at the theatre. While *Ruy Blas* did not incite audiences with the enthusiasm *Hernani* had generated eight years earlier, it is a better composed and more solid play. Its antithetical structure exemplifies more clearly than his other plays an important precept of the *Préface de Cromwell**—the alliance of the pathetic and the comic, the sublime and the grotesque—which is an essential trait of Hugo's world vision. Ruy Blas, whose very name suggests a mixture of the noble ("Ruy") and the base ("Blas"), combines the low social condition of a valet with noble character; Don Salluste, on the other hand, represents nobility of rank and depraved character. Hugo explains in the preface that the play satisfies the basic demands of an audience— action, passion, and character depiction—which are typically the separate domains of melodrama, tragedy, and comedy. He asserts that his three main characters personify those three literary forms: "Don Salluste would be the drama, don César the comedy, Ruy Blas the tragedy." In Ruy Blas, the three combine to depict the truth: "The philosophical subject of Ruy Blas is the people's aspiration toward higher spheres; the human subject, a man who loves a woman; the dramatic subject, a lackey who loves a queen."

Critics suggest at least two possible sources for the plot—an episode of J.-J. Rousseau's* *Confessions,** relating his love as a lackey for the granddaughter of the count of Gouvon, and Leon de Wailly's account in 1836 of the artist Sir Joshua Reynolds's (1723–1792) vengeful scheme to have a girlfriend who spurned him to marry a lackey disguised as a count. Hugo backed his idea with solid research into seventeenth-century Spain as well as his memories of Spain as a youth. Like *Hernani, Ruy Blas* has been criticized as melodramatic and improbable; however, it endures as Hugo's masterpiece for the beauty and eloquence of its verses, which J. B. Barrère in *Hugo* (Hatier, 1967) describes as "oratorical within bounds, of a purity sometimes classical, but enhanced with incisive strokes and dazzling imagery; the language has wit, poetry and nobility."

In act 1, the corrupt nobleman Don Salluste de Bazan is banished by the queen, Marie de Neubourg, for refusing to marry a poor servant girl whom he has seduced. He sets the wheels in motion to avenge himself, plotting to have Ruy Blas, his valet, disguised as his cousin Don César, seduce the queen and dishonor her in turn. He sells the real Don César, a bohemian who has been living under the name of Zafari, to African corsairs, then introduces Ruy Blas at court as his cousin, just returned from the Indies. In actuality, Ruy Blas loves the queen, which makes his mission all the more palatable. She spends long, lonely hours in her castle without her king, who is always hunting. In act 2, she dreams of an unknown admirer who, at great personal risk, has been sending her flowers and letters. One day, she recognizes him as Ruy Blas, her horseman. When an old friend, Don Guritan, becomes jealous of Ruy Blas and provokes a duel, the queen sends him to Neubourg, six hundred leagues away. By act 3, Ruy Blas is well established in the government. Thanks to the queen, he becomes first minister. She admits her admiration for his intellect and ability ("You seem to me to be the real king, the real master," she tells him) and begs him to save Spain, which is tottering on the brink of disaster. Ruy Blas's ecstacy is cut short by the return of Don Salluste, who humiliates him, reminding him that he is really only a servant. About to realize his plan, Salluste orders him to wait at his house in the morning; Ruy Blas obeys, but sensing danger, in act 4, has Don Guritan, who is loyal and still loves the queen, warn her not to leave the palace for three days. The arrival of the real Don César down the chimney provides comic relief. He unleashes a tirade against his cousin for sending him off, raids a pantry, drinks wine; he accepts money that is meant for Ruy-Blas/Don César, arranges a midnight rendezvous with the queen, and kills Don Guritan in a duel. Don Salluste turns him over to the authorities as Matalobos, a notorious outlaw. In act 5, Ruy Blas, confident that he has saved the queen from Salluste's trap, considers suicide; he is taken aback when she appears in the next scene, a victim of Salluste's ploy to surprise her alone at midnight in his company. Ruy Blas kills Salluste, then avowing his love for the queen, poisons himself before she forgives him.

For further information, see K. Wren, *Hugo, Hernani and Ruy Blas* (London: Grant and Cutler, 1982).

SADE, DONATIEN ALPHONSE, MARQUIS DE (1740–1814), a nobleman from one of the oldest French families, became the most radical libertine in his life as well as his literature in late eighteenth-century France. Libertinism originated with dissatisfaction against church and government and manifested itself as a political, philosophical, and social reaction against those institutions. It spawned a liberal morality that exalted sexual promiscuity and created a body of literature that reflected its values. The movement culminated in de Sade, with his novels of torture, profanation, and passion, the devastation of all social values and morality.

His youth was spent in the country estates of abbe de Sade; at age ten, he came to Paris for a Jesuit education at Louis-le-Grand. At fifteen, he was named second lieutenant in the king's infantry and later, captain of the cavalry. He fought in the Seven Years' War and married Mademoiselle de Montreuil at age twenty-three. Early on, however, de Sade dedicated himself to debauchery, crime, and destruction, earning more than thirty years in prison over the course of his lifetime. He was sentenced to death in 1772, fled, was captured and imprisoned in Vincennes and the Bastille, where a sense of persecution and claustration fed his imagination with the most revolting images of sexual freedom. In the Bastille, he wrote *Cent Vingt Journees de Sodome ou L'Ecole du libertinage* (One Hundred Twenty Days of Sodome or The School for Sodomy, posthumous, 1904), *Aline et Valcour* (1795), and the first version of *Justine ou Les Infortunés de la vertu* (*Justine or The Misfortunes of Virtue,* 1787). He was granted a reprieve during the Revolution and worked on hospital reform until reimprisoned from 1793 until 1794. He enjoyed his last years of liberty until 1804, when his writings resulted in his return to prison. He finished his days in Charenton, a mental hospital, where he organized play productions. Other works include *Justine ou Les Malheurs de la vertu* (*Justine or The Misfortunes of Virtue,* written 1788, published 1791), *La Nouvelle Justine . . . suivie de l'his-*

toire de Juliette (*The New Justine . . . Followed by the Story of Juliette,* 1797),
Le Philosophe dans le boudoir (*The Philosopher in the Boudoir,* 1795), *Les
Crimes de l'amour* (*Crimes of Love,* 1800), *Idées sur les romans* (*Ideas on
Novels,* 1800), and collections of letters.

De Sade has been variously called a monster, philosopher, victim, psychologist, pervert, and creator. Much of his work, unpublished during his lifetime,
remained unknown until the early twentieth century. His writing influenced the
surrealists (see surrealism**)—André Breton** considered de Sade an introduction to the realm of the imagination. Generally, his works elicit censure. He has
been called preromantic (see preromanticism*) for his evocation of the senses
and the imagination.

For further information, see D. Beach, "The Marquis de Sade: First Zimbabwean
Novelist," *Zambezia* 8 (1) (1980): 53–61; L. Bersani, "Representation and Its Discon-
tents," in S. Greenblatt, ed., *Allegory and Representation* (Balitmore: Johns Hopkins
University Press, 1981), 145–162; J. De Jean, "Les 120 Journées de Sodome: Disciplin-
ing the Body of Narrative," *Romanic Review* 74 (1) (January 1983): 34–45; B. Fink,
"Narrative Techniques and Utopian Structures in Sade's *Aline et Valcour,*" *Science
Fiction Studies* 7 (March 1980): 73–79; Fink, "Utopian Nurtures" [Fenelon, Mercier,
Morelly, Sade], *Transactions of the Fifth International Congress on the Enlightenment,*
vol. 2 (Oxford: Taylor Institution, 1981), 664–671; J. Gallop, "Impertinent Questions:
Irigaray, Sade, Lacan," *Sub-stance* 26 (1980): 57–67; Gallop, *A Reading of Sade with
Bataille, Blanchot and Klossowski* (Lincoln: University of Nebraska Press, 1981); S.
Kellman, "The Sadist Reader," *French Literature Series* 10 (1983): 21–31; S. Spruell,
"The Marquis de Sade: Pornography or Political Protest?" *Proceedings of the Annual
Meeting of the Western Society for French History* 9 (1982): 238–249.

SAINTE-BEUVE, CHARLES-AUGUSTIN (1804–1869), one of the outstanding literary critics of the nineteenth century and a would-be romantic (see
romanticism*) poet and novelist, was born in Boulogne-sur-mer and raised by
his mother and aunt. He came to Paris at fourteen and studied at Lycée Charlemagne. From 1824 to 1827, he studied at the Faculté des Sciences et de
Médecine, where he acquired a knack for scientific research and a spirit of
positivism,* which later influenced his criticism. In 1824, he began writing
reviews, signed "S. B.," for *Le Globe,** a liberal newspaper founded by a
former professor, Paul-François Dubois (1793–1874). After 1827, he became
one of its principal collaborators. An article on Hugo's* *Odes et Ballades* published in January 1827 won him the friendship of the young poet, who quickly
dispelled his initial reservations about romanticism. Sainte-Beuve frequented
Hugo's cénacle* and became an ardent supporter of the romantic school, both as
a theoretician and practitioner. His *Tableau historique et critique de la poésie
française et du théâtre français au XVIe siècle* (*Historical and Critical Tableau
of French Poetry and Theatre in the XVIe Century,* 1828) demonstrated that
romanticism, contrary to popular opinion, was not as much a break with seventeenth-century classical tradition as a return to the poetry of Pierre de Ronsard
(1524–1585) and the Pléiade. He showed, surprisingly, that it was the seven-

teenth century that broke with tradition and that romanticism was a return to it. He tried his hand at poetry but lacked the imagination and creativity of his contemporaries Lamartine,* Hugo, and Vigny.* *Vie, poésies et pensées de Joseph Delorme* (*Life, Poetry and Thoughts of Joseph Delorme,* 1829) expresses his mal du siècle.* One poem, "Les Rayons jaunes" ("The Yellow Rays"), is considered a precursor of Baudelaire's** "Correspondances" and the symbolist (see symbolism**) poetry of the late nineteenth century. *Les Consolations* (1830) is a collection of romantic and sentimental poems à la Chateaubriand.* Sainte-Beuve, sensing his limitations as a poet, underwent a moral crisis that led him through an affair with his best friend's wife, Adèle Hugo (1803–1868), and a religious conversion. He drifted from Saint-Simonisme* to mysticism and experienced a profound feeling of solitude, worry, and doubt. His only novel, *Volupté* (1834), a thinly disguised story of his love affair with Madame Hugo, witnesses his interior turmoil. His last volume of poetry, *Pensées d'août* (*August Thoughts*) appeared in 1837.

Sainte-Beuve found his true vocation in criticism and contributed regularly to reviews and journals. Five volumes of his *Critiques et portraits littéraires* (*Literary Criticism and Portraits*), originally published in the *Revue de Paris* and the *Revue des deux mondes,* were collected in 1832 and again from 1836 to 1839. From 1837 to 1838, he taught a course on Port-Royal at the University of Lausanne, which was the basis of an important work, *L'Histoire de Port-Royal* (7 vols., 1840–1859), a history of seventeenth-century thought, which he worked on for over twenty years. In 1840, he was named conservator of the Mazarin Library by Victor Cousin,* the minister of public instruction. He studied Greek and continued to contribute to the *Revue des deux mondes.* In 1844, he was elected to the Academy. In 1848, after the February revolution, he went to Liège, where he taught a course on Chateaubriand and his contemporaries, which was published in 1861 in two volumes. The following year, he returned to Paris, where the editor of the *Constitutionnel,* Louis Véron (1798–1867), asked him to contribute a literary article to his newspaper every Monday. These articles, plus others written for the *Moniteur* and the *Temps,* have been published as *Causeries du lundi* (*Monday Chats,* 15 vols., 1851–1862) and *Nouveaux lundis* (*New Mondays,* 13 vols., 1863–1870). He supported the Empire. In 1854, he was named professor of Latin poetry at the Collège de France, but taught only two classes because of dissatisfaction with his allegiance to the new regime. From 1857 to 1861, he taught at the Ecole Normale Supérieure. In 1865, he was elected senator but aligned himself with the liberal opposition three years later. He died in 1869, leaving volumes of correspondence and notes.

Besides the works mentioned, he wrote *Portraits littéraires* (*Literary Portraits,* 2 vols., 1844), *Portraits de femmes* (*Portraits of Women,* 1844), *Portraits contemporains* (3 vols., 1845, and 5 vols., 1869–1871), *Derniers Portraits littéraires* (*Last Literary Portraits,* 3 vols., 1852), and *P.-J. Proudhon, sa vie et sa correspondance* (*P.-J. Proudhon, His Life and Letters,* 1872).

Sainte-Beuve's early medical training endowed him with an ability to observe his fellow man that served him well as he sought to "find the man" behind the works he read. He believed that a literary work was inseparable from its author: "and I would willingly say: as is the tree, so is the fruit." He sought, through literature, to understand his literary soul-mates. He studied their religious beliefs, daily habits, economic status, and moral standards, their letters, memoirs, and novels in order to objectively discern their merits and judge their work. He brought a keen intelligence and intuition to the task and, in a scientific way, hoped to classify "families" of kindred spirits.

However, his method was not without its faults. He lacked the total objectivity required of a scientific enquiry. His deeply felt jealousy of his more creative contemporaries, Lamartine, Hugo, Vigny, Balzac,* Musset,* and Chateaubriand, surfaced in his reviews. Proust** points out in *Contre Saint-Beuve* (*Against Saint-Beuve,* posthumous, 1954) that he failed to consider that often a work is the "product of another 'moi' besides the one which we manifest in our habits, in society and in our vices." Sainte-Beuve doesn't account for that inexplicable "je ne sais quoi" of genius that lies at the heart of true art.

Nevertheless, Sainte-Beuve bequeathed posterity with an inheritance of "portraits littéraires" that capture their subject with a sensitivity and understanding which is useful even today. *Port-Royal* is a monument to Jansenism and its influence on the seventeenth century. His criticism constituted a giant step away from the classical absolutes of Malesherbes* and Nicolas Boileau (1636–1711) toward an esthetic of relativity. He believed that literature should be understood before it is judged. He sought the individual behind the work with the tools of history, biography, and later science. He tried to uncover the fundamental relationship between the work and its author. Taine* wrote that "we are all his students; today, in books and even in newspapers, his writing renovates all literary, philosophical and religious criticism."

For further information, see P. Duncan, "Pillar and Pool: the Metaphor of Amaury's Bipolar Nature in Sainte-Beuve's *Volupté,*" *Romance Notes* 23 (3) (Spring 1983): 232–237; M. Pitwood, "Sainte-Beuve and Dante," *Modern Language Review* 77 (3) (July 1982): 568–576.

SAINT-MARC-GIRARDIN (pseudonym of Marc Girardin, 1801–1873), academician, politician, and literary critic who ardently opposed romanticism,* was born in Paris, studied law and literature, and in 1826, became professor at Collège Louis-le-Grand and contributor to the *Journal des débats.* He was a professor of French poetry at the Sorbonne from 1833 until 1863 and served as deputy under the July monarchy from 1834 until 1848. He sat at the Assemblee Nationale in 1871 and contributed to the fall of Thiers* in 1873. Saint-Marc-Girardin's magnum opus is a *Cours de littérature dramatique (Course of Dramatic Literature,* 5 vols., 1843), a study of the theatre from ancient to modern times with particular emphasis on the evolution of literary treatment of feelings, such as filial love, patriotism, and religion with the aim of proving that the romantics had perverted them. As a critic, he warned youth against "the illusions and moral confusion'' of contemporary writers. His method was didactic and dogmatic, preaching the virtues of good sense, moderation, and classical absolutism. Other works include *La Fontaine et les fabulistes* (*La Fontaine and the Fabulists*, 2 vols., 1867) and *J.-J. Rousseau, sa vie et son oeuvre* (*J.-J. Rousseau, His Life and Work*, 2 vols., 1875).

SAINT-SIMON, CLAUDE-HENRI DE ROUVROY, COMTE DE (1760–1825), descendant of the eighteenth-century memorialist Louis de Rouvroy, duc de Saint-Simon,* was an economist and philosopher who founded the socialist doctrine, Saint-Simonisme.* He led an adventurous life, participating in the American Revolution against the British and travelling to Mexico as well as North America. He amassed a considerable fortune in land speculations and frequented the intellectual circles of the Directoire (1795–1799) and the industrial and financial magnates of the Restoration (1815–1830). His secretaries included Augustin Thierry* and August Comte.* However, he finished his life in abject poverty when his financial ventures failed. He attempted suicide two years before his death in 1825.

Saint-Simon outlined a new and positive reorganization of society, but he did not advocate revolution. Rather, he sought and even appealed to Louis XVIII for the formation of a new order based on science and industry. He believed in the supremacy of economics over politics, the ''administration of things'' over the ''governing of men,'' and would give the power that had historically rested with the government to ''industriels'' who would lead the people in their daily works. Government would no longer function in the hands of a nonproductive aristocracy, the church, or the military but rather through a ''meritocracy'' of artists, scientists, businessmen, bankers, and inventors. Laws would result from economics or sociology; morality would result from everyone working together for the common good. His later works pointed to a new Christian organization based on the principle that ''all men should act together as brethren.'' Saint-Simon developed his principles in several works: *L'Esquisse d'une nouvelle encyclopédie, l'histoire de l'homme* (*Sketch of a New Encyclopedia, the History of Man*, 1809–1811); *Mémoire sur la science de l'homme* (*Dissertation on the Knowledge of Man*, 1813); *L'Industrie ou Discussions politiques, morales et philosophiques, dans l'intérêt de tous les hommes livrés à des travaux utiles et indépendants* (*The Industry or Political, Moral and Philosophical Discussions in the Interest of All Men in the Service of Useful and Independent Works*, 1820–1823); *Du Système industriel* (*On the Industrial System*, 1820–1823), *Catéchisme des industriels* (*Industrial Catechism*, 1823–1824); and *Le Nouveau Christianisme* (*The New Christianity*, 1825).

SAINT-SIMON, LOUIS DE ROUVROY, DUC DE (1675–1755), nobleman, soldier, and ambassador, authored *Mémoires*, a work that presents a lively and illuminating if not totally accurate account of the final years of the reign of Louis XIV and of the Regency. His father, a court page, was named ''duc et pair,'' the highest nobility, by Louis XIII, an honor that fostered Saint-Simon's enduring feudal pride and hopes for a France ruled by the aristocracy. He was educated by the Jesuits; at seventeen, he entered the musketeers with aspirations of military glory, but left after ten years of what he viewed as unjustly slow promotions. At court, his title and merit were ignored by Louis XIV who, in sore need of military officers, disliked the young man's pride and resignation from the army. Saint-Simon, in turn, despised the Grand Dauphin, the king's son and next in line to the throne, and supported instead the duke of Burgundy, the Dauphin's son. At Burgundy's death, he aligned himself with the duke of Orleans, who became regent in 1715. Saint-Simon was appointed to the Council of Regency but held no real power. In 1721, he was appointed ambassador to Spain to arrange for Louis XV's marriage, never to take place, with the Infanta. Upon the death of the regent (1723), he retired from court and spent his remaining thirty years writing his memoirs in his chateau de la Ferté-Vidame near Chartres or in his Paris hotel on rue des Saints-Pères.

Saint-Simon's *Mémoires* originated as marginalia appended to the detailed but dull journal (which he describes with typical frankness as "fade a faire vomir"—"so insipid as to cause vomiting") of Philippe de Dangeau (1638–1720). Drawing on personal observations of court life, which he began notating at age nineteen, and interviews with women, ministers, generals, diplomats, doctors, and valets, he compiled one of the most revealing and least objective histories of the years 1691–1723. Saint-Simon witnessed all aspects of Versailles; his practiced eye recorded the details of grand events—meetings of parliament, the death of the Grand Dauphin, the marriage of the duke of Chartres—and peered into the heart and soul of their participants—the king, his courtiers, bishops, ladies. Like Jean de la Bruyère (1645–1696), he penetrates the dark underside of court life—its vanity, intrigues, and corruption. His frank evocation of the world of the court anticipates the realistic frescos of the *Comédie humaine** by Balzac,* who along with Proust,** admired and imitated him. His scope and intensity have been compared to that of Roman historian Tacitus (55?–117? A.D.) and Michelet.* Saint-Simon's fervor and impetuosity were praised by the romantics (see romanticism*). Chateaubriand* characterized his style: "Saint-Simon writes recklessly ('à la diable') for immortality." The critic Lanson (1857–1934) called him a "painter" rather than a philosopher or a moralist. Though he captured the spirit and truth of Versailles, his vision, as well as his style, is tainted by his dislike for the king and his aristocratic pretensions. His writing is at times disorganized; errors abound, along with gossip, lies, and extensive borrowing from Dangeau. Yet, despite its faults, the work remains an important chronicle of its times.

Upon his death, Saint-Simon's 173 notebooks were seized and taken to the minister of foreign affairs and viewed only by a chosen few, including Voltaire* for his *Siècle de Louis XIV*. In 1762, abbé de Voisenon (1708–1775) published extracts from it. In 1788, a three-volume edition was published, which was supplemented in 1789 and 1791. A complete edition, in twenty-one volumes, of the *Mémoires de Saint-Simon* appeared in 1829. Chéruel published a twenty-volume definitive edition in 1856; de Boislisle and Lecestre published a forty-three-volume edition from 1879 to 1930.

SAINT-SIMONISME is an early form of French socialism based on the system of Claude-Henri, comte de Saint-Simon,* who had outlined a reorganization of French society based on industry and science to assure the equal distribution of wealth and the production of goods necessary for life. Its earliest disciples included Saint-Amand Bazard (1796–1864), who in 1828 organized a series of lectures on Saint-Simon's doctrines, and Prosper Enfantin (1791–1832). By 1830, they were the acknowledged heads of the school, which had grown to include Pierre Leroux (1797–1871) (whose journal, *Le Globe,** became the principal mouthpiece for the movement), Auguste Comte,* Hippolyte Carnot (1801–1888), and others. Their goal was the elimination of man's exploitation by his fellow man. They wanted to replace the aristocratic tradition of inherited wealth with an equitable distribution according to the principle of "To each according to his capacity, to each capacity according to its works." These early Saint-Simonians organized themselves into "families," including women, and met weekly to discuss doctrine and experiment in communal living until dissension arose between the more conservative Bazard and Enfantin, who was leading the movement in a new direction advocating free love, promiscuity, and the "rehabilitation of the flesh."

Saint-Simonisme influenced the romantic (see romanticism*) literature of the time in two respects. First, it held that the "moral law of the future is equality between man and woman." Enfantin demanded her political and social liberation and her freedom in marriage. The Saint-Simonians sought an ally in George Sand,* who was sympathetic to their socialist ideals but wavered when it came to supporting free love. Secondly, it held that the artist had a sacred mission, the education and advancement of society as a whole, an ideal that saw its greatest expression in the works of Hugo.*

For further information, see L. Goldstein, "Early Feminist Themes in French Utopian Socialism: The Saint-Simonians and Fourier," *The Journal of the History of Ideas* 43 (1) (January–March 1982): 91–108.

SALAMMBO (1862), by Flaubert,* is a novel of ancient Carthage, undertaken, according to its author, in order "to live in a splendid subject and far from the modern world." Flaubert took up its composition in March 1857, shortly after having finished *Madame Bovary,** and worked on it for more than five years until April 1862. He brought to the task the same concerns about documentation and objectivity as he had to *Madame Bovary*. He haunted Paris libraries during the winter of 1856–1857, reading, researching, and planning his novel about the revolt of the mercenary troops that had served the city from 264 until 241 B.C. in its first war against Rome. He began writing in September 1857, an effort that he realized would benefit from on-site research. In April of the following year, he

set out on a journey to northern Africa, which altered the course of his work. He
came home, threw out his first efforts, and began all over again.

The novel is semiromantic and semirealist. Its subject is foreign, ancient,
monstrous. However, its lurid scenes of murder, pillage, and sacrifice, where
Flaubert gives full vent to his imagination, are tempered by his concern for
historical accuracy and detail. *Salammbô* is one of the few novels of the nineteenth century to join history with reality, imagination with documentation.

The story begins in the vast gardens of Hamilcar, a great Carthaginian general,
where an army of mercenary troops of all nations have gathered to celebrate the
anniversary of their victory over the Romans at Eryx. Their drunkenness revives
their griefs against Carthage—the government has neglected to pay them for
their services. In a fury of destruction, they burn and pillage, freeing slaves,
harming animals, and eating Hamilcar's sacred, bejeweled fish. Salammbô,
priestess of the moon goddess and Hamilcar's daughter, appeases the soldiers
with a religious hymn. Her beauty attracts two men in particular, the Numidian
chief Narr' Havas, and Mâtho, a gigantic Libyan who is assisted by Spendius, a
former Greek slave. When Salammbô offers Mâtho wine from a golden cup,
Spendius tells him that means she desires him.

The elders persuade the soldiers to leave the city for Sicca, where they say
they will receive their wages but, unsatisfied, they attack Carthage. The city
closes its gates to prevent further pillage. Mâtho, obsessed with seeing Salammbô, joins forces with Spendius, who wants to steal a sacred, mysterious veil,
supposedly the source of Carthage's invincibility. They enter the fortified city
through an aquaduct, Spendius steals the veil and Mâtho, wrapped in it, makes
his way into Salammbô's bedroom and offers it to her. She trembles at the sight
of the veil and calls for help. Mâtho is forced to flee. The people, unable to touch
the veil, permit him to escape. The loss of the veil brings misfortune to the city.
The Libyans revolt in the provinces; Narr' Havas allies himself with Mâtho, who
is now leader of the mercenaries. Hamilcar returns to Carthage and, as com-
mander-in-chief, leads his forces against the enemy in the battle of Macar. He is
surrounded, however, and his soldiers are dying of hunger. The high priest,
Schahabarim, urges Salammbô to penetrate the mercenary camp to retrieve the
veil and return it to Carthage. When an alarm calls Mâtho out of his tent, she
wraps herself in the veil and returns to her father's camp. As she arrives, Narr'
Havas announces that he is changing sides. In recompense, Hamilcar promises
him the hand of Salammbô. The increased manpower enables Hamilcar to break
the enemy lines and enter the city. Spendius cuts the aqueduct and the people die
of thirst. The mercenaries construct enormous machines and catapults to penetrate the walls. In desperation, the Carthaginians sacrifice their sons to bring
rain. Rain falls, they regain force, and after further battle, Narr' Havas captures
Mâtho and throws him in prison. Salammbô marries Narr' Havas. On their
wedding day, Mâtho is forced through the city streets, tortured by the people
who tear him apart. Weakened and falling, he makes his way to the wedding
dais. At his sight, Salammbô rises and advances, witnessing his torment, remem-

bering his past tenderness, not wanting him to die. Upon his death, the high priest slits his chest and steals his heart, raising it to the sun. As it ceases beating, the sky darkens, a cry is heard, and buildings tremble in a spasm of joy and hope. Narr' Havas drinks to the genius of Carthage. Salammbô, raising a cup also, suddenly falls over dead. "Thus the daughter of Hamilcar died, for having touched the veil of Tanit," the story concludes.

For further information, see P. Starr, "*Salammbô:* The Politics of an Ending," *French Forum* 10 (1) (January 1985): 40–56.

SAMAIN, ALBERT (1858–1900). See *Dictionary of Modern French Literature, from Naturalism and Symbolism to Post-Modernism.*

SAND, GEORGE (1804–1876), born Amantine Aurore Lucile Dupin, influential and prolific romantic (see romanticism*) novelist, was also an early feminist and socialist sympathizer who was committed to women and the working classes. Her tumultuous personal life was characterized by independence and idealism and romantic attachments to talented young men such as Frédéric Chopin (1810–1849), Musset,* and socialist thinkers. She was born in Paris, the daughter of a lieutenant in the imperial army, Maurice Dupin, who died in a riding accident when she was four. Her mother, a would-be actress and dancer of low birth, deserted her for Paris shortly after his death, leaving Sand to the charge of her aristocratic grandmother, a descendant of the king of Poland, at her estate at Nohant in Berry. As a youth at Nohant, she played with peasant children, experiencing firsthand the country scenes and country life she later immortalized in her novels. She received little formal education and was given to daydreaming. From 1818 to 1820, she attended the fashionable English Augustinian convent in Paris until thoughts of entering the convent had her grandmother bring her home. Back at Nohant, she read, especially J.-J. Rousseau* and Chateaubriand,* and rode horseback dressed as a boy. In 1821, her grandmother died. In 1822, Sand left Nohant for Paris, staying with her mother until her marriage, later that year, to Casimir Dudevant, a retired officer turned farmer whom Aurore soon found boring. They settled in a manor house at Nohant, and the following year Sand had her first child. As their love dimmed, the couple travelled about France. In 1825, they visited the Pyrennes, where Sand took a platonic lover, a young magistrate, Aurélien de Sèze. In 1828, she bore a second child, probably by Stéphane de Grandsagne, a friend of her youth. In 1831, increasingly unhappy with her husband, she left Nohant for Paris and the literary life, sharing a Left Bank garret with Jules Sandeau,* whom she had met the previous year. She published two short stories and a novel, *Rose et Blanche* (1831), written with Sandeau and signed Jules Sand. In 1832, *Indiana,* signed "J. Sand," appeared and was a success, though Sandeau had had nothing to do with it. They separated, with Sand retaining a syllable of his name to which she added the surname "George" because it "sounded Berrichon." *Valentine* followed later that year; *Lélia,* the next. All enjoyed great success.

In 1833, after a brief and unhappy affair with Mérimée,* she met Musset, already a famous poet at twenty-two, and accompanied him in December to Venice. When Musset fell ill, she betrayed him with a handsome young doctor, Pietro Pagello (1807–1898). Musset discovered her infidelity and returned to Paris by the end of March. This ill-fated affair is the source of Musset's richest poetry. Sand remained in Venice until July, where she wrote *Jacques, André,* and *Lettres d'un voyageur* (Letters from a Traveller). In 1835, after a brief reconciliation and definitive break with Musset, she nearly went mad. She returned to Nohant, where she received Franz Liszt (1811–1886) and his mistress, Marie d'Agoult (1805–1876), and met Michel de Bourges (d. 1853), a talented lawyer who gained her legal separation from her husband and won her support for his republican ideas. In 1836, after a public trial and legal separation, she travelled to Geneva and Paris. The following year, she met Lamennais* and wrote a series of five *Lettres à Marcie* (*Letters to Marcie*) for his journal, *Le Monde.* The letters advised the imaginary unwed girl of twenty-five on feminine issues, the social duties of "emancipated women," and the necessity for moral revolution. They also condemned free love. Next, Sand published *Mauprat* (1837), in favor of marriage; *Lettres d'un voyageur* (*Letters from a Traveller,* 1837); *Les Maîtres mosaïstes* (*The Master Mosaic Workers,* 1837); and various short articles.

In 1838, Balzac* came to visit her at Nohant; she met Frédéric Chopin in Paris, beginning a nearly ten-year liaison with the young composer. After *Les Sept Cordes de la Lyre* (*Seven Strings of the Lyre,* 1838), they, along with her children, travelled to Majorca, where the damp weather made Chopin gravely ill. She began *Spiridion* (1839), a religious novel written under the influence of Lamennais and Pierre Leroux (1797–1871), a romantic, utopian thinker who believed in a new Christianity based on social equality, nature, progress, and love of humanity. Upon their return to Paris, Sand wrote a play, *Cosima* (1840), which failed, and a populist novel, *Le Compagnon du tour de France* (*The Companion of the Tour of France,* 1840), influenced by Leroux's socialism. In the same vein, to expose the beauty and poetry of the proletariat, she wrote *Horace* (1841), establishing herself as France's leading social prophet. In 1841, along with Louis Viardot (1800–1895) and Leroux, she founded the Christian socialist *Revue indépendante* and began writing installments of *Consuelo* for it. *Consuelo* (1843) and *La Comtesse de Rudolstadt* (1844) popularized Leroux's ideas. Sand wrote *Jeanne* (1844), a pastoral novel partly based on Joan of Arc, for Louis Véron's (1798–1867) daily *Constitutionnel,* but he refused her next work, the communist *Le Meunier d'Angibault* (*The Miller of Angibault,* 1844), for his middle-class publication. It was finally serialized in the liberal newspaper, *Réforme.* Sand developed a short liaison with young social historian, Louis Blanc.* In 1845, she began a novelette, *Tévérino;* a novel, *Le Péché de Monsieur Antoine* (*The Sin of Mr. Antoine*); and a pastoral idyll, *La Mare au diable* (*The Devil's Pond*). By 1846, her relationship with Chopin was strained because of his steadily worsening ill health and his affection for Sand's daughter,

Solange. Her novel *Lucrezia Floriani* (1847), about her relationship with Chopin, paints a cruel portrait of the musician. Other novels from this period are *Célio Floriani* (published as *Le Château des Désertes* [*Castle of the Deserted*] in 1851) and a pastoral idyll, *François le Champi* (1850). In 1848, she lent her support to the revolution, writing manifestos to the "people" and to the "rich" which stated that France would be "communist before a century is up." From Nohant, she wrote *Lettres au peuple*. She became the government's unofficial minister of propaganda, wrote her memoirs, and started a new weekly, *La Cause du peuple* (*The People's Cause*), which lasted only three weeks. Although nominated a candidate to the constituent assembly, Sand hoped not to win, believing that guarantees of women's rights in marriage were needed before their political independence. When Leroux and other radicals were arrested, Sand returned to Nohant, where provincial opinion was against her.

Disillusioned with the events of 1848, she withdrew more often to Nohant. She wrote *La Petite Fadette* (*Little Fadette*, 1849), a pastoral novel written as a respite from the political upheaval of the revolution. With the assistance of Pierre Bocage (1797–1863), director of the Odéon theater, she transformed *François le Champi* into a play whose triumph encouraged Sand in her playwrighting. In 1852, received by Prince-President Louis-Napoleon, she pled for amnesty for imprisoned republicans. She was visited by English poets Elizabeth (1806–1861) and Robert Browning (1812–1889). In 1854, her memoirs, *L'Histoire de ma vie* (*The Story of My Life*) were first serialized in a Paris newspaper. She travelled to Italy, a trip which inspired *La Daniella* (1856), a novel written against the pope and the Italian people. She wrote more plays, *Lucie, Françoise,* and *Comme il vous plaira* (*As You Like It*), which were poorly received. In 1857, she retreated to the nearby village of Gargilesse to escape the stream of visitors invading Nohant. She did much of her later writing there, including *Elle et lui* (*She and He,* 1858), an unflattering portrait of Musset, which the poet's brother, Paul de Musset (1804–1880) countered with *Lui et elle* (*He and She,* 1859). Sand continued to write, publishing in 1859, *Narcisse, L'Homme de neige* (*The Snow Man*), *Les Dames vertes* (*The Green Ladies*), *Promenades autour d'un village* (*Walks around a Village*), *La Guerre* (*War*), and *Garibaldi. Le Marquis de Villemer,* about aristocratic salon life, and *Valdèvre* followed in 1860. In 1861, she met Alexandre Dumas fils* and a year later, she met Edmond and Jules de Goncourt** in Paris. In 1862, she published *Autour de la table* (*Around the Table*), *Souvenirs et impressions littéraires* (*Literary Memories and Impressions*), *Tamaris,* and two plays. *Mademoiselle La Quintinie,* a novel attacking church orthodoxy, and *Pourquoi les femmes à l'Académie?* (*Why Women in the French Academy?*) followed in 1863. The following year she moved to Palaiseau in the south of Paris. She enjoyed the company of Flaubert,* to whom she dedicated *Le Dernier Amour* (*The Last Love,* 1867) and *Pierre qui roule* (*A Rolling Stone,* or *Pierre,* 1870). *Le Beau Laurence* (*Handsome Lawrence,* 1870) and *Malgré tout* (*Despite Everything,* 1870) appeared on the eve of the Franco-Prussian War. In 1871, she published *Césarine Dietrich* and *Journal d'un voy-*

ageur pendant la guerre (*Diary of a Voyager during the War*), followed by *Francia* (1872), *Nanon* (1872), and *Contes d'une grand-mère* (*Grandmother's Fairy Tales,* 1873). Though increasingly ill with age, she continued to write. Her last works included *Ma Soeur Jeanne* (*My Sister Joan,* 1874), *Flamarande* (1875), and *Les Deux Frères* (*The Two Brothers,* 1875). She died on 8 June 1876, two days before the appearance of *La Tour de Percemont* (*The Tower of Percemont*).

In all, Sand wrote more than sixty novels, besides an enormous autobiography, travel works, and thousands of letters which were read across Europe and Russia and earned the praise of Balzac,* Dostoevsky (1821–1881), Matthew Arnold (1822–1888), Walt Whitman (1819–1892), and Henry James (1843–1916). Her first novels, *Indiana, Lélia,* and *Mauprat,* influenced by Rousseau and her unhappy marriage, are filled with sentimental romanticism, idealism, and lyricism. From Lamennais, Leroux, and Michel de Bourges's socialist influence, emerged the humantarian novels, *Le Meunier d'Angibault, Spiridion,* and *Consuelo,* which aspired toward a future of equality and fraternity. Her "romans champêtres" ("rustic novels")—*La Mare au diable, François le Champi, La Petite Fadette, Jeanne, Les Maîtres sonneurs, Le Meunier d'Angibault*—depicting the Berry countryside surrounding Nohant, introduced the peasant into French literature and instituted the regional novel as a viable genre for a host of writers (Loti,** Maupassant,** Daudet*) to follow. Among her last novels, the aristocratic and bourgeois *Jean de la Roche* (1859) and *Le Marquis de Villemer* mark a return to the romanesque.

Much of Sand's work has been dismissed as dated, didactic, idealistic, contrived. *Lélia,* with its attacks against the church and marriage, however, is enjoying a revival by feminists. But it is as a regional writer that Sand is most celebrated; her rustic novels of Berrichon life and nature are considered classic for their sensitive depiction of the beauty of the land and its people.

For further information, see T. Alvarez-Detrell, *"Indiana:* The Spanish Connection to George Sand," *The USF Language Quarterly* 20 (3–4) (Spring–Summer 1982): 15–17; W. Atwood, *The Lioness and the Little One. The Liaison of George Sand and F. Chopin* (New York: Columbia University Press, 1980); J. Barry, ed., *George Sand. In Her Own Words* (New York: Anchor Books, 1979); Barry, *Infamous Woman, The Life of George Sand* (Garden City: Doubleday, 1977); P. G. Blount, *George Sand and the Victorian World* (Athens: University of Georgia Press, 1979); B. Cooper, "L'envers du décor': The Space of the Fantastic in George Sand's *Consuelo,"* *Romance Notes* 25 (1) (Fall 1984): 243–248; M. Danahy, "George Sand, Women and the World of Work," *Friends of George Sand Newsletter* 3 (Spring–Summer 1980): 36–41; N. Datlof, E. Dunbaugh, F. Lambasa, G. Savet, W. Shiver, A. Szogyi, and J. Astman, eds., *George Sand Papers: Conference Proceedings, 1978* (New York: AMS Press, 1982); R. Godwin-Jones, "Where the Devil Leads: Peasant Superstitions in George Sand's *Petite Fadette* and Droste-Hulshoff's *Judenbuche,"* *Neohelicon* 10 (1) (1983): 221–238; R. B. Grant, "George Sand's *La Mare au diable;* A Study in Male Passivity," *Nineteenth Century French Studies* 13 (4) (Summer 1985): 211–223; N. Miller, "Writing from the Feminine: George Sand and the Novel of Female Pastoral," in C. Heilbrun and M. Higonnet, eds.,

The Representation of Women in Fiction (Baltimore: Johns Hopkins University Press, 1983), 124–151; N. Rogers, "Echoes of George Sand in Kate Chopin," *Revue de littérature comparée* 57 (1) (January–March 1983): 25–42; J. Sackin, "Nature Imagery as Narrative Structure in George Sand's *Indiana*," *Romance Notes* 21 (3) (Spring 1981): 313–317; A. Singer, M. Singer, J. Spleth, and D. O'Brien, eds., *West Virginia George Sand Conference Papers* (Morgantown: West Virginia University, 1981); E. Sivert, "*Lélia* and Feminism," *Yale French Studies* 62 (1981): 45–66; E. Standring, "Rossini and His Music in the Life and Works of George Sand," *Nineteenth Century French Studies* 10 (1–2) (Fall–Winter 1981–1982): 17–27; J. Vest, "Fluid Nomenclature, Imagery, and Themes in George Sand's *Indiana*," *South Atlantic Review* 46 (2) (May 1981): 43–54; P. Waddington, *Turgenev and George Sand: An Improbable Entente* (London: Macmillan, 1981).

SANDEAU, JULES (1811–1883), author of two dozen novels and several plays, was linked for a time with George Sand* and collaborated with Augier.* He was born in Aubusson in the Creuse valley. He met Sand at her country estate at Nohant; after her separation from her husband and children, she lived with him in Paris. Together they launched their literary careers with *Rose et Blanche* (*Rose and Blanche,* 1831), signed "J. Sand." After Sand, he travelled to Italy. Upon his return, he wrote an autobiographical novel, *Marianna* (1839), followed by *Le Docteur Herbeau* (1841), *Mademoiselle de la Seiglière* (1848), and others. With Augier, he wrote a realist comedy, *Le Gendre de M. Poirier* (*M. Poirier's Son-in-Law,* 1854). In 1853, he was named conservator of the Mazarin library. He was elected to the Academy in 1858. Among his recurrent themes are the depiction of the social classes and social conflict. He was not a popular novelist but is considered a talented one.

SARDOU, VICTORIEN (1831–1908), one of the most prolific and successful authors of more than fifty comedies in the latter nineteenth century, wrote, in the manner of Scribe,* with great talent in plot construction. In his comedies of manners, *Les Vieux Garçons* (*The Old Boys,* 1865) and *La Famille Benoîton* (*The Benoiton Family,* 1865); historical dramas, *Patrie* (*Country,* 1869), *Théodora* (1884), and *Tosca* (1887); melodramas; and vaudevilles; plot provides the major source of interest. Other plays include *Pattes de mouches* (*Scribblings,* 1860), about the fate of a compromising letter; *Nos Intimes* (*Our Intimates,* 1861); *Nos Bons Villageois* (*Our Good Villagers,* 1866); and *Rabagas* (1873); among others. His works have been criticized as shallow and artificial but reveal an ingenuity and imagination that were applauded by his contemporaries.

SCRIBE, EUGENE (1791–1861), popular writer of vaudeville comedies, comedies of intrigue, and opera libretti, wrote nearly four hundred plays in his lifetime. He was born in Paris, the son of a silk merchant, received a solid education, and was destined for a career in law. He began collaborating on plays at the age of twenty. *Les Dervis* (*The Dervishes,* 1811) supposedly is his first, although it is unsigned and difficult to verify. His first major success was *Une*

Nuit de garde nationale (*A Night of National Guard*, 1816). He entered the Academy in 1834. Scribe's plays are filled with sentimentality, light satire, and surprising turns of plot, which maintained his place at the helm of French theatre for thirty years. They were generally unappreciated by the romantics (see romanticism*). Gautier* wrote that Scribe understood nothing about art but wrote about money to satisfy a bourgeois audience. Nevertheless, his influence was extensive and broadened the scope of drama in the nineteenth century. His vast repertoire includes *Valérie* (1822), *La Demoiselle à marier* (*The Marriageable Lady*, 1826), *Le Mariage à raison* (*The Marriage of Reason*, 1826), *Bertrand et Raton* (1833), *La Verre d'eau* (*The Glass of Water*, 1840), and *Bataille de dames* (*Battle of Women*, 1851).

For further information, see D. Cardwell, "The Well-Made Play of Eugène Scribe," *French Review* 56 (6) (May 1983): 876–884; R. Switzer, "Medievalism in the Opera Libretti of Eugène Scribe," *West Virginia University Philological Papers* 27 (1981): 15–19.

SEDAINE, MICHEL-JEAN (1719–1797), playwright and minor poet, established, along with Diderot,* "le drame"* (drama) as an important new genre in eighteenth-century theatre. Born in Paris, the son of a master mason, he abandoned schooling for stonecutting at age thirteen to support his family after the financial ruin and death of his father. He educated himself and wrote poetry that impressed his employer, the architect Jacques Buron (remembered chiefly today as the grandfather of the painter Louis David), who became his patron. After initial attempts in "Poésies fugitives" ("Short Poems"), he achieved literary prominence in 1745 with his "Epitre à mon habit" ("Epistle to my Clothing"). He turned to the theatre with his comic opera *Le Diable à quatre* (*The Devil in Four*, 1756). As librettist for the Opéra-Comique,* he wrote *L'Huitre et les plaideurs* (*The Fool and the Suitors*, 1759); *Rose et Colas* (1764), reportedly his favorite play; *Aucassin et Nicolette* (1782); *Richard coeur de lion* (*Richard the Lion-Hearted*, 1784); *Guillaume Tell* (*William Tell*, 1791); and many more. He befriended Diderot, contributed to the *Encyclopédie,* * and voiced the ideals of the philosophes* in his comedies, operas, and opéra-comiques. He was elected to the Academy in 1786. He initially favored the Revolution but later deplored its excesses.

Sedaine is best remembered for two nonmusical plays, a one-act comedy, *La Gageur imprévue* (*The Unexpected Wager*, 1768), and the play that most successfully realizes the dramatic theories of Diderot, *Le Philosophe sans le savoir* (*The Unsuspecting Philosophe*, 1765), both performed by the Comédie-Française. *Le Philosophe sans le savoir,* hailed by the philosophes and enthusiastically greeted by the public, illustrates the dignity of doing business and the "nobility" of the bourgeoisie. The play realistically and sensitively depicts the tension of Monsieur Vanderk, whose son must defend the family's honor in a duel on his sister's wedding day. Intimate family scenes together with its social relevance distinguish the play as a significant bourgeois drama admired by

Gautier,* Hugo,* and Sand* in the following century and a work that influenced the works of Augier* and Dumas fils.*

SENAC DE MEILHAN, GABRIEL (1736–1803), political administrator and author of numerous works on French history and politics at the close of the century, while in exile in Brunswick, introduced a new and pertinent theme in his novel, *L'Emigré* (*The Emigrant,* 1794)—political emigration. In a series of letters, Meilhan portrays sensitively and realistically the life of a royalist, the Marquis de Saint-Alban, exiled from France during the Revolution. According to H. Coulet (*Le Roman jusqu' à la Révolution* [*The Novel Before the Revolution*], 1967), Meilhan lacked the penetration of the more eminent royalist emigré, Joseph de Maistre,* but he understood the importance of the Revolution. Among his other works are a philosophical novel, *Les Deux Cousins* (*The Two Cousins,* 1790); *Considérations sur l'esprit et les moeurs* (*Considerations on the Mind and Morality,* 1787); and *Portraits et caractères des personnages distingués de la fin du XVIIIe siècle* (*Portraits and Characteristics of Distinguished Individuals from the End of the Eighteenth Century,* 1813).

SENANCOUR, ETIENNE PIVERT DE (1770–1846), the melancholy author of *Obermann,** whom the romantics (see romanticism*) claimed as their spiritual father, was born in Paris to a noble family who destined him for a career in the cloth. A solitary and sickly youth, he attended Collège de la Marche where he steeped himself in the philosophes,* notably Buffon,* Helvétius,* and Nicolas de Malebranche (1638–1715). He was given to reverie and introspection and found in the forests of Fontainebleau the paths to his dreams. In 1789, when his father enrolled him in the seminary of Saint-Sulpice, he fled to Switzerland, where the following year he married Marie Daguet of Fribourg. It was an unhappy union, leaving Senancour a distaste for marriage. He returned to France frequently during the Revolution, often at great risk and settled definitively in Paris sometime, the exact date is uncertain though it was around 1794. Except for a brief visit to Switzerland in 1802, he never returned. In 1792, he published his first work, a philosophical meditation, *Les Premiers Ages* (*The First Ages*), followed by *Sur les générations actuelles* (*On the Present Generations,* 1793), written in the same vein. In 1795, he published his first novel, *Aldomen.* The pessimistic *Rêveries sur la nature primitive de l'homme* (*Reveries on the Primitive Nature of Man*), written under the influence of J.-J. Rousseau* and in praise of nature and condemning corrupt civilization, appeared in 1799. From 1800 to 1802, after living in the Valois, he earned his keep as tutor in the Hotel Beauvau to the grandchildren of Madame d'Houdetot (1730–1813), a countess who had sparked Rousseau's passion and inspired his *La Nouvelle Héloïse.** He divorced his wife in 1802, after learning that she had been unfaithful. This closed once and for all the Swiss chapter of his life. In 1804, with his masterpiece *Obermann,* which went virtually unnoticed for thirty years, he closed the door for the next fifteen years on novels and autobiography. In the following years he published

De l'amour (*On Love*, 1806), which defends divorce and considers the vanity of love; several political treatises; and a refutation of Chateaubriand* in *Observations sur "Le Génie du Christianisme"* (*Observations on the "Genius of Christianity,"* 1816). In 1819, he offered his *Libres méditations d'un solitaire inconnu sur le détachement du monde* (*Free thoughts of an Unknown Solitary Being on the Detachment of the World*), which echoed the disenchantment of *Obermann*. Impoverished by the Revolution, he lived in obscurity, earning his keep writing for popular booksellers works such as *Vocabulaire de simple vérité* (*Vocabulary of Simple Truth*, 1821), *Résumé de l'histoire de la Chine* (*Resume of Chinese History*, 1824), *Résumé des traditions morales et religieuses chez tous les peuples* (*Resume of the Moral and Religious Traditions of All People*, 1825), and a *Résumé de l'histoire romaine* (*Resume of Roman History*, 1827). He collaborated on *Biographie des contemporains* (*Contemporary Biographies*, 1829). His life took a turn for the better in 1833, when he was suddenly discovered by Sainte-Beuve* and George Sand* and hailed as a precursor of romanticism. He profitted from the new-found attention by bringing out reeditions of previous works, notably his *Rêveries* and *Libres Meditations*. In 1833, he wrote *Isabelle*, a disappointing feminine version of *Obermann*. His final years were marked with suffering and decline. Senancour, paralyzed, died in 1846.

Senancour was haunted throughout his life by the notion that he was different from others. He wrote in *Obermann*, his autobiography, "I saw that there was no accord between myself and society, neither between my needs and the things which it had done." His social isolation gave rise to feelings of boredom, lassitude, discouragement, and a mal de siècle* that he painted so poignantly in his novel. Senancour is typically preromantic (see preromanticism*) in his feelings; *Obermann* is the lyric journal of the sufferings of the romantic soul.

SIECLE DE LOUIS XIV, LE (*The Age of Louis XIV*, 1751), written and conceived by Voltaire* over a twenty-year period, constitutes a major effort to document and understand the flowering of French culture and civilization that took place under the reign of the great French king. Voltaire consulted over two hundred volumes of memoirs, scores of eyewitnesses, and royal ministers, as well as secret archives to which as historiographer he had access in researching his monumental portrait of the "spirit of the most enlightened century ever."

Voltaire states in his preface that in his view, the seventeenth century ranks among the four great ages of history along with the ages of Pericles, Julius Ceasar and Augustus, and the Italian Renaissance. Chapters 1 through 24 record military and diplomatic achievements; chapters 25 through 28 relate little-known anecdotes and particularities uncovered in his voluminous research detailing the private life of Louis XIV, his physical appearance, manners, wisdom, shortcomings, death; chapters 29 through 34 discuss internal affairs of government— justice, commerce and industry, the naval forces, the police, finances, and the fine arts. He defended Jean-Baptiste Colbert (1619–1683); praised the scientific advances of Francis Bacon (1561–1626), Sir Isaac Newton (1642–1727), and

Galileo (1564–1642); qualified the French writers as "the legislators of Europe," and celebrated Jean Racine (1639–1699) and Nicolas Boileau (1636–1711), regretting that, "Genius has but one age, after which all degenerates."

As the book evolved, however, Voltaire realized that the glory of the great Sun King was clouded with religious disputes among Calvinists, Jansenists, and Quietists, outlined in chapters 35 through 39. The book concludes with the example of the Chinese and their wise and virtuous emperor, who exiled quarreling Dominican and Jesuit missionaries.

As a historical treatise, *Le Siècle de Louis XIV* is weakened by the apparent prejudices of its author against religion and his criticism of the excesses and abuses of his own age. As a well-documented, clear, and concise literary work, however, it ranks among Voltaire's best writings.

For further information, see R. Hatton, "The Prehistory of Voltaire's *Siècle de Louis XIV,*" *Newsletter of the Society for Seventeenth Century French Studies* 5 (1982): 45–51.

LE SPLEEN BAUDELAIREN (The Baudelairian spleen). See *Dictionary of Modern French Literature, from Naturalism and Symbolism to Post-Modernism.*

STAEL, GERMAINE NECKER, BARONNE DE (1766–1817), literary theoretician and novelist whose essays on literature and Germany influenced the early development of romanticism,* was born in Paris, the daughter of wealthy Genevan banker Jacques Necker (1732–1804), who later became first minister under Louis XVI, and Suzanne Curchod (1737–1794), a gifted woman from a family of Swiss pastors. She was introduced to literature and politics at an early age in her mother's salon, where she quickly learned the art of conversation and the ideas of the eighteenth-century philosophes* such as Diderot,* Grimm,* Buffon,* Marmontel,* Raynal,* and especially her compatriot, J.-J. Rousseau.* A precocious child, she summarized Montesquieu's* *De l'esprit des lois** at age fifteen. At twenty, she married the baron of Staël-Holstein, Swedish ambassador, a cold and proper gentleman several years her senior for whom she felt no love. She opened a salon in the Swedish embassy on rue du Bac frequented by writers and politicians of liberal bent who favored the Revolution and the principles of the English constitution. In 1788, she published her first major work, *Lettre sur les écrits de Rousseau* (*Letter on the Writings of Rousseau*). For reasons political and personal, she repaired to Coppet from 1792 to 1795, the family estate on Lake Geneva. There she met Benjamin Constant* and embarked on a stormy liaison until 1808. She returned to Paris briefly in 1795 and again in 1797, reopening a salon, the most illustrious in Paris. She separated from her husband in 1798 and lived with her three children in Paris and Coppet. Constant wrote much of his discourse against tyranny, presented to Bonaparte's Tribunal in 1800, at her Paris salon. A suspicious Napoleon, who disliked the romanticism of her essay, *De la littérature considérée dans ses rapports avec les institutions sociales* (*On Literature Considered in Relation to Social Institutions,*

1800), had her watched and retaliated against her increasingly hostile salon. In 1803, the year she published her first novel, *Delphine,* Madame de Staël was permanently exiled from Paris.

Madame de Staël travelled, visiting Germany in 1803 and 1807, where she met Johann Wolfgang von Goethe (1749–1832) and Friedrich von Schiller (1759–1805), and Italy in 1804, which inspired her second novel, *Corinne* (1807). In between her voyages, Coppet, like Voltaire's* Ferney a century before, was a mecca for illustrious visitors such as Constant, Madame Récamier (1777–1849), and Mathieu de Montmorency, where theatre and conversation provided asylum from the Empire. In 1810, her masterwork, *De l'Allemagne* (*On Germany*), first appeared in Paris. It was seized by Napoleon's government and ordered burned, and Madame de Staël, banned from France, was sent to Coppet, where she was closely watched. She managed to retain one copy of *De l'Allemagne,* and the work was republished in England in 1813. Widowed since 1802, she secretly married, in 1811, a Swiss officer twenty-three years her junior, Albert de Rocca, and travelled to Vienna, Saint-Petersburg, Sweden, England, and again, Italy, not returning to Paris until the fall of Napoleon. In 1816, she married Victor de Broglie (1785–1870). She died a year later.

Madame de Staël's romanticism surfaced in 1796, with her essay, *De l'influence des passions sur le bonheur des individus et des nations* (*On the Influence of the Passions on the Happiness of Individuals and Nations*). Ever a disciple of Rousseau, she affirmed her belief in passion and enthusiasm. *De la littérature* applied Montesquieu's method in *De l'esprit des lois* to literature, seeking to show "the influence of religion, manners and laws on literature and the influence of literature on religion, manners and laws" (*Introduction*). Part 1 looks at the past. Chapters 1 through 7 show how literature and the arts developed differently in Greece, a democracy, and Rome, an aristocracy. Chapters 9 through 20 illustrate her theory of climate and the superiority of the literature of Ossian (3d century Gaelic bard) and the north (Germany, Scandinavia, the Anglo-Saxon world), which she finds more philosophical, passionate, independent and respectful of women than that of Homer and the south (the Greco-Roman civilization, Spain, Italy, France). Part 2 looks toward the future and her ideal of literature. If liberty and equality reign in France, a "republican" literature freed from the ancient models will reflect intellectual progress; women will play an essential role; philosophy, passion, and nature will replace mythology in poetry.

Both of her novels are autobiographical and illustrate the unhappiness of an intellectually superior, passionate woman in a society that constrains and condemns her. Though dated, they announce early romantic themes: passion, isolation, moral superiority, nature, God. Their feminism is unmistakable, calling for women's rights to love and happiness.

Her major work, *De l'Allemagne,* introduced German thought, imagination, and genius to France. Part 1 gives an overview of Germany, its manners and habits, its provinces, its spirit of chivalry, its conversation. Part 2 describes its literature and arts; authors Christoph Wieland (1733–1813), Friedrich Klopstock

(1724–1803), Gotthold Lessing (1729–1781), Goethe and Schiller; classical and romantic poetry; theatre; and the novel. She inaugurated the term "romantic," explaining that in Germany it designates "poetry which originated in the songs of the troubadours, in chivalry and in Christianity." Part 3 compares German and French philosophy and the influence of German philosophy on its literature, arts, science, and morality. Part 4, on religion, discusses Germany's penchant for the mystic, its concept of the infinite, the religious songs of Friedrich Novalis (1772–1801), and the necessity of enthusiasm and happiness to literature and art.

Despite Madame de Staël's love for Germany, her work is marred with error, superficiality, naiveté. *De la littérature,* with its theory of "perfectibility," contains serious flaws in literary knowledge and judgment. Her belief that one literature is superior to another merely because it follows it, as Latin followed Greek and romanticism followed classicism, is debatable. However, she brought to the eighteenth-century ideals of reason and logic, which she inherited as a child and exhibited in her work, the spirit of the coming romantic movement. In life, she was passionate, enthusiastic, troubled, and happy. Her works sought to breathe new life into a literature she feared was dying for want of inspiration and creativity. She called for a return to Christian and to medieval and national traditions. "Romantic literature," she wrote in *De l'Allemagne,* "is the only one which is still capable of being perfected, because its roots are in our own soil; it is the only one which can grow and invigorate itself again; it expresses our religion; it recalls our history." She extolled passion, enthusiasm, imagination, individualism, the mysterious, and the sublime. She failed to leave an enduring creative work of her own; that task was better met by Constant, Lamartine,* or Chateaubriand.* But, she innovated literary criticism with a concept of relativity that would judge works according to their national, political, social, even geographical circumstances, a method that would find its fullest expression in the nineteenth-century criticism of Taine.* Gone was the standard of absolute perfection of the seventeenth century. Her love of Germany widened the horizon of French literature, paving the way for a new inspiration, free expression, and a new understanding of early romanticism.

Other works include *Réflexions sur le procès de la reine, par une femme* (*Reflections on the Trial of the Queen, by a Woman,* 1793), *Réflexions sur la paix* (*Reflections on Peace,* 1794), *Essai sur les fictions* (*Essay on Fiction,* 1795), *Considérations sur les principaux événements de la Révolution française* (*Considerations on the Principal Events of the French Revolution,* 1818), and several minor short stories. *Dix années d'exil* (*Ten Years of Exile*), published posthumously in 1821, relate her life, travels, and vicissitudes with Napoleon.

For further information, see H. Borowitz, "The Unconfessed Précieuse: Madame de Staël's Debt to Mademoiselle de Scudéry," *Nineteenth Century French Studies* 11 (1–2) (1982–1983): 32–59; J. Cleary, "Madame de Staël, Rousseau and Mary Wollstonecraft," *Romance Notes* 21 (3) (1981): 329–333; E. Giddy, "Byron and Madame de Staël," in *Lord Byron and His Contemporaries: Essays from the Sixth International Byron Seminar,* C. E. Robinson, ed. (Newark: University of Delaware Press, 1982), 166–

177; M. Gutwirth, *Madame de Staël, Novelist* (Chicago: University of Illinois Press, 1978); E. Hartman, "Mme de Staël, the Continuing Quarrel of the Ancients and Moderns and the Idea of Progress," *Research Studies* 50 (1) (March 1982): 33–45; N. J. Swallow, "Portraits: A Feminist Appraisal of Mme de Staël's *Delphine*," *Atlantis* 7 (1) (1981): 65–76.

STENDHAL (1783–1842), born Henri Beyle, is best known for his novels, *Le Rouge et le noir,* * *Lucien Leuwen,* * and *La Chartreuse de Parme,* * and for his philosophy for the pursuit of happiness, known as Beylism.* He was born in Grenoble to a respectable, middle-class family but spent an unhappy childhood in the care of his father, Chérubin Beyle, an advocate in the Grenoble parliament, and his aunt, Séraphie Gagnon, both of whom he detested. His mother, Henriette Gagnon, died when he was seven. His mother was of Italian descent, a heritage that Stendhal admired for its spirit of the Renaissance. This was balanced, on the other hand, by his father's bourgeois pride and authoritativeness, which imparted to the young child a dualism that was to pervade his entire life and works. Stendhal enjoyed the company of his grandfather Henri Gagnon, who advocated the liberal ideas of the eighteenth century and imparted to the young child his love of literature. In 1792, he came under the tutelage of abbé Raillane, whom he intensely disliked—the source, perhaps, of his anticlericalism. In his autobiography, *La Vie de Henri Brûlard (The Life of Henry Brulard,* 1890), Stendhal called him "un noir coquin" ("a black rogue"). From 1796 to 1799, he attended the newly opened Ecole Centrale de Grenoble, where he distinguished himself in math and the humanities, taking first prize in each. In 1799, he prepared for the Ecole Polytechnique in Paris but never showed up for the entrance exam. Instead, under the auspices of a cousin, Pierre Daru (1767–1829), who became the general secretary of the army, he travelled to Italy, was present at the battle of Marengo, and, full of enthusiasm for Napoleon, enlisted as a second lieutenant in a dragoon regiment. He preferred Milan to Paris but soon tired of the monotony of garrison routine. In 1802, he resigned his commission and rented a garret in Paris, where he read Destutt de Tracy,* the idéologues,* and Helvétius,* one of the sources of his Beylism. He wrote comedies that he hoped would rival Molière's (1622–1673), dressed like a dandy, learned English, fell in love with a young actress, Mélanie Guilbert, and followed her to Marseille, where he became a grocer's apprentice. After she married a wealthy Russian, he followed Daru to Germany, served as secretary to Daru's brother, Martial, and filled administrative posts, mostly in supply and civil affairs. He witnessed Napoleon's siege of Berlin in 1806 and spent two years in Brunswick. In 1809, he joined the Austrian campaign, spending six months in Vienna. The following year, he was appointed auditor to the council of state and returned to Paris. In 1812, he took part in the Russian campaign and lived in Moscow; the following year, he joined the Saxony campaign. He returned to Paris in 1814, in time to witness its capture by the Allied troops.

After Napoleon's fall, Stendhal went to Milan to escape the royalists, Jesuits, and bourgeoisie who had returned to power with the Restoration. There, for the next seven years, except for a few brief excursions, he lived the life of a dilettante, haunting the theatres and museums, frequenting liberal milieux, and savoring Italian art and music. Under the pseudonym Louis-Alexandre-César Bombet, he published *Les Vies de Haydn, Mozart et Métastase* (*The Lives of Haydn, Mozart and Metastase*, 1815). *Histoire de la peinture en Italie* (*History of Painting in Italy*) followed in 1817. Both works are flawed by plagiarism. *Rome, Naples et Florence*, also published in 1817, the first signed "Stendhal," is a more original work, filled with his reflections on the psychology of Italian society.

In 1821, Stendhal was suspected by the Austrian police of Carbonarism, or working for the establishment of a unified, republican Italy. He returned to Paris for the next ten years, where he resumed the life of a dandy and frequented the salons of Destutt de Tracy, Madame Cabanis (her husband, Georges [1757–1808], was an ideologue), the Ancelots (an important literary couple, Jacques [1794–1854] and Marguerite [1792–1875]), Madame de Castellane, and art critic Delécluze. He met naturalist Victor Jacquemont (1801–1832), Augustin Thierry,* the famed actor François Joseph Talma (1763–1826), Eugène Delacroix (1798–1863), Courier,* Mérimée,* and others. Thanks to Mérimée, he met Hugo* in 1830. Love affairs during this period influenced his early writings, *De l'amour* (*On Love*, 1822), which sold a mere seventeen copies, and a romantic novel, *Armance* (1827), published anonymously. He wrote *Vie de Rossini* (*Life of Rossini*, 1823), which enjoyed a measure of success; *Racine et Shakespeare* (part one, 1823; part two, 1825), in defense of romanticism*; and *Promenades dans Rome* (*Walks in Rome*, 1829), his widely read guidebook to the Italian capital.

Before he left Paris in 1830 Stendhal, named consul to Trieste by Louis-Philippe, completed *Le Rouge et le noir*, his first success. In Trieste, he was once again suspected of Carbonarism and was transferred to Città Vecchia near Rome the following year. As a diplomat, Stendhal had decided not to publish his works, but continued to write nonetheless. In 1832, he undertook his *Souvenirs d'égotisme* (*Memories of Egotism*, posthumous, 1892), about his recent years in Paris. The following year, after a brief visit to Paris, he began but never finished another novel, *Lucien Leuwen* (posthumous, 1855, 1896). Also in 1833, he met George Sand* and Musset* in Lyon on their famous journey to Venice and travelled down the Rhône with them to Marseille. In 1835, he began his autobiography, *La Vie de Henri Brûlard*. The next year, he took leave of his post to travel to Paris and around France. *Mémoires d'un touriste* (*Memoirs of a Tourist*, 1838) captures his travel impressions. In Paris, he wrote *La Chartreuse de Parme* (*The Charterhouse of Parma*, 1839), *Chroniques italiennes* (*Italian Chronicles*, 1839), and the final works to appear during his lifetime, a collection of three short tales, *L'Abbesse de Castro* (1839).

In 1840, he resumed his post in Italy. He worked on *Lamiel* (1839–1842), but health problems plagued him. In 1841, he returned to Paris, where he died the following year of apoplexy.

Throughout the life and works of Stendhal run two opposing currents that constitute the essence of the man and his efforts—the sensitive, imaginative romantic and the analytical, critical intellectual. *De l'amour* analyzes the topic of love in a scientific, almost mathematical fashion. It distinguishes four types of love: passion, taste, physical pleasure, and vanity. Part 1 traces the development of love through seven phases from birth until its "crystalization." Part 2 studies the relativity of love according to temperament, nationality, and social customs. Chapters on marriage, divorce, and the education of women are filled with irony.

With his two-part pamphlet, *Racine et Shakespeare,* Stendhal entered the fray between the classicists and the romantics in favor of the romantics. He cries out against boring, outdated literature. The first part (1823) argues against the three unities, discusses laughter, and defines romanticism as "the art of giving to the people literary works which in the present state of their customs and beliefs are capable of giving the most pleasure possible," while "classicism, on the contrary, gives them the literature which yielded the most pleasure possible to their great-grandparents." Part 2 (1825) is largely directed against the Academy and reemphasizes the contemporaneity of romanticism. "All the great writers were romantics in their time," Stendhal writes. "It is, a century after their death, the people who copy them instead of opening their eyes and imitating nature, who are classics." Stendhal denounces French tragedy as a "series of odes mixed with epic narration" and calls for an end to the classical unities and versification, preferring historical drama in prose dealing with national topics.

Stendhal's autobiographical works, *La Vie de Henri Brûlard, Souvenirs d'égotisme,* and his *Journal* (posthumous, 1888), reveal his duality. The *Journal* primarily covers Stendhal's intellectual and emotional life from 1801 to 1815, his early manhood during the Napoleonic years. The soul searching continues in *Souvenirs d'égotisme.* As Stendhal recounts the Paris years after his return from Italy in 1821, he is looking for "something positive and which will be true for a long time for me." At nearly fifty years old, he undertook *La Vie de Henry Brûlard* in an effort to come to know himself, whether he was "happy or sad, witty or foolish, brave or fearsome, happy or unhappy." It is a sincere examination of his childhood emotions.

Stendhal's novels are historical and social portraits. *Le Rouge et le noir,* as its subtitle (*Chronique de 1830*) attests, is a "chronicle" of French life during the Restoration. *Lucien Leuwen* takes place primarily under the July monarchy. *Chroniques italiennes* are stories about criminals of the Italian sixteenth century. The novels are also autobiographical. Stendhal's heroes live in search of themselves, as he did. Julien's, Fabrice's, Lamiel's quests for happiness mirror Stendhal's own search for love and glory; their experiences and sensations illustrate Beylism in action.

Stendhal is called a romantic for his "cult" of passion and sensitivity, his worship of individuality, genius, superiority, his love of violent, passionate sixteenth-century Italy. His characters, however, unlike the typical, melancholy, uncertain romantic, are energetic and ambitious, like Stendhal's real-life hero, Napoleon. Stendhal's materialism, however, kept him firmly moored in contemporary reality. His self-knowledge and analytical ability resulted in intensely real psychological portraits. *Le Rouge et le noir* analyzes the tension of Julien Sorel, the ambitious hypocrite of 1830; the hopes, dreams, and memories of Fabrice in *La Chartreuse de Parme* are Stendhal's own.

Just as Stendhal masked his identity behind various pseudonyms throughout his literary career, he hid his emotion and sensitivity beneath a writing style that has been called classical, cold, and sparse. Much of his work was ill received. Undaunted, Stendhal wrote *La Chartreuse* "for the happy few." "I will be successful around 1880," he believed. Thus he was and is still.

For further information, see J. Booker, "Retrospective Movement in the Stendhalian Narration," *Romanic Review* 72 (1) (January 1981): 26–38; Booker, "Style indirect libre: The Case of Stendhal," *Stanford French Review* 9 (Summer 1985): 137–152; P. Comeau, "The Love Theme and the Monologue Structure in *Armance*," *Nineteenth Century French Studies* 9 (Fall–Winter 1980–1981): 37–58; J. Day, "The Hero as Reader in Stendhal," *French Review* 54 (3) (February 1981): 412–419; J. Hamilton, "Two Psychodramatic Scenes in Stendhal's *Armance*," *Kentucky Romance Quarterly* 28 (2) (1981): 121–130; B. Knapp, "Stendhal and Correggio: An Archetypal Happening," *Nineteenth Century French Studies* 12 and 13 (Summer–Fall 1984): 1–21; C. Lawson, "Hemingway, Stendhal and War," *Hemingway Review* 6 (2) (Spring 1981): 28–33; D. Miller, "Narrative 'Uncontrol' in Stendhal," in *Narrative and his Discontents. Problems of Closure in the Traditional Novel* (Princeton: Princeton University Press, 1981), 195–264; K. Muir, "Stendhal, Racine and Shakespeare," *Shakespeare Studies* 16 (1983): 1–12; I. Naginski, "The Beginning(s) of Henry Brulard: Stendhal's Metaphors for Autobiographical Writing," *French Review* 58 (5) (April 1985): 664–669; Naginski, "The Geology of Character: Stendhal and the Paradigms of Literary Vocation," *French Forum* 10 (1) (January 1985): 57–66; R. Pearson, "Stendhal's *Armance:* The Comedy of 'Une Chasse au malheur,'" *Forum for Modern Language Studies* 19 (3) (July 1983): 236–248; G. Rosa, "The Tempest and the Rock: An Intertextual Study of Two Images in Stendhal's *De l'amour*," *Romance Notes* 24 (2) (Winter 1983): 161–167; F. St. Aubyn, "Stendhal and Salomé," *Stanford French Review* 4 (Winter 1980): 395–404; "Stendhal 1783–1983," *Australian Journal of French Studies* [special issue] 20 (2) (May–August 1983).

SUE, JOSEPH (called Eugène, 1804–1857), prolific, popular novelist who created the "roman-feuilleton" (serial novel), was born in Paris, the son of a well-to-do physician in Napoleon's army and godson of Empress Josephine. He could not decide on a career between medicine and art but became a naval surgeon serving against Spain in 1823 and at the battle of Navarino in 1828. He inherited a considerable fortune upon his father's death, which enabled him to live the elegant dandy life and devote himself to literature. His naval experiences provided material for his first novels, *Plick et Plock* (1831), *Atar-Gull* (1831), *La Salamandre* (*The Salamander*, 2 vols., 1832), among others, which earned him a reputation as the James Fenimore Cooper (1789–1851) of French literature and instituted the maritime novel as a viable genre. He used his powers of observation in his "romans de moeurs" (novels of manners), *Arthur* (1838, 2 vols.), *Le Marquis de Létorière* (1839), *Le Morne au diable* (*The Devil's Bluff*, 2 vols., 1842) and *Mathilde ou Les Mémoires d'une jeune femme* (*Mathilde, or The Memoirs of a Young Woman*, 7 vols., 1841). He wrote two historical novels, *Latréaumont* (2 vols., 1837), the source of the pen name for symbolist poet Lautréamont,* and *Jean Cavalier* (4 vols., 1840). Under the influence of Fourier (see Fourierisme*) and Proudhon,* he wrote the social novels *Les Mystères de Paris* (*The Mysteries of Paris,* 10 vols., 1842–1843), the first novel to be serialized by a daily newspaper and *Le Juif errant* (*The Wandering Jew,* 10 vols., 1845–1847. Other major novels include *Les Sept Péchés capitaux* (*The Seven Cardinal Sins,* 16 vols., 1847–1849) and *Les Mystères du peuple* (*The Mysteries of the People,* 16 vols., 1849–1856). In 1848, Sue, a socialist, ran for election in the Loiret but was not elected. In 1850, he was elected to the legislative assembly in Paris; the following year, he exiled himself to Annecy, where he finished his days.

Sue's novels were lengthy and melodramatic; their style is generally considered undistinguished and monotonous. However, his realistic depictions of working-class life won the hearts of the people, who preferred him to Balzac.*

For further information, see E. Tannenbaum, "The Beginnings of Bleeding-Heart Liberalism: Eugene Sue's *Les Mystères de Paris,*" *Comparative Studies in Society and History* 23 (July 1981): 491–507.

SULLY-PRUDHOMME (pseudonym of René-François-Armand Prudhomme, 1839–1907), a Parnassian* poet because of his interest in science and pure poetic form, his best works are distinguished by their lyricism and sentiment. He was born in Paris, orphaned at an early age, and raised by an uncle, a Parisian notary, whose surname he prefixed to his own. He led a melancholy youth, attended Lycée Bonaparte, trained as an engineer, and entered the metallurgy industry in Creusot. Dissatisfied, he returned to Paris after a short time and entered law school, which he abandoned for poetry. He entered the Academy in 1881. In 1901, he became the first recipient of the Nobel Prize for literature. During his lifetime, he ranked among the most respected of the Parnassian poets.

His first works are filled with sensitivity and emotion. *Stances et poèmes* (*Stanzas and Poems,* 1865), *Les Epreuves* (*Tests,* 1866), *Les Solitudes* (1869), *Les Destins* (*Destinies,* 1872), *La Révolte des fleurs* (*The Revolt of the Flowers,* 1874), and *Les Vaines Tendresses* (Vain Tendernesses, 1875) express his fears, disillusions, religious and philosophical disappointments. His best-known poem in this vein, "Le Vase brisé" ("The Broken Vase"), compares the "invisible and sure" cracking of a vase to the slow breaking of a heart. "La Voie lactée" ("The Milky Way") depicts the solitude of the human soul as the isolation of stars, "each shining far from its sisters which seem close to her." Influenced by Leconte de Lisle,* he tried his hand at descriptive poetry with "Le Cygne"

("The Swan"), "Le Lion," and "Croquis italiens" ("Italian Sketches"). After 1875, he turned to positivism* with "Le Zénith," inspired by the balloon ascension of three Frenchmen in 1875 and its subsequent crash. Other poems celebrate man's inventiveness, including "La Roue" ("The Wheel") and "Le Monde à nu" ("The Bare Earth,"), about chemistry. *Les Destins* develops Leibnitz's theory of optimism. Two lengthy philosophical poems, *La Justice* (1878) and *Le Bonheur* (1888), written in the manner of Chénier* or Vigny,* reveal his resignation before the reality of life. He wrote a prose treatise entitled *Que sais-je? Examen de conscience* (*What do I know? A Self-Examination*, 1895), a translation of the first book of Lucretius (96?–55 B.C.), and a study of Blaise Pascal (1623–1662). He summarized his poetic principles in *Réflexions sur l'art des vers* (*Reflections on the Art of Poetry*, 1892) and *Testament poétique* (*Poetic Testament*, 1900).

Sully-Prudhomme's philosophical poems are generally considered unpoetic and dull; his reputation today rests chiefly with the beauty and simplicity achieved in his lyric poems.

T

TAINE, HIPPOLYTE (1828–1893), positivist (see positivism*) thinker and art and literary critic who established the principles of scientific determinism and prepared the way for naturalism,** was born in Vouziers, a small village in the Ardennes. Orphaned at thirteen, he came to Paris and studied first at the Collège Bourbon, then from 1848 to 1851 at the Ecole Normale Supérieure. Despite his intellectual superiority, he failed the aggregate exam because of his determinist notion that "the movements of the spiritual automaton which is our being are as regulated as those of the material world." The authorities disapproved of this belief that emotions, imagination, thought, mind, and spirit were subject to the same natural and invariable scientific laws as the liver and the gall bladder. After a short teaching stint in Nevers and Poitiers, he returned to Paris in 1853 to prepare a thesis on sensations, which the Sorbonne refused. Taine found in literary criticism the vehicle for expressing his philosophy and took his doctoral degree in 1853 with a thesis on La Fontaine. He wrote in the preface that man is a superior animal who "produces poems and philosophies almost as silkworms make their cocoons and as bees make their hives." The following year, in *Essai sur Tite-Live* (*Essay on Tite-Live*), he extolled the "faculte maîtresse" (dominant characteristic) such as Tite-Live's oratorical ability or Balzac's* imaginative powers, belonging to an author. In 1857, he published *Les Philosophes français du XIXe siècle* (*The French Philosophers of the Nineteenth Century*), which attacked the spiritualist philosophers, notably Cousin* and Simon Théodore Jouffroy (1796–1843), and collaborated on *Journal des débats* and the *Revue des deux mondes*.

Taine outlined the principles of his doctrine in the preface to his *Histoire de la littérature anglaise* (*History of English Literature*, 1863). He conceived of literature as the result of three factors or "primordial forces." First is race, the "innate and hereditary dispositions which man brings with him to the light." Second is "milieu," consisting of climate, politics, social conditions, morality.

Third, is "moment" or history. All three combine with the individual genius ("la faculte maîtresse") of the author to produce literature.

Taine applied his philosophy to art and history as well. In 1864, he was named lecturer in the history of art at the Ecole des Beaux Arts in Paris and published his teachings in *Philosophie de l'art* (*Philosophy of Art,* 1882). He turned to history to determine the causes of the defeat of 1870 and the horrors of the Paris Commune in his *Origines de la France contemporaine* (*Origins of Contemporary France,* 1875–1893). He was elected to the Academy in 1878.

Taine's philosophical system has been criticized as inaccurate and oversimplified. However, it opened new vistas for literary criticism, positivism, and the novel.

Besides those mentioned, Taine's works include his doctoral thesis, *La Fontaine et ses fables* (*La Fontaine and His Fables,* 1853); *Essais de critique et d'histoire* (*Essays on Criticism and History,* 1858–1894); *De l'intelligence* (*On Intelligence,* 1870), and various travel notes and correspondence.

For further information, see J. McNair, "P. D. Boborykin, Hippolyte Taine and the English Novel: A Russian Experiment in 'Scientific' Criticism," *Forum for Modern Language Studies* 19 (4) (October 1983): 301–320.

TENÇIN, MADAME CLAUDINE-ALEXANDRINE GUERIN DE (1685–1749), who maintained a fashionable literary salon on the rue Saint-Honoré from 1726 to 1749, was born in Grenoble, the daughter of a parliamentarian. She was a Dominican nun from 1696 to 1714 but renounced the veil for a life of love and leisure under the Regency. Her paramours reportedly were many; as mistress to the regent, Philippe d'Orléans (1674–1723) and to Cardinal Dubois (1656–1723), she secured the advancement of her brother, the abbé Pierre Guerin de Tençin, in the church hierarchy; and by the chevalier Le Camus Destouches, gave birth to and abandoned on church steps her son, who would become the famed mathematician and encyclopédist (see *L'Encyclopédie**), d'Alembert.* As a hostess, she was renowned for her grace and intelligence; her salon flourished after the death of Madame de Lambert (1647–1733). She regularly received philosophes* and writers—Fontenelle,* Montesquieu,* the abbé de Saint-Pierre (1658–1743), Marivaux,* Piron,* Helvétius,* Duclos,* and Marmontel*; visiting Englishmen, Henry Bolingbroke (1678–1751) and Philip Chesterfield (1694–1773); and the Swiss, Théodore Tronchin (1709–1781)—whom she collectively dubbed her "menagerie."

The later part of her life was occupied in writing somber novels of impossible loves, sad hearts, and ill-matched marriages, three of which were published during her lifetime under her nephew's name, Pont de Veyle—*Les Mémoires du comte de Comminge* (*The Memoirs of the Count of Comminge,*1735), a tragedy à la Romeo and Juliet about two lovers separated by family hatred; *Le Siège de Calais* (1739), the only one sporting a happy ending; and *Les Malheurs de l'amour* (*The Misfortunes of Love,* 1747). The novels have some merit in their depiction of the psychology of love and their sensitivity and morality.

THEATRE ITALIEN, the Italian Theatre in Paris, which originated in the ancient Roman commedia dell'arte with its improvisation, masks, satire, and the traditional figure of Arlequin, reached its height during the first half of the eighteenth century. The Italians, honored in 1665 with the title "Comédiens du Roi" ("The King's Comedians"), brought pantomime, parody, and caricatures—the antithesis of the classic theatre of the Comédie-Française—to the theatre. They performed wholly or partially in French from 1680 until their expulsion by the king in 1697 for an alleged impropriety toward the pious Madame de Maintenon (1635–1719) in the comedy *La Fausse Prude* (*The False Prude*). At the request of the regent in 1716, the troupe returned under the direction of Luigi Riccoboni (1675–1753) and settled in the Hotel de Bourgogne. In 1723 they were granted the title "Comédiens ordinaires du Roi de la troupe italienne" ("Comedians in Ordinary to the King from the Italian Troupe"). Riccoboni, known on stage as Lélio, along with Flaminia and Colombine (played by Madame Riccoboni*), and especially Silvia and Arlequin, provided Marivaux,* their most famous playwright, the ideal outlet for his comedies. These characters, combined with the Italian love of fantasy and free-spiritedness, distinguished the Italian Theatre from its contemporaries. When it merged with the Opéra-Comique* in 1762, it lost its identity. With it went the golden age of Italian theatre in France.

For further information, see J. Richtman, "Seven 'Canevas' for the Théâtre-Italien: Early Theatrical Ventures by Charles Antoine Coypel, Court Painter under Louis XV," in *Transactions of the Fifth International Congress on the Enlightenment,* vol. 3 (Oxford: Taylor Institution, 1981), 1175–1181.

THEATRES DE LA FOIRE, theatres of the fair, arose in the early eighteenth century after the expulsion of the Italian troupe from Paris in 1697 by Louis XIV. At the Foire Saint-Germain from February to Easter and the Foire Saint-Laurent in August and September, strolling players presented popular pieces characterized by liberties in style, tone, and inspiration—parades,* farces, comedies, and parodies of legitimate theatre. The fair theatres assimilated the Italians returning from exile in 1716, with presentations "half in French and half in Italian, interspersed with dances and intermezzos," according to Claude and François Parfaict (*Dictionnaire des Théâtres de Paris,* 6 vols., 1756). The traditional, sedate Comédie-Française, hoping to restrict the actors to mime and "knocking each other about," countered with lawsuits forbidding dialogue and spoken words in the ensuing "little theatre war." The fair theatres flourished, however, with lyrics printed on placards for the audience to read and sing. Freedom, gaiety, and improvisation reigned. Thus "vaudeville" and eventually, the opéra-comique* were born. Principal writers for the théâtres de la foire included Lesage,* Charles Simon Favart (1710–1792), and Piron.*

THIERRY, AUGUSTIN (1795–1856), historian and author of *Récits des temps mérovingiens* (*Stories from Merovingien Times,* 1840) and a history of the third estate, or the common people, represents the tendency toward narrative history in the first half of the nineteenth century. He wrote in *Considérations sur l'histoire de la France* (*Considerations on the History of France,* 1840) that rather than reason about things, he tried to present "the view of things themselves and to present man, his manners and characters in action." He wanted to "make art at the same time as science, to be dramatic with the aid of materials furnished by a sincere and scrupulous erudition."

Thierry was born in Blois to a modest family. He distinguished himself at the local college, entered the Ecole Normale in 1811, and left in 1815 to become secretary to Saint-Simon* for three years. He collaborated on liberal news-papers—*Le Censeur européen* (*The European Censor*) from 1817 until 1820 and *Le Courrier français* (*The French Courier*) the following year. From 1810 on, however, his real love was history, inspired by his reading of *Les Martyrs** while still at the college at Blois, according to the preface of *Récits des temps mér-ovingiens.* A champion of the middle classes, he sought in history a format for his political liberalism and theory of antagonism between races of people. His first important work, *La Conquête de l'Angleterre par les Normands* (*The Con-quest of England by the Normans,* 1825), explains the history of England in terms of the Norman conquest over the Saxons. It describes with sympathy and erudition the circumstances preceding the assault, the conquest itself, the reac-tion against it, and, finally, the enduring antagonism between these two nations because of it. By 1826, Thierry was blind but continued his work with the aid of his wife and secretaries. His masterpiece, *Récits des temps mérovingiens,* is a series of tableaux depicting the cruelty and beauty of sixth-century Gaul. Its first part, *Considérations sur l'histoire de France,* traces the history of France until 1840 and rectifies a previous error about the irreconcilable antagonism between the Francs and Gallo-Romans. Finally, the *Essai sur l'histoire de la formation et des progrès du Tiers Etat* (*Essay on the History of the Formation and Progress of the Third Estate,* 1853), undertaken in 1836 at the request of Guizot,* and carefully researched, is a history of the bourgeoisie and the third estate.

Today, much of Thierry's work is considered dated, his theory of the antag-onism between races rigid, his documentation weak. However, his works, es-pecially the *Récits des temps mérovingiens,* instituted an anecdotal style of history that blended art and science with a humanitarian vision and contributed to a renewed interest in history by the romantics (see romanticism*).

Besides those mentioned, Thierry's works include *Dix Ans d'études histori-ques* (*Ten Years of Historical Studies,* 1834), a collection of his works from 1817 to 1827, particularly his articles in *Le Censeur français;* and *Lettres sur l'histoire de France* (*Letters on the History of France,* 1827), a collection of twenty-five letters published in *Le Courrier français* in 1820.

THIERS, ADOLPHE (1797–1877), lawyer, journalist, orator, statesman, and gifted historian, his volumes on the Revolution and on the Consulate and the Empire contributed vastly to the understanding of French history. He was born in

Marseille, studied law at Aix, and came to Paris in 1821, where he wrote articles on art for *Le Globe** and *Le Constitutionnel* and worked on his *Histoire de la Révolution* (*History of the Revolution,* 10 vols., 1823–1827). In 1829, along with Mignet* and Armand Carrel (1800–1836), he founded *Le National,* a daily newspaper that ran from 1830 until 1851 and helped provoke the July revolution. With the revolution of 1830, he entered politics, serving as minister under Louis-Philippe in 1832, 1836, and 1840. He was elected to the Academy in 1833. Upon leaving the ministry in 1845, he undertook his masterwork, *Histoire du Consulat et de l'Empire* (*History of the Consulate and of the Empire,* 20 vols., 1845–1862). After serving as head of the executive power during the war of 1870, he was named president of the Republic until 1873. He died at Saint-Germain-en-Laye in 1877.

Thiers's works are characterized by their clarity, realistic detail, and objectivity. He drew from sources in the national archives, on-site visits to historical sites and battlegrounds, and his knowledge of geography, economics, and diplomacy. Thiers believed that the primary requisite of a historian was intelligence rather than imagination or sensitivity, which he demonstrated admirably in his works.

TOCQUEVILLE, ALEXIS, COMTE DE (1805–1859), lawyer, historian, and statesman, his *La Démocratie en Amérique* (*Democracy in America,* 1835; 1839–1840) and *L'Ancien Régime et la Révolution* (*The Old Regime and the Revolution,* 1856) represent the culmination of the study of history in the nineteenth century and are still read. He was born outside of Paris at Verneuil-sur-Seine to a distinguished family. His mother was the granddaughter of Malesherbes.* He became an assistant magistrate in 1830 and a year later was sent, with his friend Gustave de Beaumont, to examine prisons and penitentiaries in America. He returned nearly two years later with his report as well as his analysis of American democracy, the study that made his reputation. Shortly thereafter, he travelled to England and married an Englishwoman. He served as deputy under the constituent and legislative assemblies, becoming in 1849, vice president of the assembly, and for a short time, minister of foreign affairs. After the coup d'état, he retired from public life and wrote *Souvenirs* (*Memories,* written, 1850–1851; published, 1893) and his second major work, *L'Ancien Régime et la Révolution.* For health reasons, he retired to Cannes, where he died in 1859.

A legitimist and a Christian, de Tocqueville approached the study of history from a philosophical viewpoint. He considered the "gradual development of the equality of conditions" a "providential deed." America afforded him an ideal arena for the study of a nascent democracy, its principles, its functioning, its geographical and historical sources, its social and political institutions, its influence on its citizenry. He saw in the ancien régime the social and political conditions that gave rise to the French Revolution, a bold assertion that to this day has not been disproven. He believed that democracy in France was inevitable. De Tocqueville's work was serious, reminiscent of Montesquieu's* *De* *l'esprit des lois*,* and exerted a profound influence over Renan,* Taine,* and Fustel de Coulanges.*

For further information, see R. Boesche, "Tocqueville and *Le Commerce:* A Newspaper Expressing His Unusual Liberalism," *Journal of the History of Ideas* 43 (April–June 1982): 277–292; H. Brogan, "Tocqueville and the American Presidency," *Journal of American Studies* 15 (3) (December 1981): 357–375; E. Gargan, "The Silence of Toqueville on Education," *Historical Reflections* 7 (Summer–Fall 1980): 565–575; K. Hansen, "The Changing Fortunes of Tocqueville's *Democracy in America*," *Queen's Quarterly* 89 (1) (Spring 1982): 233–237; F. Litto, "Democracy and the Drama: Tocqueville and the Theatre in America," *Lingua e Literatura* 8 (8) (1979): 105–117; R. Reeves, *American Journey: Traveling with Tocqueville in Search of Democracy in America* (New York: Simon and Schuster, 1983); J. Schiefler, "Tocqueville and Religion: Some New Perspectives," *The Tocqueville Review* 4 (Fall/Winter 1982): 303–321; G. Watson, "Tocqueville and the Burden of Liberty," *The Hudson Review* 38 (3) (Autumn 1985): 365–375; D. Winthrop, "Tocqueville's Old Regime Political History," *The Review of Politics* 43 (January 1981): 88–111.

TURCARET, a five-act comedy in prose by Lesage,* was first presented at the Théâtre National in 1709. The first of the great comedies of the eighteenth century, the play is significant for its attack against a group of particularly despised people whom La Bruyère (1645–1696) had criticized earlier: the tax collectors.

Turcaret is a former lackey who has achieved power and wealth through misuse of his duties as a revenue collector. He pays his wife to remain in the country while he woos and showers a young widowed baroness with gifts and attention. She, in turn, is interested in a ne'er-do-well chevalier who claims he constantly borrows money from her to "ruin" Turcaret. Frontin, the chevalier's valet, sums it up: "We fleece the coquette; she devours the businessman; the businessman robs others: that makes for the best round of cheating in the world."

Turcaret learns of the baroness's duplicity after a resentful servant reveals all. When confronted with the truth, the baroness shrewdly denies it, casting the blame back onto Turcaret who, foolishly apologetic, offers even more gifts. Ever a cheat, the baroness convinces Turcaret to hire her comrade Frontin. Turcaret objects, "Madame, he is quite a fool," to which she replies, "He will learn a few things in your office."

Turcaret's dishonesty (he mercilessly cheats, speculates with others' funds, sells positions) clashes with the others' misdeeds in a series of deceptions and double-entendres, making the play a study in self-interest and immorality. In the fourth act, when the baroness learns that Turcaret is married and wishes to end the affair, Lisette, her servant warns, "But in the interests of your fortune, you must finish him first." After a violent scene between Turcaret, his sister, and his wife, Turcaret is arrested, the baroness sees the chevalier for the rogue he really is, and Frontin, who has outwitted and outswindled everyone, concludes, "Now the reign of M. Turcaret has finished and mine will begin."

In its presentation of the characters of Turcaret and Frontin, the play continues the seventeenth-century comic tradition of Molière (1622–1673). Turcaret emerges as ridiculous and despicable, a knave and a fool. His descent into ruin is counterbalanced by the ascent of Frontin. However, beneath the thin plot and gay repartee is an audacious depiction of corrupt financiers who had depleted France's resources and inspired its hatred during the Spanish war of succession. It portrays a world in which all are immoral—not only Turcaret, but the baroness, the chevalier, and the servants as well. Its realism* and satire modernized the genre, establishing *Turcaret* as the forerunner of realist theatre.

For further information, see G. Brereton, *French Comic Drama from the Sixteenth to the Eighteenth Century* (London: Methuen, 1977).

TURGOT, ANNE ROBERT JACQUES (1727–1781), public administrator, political economist, and *Encyclopédie** contributor, was born into an ancient and noble family and destined for a career in the church, but he changed to law. In 1750, as a student at the Sorbonne, he distinguished himself with remarkable treatises on Christianity and an optimistic assessment of human progress; two years later he was appointed substitute counsel for the attorney general and then magistrate to the parliament of Paris. He frequented the salons and enjoyed the company of d'Alembert,* d'Holbach,* Raynal,* Marmontel,* Morellet,* and Helvétius* and contributed articles on "Expansibilité" ("Expansibility") "Existence," "Fondations" ("Endowments") and "Foires" ("Fairs") to the *Encyclopédie*. Yet he gained his reputation primarily as the kind and concerned administrator of Limoges who cooperated with the clergy in a thirteen-year effort to improve the conditions of the peasants, the roads, and the agriculture and to more fairly distribute the burden of taxation. In 1774, he was named minister of finance and worked for the free trade of grain, the establishment of a territorial tax to be paid by all landowners, the abolition of forced labor, reduced expenditures at court, and improvements in agriculture and public works. Turgot's reforms were opposed by the queen, the courtiers, the nobility, and the clergy, who influenced the king to dismiss him, along with Malesherbes,* who was likewise advocating reform. Turgot retired to the study of science and poetry and enjoyed the friendship of d'Alembert, Condorcet,* and others until his death in Paris five years later.

A disciple of Quesnay* and the physiocrats,* Turgot has been called the father of political economics. His thoughts on labor, money, and agriculture are contained in his masterwork, *Réflexions sur la formation et la distribution des richesses (Thoughts on the Formation and the Distribution of Wealth,* 1766).

V

VALLES, JULES (1832–1885). See *Dictionary of Modern French Literature, from Naturalism and Symbolism to Post-Modernism.*

VAUVENARGUES, LUC DE CLAPIERS, MARQUIS DE (1715–1747), eighteenth-century moralist, continued the tradition of the great moralists of the preceding century (Jean de la Bruyère 1645–1696; François, duc de la Rochefoucauld 1613–1680), adding to their eloquence and profundity the concerns of his own era. His personal life was marked by ill health, despair, and a premature death at age thirty-two. He was born in Aix-en-Provence to an impoverished nobility, a sickly child whose reading of Plutarch (46?–120? A.D.) fired his imagination and fueled his belief in himself as a man of action and ability. He entered the army at age eighteen in hopes of glory but was quickly disillusioned. In 1733, he accompanied maréchal de Villars (1653–1734) to Lombardy as a lieutenant in the king's regiment, then turned to writing to relieve the monotony of garrison life in Verdun, Metz, and Besançon. In 1741, he fought in Bohemia, where his legs were severely frostbitten, and resigned his post a year later because of ill health. Smallpox dashed his hopes for a diplomatic career, ruined his health, and disfigured him. He spent his last days in a small Paris apartment receiving his friends Marmontel* and Voltaire,* revising his notes, and preparing his life's work, *Introduction à la connaissance de l'esprit humain suivie de Réflexions et maximes (Introduction to the Knowledge of the Human Mind followed by Reflections and Maxims,* 1746). A definitive edition of his works, published by D. L. Gilbert in 1857, contains *Conseils à un jeune homme (Advice to a Young Man), Réflexions critiques sur quelques poètes (Critical Reflections on Some Poets), Caractères (Portraits),* and several dialogues written before Vauvenargues's death in 1747.

Despite the tragedy of his life, Vauvenargues maintained an optimism, a belief in man's inherent goodness and capacity for glory, based on his observations of mankind. He found nobility in action: "No one is more prone to faults than those who act only in thought"; "Whatever merit there may be in neglecting high positions, there is perhaps more still in filling them well." Like Voltaire, he encouraged the pursuit of truth: "Truth is the light of knowledge"; "Darkness is the realm of error." However, he upheld the strength and excellence of passion: "Great thoughts come from the heart"; "If passion sometimes advises more boldly than thought, it is because it provides more strength for realizing its plans."

His self-portrait as Clazomène in *Caractères* reveals his stoicism before the pain of his existence, the "misery" of which he would never trade for the "prosperity of weak men." Other portraits, though less accomplished than those of La Bruyère, have been praised as ingenious and fine, as have his literary critiques. However, since 1746, the "brevity and energy" of his writing have earned him the highest marks.

If his work is seen as incomplete and incoherent, it is more the fault of an early death than a lack of vision. Vauvenargues sensed early on the initial stirrings of romanticism,* which later rocked the literary world in the works of Diderot* and J.-J. Rousseau.* André Maurois** called him the "type of man who made the transition between La Rochefoucauld and Stendhal."* Vauvenargues perceived the double themes of reason and sentiment that pervaded his century. His originality lies in expressing clearly and eloquently the merits of both.

VERGNIAUD, PIERRE VICTURNIEN (1752–1793), revolutionary orator and deputy to the Gironde convention, was born in Limoges, a merchant's son who impressed Turgot* with his intelligence. Thanks to the intervention of the kind economist, he received a solid education at the Collège de Plessis in Paris. In 1782, he began to practice law. In 1789, he was elected to the general council of his native Gironde; two years later, he represented Gironde at the legislative assembly in Paris, where he earned his reputation as a gifted public orator. He called for heavy taxation of property belonging to the emigrés and eventually denounced the king. However, as the Montagnard faction, led by Danton,* Robespierre,* and Jean Paul Marat (1743–1793), grew increasingly violent, Vergniaud unleashed the fury of his speech on them, exclaiming in his *Défense contre Robespierre* (*Defense against Robespierre*, 10 April 1793), "You are seeking to consummate the Revolution with terror; I would have wanted to do so with love." Other well-known speeches include *Discours sur la patrie en danger* (*Discourse on the Country in Danger*, 3 July 1792) and *Appel aux armes* (*Call to Arms*, 16 September 1792). The Montagnards, however, overthrew the Girondists. Vergniaud was arrested in June 1793 and guillotined five months later.

VERLAINE, PAUL (1844–1896). See *Dictionary of Modern French Literature, from Naturalism and Symbolism to Post-Modernism.*

VEUILLOT, LOUIS (1813–1883), Catholic writer and polemicist, virulently opposed liberal Catholics such as Lacordaire* and Montalembert* and fought for absolute monarchy and the supremacy of the church. He was born in Boynes, the eldest of five children of a wet cooper. At thirteen, as a junior clerk for Fortuné Delavigne, brother of the poet, he met a number of writers, a profession he quickly learned. In 1830 he wrote a few articles for the *Figaro*. He contributed articles, stories, and poems to *L'Echo de la Seine-inférieure* (*News from the Lower Seine*) in 1831 and edited *Mémorial de la Dordogne* (*Memoirs from Dordogne*) the following year. In Paris in 1836, he collaborated on *La Charte de 1830,* published by the government. In 1838, a trip to Rome confirmed his faith and sparked the militant Catholicism of his later articles and pamphlets. He published a number of religious novels and stories including *Les Pèlerinages de Suisse* (*Swiss Pilgrimages,* 1838), *Pierre Saintive* (1840), *Le Saint Rosaire médite* (*The Slandered Holy Rosary,* 1840), *Rome et Lorette* (1841). In 1842, he joined forces with *L'Univers religieux* (*The Religious Universe*), a Catholic daily paper, the principal organ for his attacks against liberal politics and religion. His defense of feudal privileges, the military, and the papacy was impassioned and eloquent, occasionally sarcastic, and occasionally good-natured. His chief writings have been collected in *Mélanges religieux, historiques et littéraires* (*Religious, Historical and Literary Miscellanies,* 1857–1875, 18 vols.) and *Derniers Mélanges* (*Final Miscellanies,* 1873–1877, 1908–1909).

VIE DE MARIANNE, LA (*The Life of Marianne,* 11 vols., 1728–1741), by Marivaux,* along with *Le Paysan parvenu** (5 vols., 1735–1736), is one of his most important novels. Both remain unfinished. Whether from boredom, hostile critical reception, or more academic ambitions, Marivaux abandoned Marianne's story in Book Nine for that of her religious friend, Tervire, never to definitively resolve either.

Similar to other early seventeenth-century novels, *La Vie de Marianne* is a memoir written at the request of a friend by Marianne in her maturity and ostensibly found by Marivaux in the country. Marianne, aged two, orphaned on the way to Bordeaux when brigands robbed the coach and killed all of the passengers, is raised by a country priest and his sister until their deaths. At fifteen, alone in Paris, she appeals to the church for help. Father Vincent leads her to the lecherous Monsieur de Climal, who places her in Mme Dutour's linen shop and showers her with gifts and attention. Marianne, however, is in love with the wealthy and elegant Valville, whom fate placed at her feet when she turned an ankle leaving church one day. Though a coquette, Marianne virtuously resists Climal. Humiliated and afraid, she seeks refuge in a chapel where she meets Madame de Miran, who happens to be Climal's sister and Valville's mother. The generous woman places her in a convent and eventually gives her permission to marry her son, despite Marianne's low social status. When friends and family object to the union, she returns to the convent. She refuses the hand of

Monsieur Villot, a young bourgeois chosen for her by the minister. In an emotion-laden speech, she proudly offers to renounce her marriage with Valville and sequester herself in a convent near Madame de Miran. Her victory ("Do as you like," the minister concludes, "it's your affair."), although soured by Valville's infidelity, is capped by a marriage offer from an "honnête homme" ("gentleman, or "honest man"), a retired army officer. She asks for time to consider, and there her story ends. The novel concludes with the three parts of the nun Tervire's story, which like Marianne's, remains unfinished.

Although the novel spawned numerous imitations (the most important being Samuel Richardson's [1689–1761] *Pamela*, 1740), it was not well received by contemporary critics, who viewed it as long, exaggerated, or incomprehensible. D'Alembert* decried the Tervire appendage, "Oh, my God . . . if you have enough to write two stories, write two, and don't mix and spoil them both."

The vicissitudes of Marianne's rise up the social scale interested readers of the day as had the adventures of Gil Blas* a few years earlier. In Marivaux's novel, however, psychology rather than social satire dominates. Although critical of a society based on birthright rather than personal merit, Marivaux's main interest here, as it was in the theatre, is the analysis of self-awareness and motivation. Jean Ehrard, in his *Littérature française* (1974), considers the novel not the story of a life as much as the story of a consciousness.

Besides its psychological realism, the novel is remembered for its social and historical detail, depicting village life, working-class Paris, a convent, a minister, a salon, a chateau. Its style is rich, ranging from Marianne's informed, conversational tone to the dialect of the Parisian working class.

Marivaux's characters, themes, narrative technique, psychology, and realism influenced the romanesque novels of his day. His sensitivity anticipates later eighteenth-century authors Diderot,* Sedaine,* J.-J. Rousseau,* Bernardin de Saint-Pierre* and Restif.* According to Henri Coulet (*Le Roman jusqu'à la révolution* [*The Novel Before the Revolution*], 1967) though he lacks the imagination of Prévost* and the powers of observation of Lesage,* Marivaux provides an important link to the nineteenth and twentieth centuries and Flaubert,* Proust,** and Gide,** who furthered his innovations perhaps without even recognizing in him an ancestor.

For further information, see P. Brady, *Structuralist Perspectives in Criticism of Fiction. Essays on Manon Lescaut and La Vie de Marianne* (Berne, Frankfurt, Las Vegas: P. Lang, 1978); D. Coward, *Marivaux: La Vie de Marianne and Le Paysan parvenu* (London: Grant and Cutler, 1983).

VIGNY, ALFRED DE (1797–1863), one of the three or four great romantic (see romanticism*) poets of the nineteenth century, is remembered primarily for "La Maison du berger" ("The Shepherd's Cottage") and "La Mort du loup" ("The Death of the Wolf") in *Les Destinées.* He also wrote novels (*Cinq-Mars*, 1826; *Stello*, 1832) and plays (*Chatteron*). Vigny was born in the ancient town of Loches to impoverished, aristocratic parents who inculcated in him at an early age the ideals and pride of the ancien régime. His poetry, formal, spare, and devoid of the effusion and sensitivity of his fellow romantics, bears the imprint of his noble heritage. It bears witness to his solitude and stoicism, cornerstones of the thinking that earned him the title "philosopher poet."

Vigny lived most of his life in Paris. He led an unhappy childhood raised by an elderly father and a strict mother and railed by his fellow students at the Lycée Bonaparte for his noble lineage. At seventeen, during the Restoration, he entered the army as a musketeer in the king's guard, but found his military career a disappointment. His greatest military feat occurred a year later, in 1815, when upon Napoleon's return from Elba, he accompanied Louis XVIII to the Belgian border. He was briefly interned at Antwerp, but after the Restoration, he returned to the military. In 1816, he was named second lieutenant in the infantry of the royal guard but turned to literature to relieve the boredom of barracks life in Courbevoie and Vincennes. He studied the Bible, Mme de Staël,* Chateaubri-and,* de Maistre,* Chénier,* and the English poet, Lord Byron (1788–1824). He frequented the cénacle* of Charles Nodier,* and at the salon of Emile Deschamps (1791–1871), a former school chum, met Victor Hugo,* Dumas père,* Delacroix (1798–1863), and other young romantics. He fell in love with the beautiful young poet Delphine Gay (1804-1855), but his mother opposed the marriage. He wrote poetry, contributed to Hugo's *Conservateur littéraire* (*Literary Conservator*) and, in 1822, published his first volume, *Poèmes,* and wrote his first masterpiece, "Moïse" ("Moses"). The following year, he was promoted to infantry captain and stationed first in Strasbourg and later in the Pyrennees. He was prepared to fight in the war against Spain, but to his dismay, his regiment remained at the border. During this time, he wrote "Eloa," a long epic poem in three cantos published in 1824, and "Le Déluge" ("The Flood"). In 1825, he married a wealthy young Englishwoman, Lydia Bunbury, who shortly after marriage became invalid, disfigured, incoherent, and disinherited by her cruel father. Two years later, Vigny resigned his post and sought in literature the glory that had eluded him in the military. He moved to Paris, frequented the salons, and befriended other romantics. In 1826, he published a new edition of his first poems, *Poèmes antiques et modernes** and *Cinq-Mars,* a historical novel written in the vein of Walter Scott (1771–1832), which met with great success.

Cinq-Mars, a young nobleman, proud and faithful to the duties of his rank, is an idealization of Vigny himself. He is engaged in a conspiracy against Cardinal Richelieu, a larger-than-life incarnation of cruelty and ambition. True to the theory elaborated in the novel's preface, "Réflexions sur la vérité dans l'art" ("Reflections on Truth in Art"), Vigny is exercising his rights as a poet to blend fact and fiction, to reinvent characters and refashion the truth according to his needs, since the only truth that matters is that of "human nature," not "authentic facts." Though its characters are criticized as caricatures subordinated to the theme of the novel, *Cinq-Mars* continues to be read for its faithful depiction of the mores of the time of Louis XIII, its psychology, and action.

Cinq-Mars has been called the first stanza of a "sort of epic poem on disillusionment,'' a theme picked up again in *Stello* and *Servitude et grandeur militaires* (*Military Servitude and Grandeur*, 1835), works that grew from his disillusionment with the revolution of 1830 and show the condition of two social "pariahs," which Vigny knew from first-hand experience. The novel *Stello* depicts the distress of the poet who is confronted by a society that rejects intellectual brilliance and artistic creation for mediocrity and conformity. Stello's friend, Dr. Noir, tries to cure him of his malady, advising him to "separate the poetic life from the political life. . . . solitude is holy." *Servitude et grandeur militaires,* three short stories inspired by Vigny's army experience, depicts the moral isolation of the soldier, a slave of war, who must consign his soul to the needs of humanity. His reward, often on pain of death, is dignity, honor, and freedom.

In keeping with the romantic's fascination with William Shakespeare (1564–1616) and other things English, Vigny adapted *Othello* (*Le More de Venise,* 1828), presented by the Théâtre Français in 1829. He collaborated with Deschamps on a translation of *Romeo and Juliet.* An original play, *Le Maréchale d'Ancre* (1830), achieved only moderate success. Real triumph came with *Chatterton,* which transposed the thesis of *Stello* to the stage. Vigny planned another prose work to be called either *Lamuel* or *Emmanuel,* based on a second consultation with Stello's Dr. Noir, which would apply his ideal of self-abnegation to religion. He conceived a series of "three events in three different ages, but times of religious fervor" with Emperor Julien, the reformer Melanchthon (1497–1560), and Jean-Jacques Rousseau* as heroes, but completed only the first, *Daphné,* written in 1837 and unpublished until 1912.

By 1837, Vigny's stormy relationship with actress Marie Dorval (1798–1849), for whom he wrote *Chatterton,* bitterly ended. He was tired of her infidelities, disillusioned with politics, embittered by the literary success of others and the lack of his own. After his mother died later that year, he repaired to his estate at Maine-Giraud in Charente. He turned once again to poetry, finding in his suffering and bitterness at life a source of the beautiful but somber poems initially published in the *Revue des deux mondes* and later contained in the posthumous collection published by Louis Ratisbonne (1827–1900), *Les Destinées.* He returned periodically to Paris, frequented the salons, and attempted, six times between 1842 and 1845, to enter the Academy. He finally succeeded in May 1845. Putting his trust in order, progress, and positivism,* he sought political office in 1848 and 1849 but failed. His later poems ("La Bouteille à la mer" ["Bottle at Sea"] and "L'Esprit pur" ["Pure Spirit"] convey his philosophy of hope. In 1863, Vigny died of stomach cancer a few months after his wife. He left seventy notebooks filled with his memoirs and reflections, published by Ratisbonne as *Journal d'un poète* (*One Poet's Journal*, 1867). He is buried in Montmartre cemetery.

From his earliest childhood, Vigny was stamped with nobility and pride; these were his heritage from his family and from the ancien régime. This nobility, together with his awareness of his intelligence and creativity, armed him with the stamina to overcome disappointment in love, the military, and literature. As a soldier and poet, he felt outcast and misunderstood by his contemporaries. He abandoned his belief in government, religion, nature, and love, finding in himself the ideals and strength to overcome his doubts, bitterness, and sadness and in poetry the vehicle for their expression.

Vigny's work, like that of the other romantics, is closely allied to his life. Though he intimately experienced the whole range of human emotions, his poetry reveals little of the sentimentalism or passion identified with romanticism and which he disdained. Vigny's work is subdued, formal, philosophical. Its symbolism**—the wolf, the bottle at sea, Moses—externalized his inner struggle for dignity and his compassion for mankind. Vigny pitied the weak and the humble, the struggling poet, the dedicated soldier, and sought to give them hope and inspiration in their long, slow march toward progress.

Vigny stands alone among the romantics in his philosophy of stoic resignation before the vicissitudes of life. His poetry, aspiring toward "pure spirit" is modern in its ideals, a forerunner to the poetry of the parnassians* and an inspiration to Baudelaire** and the symbolists in the later half of the century.

For further information, see M. Evans, "Mirror Images in 'La Maison du berger,' " *French Review* 56 (3) (February 1983): 393–399; H. Majewski, "The Second Consultation of the 'Docteur noir': Alfred de Vigny's *Daphné* and the Power of Symbols," *Studies in Romanticism* 20 (4) (Winter 1981): 461–474; H. Majewski, "Vigny and the Creative Experience: *le Journal d'un poète*," *The Hebrew University Studies in Literature* 7 (Spring 1979): 94–112; R. Nugent, "Vigny's *Stello* and Existential Freedom," *Nineteenth Century French Studies* 8 (Fall–Winter 1979–1980): 37–46; L. M. Porter, "Body Language in Vigny's Theatre," *Nineteenth Century French Studies* 7 (Spring–Summer 1979): 172–175; E. Rashkin, "Truth's Turn: Rereading the Fantastic in Vigny's *Véra*," *Romanic Review* 72 (November 1981): 460–471; K. Wren, "A Suitable Case for Treatment: Ideological Confusion in Vigny's *Cinq-Mars*," *Forum for Modern Language Studies* 18 (4) (October 1982): 335–350.

VILLEMAIN, ABEL-FRANÇOIS (1790–1870), brilliant academician and literary critic, broadened the scope of criticism to include the reciprocal influences between the writer and his social milieu and the relationships between the literatures of various nations. As a young man, he was thrice awarded the prize for eloquence by the Academy for his *Eloge de Montaigne* (*Praise of Montaigne*, 1812), *Les Avantages et les inconvénients de la critique* (*The Advantages and Inconveniences of Criticism*, 1814), and *Eloge de Montesquieu* (*Praise of Montesquieu*, 1816). He became a professor at the Lycée Charlemagne in 1810 and professor at the Sorbonne in 1816, where his lectures drew great crowds. In 1821, he was elected to the Academy, becoming its perpetual secretary in 1834. Under Louis-Philippe, he served two terms as minister of public education and was elected a deputy and peer of France.

As a critic, Villemain was a disciple of Madame de Staël* in his consideration of literature as the expression of civilization, social morals, and ideas. His work constitutes a movement toward relativity and cosmopolitanism in literary criticism and leads the way toward the objective criticism of Sainte-Beuve.* His principal works include *Cours de littérature française* (*Course on French Literature*, 1828–1829) comprising a *Tableau de la littérature française au XVIIIe siècle* (*Tableau of French Literature during the Eighteenth Century*) and a *Tableau de la littérature française au Moyen Age* (*Tableau of French Literature during the Middle Ages*); *Discours et mélanges littéraires* (*Literary Discourses and Miscellany*, 1823); *Tableau de l'éloquence chrétienne au IVe siècle* (*Tableau of Christian Eloquence in the Fourth Century*, 1846); *Etudes de littérature ancienne et étrangère* (*Studies of Ancient and Foreign Literature*, 1857); and a study of Chateaubriand* (1858) and Pindar (1859).

VILLIERS DE L'ISLE ADAM, AUGUSTE (1838–1889). See *Dictionary of Modern French Literature, from Naturalism and Symbolism to Post-Modernism.*

VIVANT DE NON OR DENON, BARON DOMINIQUE (1747–1825), author, playwright, courtier, engraver, and art historian, is best remembered for one short story, *Point de lendemain* (*No Tomorrow*, 1777), among the best examples of the libertine writing of the late eighteenth century. The story depicts one evening's pleasures as a woman betrays both her husband and her lover, leading the narrator to conclude, "I looked hard for the moral of all this adventure and . . . I found none at all." Still enjoyed for its style and dreamlike atmosphere, the story inspired the scenario for Louis Malle's film, *Les Amants* (*The Lovers*, 1958). A man of many talents, Denon was also a member of the Royal Academy of Painting and was named national engraver and director of National Museums. He published *Voyage dans la basse et la haute Egypte pendant les campagnes du general Bonaparte* (*Voyage in Lower and Upper Egypt during the Campaigns of General Bonaparte*, 1802), based on his travels with the emperor, and a history of art from its origins until the beginning of the nineteenth century.

For further information, see C. Reichler, "On the Notion of Intertextuality: The Example of the Libertine Novel," *Diogènes* (Spring–Summer 1981): 113–114, 205–215.

VOIX INTERIEURES, LES (*Interior Voices*, 1837), by Victor Hugo,* like *Les Feuilles d'automne,** and *Les Chants du crépuscule** which preceded it, is the intimate echo of its poet's soul, the "very confused and very feeble, but no doubt faithful" echo of the outside world that Hugo discerned within himself. The voices he heard stemmed from "the home, the field, and the street." They addressed his heart, his soul, and his mind, respectively. Politics holds a lesser place in this collection; here, once again, it is the personal Hugo, the father, the son, the sensitive artist, who is expressing his deepest thoughts in his most lyric voice.

Hugo dedicated the volume to his father, Joseph-Léopold Sigisbert, "Count Hugo, and general in the King's army," to compensate for the omission of his father's name from the Arch of Triumph. King Louis-Philippe (1773–1850) omitted Hugo's father from the names of battles and generals inscribed on the monument, because Hugo's title and rank belonged to the Spanish monarchy of Napoleon's brother, Joseph Bonaparte (1768–1844). Hugo wrote in the preface of *Les Voix interieures* that he was giving his father "this slip of paper, all that I have, and sorry that I have no granite." "A Eugène, vicomte H." ("To Eugene, Viscount H."), written six months after his death, is dedicated to Hugo's older brother. Several poems, "A quoi je songe?" ("What Am I Dreaming Of?"), "A des oiseaux envolés" ("To the Birds which have Flown Off"), and "Regardez, les enfants se sont assis en rond" ("Look, the Children are Seated in a Circle"), express Hugo's joy in family life. "A Albert Dürer," dedicated to the German painter admired by the romantics (see romanticism*) for his "visionary eye," transposes the imaginative force his paintings awaken in Hugo into a poetic tableau. "A Olympio" ("To Olympio") announces a theme that Hugo will develop in *Les Rayons et les ombres,** that of "Olympio," an imaginery brother, a twin, who incarnates his deepest thoughts.

For further information, see E. Kaplan, "Victor Hugo and the Poetics of Doubt: The Transition of 1835–37," *French Forum* 6 (May 1981): 140–153.

VOLNEY, FRANÇOIS DE CHASSEBOEUF, COMTE DE (1757–1820), historian and philosopher belonging to the idéologue* school of thought, studied law and medicine before settling into his intellectual pursuits. In 1782, he embarked on a five-year journey, which became the basis for his *Voyage en Syrie et en Egypte* (*Voyage to Syria and Egypt,* 1787), a careful description of those countries, which established his reputation as a writer. Upon his return, he was named director of agriculture and commerce for Corsica. He served as a deputy to the states general and secretary to the constituent assembly in 1790 but was imprisoned during the Terror for suspected royalist sentiment. After the fall of Robespierre* (1794), he became a history professor at the Ecole Normale, a member of the National Institute and in 1795, travelled to the United States. He was a favorite of Napoleon, who named him commander of the Legion of Honor and a count of the Empire, but Volney maintained his intellectual ties with the idéologues. His principal work, *Les Ruines ou Méditations sur les revolutions des empires* (*The Ruins or Meditations on the Revolutions of the Empires,* 1791), which was translated into several languages, served as an inspiration to Chateaubriand* and a generation of budding romanticists (see romanticism*), who derived a melancholy pleasure from the contemplation of ruins and ancient monuments. As an ideologue, Volney favored the equality of all people before the law and natural religion. He opposed despotism and called for religious toleration. His *Esquisse d'un tableau des progrès de l'esprit human* (*Sketch of a Tableau of the Progress of the Human Spirit,* 1794) summarizes the philosophical beliefs of the eighteenth century. His *Recherches nouvelles sur l'histoire ancienne* (*New Research on Ancient History,* 1814) established him as an early practitioner of critical history.

VOLTAIRE (1694–1778), born François-Marie Arouet to a family of Parisian notaries, is the poet, playwright, historian, activist, and philosophe* whose adoptive name is synonymous with the eighteenth-century quest for truth and justice. "Ecrasez l'infâme" ("Crush the infamous") was his battle cry; his wit and intelligence were his ammunition against the abuses of church and state. As publicist and polemicist, he penned poems, pamphlets, articles, stories, and histories. His *Lettres philosophiques** (1734), according to Gustave Lanson (1857–1934), constitute "the first bomb hurled against the ancien régime."

Voltaire's life, like his works, spanned most of the century, from the end of the splendiferous and authoritarian reign of Louis XIV to the dawn of the Revolution. He was born a sickly child to François Arouet, although he often denied his father, preferring to consider himself the son of a minor poet and songwriter named Rochebrune. His mother died when he was seven years old. He received his formal education at Jesuit Collège Louis-le-Grand beginning at age ten, where he was steeped for seven years in religion, humanities, and the classics. Although independent and often disrespectful, the brilliant young student with an aptitude for poetry won the lifelong regard of Fathers Porée, Tournemine, Brumoy, Thoulie, and de la Tour, as well as the later valuable friendship of fellow students—Charles Augustin de Ferriol, comte d'Argental (1700–1788), who became a lawyer and minister plenipotentiary of Parma at the French court; Armand, duc de Richelieu (1696–1788), the future marshal of France; Pierre-Robert de Cideville (1693–1776), future counselor of the Rouen parliament; Marc-Pierre, comte d'Argenson (1696–1764), who became minister of war; and his brother René-Louis de Voyer de Paulmy, marquis d'Argenson, who as eventual minister of foreign affairs assisted Voltaire in exile.

From an early age, Arouet showed an interest in literature and the life of society. In his father's salon he met poets abbé de Chaulieu (1639–1720), Charles-Auguste de la Fare (1644–1712), J.-B. Rousseau,* and aristocrats Jean-François-Paul-Le-Fèvre de Caumartin, l'abbé Servien, and the chevalier de Sully. His godfather, the epicurean abbé de Châteauneuf, introduced young Arouet to society, the salon of Ninon de Lenclos (1620–1705), and the libertines of the Society of the Temple. His father, disturbed by his lack of interest in a law career, sent him to the Hague as secretary to the Marquis de Châteauneuf, brother of the abbé, in 1713, but he was dismissed a year later because of an ill-fated love affair with a poor French refugee, Olympe Dunoyer, whom he affectionately called Pimpette. Upon his return, he worked as a clerk in the law office of Monsieur Alain but preferred the pleasures of society and writing libellous poetry. His relationship with his father at a low ebb, he was sent to Saint-Ange, the country estate of Monsieur Caumartin, where he began the first drafts of *La Henriade* and his first play, *Oedipe* (*Oedipus*). He returned after the death of Louis XIV to the pleasure-seeking Paris of the Regency period and sought the company of freethinkers at the Temple and at Sceaux with the duchess of Maine (1676–1753). In 1716, he was exiled to Tulle and Sully-sur-Loire for lampooning the regent. He returned none the wiser; the following year, he spent eleven months in the Bastille for satire directed against the reign of Louis XIV. In prison he redrafted *Oedipe* and wrote a part of *La Henriade* until released in 1718 to his father's estate in Châtenay.

His exile was soon rescinded, and *Oedipe,* a rousing success, opened on 18 November 1718 and ran for forty-five nights at the French Theatre. Arouet had his first taste of financial success, began making profitable investments, and, to advance himself in court circles, assumed a new name, Arouet de "Voltaire," an anagram taken from a number of sources, the most widely cited being "Arouet le jeune." When *La Henriade* was finally published in 1723, it capped his glory as a courtier until the fateful day two years later when the amibitious young writer, insulted by the chevalier de Rohan and beaten by his lackies, was once again imprisoned and exiled, at his own request, to England.

Rebuffed by the French aristocrats whom he wanted so desperately to equal, Voltaire found in England, from 1726 until 1729, a welcome change of pace. He was received into aristocratic and literary circles by such luminaries as Lord Bolingbroke (1678–1751), Robert Walpole (1676–1745), Thomas Pelham Holles, Duke of Newcastle, Lord John Hervey, and the rich merchant Falkener. He was received at court by the Prince of Wales. He dedicated *La Henriade* to the queen of England; he saw writers Alexander Pope (1688–1744) and Jonathan Swift (1667–1745) and philosopher George Berkeley (1685–1753), he learned to speak and write English fluently and was introduced to the thinking of John Locke (1632–1704), the science of Isaac Newton (1642–1727), and the drama of William Shakespeare (1564–1616). Above all, Voltaire found in England a social system that fostered religious and political freedoms, where a poet could be on even terms with government ministers and wealthy aristocrats.

Voltaire returned to France, gradually reestablished his ties with society, increased his wealth, and resumed his literary career with several tragedies— *Brutus* (1730), *Zaïre** (1732), *Adélaïde du Guesclin* (1734), and *La Mort de César (The Death of Ceasar,* 1731), plus a history, *Histoire de Charles XII (History of Charles XII,* 1731). At the risk of alienating himself from his fellow writers, he wrote *Temple du goût (Temple of Taste,* 1733) in prose and verse, in which the "God of Taste" judges classical and contemporary literature and art. The most important work to come from this period, however, was the *Lettres philosophiques* (1734), based on his observations of the English system. This work was condemned by parliament, the bookseller was imprisoned, and Voltaire was once again exiled.

This time Voltaire sought refuge with his friend Madame du Châtelet (1706–1749), a wise and intelligent woman, at her estate at Cirey in Lorraine, where he remained for ten years. Here Voltaire was removed from the rigors and temptations of society, and the Cirey years are rich in study, literary output, and visits from friends. He wrote the tragedies *Alzire* (1736), *Zulime* (1740), *Mahomet (Mohammed,* 1742), and *Mérope** (1743); the satirical poem, *Le Mondain (The Worldly One,* 1737), followed shortly by *La Défense du mondain (In Defense of 'The Worldly One')*; and *Discours sur l'homme (Discourses in Verse on Man,*

1738). He began the mock-heroic poem on Joan of Arc, *La Pucelle* (*The Maiden*, 1755), *Siècle de Louis XIV* (*Age of Louis XIV*, 1751), and *Essai sur les moeurs* (*Essay on Manners*, 1756). The Cirey estate contained a theatre where comedies and operas were performed and a laboratory where the "divine Emily," as Madame du Châtelet was affectionately called by Voltaire, and the writer himself performed experiments and studied Newton and astronomy. They made short trips to Paris, Belgium, Holland, and Prussia; Voltaire wrote short pamphlets against the poet J.-B. Rousseau and abbé Desfontaines (1685–1745); he maintained a vast correspondence with his Parisian allies.

When his former school chum, René d'Argenson (1694–1757), became minister of foreign affairs in 1744, Voltaire once again enjoyed the favor of the court. As royal historiographer, he wrote operas and light verse for royal occasions; he celebrated the royalty in his *Poème de Fontenoy* (*Poem on Fontenoy*, 1745) and was elected to the Academy in 1746. Appointed ordinary gentleman of the king's chamber, he was able to protect Marmontel,* d'Alembert,* and Vauvenargues.* By 1747, however, his wit and satire forced his retreat to Sceaux, where, drawing upon his experiences at court, he wrote *Zadig** (1747).

From Sceaux, he and Mme du Châtelet travelled to Lunéville and Commercy, the estates of former Prussian ruler King Stanislas (1677–1766), which Voltaire found mediocre. The shocking death in 1749 of Mme du Châtelet, while bearing the child of Saint-Lambert (1716–1803), an officer of the king's guard, coupled with his continued disfavor at the French court, led Voltaire to Berlin and King Frederick (1712–1786) in 1750 where, as chamberlain, he entertained hopes of becoming a minister. Tension mounted between the two men, however, and Voltaire tired of correcting the king's verses ("his dirty laundry"); he quarreled with Maupertuis,* president of the Prussian academy, and took him to task in his *Diatribe sur Docteur Akakia* (*Diatribe on Doctor Akakia*, 1752), which Frederick ordered burned. However, Voltaire did produce some good in Prussia—his *Age of Louis XIV* was published in 1751, and he wrote *Poème sur la loi naturelle* (*Poem on Natural Law*) and *Micromégas** in 1752. He slowly retreated toward France but was apprehended in Frankfurt and forced to relinquish samples of the king's poetry, with which he had hoped to embarrass him before all of Europe.

Voltaire spent two years in Alsace before installing himself in the beautiful Swiss countryside at Les Délices outside of Geneva in 1755 with his niece, Madame Denis (c.1710–1790). There he admired nature, received friends, and built a theatre, where he presented his tragedy, *L'Orphelin de la Chine* (*The Orphan of China*, 1755). *La Pucelle* also appeared in 1755. The Lisbon earthquake, occurring later that year, shook his faith in God and nature and resulted in the pessimistic "*Poème sur le désastre de Lisbonne*" ("*Poem on the Lisbon Disaster*," 1756) and his most famous work, *Candide** (1759). He completed his *Essai sur les moeurs et l'esprit des nations** and collaborated on Diderot's* *Encyclopédie.** Finding Swiss pastors more liberal than the French curés, Voltaire dreamed of a possible reconciliation with the church and hoped to found a religion without superstition, fanaticism, or sentimentalism. The Swiss, however, insulted by d'Alembert's article "Genève" in the *Encyclopédie,* believed Voltaire had unjustly portrayed Jean Calvin (1509–1564) in his *Essai sur les moeurs* and prohibited his theatrical productions. Voltaire had dreamed in vain. He quarreled with Jean-Jacques Rousseau* on the nature of civilization, God, and the theatre. He launched a series of satires and pamphlets against the anti-philosophes—Fréron,* Pompignan,* and the *Journal of Trévoux.*

In 1760, Voltaire moved to Ferney, just inside the French border, where he remained until his triumphant return to Paris in the spring of 1778. With Voltaire as chatelain, the sleepy country village grew to a thriving community of 1,200. Voltaire planted crops and trees, built houses, a church, a stocking factory, a tannery; he worked for the improvement of peasants' conditions while at the same time corresponding with all of Europe—Frederick II (1712–1786), Catherine of Russia (1729–1796), and the kings of Poland, Sweden, and Denmark. Europe, in turn, visited Voltaire, who, calling himself the "innkeeper of Europe," often housed as many as a hundred guests a night. While at Ferney, he wrote ten more tragedies, published a new volume of Pierre Corneille (1606–1684) for the great-granddaughter of the playwright, attacked the Jesuits in the *Précis du siècle de Louis XV* (*Precis of the Age of Louis XV,* 1769), outlined the errors of parliament in a history of the Parisian parliament (1769), and turned out philosophical stories—*Jeannot et Colin* (1764), *L'Ingénu* (*The Ingenu,* 1767), *L'Homme aux quarante écus* (*The Man with Forty Crowns,* 1768), and *La Princesse de Babylone* (1768).

Voltaire spent his final years as a champion of justice, tirelessly writing pamphlets against parliaments, torture, and especially against religious superstition and intolerance. *Extraits des sentiments de Jean Meslier* (*Extracts of the Sentiments of Jean Meslier,* 1762) attacks Christian dogma; *Le Sermon des cinquante* (*The Sermon of the Fifty,* 1762) preaches natural religion. He intervened on behalf of victims of injustice, undertaking the defense of Jean Calas (1762), who was condemned and executed for supposedly having hung a son who wanted to convert to Catholicism. Voltaire defended the family, harbored them at Ferney, and after three years of efforts, established their innocence. Likewise, he defended the Sirvens, Protestants condemned to death for having killed their daughter. Among others, he defended the nineteen-year-old Chevalier de la Barre, executed for blaspheming and mutilating a crucifix. Two important philosophic works to come from this period include the *Traité sur la tolérance* (*Treatise on Tolerance,* 1763), inspired by the Calas affair, and the *Dictionnaire philosophique portatif** (1764).

In 1778, Voltaire returned to his beloved Paris for a presentation of his tragedy, *Irène.* Paris thronged to greet him; the Academy elected him director; his bust was crowned on stage. Two months later he died.

Though Voltaire is remembered primarily for his philosophical stories and histories, in his own time, he made his mark first as a poet. An admirer of Homer (8th century B.C.) and Virgil (70–19 B.C.), Voltaire combined his love of history and philosophy with the epic form of the classics in his first attempt at serious poetry, *La Henriade*. Originally entitled *Poème de la ligue* (*Poem of the League*) and published in England, it was hailed as a masterpiece and brought fame and fortune to its young author. Eloquent and forceful, its ten cantos recount in truth and fiction, history and allegory, the final wars of religion that led Henri IV to the French throne. More important, however, are the attacks levelled against religious fanaticism and intolerance. Other poems vented Voltaire's satire against his contemporaries. *Le Pauvre Diable* (*The Poor Devil*, 1758) attacks his enemies Fréron and Desfontaines (1685–1745); *La Vanité* (*Vanity*, 1760), Pompignan.

Like the other genres Voltaire practiced, poetry served primarily as a vehicle for his ideas. *Epitre à Uranie* (*Epistle to Urania*, 1722), rejecting Christian orthodoxy, promoting instead a natural religion based on virtue and justice, declares his religious principles; *Temple du goût* (*Temple of Taste*, 1733), depicting in prose and poetry a "beauteous structure" into which writers, artists, and critics seek to enter but often do not succeed, reveals Voltaire's literary ideals— classical unity, clarity, simplicity, and naturalness. *Essai sur la poésie épique* (*Essay on Epic Poetry*, 1727), written in English to promote the *Henriade*, which followed the next year, surveys the art of the epic poem historically and critically. *Le Mondain* (*The Worldly One*, 1736), an apologia for his belief in progress and love of material comfort and luxury, along with the seven *Discours en vers sur l'homme* (*Discourses in Verse on Man*, 1738), expresses the epicureanism of his early years. Twenty years later, *Poème sur le désastre de Lisbonne* (*Poem on the Disaster of Lisbon*, 1756), recounting the earthquake of the previous year, reveals his mounting pessimism and attacks the Leibnitzian idea that all is well in the world; *Poème sur la loi naturelle* (*Poem on Natural Law*, 1752) upholds the theory of the existence of a morality that is universal and exists independently of all religion. *Epitre à l'auteur du livre des trois imposteurs* (*Epistle to the Author of the Book of the Three Imposters*, 1769) combats atheism and demonstrates the existence of God.

La Henriade today is considered contrived and unimaginative; the philosophical poems, flat and uninspiring. As a poet, Voltaire achieved enduring success with his lighter verse, his epigrams, odes, elegies, and epistles, which sparkle yet with spirit, vigor, and often with maliciousness and continue to be read.

The theatre was the focus of Voltaire's creative energy throughout most of his life. His first and most famous play, *Oedipe* (*Oedipus*, 1718), met with resounding approbation, despite its antimonarchical and anticlerical tone, and established Voltaire at the forefront of French literature. His homes in Cirey, Potsdam, Les Délices, and Ferney all contained stages where he and his friends performed. He brought to the theatre, as he had to his poetry, his love of the classics. He strove to emulate the purity, the simplicity, the naturalness, of Corneille and Jean Baptiste Racine (1639–1699), preferring them to the Greek playwrights. Performances of Shakespeare he had observed on the English stage energized Voltaire's plays with scenery, costumes, and action. Besides his comedies and operas, he wrote about twenty tragedies, of which the most famous are *Zaïre* (1732) and *Mérope** (1743). His first plays, *Oedipe* (1718), *Artémire* (1720), and *Mariamne* (1725) are direct imitations of the tragedies of the seventeenth century. *Brutus* (1730) and *La Mort de César* (*The Death of Caesar*, written, 1731; presented, 1743) were influenced by Shakespeare; *Brutus, La Mort de César*, and *Rome Sauvée* (*Rome Saved*, 1752) are inspired from classical antiquity; *Adélaïde du Guesclin* (1734) and *Tancrède* (1760) depict French history—the crusades, the age of chivalry, and the Hundred Years' War. Others are more exotic. *Zaïre* is set in Jerusalem; *Alzire*, in Peru; *Mahomet* in Mecca; *Sémiramis* (1748), in Assyria; and *L'Orphelin de la Chine*, in China.

Voltaire felt that emotions other than romantic love should motivate the action on stage and explored maternal love in *Mérope*, religious fanaticism in *Mahomet*, and political ambitions and civic duty in *Brutus* and *La Mort de César* (which has no female characters). His final plays, *Les Guèbres* (*The Guebres*, 1769), *Les lois de Minos* (*The Laws of Minos*, 1772), and *Don Phèdre* (1774), all called "pamphlets in five acts" by the critic Ch.-M. Des Granges (*Histoire illustrée de la littérature française* [*Illustrated History of French Literature*], 1918), are mouthpieces for his ideas on tolerance, royalty, and parliament.

Despite innovations in costume, staging, theme, and melodrama, which helped prepare the way for early romantic drama, Voltaire's plays lack the psychological depth and emotional impact of those of the classical masters he so admired. Except for *Zaïre*, they remain largely unread and unperformed today.

As a historian, Voltaire revolutionized the total concept of history—its method, its subject matter, its style. He separated fact from fiction, applying the systematic approach of Bayle,* Fontenelle,* and Montesquieu,* in a detailed investigation of primary and secondary sources—memoirs, letters, historical records, and firsthand reports. He interviewed statesmen, ministers, and political refugees in his search for truth, objectivity, and credibility. He eliminated unnecessary details and uncovered the underlying causes for historical events, minimizing the role of Providence and emphasizing that of man and nature. As a philosophe, Voltaire colored history according to his own particular view, never missing a chance to denounce intolerance and religious fanaticism, always pointing to reason as the only sure road to the future. As an artist, he added style and drama to the writing of history, claiming, "It is necessary in a history, as in theatre, to have an exposition, a problem and a denouement."

For his first work, *Histoire de Charles XII* (*History of Charles XII*, 1731), Voltaire consulted Chaplain Nordberg's history and the firsthand observations of Stanislas Leczinski (1677–1766), king of Poland; former ambassadors Colbert de Croissy (1626–1696), de Fierville, and Roland Puchot, chevalier des Alleurs; Johann Albert Fabricius, chamberlain of King George I of England, who spent seven years in Sweden; and Baron Georg Heinrich Goertz, the Swedish minister. Besides relating the dramatic conquests of this extraordinary man's life in eight books that read like a novel, Voltaire hoped to cure the sovereigns of his day of their "madness for conquests" and show how a "peaceful and happy government is preferable to so much glory." Though its printing was prohibited in Paris, the book enjoyed great popular success.

Voltaire enlarged the scope of history to include the entire nation in his historical masterpiece, *Le Siècle de Louis XIV*. Unfortunately, his monument to the golden age of French culture was interpreted as a criticism of Louis XV and banned by the government. Its thirty-nine chapters formed part of the immense *Essai sur les moeurs* (1756), which Voltaire undertook for Mme du Châtelet. Both works present a global view of history, from the age of Charlemagne to Louis XIV, emphasizing not kingly deeds and battles, but civilization, daily life, and manners, which Voltaire considered more important. He wrote to Nicolas-Claude Thieriot (1696–1792) in 1735, "A canal-lock joining two seas, a painting by Poussin, a beautiful tragedy, a truth discovered are things a thousand times more precious than all accounts of military campaigns."

Voltaire's lesser historical works include *Histoire de la Russie sous Pierre-le-Grand* (*History of Russia under Peter the Great*, 1759), a counterpart to his earlier *Histoire de Charles XII; Précis du siècle de Louis XV* (*Précis of the Age of Louis XV*, 1769), undertaken as king's historiographer; and *Histoire du Parlement de Paris* (*History of the Parliament of Paris*, 1769).

Despite his poetic, dramatic, and historic importance, Voltaire is remembered primarily as the leading social, political, and religious reformer, the "philosophe par excellence," of his day. Criticism of religious fanaticism and persecution; hatred of bloodshed and violence; deism, empiricism, skepticism, and humanism pervade his literature.

Voltaire promoted a natural religion based on tolerance and reason rather than illusion or sentimentality; his "clockmaker," "eternal geometrist," "eternal architect," God was the only rational explanation for the world and its social and moral systems. Morality, according to Voltaire, exists independently of God and applies to all people; a moral man is a good father, good citizen, charitable, and just. *Lettres philosophiques* is concerned chiefly with English government and society, which Voltaire found more tolerant; *Traité de métaphysique* (*Treatise on Metaphysics*), written but not published in the same year, attacks blind metaphysical speculation. Inspired by Locke, the *Treatise* debates the existence of God, establishes the probability of his existence, questions the existence of the soul and immortality, and considers man's limited freedom and morality. The *Dictionnaire philosophique*, a storehouse of his ideas ranging from "Abraham" to "Virtue," bristles with contempt for organized religion and criticizes biblical texts and religious dogma as superstitious, false, divisive, and inspired by man rather than God. Voltaire lashed out against religious intolerance, injustice, and wars in his *Traité sur la tolérance* (*Treatise on Tolerance*, 1763), in which he pleads "Aren't we all children of the same father and creatures of the same God?"

Believing man to be naturally free and equal, Voltaire fought for his political as well as his religious liberty. Though a political conservative, he attacked the capriciousness and despotism of the absolute monarchy as well as its consequences—slavery, persecution, hypocrisy and war—and campaigned for justice with countless pamphlets. He praised democracy, but like J.-J. Rousseau, considered it practical only for small states, preferring an enlightened, tolerant "philosopher" king or England's constitutional monarchy. An aristocrat, he disdained the people, whom he termed "the canaille" or "the riff-raff," but for whom he provided, especially in his latter years, a living example of his ideals. He worked tirelessly for the peasants at Ferney, teaching them to work according to their abilities, to rely on themselves rather than on an indifferent God, to "cultivate" their gardens and to prosper.

Mankind, his destiny, and his relationship with God, are the themes of Voltaire's philosophical stories and novels. Inspired by the Orient, they mix fact with fantasy; ideas mingle with irony and imagination to expose man's foolishness, ignorance, cruelty, pride, and fanaticism as the hero, always young and pure, searches for the truth through a maze of adventures, abductions, and pursuits across continents, imaginary lands, and through past and present history. Inevitably, he fails yet eventually attains his quest.

Le Monde comme il va, vision de Babouc (*The World as It Is, Babouc's Vision,* 1746), the earliest of the stories, recounts Scythian Babouc's verdict on the fate of the city of Persepolis. Though he finds it rampant with evil and madness, he decides to let "the world as it is," since "if all is not well, all is passable." The questions of destiny and free will dominate *Zadig* (1747), in which the hero, constantly thwarted in his pursuit of happiness, falls from favor at court and flees to Egypt, Arabia, and the island of Serendib before ruling Babylon as a happy king. In *Micromegas,* a young Sirien, and his companion judge mankind as they traverse the planets. *Les Deux Consolés* (*The Two Comforters,* 1756) tells the story of a philosopher who attempts to console a woman with tales of others similarly afflicted; when he, in turn, loses a son, she sends him a list of other men who have lost sons. Neither succeeds in helping the other. Candiote, in *Histoire de Scarmentado* (*The Story of Scarmentado,* 1756), meets horror, perversion, and foolishness before returning to his island. *Candide,* the most famous, pessimistic, and skeptical of the stories, is a story of paradise lost as its young hero, exiled from the best of all possible worlds, experiences the evils and absurdities of mankind until finally achieving a measure of happiness in his own little garden. *Jeannot et Colin* (*Jeannot and Colin,* 1764), on the other hand, directed against the nobility, is a more encouraging tale of friendship and happiness. Jeannot, whose father strikes it rich, becomes the foolish and pretentious Monsieur de la Jeannotière, who scorns his former friend, the modest metalworker, Colin, who nevertheless remains true. The unspoiled goodness of nature is contrasted with the evils of civilization in *L'Ingénu* (*The Ingenu,* 1767), where in Lower Brittany, an Indian is adopted by a prior who turns out to be his uncle. Civilization is satirized again in *La Princesse de Babylone* (*The Princess of Babylon,* 1768) as Princess Formosante searches across continents for her lover.

Other philosophical tales include *Cosi-Sancta* (1746), *Memnon* (1749), *Le Songe de Platon* (*Plato's Dream,* 1756), *Le Blanc et le noir* (*The White and the Black,* 1764), *L'Homme aux quarante écus* (*The Man with Forty Crowns,* 1768), *Lettres d'Amabed* (*Amabed's Letters,* 1769), *Le Taureau blanc* (*The White Bull,* 1774), *Histoire de Jenni* (*Jenni's Story,* 1775), and *Les Oreilles de Lord Chesterfield* (*Lord Chesterfield's Ears,* 1775).

Voltaire's fiction has been criticized as unrealistic, melodramatic; his characters, mere puppets or mouthpieces for his ideas. On the other hand, the stories have been praised for their originality, their clarity, their vivacity, their irony, their satire, their vision of man's mediocrity and his destiny, and especially their insights into the mind and spirit of Voltaire. In all, adventure, irony, fantasy, and philosophy abound.

Besides his multifarious plays, dialogues, novels, stories, poems, essays, and papers—enough, according to Theodore Besterman (*Voltaire* [London: Longmans, 1969]), to fill twenty Bibles, Voltaire wrote more than 20,000 letters to kings and commoners on matters of state, everyday life, and his larger concerns in French, English, Italian, Latin, German, and Spanish. They merit a place in French literature for their historical importance as well as for their insights into Voltaire's personality.

In his eighty-four years, Voltaire led a life rich in personal and intellectual triumphs. He overcame the limitations of ill health and bourgeois birth to become a bona fide French aristocrat. His keen intelligence and indefatigable curiosity rapidly assured his place among the intellectual giants of all time. His unremitting devotion to the cause of truth, justice, and reason not only shook the foundations of French society, but sparked a revolution in thought that ushered in the modern age and gave birth to its ideal of freedom.

For further information, see A. Ages, "Voltaire and the Geography of Philosophy: the Testimony of the Correspondence," in W. Hemple, ed., *Französische Literatur im Zeitalter der Aufklärung* (Frankfurt: Klostermann, 1983), 1–14; A. Ages, "Voltaire's philosophical modernity: the Testimony of the Correspondence," *Romance Notes* 21 (Winter 1981): 338–342; A. Aldridge, "Swift and Voltaire," *Actes du VIIIe congrès de l'Association internationale de littérature comparée,* Budapest, 1 (Stuttgart: E. Bieber, 1980), 283–289; W. Andrews, *Voltaire* (New York: New Directions, 1981); R. P. Bartlett, "Catherine II, Voltaire and Henry IV of France," *Study Group on Eighteenth-century Russia Newsletter* 9 (September 1981): 41–50; A. Bingham and V. Topazio, eds., *Enlightenment Studies in Honor of Lester G. Crocker* (Oxford: Voltaire Foundation, 1979); T. Braun, "Alzire and The Indian Emperor: Voltaire's Debt to Dryden," *Studies on Voltaire and the Eighteenth Century* 205 (1982): 57–63; Braun, "Voltaire and His Contes: A Review Essay on Interpretations Offered by Roy S. Wolper," *Studies on Voltaire and the Eighteenth Century* 212 (1982): 312–317; M. Carozzi, *Voltaire's Attitude toward Geology* (Geneva: Societe de physique et d'histoire naturelle, 1983); M. Cartwright, "From *Adélaïde du Guesclin* to *Alamire:* the Transmutations of a Dramatic Text and Their Importance in an Appreciation of Voltaire's Theatre," *Transactions of the Fifth International Congress on the Enlightenment,* vol. 3 (Oxford: Taylor Institution, 1981), 1515–1517; C. Cherpack, "Positivism, Piety, and the Study of Voltaire's Philosophical Tales," *The Eighteenth Century: Theory and Interpretation* 24 (1) (Winter 1983): 23–27; D. Fletcher, "Three Authors in Search of a Character: Julius Caesar as Seen by Buckingham, Conti and Voltaire," in *Mélanges à la mémoire de F. Simone,* vol. 2 (Geneva: Slatkine, 1981), 439–453; G. Gargett, *Voltaire and Protestantism* (Oxford: The Voltaire Foundation at the Taylor Institution, 1980); L. Gossman, "Ce beau génie n'a point compris sa sublime mission—An Essay on Voltaire," *French Review* 56 (October 1982): 40–50; A. Gunny, "Some Eighteenth Century Reactions to Play on the Life of Cato," *The British Journal for Eighteenth-Century Studies* 4 (Spring 1981): 54–65; Gunny, *Voltaire and English Literature, a Study of English Literary Influences on Voltaire* (Oxford: Voltaire Foundation, 1979); W. Hanley, "The Question of a Royal Edition of Voltaire's *Précis de l'Ecclésiaste,*" *Papers of the Bibliographical Society of America,* 77 (1) (1983): 47–52; Hanley, "Vicissitudes of the Literary Inquisition: The Case of Voltaire's *Mahomet,*" in J. D. Browning, ed., *The Stage in the Eighteenth Century* (New York: Garland, 1981), pp. 87–107; D. Howarth, "Voltaire, Ninon de L'Enclos and the Evolution of a Dramatic Genre," in *Studies on Voltaire and the Eighteenth Century* 199 (1981): 63–72; F. Keener, *The Chain of Becoming. The Philosophical Tale, the Novel, and a Neglected Realism of the Enlightenment—Swift, Montesquieu, Voltaire, Johnson, Austin* (New York, Columbia University Press, 1983); O. Kenshur, "Fiction and Hypothesis in Voltaire," *The Eighteenth Century: Theory and Interpretation* 24 (1) (Winter 1983): 39–50; H. Mason, *Voltaire. A Biography* (London/Granada: P. Elek, 1981); *Melanges à la memoire de Franco Simone: France et Italie dans la culture européene,* vol. 2: Seventeenth and Eighteenth Century (Geneva: Slatkine, 1981); W. M. Mudrick, "Truth, Justice, and Other Spice for the Immature," [Voltaire and his Biographers], *The Hudson Review* 34 (Winter 1981): 525–548; R. Nablow, "Some Reflections on Voltaire's Poetic Imagery," *Romanic Review* 74 (1) (January 1983): 16–33; Nablow, "Was Voltaire Influenced by La Fontaine in *Thélème et Macare?*" *Romance Notes* 24 (3) (Spring 1984): 259–261; Nablow, "Was Voltaire Influenced by Rabelais in Canto V of the *Pucelle?*" *Romance Notes* 21 (Winter 1981): 343–348; P. M. Rattansi, "Voltaire and the Enlightenment Image of Newton," in H. Lloyd-Jones, V. Pearl, and B. Worden, eds., *History and Imagination: Essays in Honor of H. R. Trevor-Roper* (New York: Holmes and Meier, 1982), 218–231; S. Roe, "Voltaire Versus Needham: Atheism, Materialism and the Generation of Life," *Journal of the History of Ideas* 46 (1) (January–March 1985): 65–88; G. Sheridan, "Voltaire's *Henriade:* A History of the 'Subscriber' Edition, 1728–1741," *Studies on Voltaire and the Eighteenth Century* 215 (1982): 77–90; H. Stavan, "Are Voltaire's Tales Narrative Fantasies? A Reply to Wolper," *Studies on Voltaire and the Eighteenth Century* 215 (1982): 281–287; *Studies on Voltaire and the Eighteenth Century* (Oxford: Taylor Institution, 1981 to the present); O. Taylor, "Voltaire Iconoclast: An Introduction to *Le Temple du goût,*" *Studies on Voltaire and the Eighteenth Century* 212 (1982): 7–81; S. B. Taylor, "Voltaire's Humor," *Voltaire and the English* 2940 (1979): 101–116; W. H. Trapnell, *Christ and His 'Associates' in Voltairian Polemic: An Assault on the Trinity and the Two Natures* (Saratoga, Cal.: Anma Libri, 1982); Trapnell, *Voltaire and the Eucharist* (Oxford: Taylor Institute, 1981); J. Undank, "The Status of Fiction in Voltaire's Contes," *Degré Second* 6 (July 1982): 65–88; R. Vigne, "The Killing of J. Calas: Voltaire's First Huguenot Cause," *Proceedings of the Huguenot Society of London* 23 (5) (1981): 280–294; *Voltaire and the English, Studies on Voltaire and the Eighteenth Century,* vol. 179 (Oxford: Voltaire Foundation, 1979); R. Walters, ed., *Colloque 76: Voltaire* (London, Ont.: University of Western Ontario, 1983); R. Wolper, "The Toppling of Jeannot," *Studies on Voltaire and the Eighteenth Century* 183 (1981): 69–82.

Z

ZADIG OU LA DESTINEE (*Zadig or Destiny*, 1747), by Voltaire,* originally published in Amsterdam as *Memnon* (but not to be confused with a shorter work of the same title published three years later), ranks among the earliest and best of Voltaire's more than twenty-five philosophical tales and novels. Tradition has it that the tale was written in Sceaux, at one of the duchess of Maine's (1670–1736) famous ''white night'' lotteries when Voltaire, drawing the letter Z, proposed his ideas on mankind and human destiny in the form of a fable from *A Thousand and One Nights*.

The story begins in Babylon, where Zadig, who is young, rich, talented, and wise, dreams of finding happiness. However, he fails in love—his fiancee, Sémire, abandons him for his rival when she believes him blinded in one eye, and later his wife, Azora, is unfaithful—and in science, for his knowledge and reason are punished. Nonetheless, his wisdom wins the favor of King Moabar and Queen Astarté, who name him first minister, a post that he fulfills happily and wisely until his love for the queen angers the king and forces him to flee. Although enslaved in Egypt for freeing a woman from her brutal lover, his knowledge and wisdom soon earn the friendship of his master, put an end to the senseless tradition of the ''bûcher'' (in which a man's widow publicly burns herself and his dead body), and reconcile a religious argument. Eventually freed, Zadig is sent on a mission to the king of Serendib, whom he assists in locating a treasurer (only one in sixty-four was honest enough) and a wife (unfortunately, she had blue eyes and was therefore unacceptable). Victimized by the clergy for his wisdom, he flees again, falls into the hands of a merry thief, who informs him of Moabar's death, civil war in Babylon, and the uncertainty of Astarté's fate. Free once more, Zadig departs for Babylon, meets an unhappy Babylonian cheesemaker along the way, and finally discovers Astarté, now a slave. Zadig wins her freedom and arranges for her triumphant return to Babylon, where he returns incognito to participate in the trials, contests, and riddles that will determine the next king. Though he wins, his victory armor is stolen while he sleeps. More desolate than ever, he leaves the city for the banks of the Euphrates, where the angel Jesrad appears disguised as a hermit reading from the book of destinies, of which Zadig can decipher not a single letter. "Men," Jesrad informs him, "judge everything without knowing anything: you were the one man of all men who was most worthy of enlightenment." Jesrad explains that all is determined, there is no such thing as chance, and that one must submit to God's plan. "Feeble mortal," he implores, "stop arguing with what you must adore." Knowing thus the secrets of the universe, Zadig returns to Babylon, answers the riddles, is recognized as king, and reigns happily at last with his beloved Astarté.

With typical Voltairian wit, Zadig satirizes human nature (Zadig was wealthy and therefore had many friends), metaphysics (Zadig knew all there was to know on the subject—very little), women, doctors, marriage, justice, priests, and religion. However, when considering the larger issue of man and his destiny, the optimisim expressed in earlier works (*Le Mondain* and *Babouc*) has been qualified. The wise and virtuous Zadig is constantly thwarted by man and his irrationality in his search for happiness. "Knowledge, custom, courage have never served but my misfortune," he cries in chapter 19, while "secretly accusing Providence who persecuted him always." To achieve his goal, he must submit to the will of God. At this point, Voltaire still believes in the order of the universe—"Nothing happens by accident; all is a test, or punishment, or reward or precaution." However, by 1759, Voltaire's limited optimism will have developed into the full-blown pessimism of his masterpiece, *Candide.**

For further information, see U. Eco, "Horns, Hooves, Insteps: Some Hypotheses on Three Types of Abduction," in U. Eco and T. Sebeok, eds., *The Sign of Three: Dupin, Holmes, Peirce* (Bloomington: Indiana University Press, 1983), 198–220; M. Gertner, "Five Comic Devices in *Zadig*," *Studies on Voltaire and the Eighteenth Century* 117 (1974): 133–152; N. Senior, "The Structure of *Zadig*," *Studies on Voltaire and the Eighteenth Century* 135 (1975): 135–141; C. Sherman, "Voltaire's *Zadig* and the Allegory of (Mis)reading," *French Review* 58 (1) (October 1984): 32–40; P. L. Smith, "A Note on the Publication of *Zadig:* Why Voltaire Cried Slander," *Romance Notes* 16 (Winter 1975): 345–50; R. Wolper, "*Zadig,* a Grim Comedy," *Romanic Review* 65 (November 1974): 237–248.

ZAIRE (1732), a tragedy in five acts by Voltaire,* is the best and most enduring of his more than twenty tragedies. Inspired in part by William Shakespeare's *Othello* (1604), the play is written in the classic style of Racine (1639–1699), which Voltaire upheld as a model of perfection. Situated in the thirteenth century, in a harem in Jerusalem, the play relates the story of Zaïre, a beautiful Christian slave who has been held captive since birth. She loves Orosman, the young sultan who loves her in return and plans to marry her. However, Nerestan, a Christian knight, reappears on the scene to ransom Zaïre, her friend Fatima, and ten Frenchmen, and to surrender himself to captivity. Orosman grants him his freedom and that of one hundred knights but will release neither Zaïre nor

Lusignan, an old French descendant of the kings of Jerusalem, who reveals himself as the father of Zaïre and Nerestan. As her father dies, Zaïre promises to be baptized but finds herself torn between her vow and plans to marry Orosman. Orosman, who becomes suspicious, intercepts a letter fixing a rendezvous between Zaire and Nerestan. Believing himself betrayed, Orosman appears in Nerestan's place and stabs Zaïre. When he finally realizes his mistake, Orosman releases the Christian captives and kills himself.

This tragedy, described by the critic Theodore Besterman (*Voltaire* [London: Longmans, 1969]) as "perhaps the least Voltairean and consequently the most popular of his tragedies," survives because of its sensitivity, rare in Voltaire's writings, and its vivacity and passion.

For further information, see T. Braun, "Subject, Substance and Structure in *Zaïre and Alzire*," Studies on Voltaire and the Eighteenth Century 102 (1973); pp. 7–52; C. Cherpack, "Love and Alienation in Voltaire's *Zaïre*," *French Forum* 2 (January 1977): 47–57; L. B. Price, "Spatial Relationships in Voltaire's *Zaïre*," *French Review* (December 1976): pp. 251–259.

ZOLA, EMILE (1840–1902). See *Dictionary of Modern French Literature, from Naturalism and Symbolism to Post-Modernism.*

Historical and Literary Events

THE EIGHTEENTH CENTURY

History

1715–1774 Reign of Louis XV

1715–1723 Regency of the Duke of Orleans

1726 Cardinal Fleury, Prime Minister

1733–1738 War of Polish succession; Louis XV's first war

1743 Death of Fleury

1755 Lisbon earthquake

1756–63 Seven Years' War

1766 Lorraine returned to France

1768 France acquires Corsica

Literature

1715–1735 Lesage, *Gil Blas*

1721 Montesquieu, *Lettres persanes*

1730 Marivaux, *Le Jeu de l'amour et du hasard*

1731 Prévost, *Manon Lescaut*
Voltaire, *Histoire de Charles XII*

1732 Voltaire, *Zaïre*

1734 Voltaire, *Lettres philosophiques*

1734–1753 Saint-Simon, *Mémoires*

1747 Voltaire, *Zadig*

1748 Montesquieu, *L'Esprit des lois*

1749–1788 Buffon, *Histoire naturelle*

1751–1772 *L'Encyclopédie*

1759 Voltaire, *Candide*

1761 Rousseau, *La Nouvelle Héloïse*

1762 Rousseau, *Le Contrat social*
Rousseau, *Emile*
Diderot, *Le Neveu de Rameau*

1765–1770 Rousseau, *Confessions*

1773 Diderot, *Jacques le Fataliste et son maître*

History

1774–1791 Reign of Louis XVI

1776 American Declaration of Independence

1789–1799 French Revolution

1789 Etats généraux (states general) convened; Tiers Etat (Third Estate) forms the Assemblée nationale (National Assembly); Tiers Etat takes the Oath of the Jeu de Paume (Oath of the Tennis Court), 28 June to provide France with a new constitution; Assemblée nationale becomes the Assemblée Constituante (Constituent Assembly); Storming of the Bastille, 14 July; Declaration of the Rights of Man

1791 Assemblée législative (Legislative Assembly) succeeds the Constituante (Constituent)

1792 Convention nationale (National Convention) succeeds the Assemblée législative (Legislative Assembly) and abolishes the monarchy; First Republic proclaimed

1793 Louis XVI executed, 21 January

1793–1794 Reign of Terror under Maximilien de Robespierre

1794 Fall of Robespierre on 27 July (9 Thermidor on the Republican calendar)

1795–1799 The Directoire (Directory) replaces the Convention nationale (National Convention)

1799 Napoléon Bonaparte's (1769–1821) coup d'état on 9 November (18 Brumaire on the Republican calendar)

Literature

1775 Beaumarchais, *Le Barbier de Séville*

1776–1778 Rousseau, *Rêveries du promeneur solitaire*

1784 Beaumarchais, *Le Mariage de Figaro*

1785 Chenier, *Idylles, Elégies*

1787 Bernardin de Saint-Pierre, *Paul et Virginie*

THE NINETEENTH CENTURY

History	Literature
1799–1804 Le Consulat (The Consulate) established on 13 December; Napoléon as First Consul	
1801 Le Concordat establishes Roman Catholicism as official religion	1801 Chateaubriand, *Atala*
	1802 Chateaubriand, *Le Génie du Christianisme*
1804–1814 First Empire, Napoléon I	
1805 Austerlitz victory	
1806 Iena victory	
1809 Wagram victory	
1812 Russian invasion and retreat	
1814 France invaded; monarchy restored; Napoléon exiled to Elbe	
1815 Napoléon rules again for 100 days but is defeated at Waterloo	
1815–1830 The Restoration	
1815–1824 Louis XVIII	1820 Lamartine, *Les Méditations poétiques*
1821 Death of Napoléon	1822 Hugo, *Les Odes et Ballades*
1824–1830 Reign of Charles X	1826 Vigny, *Les Poèmes antiques et modernes*
	1827 Hugo, *Cromwell*
1830 Revolution	1830 Hugo, *Hernani*
1830–1848 Reign of Louis-Philippe	Stendhal, *Le Rouge et le noir*
	Hugo, *Notre-Dame de Paris*
	1833 Balzac, *Eugénie Grandet*
	1834 Balzac, *Le Père Goriot*
	1835 Musset, *La Nuit de mai*
	Vigny, *Chatterton*
	1836 Tocqueville, *De la Démocratie en Amérique*
	1839 Stendhal, *La Chartreuse de Parme*
1840 François Guizot, prime minister, February–March	1840 Proudhon, *Qu'est-ce que la propriété*
	1844 Dumas, *Les Trois Mousequetaires*
	1845 Mérimée, *Carmen*
1848 Revolution, 22–24 February	1848 Chateaubriand, *Les Mémoires d'outre-tombe*

1848–1851 Second Republic declared 24 February; Louis-Napoléon elected president

1851 Coup d'état of 2 December

1852–1870 Second Empire, Napoleon III

    1854–1855 Crimean War

    1860 La Savoie and Nice given to France by Italy

1851–1870 Sainte-Beuve, *Lundis*

1853 Hugo, *Les Châtiments*

1857 Flaubert, *Madame Bovary*
        Baudelaire, *Les Fleurs du mal*

1862 Hugo, *Les Misérables*

1865 Goncourt, *Germinie Lacerteux*

1869 Baudelaire, *Petits Poèmes en prose*

1869 Daudet, *Les Lettres de mon moulin*

1870 War declared against Prussia, 19 July; Third Republic proclaimed, 4 September, until 1940; Paris sieged, 19 September

1871 Treaty of Frankfurt ends Franco-Prussian War; Alsace and Lorraine ceded to Prussia; Adolphe Thiers elected President; Paris Commune, March–May;

1873–1879 Patrice, comte de Mac-Mahon, president of the Republic

1873 Rimbaud, *Une Saison en enfer*

1874 Verlaine, *Romances sans paroles*

1875 Mallarme, *L'Après-midi d'un faune*

1877 Zola, *L'Assommoir*
        Flaubert, *Trois contes*

1880 Maupassant, *Boule de suif*

Entries Grouped by Subject Matter or Chronological Period

INSTITUTIONS

Arsenal, Bibliothèque de l'

LITERARY TERMS

Beylism

Bovarysme

Cénacle

Comédie larmoyante

Drame

Frénétique

Mal du siècle

Marivaudage

Opéra-Comique

Parades

Proverbes dramatiques

Théâtre Italien

Théâtres de la foire

MOVEMENTS, SCHOOLS, AND PERIODS

Art pour l'art, l'

Fourierisme

Idéologues

Parnassians

Philosophe

Physiocrat

Positivism

Preromanticism

Realism

Romanticism

Saint-Simonisme

JOURNALS

Globe, le

Muse française, la

EIGHTEENTH-CENTURY POETS, PLAYWRIGHTS, AND NOVELISTS

Baculard d'Arnaud

Beaumarchais

Berquin

Carmontelle

Cazotte

Challes or Chasles

Chénier, André

Chénier, M.-J.

Collé

Collin-d'Harleville

Crébillon

Crébillon fils

Dancourt

De Belloy

Delille

Destouches

Ducis

Dufresny

Dulaurens

Fabre d'Eglantine

Florian

Fougeret de Monbron

Graffigny, Madame de

Gresset

Hamilton

La Chaussée

Laclos

La Harpe

Lebrun

Lemierre

Lesage

Louvet de Couvray

Marivaux

Pompignan

Prévost

Regnard

Restif de la Bretonne

Riccoboni, Madame

Rousseau, J.-B.

Rousseau, J.-J.

Sade

Sedaine

Tençin, Madame de

Vivant de Non or Vivant Denon

Voltaire

EIGHTEENTH-CENTURY MEMORIALISTS, PHILOSOPHERS, NATURALISTS, MORALISTS, AND HISTORIANS

Bachaumont

Bayle

Buffon, Comte de

Cabanis

Casanova di Seingalt

Chamfort

Courtilz de Sandras

Duclos

Fénelon

Fontenelle

Maine de Biran

Malesherbes

Marmontel

Maupertuis

Mercier

Rivarol

Roland, Madame

Saint-Simon, Duc de

Senac de Meilhan

Vauvenargues, Marquis de

PHILOSOPHES

Alembert

Condillac

Condorcet

Diderot

Grimm

Helvétius

Holbach, Baron de

Jaucourt, Chevalier de

La Mettrie

Mably

Montesquieu

Morellet

Morelly

Quesnay

Raynal

Rousseau, J.-J.

Turgot

Voltaire

ANTI-PHILOSOPHES

Fréron

Palissot de Montenoy

REVOLUTIONARY ORATORS, JOURNALISTS, POETS, AND PLAYWRIGHTS

Danton

Desmoulins

Mirabeau, Comte de

Robespierre

Vergniaud

EIGHTEENTH-CENTURY WORKS

Barbier de Séville, Le, ou La Précaution Inutile

Candide

Confessions, Les

Contrat social, Le

Dialogues ou Rousseau Juge de Jean-Jacques

Dictionnaire philosophique portatif

Discours sur les sciences et les arts

Discours sur l'origine de l'inégalité

Emile

Encyclopédie, L'

Esprit des lois, De l'

Essai sur les moeurs et l'esprit des nations

Fausses confidences, Les

Gil Blas de Santillane, L'Histoire de

Jacques le fataliste et son maître

Jeu de l'amour et du hasard, Le

Lettre à d'Alembert sur les spectacles, La

Lettres persanes, Les

Lettres philosophiques

Lettre sur les aveugles, La

Manon Lescaut

Mariage de Figaro, Le, ou La Folle Journée

Mérope

Micromégas

Neveu de Rameau, Le

Nouvelle Héloïse, Julie ou la

On ne badine pas avec l'amour

Paradoxe sur le comédien, Le   *Turcaret*

Paysan parvenu, Le   *Vie de Marianne, La*

Rêve de d'Alembert, Le   *Zadig*

Rêveries du promeneur solitaire, Les   *Zaïre*

Siècle de Louis XIV, Le

NINETEENTH-CENTURY NOVELISTS AND STORYWRITERS

Balzac   Mérimée

Barbey d'Aurevilly   Nerval

Champfleury   Nodier

Chateaubriand   Sand, George

Constant   Sandeau

Dumas père   Senancour

Flaubert   Stendhal

Fromentin   Sue

Gobineau, Comte de   Vigny

Hugo

NINETEENTH-CENTURY PLAYWRIGHTS

Augier   Pailleron

Becque   Pixerécourt

Dumas fils   Ponsard

Halévy   Sandeau

Labiche   Sardou

Meilhac   Scribe

Musset   Vigny

NINETEENTH-CENTURY HISTORIANS AND PHILOSOPHERS

Ballanche   De Maistre

Barante, Baron de   Destutt de Tracy, Comte

Blanc   Fustel de Coulanges

Bonald, Comte de   Guizot

Comte   Lacordaire

Courier   Lamennais

Cousin   Martin

Michelet

Mignet

Montalembert, Comte de

Proudhon

Quinet

Renan

Royer-Collard

Saint-Simon, Comte de

Taine

Thierry

Thiers

Tocqueville, Comte de

Veuillot

Volney, Comte de

NINETEENTH-CENTURY POETS

Gautier

Hugo

Lamartine

Lautréamont

Musset

Nerval

Vigny

NINETEENTH-CENTURY PARNASSIAN POETS

Banville

Coppée

Dierx

Glatigny

Heredia

Leconte de Lisle

Ménard

Mendès

Sully-Prudhomme

NINETEENTH-CENTURY CRITICS AND LITERARY THEORISTS

Janin

Nisard

Saint-Marc Girardin

Sainte-Beuve

Staël, Baronne de

Taine

Villemain

PREROMANTICS

Bernardin de Saint-Pierre (18th century)

Constant

Rousseau, J.-J. (18th century)

Senancour

Staël, Barrone de

ROMANTICS

Arvers

Barbier

Béranger

Bertrand

Borel

Brizeux

Chateaubriand

Desbordes-Valmore

Dumas père

Guérin

Hugo

Lamartine

Moreau

Musset

Nerval

O'Neddy

Vigny

REALISTS

Balzac

Champfleury

Flaubert

Sue

NINETEENTH-CENTURY WORKS

Adolphe

Atala

Carmen

Chants du crépuscule, Les

Chartreuse de Parme, La

Châtiments, Les

Chatterton

Colomba

Comédie humaine, La

Contemplations, Les

Corbeaux, Les

Destinées, Les, Poèmes Philosophiques

Dominique

Education sentimentale, L'

Eugénie Grandet

Feuilles d'automne, Les

Génie du Christianisme, Le

Harmonies poétiques et religieuses

Hernani

Jeanne d'Arc

Jocelyn

Légende des siècles, La

Liaisons dangereuses, Les—see Laclos

Lorenzaccio

Lucien Leuwen

Madame Bovary

Martyrs, Les

Mateo Falcone

Méditations poétiques, Les

Mémoires d'outre-tombe, Les

Misérables, Les

Notre-Dame de Paris

Obermann

Orientales, Les

Père Goriot, Le

Poèmes antiques et modernes, Les

Préface de Cromwell, La

Rayons et les ombres, Les

René

Rouge et le noir, Le

Ruy Blas

Salammbô

Voix intérieures, Les

Index

Page numbers in *italics* refer to main entries in the dictionary.

Labiche, Eugène, *161*
La Bruyère, Jean de, 43, 96, 124, 132, 176, 195, 245, 246, 290, 316, 319, 320
Lacépède, Etienne de la ville, comte de, 32
La Chaussée, Pierre-Claude Nivelle de, 61, 85, *161–62*
Laclos, Pierre Choderlos de, 77, *162–64*, 180
Lacordaire, Jean-Baptiste-Henri, 137, *164*, 168, 215, 321
Ladvocat, Charles, 49
Lafayette, Madame de, 192
Laffitte, Pierre, 26
La Fontaine, Jean de, 123, 198
La Harpe, Jean-François de, 47, *164–65*, 194
La Hire, Philippe de, 123
Lamarck, Jean-Baptiste, 32, 87
Lamartine, Alphonse de, 6, 50, 139, 140, 146, 148, 149, 158, *165–68*, 169, 173, 190, 201, 219, 221, 222, 252, 287, 288, 303
Lambert, Madame de, 123, 144, 194, 215, 312
Lamennais, Félicité-Robert de, 26, 29, 49, 105, 137, 215, 164, *168–69*, 294, 296
La Mettrie, Julien Offray de, *169–70*, 200, 246
Lamotte-Houdart. *See* Houdar de la Motte, Antoine
Lanson, Gustave, 132, 192, 290, 328
La Place, Pierre-Antoine de, 95
La Platière, Roland de, 273
Laprade, Victor-Richard, 241
Larivière, Mercier de, 248, 259
La Rochefoucauld, François duc de, 319, 320
Latouche, Henri de, 82
La Tour, Maurice Quentin de, 88
Lautréamont, *170–71*, 308
Law, John, 162, 195
Le Breton, André-François, 87, 107, 108
Lebrun, Ponce-Denis Echouard, 47, 54, *171*

Leclerc, Théodore, 257
Leconte de Lisle, Charles-Marie, 18, 72, 91, 130, 133, 141, *171–73*, 203, 238, 241, 252, 308
Lecoq, Charles, 139
Le Coulteux, Madame, 53
Leczinski, Stanislas, 330, 333
Légende des siècles, La, 51, 117, 118, 149, 150, 151, *173–75*, 214, 249
Leibnitz, Gottfried Wilhelm, 5, 35, 62, 124, 132, 211, 309
Lemaître, Jules, 197
Lemerre, Alphonse, 241
Lemierre, Antoine-Marin, *175*
Lenclos, Ninon de, 328
Lenin, Nikolai, 15
Le Poitevin, Auguste, 11
Le Poittevin, Alfred, 119, 121
Leprince de Beaumont, Madame, 198, 205
Leroux, Pierre, 291, 294, 296
Lesage, Alain-René, 79, 84, 96, 132, 133, *175–77*, 196, 237, 313, 316, 322
Lespinasse, Mademoiselle de, 5, 64, 252, 269
Lessing, Gotthold, 303
Le Tourneur, Pierre, 95
Le Trosne, Guillaume-François, 248, 259
Lettre à d'Alembert sur les spectacles, 94, *177*, 278
Lettres d'une Péruvienne, 135
Lettres persanes, 135, 215, *245–46*
Lettres philosophiques, 95, *177–79*, 328, 329, 334
Lettre sur les aveugles, 87, 92, *179*, 278
Leuven, Adolphe de, 98
Levasseur, Thérèse, 278
Liaisons dangereuses, Les, 162, 163, 180
Libertinism (libertines), 96–97, 125, 182, 268, 269, 285, 326
Liszt, Franz, 294
"Littérature facile," 229
Littré, Emile, 62
Locke, John, 5, 62, 178, 179, 216, 246, 329, 334
Lorenzaccio, 180–81, 220, 222
Loti, Pierre, 296

About the Author

SANDRA W. DOLBOW is a freelance writer. A former French teacher on levels ranging from junior high school to college, she currently writes a monthly book review column and has worked for numerous publications, including the *Indianapolis Star Magazine, Action for the Arts,* and *Focus.*